PRENTICE HALL

Introduction to Computers and Information Technology

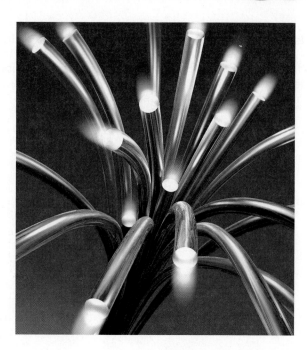

Taken from:
Prentice Hall Technology Applications Student WorkText, Level I Revised Edition
Prentice Hall Technology Applications Student WorkText, Level II Revised Edition
Prentice Hall Technology Applications Student WorkText, Texas Grade 8 Revised Edition

Cover Art: Courtesy of Shutterstock.

Taken from:

Prentice Hall Technology Applications Student WorkText, Level I Revised Edition
Copyright © 2008 by Pearson Education, Inc.
Published by Prentice Hall
Upper Saddle River, New Jersey 07458

Prentice Hall Technology Applications Student WorkText, Level II Revised Edition
Copyright © 2008 by Pearson Education, Inc.
Published by Prentice Hall
Upper Saddle River, New Jersey 07458

Prentice Hall Technology Applications Student WorkText, Texas Grade 8 Revised Edition
Copyright © 2008 by Pearson Education, Inc.
Published by Prentice Hall
Upper Saddle River, New Jersey 07458

Pearson Learning Solutions, 501 Boylston Street, Suite 900, Boston, MA 02116
A Pearson Education Company
www.pearsoned.com

Printed in the United States of America

2 3 4 5 6 7 8 9 10 V382 16 15 14 13 12 11

0002000102746574

JH

ISBN 10: 1-256-05024-5
ISBN 13: 978-1-256-05024-7

Table of Contents

Table of Contents

Table of Contents

Table of Contents

Table of Contents

Table of Contents

To the Student

USING YOUR TEXTBOOK

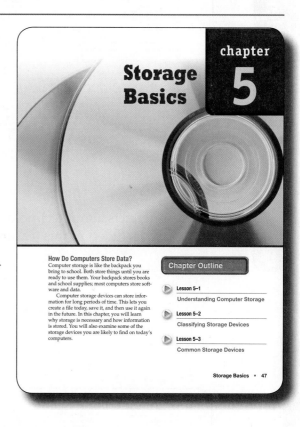

Chapter Overview

Each chapter begins with an introduction to concepts and a chapter outline.

Lesson Overview

At the start of each lesson you will find helpful tools that guide you through the learning process.

As You Read Ideas for how you can best organize information for maximum learning.

Objectives Tasks you should be able to complete by the end of the lesson.

Key Terms Key words you should know after you complete the lesson.

Sidebar Features

Additional features in each chapter enhance and support the text.

Sequential Versus Random Access When equipped with a tape drive, business computers can store data on a long piece of tape, similar to an old-fashioned cassette tape. A tape drive is an example of a **sequential storage device**, which requires the computer to scan from one beginning of the medium to the end until it finds the data it needs. While cheaper and slower than other types of storage, the highest capacity tape cartridges can hold five terabytes of uncompressed data. Because it can take several minutes to locate a piece of data on a high-capacity tape, tapes are used chiefly by businesses that want to back up their computer systems—often after the business day is over.

A **random access storage device** lets a computer go directly to the needed information. The device does not have to search the entire medium to find data. For this reason, random access storage devices are much faster, and more expensive, than sequential devices. A hard drive is an example of a random access storage device.

Magnetic Versus Optical Storage Magnetic storage devices are specially treated disks or tapes, such as those mentioned above, that record information using magnetically sensitive materials. These devices use electricity to shift magnetic particles so they form a pattern that the computer reads and stores as information. Common magnetic storage devices include hard drives and tape drives

Other storage devices use laser beams to read information that has been stored on the reflective surface of a disc. These are called **optical storage devices**. Popular types of optical storage devices for computers include CD-ROM and DVD-ROM drives.

Technology@School

In addition to hardware, software, and peripherals, schools use storage devices such as hard drives and CD-ROMs/DVDs. Some schools have a dedicated computer "lab," but more and more schools have computers in every classroom. It's important for all students to treat computer equipment with care and use good, respectful conduct when doing tasks on school—or any—computers.

Think About It!

Rate the computer equipment that you think is most sensitive to mishandling and needs the most care. On a scale of 1 to 5, use 1 for most sensitive and 5 for least.

▷ CD-ROM/DVD
▷ Flash drive
▷ Hard drive
▷ Power cord
▷ Laser printer

Technology@Home
Technology@School
Technology@Work

These include relevant information on how you can use the technology that you are learning about. They put the topics being discussed into real-world context.

Did You Know?

Interesting facts about technology are included in this feature.

Did You Know? Most computers only have enough RAM to store programs and data while a computer is using them. This is because RAM is relatively expensive to make and buy. As a result, makers of computers limit the amount of RAM in their machines to help lower initial computer costs and to allow users who want more RAM to purchase it separately.

Storage Versus Memory New computer users sometimes get confused about temporary memory (RAM) and permanent storage (disks and disk drives). They will say "memory" when they actually mean to say "storage." To avoid this problem, remember two key differences between storage and memory:

- The two work differently. Remember that RAM uses chips to temporarily store information. These chips depend on a constant supply of power to keep their contents; when the power is lost, the chips lose their contents. Storage uses different methods to store data permanently, so it isn't lost when the power is turned off.
- A PC has more storage capacity than memory. Even though some PCs have several gigabytes of RAM, their hard drives will be many times larger.

Storage Media and Storage Devices

Storage has two components: storage media and storage devices.

Storage Media In terms of storage, a medium is an object that physically holds data or program instructions. Flash drives, magnetic tapes, compact discs, and DVDs are examples of storage media. (The word *media* is the plural of *medium*.)

Storage Devices A storage device is a piece of hardware that holds the storage medium, sends data to the medium, and retrieves data from the medium. Hard drives, flash drives, and CD drives are all examples of storage devices.

Magneto-Optical (MO) Drives One of the most popular methods of data storage for many businesses, this type of drive combines both magnetic and optical drive technologies. A magneto-optical drive uses a removable disk that is inserted via a slot in the front of the drive. These drives can be internal or external. Their disks can store several gigabytes of information.

Online Storage Many online—or cloud—storage sites are available where you can store files on a network server at a remote location. You access your data by logging in through the Internet using a secure password. Some programs, including Microsoft Office 2010, come with free online storage space. You can also pay a storage service provider (SSP) for space. Online storage offers these three benefits: 1) it is expandable; 2) it allows you to share files with others; and 3) data stored in a remote location is protected if your computer is stolen or damaged.

Capacities of Common Storage Devices	
Device	**Capacity**
Internal hard drive	500 GB and more
External hard drive (USB or Firewire connection)	500 GB–8 TB and more
MP3 player	16 GB–64 GB and more

Career Corner

Computer Security Specialist Today, security specialists are in demand to work with various computer storage systems, such as tape warehouses and online storage companies.

Computer security specialists study ways of improving the overall security of their systems. For example, some goals include improving recording or access time or the safety of the protected information in case of a natural disaster.

Figure 5.3.2 A USB flash drive has a USB connector, a flash memory chip, a mass storage controller, and a crystal oscillator that allow the device to communicate with the computer.

Career Corner

This feature includes information on related careers that use the technology being discussed in the chapter.

Connections

This cross-curricular feature explains how the technology covered in the chapter is used in other areas, including the arts, science, social studies, language arts, and mathematics.

Connections

Mathematics In math class, you are accustomed to a system that combines ten possible digits, or numbers, in a certain order to represent larger numbers. In binary code, only 0 and 1 are used.

- In math class, you carry a number over to the next column when numbers in a column add to 10 or more. With binary numbers, a number is carried if the items add to 2. In an eight-bit example, the number 35 would be written as 100011.
- While numbers in math class refer to specific quantities, binary code numbers refer to specific actions. A 1 turns a circuit on, while a 0 turns a circuit off.

Solid State Disks Solid state disks or drives, or **SSDs**, are a mass storage device similar to a hard disk drive. Even though SSDs serve the same purpose as hard drives, their internal parts are much different. SSDs do not have any moving parts, like the hard drive's magnetic platters; they store data using flash memory. SSDs have better read performance because the data does not get fragmented into many locations, and, since they are not magnetic, SSDs do not lose data when next to a strong magnetic field.

SSDs do have disadvantages, though. This newer technology costs about ten times more per gigabyte, so people tend to buy SSDs with smaller capacity than most hard drives. Their limited number of write cycles means their performance declines over time. Yet, with improvements in SSD technology, these devices will advance, and the prices may come down.

Flash Memory Devices Several types of storage devices using flash memory offer the speed of memory with the high capacity of a magnetic storage device. Flash memory drives work faster than magnetic drives, because they have no moving parts, and they do not require battery power to retain their data. Flash drives installed inside computers resemble magnetic hard drives in size and shape.

A **USB flash drive** is a portable, self-contained storage device that uses **flash memory**. In addition to portability, these drives offer the advantages of speed, capacity, and cost. A USB flash drive has a USB connector that plugs into the USB port on a computer.

Additional Chapter Features

Throughout the text are Spotlight on. . . and Real-World Tech features.

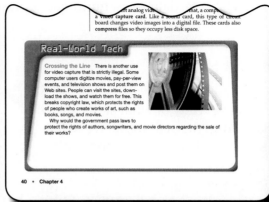

▲ **Spotlight on . . .**

There are so many individuals who have made a difference in the technology that we use today. Spotlight on . . . highlights some of these people.

▲ **Real-World Tech**

This is a technology-awareness feature that introduces a technology concept relating to the current topic.

At the End of Each Chapter

▼ **Use the Vocabulary**

Matching exercises to check your understanding of key terms in the chapter

▼ **Thinking Critically**

Short-answer questions to demonstrate your understanding of concepts

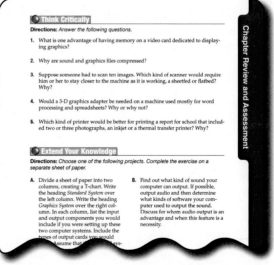

▲ **Check Your Comprehension**

Questions to self-check your reading comprehension

▲ **Extend Your Knowledge**

Projects incorporating all the skills you have learned in a fun and challenging activity

Hands-on Application Activities

In chapters where application skills are discussed, hands-on activities are included. These projects give you the opportunity to use the operating system, create documents, spreadsheets, databases, multimedia presentations, Web pages, and e-mail messages.

Activity Directions

An overview of what skills are to be used in the activity, along with a scenario of what you'll be creating

▶

Activity Steps

Step-by-step directions indicate what needs to be done in order to complete the project

▶

Illustrations

Activity illustrations help you check your work

▶

What's on the Student CD-ROM

The CD-ROM that accompanies your text includes data files and data record sheets to be used in some of the hands-on activities, cross-curricular projects, Microsoft Office 2010, 2007, and 2003 procedure reference, and puzzles.

part **1**

Computing Fundamentals

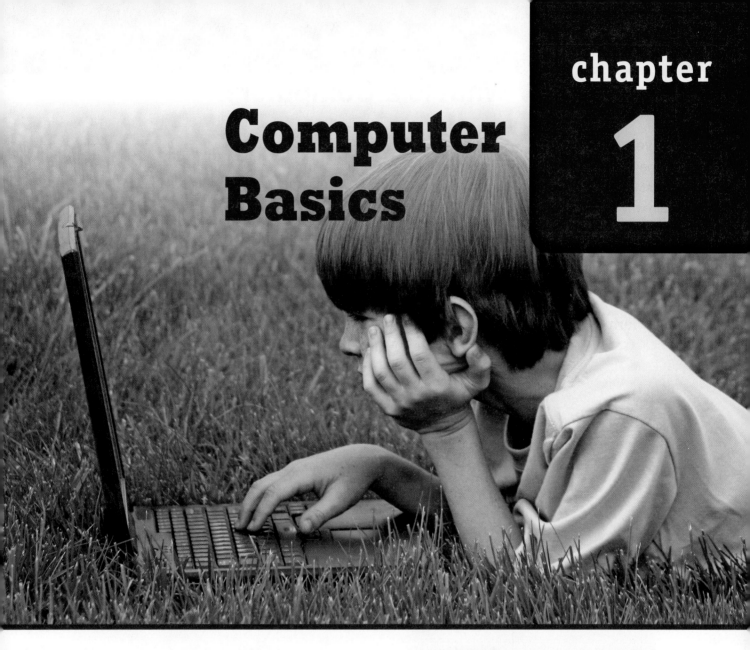

Computer Basics

How Do Computers Work? The answer to this question can be very long and complicated, even though computers work in a fairly simple way. At its core, a computer contains a set of on/off switches; by turning these switches on and off very rapidly, the computer can represent information. Imagine a wall covered with a thousand light bulbs, each with its own on/off switch. By turning switches on and off in a certain way, you could use the lights to spell words or create pictures. Computers work in a similar way.

But a computer cannot use its switches without instructions. That's where software and you, the user, come into play. By giving the computer instructions and data to work with, you and your software programs tell it how to work its switches—turning them on and off millions of times each second.

Chapter Outline

 Lesson 1–1

What Is a Computer?

 Lesson 1–2

What Is Computer Hardware?

 Lesson 1–3

What Is Computer Software?

What Is a Computer?

Objectives

- Describe the four operations of computers.
- Contrast analog and digital computers.
- Explain why data and instructions for computers are coded as 0s and 1s.
- Identify three benefits of computers.

As You Read

Sequence Information   Use a sequence chart to help you organize the four operations of computers as you read the lesson.

🔑 Key Terms

- bit
- byte
- computer
- input
- output
- processing
- storage

Computer Basics

A **computer** is a machine that changes information from one form into another by performing four basic actions. Those actions are input, processing, output, and storage. Together, these actions make up the information processing cycle. By following a set of instructions, called a program, the computer turns raw data into organized information that people can use. Creation of usable information is the primary benefit of computer technology. There are two kinds of computers:

- Analog computers measure data on a scale with many values. Think of the scales on a mercury thermometer or on the gas gauge of a car.
- Digital computers work with data that has a fixed value. They use data in digital, or number, form. The computers that run programs for playing games or searching the Internet are digital computers.

Input

Input is the raw information, or data, that is entered into a computer. This data can be as simple as letters and numbers or as complex as color photographs, videos, or songs. You input data by using a device such as a keyboard or digital camera.

Bits of Data   Data is entered into a computer in a coded language. The building blocks of that language are units called **bits**. *Bit* is short for *b*inary dig*it*. Each bit is a number, or a digit. A bit can have only two possible values—0 or 1.

Bits into Bytes   Every letter, number, or picture is entered into the computer as a combination of bits, or 0s and 1s. The bits are combined into groups of eight or more. Each group is called a **byte**. Each letter or number has a unique combination of bits. For instance, on most personal computers, the letter *A* is coded as 01000001. The number *1* is 00110001.

Even images are formed by combinations of bytes. Those combinations tell the computer what colors to display and where to put them.

Processing

The second step of the information processing cycle is called **processing**. In this step, the computer does something to the data.

Coded Instructions   What the computer does depends on the instructions, or program, given to the computer. The instructions are also written in binary code, using combinations of 0s and 1s. They might tell the computer to add two numbers, or they might have the computer compare two numbers to see which is larger.

Speed of Processing   Computers can process data very rapidly, performing millions of operations every second. The ability to process data with lightning speed is another reason computers are so valuable.

 Connections

Math   You ordinarily count using the decimal, or base 10, system. That system has 10 values, 0 through 9. But you can express many numbers using those values. You simply add additional places—the 10s, the 100s, and so on. Each place is 10 times larger than the previous place. In a binary system, the quantity represented by each place is 2 times the previous quantity. In an 8-digit binary number, the places are the 1s, 2s, 4s, 8s, 16s, 32s, 64s, and 128s.

Figure 1.1.1 Each computer component plays a role in one of the system's four primary functions.

In some schools, students' work is collected over the year in electronic portfolios. These portfolios reflect a range of the students' work on many projects during the school year. The computer's ability to store this information is perfect for portfolio work.

Think About It!

Think about how an electronic portfolio might be used. Circle each item that you think could be in an electronic portfolio.

➤ multimedia presentations

➤ maps

➤ paper-and-pencil homework

➤ poetry

➤ lab report

Output

The third step shows what happens after the computer processes the data. This is the **output** step. If the program tells the computer to add two numbers, the output stage displays the result. To create output, the computer takes the bytes and turns them back into a form you can understand, such as an image on the screen or a printed document.

Output can take many forms. A program might convert the 0s and 1s into a report. It might become an image you are drawing on the computer. If you are playing a game, the output might be a car zooming along a road and the sound of its engine. A computer provides output through a device such as a monitor, speaker, or printer.

Storage

The fourth operation is **storage**, in which the computer saves the information. Without storage, all the work you do on the computer would be lost. Computers have a temporary memory that is used during the processing stage. When the computer is turned off, however, any data in that temporary memory is lost.

By storing the data in a permanent form, you can access the information over and over. This is another great advantage of computers—what you do one day can be saved and reused on another day.

Real-World Tech

Robots at Work Some output is very unusual. Computer-controlled robots work in some auto factories. Their output is cars. The robots are perfect for the tasks that take place on an assembly line. These tasks are done over and over again without change. For instance, robots weld parts together and paint car bodies.

What is a disadvantage to workers of bringing in robots to do tasks such as factory work? What can businesses and workers do to make that less of a problem?

What Is Computer Hardware?

Objectives

- Summarize how a CPU and RAM work together.
- Contrast primary and secondary storage.
- Compare the features of four secondary storage devices.
- Identify three types of connectors and the peripherals that use each.

As You Read

Compare and Contrast Use a chart to help you compare and contrast computer hardware as you read.

What Is Hardware?

When you think about a computer, you probably picture its **hardware**, the computer's physical parts. You use hardware devices such as a keyboard or mouse to input data. The processor is a hardware device that turns the raw data into usable information. Hardware devices such as a monitor or a disk drive show output and store data for later access.

Inside the Case

Much of a computer's hardware is found inside the computer case, hidden from view. Most of this hardware is used for processing and storing data.

Processing Devices Perhaps the most important piece of hardware in a computer is the **central processing unit**, or **CPU**. This is the device that processes data. The CPU is a small, thin piece of silicon attached to a circuit board. The CPU is covered with tiny electrical circuits. By moving data along these circuits in specific ways, the CPU can do arithmetic and compare data very quickly.

Primary Storage Some hardware used to store data is inside the computer case near the CPU. The computer uses **random access memory**, or **RAM**, to store data and instructions while the computer is working. In this way, the CPU can quickly find the data it works with. This type of storage is called primary storage. Data in RAM is lost when the computer is turned off.

Secondary Storage Devices Other pieces of storage hardware are secondary storage. The following devices let you store data permanently—even when the computer is turned off.

Key Terms

- central processing unit (CPU)
- cloud storage
- hardware
- peripheral
- random access memory (RAM)
- universal serial bus (USB)

Figure 1.2.1 Intel's Core 2 Duo is one type of processor.

- Hard drives use a stack of disk platters to store large amounts of information permanently on the computer. External hard drives, which are plugged into the computer, are used to store back-ups of your data. They can be desktop or portable devices. They usually connect to the computer via a **universal serial bus**, or **USB**, port.

- Flash, jump, thumb, or pen drives—all names for the same kind of storage device—connect to the computer through a USB port. They hold anywhere from 4 gigabytes to as many as 32 gigabytes or more.

- Compact Discs (CDs) and Digital Video Discs (DVDs) are optical storage devices. You insert the CD or DVD into your computer through the disc drive. A CD can store 650 to 700 megabytes of data. DVDs can store anywhere from 4.7 gigabytes to double that amount if the DVD is double-sided. We'll learn more about different types of CDs and DVDs in Chapter 5.

- **"Cloud" storage** is online storage offered on various Web sites. Most of them will give you a few gigabytes for free, but then require you to pay for more space.

Secondary Storage Capacity Hard disk drives hold the most data. Many computers now have hard drives that can store several hundred gigabytes. A gigabyte is just over a billion bytes. Thumb or flash drives hold the next largest amount of data, sometimes going over 32 gigabytes. CDs and DVDs hold the least amount of data—from around 700 megabytes to almost 10 gigabytes. A megabyte is just over a million bytes, but still several hundred of them on a CD can store entire encyclopedias, including images, maps, and sound.

Figure 1.2.2 Today, nearly all computers feature a built-in hard drive, with capacities of 400 gigabytes or more.

Peripherals

For most desktop systems, input devices, such as the keyboard and mouse, are separate from the case. So are output devices, such as monitors and printers. Hardware that is separate but can be connected to the case is called a **peripheral**.

Not all computers have all this equipment as peripherals. Apple's iMac® computers include the monitor as a physical part of the main system. Other computers may have built-in storage devices. Portable computers have the keyboard, a type of mouse, and a monitor all attached to the main unit.

Cables Peripherals need to be connected to the computer so that data can be moved back and forth. Each peripheral is linked to the computer by a cable with a plug. The plug joins the computer at a connector on the computer case.

Connectors There are several main types of connectors, or ports:

- Serial ports move data one bit at a time. For example, they connect computers to modems for Internet access.
- Parallel ports move data in groups. They are typically used to connect printers to computers.
- Multiple device ports, such as Small Computer Systems Interface (SCSI) and Universal Serial Bus (USB) ports, connect several peripherals to a computer at one time. They all move data faster than serial ports can.

Mouse
Keyboard
USB ports
Serial port
Parallel port
Speakers
Monitor
Power cord

Figure 1.2.3 Personal computers have a variety of special ports, so you can connect many different devices to them.

What Is Computer Software?

Objectives

- Describe what an operating system does.
- Summarize why compatibility is an issue for computer users.
- Explain what utility software does.
- Identify four types of application software and ways to obtain them.

As You Read

Classify Information   Use a concept web to help you classify different types of computer software as you read.

Key Terms

- application software
- operating system (OS)
- software
- system software
- utility software

What Is Software?

Hardware includes all the physical pieces that make up a computer. Hardware is useless without software, however. **Software** includes all of the programs that tell a computer what to do and how to do it. Think of a computer as a sports team. Hardware is the players, and software is the coach. No matter how talented the players are, the team will only perform properly if the coach gives it the right instructions.

Figure 1.3.1 MacOS™, which runs Apple computers, is an example of system software.

Types of Software

Software is divided into two main types: system software and application software. **System software** includes programs that help the computer work properly. You are probably more familiar with **application software**, which are programs designed to help you do tasks such as writing a paper or making a graph. This type of software also includes programs that allow you to use the computer to listen to music or play games.

System Software

There are two types of system software: operating systems and system utilities. Both help computers run smoothly.

Operating Systems   The **operating system (OS)** lets the hardware devices communicate with one another and keeps them running efficiently. It also supports the hardware when applications programs are running. The two most widely used operating systems are the Macintosh® OS and Microsoft® Windows®.

System Utilities   Programs that help the computer work properly are called **utility software**. They usually do maintenance and repair jobs that the operating system cannot do itself. Some utility programs repair damaged data files or save files in certain ways so they take up less space. Others translate files created in one OS so they can be read and worked on in another.

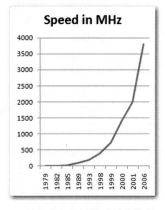
Spotlight on...

BILL GATES

❝ Bill Gates has the obsessive drive of a [computer] hacker working on a tough technical dilemma, yet [he also] has an uncanny grasp of the marketplace, as well as a firm conviction of what the future will be like and what he should do about it. ❞

Steven Levy
Writer

Bill Gates has a simple idea about the future of computing. "The goal," he says, "is information at your fingertips." It will not surprise anyone

if Gates and his company, Microsoft, play a major role in making that goal become a reality. Gates started writing software in high school. He and a childhood friend, Paul Allen, wrote a programming language to run on a machine called the Altair, the first personal computer. Allen and Gates then formed Microsoft, which is now one of the leading software companies in the world.

Technology @ Work

A software program's version is usually indicated by a number, such as "Version 4" or "Version 8.5." Software is upgraded to remove programming errors and to add new features. Some revisions are major, and the version number jumps from, for example, 9.0 to 10. Minor fixes typically change the number after the decimal point, such as 10 to 10.2.

Think About It!

For which items below would it be worthwhile for you to buy the new version of the program?

➤ a program you use all the time that is moving from 4.3 to 5.0

➤ a program you rarely use that is moving from 2.2 to 2.3

➤ a program you often use that is moving from 5.1 to 5.2

➤ a program you often use that is moving from 1.0 to 3.0

Figure 1.3.2 You can buy off-the-shelf software in many places, from computer stores to department stores.

Application Software

There are many different applications. They can be grouped into four main categories:

- Productivity software helps people be more productive at work. People use these programs to write reports, prepare financial plans, and organize data.

- Graphics software makes it possible to draw, paint, and touch up photos.

- Communication software allows computers to connect to the Internet and to send e-mail.

- Home, education, and entertainment software helps people manage their money or figure their taxes. Other products can be used to learn new skills or simply to have some fun.

Custom Software   There are two ways to obtain application software. Some organizations need software programs to do very specific jobs. They hire people to write custom software designed to do those jobs. Because these programs are custom written, they are usually quite expensive.

Off-the-Shelf Software   Most people use software to do standard jobs. They might want to write letters or keep track of their CD collection. They can choose from many ready-made programs to handle these common tasks. These are called "off-the-shelf" programs because stores and companies that sell software from the Internet stock them. Because software publishers can sell many copies of this software, it is less expensive than custom software.

Use the Vocabulary

Directions: *Match each vocabulary term in the left column with the correct definition in the right column.*

_____ 1. input
_____ 2. bit
_____ 3. byte
_____ 4. output
_____ 5. hardware
_____ 6. central processing unit
_____ 7. random access memory
_____ 8. peripheral
_____ 9. software
_____ 10. utility software

a. program that tells the computer what to do

b. group of 8 bits

c. area where data and instructions are stored while the computer is working

d. physical parts of a computer

e. raw data entered into a computer

f. program that does maintenance or repair tasks

g. part of a computer that processes data

h. basic unit of data a digital computer can understand

i. hardware separate but connected to the computer

j. the results of the computer's processing

Check Your Comprehension

Directions: *Complete each sentence with information from the chapter.*

1. A(n) _____ is a machine that changes information from one form into another.

2. _____ is a basic operation of computers.

3. Data and instructions in computers are coded with a(n) _____ because computers only understand two values.

4. The CPU uses _____ to hold data it is working on.

5. Data in RAM is _____ when the computer is turned off.

6. A(n) _____ is an example of a connector that works with only one kind of peripheral.

7. SCSI and USB connectors connect _____ peripherals at the same time.

8. Some organizations need _____ software programs to do very specific jobs.

9. _____ software is used to connect to the Internet and send e-mail.

10. Off-the-shelf software is _____ expensive than custom software because publishers sell more units.

Think Critically

Directions: *Answer the following questions.*

1. How do analog and digital computers differ?

2. Which benefit of computers—the ability to use any kind of data, the ability to work rapidly, or the ability to access stored data again and again—do you think is the most important? Why?

3. What are the differences between primary and secondary storage?

4. Why might the operating system be called a computer's most important software?

5. What type of application software do you use most? Explain.

Extend Your Knowledge

Directions: *Choose one of the following projects. Complete the exercise on a separate sheet of paper.*

A. Look at a computer. Create a five-column chart. In the first column, list all the hardware that you can identify. In the remaining columns, state whether each item is used for inputting, processing, outputting, or storage. Examine how the different pieces are connected to the computer. What other hardware do you think the computer has that you cannot see? What kinds of hardware were usually peripherals? Which were usually in the computer's case? What exceptions did you identify? Share your findings with the class.

B. Using the Internet or library resources, research at least three types of processing devices used in laptop computers. Create a chart that compares and contrasts the price, top speed, and number of operations per second each one can perform. Determine which device would be most appropriate for working with text, graphics, and math. Using a computer and an appropriate processing device available in class, do an example of each of these types of work. Then, visit a computer store and repeat this work using at least two of the appropriate processing devices you researched. Share your findings in a report to your class.

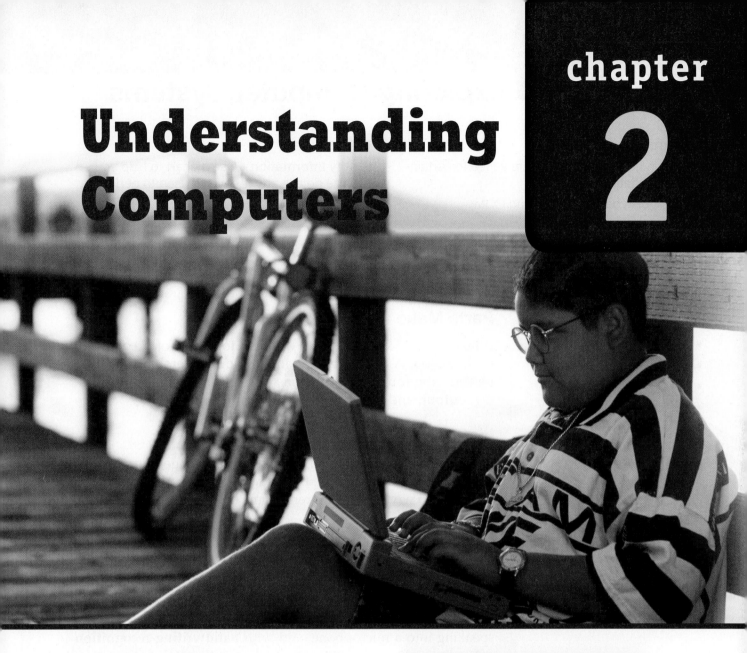

Understanding Computers

Working Together Computers come in many different shapes and sizes. Some are large enough to fill a room. Others can be held in the palm of your hand. Whatever their size and capabilities, all these computers have something in common. They use electronic parts and instructions to perform specific tasks.

The electronic parts or components are called hardware. Hardware includes things like computer chips, circuit boards, hard drives, keyboards, monitors, and speakers. These hardware pieces, however, cannot perform the tasks by themselves. They require power and instructions. Electricity provides the power and software provides the instructions to work. Software programs unlock the potential of the hardware so that you can use the computer to do amazing things.

Chapter Outline

 Lesson 2–1

Exploring Computer Systems

 Lesson 2–2

Making Computers Work

 Lesson 2–3

Group and Individual Computing

Exploring Computer Systems

Objectives

- Explain how input devices are suited to certain kinds of data.
- Distinguish between RAM and ROM.
- Identify an appropriate output device for different types of data.

As You Read

Identify Information   Use a chart to help you organize details about devices used to perform computing functions as you read the lesson.

🔑 Key Terms

- command
- computer system
- flash drives
- handwriting-recognition software
- motherboard
- read-only memory (ROM)
- speech-recognition software
- stylus

Parts Make a Whole

It takes many different parts working together for a computer to do its job. A **computer system** includes several devices that perform the four basic functions of computing: input, processing, output, and storage.

Input Devices

Input means entering data, such as text, images, or sounds. Computer users can choose from several different input devices designed to work with different forms of data.

Text and Commands   Perhaps the most basic input device is the keyboard. You can type on it to input text (letters, numbers, and symbols) and commands. A **command** is an instruction for the computer to perform some action. For example, the Print command tells the computer to send the file you are working on to a printer. With **speech-recognition software**, users can input text by speaking into a microphone, and with **handwriting-recognition software**, users can input text by writing with a **stylus** directly on a device such as a tablet or screen. The software changes the words into digital data the computer can read. This software can be used by people with disabilities that prevent them from typing.

A mouse moves a pointer on the monitor, which allows you to move around a document, or to select commands. Some individuals cannot use a mouse. For them, keyboard equivalents for mouse commands provide access to the data. Adaptive devices can help users type without using their fingers on the keyboard.

Two other input devices, a trackball and a touchpad, or trackpad, function similarly to a mouse. A joystick, often used in computer games, is yet another input device.

Images   A mouse can also be used to input images. You can create pictures in draw and paint programs by moving the mouse to make the patterns you want. You can also bring existing images into a computer as input. Digital cameras and scanners, for example, allow you to input images that are stored on a storage device. You can also input images found on the Internet.

Sounds   Microphones can be used to input sounds. As with images, sounds stored on a storage device or on the Internet can also be brought into the computer as input.

Processing Devices

Inside the computer, data travels from one device to another through the computer's **motherboard**. This board is covered with electrical circuits and switches, and it connects vital pieces of hardware such as the CPU and memory.

The CPU   The main processing device in a computer is the central processing unit, or CPU. The CPU is a chip inside the computer that receives data from input devices and changes it into a form that you can use, such as text, pictures, or sounds. The processor also follows your commands to do something to that data, such as change a word or move a picture.

CPUs can carry out fewer than 1,000 instructions. However, they can perform millions of these operations every second. That ability is what makes computers able to work so quickly.

RAM   The CPU temporarily stores the instructions and data it is using on chips called random access memory, or RAM. Once the computer is turned off, RAM no longer stores any data. Reading information from RAM takes very little time—just billionths of a second. Because programs today are complex, they need a large amount of RAM to run properly.

ROM   A second kind of memory is called **read-only memory**, or **ROM**. These chips contain the instructions that start the computer when you turn it on. The instructions in ROM typically do not change once this memory is placed on the motherboard.

Output Devices

A computer needs output devices to display the results of its processing. Different types of data are sent to different devices. Text and images are displayed on a computer screen. They can also be printed by a printer. Sound data is sent to speakers inside, or connected to, the computer. You can also connect headphones to a computer to listen to sounds.

Storage Devices

Because memory is temporary, a computer needs a secondary location for storing data permanently. Devices such as hard disk drives, **flash drives**, CDs/DVDs, and online storage are all popular types of secondary storage.

Technology@Home

A sudden loss of power that shuts down a computer may result in the loss of unsaved work. Users can prevent that loss by buying a backup device that runs a battery if the power shuts down. The battery can keep the computer running for 20 to 45 minutes, which gives the user enough time to save valuable data.

Think About It!

Think about what would be harmed by a loss of power. Which kinds of data listed below would suffer from a loss of power?

➢ data on a hard drive

➢ data on a DVD

➢ unsaved data in RAM

➢ data in ROM

➢ data on a CD-ROM encyclopedia

Figure 2.1.1 The motherboard houses all the chips and circuits a computer needs in order to function.

Making Computers Work

Objectives

- Explain the binary system used by computers.
- Describe how software is written and translated.
- Summarize the tasks of operating systems.
- Identify two leading operating systems and explain why compatibility is an issue.

As You Read

Outline Information   Use an outline as you read to help you organize information about how software makes computers work.

Key Terms

- ASCII
- character set
- compiler
- intepreter
- object code
- object-oriented programming
- procedural programming
- programmer
- screen-magnifier software
- source code
- Unicode

Digital Computing

The computers widely used today are digital machines. Each piece of information used in the computer is identified by a distinct number. As a result, the computer acts on each piece of data by comparing its value to the value of other data or by performing a mathematical operation on it.

The Binary World   Most computers are not just digital but binary, too. That is, they only recognize two possible values. Think of a television's power switch. It, too, is binary: The switch is either on or off. There are no other possibilities.

Computers break data into pieces called bits and give each bit a value of either 0 or 1. A byte is a group of bits—usually 8. Using 8 bits in different combinations, each byte can represent a different value. For example, one byte might be 00000000, another might be 01010101, and another might be 00110011. There are 256 possible combinations!

Data in Bytes   Every piece of data that a computer works on, therefore, must be expressed in 0s and 1s and organized into bytes.

Digitizing Text   Programmers use 0s and 1s arranged in 8-digit bytes to represent the letters of the alphabet and many standard punctuation marks. American Standard Code for Information Interchange (**ASCII**) is a common system, or **character set**, for coding letters that uses 8 bits. **Unicode**, which uses 16 bits, is another.

Software Provides Directions

How does a computer know what to do with data in digital form? Software gives it the instructions it needs. Experts called **programmers** write the instructions that become software. Programmers write these instructions, called **source code**, using a programming language.

Procedural or Object-Oriented Programming There are two basic categories of programming, procedural and object-oriented. **Procedural programming** uses step-by-step instructions to tell a computer what to do. Procedural programming languages include C, Fortran, Pascal, and Basic. **Object-oriented programming** provides rules for creating and managing objects, which are items that include both data and how to process the data. Object-oriented programming languages include Java and VBScript. Some programming combines the two. C++ is an example of a programming language that uses both procedural and object-oriented programming.

Compilers and Interpreters Special programs called **compilers** translate the source code into binary form, using only 0s and 1s. The result, called **object code**, can be read and acted on by a computer. Sometimes, programs called **interpreters** are used to translate the source code directly into actions, by-passing the need for a compiler.

Representing Data Some programming languages require the programmer to define a data type to variable data. Some common data types include string, which is a sequence of characters that does not contain numbers used for calculations; numeric, which is numbers or amounts that are used in calculations; character, which is text; integers, which represent whole numbers; and date, which is the method of coding dates.

By backing up your data, you make copies of data stored on your computer's hard drive to an external hard drive, USB flash drive, online storage service, or CDs/DVDs. Using an external hard drive with backup software or an online service lets you backup automatically. If you use CDs/DVDs or flash drives, you must back up data on your own.

Think About It!

Before deciding *how* to back up your hard drive, think about *why* it is important to back up. Sequence the importance of backing up each item in the list below using a scale of 1 (lowest) to 5 (highest):

- ➤ A program you can download from the Internet
- ➤ A report that you spent four hours on
- ➤ A file not used for a year
- ➤ Photos of friends
- ➤ Stored files of a game

Spotlight on...

GRACE MURRAY HOPPER

66 *[Everyone will have quick access to information] in the next generation—when our bright youngsters take over. I watched third-grade students. . . write programs in BASIC and debug them. They'll be able to handle the computers when they grow up. . . .* 99

Grace Murray Hopper

Grace Hopper was a talented mathematician who joined the Naval Reserve during World War II. She

worked on a computer the Navy was building, and she became the computer's first programmer. She also was a key figure in the development of compilers. Hopper's work helped make computers what they are today—tools that process text as easily as numbers.

Software Controls the System

Recall that the software that tells a computer how to do its work is the operating system, or OS. The OS does many different jobs:

- Working with peripherals: moving data and commands between the CPU and monitors, printers, and disk drives
- Managing data: finding the needed programs and files
- Using memory: storing data and programs in RAM or on the hard drive
- Coordinating data processing: doing many tasks at once without interfering with one another
- Providing the user interface: organizing and displaying the options you see on your screen when you turn on your computer

Systems Compatibility   The two most popular operating systems are Microsoft® Windows® and the Macintosh OS®. Both use text and images to represent data and programs. The Macintosh OS runs on Apple® computers. Earlier versions of Mac OS ran only on computers with Motorola® processors. The latest versions of Mac OS run on computers with either Motorola or Intel® processors. Windows also runs on computers that have Intel processors or processors that are made to work like Intel chips.

For many years, the two systems were not compatible. That is, programs written for one OS did not run on the other. Also, files saved in one OS had formats that could not be read by the other OS. Today, some programs are written for both systems. Most files can be written, saved, and read in formats usable in both systems. Also, utility programs can translate files that previously may have been unreadable.

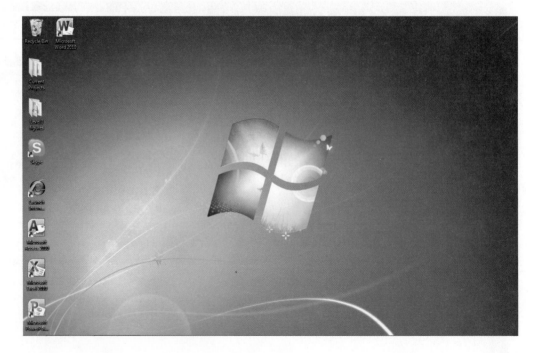

Figure 2.2.1 This is a Windows Vista desktop, which is the main starting place for working with Windows and programs.

Output Devices

Output is the results of the computer's processing. The output that users see or hear can lead them to give the computer new instructions for processing their data. Some output devices and features help make computers more accessible to users with disabilities.

Monitors Both text and images are displayed on the monitor. **Screen-magnifier software** can make images on the monitor much larger for people who have difficulty seeing. The program enlarges the area where the cursor is. The user can also change the colors on the monitor to make text easier to see.

Printers Another form of output for text and images is print. A high-quality output at a large font size may help some people with poor vision read printed text more easily. Braille printers can also provide output in a format some people with visual disabilities can read.

Speakers To hear recorded voices, sounds, and music, you need external speakers or headphones. Software lets you choose which recording to hear and adjust the volume. Windows has a feature called Show Sounds. When activated, this feature shows a visual symbol when it plays a sound and displays spoken words as text. This feature can help people who have hearing difficulties. Many programs can display audio as printed text so people with hearing difficulties can see the spoken words.

Purchasing and maintaining a computer system is costly for both individuals and companies. It is important to research all available options to make sure the investment will pay off in terms of productivity, ease of use, and efficiency.

Think About It!

Although the decision-making process is similar for both individuals and companies, there are some differences. Which of the following factors do you think is more important for an individual or for an organization?

➤ How much does it cost?

➤ Is it easy to use?

➤ Does it work with existing software and hardware?

➤ Does it meet current needs ?

➤ Will it meet future needs?

➤ Is it expandable?

➤ Does it come with a warranty?

➤ Is it easy to maintain?

➤ Is it durable?

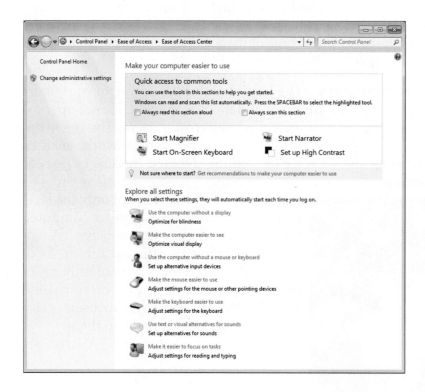

Figure 2.2.2 Operating systems such as Windows 7 offer Ease of Use settings for customizing the interface for people with special needs.

Group and Individual Computing

Objectives

- Compare and contrast different kinds of computers used in organizations.
- Compare and contrast different kinds of computers used by individuals.

As You Read

Compare and Contrast   Use a Venn diagram to help you compare and contrast information about the types of computers as you read the lesson.

🔑 Key Terms

- desktop computer
- handheld computer
- mainframe
- netbook
- server
- smart phone
- supercomputer
- tablet computer

A Dizzying Variety

Computers range in size from huge machines as big as a room to devices so small they can fit in your pocket. Each type of computer is suited to handling a particular set of jobs in particular settings. When thinking about this great variety of computers, it is helpful to look at them in two groups: those used by organizations and those used by individuals.

Computers for Organizations

Companies and other organizations use the full range of computers. Large organizations can afford the largest and most expensive machines, and such companies are more likely to need all the processing power that these huge machines have. Many companies also want some of their workers, such as salespeople, to have small handheld computers.

Supercomputers   The largest and most powerful computers can process huge amounts of data very quickly. These superfast scientific computers are called **supercomputers**. The organizations using supercomputers do very complex work, such as forecasting the weather or creating detailed models of nuclear reactions.

Supercomputers are not only the largest and most powerful type of computer, they are also the most expensive. A single supercomputer can cost hundreds of thousands of dollars or tens of millions of dollars. They are also extremely rugged and dependable systems, so users place constant heavy workloads on them.

Figure 2.3.1 Some organizations use very large computer systems and house them in their own special environments.

Mainframes   The **mainframe** is another type of computer used by government agencies and large corporations. Mainframes are designed so that many people can use the same secure data at once. For example, airline company employees use mainframes to store and process reservations. In this way, reservations agents and travel agents all around the world can locate and use the same information at the same time.

Minicomputers   Minicomputers are also known as midrange computers as they fall between mainframes and microcomputers (personal computers). However, today's microcomputers are so powerful that they have replaced minicomputers in most cases.

Many users connect to mainframes or minicomputers through terminals, a keyboard, and a monitor. This hardware, sometimes called a "dumb" terminal, can connect to a computer and use the computer's processing power and storage. The terminal cannot process or store the data on its own, however.

Servers   Many organizations connect their computers together in a network. All the computers that are part of the network are connected to a computer called a **server**. The server holds data and programs that people on the network can use on their personal computers. A computer connected to a network uses a special program to contact the server and get data from it. Unlike terminals, computers on a network can have their own disk storage, but the main source of data for the network is still the server.

Real-World Tech

The Intelligent Room   Some businesses are using a powerful new approach to working together called the Intelligent Room. The room looks like a normal conference room, but computer-controlled microphones and cameras placed around the room make sure that the speaker is always in view. This is especially helpful for video conferencing, in which a video of a meeting in one room is sent to another group of workers in another room. Screens mounted on the wall can be used to display data from computers simply by touching the screen.

Why is the camera's ability to follow the speaker useful for video conferencing?

Career Corner

Computer Engineer Designing compact, powerful machines like subnotebooks and PDAs is the work of computer engineers. They design and test components and then put them together to make sure they work properly. Engineers need to know software and programming as well as understand the workings of hardware. Demand for computer engineers is expected to be good in the coming years.

Computers for Individuals

Most individuals do not need as much computing power as organizations do. They typically choose from among four types of computers:

Workstations The most powerful and expensive personal computers are workstations. Architects, engineers, designers, and others who work with complex data use these machines for their power and speed.

Desktop Computers Most individuals use personal computers, or **desktop computers**, to do everyday jobs more quickly and easily. They are also used to connect to computer networks such as the Internet.

Portable Computers Some computers are powerful enough to do the work of desktop computers but can be easily moved. Laptop and notebook computers fit in a briefcase or backpack. Smaller still are **netbook** computers, also called subnotebooks or mini laptops. A mini netbook is only 10" across, but does not have a CD-ROM drive. **Tablet computers**, such as Apple's iPad, are also portable. The iPad2 measures only 9.56" × 7.47" and is only 1.5 pounds and ½" thick.

Handheld Computers Computers small enough to fit in your pocket are called **handheld computers**, personal digital assistants (PDAs), or, with phone service, a **smart phone**. Handhelds provide basic organizational features such as address/phone books, to do lists, and calendar functions, but can also be used with a wide variety of "apps" to run programs, play games, and interface with a PC.

Figure 2.3.2 The Apple iPad is an example of a portable computer.

Use the Vocabulary

Directions: *Match each vocabulary term in the left column with the correct definition in the right column.*

_____ **1.** command
_____ **2.** motherboard
_____ **3.** read-only memory
_____ **4.** programmer
_____ **5.** compiler
_____ **6.** supercomputer
_____ **7.** mainframe
_____ **8.** server
_____ **9.** desktop computer
_____ **10.** handheld computer

a. computer made for working with large amounts of data

b. instruction for the computer to do something

c. another name for a personal digital assistant

d. where the CPU is located

e. high-speed computer for complex work

f. another name for personal computer

g. set of chips that starts the computer when it is turned on

h. language that translates source code into binary form

i. writes instructions for a computer to follow

j. computer accessed by users on a network

Check Your Comprehension

Directions: *Determine the correct choice for each of the following.*

1. What would you most likely use a microphone to input?
   a. commands
   b. images
   c. sound
   d. text

2. Data from which part of a computer is lost when it is turned off?
   a. the CD-ROM
   b. the hard drive
   c. RAM
   d. ROM

3. What kinds of data use printers for output?
   a. text and commands
   b. text and images
   c. images and commands
   d. images and sounds

4. Which is an example of a binary number?
   a. 10011001
   b. −342
   c. 67439622
   d. .0000002

5. Which of the following is NOT a task performed by operating systems?
   a. controlling a printer
   b. managing memory
   c. coordinating how programs run
   d. compiling a program

6. What kind of machine is more powerful than a server?
   a. desktop computer
   b. portable computer
   c. mainframe
   d. handheld computer

Think Critically

Directions: *Answer the following questions.*

1. What are the advantages and disadvantage of using a portable computer versus a desktop computer?

2. Why do programmers have to carefully write every step in a process when writing instructions for a computer?

3. How would you bring files created in one operating system into another if they were not compatible?

4. Why do organizations link computers together more than individuals do?

5. Ed sells sweaters and shirts in a clothing store. Edna sells office machines to businesses in a three-state area. She works in her office one day a week, works at home one day a week, and travels to visit her customers three days a week. Which person is more likely to need a PDA for work? Why?

Extend Your Knowledge

Directions: *Choose one of the following projects. Complete the exercise on a separate sheet of paper.*

A. Make a chart to contrast different storage media. First, divide the chart into two columns, one for primary media and one for secondary. Then divide the section on secondary media into two parts to cover the two types. List each different component under the appropriate heading. For each component, list two key facts.

B. Collect three advertisements for home computer systems. List the components that are offered in each ad. Compare the three systems for their appropriateness for inputting and outputting text, images, and sounds. Compare their capacity to store data. Based on the features, write an explanation of which machine you think is best and why.

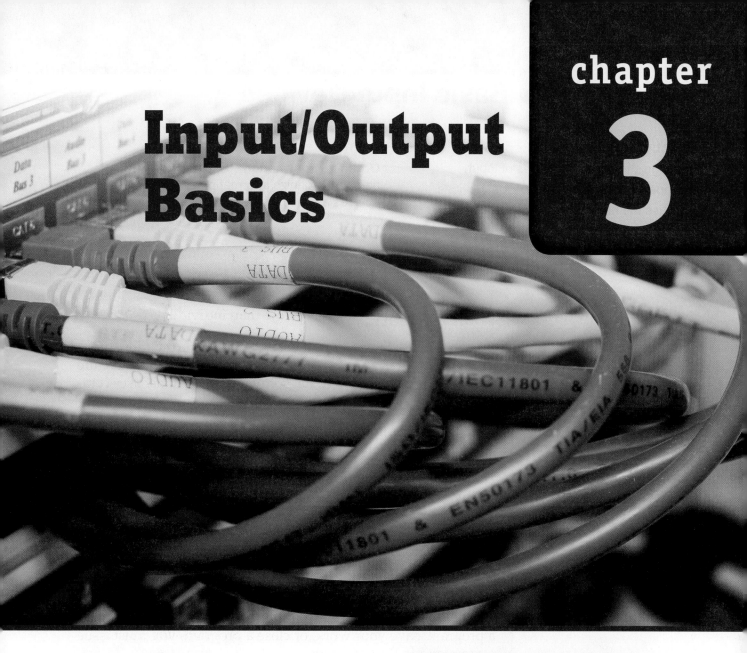

Input/Output Basics

Input and Output If you think of the computer as a person, its brain would be the central processing unit, or CPU. Like a brain, a CPU receives and organizes data from many different sources into useful information.

Also, like a person, a computer needs more than just a brain to work properly. It needs a way to receive the unorganized data and to show the results of its processing of the data. The brain receives data through the senses: sight, hearing, smell, taste, and touch. It shows the results of its processing of the data through speech, movement, and writing. The CPU receives its data from input devices such as the keyboard and mouse. It shows the results of its processing through output devices such as a monitor, printer, or speakers.

Chapter Outline

 Lesson 3–1

Basic Input Devices

 Lesson 3–2

Basic Output Devices

Basic Input Devices

Objectives

- Distinguish among four types of input.
- Compare and contrast basic input devices.
- Discuss the health risks of using some input devices.

As You Read

Organize Information   Use a concept web to help you organize information about basic input devices as you read.

 Key Terms

- command
- digital camera
- ergonomic
- pointer
- pointing device
- repetitive strain injury (RSI)
- scanner

What Is Input?

As you already learned, input is any kind of information, or instructions, that is entered into a computer's memory. There are four basic types of input: data, software instructions, user commands, and responses.

Data   Words, numbers, images, and sounds that you enter into a computer are data. This is the raw material that a computer processes.

Software Instructions   To perform any job, a computer must follow instructions from a software program. Software typically is installed from a CD onto the hard drive. Launching a program moves it into the computer's RAM. That makes the program available to the CPU—and to you.

User Commands   A **command** is an instruction that tells a software program what action to perform. For example, to open a program, save your work, or close a program, you must issue a command to the computer.

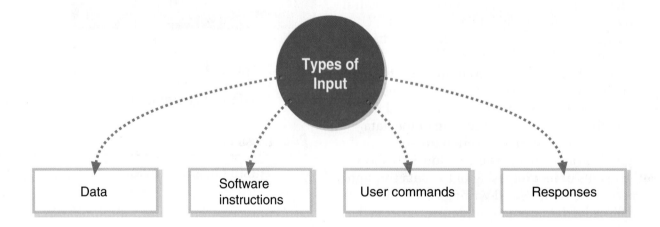

Responses Sometimes a program asks you to enter information or make a choice so that it can carry out a command or process data. For example, if you try to close a program without saving your work, the program will ask if you wish to save it. Before you can continue, you must input a response.

What Is an Input Device?

An input device is any hardware used to input data. Recall from Chapter 2 that two common input devices are the keyboard and the mouse. A mouse is a type of **pointing device**. Moving the mouse over a surface moves a **pointer** on the screen. Small computers, such as notebooks, often use a touchpad, or trackpad, as the pointing device. It is built into the computer. Moving your finger on the touchpad moves the pointer. There are also specialized input devices.

Joystick The joystick is a lever that can be moved in all directions to move objects on the screen. The programs that use the joystick the most are computer games or those that simulate flying a plane. Joysticks typically have buttons that are used to input commands.

Figure 3.1.1 Joysticks are often used for computer games and flight simulators.

Spotlight on...

DOUG ENGELBART

66 *We were looking for the best—the most efficient—device. We . . . said 'let's test them,' and determine the answer once-and-for-all. . . . It quickly became clear that the mouse outperformed all the [other devices].* 99

Doug Engelbart

In the 1960s, Doug Engelbart created the mouse—a device that could be used to move a cursor around a computer screen.

The first mouse was a crude wooden box with two round discs on the bottom and a button on the top. The long cord that connected it to a computer looked like a tail.

A visionary, Engelbart also thought computers could be used as writing machines, or word processors.

Figure 3.1.2 Specially designed keyboards, like this one, can reduce the risk of repetitive strain injuries.

Microphone   To input sounds, you can use a microphone or a sound card (inside the computer) to record and play back sounds.

Digital Cameras, Webcams, and Scanners   Digital cameras connect to the computer by a cable or a wireless link to input photos. When you video chat with a friend you're using a webcam, a small camera that either attaches to the computer monitor, sits on your desk, or—like Apple's iSight—is built into the computer. Webcams usually come with software that enables you to record video or stream the video on the Web. **Scanners** are devices that let you copy printed images into a computer and can be stand-alone or part of your printer. The scanner changes the printed image into a digital form.

Modem   A modem allows one computer to input data into another computer. Computers must be connected by cables or phone lines. Many people use modems to connect their computers to the Internet.

Health Risks of Some Input Devices

When you use a keyboard or mouse a lot, you make the same hand movements over and over again. This can cause damage to nerves in the hand. The problem is called **repetitive strain injury**, or **RSI**. New, **ergonomic**, keyboards have been designed to reduce RSI. Some people who suffer from this problem use a mouse controlled by foot pedals or some other kind of pointing device.

Basic Output Devices

Objectives

- Distinguish among the four types of output.
- Compare and contrast basic output devices.
- Explain how visual display systems work.
- Summarize printing technology.

As You Read

Outline Information   Use an outline format to help you organize information about output as you read.

What Is Output?

As discussed in Chapter 2, after a computer has processed data, it provides the results in the form of output. There are four types of output: text, graphics, video, and audio.

Text   Characters such as letters, symbols, and numbers are called text. To be considered text, the characters must be organized in a coherent way. For example, random letters on a page are not considered text, but paragraphs in a book report are text.

Graphics   Drawings, photographs, and other visual images are called graphics.

Video   Moving images are known as video. Images captured by a digital video camera, and which can be played on a computer, are one example of video. The use of animation is another example.

Audio   Sound output is called audio. This includes music or speech that the computer plays through its speakers or headphones.

Key Terms

- All-in-One printer
- cathode ray tube (CRT)
- impact printer
- liquid crystal display (LCD)
- nonimpact printer
- output device

Figure 3.2.1 This is a CRT monitor—an output device for displaying text and graphics.

Technology @ School

Some schools have a special kind of monitor that is an educational tool. The SMART Board™ allows teachers and students to project text and images onto a special monitor mounted on the wall. Not only is the image visible to all students, but it can also be manipulated and changed, making learning more interactive.

Think About It!

Think about ways the SMART Board can be used at school. For which examples below do you think the SMART Board would be useful?

➤ solve math problems

➤ play music

➤ edit text

➤ display reports

➤ meet in groups

What Is an Output Device?

An **output device** is any piece of hardware that displays or plays back the result of computer processing in one of the four forms of output. For example, monitors and printers create a visual record of the processing completed by the computer.

Monitors

The computer displays information on a monitor, a hardware device that receives and shows images on a screen. The images the monitor displays change as the computer processes data.

CRTs One type of monitor is the **cathode ray tube**, or **CRT**. In a CRT, the monitor receives electrical signals from the computer. The signals cause "guns" in the CRT to shoot a stream of electrons at the back of the screen. The electrons strike materials called phosphors, which begin to glow. The glowing phosphors appear as points of light on the screen.

Color monitors have three electron guns, each one shooting a beam of a different color: red, blue, or green. CRTs today are now capable of producing thousands of colors, and they are affordable. However, these monitors are not only heavy and take up a lot of desk space, but they also heat up easily.

LCDs Portable computers, like notebooks, use the lighter **liquid crystal display**, or **LCD**. In an LCD, two transparent surfaces are placed on either side of a layer of cells containing tiny crystals. Electrical signals sent to the crystals cause them to form images on the surface.

LCDs use less power than CRTs and can even be operated just using batteries. They are becoming less expensive and more common on desktops. Also, there are now two different techniques for producing color: thin film transistor (TFT) and passive matrix technology. TFT produces sharper color and images, so it is becoming the standard.

Printers

A printer makes a paper copy of the display shown on a monitor. The most common types of printers are nonimpact printers, which have made impact printers almost obsolete.

Nonimpact Printers Most computer users today use these inkjet and laser printers to produce paper copies. Inkjet printers make images by spraying a fine stream of ink onto the paper. Laser printers use a powder called toner and operate like a copier machine. Heat fuses the toner to the paper to create the image. Laser printers create more crisp images than inkjet. Both inkjet and laser printers are available in **All-in-One** versions that add fax, copier, and scanner capabilities at a very low cost.

Impact Printers Dot matrix printers are a kind of impact printer that uses hammers or pins to press an ink-covered ribbon. They are noisy and the image quality is poor, but some are still used in businesses to provide copies of multi-part forms, like invoices.

Figure 3.2.2 An inkjet printer is a good choice for printing photographs.

Use the Vocabulary

Directions: *Match each vocabulary term in the left column with the correct definition in the right column.*

_____ **1.** command
_____ **2.** pointer
_____ **3.** output device
_____ **4.** digital camera
_____ **5.** scanner
_____ **6.** repetitive strain injury
_____ **7.** All-in-One printer
_____ **8.** liquid crystal display
_____ **9.** impact printer
_____ **10.** nonimpact printer

a. produces images by sending electrical signals to crystals

b. any piece of hardware that displays or plays back the result of computer processing

c. device with hammers or pins that strike a ribbon to leave ink on paper

d. lets you input printed images into a computer

e. a printer that contains fax, copier, and scanner capabilities

f. follows a mouse's movements

g. device such as an inkjet or laser printer

h. takes photographs that a computer can read

i. condition caused by making the same movements again and again

j. instruction to a software program to take an action

Check Your Comprehension

Directions: *Determine the correct choice for each of the following.*

1. Which type of input provides answers to questions issued by programs?
   a. commands
   b. data
   c. responses
   d. software

2. Which device can be used to connect a computer to the Internet?
   a. keyboard
   b. modem
   c. pointing device
   d. scanner

3. Which of the following devices can be designed to reduce the problem of RSIs?
   a. scanner
   b. digital camera
   c. monitor
   d. keyboard

4. What do output devices provide?
   a. data to be processed
   b. software code
   c. text and images only
   d. results of processing

5. Which of the following is NOT descriptive of a CRT?
   a. heavy
   b. uses little power
   c. heats up easily
   d. affordable

6. What kind of output device would NOT be used to output images?
   a. CRT
   b. LCD
   c. printer
   d. speaker

Think Critically

Directions: *Answer the following questions.*

1. Why are microphones or digital cameras unlikely to cause the damage that is found in repetitive strain injury?

2. Are you likely to use a joystick to complete schoolwork? Why or why not?

3. What type(s) of monitor(s) do use at school? What are the advantages and disadvantages of the different types of monitors?

4. How is video similar to ordinary graphics? How is it different?

5. Why have nonimpact printers all but replaced impact printers?

Extend Your Knowledge

Directions: *Choose one of the following projects. Complete the exercise on a separate sheet of paper.*

A. Open a word-processing program. Use the keyboard to input the definition of the word "Text" on page 31. Input the paragraph a total of five times. Each time you do so, time yourself. Print the five paragraphs. Compare the five times. Determine whether you were able to type faster and more accurately with practice.

B. Open a word-processing program. Find a file that you created and saved previously. Open the file. Use both the keyboard and the mouse to move around in the document and to print it. Write a paragraph explaining which device you thought was easier to work with and why.

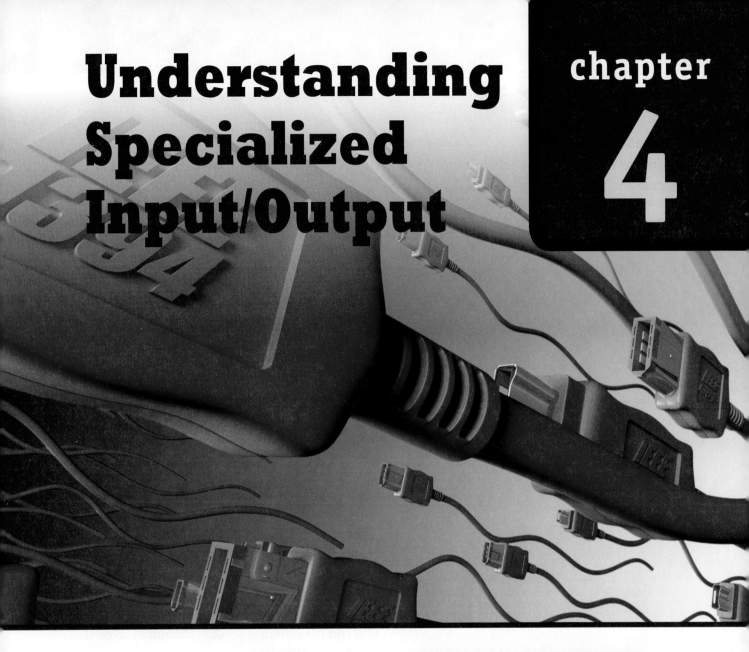

Understanding Specialized Input/Output

From Text to Moving Pictures Modern personal computers work in basically the same way that early personal computers did. Both perform the same four operations: input, processing, storage, and output. Both turn different sources of data into useful information. There is a major difference between what earlier and more recent computers can do, however.

Early personal computers could work with text and numbers. Today's computers can also handle different types of data, such as still images, sound, and video. Hardware makers have designed new devices to allow users to input data and output information in new ways. These devices have taken computers from the still and silent world of text and numbers into a dazzling multimedia world of sound, images, and motion.

Chapter Outline

 Lesson 4–1

Specialized Input Devices

 Lesson 4–2

Specialized Output Devices

Specialized Input Devices

Objectives

- Explain how sound cards process sound.
- Compare and contrast traditional and digital cameras.
- Compare digital cameras, scanners, and digital video cameras.

As You Read

Organize Information   Use a concept web to help you organize information about devices used to input sound, still images, and video as you read.

🔑 Key Terms

- compress
- digital video camera
- fax machine
- optical character recognition (OCR)
- video capture card

Inputting Sound

As you learned in Chapter 3, the microphone is the most basic device for inputting sound into a computer. You use it for all types of sound, including music, narration, and speech for voice recognition software. Microphones capture sounds in analog form—as a series of rapidly changing waves or vibrations. To be usable by a computer, sounds must be in digital form, that is, the waves must be converted to binary code (1s and 0s) that the computer can recognize. The sound card does this work.

A sound card is a circuit board that processes sounds in multiple ways. First, it digitizes sounds by changing them from analog to digital form. Then, it processes the digital sounds by following a set of built-in instructions. For example, it can prepare the digital sound files for use with voice recognition software. Sometimes the sound card reduces the size of sound files by compressing the data. That way, the files take up less space in memory. Finally, the sound card reverses the digitizing process so you can play analog sounds through the computer's speakers.

Figure 4.1.1 A sound card handles the audio-processing tasks in a computer.

Inputting Still Images

There are several different ways to input still images into a computer. The most popular include facsimile (fax) machines, digital cameras, and scanners.

Facsimile Machines A **fax machine**, or facsimile machine, scans printed documents and sends them over phone lines to another fax machine. Most home printers now have fax capabilities, so while fax machines are still used in businesses, individuals are less likely to have stand-alone fax machines.

Digital Cameras A digital camera, like a traditional camera, takes pictures. In a traditional camera, light enters the lens and strikes a piece of film coated with chemicals that are sensitive to light. The chemicals produce an image on the film. In a digital camera, a computer chip takes the information from the lens and records it as pixels, or small dots, that form the image. A digital camera has memory to store the pictures you take.

Some digital cameras store images on a memory card that can be removed. If a computer has the correct device, it can read the images from the memory card. Many digital cameras can connect to a computer via a cable or wireless link. When the camera is connected, the computer treats it like a disk drive and the pictures can be copied to the computer.

The Arts A digital camera can take pictures that use from 4 to 12 million dots (pixels) to make the picture. The more dots it uses, the sharper the image is. But more dots also take up more space on the memory card where the pictures are stored in the camera.

Photographers can choose to take photos of lesser quality to save space. They can also delete photos from the camera's memory to make space for new ones.

Figure 4.1.2 Digital cameras capture and store images electronically. Most smart phones have a built-in digital camera. Apple's iPhone 4 smart phone (left) and Cannon PowerShot 10 Megapixel digital camera (right) are shown below.

Technology @ Work

Scientists use an input device called a sensor to record many different kinds of data. Sensors can detect physical phenomenon, such as humidity, air pressure, and temperature.

Think About It!

For which examples below could a sensor be used?

➤ weather forecasts

➤ climate control

➤ monitor of medical patients

➤ work by robots

Scanners Photos taken by a traditional camera, drawings, or other printed documents can be digitized by using a scanner. Scanners shine a light onto the material to be copied and change the image into pixels. This creates a digital image that can be input.

Most scanners have **optical character recognition**, or **OCR**, software. When you scan printed text using this software, the text is turned into a digital file. In this way, you can input printed text, including handwriting, without having to type it.

There are different types of scanners:

- With a sheetfed scanner, you insert the pages you want copied and the scanner pulls them through one at a time.

- Flatbed scanners work more like copy machines. You lay material on a flat glass panel to make the copy. All-in-one printers have flatbed scanner capability.

- Handheld scanners are portable models that you hold in your hand. They are useful for copying small originals.

Inputting Video

Most computers today can show full-motion videos as well as still images. Like all other forms of input, the videos must be in digital form. **Digital video cameras** record moving images in digital form.

To convert analog videos to digital format, a computer needs a **video capture card**. Like a sound card, this type of circuit board changes video images into a digital file. These cards also **compress** files so they occupy less disk space.

Real-World Tech

Crossing the Line There is another use for video capture that is strictly illegal. Some computer users digitize movies, pay-per-view events, and television shows and post them on Web sites. People can visit the sites, download the shows, and watch them for free. This breaks copyright law, which protects the rights of people who create works of art, such as books, songs, and movies.

Why would the government pass laws to protect the rights of authors, songwriters, and movie directors regarding the sale of their works?

Specialized Output Devices

Objectives

- Distinguish among different video adapters.
- Compare and contrast different printers.
- Compare and contrast other output devices.
- Identify kinds of audio output.

As You Read

Gather Information Use a chart to help you gather information about output and output devices used for still images, video, and sound as you read.

Video Adapters

The images you see on your monitor are created by a **video adapter**. The adapter is a circuit board that receives data from an operating system or software application. It changes that data into electrical currents and sends them to the monitor. In a color monitor, the amount of current sent by the video adapter determines the color the monitor will produce. Like a sound card, a video adapter processes data so that the computer's CPU can take care of other jobs. It also has its own memory, called **video memory**, or **VRAM**, to free up space in the computer's memory.

Special Video Adapters Some video adapters send images to the monitor very quickly. They are called video accelerators.

Key Terms

- data projector
- high-definition television (HDTV)
- Musical Instrument Digital Interface (MIDI)
- OLED
- speech synthesis software
- thermal transfer printer
- video adapter
- video memory (VRAM)

Figure 4.2.1 The video adapter processes video data for display on the monitor, allowing the CPU and RAM to handle other tasks.

Most computers today have highly specialized video adapters, called 3-D video adapters. Images on a monitor have only two dimensions—height and width. 3-D video adapters add a third dimension to an image—depth.

Outputting Images with Printers

As you learned in Chapter 3, image quality varies based on which type of printer is used to output an image. Both impact and non-impact printers create images by printing tiny dots on the paper. Inkjet and laser printers have much higher print quality. Therefore, they are more often used for printing graphic images.

The best printer for printing color images is a **thermal transfer printer**. These printers use heat to transfer color dyes or inks onto paper. Thermal transfer printers do not make pictures out of tiny dots. Instead, the colors actually blend together on the paper. These printers only work with glossy paper.

Outputting Video

You can use three types of devices to output video.

Data Projectors You may be familiar with **data projectors**, which show a computer's video output on a projection screen so many people can view it at once. These projectors are often used to display presentations for educational or business meetings.

Digital light processing, or DLP, projectors use millions of tiny mirrors to create a very sharp image. That image is then projected through a lens and onto a screen. Because the image they produce is so sharp, DLP projectors can be used with large audiences. They can even be used in brightly lit rooms.

Televisions Some devices let you send video from a computer to a television, but the image is usually very poor. As **high-definition television**, or **HDTV**, has become more widely used, more people are using their television as an output device. HDTV uses only digital audio and video and produces a much sharper image than regular television.

Figure 4.2.2 Digital television systems produce much higher quality output than standard televisions.

Headsets   A headset, which has two LCD panels, is worn over the head. The computer sends video images to each panel. To the person wearing the headset, it seems as if he or she is walking in a three-dimensional space.

A similar but larger device is the Cave Automated Virtual Environment, or CAVE. This is a room in which three-dimensional images are shown on the floor, walls, and ceiling. A person in the room wears 3-D glasses. The glasses and images create the illusion of interacting in three-dimensions.

Outputting Sound

To output sound to headphones or speakers, your computer must have a sound card and speakers. The sound card changes digital sound files stored in the computer's memory into an electrical current. It sends that current to the speakers to produce audio output.

The sound a computer can produce depends on the computer's software. Two kinds of software allow audio output:

- **Speech synthesis software** allows the computer to read text files aloud.
- **Musical Instrument Digital Interface (MIDI)** software allows the computer to create music. With this software, you can send instructions to a digital musical instrument called a synthesizer. This device then sounds the notes it has been instructed to play.

Spotlight on...

RAYMOND KURZWEIL

66 The Kurzweil Reading Machine was a breakthrough that changed my life. With the Kurzweil Reading Machine, I could read anything I wanted with complete privacy . . . . It gave blind people the one thing that everyone treasures, which is independence. 99

Stevie Wonder
Singer and songwriter

Raymond Kurzweil's reading machine turned printed text into spoken language, opening a world of information to people with visual impairments.

Kurzweil also devised the first electronic musical instrument. After Kurzweil spoke with singer and songwriter Stevie Wonder, he had the idea of making a better music synthesizer. Kurzweil's synthesizer could make the music of an entire orchestra.

Use the Vocabulary

Directions: *Match each vocabulary term in the left column with the correct definition in the right column.*

_____ **1.** compress

_____ **2.** fax machine

_____ **3.** optical character recognition

_____ **4.** digital video camera

_____ **5.** video capture card

_____ **6.** video adapter

_____ **7.** VRAM

_____ **8.** thermal transfer printer

_____ **9.** speech synthesis software

_____ **10.** MIDI

a. turns text into audio

b. prints high-quality output suitable for photos

c. software that lets the computer play like an electronic instrument

d. software that scans text and turns it into a digital file

e. memory on a video adapter

f. to make files smaller

g. captures still images, which are then shown rapidly

h. controls video output to the monitor

i. converts analog video into digital

j. scans documents and sends them over phone lines

Check Your Comprehension

Directions: *Complete each sentence with information from the chapter.*

1. To play sound that has been stored in a computer, it must be converted to _____ format.

2. Digital photos can be input from a camera by transporting them on a disk or sending them to the computer using a(n) _____.

3. _____ software allows people to scan text instead of rekeying it.

4. Photos that haven't been taken with a digital camera can still be input into a computer using either a fax machine or a(n) _____.

5. The amount of current that a video adapter sends to the monitor determines the _____ display on the monitor.

6. Three-dimensional graphics include height, width, and _____.

7. DLP projectors are better than LCD projectors for giving a presentation to many people because the _____ appear sharper.

8. Standard printers create output by printing tiny _____ on paper.

9. Headsets and the room-sized _____ create virtual three-dimensional environments.

10. Audio can be output to headphones or _____.

Think Critically

Directions: *Answer the following questions.*

1. What is one advantage of having memory on a video card dedicated to displaying graphics?

2. Why are sound and graphics files compressed?

3. Suppose someone had to scan ten images. Which kind of scanner would require him or her to stay closer to the machine as it is working, a sheetfed or flatbed? Why?

4. Would a 3-D graphics adapter be needed on a machine used mostly for word processing and spreadsheets? Why or why not?

5. Which kind of printer would be better for printing a report for school that included two or three photographs, an inkjet or a thermal transfer printer? Why?

Extend Your Knowledge

Directions: *Choose one of the following projects. Complete the exercise on a separate sheet of paper.*

A. Divide a sheet of paper into two columns, creating a T-chart. Write the heading *Standard System* over the left column. Write the heading *Graphics System* over the right column. In each column, list the input and output components you would include if you were setting up these two computer systems. Include the types of output cards you would want. Assume that the standard system will be used for word processing and spreadsheet work. Assume that the graphics system will be used for high-quality photographs.

B. Find out what kind of sound your computer can output. If possible, output audio and then determine what kinds of software your computer used to output the sound. Discuss for whom audio output is an advantage and when this feature is a necessity.

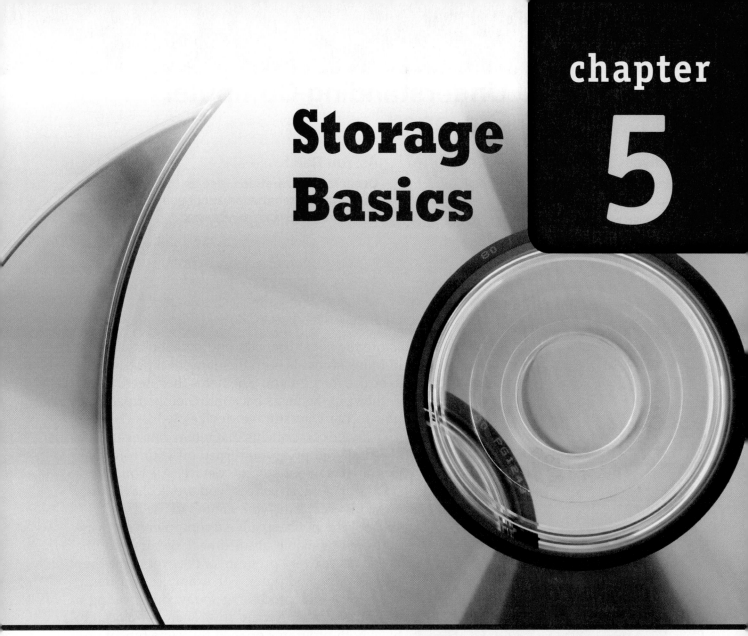

Storage Basics

How Do Computers Store Data?

Computer storage is like the backpack you bring to school. Both store things until you are ready to use them. Your backpack stores books and school supplies; most computers store software and data.

Computer storage devices can store information for long periods of time. This lets you create a file today, save it, and then use it again in the future. In this chapter, you will learn why storage is necessary and how information is stored. You will also examine some of the storage devices you are likely to find on today's computers.

Chapter Outline

 Lesson 5–1

Understanding Computer Storage

 Lesson 5–2

Classifying Storage Devices

 Lesson 5–3

Common Storage Devices

Understanding Computer Storage

Objectives

- Explain the need for storage devices for computers.
- Distinguish between memory and storage.
- Distinguish between storage devices and media.

As You Read

Organize Information   Use an outline to help you organize information about computer storage and storage devices as you read.

🔑 Key Terms

- Basic Input/Output System (BIOS)
- file
- memory
- storage device

Computer Storage Devices

Where do you store the books, pencils, and notebooks that you need for school? Many students keep them in a backpack. When class is about to begin, they pull out the items they need. When class is finished, they put the items back into their backpacks.

This is similar to the way **storage devices** work. They are the computer's hardware components that retain data even after the power is turned off. Suppose you turned off your computer without saving your work to a storage device. All your work would be lost. Without storage devices, you would have to re-create all of your work every time you wanted to use it.

Why not keep all of a computer's software and data available at all times? Because no one needs to use every program or file every time they work on the computer. For example, you might be doing word processing today, but creating a computer drawing tomorrow. There is no need to have both programs open at the same time if you are not using both of them.

Files   A computer stores data and program instructions in files. A **file** is a collection of related information or program code, which has been given a unique name.

Figure 5.1.1 Like a backpack, a computer's storage devices hold things until you need them.

The type of file people most often use is called a document. A document can be any kind of file that a user can create, save, and edit. For example, you can use a word-processing program to create a letter, which is one type of document. A digital photo is another type of document.

System Startup Computer storage devices are a key part of a computer's startup process. Without a storage device to hold startup information permanently, a computer would not know what to do when you turned it on.

When you start a computer, it looks for information that tells it what to do. The **Basic Input/Output System**, or **BIOS**, is a set of programs that tells the computer equipment how to start up. When a computer is built, the BIOS is set up with this basic information. The BIOS is permanently stored in special memory chips called read-only memory, or ROM. Usually, the BIOS instructs the computer to look for the operating system. The operating system contains all the commands required to run the computer. It provides the tools to operate the system and to run programs.

Memory and Storage

When people talk about computer **memory**, they usually mean a set of chips that acts as a temporary workspace in the computer. This memory, called random access memory, or RAM, stores data and program instructions needed by the CPU.

RAM and ROM are different in two important ways, as the following chart shows. First, ROM stores its contents permanently, even when the computer is turned off. RAM, on the other hand, only stores its contents temporarily; if the computer loses power, RAM's contents are lost.

Second, because ROM stores instructions that are needed only by the computer, you seldom need to think about ROM or the information it holds. But RAM holds data and programs while they are being used. As you use the computer, you constantly work with the contents of RAM.

Connections

Science Nanotechnology is a field of science and technology that studies how to make things by arranging individual atoms and molecules. Nanotechnology has contributed to advances in computer technology.

For example, nanotechnology has made it possible for computer hard drives to hold ever larger amounts of data. They can do so because the parts that retrieve and record data—called the read/write heads—are made from an extremely thin layer of magnetic material. The material is less than one billionth of a meter thick, or close to 7,000 times thinner than a strand of a spider web.

ROM and RAM

	Storage	Holds
ROM	Permanent	Startup instructions and configuration information for the computer
RAM	Temporary	Program instructions and data that are being used by the CPU

Storage Versus Memory   New computer users sometimes get confused about temporary memory (RAM) and permanent storage (disks and disk drives). They will say "memory" when they actually mean to say "storage." To avoid this problem, remember two key differences between storage and memory:

- The two work differently. Remember that RAM uses chips to temporarily store information. These chips depend on a constant supply of power to keep their contents; when the power is lost, the chips lose their contents. Storage uses different methods to store data permanently, so it isn't lost when the power is turned off.

- A PC has more storage capacity than memory. Even though some PCs have several gigabytes of RAM, their hard drives will be many times larger.

Storage Media and Storage Devices

Storage has two components: storage media and storage devices.

Storage Media   In terms of storage, a medium is an object that physically holds data or program instructions. Flash drives, magnetic tapes, compact discs, and DVDs are examples of storage media. (The word *media* is the plural of *medium*.)

Storage Devices   A storage device is a piece of hardware that holds the storage medium, sends data to the medium, and retrieves data from the medium. Hard drives, flash drives, and CD and DVD drives are all examples of storage devices.

Figure 5.1.2 Nearly all PCs use the storage devices and media shown here.

CD-ROM drives are storage devices. USB ports accept flash drives.

Flash drives, DVDs, and compact discs are examples of storage media.

A hard drive is a storage device with its storage media built into it.

Classifying Storage Devices

Objectives

- Explain how computer storage devices are classified.
- Compare and contrast primary, secondary, and archival storage devices.
- Describe the categories of storage devices.

As You Read

Classify Information   Use a spider map to help you classify storage devices as you read.

Hierarchy of Storage Devices

Computer storage devices are sometimes classified in a hierarchical structure—that is, primary or secondary.

Primary Storage Devices   The term **primary storage** is sometimes used to describe the main memory, or RAM, in a computer. This is because when the CPU needs data or instructions, it looks in memory before looking anywhere else.

Most knowledgeable computer users, however, avoid using the term *storage* when talking about RAM. This is because RAM works very differently from storage devices such as disks or tapes. RAM also loses any data it contains when the computer is turned off, while disks and tapes can hold data permanently.

Secondary Storage Devices   The term **secondary storage** is sometimes used to describe devices that can store data permanently, such as a hard drive, flash drive, compact disc, DVD, or external hard drive. This is because the computer will look for data on one of these devices if the data is not in RAM.

Many kinds of secondary storage devices can hold much more data than a computer's RAM can. For example, while most of today's PCs have from 128 megabytes to 1 gigabyte of RAM, they have hard drives that can store up to several hundred gigabytes.

Because they can store data permanently (or until you erase it), secondary storage devices are sometimes called **archival storage devices**. This refers to the fact that you can store data on a drive or disk and then put it away for a long time, only using it again when you need it.

Key Terms

- archival storage device
- optical storage device
- primary storage
- random access storage device
- read/write device
- read-only device
- secondary storage
- sequential storage device
- smart phones

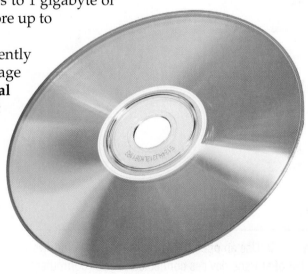

Figure 5.2.1 Compact discs and digital video discs are popular storage media.

You probably use a variety of storage devices in your home. Some of these may be computerized, while others are not.

Think About It!

Some of the devices listed below are based on read-only technology, while others are based on read/write technology. Which storage devices in the list do you think are based on read-only technology?

➢ Smart phone

➢ CD-ROM drive

➢ CD burner

➢ DVD-ROM drive

Categories of Storage Devices

Storage devices (but not RAM) are divided into three categories. Each category has two options based on the device.

Read-Only Versus Read/Write   A **read-only device** can only read data from the storage medium. You cannot change the data on the medium or save new data onto it. A CD-ROM drive is an example of a read-only device, because it does not have the capability to write data onto a disc.

The media used with read-only devices come with data already saved on them. Music CDs or software programs on CDs are CD-Rs. Your CD-ROM drive will be able to play the music or read the program instructions from the disc, but you can't change the disc's contents. Standard DVD players are another example of a read-only device.

A **read/write device** not only can read data from the storage medium, but can write data onto the medium, as well. These devices let you read data from a disk or tape, make changes to the data, and save new data onto the medium. Hard drives, USB flash drives, CD-Rewritable drives (CD-RW), and DVD-RAM drives are commonly used examples of read/write devices.

Figure 5.2.2 Use an operating system such as Windows 7 to view a list of storage devices connected to your computer.

Sequential Versus Random Access   When equipped with a tape drive, business computers can store data on a long piece of tape, similar to an old-fashioned cassette tape. A tape drive is an example of a **sequential storage device**, which requires the computer to scan from the beginning of the medium to the end until it finds the data it needs. While cheaper and slower than other types of storage, the highest capacity tape cartridges can hold five terabytes of uncompressed data. Because it can take several minutes to locate a piece of data on a high-capacity tape, tapes are used chiefly by businesses that want to back up their computer systems—often after the business day is over.

A **random access storage device** lets a computer go directly to the needed information. The device does not have to search the entire medium to find data. For this reason, random access storage devices are much faster, and more expensive, than sequential devices. A hard drive is an example of a random access storage device.

Magnetic Versus Optical Storage   Magnetic storage devices are specially treated disks or tapes, such as those mentioned above, that record information using magnetically sensitive materials. These devices use electricity to shift magnetic particles so they form a pattern that the computer reads and stores as information. Common magnetic storage devices include hard drives and tape drives

Other storage devices use laser beams to read information that has been stored on the reflective surface of a disc. These are called **optical storage devices**. Popular types of optical storage devices for computers include CD-ROM and DVD-ROM drives.

Technology @ School

In addition to hardware, software, and peripherals, schools use storage devices such as hard drives and CD-ROMs/DVDs. Some schools have a dedicated computer "lab," but more and more schools have computers in every classroom. It's important for all students to treat computer equipment with care and use good, respectful conduct when doing tasks on school—or any—computers.

Think About It!

Rate the computer equipment that you think is most sensitive to mishandling and needs the most care. On a scale of 1 to 5, use 1 for most sensitive and 5 for least.

➤ CD-ROM/DVD

➤ Flash drive

➤ Hard drive

➤ Power cord

➤ Laser printer

Spotlight on...

HIGH-CAPACITY PORTABLE STORAGE

Devices such as Apple's iPod Touch, Microsoft's Zune HD, and Sony's X-Series Walkman function as both MP3 players and as high-capacity, portable storage devices.

By plugging them into a computer, you can use these tiny storage devices to download files or transfer information from one computer to another. They can store 32 GB of data. (That's at least 7,000 songs or up to 40 hours of continuous video!) Yet, they are the size of a deck of cards and weigh 2–4 ounces, and they are getting smaller in size and larger in storage all the time.

Smart phones, such as Apple's iPhone or Motorola's Droid, offer storage capabilities along with phone service.

Common Storage Devices

Objectives

- Differentiate between internal and external storage devices.
- List commonly used magnetic storage devices.
- Summarize optical storage options.

As You Read

Classify Information   Use a T-chart to help you classify information about magnetic and optical storage devices as you read.

Key Terms

- CD-ROM drive
- hard drive

Internal and External Storage Devices

Storage devices can be installed in your computer or connected to it. A storage device installed inside your computer is called an internal storage device. One that is positioned outside your computer is referred to as an external storage device.

Magnetic Storage Devices

The most common magnetic storage device installed in computers is a **hard drive**. You cannot see the hard drive because it is installed inside your computer. Often, a small flashing light on the front of a computer shows when the hard drive is in use. Hard drives hold a great deal of data, but they are not portable.

External Magnetic Devices   Other forms of magnetic storage devices include a variety of USB- or firewire-connected external hard drives. These can hold up to as much as 8 terabytes of data, and they are portable. External drives communicate with the computer via a high-speed interface cable. By using the external hard drive with an automatic backup program, like the Mac's TimeMachine, computer users have peace of mind. They know their data is always recoverable if their computer crashes or is hit by a virus.

Figure 5.3.1 If you removed your PC's internal hard drive, it would look something like this.

Magneto-Optical (MO) Drives One of the most popular methods of data storage for many businesses, this type of drive combines both magnetic and optical drive technologies. A magneto-optical drive uses a removable disk that is inserted via a slot in the front of the drive. These drives can be internal or external. Their disks can store several gigabytes of information.

Online Storage Many online—or cloud—storage sites are available where you can store files on a network server at a remote location. You access your data by logging in through the Internet using a secure password. Some programs, including Microsoft Office 2010, come with free online storage space. You can also pay a storage service provider (SSP) for space. Online storage offers these three benefits: 1) it is expandable; 2) it allows you to share files with others; and 3) data stored in a remote location is protected if your computer is stolen or damaged.

Capacities of Common Storage Devices

Device	Capacity
Internal hard drive	500 GB and more
External hard drive (USB or Firewire connection)	500 GB–8 TB and more
MP3 player	16 GB–64 GB and more
Smart phones	64 GB flash storage
Magneto-Optical (MO) drives	100 MB–several GB
Flash memory cards and drives	4 GB–32 GB and more
CD-ROM	650 MB–700 MB
DVD	9.5 GB

Figure 5.3.2 A USB flash drive has a USB connector, a flash memory chip, a mass storage controller, and a crystal oscillator that allow the device to communicate with the computer.

Flash Memory Storage Devices

Flash media use a non-magnetic storage medium called flash memory. Flash memory is a special kind of storage used in ROM chips within your computer itself to store basic information about the computer's configuration. It is also used in memory cards and memory sticks for digital cameras that require removable, reusable storage and in USB flash drives (also called jump, pen, and key drives). Flash drives connect to the computer through a USB (universal serial bus) port.

Most removable flash memory devices include a chip that stores data and a microcontroller that permits the operating

Businesses protect their data by backing up their saved files. Experts recommend having two backups—one at the worksite and one in a different location.

Think About It!

Think about why a business might need to store its backups at a completely different site. Which disasters listed below might destroy a backup if it were kept on-site?

➤ fire

➤ flood

➤ earthquake

➤ break-in

➤ tornado

system to communicate with the chip. As the technology of flash memory improves, the capacity of flash devices increases significantly. Early flash devices only held 32–256 MB, but capacities of 32 GB are now available. The small size, increasing capacity, and ease of connection of these removable devices make them widely used.

Optical Storage Devices

Optical storage devices store data by etching tiny pits onto a disc. A laser then scans the disc and changes the data into a form the computer can work with. CDs and DVDs are the most common types of optical storage media. On a PC, a button on the front of the drive opens a tray on which you insert a CD. You push the button to close the tray so you can read the disc's contents. On Macs the **CD-ROM drive** is simply a slot into which you insert a disc, and you can eject it electronically by moving the disc icon into the "trash."

Standard CD-ROM and DVD drives can only read data stored on an optical disc. Only optical drives labeled CD-R, CD-RW, or DVD/CD-RW can be used to record data onto blank discs.

A standard CD can store 650 megabytes of data, or around 74 minutes of audio. Newer CDs can store 700 megabytes of data, or about 80 minutes of audio. Digital video discs can store about 4.7 gigabytes of data on each side. These discs are used for storing programs, games, data, and movies.

Figure 5.3.3 CDs and DVDs are popular components in both computers and home entertainment centers.

Use the Vocabulary

Directions: *Match each vocabulary term in the left column with the correct definition in the right column.*

_____ **1.** storage device
_____ **2.** memory
_____ **3.** primary storage
_____ **4.** secondary storage
_____ **5.** read/write device
_____ **6.** random-access storage device
_____ **7.** optical storage device
_____ **8.** hard drive
_____ **9.** read-only device
_____ **10.** CD-ROM drive

a. temporary workspace on a computer

b. sometimes used when referring to a computer's RAM

c. uses laser to read information

d. users access from and save information to this type of device

e. common secondary storage device

f. computer component that retains data even after power is shut off

g. storage device that lets computer go directly to the needed information

h. read-only optical device

i. can only read data from the storage medium

j. any type of storage device that holds data permanently; not RAM

Check Your Comprehension

Directions: *Complete each sentence with information from the chapter.*

1. Storage devices _____ information even when a computer is turned off.

2. Information saved as a(n) _____ is identified by a unique name.

3. The _____ is a set of programs that directs a computer to start up.

4. RAM stores its contents _____ and is cleared when the computer is shut down.

5. A computer's BIOS is usually stored in a special memory chip, called _____.

6. Apple's iPod or Microsoft's HD Zune are examples of _____ that store data in the popular _____ format.

7. The most common secondary storage device is a(n) _____.

8. _____ storage allows users to access rarely used computer files.

9. A magnetic tape is an example of a(n) _____ storage device.

10. _____ lets you store data on a remote computer.

● Think Critically

Directions: *Answer the following questions.*

1. Which type of secondary storage device do you use most at school? Do you think this will change in the near future? If so, why?

2. What can you do with a CD-RW that you cannot do with a CD-R?

3. Why do you think computer hard drives locate information directly, rather than sequentially?

4. What are the ways in which computer users would use a CD-ROM drive at home? At work? At school?

5. Where do you think users of computer games sold on CDs and DVDs store their information? Why?

● Extend Your Knowledge

Directions: *Choose one of the following projects. Complete the exercise on a separate sheet of paper.*

A. Look at your computer at school and find out how much memory it currently has. Next, use online documentation or other resources, such as the manufacturer's Web site, to compare your computer memory to the maximum amount of memory your computer can hold. Identify advantages to having more random access memory and compare this to the cost. As a class, conclude whether or not your school computers have sufficient memory to meet students' needs.

B. Go online and do research on storage service providers. What services and features do they offer? How do they protect the data they store? How easy is it for customers to access their data once they have given it to the service? Can customers share the stored data with other people? What fees do these services charge? Do you think such services can be useful to individuals as well as to companies?

Understanding How Data Storage Works

Why Is Computer Storage Important?

Once you understand the basics of computer storage, you can begin to understand why storage is so important. In fact, the true power of a computer is its ability to store data for future use. Without storage, a computer would be similar to a calculator; useful for a one-time task, but not much more than that.

In this chapter, you will examine how different types of storage devices work. You will learn more about the advantages and drawbacks of storage devices, and the steps you can take to protect your data.

Chapter Outline

 Lesson 6–1

Understanding Hard Drives and Flash Drives

 Lesson 6–2

Optical Storage Devices

 Lesson 6–3

Storage Trends

Understanding Hard Drives and Flash Drives

Objectives

- Identify the parts of a hard drive.
- Explain the role platters play in storing information.
- Compare and contrast the access time of different storage devices.

As You Read

Organize Information   Use a concept web to help you organize key concepts related to hard-drive storage as you read.

🔑 Key Terms

- access time
- cylinder
- data loss
- flash memory
- platter
- property
- read/write head
- sector
- solid state disks (SSD)
- storage media
- track
- USB flash drive
- write
- write-protect switch

Figure 6.1.1 In a stack of platters, the same track creates a cylinder.

Parts of a Hard Drive

Recall from Chapter 5 that a hard drive is a storage device that is usually installed inside a computer, although some hard drives are external. Its main function is storing information. Several rigid disks, coated with a magnetically sensitive material, are enclosed with recording heads in a hard metal container that is sealed to protect it from dirt and other damaging items.

Platters   Inside the sealed container is a stack of metal disks, known as **platters**, that store information. The platters rotate around a spindle inside the sealed container. These platters are so close together that only a thin layer of air separates them. The platters are **storage media**, coated with a special material that allows information to be saved on them.

Each platter is divided into **tracks**, or a set of circles on the surface of the platter, on which the data is recorded. A **cylinder** is the same track location on all the stacked platters. Each track is divided into segments, called **sectors**.

The process of storing information on storage media is called **writing**. Information can also be deleted from the platters. This is done when you no longer need a file or want to make room for another one.

Read/Write Heads   A hard drive has a motor that spins the platters at a high speed. Usually, these platters spin continuously when your computer is on. A small, needle-like component, called the **read/write head**, travels back and forth across the surface of each platter, retrieving and storing data. Most hard drives have at least one head on the top and one on the bottom of each platter for storage on each side of the platter.

Storing Data on a Hard Drive

When a file is saved to the hard drive, the read/write head locates a spot on a platter. It then generates a magnetic field on the surface of the platter. The magnetic field records a string of 1s and 0s, or binary code, to generate the information a computer can read.

If the hard drive is damaged or if the read/write head changes the field in order to modify or delete the file, the magnetic field will not remain intact. A head crash, or the collision of a read/write head with the surface of the disk, could occur. If this were to happen, data could no longer be stored on the damaged sector of the drive.

Limitations of Hard Drives

The amount of information a hard drive can hold depends on several factors. One factor is the number of platters contained in the hard drive. The greater the number of platters, the more information a drive can store.

Another factor is the number of read/write heads. Generally, there is a read/write head for each side of each platter. However, sometimes one side of one platter will not have its own read/write head. That means information cannot be stored on that side.

Effects of Performance   The performance of your hard drive directly affects how fast your computer works. The faster the hard drive, the faster your computer will read and write data. Because the platters in a hard drive are rigid, they can spin at very high speeds. The platters in most hard drives can spin at a rate of 7,500 rpm (revolutions per minute), but some can spin at rates as high as 15,000 rpm.

Hard Drive Speed   A storage device's most important performance characteristic is the speed at which it locates the desired data. This is measured by its **access time**, the amount of time it takes for the device to begin reading the data. For hard drives, the access time includes the time it takes the read/write head to locate the data before reading begins.

The speed of storage devices varies considerably, but all storage devices are significantly slower than RAM. RAM speed is measured in nanoseconds, or billionths of a second. A storage device's speed is measured in milliseconds, or thousandths of a second.

Hard Drive Capacity   The first PC hard drives held only about 10 MB of data and program instructions. In the early 1980s, that seemed like an enormous amount of storage space!

Recent personal computers feature hard drives with capacities of 500 GB and higher—you can even buy hard drives with capacities of 1,000 GB.

Alternative Storage Options

Manufacturers of computer chips are working to provide faster alternatives to magnetic storage.

Mathematics In math class, you are accustomed to a system that combines ten possible digits, or numbers, in a certain order to represent larger numbers. In binary code, only 0 and 1 are used.

- In math class, you carry a number over to the next column when numbers in a column add to 10 or more. With binary numbers, a number is carried if the items add to 2. In an eight-bit example, the number 35 would be written as 100011.

- While numbers in math class refer to specific quantities, binary code numbers refer to specific actions. A 1 turns a circuit on, while a 0 turns a circuit off.

Solid State Disks **Solid state disks** or drives, or **SSDs**, are a mass storage device similar to a hard disk drive. Even though SSDs serve the same purpose as hard drives, their internal parts are much different. SSDs do not have any moving parts, like the hard drive's magnetic platters; they store data using flash memory. SSDs have better read performance because the data does not get fragmented into many locations, and, since they are not magnetic, SSDs do not lose data when next to a strong magnetic field.

SSDs do have disadvantages, though. This newer technology costs about ten times more per gigabyte, so people tend to buy SSDs with smaller capacity than most hard drives. Their limited number of write cycles means their performance declines over time. Yet, with improvements in SSD technology, these devices will advance, and the prices may come down.

Flash Memory Devices Several types of storage devices using flash memory offer the speed of memory with the high capacity of a magnetic storage device. Flash memory drives work faster than magnetic drives, because they have no moving parts, and they do not require battery power to retain their data. Flash drives installed inside computers resemble magnetic hard drives in size and shape.

A **USB flash drive** is a portable, self-contained storage device that uses **flash memory**. In addition to portability, these drives offer the advantages of speed, capacity, and cost. A USB flash drive has a USB connector that plugs into the USB port on a computer; a flash memory chip that stores data; a USB mass storage controller that allows the computer to read, write, and erase data on the drive; and a crystal oscillator that controls the speed with which the drive works.

The electronic parts of the flash drive are protected by a hard plastic or metal case. The USB connector usually has a cover to protect it as well. Most USB flash drives have a light that comes on when the drive is plugged in. The drive may have a **write-protect switch**. When the switch is in the on position, the computer can read from the drive but cannot write to it or delete data from it.

Protecting Your Information

The information saved on computer storage media is important to the individuals, schools, businesses, and government agencies that wanted to keep it. Computers store information about virtually every aspect of life. We use them to store school grades, lists of business contacts, names of registered voters, bank account balances, and many other kinds of crucial data. Since this information can be so important, computer users should be aware of data loss and protection.

Data Loss   When a storage device experiences **data loss**, the data is damaged or made unusable. Storage devices and computers can also be lost, stolen, or destroyed, resulting in data loss. The data may be gone forever. It may be time-consuming or impossible to reconstruct the information that had been stored.

Data Protection   One way to reduce the impact of data loss is to back up your data. Storing information on removable storage media, which may be locked in high-security areas or stored at a different location, makes it difficult for people to steal the information, or to lose it due to a disaster such as fire, flood, or system failure. Many businesses use magnetic tape to back up large amounts of data, because it is relatively inexpensive and reliable. Some organizations hire storage service providers, or SSPs, to store data on offsite computers, and online storage is becoming increasingly popular.

Information can also be accidentally deleted, overwritten, or stolen by unauthorized users. One way to protect data is to apply password protection to a file or drive so only authorized users can access it, or to set a read-only property so the data may be read but cannot be changed. A **property** is a piece of data, sometimes called metadata, attached to or associated with a file, program, or device. Typical properties include name, type, storage location, and size. You can view and customize properties in the Properties dialog box.

Natural disasters present a threat to computer information stored at home. Even if you back up your information using standard methods, backups typically are stored in the home and are likely to have suffered the effects of the disaster.

Think About It!

Choosing the right backup system can mean the difference between being able to retrieve lost information and never being able to find it. Which backup storage methods below might survive a fire at home?

➢ store in a home safe
➢ store in a drawer at work
➢ store next to the computer
➢ send as e-mail attachments to a remote computer
➢ store on the hard drive in a different folder

Figure 6.1.2 To keep a file from being changed or overwritten, you can set its properties to Read-only.

Optical Storage Devices

Objectives

- Compare and contrast CD-ROM and DVD-ROM drives.
- Summarize how compact discs and digital video discs store data.

As You Read

Organize Information Use a spider map to help you organize information about optical storage devices and how they work as you read.

 Key Terms

- data transfer rate
- land
- laser sensor
- pit

CD-ROM and DVD-ROM Drives

The most recent advancements in storing data are in optical storage. These include CD-ROM (compact disc read-only memory), DVD-ROM (digital video disc read-only memory), laserdiscs, PhotoCDs, and similar storage devices. Optical storage media—the discs themselves—are easy to transport and can store large amounts of information. Most new computers have an internal CD-ROM, CD-Recordable (CD-R), CD-Rewritable (CD-RW), or DVD-ROM drive. Newer computers may be equipped with both a CD-RW and a DVD-ROM drive. In part to distinguish optical media from magnetic media, some people prefer changing the spelling of disc (optical) to disk (magnetic).

Compact Disc Media Optical drives are storage devices into which you insert a compact disc, or CD. When you look at an optical disc, it looks like a shiny, circular mirror. Optical discs are made up of three layers. The bottom layer is a clear plastic. The middle layer is a thin sheet of aluminum. The top layer is a lacquer coating that protects the disc from scratches and dust.

Figure 6.2.1 If a computer has a built-in CD drive, you can use it to watch movies.

Reading Optical Information

All storage devices read information at a speed measured by the unit's **data transfer rate**, or the number of bits of data the device can transfer to memory or to another device in a single second. In CD-ROM drives, the speed is measured in a multiple of 150,000 bits—the speed per second of the first CD-ROM drives. A 2X drive transfers data at double speed, or 300,000 bits per second. Some drives transfer data at 7.8 million bits per second, about as fast as slower hard drives.

Laser Sensors   A **laser sensor**, a laser-operated tool that reads information, is housed inside the optical drive. Optical drives read information by shining a laser on the disc in the drive. A laser sensor starts to read from the center of the disc's spirals and moves outward. The sensor notices changes in the physical properties of the disc and reads these changes as binary code: 0s and 1s.

Lands and Pits   The surface of an optical disc stores data as a series of lands and pits. A **land** is a flat, reflective area on the surface of a disc. Lands reflect light from a laser's sensor and are recorded as a 1 by a computer. A **pit** is an indented area on the surface of a disc that scatters the light from a laser's sensor. Since no light is reflected by a pit, it is recorded as a 0. The binary code represents the information encoded on the surface of the disc.

Figure 6.2.2 How an optical drive reads data on an optical disc.

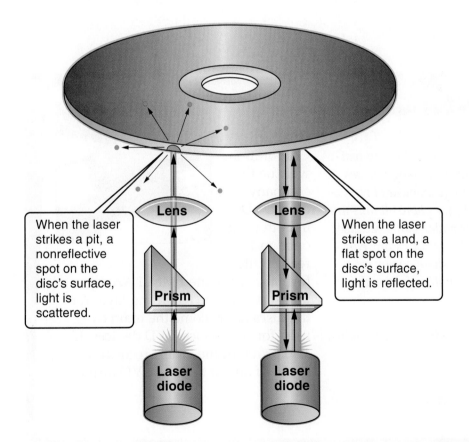

When the laser strikes a pit, a nonreflective spot on the disc's surface, light is scattered.

Lens

Lens

When the laser strikes a land, a flat spot on the disc's surface, light is reflected.

Prism

Prism

Laser diode

Laser diode

Storing Optical Information

CD-ROM, laserdisc, and DVD-ROM drives are read-only devices. CD-R, CD-RW, and DVD-RAM drives read *and* write information.

CD-R Drives These drives let you insert a blank recordable CD and then save data to it. After the information is stored, the disc's surface is changed so that the recorded information cannot be changed or erased.

CD-RW, DVD-RAM, DVD-R/RW, and PhotoCDs Optical devices that let you record, change, or overwrite data multiple times are called read/write storage devices. CD-RW, DVD-RAM, and DVD-R/RW drives provide read/write capabilities using erasable discs. The information on that disc can be deleted after it is written, and additional information can be added. PhotoCDs can save photographs from the Internet and from digital cameras.

Storage Trends

Objectives

- List limitations of current storage technologies.
- Compare solid-state storage devices to magnetic and optical storage devices.

As You Read

Identify Key Concepts   Use a spider web to help you identify key concepts about future storage devices as you read.

Limitations of Storage Devices

All technologies change over time. Technological breakthroughs have helped correct these common storage-device problems:
- slow retrieval
- data decay
- friction

Slow Retrieval   Tape devices are limited by slow retrieval speeds. Because devices must search from the beginning to the end of the tape to find the data, and magnetic tape cannot spin as fast as hard drives, it can take several minutes or even hours to locate information. Also, because tapes are usually stored in a remote location, you must first retrieve them.

Data Decay   One limitation of current storage devices is the possibility of **data decay**, or the loss of information resulting from the gradual wearing down of a storage medium. Information stored on magnetic tapes and disks will, over time, become unusable. Air, heat, and humidity can break down the surface of magnetic storage media. As this breakdown occurs, the information stored may be lost.

People once thought optical storage devices did not decay. However, studies have shown that user-recorded discs can lose information in as few as five to ten years. Factory-recorded, or pressed, compact discs may decay in 10 to 25 years. In addition to being vulnerable to gradual decay, magnetic storage devices can lose data in an instant if exposed to a strong magnetic field.

Friction   As a magnetic tape travels through the tape heads, friction is created. This causes heat, which can stretch and burn a tape. Companies are trying to develop read/write heads that decrease this friction and preserve magnetic media.

Key Terms
- cloud computing
- data decay
- data integrity
- enterprise storage system
- holographic data storage system (HDSS)
- storage area network (SAN)
- virtualization

Figure 6.3.1 Time and environmental conditions can take their toll on any storage medium.

Science You may have learned about solid-state technology in science class. However, that definition may be different from what you associate with solid-state storage devices.

- One definition of *solid state* refers to the properties of solids. These can include the electrical forces of solids as well as their magnetic currents.

- A second definition refers to the levels of heat inside a piece of equipment, which are controlled by electronic devices, such as semiconductors.

Devices such as digital recording equipment and laptop computers have their heat levels controlled by electronic devices, thereby fitting the second definition of *solid state*.

Data Integrity

When information is stored, it must be maintained correctly. **Data integrity** means that stored information is usable and available in the location in which you expect to find it. Data integrity can be maintained using RAID, Redundant Array of Inexpensive Disks.

RAID is a term used to describe a collection of drives or disks that run together to store data. For example, a computer using RAID may have two or more hard drives installed. The hard drives work together as one to read data from and write to the drive at the same time. This backup process ensures that copies of files can be retrieved in case one drive fails.

Enterprise Storage

Computers linked together by a cable or wireless medium are called networked computers. In a network environment, computers can share data using an **enterprise storage system**. This technology allows networked computers to access storage devices linked to the network, such as servers, RAID systems, tapes, and optical disc systems.

New and Future Technologies

As computer use increases, the need also grows for faster, more reliable, and higher capacity storage.

Cloud Computing and Virtualization Both cloud computing and virtualization make computers more efficient by using centralized storage, memory, and processing. **Cloud computing** uses the Internet and central remote servers to host data and applications.

Figure 6.3.2 Solid-state devices store large amounts of data, despite being very small.

Virtualization is when physical storage is pooled from multiple network storage devices into what seems to be one single storage device managed from a central console. Storage virtualization is usually used in a **storage area network (SAN)**, a network of storage devices that can be accessed by multiple computers. Many businesses use virtualization to consolidate many different servers onto one piece of physical hardware that then provides a simulated set of hardware to two or more operating systems. While cloud computing and virtualization are two distinct storage options, many cloud computing providers use virtualization in their data centers.

New Magnetic Media   In the future, by manipulating molecules and atoms, magnetic hard drives will store as much as 1 terabyte (TB) per square inch of disk space. That's an increase of 100 times the 10 gigabytes per square inch of current hard drives.

New Optical Media   FMD-ROM, or fluorescent multilayer disc read-only memory, discs contain multiple layers of a fluorescent material that stores information on each layer. A disc can hold 1 terabyte of data.

Holographic Media   A **holographic data storage system**, or **HDSS**, stores data in images called holograms on optical cubes. These devices will hold more than 1 terabyte of storage and will be ten times faster than today's hard drives.

Spotlight on...

MARVIN THEIMER

After a major earthquake hit California in 1989, many file storage systems were not working, and even backup data had been destroyed. It was then that Marvin Theimer started thinking about creating a disaster-tolerant storage system.

As a result, Theimer has been developing Farsite, a system which will let people back up their data on a system of networked computers. The exciting news about Farsite is that it uses the additional hard drive space that machines aren't using. That way, even if 99 out of 100 machines in the network are destroyed, people will still be able to retrieve their information from the machine that is still working.

Use the Vocabulary

Directions: *Match each vocabulary term in the left column with the correct definition in the right column.*

_____ **1.** storage media
_____ **2.** platter
_____ **3.** write
_____ **4.** read/write head
_____ **5.** access time
_____ **6.** USB flash drive
_____ **7.** SSD
_____ **8.** data transfer rate
_____ **9.** laser sensor
_____ **10.** pit

a. amount of time it takes storage device to begin reading data

b. one of the disks in a hard drive

c. removable, portable storage device inserted into a USB slot

d. save information on a storage medium

e. indentation on optical disc that does not reflect light

f. a mass storage device, similar to a hard disk drive that uses flash memory

g. needle-like device that retrieves and stores data on a magnetic disk

h. tool in optical drive that reads information

i. number of bits per second at which data is moved from a storage device to RAM

j. material that retains stored information saved by a computer storage device

Check Your Comprehension

Directions: *Determine the correct choice for each of the following.*

1. What type of media are used in a computer hard drive?
  a. magnetic
  b. optical
  c. solid state
  d. photo

2. What does the performance of a hard drive affect?
  a. if a read/write head can store data
  b. where a read/write head stores data
  c. how fast a computer reads and writes data
  d. the computer's memory

3. Which medium stores the least amount of information?
  a. DVD
  b. CD
  c. hard drive
  d. USB flash drive

4. Optical drives read information by using a _____.
  a. memory chip
  b. magnetic sensor
  c. laser sensor
  d. binary code

5. How many layers of material make up an optical disc?
  a. one
  b. two
  c. three
  d. four

6. Which of the following storage devices allow you to write data to a medium multiple times?
  a. CD-Rs
  b. read/write storage devices
  c. DVD-ROMs
  d. laserdiscs

Think Critically

Directions: *Answer the following questions.*

1. Why are disks (and discs) considered secondary—and not primary—storage devices?

2. Briefly explain why USB flash drives are now the most popular portable storage device?

3. What can happen if a read/write head is disturbed?

4. How are magnetic storage devices organized?

5. If USB flash drives and CD-Rs cost about the same per megabyte of storage, which do you think is more advantageous? Why?

Extend Your Knowledge

Directions: *Choose one of the following projects. Complete the exercise on a separate sheet of paper.*

A. Find out the age and the storage capacity of the hard drive on the computer you use at school. By using computer ads or visiting a local retailer, find out what improvements have been made to hard drives currently on sale. What conclusions can you draw about today's computers?

B. What kinds of storage devices do you think computers will have in five to ten years? What trends, if any, do you predict?

System Software Basics

What Is an Operating System? Have you ever wondered what happens when you turn on your computer? For many users, just seeing that the computer starts and that they can begin working is enough to meet their needs. But to become a more knowledgeable user, you should know how your computer works. One of the main behind-the-scenes contributors is the operating system.

The operating system is like the control center of your computer: it controls everything that happens with your computer. The operating system makes sure that files are stored properly on storage devices, software programs run properly, and instructions to peripherals are sent, among other jobs. Without an operating system, your computer would not be able to perform even basic tasks.

Chapter Outline

 Lesson 7–1

Introducing the Operating System

 Lesson 7–2

Operating Systems and Utilities

Introducing the Operating System

Objectives

- Explain what an operating system is and what it does.
- Identify types of operating systems.
- Describe a graphical user interface.

As You Read

Organize Information   Use a concept web to help you collect information about operating systems as you read.

 Key Terms

- crash
- desktop
- graphical user interface (GUI)
- icon
- interface

What Operating Systems Do

An operating system (OS) is a set of instructions designed to work with a specific type of computer, such as an IBM® PC or a Macintosh® computer. The OS controls all the computer's functions. It also provides an **interface**, the on-screen tools you use to interact with the computer and your programs. The operating system performs several tasks:

- manages the central processing unit (CPU) so that processing tasks are done properly
- manages computer memory
- manages files stored on the computer's disks
- manages input and output devices
- loads application programs into memory

Avoiding Conflicts   In most computers, especially personal computers, the operating system is stored on the hard drive. Before you can use the computer, a portion of the operating sytem must be loaded into memory. This is true of all programs; they may permanently reside on a disk but must be copied into RAM before you can use them.

Some operating systems enable a computer to run more than one program at a time. To do this, the operating system has to assign each program some space in RAM, and then protect that space. Otherwise, conflicts can occur when two programs try to occupy the same space in RAM. When this happens, one or both of the programs may **crash**, or stop working, until the conflict is resolved.

Types of Operating Systems

All computers require an operating system. There are four kinds of operating systems.

Real-Time Systems Real-time operating systems are used to control large equipment, such as heavy machinery and scientific instruments, and to regulate factory operations. In order for these systems to run, they require very little user interaction.

Single-User/Single-Task Systems This kind of system lets one person do one task at a time. An example is the operating system that controls a handheld computer.

Single-User/Multitasking Systems A multitasking system allows the computer to perform several jobs, either one after the other or at the same time. For example, you could use your computer to write a letter as it downloads a page from the Internet and prints another letter. Most desktop and laptop computers today use this kind of system. Windows and the Macintosh OS are examples of this type of operating system.

Multi-User Systems These systems allow many individuals to use one large computer. The OS balances all the tasks that the various users ask the computer to do. UNIX® is an example of this type of operating system.

Real-World Tech

An Operating System—in Your Dog? Robots are devices that can move and react to input from sight, hearing, touch, and balance. How are those "senses" and those reactions controlled? Through an operating system, of course! Robots are used to explore outer space and to do factory jobs. Now, however, they're also available as pets. Some robotic "dogs" can learn their own name and your name. They can show joy, anger, and surprise through lights, sounds, and gestures.

For what purposes do you think robots would be useful or fun?

Technology @ Work

Fingerprint identification programs allow scanned fingerprints to be matched to electronic fingerprints stored in the computer.

Think About It!

For which activities below do you believe such a fingerprint identification system would be an advantage at school?

➢ paying for a school lunch

➢ checking out a library book

➢ taking attendance

➢ turning in homework

➢ accessing computer files

The User Interface

The operating system's user interface lets you start programs, manage disks and files, and shut down the computer safely. To start the OS, you turn the computer on. During the startup procedure, the OS places part of itself into the computer's memory.

Desktop Nowadays, computer operating systems are based on visual displays. The **graphical user interface**, or **GUI** (*GOO-ee*), lets you use a mouse to interact with the workspace on the computer screen, called a **desktop**.

Icons On the screen, pictures called **icons** represent various resources on the computer. An icon might represent a program, a document, a hardware device, or a Web site. You click or double-click an icon to perform an action, such as starting a program or opening a file.

Options The operating system lets you change some features of the desktop, such as the look of the background or the placement of the icons. You can also change how other things work on your computer, such as keyboard functions and the speed at which the cursor blinks on the screen. The computer's manual or the Help feature allows you to explore these options.

Figure 7.1.1 Customizing the display with Microsoft Windows 7.

Operating Systems and Utilities

Objectives

- Examine different operating systems.
- Discuss the function of the file manager in an operating system.
- Describe how system utilities help operating systems function.

As You Read

Outline Information   Use an outline to help you note details about operating systems and system utilities as you read.

Popular Operating Systems

Three operating systems dominate the computer world—Microsoft Windows®, the Macintosh OS, and UNIX. The computer you use at school or at home probably has a version of Windows or the Macintosh OS installed. UNIX, and adaptations of it, is most often found running on large business or scientific networks.

Mac OS X®   In 1984, Apple® became the first computer maker to sell consumers a personal computer equipped with a graphical user interface (GUI). *Macintosh* names both the computer and its operating system. Easy for beginners to use, some version of the Mac OS runs all Macintosh computers.

Microsoft Windows   Although Microsoft Windows was not the first OS to have a GUI, the Windows OS is currently the market leader, installed on more than 90 percent of personal computers.

UNIX and Linux™   UNIX was one of the first operating systems ever written. It was designed to work on powerful business and scientific computers. Later versions of UNIX have been developed to work on microcomputers, or personal computers.

One of these versions of UNIX, a system called Linux, has become very popular. Linux works with an optional GUI and is very fast compared to other operating systems. It is also unique in that it is an open-source operating system, in which the source code (programming language) used to create it is available to the public. Programmers from across the globe constantly work on Linux to test and improve it. Linux is also free and can be downloaded from the Internet, but most users buy it with other features on a disc. It is now challenging Apple and Microsoft for a share of the OS market—with 18% of market share as of 2011.

Key Terms

- backup utility
- driver utility
- file compression utility
- Plug and Play (PnP)

GUI designers choose icons that most people recognize.

Think About It!

Which items below are represented by an icon on a home computer?

➤ music files

➤ e-mail

➤ Internet browser

➤ printer

➤ text files

➤ antivirus software

Figure 7.2.1 Use an operating system such as Windows 7 to organize and manage files and folders.

System Utilities: File Management

Utility software is a collection of programs that help you maintain and repair your computer. Today, many types of utilities are built into the operating system. Probably the most important utilities are file managers, which let you work with data stored on your computer.

Organizing Files The operating system, programs, and data are all stored in files, each with a name. Files can be grouped together into folders. Folders are also called directories. A folder can be divided into subfolders.

Using Files You can use an operating system's file manager to perform several tasks:

- create new folders or subfolders
- move or copy items between folders or to other disks
- delete files and folders
- launch applications

Finding Files You can use the file finder utility from your operating system to help you look for a file. This utility can search for a file by its name, type, date, or even by looking for specific data inside the file.

System Utilities: Other Jobs

Your operating system probably has utilities that can help with routine maintenance and other jobs.

Driver Utilities   A **driver utility** contains data needed by programs to operate input and output devices such as a mouse and printer. Operating systems that have **Plug and Play (PnP)** capability can automatically detect new PnP-compatible devices.

Otherwise, you will be prompted to insert the disc that came with the equipment to load the driver.

Program Utilities   Before you can use a program, you must install it on your hard drive. In Windows, you can use the Add/Remove Programs utility to ensure that your program installs properly. You can use the same utility to remove a program you no longer need.

Backup Utilities   **Backup utility** programs automatically copy data from the computer's hard drive to a backup storage device, such as an external hard drive or a CD. Businesses and individuals routinely use backup utilities to ensure data is not lost if a computer or disk drive fails. You, too, should regularly back up your computer data.

File Compression Utilities   **File compression utilities** are programs that reduce the size of files without harming the data. These programs make it easier to copy and send files.

Science   If your science teachers have not yet done so, they may soon add to your computer a microscope and a driver to control it. Computer microscopes allow an enlarged image to appear on the monitor or on a wall screen, making it easier for groups to see. Students can also capture images to study and use in reports and presentations.

Figure 7.2.2 Microsoft Windows comes with a backup and restore utility.

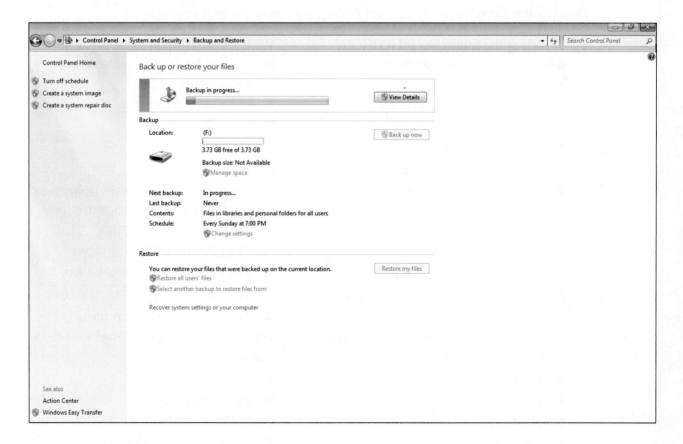

Use the Vocabulary

Directions: *Match each vocabulary term in the left column with the correct definition in the right column.*

_____ **1.** interface
_____ **2.** crash
_____ **3.** graphical user interface
_____ **4.** desktop
_____ **5.** icon
_____ **6.** driver utility
_____ **7.** Plug and Play
_____ **8.** backup utility
_____ **9.** file compression utility

a. area on a computer screen where you perform work

b. to stop working

c. program that controls input/output devices

d. picture that represents something on a computer

e. on-screen tools that let you use the computer

f. program that copies a file onto another medium

g. lets you use a mouse to work with the computer

h. capable of detecting compatible devices

i. reduces file size without harming data

Check Your Comprehension

Directions: *Determine the correct choice for each of the following.*

1. Which of the following is NOT usually handled by the operating system?
   a. managing programs
   b. dealing with input/output devices
   c. publishing Web pages
   d. interacting with the user

2. Which kind of computer operating system usually requires the least amount of user interaction?
   a. real-time systems
   b. single-user/single-task systems
   c. single-user/multitask systems
   d. multi-user systems

3. Which of the following is a key part of a graphical user interface?
   a. command words
   b. cursors
   c. memory
   d. icons

4. Which operating system is found most often on large business and scientific computers?
   a. Microsoft Windows
   b. Mac OS
   c. UNIX
   d. Linux

5. Which of the following do operating systems, application programs, and user data have in common?
   a. They are all system utilities.
   b. They are all Windows-based.
   c. They are all created by the user.
   d. They are all stored in files.

6. What kind of utility is used to reduce the size of a file?
   a. driver utility
   b. program utility
   c. backup utility
   d. file compression utility

● Think Critically

Directions: *Answer the following questions.*

1. What kind of computer operating system do you think small, sophisticated devices such as PDAs use? Why?

2. What effect do you think the development of graphical user interfaces had on the number of people using computers? Why?

3. Which kind of utility program do you think is most important to your computer? Why?

4. What are two ways that you can launch an application program?

5. Why is it a good idea to back up your important files?

● Extend Your Knowledge

Directions: *Choose one of the following projects. Complete the exercise on a separate sheet of paper.*

A. Go to Help in a Microsoft Windows operating system. Find out how it is organized, but make no changes to the system settings. Follow the same process on a Macintosh computer. Which Help section was easier to use? Provide reasons for your preference. Discuss your conclusions as a class.

B. Find ads in computer magazines or on the Web that are sponsored by companies that sell backup and file compression utilities. Make a chart to summarize the features of three products in each category. Note which operating system each product works with and its price. Summarize your findings in a brief report.

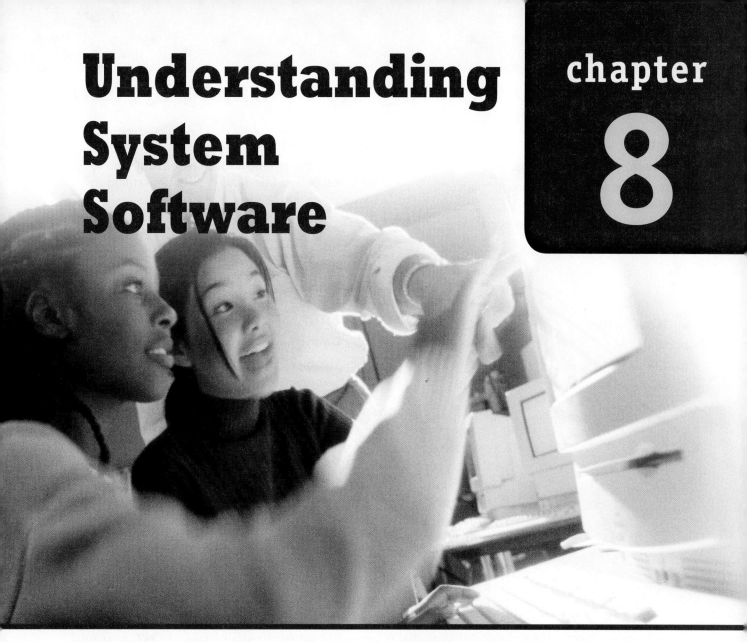

Understanding System Software

chapter

8

What Is the Purpose of an Operating System?
When you use a computer program, most of the activity you see on the screen is conducted by the operating system. An application, such as a word processor, asks the operating system to perform actions, such as opening a file, printing a document, or showing a list of recently used documents.

To fulfill these requests, the operating system needs to know how to handle different **file formats**, or standards used to save data on a disk. Those formats determine how text documents, graphics, audio, and video files are stored and used. In this chapter, you will learn more about what the functions that the operating system and its utilities perform, and how you use them.

Chapter Outline

 Lesson 8–1

Exploring the Operating System

 Lesson 8–2

Exploring System Utilities

Exploring the Operating System

Objectives

- Summarize the boot process.
- Describe the features of a graphical user interface.
- Explain how operating systems can be configured and changed.

As You Read

Organize Information Use a concept web to help you collect information about operating systems as you read.

🔑 Key Terms

- boot
- file format
- pop-up menu
- power-on self test (POST)
- pull-down menu
- Ribbon
- screen saver
- system administrator
- window

Loading the Operating System

The operating system, or OS, controls the computer and manages its work. The OS also provides an interface which enables you to interact with the computer.

The Boot Process When you turn the computer on, you **boot** it. That is, you start the computer, and it responds by loading the operating system. If your computer is set to show it, the first thing you see is the BIOS screen. As you learned in Chapter 5, *BIOS* stands for basic input/output system, and it manages and configures the computer's hardware. This means that the computer will be able to accept input from the keyboard and display information.

The Power-On Self Test As a computer boots, it performs a series of tests called the **power-on self test**, or **POST**. During POST, the BIOS checks the major components of the system, such as its memory, keyboard, and hard drive.

If your BIOS screen is set to display during POST, you will see text messages telling you what is happening. If there is a problem, a written message or a sound alerts you. If this happens, the computer may need repair. If no problem is detected, parts of the operating system are loaded from storage into memory and take control of the computer.

The Login As the operating system starts, you may see a screen that asks you for a username and password. This is called the login screen. Businesses and schools often use this process to control who has access to the computer.

Exploring the GUI

When the operating system is loaded into RAM, it displays the desktop provided by the graphical user interface, or GUI. The desktop is where all work is done, including opening and closing programs, modifying system settings, and managing files. Icons on the desktop allow you to launch programs by clicking or double-clicking them. You also can click Start (on a PC) or Finder (on a Macintosh®) and then the name of the program you want. A taskbar on the desktop identifies which programs or files are open. To switch back and forth among applications, just click what you want to work on next.

Using Windows The operating system in today's PCs and Macintosh computers displays documents in **windows**, or rectangular, on-screen frames that can be opened, closed, resized, and rearranged to view programs or documents. Each window provides commands and options. Some programs have **pull-down menus** that list commands when you select an item from the menu. Sometimes menus have submenus with additional commands. In Microsoft Office 2010, the window provides commands on the **Ribbon**, a series of tabs at the top of the window. Each tab has a group of related commands for specific tasks. A command may display a dialog box that lets you set several options at the same time.

Pop-up menus, or lists of shortcut commands that appear when an area of the screen is clicked or right-clicked or the mouse button is held down, can appear anywhere in a window. Pop-up menus can be context-sensitive, providing options that relate to tasks you are doing at that moment.

Today, a number of operating systems use voice recognition, which allows you to say, for example, "Computer, start word processing," or "Computer, check e-mail," and the computer will know what you mean. However, you must know the right commands. If you say, "Ditch that file," instead of "Delete that file," the computer will not know how to process the command.

Figure 8.1.1 Many programs have dialog boxes you use to select options, such as number formats in a spreadsheet.

Exploring Configuration Options

Every operating system includes default settings, the settings a program automatically uses unless others are selected. Operating sytems provide configuration options, which let you change some of the default settings and make the computer work in a way that best suits your needs. For example, you can:

- change keyboard and mouse settings
- change the volume of sounds and audio equipment
- change the system date or time
- set up or change your Internet connection
- add new hardware, such as a printer or scanner
- add or remove programs
- schedule a task to run automatically, such as an antivirus program

Changing system settings lets you customize your computer, but it can also cause your computer to malfunction. Most operating systems have a feature that lets you restore settings to a previous configuration.

Desktop Changes Your operating system lets you change the desktop display. Among your choices are these:

- change the background appearance of the desktop, sometimes called the wallpaper
- change the **screen saver**, a utility program that changes the screen display after a preset period of nonuse
- add or eliminate desktop icons for various programs
- display or hide the taskbar

Real-World Tech

Offering a Free Operating System

As discussed in Chapter 7, the operating system Linux® is based on a powerful scientific system called UNIX®. Linux is freeware, or open-source software, which means programmers can freely modify its code. To help expand computer use in schools in Mexico, Miguel de Icaza, while still in his 20s, developed GNOME, one of the Windows-based, easy-to-use desktop graphical user interfaces for Linux.

What are some of the advantages and disadvantages of a freeware operating system?

Managing User Accounts

Since computers are used for many different tasks, from playing games to writing reports and calculating numbers, businesses may want to restrict the use of some programs and files to designated users. This may also be true in schools, homes, and other settings where several people can use the same computer.

Usernames and Passwords   One way to protect data is to set up user accounts that identify who can access a computer. Each user is assigned a username and a password that he or she must provide in order to gain access. User accounts are set up using a system tool provided by the operating system. The **system administrator** is the person responsible for maintaining the computer system and for setting up user accounts.

Other Protections   Besides the username and password, a user account can also include the following properties:

- file access rights that specify which files a user can access and what he or she can do with these files
- installation rights that specify whether a user can install or remove programs
- hardware rights that specify whether a user can add or remove hardware
- configuration rights that specify whether a user can change operating system settings

Real-World Tech

See It on the Big Screen   One fascinating task that computers do is create some of those dramatic special effects you see in movies. The Linux operating system, authored by Linus Torvalds (pictured at right), has been especially influential in this area in recent years. Linux was used in the filming of *Titanic* to make a model of the ship look real; in *The Fellowship of the Ring* to make human actors look small and a computer-generated troll look huge; and in *Shrek* to combine models and animation with startlingly lifelike effects.

What movie have you seen recently in which the special effects caught your attention?

Exploring System Utilities

Objectives

- Analyze file names and file formats.
- Explain cross-platform compatibility issues.
- Identify and discuss system maintenance utilities.

As You Read

Draw Conclusions   Use a chart to help you draw conclusions about system utilities as you read.

🔑 Key Terms

- corrupted
- cross-platform compatibility
- disk scanner
- file extension
- file fragmentation

Managing Files and Folders

As you learned in Chapter 7, system utilities help users complete various tasks. Among the most important system utilities is the file manager, called Explorer in Windows. This utility allows you to organize, view, copy, move, rename, and delete files. You can even use it to create certain types of files. The commands for these tasks are available on a menu. For example, to delete a file, right-click it, click Delete on the shortcut menu, and then click OK.

Naming Files and Folders   When you create a new file or folder, you give it a name. Using descriptive names helps you identify the contents and keep your data organized. For example, the name *2012 Annual Report* is more descriptive than *Report*. It also helps keep you from accidentally deleting or overwriting files and folders that have the same name. Most operating systems let you use file and folder names with up to 255 characters, including spaces and punctuation. You cannot use <. >/ :. ", /, \, |, ?, or *.

File Extension   Some operating systems, such as Windows, automatically add a period and a file extension to file names. A **file extension** is a short series of letters that indicate the application used to create the file and the file format. For example, a Microsoft Word document has the extension .doc or .docx. You can set options to display file extensions when you view a file list.

Figure 8.2.1 You can display file extensions when viewing files with Windows 7.

Name	Type	Size
Current Science Projects	File folder	
Article.docx	Word 2007 Document	18 KB
Astronomy Presentation.pptx	Microsoft Office PowerPoint 2007 Presentation	3,793 KB
Book Report Presentation.ppt	Microsoft PowerPoint 97-2003 Presentation	6,857 KB
Drawing.gif	GIF image	222 KB
Invitation Back.pub	Microsoft Publisher Document	113 KB
Invitation Front.pub	Microsoft Publisher Document	148 KB
Lion.jpg	JPEG image	200 KB
Mayans.docx	Word 2007 Document	27 KB
Scanned Image.tif	TIF File	1,970 KB
Schoolwork Compressed.zip	Compressed (zipped) Folder	10,571 KB

Using Files on Different Operating Systems

As previously discussed, the two most widely used operating systems are Microsoft Windows on PCs and Mac OS on Apple Macintosh computers. Many times, a file created on one OS can work on another. This is because the OS associates files with specific programs.

Cross-Platform Compatibility Sharing files across operating systems is called **cross-platform compatibility**. There are two keys to compatibility. First, both operating systems must have the same program installed in a compatible version that has been written for each operating system. Second, the application must allow its file formats to be shared across different operating systems.

Using System Maintenance Utilities

Like any machine, a computer needs routine maintenance. System maintenance utilities do these jobs and more.

Disk Scanner Computer files can be **corrupted**, or damaged to the point at which data is unrecoverable, in different ways. One way is by being stored on a damaged part of the hard drive. Running a utility called a **disk scanner**, which checks magnetic disks for errors, can fix this problem. A disk scanner looks for and tries to correct irregularities on a disk's surface.

Spotlight on...

STEVE JOBS

❝ *I know if I got run over by a bus tomorrow, Apple's going to keep on going—because the engines have been put in place and cultures have been put in place to keep innovating, to keep doing things at this level of quality.* **❞**

Steven Jobs
Founder, Apple computers

At age 21, Steven Jobs and his friend Stephen Wozniak founded Apple Computer Company in the Jobs' family garage. A year later, Apple released the first mass-market personal computer. In 1984, Apple released the Macintosh computer, the first personal computer to use a GUI. Jobs left Apple in 1985 but rejoined the company in 1997. One of the company's newest ventures is the iPad tablet computer.

Figure 8.2.2 Scanning a disk for viruses with the McAfee® Security Center.

Disk Defragmenter

As you add, move, and delete files on your computer, parts of files end up saved in different areas of the hard drive. **File fragmentation** occurs when a file is broken into pieces that are saved in different places on a hard drive.

File fragmentation reduces disk efficiency because the read/write head must travel longer distances to retrieve parts of a file that are scattered across a disk than if the files were stored close together. A disk defragmentation program can gather all the file pieces and place them together, thus improving the efficiency of the disk or hard drive.

Virus Detection

Viruses can get into your computer through a number of ways. Once there, they can destroy or corrupt data. Running updated versions of antivirus programs can detect and get rid of computer viruses.

Antivirus software is essential to keeping your computer running and protecting your files and programs. This is because viruses can do all sorts of damage once they infect a computer. For example, many viruses look for certain types of files and then damage or delete them.

Antivirus programs check your computer's memory and disks, looking for virus code. Newer programs can also check e-mail and files as they are downloaded to your computer from the Internet. If the program finds a virus, it alerts you and then attempts to disable and remove the virus.

Use the Vocabulary

Directions: *Match each vocabulary term in the left column with the correct definition in the right column.*

_____ **1.** boot
_____ **2.** POST
_____ **3.** window
_____ **4.** pull-down menu
_____ **5.** pop-up menu
_____ **6.** screen saver
_____ **7.** file extension
_____ **8.** cross-platform compatibility
_____ **9.** disk scanner
_____ **10.** file fragmentation

a. to start the computer and load the operating system

b. option that appears when an item is selected from the menu bar

c. utility that looks for errors in magnetic media

d. changes the display on the desktop

e. two or three letters that identify a file's format

f. series of tests run during the boot process

g. ability to share files across operating systems

h. shortcut command that appears anywhere in a window

i. frame that displays a document or file

j. having parts of files stored on different areas of a disk or hard drive

Check Your Comprehension

Directions: *Determine the correct choice for each of the following.*

1. Which of the following indicates that the computer can accept input from the keyboard and display information on the monitor?
  a. POST
  b. BIOS screen
  c. GUI
  d. cross-platform application

2. At what point in the boot process can users be asked their username and password?
  a. at the control panel
  b. in a screen saver
  c. in a file manager
  d. at login

3. If a pop-up menu is context-sensitive, what is it related to?
  a. file format
  b. printer settings
  c. what you are doing
  d. operating system

4. Which of the following is NOT a system change most users should attempt?
  a. moving the operating system
  b. adding a scanner
  c. changing mouse settings
  d. removing a program

5. Along with the data itself, which of the following is saved with a file?
  a. login procedure
  b. code for the application that created it
  c. icon that describes it
  d. maintenance utility

6. Which of the following is one way that a file can be corrupted?
  a. by deleting it
  b. by appearing on the desktop
  c. by moving it to a new folder
  d. by storing it on a damaged disk

Think Critically

Directions: *Answer the following questions.*

1. What feature would you like to see in the next generation of graphical user interfaces? Why?

2. After you add a peripheral to your computer or change a preference, you are asked to reboot the computer. Why do you think this is necessary?

3. Why do most operating systems let users make system changes?

4. Suppose some of the reporters and photographers for your local newspaper work from home and are networked. What is an example of one application that would allow them to work without concern for the operating system they use?

5. Which system maintenance utility do you think requires the most user interaction? Why?

Extend Your Knowledge

Directions: *Choose one of the following projects. Complete the exercise on a separate sheet of paper.*

A. With a partner, interview three adult computer users: one who uses Microsoft Windows, one who uses a Macintosh, and one who has experience with both operating systems. Prepare written questions related to ease of learning the operating system, ease of use, availability of programs, and overall satisfaction with the operating system. Add your findings to your own experiences and write a conclusion about the user preferences of the two major operating systems.

B. Explore the desktop on your computer. Identify the icons on the desktop and explain what each launches. Use the taskbar to identify files or programs that are open and the file formats they are in. How does the desktop help you manage your work on the computer? Using a text editor, word-processing application, or on paper, write a paragraph explaining the concept of a computer desktop. Then, write step-by-step instructions that someone could use to arrange items on the desktop. With your teacher's permission, print or publish the document and exchange it with a classmate. Read your classmate's work. As a class, discuss why step-by-step instructions are useful.

DIRECTIONS: *You will use your operating system to navigate to a storage location where you will create a folder. You will then create, copy, move, rename, and delete files and subfolders. You will also display file properties and change the folder view. Windows 7 procedures required for this activity can be found in Appendix A.*

1. Start your computer, and log in to your user account, if necessary.
2. Use your operating system to navigate to the location where your teacher instructs you to store the files for this activity. For example, plug a flash drive in to a USB port, and display the contents of that drive in a program window.
3. In the storage location, create a new folder named **OS-1_folder1_xx**. Replace *xx* with your own initials or name, as directed by your teacher.
4. In the same storage location, create a new text document named **OS-1_text1_xx**.
5. Copy **OS-1_text1_xx** in to **OS-1_folder1_xx**.
6. In **OS-1_folder1_xx**, rename **OS-1_text1_xx** to **OS-1_text2_xx**.
7. Navigate back to the original storage location.
8. Rename **OS-1_folder1_xx** to **OS-1_folder2_xx**.
9. Move **OS-1_text1_xx** in to **OS-1_folder2_xx**.
10. Open **OS-1_folder2_xx** and, if not already selected, change the folder view to Large Icons.
11. On your keyboard, press ALT + PRTSC to capture an image of the folder window.

12. Start a graphics or paint program, such as Paint, and paste the screen capture image in the program window. It should look similar to Illustration A.
13. Save the file as **OS-1_image1_xx** in **OS-1_folder2_xx**.
14. With your teacher's permission, print the file, and then exit the program.
15. In **OS-1_folder2_xx**, change the folder view to Content.
16. Change the folder view to Details.
17. Display the properties for **OS-1_image1_xx**, and then close the Properties dialog box.
18. Delete **OS-1_text2_xx**.
19. In **OS-1_folder2_xx**, create a new folder named **OS-1_folder3_xx**.
20. Copy **OS-1_text1_xx** into **OS-1_folder3_xx**.
21. Delete **OS-1_folder3_xx**.
22. Navigate to the original storage location, and close it.
23. If necessary, safely remove or eject the storage device.
24. With your teacher's permission, log off and/or shut down the computer.

Illustration A

Activity 2: Exploring the Operating System

DIRECTIONS: *You will explore the features of your operating system. You will identify storage devices, network components, and installed printers, and you will locate information about the amount of installed RAM and processor speed for your system. You may complete this activity alone, or work as a team. Windows 7 procedures required for this activity can be found in Appendix A.*

1. Start your computer, and log in to your user account, if necessary.
2. Create a new text file named **OS-2_wp1_***xx* in the location where your teacher tells you to store the files for this activity.
3. Start a text editor or word-processing program, and open **OS-2_wp1_***xx*.
4. Maximize the program window, if it is not already maximized.
5. Type your name and today's date in the file, and save the changes.
6. Minimize the program window.
7. Use your operating system to display available storage devices.
   - ✔ *In Windows, click Start, and then click Computer.*
8. Count the number of available storage devices.
9. Make the text editor or word-processing program window active.
10. Arrange the two open windows side by side. Your desktop should look similar to Illustration B.
11. Cascade the two open windows.
12. Maximize the text editor or word-processing program window.
13. In the text file, press Enter to start a new line, type **Storage devices:**, and then type the total number of available devices you counted in step 8. Save the changes.
14. Restore down the program window.
15. Make the Computer window active.

16. Display the contents of a storage device. For example, double-click Local Disk (C:) or a removable device.
17. Display the components of your current network.
    - ✔ *In the Windows Navigation pane, click Network, or click Start and then click Network.*
18. Close all Explorer windows, leaving the word-processing program open.
19. Display a list of available printers.
    - ✔ *In Windows 7, click Start > Devices and Printers.*
20. Count the number of available printers.
21. Make the text file active, press Enter, type **Printers:**, and then type the total number of available printers you counted in step 20. Save the changes.
22. Display system information, including the amount of installed RAM and processor speed.
    - ✔ *In Windows 7, Click Start > Control Panel > System and Security > View amount of RAM and processor speed.*
23. Switch to the text document, press Enter, type **RAM:**, and type the amount of installed RAM.
24. Press Enter, type **Processor speed:**, and type the processor speed. Save the changes.
25. Close all Control Panel windows.
26. With your teacher's permission, print **OS-2_wp1_***xx*, then close it and exit the program.
27. Close all open windows. With your teacher's permission, log off and/or shut down the computer.

Illustration B

DIRECTIONS: *You will personalize your operating environment by customizing desktop icons and by changing the theme, desktop background, and window colors. You will capture an image of the desktop and paste it into a graphics file. Finally, you will reset all options to the previous configuration. Windows 7 procedures required for this activity can be found in Appendix A.*

1. Start your computer, and log in to your user account, if necessary.
2. If necessary, change the desktop display to show large icons.
3. Sort the icons on the desktop by name.
4. Sort the icons on the desktop by type.
5. Personalize the desktop using a built-in theme. For example, if you are using Windows 7, apply the United States theme.
6. Personalize the desktop by applying a different picture to the background. For example, if you are using Windows 7, apply one of the Nature pictures.
7. Personalize the desktop by changing the color of window borders. For example, if you are using Windows 7, change the color to Ruby.
8. Display options for changing the date and time display.
9. Synchronize the clock with Internet time.
10. Select to display an additional clock, showing the time in Beijing, China. Name the clock **Beijing**.
11. Make sure the Beijing clock is displayed. (In Windows 7, rest the mouse point over the clock/calendar in the taskbar to display a ScreenTip.) Then, capture an image of the desktop.

12. Start a paint or graphics program, such as Paint, and paste the captured image into the new blank file. Scroll the window so you can see the clock. It should look similar to Illustration C.
13. Save the file as **OS-3_image1_xx** in the location where your teacher tells you to store the files for this activity.
14. With your teacher's permission, print the file, and then close it and exit the program.
15. On the desktop, create a shortcut to the **OS-3_image1_xx** file, and then use the shortcut to open the file.
16. Resize the program window so it is about 4" high by 4" wide.
   ✔ *If the window is maximized, you must restore it before you can resize it.*
17. Close the file, and exit the program.
18. Mute the speaker volume.
19. Restore the desktop settings, clock, and speaker volume to the way they were at the beginning of this activity.
20. With your teacher's permission, log off and/or shut down the computer.

Illustration C

Operating System Activities

Operating System Activities

DIRECTIONS: *You will use your operating system to set up an electronic portfolio. You will read about how to create a useful and effective portfolio, and then you will create a folder with subfolders where you can store items you select to include. You will convert printed items into digital files, and you will copy or move digital files into the portfolio. Windows 7 procedures required for this activity can be found in Appendix A.*

1. Open the .pdf file **OS-4_Portfolio**, which is located on the student CD. This file contains information about electronic portfolios.
2. Read the information to learn about electronic portfolios.
3. In your operating system, navigate to the location where you want to store the electronic portfolio.
4. Create a new folder, and name it **OS-4_Portfolio_xx**.
5. In the folder, create one subfolder named **Academic Achievement**, a second named **Personal Information**, and a third named **Career Information**.
6. Select an application that you can use to create a list of artifacts and other items you will include in your portfolio. This might be a word-processing program, a spreadsheet program, or a database program.
7. Use the application to create a new file. Save the file in the **Personal Information** subfolder, with the name **OS-4_List of Artifacts_xx**.
8. In the file, list the name and a description of each artifact and item you want to include in the portfolio. (Refer to the list in the **OS-4_Portfolio.pdf** file.)
9. In the file, include whether each artifact already exists, or if it is something you will create in the future.
10. In the file, also include the name of the subfolder in which you will store the artifact. For example, you might store a resume and list of references in the **Career Information** folder and an example of a word-processing document you typed and formatted in the **Academic Achievement** folder.

11. Save the file. You can modify it and refer to it as you develop your portfolio.
12. Locate existing artifacts and items you have stored in digital format and copy or move them into the appropriate subfolder in your **OS-4_Portfolio** folder.
13. Locate printed artifacts and items, and use appropriate technology, such as a scanner or digital camera, to convert them into digital files. Store them in the appropriate subfolder in your **OS-4_Portfolio_xx** folder.
14. Select an application, and use it to create new items to include, such as a contact information sheet, a personal academic plan, and guidelines for assessment. Store the items in the appropriate portfolio subfolders.
15. Select an application, and use it to create reflections for your artifacts. Store the reflections with the artifacts in the portfolio.
16. Select an application, and use it to create a table of contents for your portfolio. Format the items as hyperlinks that link to the digital artifacts and items.
17. Practice presenting the portfolio to your class.
18. Continue to review, update, and add new artifacts and items to your portfolio on a regular basis.

Activity 5: Identifying Screen Elements

DIRECTIONS: *You will use your operating system to capture images of different program windows and insert the images into a word-processing file. You will then print the file and label the elements on each image. Windows 7 procedures required for this activity can be found in Appendix A.*

1. Start your computer, and log in to your user account, if necessary.
2. Start a word-processing application, such as Microsoft Word or Google Documents.
3. Save the default blank document with the name **OS-5_wp_xx** in the location where your teacher instructs you to store the files for this activity.
4. Maximize the application window.
5. On the first line of the word-processing file, type your first and last names and today's date.
6. Press Enter to start a new line.
7. Capture an image of the screen.
8. Paste the image from the Clipboard into the word-processing document.
9. Save the document, and then minimize the application window.
10. Capture an image of your computer desktop.
11. Restore the word-processing program window.
12. Press CTRL + ENTER to start a new page.
13. Paste the captured image into the word-processing document.

14. Save the document, and then minimize the application window.
15. Start a spreadsheet application.
16. Maximize the spreadsheet application window.
17. Capture an image of the spreadsheet application window.
18. Exit the spreadsheet application.
19. Make the word-processing application window active.
20. In the word-processing document, press CTRL + ENTER , to start a new page.
21. Paste the captured image into the word-processing document.
22. Save the word-processing document.
23. With your teacher's permission, print the word-processing document and label the parts of all three screens. Alternatively, use drawing tools to insert callouts or text boxes in the word-processing document to label the parts of the screens. Page 1, the word-processing screen, might look similar to Illustration D.
24. Close the word-processing document, saving all changes, and exit the application.

Illustration D

DIRECTIONS: *You will use a Help program to locate and review security settings. You will also access the command prompt and display a directory. Windows 7 procedures required for this activity can be found in Appendix A.*

1. Start your computer, and log in to your user account, if necessary.
2. Start your operating system's Help program, and maximize the window.
3. Search for **managing security settings**.
4. Click a link for information about understanding security and safer computing.
5. Read the information, scrolling down in the window until you reach the end.
6. Click the Back button to return to the previous window.
7. Search for information about where you can view your security settings. For example, in Windows 7, search for **Action Center**.
8. Click a link for more information, such as the link *What is Action Center?*.
9. Click a link to open the Action Center. If you are using an operating system other than Windows 7, click a link to open the window where you can view security settings.
10. If necessary, expand your security settings.
11. With your teacher's permission, use the links on the page to view your installed security programs, such as you firewall program and your antivirus program.

12. Close the security settings window.
13. Close the Help program window.
14. If you are on a Windows OS, open the Command Prompt. If you are on a Mac OS, skip to step 22.
    ✔ *Click Start > All Programs > Accessories > Command Prompt.*
15. Type **dir**, and press [ENTER] to display a directory list of files.
16. Capture an image of the command prompt window.
    ✔ *Press* [ALT] + [PRTSC] .
17. Start a paint or graphics program and paste the screen capture into the file. It should look similar to Illustration E, although the actual directory contents depend on the contents of your system.
18. Save the file as **OS-6_image1_*xx***.
19. Close the Command Prompt window.
20. With your teacher's permission, print **OS-6_image1_*xx***.
21. Close the file, and exit the program.
22. With your teacher's permission, log off and/or shut down the computer.

Illustration E

part **2**

Applications

Application Basics

What Is Application Software?

Application software is a type of program, such as word-processing or spreadsheet software, that directs a computer to perform one or more tasks. Think about all the things a computer can help you do. You can write letters and reports. You can look up information, record songs, play games, chat with friends, and more. Application software makes it possible for your computer to perform such tasks.

There are many different types of application software (sometimes called applications), each best suited for a certain purpose. Some programs perform specific jobs. Others do many different tasks. Once you become familiar with application software, you can make choices to help your computer work faster and more efficiently.

Chapter Outline

 Lesson 9–1

Selecting Application Software

 Lesson 9–2

Obtaining Application Software

 Lesson 9–3

Getting Started with an Application

Selecting Application Software

Objectives

- Identify widely used types of application software.
- Compare and contrast three types of application software.
- Decide what kinds of applications will work best for you.

As You Read

Compare and Contrast   Use a three-column chart to compare three different types of application software. Write each type as a column header and list the features below the header.

🔑 Key Terms

- application software
- apps
- integrated software
- personal information manager (PIM) program
- productivity suite

Why Use Application Software?

Application software performs a specific job or task. For example, some applications help astronomers research stars. Others help doctors care for their patients. It is important to choose applications that can do the jobs you want done. The most common types of application software include:

- word processors for writing letters and reports
- spreadsheets for working with numbers and doing math
- databases for storing and finding information
- presentation graphics for creating slide shows
- telecommunications for using the Internet and e-mail
- **personal information manager (PIM)** programs for storing phone numbers and addresses and creating schedules

Types of Application Software

Application software falls into three basic categories: stand-alone programs, integrated software, and productivity suites. These forms differ in their features (the tasks they do) and in cost. Wise computer users choose the type of software that best fits their needs, their computers, and their budgets.

Why Use Application Software?

Application	Purpose
Word-processing	Create text-based documents such as reports and letters
Spreadsheet	Display and analyze business, personal, or financial data
Database	Store and organize information
Presentation	Create and deliver multimedia slide shows
Desktop-publishing	Create publications such as brochures and invitations
E-Mail	Create, send, receive, and organize electronic mail messages

Stand-alone Programs   Software that specializes in one task is called a stand-alone program. Because each program—such as a word processor, database, or spreadsheet—is dedicated to just one application, stand-alone programs can have many useful and advanced features. However, stand-alone programs may cost more than other forms of application software.

Because they focus on one kind of job, stand-alone programs usually have many very specialized features. Word processors, for example, give users tools to print labels and envelopes.

Integrated Software   Buying multiple stand-alone programs might require too much memory in your computer or may cost too much. You might want to do more with the software than a stand-alone program is capable of handling.

Integrated software programs combine the basic features of several applications into one package. They are not as powerful or as complete as their stand-alone counterparts, nor do they specialize in one application. However, integrated software usually is less costly and is fairly easy to use. These programs let you do basic work in several applications such as word processors, databases, spreadsheets, graphics, and more.

People use integrated software programs because the applications work in similar ways. That is, you often can use many of the same commands. You also can use data from one program in another. Popular integrated programs include AppleWorks® and Microsoft Works.

Spotlight on...

APPS FOR ALL

With its iPhone, Apple Computer pioneered the development of **apps**, third-party software programs developed specifically for smart phones, tablet computers such as iPad, and other handheld devices such as iPod Touch. These software applications usually cost as little as $2.00 each and take up very little space—usually around 6–10 megabytes.

As of 2011, Apple had 350,000 apps in its store—ranging from popular games like "Angry Birds," to practical apps that let you locate restaurants or count your calories. And there are some apps that are just plain silly, like the "Zombie" app that includes a Zombie weatherman who always forecasts doom and destruction "five days from now."

There are many advantages to using the same software at school and at home. For example, some programs allow you to use one computer to access files stored elsewhere.

Think About It!

For which reasons listed below would it be helpful to have the same programs at school and at home?

➤ I can work on my school projects at home.

➤ I can practice using the programs that I need at school.

➤ I can e-mail files to my teacher.

Productivity Suites   What if you need to use the advanced features of several stand-alone programs? You might select a productivity suite. Although one suite may differ from another, in general **productivity suites** combine several programs such as word-processing, spreadsheets, databases, and graphics. Like integrated software, the programs in productivity suites have a common look and feel. But productivity suites contain more than the basic software found in integrated programs. They contain the actual stand-alone programs with all their features.

Productivity suites generally cost more than integrated software, but usually they are cheaper than buying the stand-alone programs separately. Some common productivity suites include:

- Microsoft Office (with Word, Excel, PowerPoint, Outlook, and Access in the Windows version)
- Corel WordPerfect Office (with WordPerfect, Quattro Pro, Paradox, Corel Presentations, and Corel CENTRAL)
- Lotus SmartSuite (with WordPro, Lotus 1-2-3, Approach, Freelance Graphics, and Organizer)
- Adobe Creative Suite Design Premium (with Photoshop, Illustrator, InDesign, Dreamweaver, and Flash)

New Types of Applications

New types of software are always emerging. Current trends include applications that reside on Internet servers and applications that give everyday objects computing power.

Software as a Service   Some companies are now making applications available for use online. For example, Microsoft offers a version of its Microsoft Office suite online, and Google offers Google docs. For free, or low cost, users can access the applications using an Internet connection instead of installing the program on their own computer.

Pervasive Computing   Now that so many objects have embedded computer chips, applications are emerging that let users interact with their things. For example, applications make it possible for you to use voice activated telephone calling in your car and to program your dishwasher to alert you when it is full. programmable washing machines, pervasive computing

Which Type of Software Is Right for You?

The type of application software you choose depends on what you want it to do, how much you are willing to spend, and how easy the programs are to learn. It also depends on whether the software will work on your computer and how much space each program will take up on your hard drive. You might want to match the software you use at home with the programs you use at school so you can work on documents in both locations.

While most computers are sold with some application software installed, your computer may not have the software you need. Your needs will also change over time. Consider how problems could arise if you use the wrong software product when you try to complete a specific task—like attempting to performing advanced mathematical calculations using a word-processing program. Whether you consider upgrading your existing software, buying new programs, or downloading free software from the Internet, you should consider the following:

- Reviews of the software. Consumer reviews are usually a great source of information.
- User-friendliness. What kind of support is available? Is there live help included?
- Licensing agreements (see Lesson 9–2). Can you agree to the licensing requirements? Remember that copying a friend's program is piracy.

Figure 9.1.1 Popular productivity suites include Microsoft Office Home and Student 2010 and Adobe Creative Suite 5 Design Premium.

Obtaining Application Software

Objectives

- Explain why computer hardware and software must be compatible.
- Identify sources for obtaining application software.
- Summarize the best way to install or uninstall application software.
- Analyze how piracy affects makers and users of computer software.

Key Terms

- commercial software
- freeware
- install
- public domain software
- shareware
- software license
- system requirement
- uninstall

As You Read

Organizing Information Make an outline of the lesson. Use Roman numerals for main headings. Use capital letters for subheadings, and use numbers for supporting details.

Minimum System Requirements

Each software program has minimum **system requirements**. The computer must meet the minimum hardware and software needs of the program for it to work properly.

To get the most from your computer, it is important to choose software that will work with the following:

- your type of computer (Macintosh or PC compatible)
- microprocessor speed
- operating system (such as Linux, MAC OS X, or Windows 7)
- available amount of memory (RAM)
- available hard drive space
- special equipment, such as a DVD drive

Obtaining Application Software

Some application software is usually loaded on new computers. You can also obtain additional software in multiple forms.

Commercial Software Companies own the copyrights to the application software they sell to the public. This prevents you from legally copying it to sell it to others, giving it away, or sharing it. **Commercial software**, which may also be called proprietary software, is copyrighted software that you must buy before using it. Usually, you must agree to or sign a license, as well.

Shareware Copyrighted software that you can use on a try-before-you-buy basis is called **shareware**. If you decide to keep using it after that, you must pay a registration fee to the company. You are also allowed to copy shareware and give it to your friends. They, then, must follow the same process to acquire the software.

Freeware   Some companies give away their copyrighted software for free. This is known as **freeware**. The companies allow users to install the program as long as they do not resell it.

Open-Source Software   This kind of software makes the source code available to the public. The idea is that the software will improve and benefit from the innovations of users, who troubleshoot weak points and expand features. Critics, however, say that developers are not fairly compensated for their work (open source is not automatically "free") and also that the software development suffers if there is no central organizer.

Creative Commons   A creative commons license lets software copyright holders open some of their work for public use while letting them hold onto other parts of their work. As with open-source software, there are critics who complain that creative commons licenses eat away at intellectual property rights. Yet, several million pages of Web content are "brought to you" by Creative Commons licenses, such as The Library of Public Science, Garageband.com, and Flickr, the popular photo sharing sight.

Public Domain Software   On occasion, program authors allow you to use programs, share them, give them away, or even alter them to meet certain needs. This is called **public domain software**. Beware: the quality of these programs can vary widely, and they may contain more errors than other types of software.

Technology @ Work

Shareware companies make money by collecting fees for the products they send out on a free trial basis.

Think About It!
Shareware has many advantages for its producers. Identify each benefit of shareware listed below as either true or false.

➤ A user might try shareware rather than opting to buy a commercial program.

➤ Shareware companies do not have to pay for distribution.

➤ Users who do not like the product still have to pay for it.

Real-World Tech

Authoring Shareware   California-based Tenadar Software develops adventure games and distributes them as shareware. To play the game more than once, you send the requested royalty to the copyright holders. Who are they? Tenadar employees are all between 10 and 12 years old. What started as a fifth-grade project has grown into a business of several employees offering a variety of computer games for the Macintosh. The company's motto is "Great Software for Kids, by Kids."

   If you were to create shareware, what might you choose to develop?

Installing and Uninstalling Programs Application software must be **installed**, or prepared to run on a computer, before it can be used. You must copy it from a location such as a disk, a CD, or the Internet to the computer's hard drive.

Most programs come with an installation, or setup, program that prompts you to load the software onto the computer. Companies that make commercial software often provide printed or online guides, or telephone support, to help solve users' problems.

To delete a program from the computer, you must run a special removal program to properly remove, or **uninstall**, it. Otherwise, parts of the program can remain on the computer and may interfere with its operation.

Using Software Legally

Buying proprietary, copyrighted software usually permits the buyer to install and use that software on only one computer. This permission is contained in a document known as the **software license**. Typically, agreeing to the licensing agreement is part of the installation and registration process.

Software Piracy People who copy copyrighted software to install on other computers, give away, or sell are guilty of copyright violation and stealing, called software piracy. Violating a copyright and pirating software are both morally wrong and illegal. These activities discourage the authors of good software from writing new and better programs because they may not get paid for their work. Pirated software cannot be registered, so users do not get the support services they may need.

Figure 9.2.1 Most software programs come with a license agreement, like the one shown here for Windows 7 Professional.

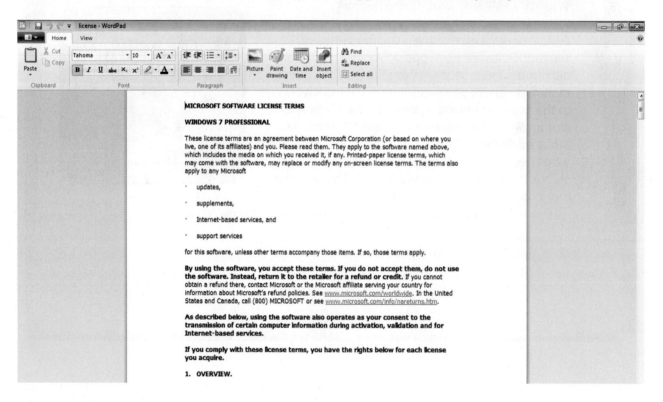

Getting Started with an Application

Objectives

- Describe how to launch a program.
- List common features of application software windows.
- Explain how to maximize and minimize a program window.
- Explain how to create, open, save, and close a file.
- Explain how to exit an application.

As You Read

Draw Conclusions Use a conclusion chart to help you understand how to use application software as you read.

Launching an Application

To get started with an application program, you open it using the operating system on your computer. Most applications use similar commands to accomplish basic tasks, such as starting, exiting, and saving. Once you learn these tasks in one program, you can easily transfer the knowledge so you can use other programs, too.

Starting a Program When a computer is turned on, it typically starts its operating system. You can then **launch**, or start, any application installed on the computer. You can launch an application in two ways: a menu or a desktop icon.

Menu In Windows, clicking the Start button displays a list of programs installed on the computer.

Desktop Icon Desktop icons are on-screen symbols that stand for a computer function or program. Because they are shortcuts to programs, it is helpful to customize your PC or Macintosh desktop to include icons for the programs you use most often.

Exploring Application Windows

A launched application appears in a frame called a window. You can work in any size window, but it is usually best to **maximize** the window, or make it as large as it can be. Sometimes you will want to use another program without closing the first one. You can **minimize** a program window, or make it as small as possible, so it remains out of the way while you use the other program.

Key Terms

- command
- groups
- launch
- maximize
- menu bar
- minimize
- Ribbon
- scroll
- tab
- title bar

Figure 9.3.1 The Windows 7 Start menu.

Figure 9.3.2 Applications in the Microsoft Office software suite share these basic elements.

The largest portion of an application window is the space for your work. The rest of the window contains tools that you use to develop your files.

Title Bar   The top row of an application window is called the **title bar**. The title bar shows the program's name and, in some cases, the name of the document you are working on.

The Ribbon   In Microsoft Office 2010, the **Ribbon** is the control center for using the application. The Ribbon has three parts:

- **Tabs.** Each **tab** contains important tasks you do within an application. For example, the Home tab in Excel offers formatting and formula options.
- **Groups.** Each tab contains **groups** of related tasks. For example, in Excel 2010, the Number group on the Home tab offers number formatting options.
- **Commands.** A **command** is a button, a box for entering information, or a menu. For example, the % button formats a number as a percentage.

The Menu   A **menu bar** lists sets of commands. On a Macintosh, it appears at the top of the screen. In Windows applications, the menu generally appears under the title bar.

Creating, Opening, Saving, and Closing

Application software lets you create new documents, save them for future use, or work on documents you have saved. You can close the application when you are done working. Most applications have a File menu (see below)—though the old 2007 version of Microsoft Office has an "Office" button—which includes these commands:

- New—creates a file into which you can enter data
- Open—finds a document that was previously saved as a disk file and displays it in a window
- Save—saves the document in the current window to a disk file
- Close—closes an open file
- Exit or Quit—closes the application and removes its window from the screen

Moving in the Application Window

Some tools allow you to **scroll**, or move from one part of a window to another. The scroll bars usually appear at the right side of the window and at the bottom. Boxes appear in these bars to show whether you are at the beginning or end of the file or somewhere in the middle. You can move from one place to another by either dragging these scroll boxes or clicking the scroll arrows at each end of the scroll bars.

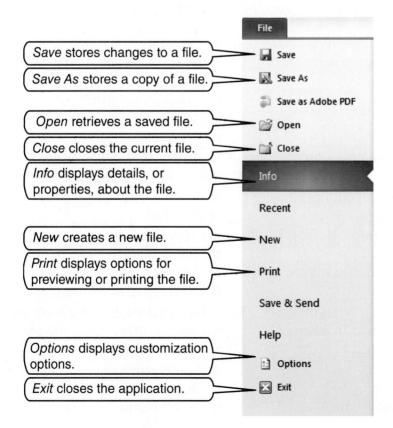

Save stores changes to a file.

Save As stores a copy of a file.

Open retrieves a saved file.

Close closes the current file.

Info displays details, or properties, about the file.

New creates a new file.

Print displays options for previewing or printing the file.

Options displays customization options.

Exit closes the application.

Figure 9.3.3 In Microsoft Office 2010, use the File menu in Backstage view to access commands for creating, saving, printing, and managing documents.

Use the Vocabulary

Directions: *Match each vocabulary term in the left column with the correct definition in the right column.*

_____ **1.** personal information manager
_____ **2.** integrated software
_____ **3.** productivity suite
_____ **4.** shareware
_____ **5.** freeware
_____ **6.** public domain software
_____ **7.** uninstall
_____ **8.** maximize
_____ **9.** apps
_____ **10.** scroll

a. software that you can try before purchasing
b. uncopyrighted software that is given away without cost
c. software that stores phone numbers and creates schedules
d. software that combines several different applications
e. third-party software programs developed specifically for certain smart phones
f. to delete a program from the computer
g. software that combines several applications
h. move from one place in a window to another
i. to make a window as large as possible
j. copyrighted software that is given away without cost

Check Your Comprehension

Directions: *Determine the correct choice for each of the following.*

1. Which of the following items is NOT an example of application software?

  a. spreadsheet
  b. database
  c. operating system
  d. word processor

2. Which of the following types of application software combines the basic features of several applications?

  a. stand-alone program
  b. integrated software
  c. office suite
  d. personal information manager (PIM) program

3. Which of the following types of software must be purchased in advance?

  a. commercial software
  b. shareware
  c. freeware
  d. public domain software

4. Which of the following types of software is available on a try-before-you-buy basis?

  a. commercial software
  b. shareware
  c. freeware
  d. public domain software

5. Which of the following features allows the user to launch an application?

  a. Help menu
  b. menu bar
  c. title bar
  d. desktop icon

6. Which of the following tools allows the user to move from one part of a window to another?

  a. scroll arrows
  b. scroll icons
  c. scroll menu
  d. scroll file

Think Critically

Directions: *Answer the following questions.*

1. Why might a computer user choose to purchase an integrated software program instead of a productivity suite?

2. Why should you check a program's system requirements before purchasing it?

3. Why is it important to uninstall a program you no longer use?

4. What is the difference between the New and Open commands on the File menu?

5. Why does an application window include tools such as scroll bars, scroll boxes, and scroll arrows?

Extend Your Knowledge

Directions: *Choose one of the following projects. Complete the exercise on a separate sheet of paper.*

A. The computer desktop shows many different types of icons. Icons can represent applications, files, or file folders. Experiment with a Macintosh or Microsoft Windows operating system. Make a three-column chart of the icons that appear on the desktop. Include a description of what happens when each icon is clicked, and identify what type of file or program the particular icon represents.

B. Several types of application software are listed in this chapter. They include word processors, spreadsheets, databases, presentation graphics, telecommunications, and personal information managers. Using the Internet or other resources, prepare a report that evaluates and compares two types of application software that you may use based on their appropriateness for a task, licensing agreements, and available support. Share your reports with the class.

Understanding Applications

How Can an Application Help You?

Application software provides the tools you need to get a job done. When you select the right program for the job, you can accomplish the task quickly and efficiently.

Applications are designed to meet different needs. Some are designed for one specific purpose, such as managing medical records or product inventory. Some are designed for multiple purposes, such as creating presentations on any subject.

In this chapter, you examine application software more closely. You learn more about types of applications, and how to use an application program to complete a task.

Chapter Outline

 Lesson 10–1

Examining Types of Application Software

 Lesson 10–2

Application Documentation and Versions

 Lesson 10–3

Using Application Software

Examining Types of Application Software

Objectives

- Compare and contrast horizontal and vertical applications.
- List examples of horizontal and vertical applications.
- Describe the role of beta versions in the software-testing process.

As You Read

Organize Information Use an outline to organize information about application software as you read.

🔑 Key Terms

- beta version
- copy protection
- horizontal application
- personal productivity program
- time-limited trial
- vertical application

Which Direction Is Right for You?

As discussed in Chapter 9, application software can be classified as a stand-alone, integrated, or productivity suite program. These types of software differ in the number of tasks they perform. Another way to classify application software is based on whether it is developed for a few users with very specific needs or whether it appeals to many users with shared needs.

Vertical Application A **vertical application** is designed for a very limited purpose, such as restaurant management or medical billing. Although the software is very useful to one field or business, it is of little interest to others.

Horizontal Application A **horizontal application** is a general-purpose program that meets the needs of many different users. It can be applied to many tasks. It also tends to be less expensive. It is likely that you will use horizontal, not vertical, applications for schoolwork you do on the computer. Horizontal applications are also used in many households to track finances and prepare tax forms.

Application Software → Vertical Application / Horizontal Application

Figure 10.1.1 Vertical application software is very specific—such as the computer-aided design programs used by architects—and horizontal application software—such as Microsoft Word—can be used by all types for everyday computing tasks.

Types of Horizontal Applications

Horizontal applications can be divided into several categories depending on the focus of the program.

Personal Productivity Programs The most popular horizontal applications are known as **personal productivity programs**. They help people work more effectively and include common applications such as word processors and database systems.

Multimedia Applications Some horizontal applications combine text, graphics, video, and sound. These include:

- desktop publishing—to combine text and graphics to produce newsletters and brochures

- graphics—to create and edit pictures
- Web page design—to create Web pages using sound, graphics, animation, and text

Internet Applications Some horizontal applications help computer users communicate over the Internet, including:

- Web browsers—to access data from the World Wide Web

- e-mail—to send and receive electronic messages

Testing Software

Beta versions, or early working copies of application software, are often sent to selected users to test the program. They use it for a period of time and report errors or problems to the developer. Beta versions help ensure that the final software will work correctly and offer customers the best tools possible.

Limited Trials To protect their work and guard against illegal copying, companies may set their beta software to expire after a certain date. These **time-limited trials** stop working after a certain number of uses or days.

Copyright Concerns Developers sometimes add **copy protection**, a physical device or software tool to keep users from making unauthorized copies of the beta software. These copyright safeguards can protect the sellers' property from illegal copying—a serious crime. Copy protection prevents beta software, which is still in development, from being widely distributed.

Real-World Tech

Protecting Digital Media Copy protection extends beyond software. Any form of information that is stored digitally is at risk of being illegally copied, including CD music and DVD movies. An early attempt by Sony Corporation to copy-protect CDs sold across Europe failed. It turned out that consumers could defeat the copy-protection method too easily.

Why do you think companies continue to research new and better ways to copy-protect their work from unethical and illegal duplication?

Application Documentation and Versions

Objectives

- Compare and contrast types of documentation.
- Explain the purpose of versions and version numbers.
- Describe why it is important to register your software.

Cause and Effect Use a cause-and-effect chart to help you understand the results of various software elements.

Key Terms

- documentation
- maintenance release
- site license
- troubleshoot
- version

Software Documentation

Most software packages provide directions on how to install the program, to use the application, and to **troubleshoot**, or correct, problems. These instructions, called **documentation**, are typically available in three forms:

- printed tutorials and reference manuals
- electronic help screens in the program or on CD-ROM
- information available on the publisher's Web site

Printed Documentation Installation instructions may be a single sentence printed on the software disk or CD. Other instructions may take the form of a booklet. Some programs include encyclopedia-type references that detail the software features.

Electronic Help Screens Application software frequently provides reference materials in electronic form as part of the program or on a separate CD-ROM. Opening the program's Help menu lets you troubleshoot problems as they happen and find out how to perform certain operations or tasks.

Figure 10.2.1 Most software programs provide help screens, like this one.

Web Sites Software documentation sometimes may be found on the software publisher's Web site. These sites often include answers to users' frequently asked questions (FAQs) and give other helpful hints. Files, sometimes called patches, may be available to fix, or patch, problems with the software. More so than other types of support, Web documentation can be updated quickly by the publisher and shared with users who need it.

Other Sources If you need more information than is provided by the software's documentation, telephone support may be an option. In addition, many helpful application software references and tutorials are available in libraries, online, or at bookstores.

Versions of Software

Successful software can lead to multiple **versions**, or releases. Companies typically identify their new software with a version number. A version can be identified by the year it was released, such as Microsoft Word 2010. Sometimes the version number is a whole number followed by a decimal or a letter, such as 5.D or 6.22. Smaller numbers such as 1.2 or 1.2a indicate a **maintenance release**—a minor revision to correct errors or add minor features. A larger number indicates that the software has significant revisions with new features.

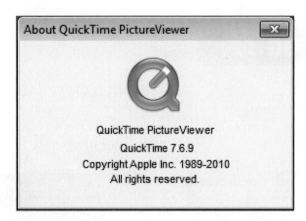

Figure 10.2.2 In most programs, you can find the version number and other information through the Help menu.

There is a gradual but steady shift in most companies away from outputting files in hard copy (printed) to outputting soft copy (digital or electronic files). Digital output includes any information displayed on a computer, including application files, e-mail, e-mail attachments, and Web pages

Think About It!

Outputting files electronically is convenient, fast, and can save costs related to printing and mailing. It also poses some risks. Which of the following issues do you think poses the greatest risk to companies and individuals?

▷ lack of hard copy documentation

▷ risk of unauthorized access to data

▷ risk of loss or damage to data

▷ inability to open or read incompatible files

Technology @ Home

One type of software sees seasonal increase in sales. Every spring, many families purchase tax preparation software to assist in preparing annual federal tax returns to send to the Internal Revenue Service by April 15, the filing date.

Think About It!

Some revisions in tax preparation software are out of the control of the programmers. Of the reasons listed below for a revision, which do you think developers could not have predicted?

➢ bugs in the program

➢ changes in tax laws

➢ changes in the data user's input

The version number may not be obvious when an application launches. However, most software manufacturers locate the version number in the Help menu, where you can select the About command. This will open a window with useful information about the software—including its version and revision number.

Software Registration and Protection

When you install software, you are typically asked to register, or be recorded as the owner of your copy, with the publisher. You can register by faxing or mailing a printed form that comes with the package or by completing an online form that can be sent to the software manufacturer.

Registration allows you to use the software legally. Since the software company knows you have a legal copy of its product, it may offer services such as free technical support. The company may also send notices of new version releases or upgrades offered at no cost or at a discounted price.

Organizations that have many computers—such as schools, businesses, or government agencies—may purchase a **site license** instead of registering individual copies of the software. A site license gives permission to install the software on a specific number of computers for the organization's internal use only.

 Spotlight on...

NORAH SCHOLL
❝*Easter Seals' award-winning Assistive Technology program . . . makes me more independent.*❞

Norah Scholl

She is the fastest typist in her grade. Why is that so special? Well, Norah Scholl cannot use her hands. Thanks to upgraded software provided by Easter Seals and special hardware, she does many of the things other middle-school students do.

Norah is the youngest person ever to master the special software that now allows her to speak into her computer to operate it.

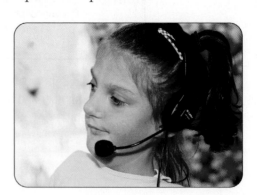

Using Application Software

Objectives

- Identify and describe common features of application software.
- Explain how default settings can be changed to suit a user's needs.
- Explain the benefits of multitasking.

As You Read

Summarize Use a chart to summarize the purpose of each common feature of application software as you read.

Working in an Application's Window

There are several common features you are likely to find in your application windows. You use a mouse or keyboard to navigate in the window, to make selections, and input commands.

Application Workspace The largest area of a program's window is called the **application workspace**. It displays the file in which you are working. You can enter text, graphics, or other data into the workspace. You also can locate and open a saved file into the application workspace. The workspace looks different depending on the application. For example, a word-processing application workspace looks like a page; a spreadsheet workspace looks like a grid of columns and rows.

Title Bar The title bar usually displays the name of the application and the name of the file you are in. If this is a new document, you will see a placeholder name, such as *Untitled* or *Document 1*.

Toolbar and Command Buttons Most applications have a **toolbar** or **command buttons** that you use to select a command. A toolbar is a row of icons or buttons. Clicking a toolbar icon or command button tells the application to execute that command.

Key Terms

- application workspace
- command button
- default
- menu
- multitask
- preference
- Print Preview
- status bar
- tab
- toolbar
- zoom

Figure 10.3.1 The Ribbon in Microsoft Office 2007 and 2010 programs provides easy access to commands. Other programs may use toolbars or menus.

Some applications have more than one toolbar. Many toolbars can be dragged to a different location, if desired, or even "floated" in the application workspace.

Menus and Tabs   **Menus** and **tabs** give you access to the program's commands. They present a list—or menu—of choices so you can select the one you need.

Viewing a Document   Many programs let you change how a document is displayed in the application workspace. Changing the view can help you accomplish specific tasks. For example, you might change to **Print Preview** to see how a file will look when it is printed, or change to Draft view when you do not need to see features such as graphics or columns.

Adjusting the Display   You can adjust the display of the data in the workspace by using the **zoom** control. This option magnifies the view of the document. You typically can set it to any size you prefer between 10 percent and 500 percent. Zoom options do not affect the printing size, only how you see your document on the screen. A 100 percent magnification shows the document at the same size that a printed copy will be.

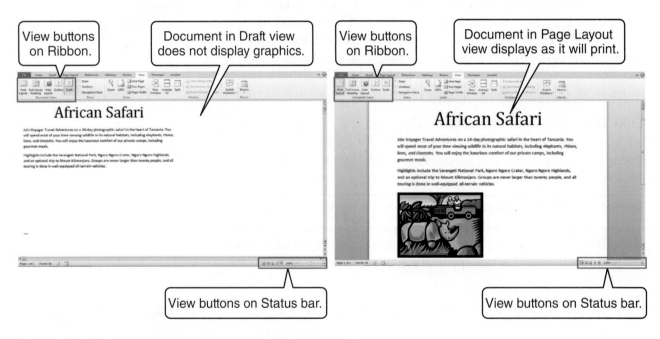

Figure 10.3.2 The same document displayed in Draft view (left) and Page Layout view (right) in Microsoft Office 2010.

Checking Your Status Many software programs display a **status bar** below the application workspace. A status bar shows information about the program and other useful messages. For example, the status bar in Word displays the current page number, total page count, and the number of the line on which you are currently typing.

Setting Options and Preferences

Software applications come with **default** settings. These are options preset by the software maker, based on what most users prefer. Most applications let you select options or **preferences** and change them to suit your way of working. Changing an option or preference replaces the default setting.

You can change such features as how the screen looks, how the spelling checker works, and the preferred location for saving documents. You can choose to apply a preference to a current document only, or save it in the computer as a new default setting. Many programs also allow you to reset the revised default settings back to their original settings.

Language Arts Settings in the Proofing section of Microsoft Word's Options can help you check and correct your spelling and grammar as you type. See which options are set as program defaults. Customizing these settings may enable you to write better and more clearly.

Figure 10.3.3 Changing default Display settings in Adobe Reader.

Working with Two or More Programs

The term **multitasking** means working with more than one computer application at the same time. Computer operating systems allow you to multitask by giving sections of memory to each application that is running. You can then switch among them as needed.

To multitask, open the desired programs, such as a word processor and a spreadsheet. Each application appears in a separate window. Select one window by clicking its button on the taskbar, and begin to work. You can move from one window to another. If you create a chart in a spreadsheet, you can cut or copy and paste it into the word processor. When you are done, exit each application to close your programs.

Figure 10.3.4 Multitasking means using more than one program at a time.

Use the Vocabulary

Directions: *Match each vocabulary term in the left column with the correct definition in the right column.*

_____ **1.** vertical application
_____ **2.** horizontal application
_____ **3.** beta version
_____ **4.** copy protection
_____ **5.** documentation
_____ **6.** version
_____ **7.** site license
_____ **8.** application workspace
_____ **9.** zoom
_____ **10.** preference

a. permission to install software on multiple computers
b. main area of a program window
c. a program designed for a limited purpose
d. a general-purpose program that can be used by a variety of users to change the size of the data on the screen
e. tool that keeps a user from making unauthorized copies of software
f. instructions that make using software easier
h. test copy of software that companies use to find errors
i. setting defined by the computer user
j. copy of software that may have new features

Check Your Comprehension

Directions: *Determine the correct choice for each of the following.*

1. Which of the following is an example of a vertical application?

  a. an Internet browser
  b. a library card catalog
  c. a popular personal information manager
  d. an inexpensive spreadsheet

2. Which of the following is NOT an example of multitasking?

  a. switching from one program to another
  b. moving data to a different document
  c. keeping your desktop clear
  d. working in three or four applications at once

3. Software documentation can help you do which of the following?

  a. troubleshoot problems
  b. obtain a site license
  c. make an application vertical
  d. create a new version

4. Which of the following is NOT a characteristic of a maintenance release?

  a. minor revisions to existing features
  b. minor features added
  c. letter added to the version number
  d. significant improvements

5. Changing the zoom controls allows you to do which of the following?

  a. change the font of the data on the screen
  b. adjust the size of the data on the screen
  c. change the order in which the data is displayed on the screen
  d. adjust the document's margins

6. Which of the following menus would a word processor most likely have?

  a. Calculate
  b. Message
  c. Sound Controls
  d. Edit

◯ Think Critically

Directions: *Answer the following questions.*

1. What are some consequences of violating copyright laws to both software companies and to users?

2. In what ways do beta versions help improve new software applications?

3. Why is good documentation important?

4. Why might a user choose to upgrade to a newer version of a particular software application?

5. How are the terms *default* and *preferences* related?

◯ Extend Your Knowledge

Directions: *Choose one of the following projects. Complete the exercise on a separate sheet of paper.*

A. Horizontal applications are popular types of software, such as word processors and Internet browsers, with which most computer users work. Vertical applications are designed for more specific activities. Interview two adults who use computers for their jobs. Identify the types of applications they use at work. What programs do they use that are specific to their careers or businesses? How do they use popular applications differently? For both types of software, to what extent do licensing agreements and customer service/ technical support influence their purchasing decisions? Create a Venn diagram comparing your findings.

B. Several types of documentation are listed in this chapter, including printed material, help screens, and Web sites. Using the Internet or other resources, prepare a report that discusses documentation. Discuss the purpose of each type of documentation. How and when might you need to use each—now and in the future? What are some of the different features available in each type of documentation? Share your reports with the class.

Word-Processing Basics

What Is Word Processing? In 1968, IBM first used the term *word processing*. The term described machines that could be used to type a document, remember the typist's keystrokes, and produce more than one copy. With this new tool, workers saved time.

That was just the beginning. Today's word-processing programs do much more. Suppose you were writing something by hand and made a mistake or changed your mind about what you wanted to say. If you were using a pen, you would probably cross out the words you wanted to change. Doing that leaves the page messy, though. With word-processing software, you can change the text and still create neat pages. You can even save what you typed and use it again a day, a week, or even a year later.

Chapter Outline

Creating a Document

Objectives

- List the four basic functions of word-processing programs.
- Name two tools used to navigate a word-processing document.
- Summarize four key features of word-processing programs.
- Identify three standards for word-processing documents.

As You Read

Organize Information   Complete a spider map to help you organize basic facts about word processing as you read.

Key Terms

- AutoCorrect
- autosave
- insertion point
- pagination
- word-processing program
- word wrap

Functions of Word-Processing Programs

Word-processing programs are used for creating and printing text documents. These programs have four functions:

- writing—entering text and symbols into a document
- editing—revising or reorganizing the text
- formatting—changing how the text looks on the page
- printing—producing a printed copy

These tasks do not need to be done all at once or even in the order shown here. Whatever the order, these four functions are at the heart of word processing.

Writing

Editing

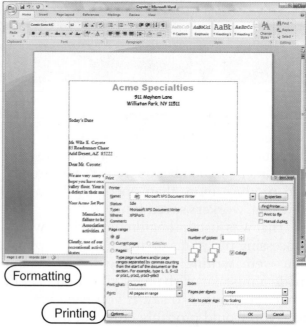

Formatting

Printing

Figure 11.1.1 The four main functions of a word-processing program.

Uses of Word Processing

Word-processing programs can be used to create almost any kind of printed document, such as letters, reports, and brochures. They can also be used to create calendars, return-address labels, and labels for homemade CDs. It is no surprise that word-processing software is the application that people use more than any other application.

Working with a Word-Processing Document

When you open a word-processing program, a new, blank document is created. It looks like a blank piece of paper on the screen. The program is ready for you to start writing. In Word 2010, you can create another document at any time by clicking the File tab, clicking the New command, selecting Blank Document, and clicking the Create button. In Windows OS, most word-processing programs allow you to create a new document by pressing Ctrl+N (hold the Ctrl key and press N). In Mac OS, this is similarly done by pressing Command+N.

Every time you create a new document you need to save it. Click the Save button on the Quick Access toolbar. When the Save As dialog box opens, name your document.

Insertion Point The **insertion point** shows where the text you type will appear. It moves as you type.

Scrolling As you write, you might want to reread or change something you wrote earlier. That is made easy by scrolling—using the mouse or keyboard to move through the document.

Technology @ School

Some students sharpen their word-processing skills by writing to pen pals in other countries.

Think About It!

Before writing a letter, think about the topics you could cover. Which items listed below would you discuss in a pen-pal letter?

➤ your family

➤ your school

➤ your hometown

➤ your math class

➤ your favorite movie

Figure 11.1.2 All word-processing programs share basic features, but commands may be located on a different toolbar or menu.

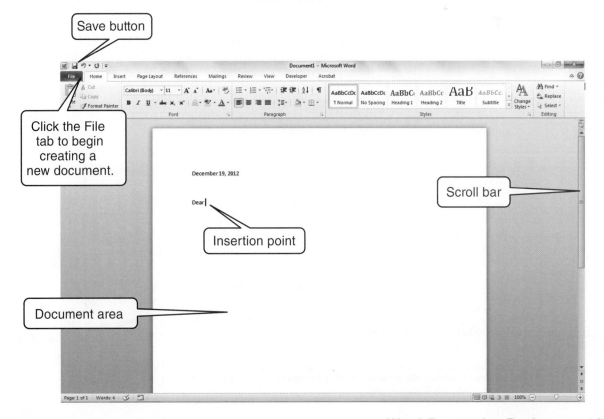

Save button

Click the File tab to begin creating a new document.

December 19, 2012

Dear

Insertion point

Scroll bar

Document area

You can scroll up or down by using the mouse to click the scroll bar or drag the scroll box at the right of the document window. Many mouse devices have scrolling wheels. You can also use the Up and Down arrow keys or the Page Up, Page Down, Home, and End keys to move around in the document.

Basic Features

Most word-processing programs have these features to help you write, edit, and save your work.

- With **word wrap**, the program automatically starts a new line, or "wraps" the text, when the current line is full. If you wish to force text onto a new line, press Enter or Return.

- When a page is full, the **pagination** feature automatically starts a new page. You can also force a new page by inserting a special character, called a page break.

- The **AutoCorrect** feature fixes common spelling mistakes as they are typed. You can turn off this feature or modify it to accept unusual words that you often use.

- The AutoRecover or **autosave** feature protects you from losing work. It does so by automatically saving a document as often as you want. If the computer shuts down accidentally, you can retrieve the most recently saved version.

Typing Standards for Word-Processing Documents

As you write, keep in mind three standards of style to make your work look professional.

- Two standards are met automatically by many programs. They change two hyphens (--) to an em dash (—). They also convert quotation marks to curly quotation marks, or "smart quotes."

- The other standard is not automatic—you have to remember to do it. This standard is to type one space, not two, between sentences.

Figure 11.1.3 Word wrap and pagination are two of the basic word-processing features.

Editing a Document

Objectives

- Explain how to identify document files in a list of files.
- Describe the benefits of selecting text.
- Contrast different editing tools, such as the Cut and Copy commands, and the Undo and Redo commands.

As You Read

Identify Cause and Effect Complete a cause-and-effect chart to help you identify what happens when word-processing functions are applied as you read.

Opening a Document for Editing

Editing can take place at any time after you have created the document. You can go back and edit text you recently entered, or you can edit a document you created, saved, and closed. To do so, you need to open the file you created so you can work on it again.

You can use a word-processing program's Open command to open a file, or you can use your operating system's file management features to find files on a disk. In Windows, file names have extensions, such as .txt, .rtf, .docx, or .wpd, although these extensions may be hidden from view. On a Macintosh computer, documents are simply listed by file name.

Word-processing programs make editing easy. You can add words simply by typing them. You can delete characters by pressing the Delete or Backspace keys. Powerful features in these programs help you do even more.

Selecting Text

Usually, people edit more than one character at a time. The **select text** feature lets you highlight anything from a word to a whole document. Then you can delete it, move it, copy it, or change its formatting.

To select text, simply click and drag the mouse over the text you want (see Figure 11.2.1 on the next page). Most programs also let you select text by using the keyboard. You hold down the Shift key while you use the arrow keys and other keys to select the text. Selected text is highlighted on the screen; that is, it appears with a different background color.

Key Terms

- Clipboard
- Copy
- Cut
- data source
- mail merge
- Paste
- Redo
- select text
- Undo

Cutting, Copying, and Pasting

Two common reasons for selecting text are cutting and copying. Both actions place the text in the Clipboard.

The Clipboard   The **Clipboard** stores cut or copied text while you work. Once you close the program or shut down the computer, items on the Clipboard are no longer available. Some programs store only one item at a time, so cutting or copying new text replaces what was held before. Some programs can hold many items on the Clipboard.

- The **Cut** command removes the selected text from a document and places it on the Clipboard.

- The **Copy** command places a duplicate of the selected text on the Clipboard.

Pasting   Use the **Paste** command to insert an item copied or cut to the Clipboard. Simply place the insertion point where you want the item to appear. Then, click the Paste icon on the Clipboard group of the Home tab and press Ctrl+V. The copied item or text appears where you want it.

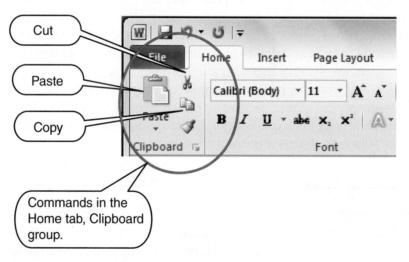

Commands in the Home tab, Clipboard group.

Figure 11.2.1 The Cut, Copy, and Paste buttons in the Clipboard group in Microsoft Word 2010.

Using Cut and Paste Moving a sentence from the middle of a paragraph to the beginning can be done by selecting and dragging it. You can use Cut and Paste to move that sentence farther—for example, to another page—or to move text or a graphic from one document to another. You can even open a new window, paste the text you cut from another document, and save the pasted text as a new document.

Using Copy and Paste Copying and pasting saves time when you need to repeat some text. You can also copy and paste to bring a graphic from one document into another.

Undoing and Redoing

Word-processing programs have commands that can undo or cancel an edit. If you delete a word by mistake, you can use the **Undo** command to put it back. Many programs also have a **Redo** command. You can use this feature to put a change back in effect after cancelling it with Undo.

Figure 11.2.2 The Undo and Redo commands are on the Quick Access toolbar in Microsoft Office 2010.

Merging

Most word-processing programs have a **mail merge** feature you can use to generate customized form letters, mailing labels, envelopes, and even e-mails. You create a word-processing document that includes the content you want everyone to receive and then merge it with a **data source** of customized information, such as names and addresses.

The Copy command isn't suitable if the copied text will change.

Think About It!

Think about what the Copy command does. For which items below would the copy command be useful? For which would it not be useful?

➤ the delivery address for letters to different people

➤ the cook's name on the top of recipe cards

➤ the title of a CD in a list of CDs

➤ a paragraph to appear in two different letters

Formatting a Document

Objectives

- Explain what default formatting is.
- Identify four parts of any document that can be formatted.
- Summarize the advantages of dividing a document into sections for formatting.
- Compare portrait and landscape orientation.

As You Read

Summarize Complete a summary chart to help you identify different features that can be formatted as you read the lesson.

🔑 Key Terms

- default
- page formatting
- sans serif
- section
- serif

Figure 11.3.1 Dialog boxes like these let you change all sorts of formatting options.

Appearance Is Important

A document's formatting—its appearance—is sometimes as important as its contents. This is why word-processing programs have so many tools to format documents.

Word-processing programs include many preset formats, called **defaults**. The program applies these formats automatically, unless you change them. For example, many word processors use Times New Roman as the default font. Word 2010, however, uses Calibri, but you can change to a different font whenever you want.

You can format four distinct parts of a document: characters, paragraphs, sections, and pages.

The Font dialog box lets you format individual characters or groups of characters.

The Paragraph dialog box lets you change spacing, indentations, and other features of a paragraph.

Formatting Characters

Character formatting lets you change the look of letters. Three primary formats are applied to characters:

- The **font** is the family of characters used. A font is a named set of characters that have the same appearance.
- Font size is the height of characters, measured in **points**. One point equals 1/72 inch.
- Font styles are characteristics such as boldface and italic.

There are four general categories of fonts. **Serif** fonts, such as Times New Roman, have serifs, or lines projecting from the ends. They are easy to read and are often used for document text. **Sans serif** fonts, such as Arial, do not have serifs, and are often used for headings. Script fonts are used to simulate handwriting. Decorative fonts have embellishments such as curlicues.

Formatting Paragraphs

A paragraph is any text that ends with the press of the Enter key. Whenever you press Enter, you create a paragraph. You can change many paragraph formats, including:

- Alignment—This is the way a paragraph lines up between the page's left and right margins.
- Line spacing—This is the amount of space between the lines of text in a paragraph.
- Indentation—This is added space between a margin and the text.
- Tabs—These are stops placed along a line. Pressing the Tab key moves the insertion point to the next stop. Tabs can be used to align text in tables or columns.

You can apply these paragraph formats through dialog boxes, but you also can apply some of them by using ruler settings. In Word 2010, for example, you can create a tab stop by displaying the ruler and then clicking the horizontal ruler at the point where the tab stop should appear. You can change a paragraph's indentation by dragging indent markers, which normally are found at each end of the ruler. Ruler settings apply only to the paragraph that contains the insertion point, or to selected paragraphs.

Figure 11.3.2 A key feature of a word-processing program is the ability to align and position text on the page.

In Wallace County, the number of youth soccer teams is growing very quickly. In 1995, each township had only two or three teams. Today there are nearly three dozen teams in the Kids Community Soccer League, with new ones created every day.

WALLACE COUNTY YOUTH SOCCER TEAMS: 1995 AND TODAY

Township	1995	Today
Boscoe	3	7
Clements	2	9

Ruler

This paragraph is left-aligned, and its first line is indented.

Left margin

This text is aligned in column using tabs.

This paragraph is centered between the margins.

Right margin

Figure 11.3.3 Word-processing programs let you print documents in portrait and landscape orientations.

Formatting Sections

In some word processors, a **section** is part of a document that contains specific format settings. A document begins as one section, but you can insert section breaks to divide the document into more than one section. You can format each section in its own unique way. For example, in a most newsletters, the first section is one column, so the title spans the width of the page, but the next section is two columns, allowing more articles to fit on the page.

Formatting Pages

Page formatting affects how and where text is positioned on the page. The main features in page formatting are:

- Paper size—Various sizes of paper can be used to create documents.

- Orientation—Text can be printed in one or two directions, or orientations. In portrait orientation, text is printed down the page's long edge, creating a page that is taller than it is wide. In landscape orientation, text is printed down the page's short edge, creating a page that is wider than it is tall.

- Margins—This is the space between the four paper edges and the text. This open space frames the page and can make the text easier to read.

- Headers and footers—This is special information placed at the top of the page—headers—or at the bottom—footers. These placeholders can show page numbers, the date, or the document's title.

- Graphics—These include drawings, photographs, or other images. Some graphics, like charts and graphs, are informative. Others are decorative. Many word-processing programs let you create or add graphics.

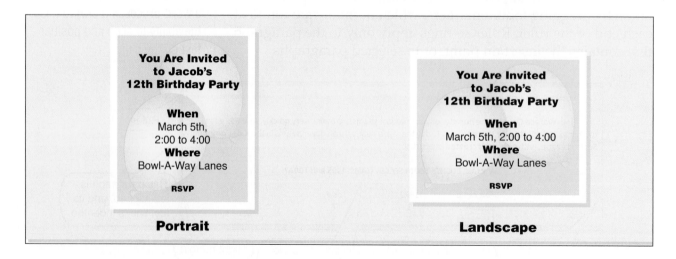

You Are Invited
to Jacob's
12th Birthday Party

When
March 5th,
2:00 to 4:00
Where
Bowl-A-Way Lanes

RSVP

Portrait

You Are Invited
to Jacob's
12th Birthday Party

When
March 5th, 2:00 to 4:00
Where
Bowl-A-Way Lanes

RSVP

Landscape

Basics of Desktop Publishing

Objectives

- Describe the benefits of creating documents in a desktop-publishing program.
- Compare word-processing and desktop-publishing programs.
- Summarize the basic steps in desktop-publishing.

As You Read

Organize Information   Complete a sequence chart to help you organize basic facts about desktop publishing as you read the lesson.

Publishing from a Desktop

Desktop-publishing (DTP) programs are used to create high-quality publications that look as if they were produced on a printing press. They can be used to do some of the same tasks as word-processing programs, but they greatly expand design options so you can create high-quality documents.

Word-processing and DTP programs complement each other. In fact, they are often used together. Text is frequently created and edited in a word processor, and then that text is brought into a DTP program to be formatted for publishing.

Benefits of DTP   Desktop-publishing software gives you tools you can use to produce the files and fonts for large projects, such as books, magazines, and other complex printed materials. DTP software also gives you more control over the final product than you would have if you hired a professional contractor or other "outside" source.

Drawbacks of DTP   Desktop publishing is not without its problems. Often it is a team effort, which means that the work of writers, editors, artists, and layout specialists has to be carefully coordinated. These complex programs can also be more difficult to learn than word-processing software.

Creating a Document with Desktop Publishing

Some popular desktop-publishing programs include Microsoft Publisher, Adobe® PageMaker®, QuarkXPress®, and InDesign®. Using any of these programs to publish a document involves six steps. While you can move back and forth among these different steps, separating them makes it easier to see what each one involves and how they fit together.

🔑 Key Terms

- crop
- frame
- master page

The Arts Desktop-publishing programs let you enhance a document in many ways. You can use color, large type, bold and italic type, drawings, and special effects to make the pages interesting. Experienced designers offer the following guidelines for using these tools:

- Use only a few fonts and choose appropriate ones for the task.

- Don't overuse color, bold, or italic type. Too much can make a document difficult to read.

- Use type size, space, and other elements to emphasize the most important parts of the document.

- Keep the reader in mind. Design a document so that it is easy to read and use.

Designing the Layout The most important task—and the one that is done first—is designing the document's layout. A designer plans how each page will look by creating a **master page**. This provides the pattern for all the pages to follow and sets the basic features of the document's look, including:

- page size and margins

- number of columns, width of columns, and space between columns

- type font, size, and treatment for all the major elements that will be repeated in the document, such as titles, headings, text, and headers and footers

- rules that will be followed in placing, sizing, and treating images

The columns on the master page create areas called **frames**. Frames are simply empty containers that will eventually hold text or graphics. They will be filled as you add text and images to the document.

Entering Text Text can be placed in the frames by typing it, but desktop-publishing software is not well suited to entering text. Therefore, text is usually created and edited in a word-processing program. Then, that text is automatically placed in the DTP frames, filling as many pages as needed.

If the writer has formatted the text by using styles in the word processor, the DTP software may be able to use those styles to identify and format different parts of the document automatically.

Comparing Word-Processing and Desktop-Publishing

Word-Processing Programs	Desktop-Publishing Programs
Emphasizes content—the text	Emphasizes appearance—layout and the mix of text and graphics
Can import many kinds of graphics	Can import many kinds of graphics
Can format text in many ways	Has more tools for formatting text and for combining text and graphics
Can produce relatively simple documents, such as brochures and newsletters	Can produce very complex documents, including magazines and books
Effective at black-and white documents; not effective with full-color documents	Effective with both black-and-white and full-color documents
Prints on standard office machines such as laser and inkjet printers	Prints on high-quality printers

Importing Graphics After the text has been imported, images can be added. A location for each image is found. The text then wraps around the art.

Laying Out the Document A DTP user then formats the document by adjusting the size of art and the use of space to make the page attractive and easy to read. Program tools make it easy to change an image's size or shape. Other tools can be used to **crop** the image, or trim it to focus only on certain parts.

Checking and Revising DTP documents are often printed several times before they are finished. Editors review these versions, called proofs, to make sure that no text has been lost and that the text reads correctly. Designers check design elements. Then DTP users make changes to the document.

Printing After the document is final, it is printed. Sometimes, DTP documents are published on the Web or are printed on powerful color laser printers. Items such as books and magazines are sent to printers who print and bind finished copies. For color documents, the DTP program can prepare color separations, which are separate versions of the document's pages. Each version contains a specific set of colors; each of which is applied in a separate pass through the printer. When the colors are combined, the full-color document is finished.

Career Corner

Workers who do desktop publishing are called graphic designers. There are about 200,000 graphic designers in the United States. Most work for companies, but about one third work for themselves.

The Bureau of Labor Statistics says that in the next few years the number of jobs for desktop publishers will grow by a huge amount—about 67 percent.

Interested students can take courses in design at some colleges and professional schools. Of course, experience in using computers is a great plus!

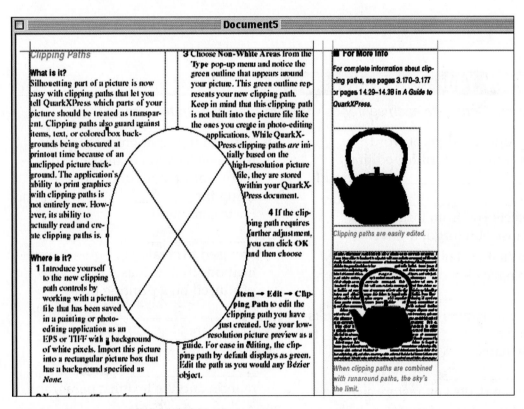

Figure 11.4.1 Designing a page in a desktop publishing program.

Use the Vocabulary

Directions: *Match each vocabulary term in the left column with the correct definition in the right column.*

_____ **1.** insertion point
_____ **2.** word wrap
_____ **3.** pagination
_____ **4.** AutoCorrect
_____ **5.** select text
_____ **6.** Clipboard
_____ **7.** default
_____ **8.** section
_____ **9.** page format

a. features that identify how and where text is positioned

b. a separate part of a document with its own formatting

c. area where cut or copied text is temporarily stored

d. fixes common spelling mistakes as they are typed

e. shows the place in a document where text will be added or deleted

f. automatically moves text to a new line

g. the automatic division of a document into pages

h. action made on a block of text before changing it

i. preset formats

Check Your Comprehension

Directions: *Complete each sentence with information from the chapter.*

1. The four functions of word processing are writing, editing, _____, and printing.

2. The _____ feature protects you from losing work because you forgot to save.

3. One standard of word processing is to have only one space after each _____.

4. Some programs add extra characters, called a(n) _____, to a file name.

5. The _____ command lets you restore a change that you have just undone.

6. You can repeat a sentence in more than one location in the same document—or in other documents—by using the _____ and Paste commands.

7. _____ programs are used to create high-quality publications that look as if they were produced on a printing press.

8. One _____ equals 1/72 inch.

9. Indentation refers to the _____ between a margin and the text in a paragraph.

10. An example of a(n) _____ is a page number that appears at the bottom of every page in a report.

Directions: *Answer the following questions.*

1. What is the difference between a serif font and a sans serif font? Give examples of each.

2. Why is selecting text an important function in word processing?

3. Why are there both mouse and keyboard methods for performing actions such as selecting, cutting, copying, and pasting?

4. What is the difference between landscape and portrait orientation?

5. Why might a student type his or her name and the class period in the header of a homework assignment?

Extend Your Knowledge

Directions: *Choose one of the following projects. Complete the exercise on a separate sheet of paper.*

A. Open a word-processing program and type these directions in full. Add the heading *Formatting Sample* above the first line of text. Then do the following: (1) Copy your text and paste the copy below the first paragraph; (2) Format the text by changing fonts and type size; (3) Change the page to landscape orientation; (4) Add a header; and (5) Print your document. Remember to save your file.

B. Open a word-processing program. Choose one of the menus on the menu bars or tabs on the Word 2010 Ribbon. Write down the items listed on the menu or the groups listed on the tab. Choose two of the menu items or one of the groups. Look up the commands in the Help system. Take notes on what you read. Make a presentation to the class describing which actions result from choosing each command. Identify a way that someone could use the commands in working on a document.

Using a Word-Processing Application

What Does Word Processing Do? In 1875, Mark Twain sent his publisher a historic manuscript. It was the first time that an author submitted a manuscript that had been written using a typewriter. Now, more than 125 years later, word-processing software does far more than a typewriter ever could. As discussed in Chapter 11, you can format text, add graphics, and even print documents in color.

In this chapter, you learn more about the word-processing tools you can use to create neat and professional documents. You learn how to select a view, how to insert pictures and symbols, and how to prepare a document for printing. Finally, you explore the options for collaborating with others to improve your work.

Chapter Outline

 Lesson 12–1

Viewing a Document

 Lesson 12–2

Enhancing a Document

 Lesson 12–3

Formatting and Printing

 Lesson 12–4

Making and Tracking Edits

Viewing a Document

Objectives

- Compare different document views in a word-processing program.
- Describe the benefits of using split windows.
- Explain how to use a document map to move through a document.

As You Read

Compare and Contrast Complete a conclusion chart to help you compare the different ways of viewing a word-processing document as you read.

Key Terms

- document map
- pane
- Print Layout view
- Web Layout view

Figure 12.1.1 A Word 2010 document in Page Layout view.

Changing Views

Word-processing software lets you look at your documents in several different views.

Basic View The most basic view, called Normal view or Draft view, shows text in the correct font and has character formatting like bold and italic. The basic view does not display certain parts of a document, such as margins, headers and footers, or columns.

Print Layout View The **Print Layout view** shows how a document will look when it is printed. This view may be called Page Layout view, Layout view, or Page view. It includes all text, graphics, margins, and other elements that will appear on the printed page. In this view, you can edit headers and footers, change margins, and work with columns and graphics.

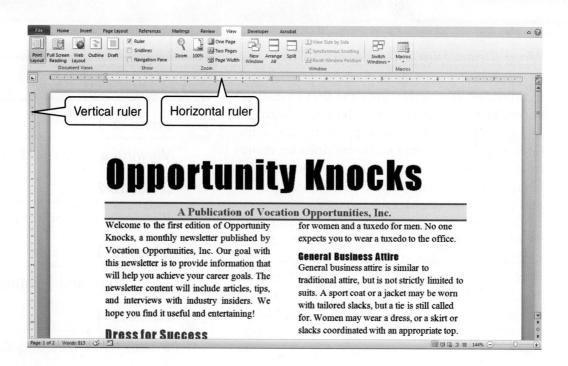

Web Layout View Some word-processing programs have a **Web Layout view**, which shows how a document will appear when published on the World Wide Web.

Outline View An Outline view reveals the structure of a document. It breaks down the document into its major headings, subheadings, and text. You can choose to view only the main headings, both the headings and subheadings, or everything, including the entire text. This view is useful when editing a large document. Some programs let users rearrange large amounts of text simply by dragging outline headings from one place to another.

Ruler Settings Some views display a horizontal ruler—a guide at the top of the document window, showing you where each paragraph's tab stops and indents are located. In Word's Page Layout view, you also see a vertical ruler on the left side of the screen. You can use rulers to set margins, tabs, indents, and other paragraph formats.

Changing Views It's easy to change from one view to another. Just go to the View menu and select the option you want. Some programs also have small icons representing different views near the status bar. Clicking an icon changes the view.

Zooming In and Out

The Zoom feature changes the size of the text displayed on the screen. While larger text is more readable, smaller text allows you to see more at once. But only at 100 percent will you have an accurate picture of the text as it will appear when it is printed. At this percentage, you get the benefit of a program's WYSIWYG (What You See Is What You Get) display, which means that the screen shows how the printed page will look.

Language Arts A writing style is a set of guidelines for the language, punctuation, and formatting of a document. There are a number of accepted styles, but many teachers prefer the Modern Language Association (MLA) style. Some examples of MLA style rules include double-spaced lines, 1" margins on all sides, and in-text citations of sources. Other commonly used styles include the *Chicago Manual of Style*, which does not require in-text citations, and American Psychological Association (APA) style, which is usually preferred for papers written about the social sciences. Before writing a research paper, ask your teacher which style you should use.

Figure 12.1.2 Use Zoom controls to change the magnification of a document display.

100% magnification

120% magnification

Career Corner

Technical Writer A technical writer creates text-based documentation, such as user manuals for software, online help sites, guides for machinery, and design specifications for construction projects. In addition to being able to use words in a clear and concise manner to convey information, a technical writer must understand the topic about which he or she is writing.

Multiple Views of the Same Document

Some word-processing programs allow you to split the document window into two sections, or **panes**. This split screen lets you view two parts of a document at the same time. You can scroll through each pane separately to display any part of the document. This feature makes it easy to move or copy text from one part of a large document to another. You can also use this feature to compare discussions of the same topic in two different parts of a document.

Mapping the Document

Some programs also split the screen by showing text in one pane and a list of the document's headings in the other. This list is called a **document map**, or navigation pane. You can use the document map to move about in the document simply by clicking a heading. In some programs, you can change the display in the navigation pane to show thumbnails, or icons representing each page. You can click a page to display it in the main document area.

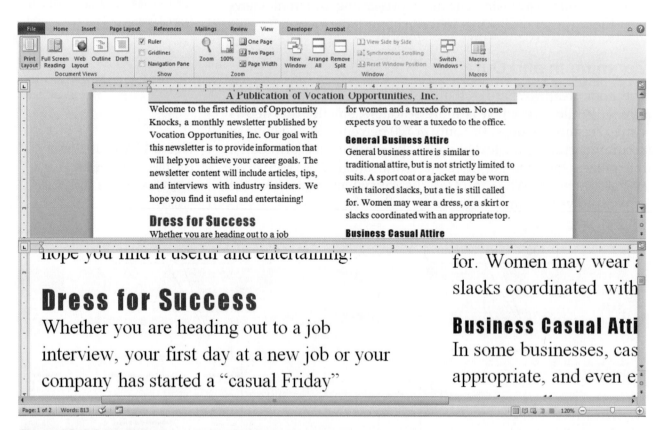

Figure 12.1.3 Some programs let you split a document so you can see different sections at the same time using different views.

Enhancing a Document

Objectives

- Identify the advantages of using keyboard shortcuts.
- Explain how to insert special characters or symbols.
- Describe the process for adding clip art.
- Describe uses for the find and replace features.

As You Read

Organize Information   Complete a spider map to help you organize details about different editing features as you read.

Keyboard Shortcuts

Usually, you move the insertion point and select commands using the mouse. Sometimes you may find it easier and faster to keep the fingers of both hands on the keyboard. You may be able to use the keyboard to type, issue commands, and select options quicker than you can move a mouse through a series of menus.

Most programs offer **keyboard shortcuts**, combinations of keys that can carry out some actions. Usually, issuing these commands requires pressing the Control (Ctrl) key in Windows or the Command key in Macintosh in combination with some other key. Ctrl + C, for example, is a Copy shortcut on Windows computers. Some of the shortcuts use a **function key**, one from the row of keys at the top of the keyboard that are labeled F1, F2, and so on.

 Key Terms

- find and replace
- function key
- keyboard shortcut

Common Keyboard Shortcuts

Command	Windows	Macintosh
Boldface	Ctrl + B	Command + B
Italic	Ctrl + I	Command + I
Underline	Ctrl + U	Command + U
Cut	Ctrl + X	Command + X
Copy	Ctrl + C	Command + C
Paste	Ctrl + V	Command + V

Using Special Characters and Symbols

Most word-processing programs allow you to insert special characters and symbols. These are symbols and characters that cannot be created simply by pressing one key. Common symbols can be made using a combination of keys. For example, in some programs you can type (c) to make the copyright symbol ©.

There are too many special characters to have keyboard shortcuts for all of them. Many word-processing programs provide a dialog box that displays all the characters they offer. In Word 2010, to choose a symbol, click the Insert tab and click the Symbol command in the Symbols group.

Adding Art

Suppose you are making a birthday card and want to add a piece of art to decorate it. Many word-processing programs make that easy by providing a collection of ready-to-use drawings called clip art. In Word 2010, go to the Insert tab and select the Clip Art command button. A pane opens on the right side of the window that lets you select art from as many as three different places:

- the computer's hard drive
- a CD-ROM
- a linked Web site

Once you find an image, you can place it in the program by either dragging it into the document or clicking it. After adding a clip art image to a document, you can resize it, change its colors, and edit it in other ways. You can also insert other types of graphics, including pictures, shapes, charts, and diagrams.

Figure 12.2.1 Word-processing programs, such as Microsoft Word, offer a wide selection of clip art images.

Finding and Replacing

Suppose you had written an essay about President George W. Bush. After finishing, you realized you had to make clear that you were writing about George W. Bush and not his father, George Herbert Walker Bush, who also had been president. You can use a powerful word-processing feature to search your essay for every time the name *George Bush* appears. You can even use the program to automatically replace every occurrence of *George Bush* with *George W. Bush*.

Using Find and Replace   The **find and replace** (or search and replace) feature lets you:

- locate a word or combination of words
- change those words to other words
- search for text characters, including spaces, punctuation, and symbols
- search for text that is formatted a certain way

In most programs, you select the command for Find and Replace, and then use a dialog box to enter the text to find and then the replacement text.

Cautions   Use the search and replace feature very carefully. The feature looks for a specific set of letters, not just the word containing that set of letters. Suppose you type *his* as the search term and *hers* as its replacement. Since the program will replace every instance of *his* with *hers*, it will change *history* to *herstory* and *this* to *thers*.

You can avoid this problem by making sure you search for the word *his*, not just the letters *his*. The dialog box typically has an option for searching only for the whole word. Be sure to choose this option to avoid such errors.

Technology @ Work

Some businesses mail the same letter to many different customers. In these letters, all the text is exactly the same. Only the name and address changes.

Think About It!

Think about a word-processing feature that automatically makes the changes needed in these letters. Which features listed below would be useful for this purpose?

➤ changing document views
➤ formatting text
➤ inserting special characters
➤ find and replace
➤ merge

Figure 12.2.2 The Find and Replace feature can locate text anywhere in a document and replace it with different text.

Formatting and Printing

Objectives

- Explain how to use styles to format a document.
- Describe how tables can be used to display information.
- Describe the benefits of previewing a document.
- Compare print options.

As You Read

Outline Information Complete an outline to help you identify different ways of creating a professional-looking word-processing document.

Key Terms

- paragraph
- Print Preview
- style
- style sheet

Applying Styles

A **style** is a set of formats that is applied all at once. For example, you can apply a style to a heading to quickly format the heading with a set of formats, such as bold, large font size, and an underline. Using styles to apply consistent formatting gives your document a professional look.

Using Styles Styles can be applied to selected characters or to **paragraphs**. Character styles include font formatting, such as font, font size, and font style. Paragraph styles include font formatting and paragraph formatting, such as alignment, line spacing, and tabs.

To apply a paragraph style, place the insertion point in a paragraph, and select the style.

Figure 12.3.1 A document before and after styles were applied.

Some programs display each style in the correct font and type size so you can quickly see what it looks like. You simply choose the style you want for the selected paragraph. The program then assigns a set of formats to the paragraph.

Modifying Styles   You can easily change the look of all paragraphs that have the same style. For example, to make all main headings larger, simply edit the *Heading 1* style and change the type size. The program automatically changes the size of all those headings.

Using Style Sheets   Most programs provide a standard **style sheet**, a collection of predefined styles that go together. For instance, there are styles for text, headings, page numbers, headers, lists, and so on.

You can probably find styles you want to use in the standard set of styles. If not, you can modify existing styles or even design new ones.

Presenting Information in Tables

Suppose you wanted to show the batting averages of the players on your school's baseball team. You could do this by writing a paragraph, but tables let you compare this information more easily by placing it in columns and rows. Columns run down the table; rows go across.

In some programs, you insert tables by using the Insert menu. Others have a special Table menu. In Word 2010, the Tables group is on the Insert tab. These methods make it easy to add a table to your document and format it. You can even add color and shading so different parts of the table stand out.

Printing a Document

Although some documents are designed to be viewed on a monitor, people usually print the reports, greeting cards, letters, and posters they create.

Print Preview   Before printing a document, you can see how it will look by selecting the feature called **Print Preview**. Print Preview shows everything in a document—margins, graphics, headers, page numbers, and text. If you change margins and edit text while in Print Preview, you will immediately see these changes on your document.

Print Options To print, you typically go to the File menu and then select Print. This opens a dialog box that gives you several options:

- Printer—If the computer is connected to more than one printer, you can choose which one to use.
- Page range—You can choose to print every page in the document, the current page, or a group of pages.
- Number of copies—You can print one copy of the document, hundreds of copies, or any number in between.
- Print quality—You may be able to print in a faster "draft" mode or in a slower, high-quality mode.

Depending on your printer, you might have other options. For example, if you have a color printer, you may have the option to print documents in black-and-white or grayscale modes. If your printer can print in duplex (using both sides of the paper), you can set options to control this feature, too.

Figure 12.3.2 Many programs let you select options for printing in a Print dialog box.

Making and Tracking Edits

Objectives

- Explain how to check spelling, grammar, and style.
- Describe the benefits of tracking editing changes.
- Outline the steps for adding comments to a document.

As You Read

Organize Information Complete a chart to help you organize basic facts about checking tools and workgroup editing functions in word-processing programs.

Tools for Correcting Errors

Most word-processing programs offer tools to help with your writing. These tools check spelling, grammar, and writing style.

Spelling Checker The **spelling checker** matches each word in the text against a word list built into the program and gives you options for correcting a misspelling. You can accept one of the spellings or ignore the suggested change. You can also add a word to the word list so the program will accept it in the future. You can use the spelling checker in two ways:

- Check spelling as you type. The program highlights possible errors as they occur. In some programs, you can click the error to find different spellings and then quickly choose one.
- Check a word, a selection, or a whole document. As each possible spelling error is displayed, you decide whether to keep the original spelling or change it.

Spelling checkers are useful, but they accept words as long as they are spelled correctly—even if they are used incorrectly. You need to proofread your documents carefully even if you use the spelling checker.

Key Terms

- grammar checker
- spelling checker
- style checker
- Track Changes

Figure 12.4.1 Use the spelling checker to check spelling in a document.

Figure 12.4.2 Checking grammar in a document.

Grammar and Style Checkers You can run grammar and style checks as you type, or you can check a selection or the entire document at once. Either way, the program highlights potential errors. You can examine each one and accept or ignore the suggested correction.

Grammar checkers look for problems such as errors in the use of verb tenses, pronouns, punctuation, and capitalization. For instance, the program would suggest fixing the sentence "He had ran yesterday." The grammar checker also finds sentence fragments (incomplete sentences) and run-on sentences (two sentences joined together incorrectly).

Style checkers suggest ways to improve the writing style in a document. They let you know whether a sentence is unclear or too wordy or long. They offer alternatives to the use of contractions or language that is too informal.

Most programs also include a **Thesaurus** feature that lets you look up definitions, synonyms, and antonyms for words. You can use a thesaurus to improve your writing by replacing overused or boring words.

Collaborative Writing

Many documents are produced by several people working together. Often, one person creates a first draft, which other members of the group review. The draft author then reviews the group's suggestions and accepts or rejects them. This way, workers who have expert knowledge can make sure that a document is accurate. Many word processors have features that help groups carry out this kind of work.

Track Changes One feature that is helpful for working in groups is called **Track Changes** in Microsoft Word. A similar feature in WordPerfect is the red-line method of document review. This feature marks each editing change made by each member of the group. This is done by adding specific marks to the document at the point where the changes were made.

- Inserted text is shown in a specific color assigned to each group member.
- Deleted text is not removed but appears in the assigned color with a line running through the words.
- In some programs, special boxes name the person who made the change.

When the original author reviews the document, he or she can choose to accept or reject each suggested change.

Comments Some programs let group members add notes to a document without changing the document's text. Microsoft Word does so using the Comment feature. In most programs, including Microsoft Word, to insert a comment, click Review and then click New Comment. A special pane appears at the bottom or edge of the screen, ready for you to type your comment.

Several people can add comments to a document, and the program tracks each person's comments. That way, the author can see who added what remarks to the document. Comments can be hidden or deleted, and a comment's text can be formatted and edited just like normal text.

Document Protection Most programs let you protect a document from unauthorized changes. Protection options range from allowing users to read but not edit or format a document to allowing only those with a password to open the document.

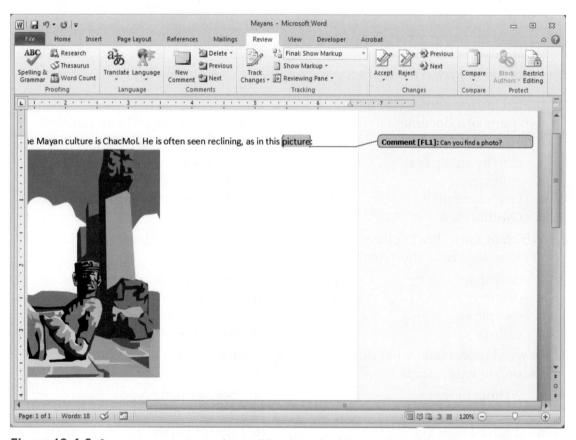

Figure 12.4.3 Comments can appear in small boxes in the document's margins.

Use the Vocabulary

Directions: *Match each vocabulary term in the left column with the correct definition in the right column.*

_____ **1.** Print Layout view
_____ **2.** Web Layout view
_____ **3.** pane
_____ **4.** document map
_____ **5.** keyboard shortcut
_____ **6.** function key
_____ **7.** find and replace
_____ **8.** paragraph
_____ **9.** style sheet
_____ **10.** Print Preview

a. text in a document up to a forced new line

b. screen that shows a document's text and a list of its headings

c. feature that finds a word and puts another in its place

d. document display that shows how page elements will look when published on the Web

e. print feature that shows everything in a document as it will look when printed

f. holds formats for all elements in a document

g. document display that shows how page elements will look when printed

h. a special key labeled F1, F2, and so on

i. combination of keys that carry out an action

j. partial window seen in split screen

Check Your Comprehension

Directions: *Determine the correct choice for each of the following.*

1. Which feature allows you to look at two parts of a document at the same time?

  a. side-by-side pages
  b. split screen
  c. Document view
  d. Outline view

2. Which of the following keys is used in many keyboard shortcuts?

  a. backspace
  b. delete
  c. escape
  d. control

3. In word processing, what determines the end of a paragraph?

  a. 20 lines of text
  b. 400 words of text
  c. a forced new line
  d. a forced new page

4. By choosing "Whole Word" when searching, what will you replace?

  a. every case where the letters appear
  b. those letters and no others
  c. all paragraphs with those letters
  d. the letters only when they make a word

5. How does a document look in Print Preview?

  a. as it appears when printed
  b. as it appears on the Web
  c. as it appears on the monitor
  d. as it appears in computer code

6. Which options are provided in the Print dialog box?

  a. bold or italic type
  b. number of copies
  c. size of paper
  d. inserting graphics

Think Critically

Directions: *Answer the following questions.*

1. Why is the document map feature useful for editing large documents?

2. What is the difference between using the mouse to carry out basic commands and using keyboard shortcuts? Which do you think is easier? Why?

3. How do you insert special characters?

4. What do you need to do to bring clip art from a CD into a word-processing document?

5. Suppose you want to create a table to keep track of your test scores in math class. How would you design your table?

Extend Your Knowledge

Directions: *Choose one of the following projects. Complete the exercise on a separate sheet of paper.*

A. Open a word-processing program and create a new document. Input any two paragraphs from this chapter. After you input the text, change the font of the paragraphs. Create a left tab setting for the paragraphs and indent the first lines using that setting. Type "Formatting Practice" as the title at the top, and center that line. Adjust the page setup to use different margins. Add a header at the top of the page that gives your name and the date. Review and save your document. Then, print it for your teacher to review.

B. Interview a student your age and two adults. Ask them what kinds of character, paragraph, and page formatting they have used in a word-processing program. Ask them how they learned how to apply these features. Ask the adults whether they learned on the job or in special computer classes. Share your findings with the class. Discuss with your classmates how adults continue to learn new skills throughout their lives.

Word-Processing Activities

DIRECTIONS: *You will use a word-processing program to make changes to the text of an advertising poster. Microsoft Word 2010 procedures required for this activity can be found in Appendix A.*

1. Start your word-processing program.
2. Open the data file **WP-1_Jump**, which is on the student CD. Save it as **WP-1_Jump_***xx* in the location where your teacher instructs you to store the files for this activity. Replace *xx* with your own initials or name, as directed by your teacher. The document is an advertisement for a trampoline.
3. Insert a footer that includes your name and the current date. Read the advertisement. Notice that it contains several typographical and grammatical errors.
4. Correct the capitalization error in the first line of text.
5. Replace the incorrect adjective, *Better*, in the second line of text with the correct adjective, *Best*.
6. Insert an exclamation point after the word *Difference* at the end of the third line of text.
7. Locate and correct the spelling error in the fourth line of text.
8. The fifth line of text contains a singular verb that should be plural. Locate and correct the incorrect verb usage.
9. The last line of text—the address—is missing punctuation. Identify and insert the correct punctuation.
10. Change the page orientation to landscape.
11. Format the font in the first line of text in 48-pt. bold Impact with a shadow effect.
12. Format the font in the second line of text in 26-pt. Arial Black.
13. Select lines three through six of text, and apply 14-pt. Arial Black font formatting.
14. Select lines four through six of text, and apply the default bullet list formatting.
15. Change the font of the last line of text on the page to Arial.
16. Select all text in the document, and center it horizontally.

17. Identify at least one statement in the text that is an opinion, and format it using italics.
18. Add the button for checking spelling to a toolbar. For example, add the Spelling & Grammar button to the Quick Access Toolbar.
19. Create a new menu, toolbar, or tab named **Printing** that contains the Page Setup, Preview and Print, and Quick Print commands. The customized toolbars and/or menu should look similar to Illustration A.

Illustration A

20. Using the customized toolbar and/or menu, check the spelling in the document.
21. Using the customized toolbar and/or menu, preview the document. Make modifications to the text and formatting as necessary.
22. With your teacher's permission, print the advertisement.
23. Restore the toolbar and/or menu to their default configuration.
24. Save the document, then close it, and exit your word-processing program.
25. As a class discuss how language can be used to influence someone's actions and thoughts. List the places where you see advertisements, and what makes some ads more effective than others.

DIRECTIONS: *You will examine the results of a survey. Then, you will use a word-processing program to create a tabular summary of the survey results. Microsoft Word 2010 procedures required for this activity can be found in Appendix A.*

1. Start your word-processing program.
2. Open the data file **WP-2_Survey**, which is on the student CD. Save it as **WP-2_Survey_xx** in the location where your teacher instructs you to store the files for this activity. This document contains the results of a survey.
3. Read the results, and then minimize the **WP-2_Survey_xx** document.
4. Open the data file **WP-2_Summary**, which is on the student CD. Save it as **WP-2_Summary_xx** in the location where your teacher instructs you to store the files for this activity. This document contains a paragraph summarizing the results of the survey. You will use tabs to insert some of the survey results data in the document.
5. Insert a footer that includes your name and the current date.
6. Move the insertion point to the last blank line in the document, and press Enter. Set a center tab at the 3" mark.
7. Tab to the tab stop, and type **Student Survey**. Reveal the formatting of the heading at the top of the page, and then apply the same formatting to the text *Student Survey*.
8. Press Enter.
9. If necessary, clear the center tab stop and then set two left tab stops at the 4½" and 5½" marks.
10. Type **Question**, press Tab, type **Yes**, press Tab, and then type **No**. Apply bold to the line.
11. Press Enter, and toggle off the bold font style.
12. Type **Do you plan to go to college after high school?**. Press Tab.
13. Arrange the two word-processing documents so you can see them both at the same time.
14. Make the **WP-2_Survey_xx** window active.

15. Increase the zoom magnification, then count the ticks under Yes for question 1, and then count the ticks under No.
16. Make the **WP-2_Summary_xx** window active, and type the correct number of Yes responses. Press Tab, and type the number of No responses.
17. Press Enter.
18. Type **Do you plan to live in the same state after you finish school?**. Press Tab.
19. Go to the **WP-2_Survey_xx** window. Count the ticks under Yes for question 2, and then count the ticks under No.
20. Return to the **WP-2_Summary_xx** window, and type the correct number of Yes responses. Press Tab, and enter the number of No responses.
21. Select the two questions and their respective number of responses. Apply a dotted tab leader between the tab stops.
22. Check the spelling and grammar, and correct any errors you find.
23. Preview the document. Make modifications to the text and formatting as necessary.
24. Add the following tag properties to the file: **college plans**; **survey**; **staying in state**. For example, in Word 2010, click the Info tab in Backstage view, click Tags in the right pane, and type the tag text.
25. With your teacher's permission, print the document.
26. Close both open documents, saving all changes, and exit your word-processing program.
27. As a class, discuss the survey results. If possible, use the survey questions in your class and compare the results with the sample used in this activity.

Word-Processing Activities

DIRECTIONS: *You will use a word-processing program to create a table that classifies scenarios as legal or illegal under current copyright laws. Microsoft Word 2010 procedures required for this activity can be found in Appendix A.*

1. Start your word-processing program.
2. Open the data file **WP-3_Copy**, which is on the student CD. Save it as **WP-3_Copy_xx** in the location where your teacher instructs you to store the files for this activity. This is a two page document that contains information about copyright laws.
3. Insert a footer that contains your name and the current date. Read the entire document, and then scroll up to the top of page 1.
4. In the first paragraph, select the sentence that best describes the main idea and apply the underline format.
5. Repeat step 4 to identify and underline the sentence that best describes the main idea in the remaining paragraphs.
6. Save the changes. Preview the document, and, with your instructor's permission, print it.
7. Open the data file **WP-3_Legal**, which is on the student CD. Save it as **WP-3_Legal_xx** in the location where your teacher instructs you to store the files for this activity. This document lists examples of how different individuals use copyrighted materials. Some of the examples are legal and some are illegal.
8. Insert a footer that contains your name and the current date.
9. In the title at the top of the page, insert the copyright symbol after the word *Copyrighted*.
10. Move the insertion point to the last blank line of the document, and insert a table with 2 columns and 6 rows.
11. Type **Legal** in the first column of the first row, and center the text in the cell.
12. Press Tab, type **Illegal** in the second column of the first row, and center the text in the cell.
13. Format the text in the first row in 14-pt. bold. The table should look similar to Illustration B.

14. Read example 1 in the list. Use the information you learned reading the **WP-3_Copy_xx** document to determine whether example 1 describes a legal or illegal use of copyrighted materials.
15. Select the text in example 1—excluding the number at the beginning and the paragraph mark at the end—and cut it to the Clipboard. If necessary, display nonprinting characters in order to see the paragraph marks on-screen.
16. Paste the selection into the appropriate column in the second row of the table.
17. Repeat steps 14 through 16 to move the text from the second example into the appropriate column in the third row of the table.
18. Continue cutting and pasting each example until all of the items in the list have been moved to the table.
19. Delete the numbers that remain in the document above the table.
20. Check the spelling and grammar in the document, and then preview it. Make modifications and corrections as necessary.
21. With your teacher's permission, print the document.
22. Protect the document by applying the password **!copyright?** and then close it.
23. Open the document by entering the password.
24. Save a copy of the document as **WP-3_Legal2_xx** in the location where your teacher tells you to store the files for this activity.
25. Remove the password from **WP-3_Legal2_xx**.
26. Format the table in **WP-3_Legal2_xx** to enhance its appearance and make it easier to read. For example, apply a table style, or apply borders and fills. Delete unnecessary columns and rows.
27. With your teacher's permission, print the document. Close all open documents, saving all changes, and exit your word-processing program.
28. As a class, discuss why it is important to respect the copyright laws.

Illustration B

Legal	Illegal

DIRECTIONS: *You will create and format a letter about the stages of the water cycle. Microsoft Word 2010 procedures required for this activity can be found in Appendix A.*

1. Start your word-processing program, and create a new document. Save it as **WP-4_ Water_xx** in the location where your teacher instructs you to store the files for this activity.
2. Set the document margins to .75" at the top, and 1" for the left, right, and bottom.
3. On the first line of the document, insert the date in *month dd, yyyy* format. Do not set the date to update automatically.
4. Set line spacing to single and paragraph spacing to 0 points before and after, or apply a No Spacing style. Insert three blank lines, and then input the following name and address using an available input device and software that converts words into digital text. For example, you may type on a keyboard, use voice-recognition software, or use handwriting-recognition software.

   Dr. Sandra Phipps
   Science Department
   Watertown University
   1 Watertown Blvd.
   Anytown, MI 48000
5. Press Enter twice to leave a blank line and type the salutation, **Dear Dr. Phipps:**. Press Enter twice, and save the document.
6. Open the data file **WP-4_Letter**, which is located on the student CD. The document contains the text of the letter that you will send.
7. Select all the text in the document and copy it. Close the **WP-4_Letter** document without saving any changes.
8. In the **WP-4_Water_xx** document, make sure the insertion point is on the last line of the document, and paste the selection.

9. Identify the headings and descriptions of the four stages of the water cycle—Evaporation, Condensation, Precipitation, and Runoff and Groundwater—and format them as a multilevel list. The name of each stage should be a top level. The two sentences that describe each stage should be formatted as a second level (refer to Illustration C).
10. Read the paragraph following your multilevel list. Click at the beginning of the third sentence in the paragraph (*If this is so . . .*), and press Enter to start a new paragraph. Then, click at the beginning of the second sentence (*Isn't all of . . .*) in that new paragraph, and press Enter.
11. Select the two new paragraphs and apply number list formatting using numbers followed by a period (refer to Illustration C).
12. Replace the line *Your Name* with your own name. Then, replace the school name and address with your school's name and address.
13. Exchange documents with a classmate according to your teacher's instructions. For example, you might send it electronically by e-mail or print it. Proofread your classmate's document carefully. Check the spelling and grammar and insert comments to mark any errors that you find.
14. Exchange documents back, and respond to your classmate's comments.
15. With your teacher's permission, print the document.
16. Close the document, saving all changes, and exit your word-processing program.

My sixth grade science class is currently studying the water cycle. We learned that there are four steps in the cycle:

1) Evaporation
   a) During evaporation, sun heats up water in lakes, rivers, or oceans and turns it into vapor or steam.
   b) The vapor or steam then enters the atmosphere.
2) Condensation
   a) During condensation, water vapor in the air cools.
   b) As it cools, it turns back into liquid, forming clouds.
3) Precipitation
   a) During precipitation, the condensed liquid becomes too heavy for the air.
   b) Water falls back to Earth in the form of rain, sleet, snow, and hail.
4) Runoff and Groundwater
   a) Some of the precipitation runs off along the surface of the ground.
   b) Some soaks into the soil to become groundwater.

Because of the water cycle, Earth constantly recycles the same water to be used over and over again. Our teacher told us that this cycle has been going on for millions of years and that the amount of water on Earth has remained fairly constant over that entire time.

1. If this is so, why should we conserve water?
2. Isn't all of the water on Earth eventually reused as part of the water cycle, whatever we do with it?

Illustration C

DIRECTIONS: *You will create a newsletter by writing three articles about recent events in your family or community. You will revise and edit your work and arrange it in a newsletter format. Microsoft Word 2010 procedures required for this activity can be found in Appendix A.*

1. Open the .pdf file **WP-5_News**, which is located on the student CD. With your teacher's permission, print the Data Record Sheet. Close the file, and exit the pdf reader program.

2. Use the space provided on the Data Record Sheet to plan a newsletter. Write a name for your newsletter in the space for the title. Think of three articles about upcoming special occasions, recent vacations, family outings, or any other exciting news you might have. Write a headline and text for each article.

3. Think of a photograph or an image that relates to one of the articles. Write a description of the image in the space provided on your Data Record Sheet.

4. Determine the best method for creating or obtaining the image, and then do so. For example, you could scan an existing photograph, take a new photograph with a digital camera and then import it, or create an image file using drawing tools. Save the image file with the name **WP-5_Images_***xx* in a format that is compatible with your word-processing program (such as .jpg), in the location where your teacher instructs you to store the files for this activity. Add appropriate tags to help identify the image.

5. Start your word-processing program, and create a new document. Alternatively, you may choose to use a desktop-publishing program. Save the file as **WP-5_Newsletter_***xx* in the location where your teacher instructs you to store the files for this activity.

6. Insert a header that includes your name and today's date. Insert a page number in the footer.

7. If available in your word-processing program, apply a theme and a style set.

8. At the top of the page, type the newsletter title, and apply formatting that is appropriate for a title.

9. Type the three articles from your Data Record Sheet, including a headline for each one. Be sure to use one space after punctuation, smart quotes instead of straight quotes, and en dashes and em dashes as needed.

10. Format the paragraph with single line spacing, first-line indent, and justified alignment.

11. Read the articles and revise them as necessary. Look for places to add transition words to improve the flow of the text. Use the thesaurus to select interesting and descriptive words that improve the text.

12. Apply formatting, such as styles and fonts, to improve the readability of the text. For example, use a style to format headlines, or apply a larger font size to make headlines stand out.

13. Insert a section break below the title and format the second section of the newsletter into two columns.

14. Make sure the text alignment is justified in all three articles.

15. Insert the image file that you created earlier. Format it so that text will wrap around it.

16. Resize and position the image to create an attractive layout for your newsletter, and format it using a style or other formatting options.

17. Insert a text box, and type the headline **Birthdays**.

18. Type the names and birthdays for at least five people. Format the text as a bulleted list. Format the text box so that text will wrap around it. Resize and position it on the page so it looks good and is easy to read.

19. Adjust the zoom so you can see the entire page on the screen, and make any changes or adjustments necessary to improve the page layout and design.

20. Save the document, and then exchange documents with a classmate according to your teacher's instructions. For example, you might send them electronically as an attachment to an e-mail message, or you might print them and exchange the printed copies. Check the spelling and grammar in your classmate's document and mark any errors that you find. Insert comments to make suggestions or praise good work.

21. Exchange documents to get your own back, and make the changes and corrections as necessary.

22. Preview the document, and, with your teacher's permission, print it.

23. Save the document in .pdf format with the name **WP-5_Newsletter_***xx* in the location where your teacher instructs you to store the files for this activity.

24. Close all open files, saving changes, and exit all open programs.

25. As a class, discuss other ways in which a computer can help you communicate with friends and family. What are the benefits and drawbacks of written or online communication versus face-to-face communication?

Spreadsheet Basics

What Is a Spreadsheet? Suppose you wanted to keep track of all your grades in one of your classes so you could figure out your final average for the class. Spreadsheet programs are the perfect software for doing this kind of work.

Spreadsheets are set up like tables with information running across rows and down columns. You could enter your assignments in one vertical column. Then you could enter the grade or score you received on each assignment in the next column. The spreadsheet could add up all the scores and calculate your average. When an assignment is returned to you, you could add it to the spreadsheet, and your average would be updated automatically. Just think how long it would take you to do this if you did it by hand!

Chapter Outline

Exploring Spreadsheets

Objectives

- Explain the purpose of spreadsheet software.
- Identify and describe parts of a worksheet.
- Summarize key features of spreadsheet software.

As You Read

Organize Information Use a concept web to help you organize basic facts about spreadsheets as you read the lesson.

🔑 Key Terms

- active cell
- cell
- cell address
- formula
- function
- spreadsheet
- worksheet

Spreadsheet Basics

A **spreadsheet** is a program that processes information that is set up in tables. Spreadsheets can be used to:

- place numbers and text in easy-to-read rows and columns
- calculate numbers and show the result
- calculate new results when the numbers are changed
- create charts to display data
- create models and simulations
- make predictions by adding inputs and reviewing results
- analyze trends and forecasting possibilities

These features make spreadsheets perfect for tracking information that involves numbers. Suppose you work at a company that needs to decide what price to charge for a product. You can create a spreadsheet that shows how much profit your company will make by charging several different prices. The spreadsheet finds the results quickly. Those results can be used to set a price.

Understanding Worksheets When you use a spreadsheet program, your data goes into a special kind of document called a **worksheet**, a grid made of vertical columns and horizontal rows. Columns are labeled with letters, and rows are labeled with numbers.

Each column and row meets to make a box called a **cell**. Each cell in the grid is identified by a unique name—its **cell address**. The address is made simply by taking the letter of the column and the number of the row that meet to make the cell. For example, column C and row 3 create the cell address C3.

Figure 13.1.1 A worksheet includes rows and columns, which create a grid of cells that hold data.

Cell address: C3

Column

Cell

Row

Parts of a Worksheet

Most worksheets look similar. The parts of a worksheet include:

Frame   The frame forms the top and left borders of the worksheet. It includes the column and row headings.

Active Cell   The **active cell** is the cell currently in use. A rectangle appears around this cell to highlight it and make it easy to spot.

Cell Identifier   Located in the upper-left corner, just above the frame, the cell identifier is an area that shows the cell address of the cell that is active.

Formula Bar   The formula bar displays what you type. This data will be entered into the active cell when you are done. The formula bar is like a one-line word-processing program. Pressing Enter, Return, or Tab completes the entry and places the data in the cell.

Scroll Bars   Scroll bars appear on the worksheet's right and bottom edges. You can click on the arrows or slide the scroll box to see another part of the worksheet.

Worksheet Tabs   On the same line as the horizontal scroll bar are tabs that show the other worksheets that belong to the same spreadsheet file. If you click on one of these tabs, you switch to that worksheet.

Status Bar   The status bar appears below the scroll bar at the very bottom of the worksheet. Messages from the program are displayed here.

Figure 13.1.2 All spreadsheet programs share basic elements.

Connections

Language Arts Some teachers use a spreadsheet program to create vocabulary tests. They place vocabulary words in one column and the definitions in the next. By scrambling the definitions, vocabulary matching tests are made quickly and easily.

Working with a Spreadsheet

Spreadsheet programs share many features. You can perform many similar actions, regardless of the program.

Moving Around You can use the Home, End, Page Up, and Page Down keys, along with the scroll bars, to move large distances within the worksheet. You can use the Tab key to move one cell to the right or the arrow keys to move one cell at a time in any direction.

Selecting Cells and Entering Data To make a cell active, click on that cell. Then, type to enter data in the cell. Data can be text, numbers, dates, or formulas.

Formulas **Formulas** are mathematical expressions. In a spreadsheet, most formulas reference the data entered in one or more cells. A simple formula might add the numbers in two cells. The formula appears in the formula bar but not in the active cell. The active cell shows the result of the formula—in this case, the sum of the two numbers. **Functions** are built-in formulas for performing calculations, such as addition, in a table. See Chapter 14 for more on functions.

Formatting the Worksheet You can change the look of a worksheet in many ways. You can add or remove rows or columns or change their size. You can change the font or type size of the data. You can also add color, borders, or shading and change how the data is aligned in the cell.

Spotlight on...

DAN BRICKLIN

❝*In terms of the success of VisiCalc . . . it is nice to be able to realize you've done something very worthwhile. . . . I feel that I've made a change in the world. That's a satisfaction that money can't buy.* **❞**

Dan Bricklin
Software developer

When Dan Bricklin was a business school student in the late 1970s, he had to do his calculations for class on a calculator and then write them down. Bricklin wanted to develop a computer program that could calculate and display the work automatically. He and his friend Bob Frankston created such a program. They called it *VisiCalc*®—short for visible calculator. It was the first computer spreadsheet. Although VisiCalc is not sold anymore, today's spreadsheets are all based on Bricklin's original idea.

Entering and Editing Data

Objectives

- Describe types of data you can enter in a worksheet.
- Compare and contrast values and labels in a worksheet.
- Describe ways to edit and format data in a worksheet.
- Use a spreadsheet to create a chart.
- Evaluate the benefit of printing options.

As You Read

Sequence Steps Use a sequence chart to help you sequence the steps in working with spreadsheets as you read the lesson.

Entering Data

In addition to formulas, you can enter three types of data in a worksheet: values, labels, and dates and times.

Values A **value** is a number, such as a whole number, a fraction, or a decimal. The program automatically formats values to align to the right in a cell. If a value is too large for the width of the cell, you may see a set of symbols such as ###### or *******. You can change the column width so that the full number shows. Click the right edge of the column heading and drag it to the right.

Labels A **label** is text or a combination of numbers and text. Labels are typically used for headings or explanations. By default, labels are aligned to the left in a cell. Labels that are too wide will overlap into the next cell to the right—if that cell is empty. If that cell already has text, the long text in the first cell will appear cut off. Again, you can widen the column to show the entire label.

Key Terms

- chart
- label
- print area
- value

Figure 13.2.1 If data doesn't fit in a cell, it might not display correctly.

Many people use spreadsheets at home to track monthly income and expenses. They can set up a worksheet to show regular monthly costs. Then, they only need to copy and paste it on other blank worksheets to create budgets for other months.

Think About It!

Before you set up a budget, think about which expenses arise each month. Which items listed below do you think would be a regular monthly expense?

➤ housing payment

➤ vacation

➤ telephone

➤ holiday presents

➤ food magazine subscription

Dates and Times   Data typed as dates or times are displayed in the format you choose. For example, November 1, 2012, can be typed as 11/01/12 or 01-Nov-12. Times can simply be typed as the hour and minute—07:45 or 12:52, for instance.

Editing Data

You can easily change data to correct an error or reflect new information in a spreadsheet.

Editing Cell Data   To edit data, click the desired cell. Then click within the formula bar to place the insertion point where you want to make the change. Press Backspace or Delete to remove characters, or type to add them. Press Enter to place the edited information in the cell.

Moving or Copying Data   To move information from one cell to another, select the cell and drag its contents to the new cell. You can also go to the Edit menu, and select Copy or Cut. Click the new location, and then go to the Edit menu and select Paste.

Removing Data   To remove data, select the cell and press Delete. You can also go to the Edit menu, and select Delete. A dialog box will ask if you wish to delete the entire row or column or just those cells.

Formatting Data   You can change the appearance of the data in the cells. You can show data in bold or italic type and change its type size. You can also change the format of numbers.

Program	Click	Then click	Next step
Excel	Home tab	Number group	Click the desired format button or activate the Format Cells dialog box and select the desired format.
Quattro Pro	Format menu	Selection	Select the Numeric Format tab and select the desired format from the dialog box.
iWork Numbers '09	Inspector button	Cell format drop-down	Select the desired format.

Figure 13.2.2 The steps for formatting data in spreadsheet programs vary slightly depending on the software you are using.

Creating a Chart

With a spreadsheet program, you can create **charts**, which are also called graphs. Charts show data in ways that are visually more interesting than tables, and make it easier to analyze trends such as changes over time. Simply select the cells that have data you want to graph. Then, choose the command for creating a chart.

Next, you select a type of chart. Bar charts compare different amounts, such as how many students there are in each grade in a school. Pie charts show how parts relate to the whole. For instance, a pie chart would show what percentage of all students are in each grade. Line charts show change over time, such as the number of students in a grade each year. Once you have chosen the type of chart to create, dialog boxes help you through the rest of the process. After you have made a chart, you can copy it and paste it into another document.

Previewing and Printing a Worksheet

Before you print, preview your worksheet to make sure the data displays the way you want. Most spreadsheets have special features for printing. For example, you can specify a portion of a worksheet called a **print area** before you instruct the program to print. Headings for columns and rows normally only print on the first page, but you can choose to print the headings on every page. You can also add headers and footers, change the page margins, and switch from portrait to landscape orientation.

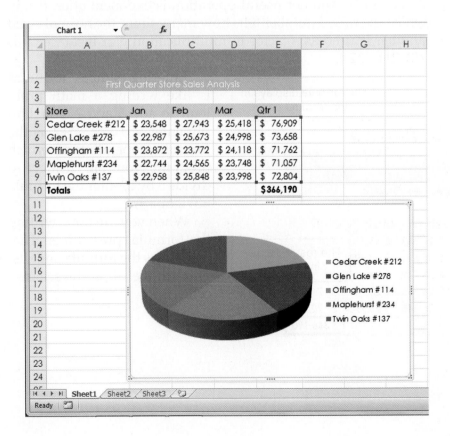

Figure 13.2.3 Creating a chart from data in a worksheet.

Using Formulas

Objectives

- Construct a simple formula using one or more operators.
- Explain the importance of the order of evaluation.
- Evaluate the benefit of building formulas using cell references.

As You Read

Enter Information   Use a concept web to help you enter formulas in a worksheet as you read the lesson.

 Key Terms

- cell reference
- order of evaluation

Entering Formulas in Worksheets

The power of a spreadsheet is its ability to use formulas to represent data in different cells.

Entering Formulas   To enter a formula, click the cell where you want the result of the formula to appear, and type the formula in the formula bar. You need to begin the formula with a symbol to signify that you are typing a formula. In Excel and AppleWorks, that symbol is an equal sign (=). In Quattro Pro and Lotus 1-2-3, formulas start with a plus (+) or minus (–) sign.

Simple Formulas   Many formulas use the basic arithmetic operations of addition (+), subtraction (–), multiplication (*), and division (/). Another useful operation is exponentiation (^), in which the raised number tells how many times the normal sized number is used as a factor in multiplication. For instance, 2^2 is 2*2; 2^3 is 2*2*2.

Entering simple formulas is like writing a math problem. To add 5 and 2, you simply enter =5+2 or +5+2 as the formula, depending on which program you are using. To divide 5 by 2, enter the formula =5/2 or +5/2.

When you are done writing the formula, press Enter. That completes the formula and displays the result in the selected cell.

Figure 13.3.1 Using a formula in a worksheet.

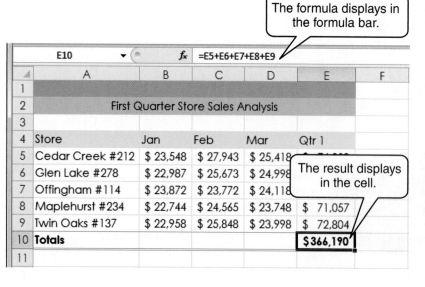

Complex Formulas

You can enter more complex formulas as well. Formulas can include many numbers, such as =1+2+3+4+5. They can also include more than one mathematical operation. For instance, suppose you owned a store that sold 50 copies of a game one month and 56 copies the next. You want to know by what percentage your sales of that game increased. You could find out by writing this formula: =(56–50)/50. In this formula, you subtract 50 from 56 to find the number of additional games you sold. Then, you divide the result by 50, the number of games sold the first month, to find the percentage increase. The answer is .12, or 12 percent.

Working with Complex Formulas Many formulas, like =(56–50)/50, have two or more operations. How does the program know which one to do first? It uses the **order of evaluation**. This rule tells the program to do the most important operation first. Then, it does the others in order, from most to least important.

Ranking Operations Operations within parentheses are the most important. Exponentiation comes next, followed by multiplication or division, then addition or subtraction. Use the sentence, "Please excuse my dear Aunt Sally" to remember the order. The first letter of each word (P-E-M-D-A-S) matches the first letter of each operation in the right order.

Using Order of Evaluation Suppose you want to write an Excel formula to average the numbers 29, 34, and 27. The formula =(29+34+27)/3 is correct. The parentheses tell the program to add the three numbers first. The sum, 90, is then divided by 3 to find the average, which is 30.

The formula =29+34+27/3 is not correct. In this case, the program would first divide 27 by 3 because division is performed before addition. It would then add the result, 9, to 29 and 34 for an answer of 72.

Some formulas have more than one operation with the same importance, such as addition and subtraction. In this case, those operations are done in the order in which they appear from left to right.

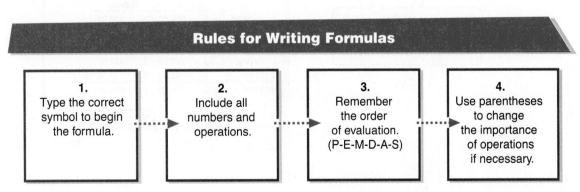

Rules for Writing Formulas

| 1. Type the correct symbol to begin the formula. | 2. Include all numbers and operations. | 3. Remember the order of evaluation. (P-E-M-D-A-S) | 4. Use parentheses to change the importance of operations if necessary. |

Career Corner

Statistician People who work with statistics, or facts expressed as numbers, are called statisticians. They study information about the number and ages of people in a population, the economy, the number of people who tune in to radio and television shows, and so on.

Statisticians rely heavily on computers, as the information they work with can be very complex. Spreadsheets are very useful for them because of their power to store and process numbers.

Using References, Not Values

The formulas discussed so far have used values. But formulas can also use **cell references**, or cell addresses. For example, suppose you wanted to multiply 5 times 3. If the value 5 is entered in cell A1, and the value 3 is entered in cell B2, you could enter the formula =A1*B2. It is better to use cell references for the two reasons listed below.

Avoiding Errors You might accidentally type the wrong value and not realize it, as the formula does not always show in the cell. If you insert a cell reference, however, the formula will always use the correct value.

Reflecting Changes A value in a formula never changes. The formula =5*3 will always produce 15. But if you use a cell reference, the formula uses whatever value is entered in the cell. If the cell value changes, so will the result calculated by the formula. By using cell references, you make sure that your worksheet remains up-to-date even if data changes.

Functions

Spreadsheet programs come with built-in functions, which are formulas used to perform common tasks. For example SUM is the function used to find a total and AVERAGE is used to find the average of a range. Using a function can make it easier to enter formulas. Using functions is covered in Lesson 14–4.

Figure 13.3.2 Examples of a formula and a function in a worksheet.

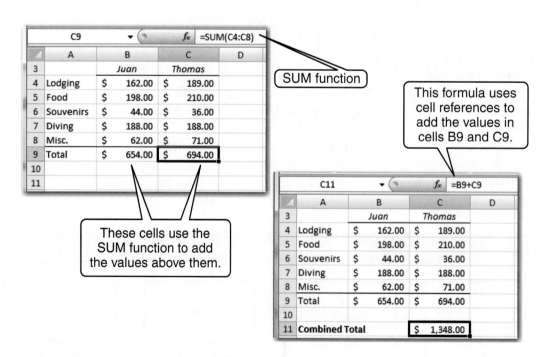

SUM function

This formula uses cell references to add the values in cells B9 and C9.

These cells use the SUM function to add the values above them.

Sharing Data Among Programs

Objectives

- Explain benefits of sharing data among programs.
- Contrast embedding and linking data.
- Summarize how to import data from a word-processing program into a spreadsheet.

As You Read

Compare and Contrast Use a Venn diagram to compare and contrast ways to share data as you read.

Sharing Data

Many spreadsheet programs are not used alone. In fact, many are part of a productivity suite—a set of separate programs that are similar in look and are sold together as a package. As a result, the programs have features that allow them to export data, or send it to other programs in the package. They can also import data from other programs that are not in the package.

Using Strengths By sharing data, you let each program perform its strengths. For example, suppose you are writing a report about the American economy. You want to include a chart that shows the growth of the economy in one period. It makes sense to use a spreadsheet to create the chart because spreadsheets have powerful charting features. Then, you can import that chart into your word-processing document.

Saving Time Importing data from another program also can save you time. Suppose you had created a worksheet containing the data on American economic growth before you started writing your report. Instead of typing the data again, it is much easier to simply copy it from the spreadsheet into the other application.

Key Terms

- destination file
- embed
- link
- source file
- parse

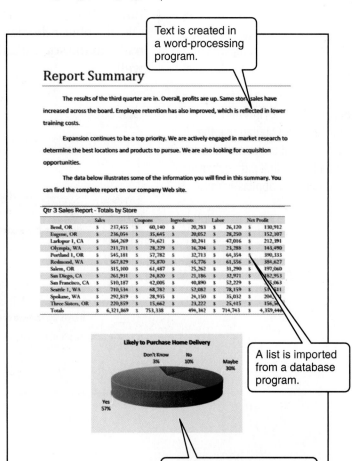

Text is created in a word-processing program.

A list is imported from a database program.

The chart is imported from a spreadsheet program.

Figure 13.4.1 A single document can include data from several different applications.

Ways to Share Data

There are two basic methods of sharing data between applications. In one you **embed** the data. In the other, you **link** it. In both, the file that contains the original data is called the **source file**, and the file where you place the shared data is called the **destination file**.

Embedding The simplest way is to copy the data in the source file and paste it into the destination file. This process is called embedding. For example, you could select a chart in a spreadsheet, and choose the Copy command. Then, position the insertion point in a word-processing document, and choose the Paste command.

Embedding is useful if you do not need to keep the pasted data up-to-date. Even if the data in the spreadsheet changes, the data pasted in the document will not change.

Linking There is a way to export data that keeps objects up-to-date. This is called linking. To link data, you begin in the same way—by copying the data from the source. However, instead of using the Paste command in the destination, you use Paste Special.

When you choose the Paste Special command, a Paste Special dialog box appears. In that box, click the button for Paste Link. Then, select the type of object you want. When you click OK, the object displays in your destination file. Any changes you make to the source data will be updated in the destination file as well.

Figure 13.4.2 In Windows applications, you can use the Paste Special command and this dialog box to link data between documents or applications..

Importing Data into Spreadsheets

You can use embedding and linking to copy data from other files into a spreadsheet. If the data is in a table format, it is pasted into the spreadsheet cells. Problems might arise, however, if you paste paragraphs of text. When text from a word-processing file is pasted into a spreadsheet, the continuously flowing text will be split into chunks that fit in the columns. The spreadsheet breaks up the file using its **parse** feature.

Importing text files works best if the text is formatted in a way that lets the spreadsheet program identify where to break for each column. You can do this using tabs. For example, suppose that you had a word-processing document with a list of addresses. Entries might read as follows ("[Tab]" stands for a tab entered between address parts):

Kim [Tab] Chang [Tab] 4444 Adams Street [Tab] Springfield [Tab] AR

Austin [Tab] Sinclair [Tab] 522 Jefferson Street [Tab] Springfield [Tab] AZ

Maria [Tab] Torrez [Tab] 111 Washington Street [Tab] Springfield [Tab] TX

Tempest [Tab] Withers [Tab] 3567 Madison Street [Tab] Springfield [Tab] TX

To import the data into Excel 2010, go to the Data tab, click the Get External Data command, and select From Text. The program lets you choose how to break up the data. In this example, it would convert the tabs into column breaks. The result would be a spreadsheet with data in five columns—one each for the first name, the last name, the address, the city, and the state.

Spotlight on...

HOOD RIVER, OREGON

66 *As a P.E. teacher, . . . this gives me time to communicate with [parents]. I try to write a personal note on each graph that I send home.* 99

Stephanie Perkins
Physical Education Teacher

Teacher Stephanie Perkins in Hood River proves that computers and Physical Education classes really do go together. Physical fitness progress reports are sent home with report cards several times a year in this Oregon school district. Spreadsheet data is input by the students to create the charts and graphs that reflect their fitness progress. The data is then interpreted to help students improve their level of fitness and set goals.

Use the Vocabulary

Directions: *Match each vocabulary term in the left column with the correct definition in the right column.*

_____ **1.** cell
_____ **2.** cell address
_____ **3.** active cell
_____ **4.** formula
_____ **5.** function
_____ **6.** value
_____ **7.** label
_____ **8.** destination
_____ **9.** print area
_____ **10.** order of evaluation

a. rules followed for carrying out the order of more than one mathematical operation
b. mathematical expression that might link numbers in cells
c. part of a spreadsheet to which printing can be limited
d. place where a column and row meet
e. number in a cell
f. file where you paste shared data
g. highlighted cell in use, where data or a formula will be entered or edited
h. text or text and numbers in a cell
i. shortcut to a formula that is used frequently
j. identifies each individual cell

Check Your Comprehension

Directions: *Determine the correct choice for each of the following.*

1. Tables in spreadsheets are better than tables in word processors because they
   a. use numbers only
   b. will have unchanging formats
   c. can be easily updated
   d. have accurate data

2. All changes to values, labels, or formulas in a spreadsheet are made in the
   a. formula bar
   b. cell
   c. frame
   d. function line

3. Values, by default, are aligned
   a. to the left
   b. to the right
   c. centered in the cell
   d. at the top of the cell

4. How does an Excel spreadsheet know that =10/12 is a formula and not the date October 12?
   a. The equal sign (=) signals it.
   b. The division (/) sign signals it.
   c. Dates cannot be shown that way.
   d. It would not know.

5. Operations are carried out in the following order:
   a. A-D-E-M-P-S
   b. M-D-E-P-S-A
   c. P-M-D-A-S-E
   d. P-E-M-D-A-S

6. It is best to write formulas using cell references so that a spreadsheet
   a. has no hidden information
   b. has all correct values
   c. can be updated easily
   d. can be more easily graphed

Think Critically

Directions: *Answer the following questions.*

1. How do values and labels differ in the way they treat data that is too wide for the cell?

2. If you were preparing a budget for a business, how would you indicate that the numbers represent dollar amounts in the worksheet?

3. In what situations do you think it would be useful to repeat column headings in a printed worksheet? Why?

4. What type of graph would be best for showing how much a child grew in inches over the years? Why?

5. Look at the formulas =B1/B2+B3 and =B1/(B2+B3). Would these formulas give the same result? Why or why not?

Extend Your Knowledge

Directions: *Choose one of the following projects. Complete the exercise on a separate sheet of paper.*

A. Open a spreadsheet program and create a new worksheet. Place the title "Cupcake Café Sales" in cell A1. Enter the days of the week in cells A2 to A8. Enter the following values in cells B2 to B8: $10,000; $11,500; $13,000; $9,500; $12,000; $13,000; $8,000. Write a formula that places a total in B9. Create a chart that compares sales for each of the seven days. Save the file, and, with your teacher's permission, print it.

B. Think of three ways spreadsheets could be used. Identify one use that is suitable for each of the following people: a 12-year-old student; a 35-year-old businesswoman; and a 70-year-old man. Describe each use, and explain how it is suitable to the person's age. If possible, create one of the spreadsheets using made-up data to show what it would look like.

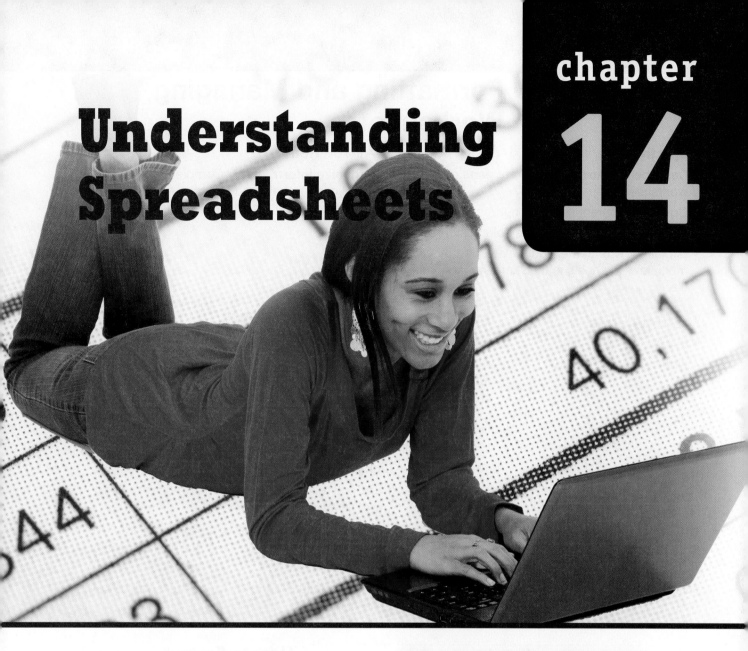

chapter 14

Understanding Spreadsheets

What Do Spreadsheets Do? For many years, businesses tracked financial data on large pieces of paper called ledgers. For instance, a business owner might list each worker's weekly pay, then add the numbers to find the total weekly payroll. The process could take many hours. If there were any changes, a lot of work would have to be redone.

Today's businesses use spreadsheet programs to do this work automatically. They enter information into an electronic table. Then, the spreadsheet program makes the calculations. If information changes, as when a new employee is added, the program creates a new result. These programs can save hours of work, and the calculations are often more accurate than those done by hand.

Chapter Outline

Formatting and Managing Worksheets

Objectives

- Describe how to select different parts of a worksheet.
- Compare different data and number formats.
- Explain how to add or delete columns or rows.
- Explain how to name, add, delete, and move multiple worksheets in the same spreadsheet file.

As You Read

Organize Information Complete a main idea/detail chart to help you learn the options for formatting spreadsheets as you read.

🔑 Key Terms

- range
- worksheet tab

Figure 14.1.1 Apply formatting to worksheet cells to improve the appearance and readability of the data.

Formatting Data in Worksheets

As you learned in Chapter 13, a spreadsheet is a program that displays data—text and numbers—in a table called a worksheet. After you have entered data and formulas, you can make a worksheet look better by changing various formats.

Selecting Cells to Format The first step in formatting is to select the cells to format. To select:

- One cell—Click the cell.
- An entire column or row—Click the column or row heading in the frame.
- Neighboring cells—Click a cell and drag the mouse over additional cells you want to select. This defines a **range**, a group of cells next to each other.
- Cells that are not connected—Hold down the Control key while you select each cell.

	A	B	C	D	E	F
					A1 ▼	fx Hourly Employees
1		**Hourly Employees**				
2		Employee Name	Employee ID	Rate		
3		Thomas Cortese	21875	$ 8.25		
4		Javier Cortez	21154	$ 7.75		
5		Allen Gaines	23455	$ 7.25		
6		Freda Gage	27855	$ 8.00		
7		Vickie Helms	31851	$11.25		
8		Isiah Herron	33252	$10.95		
9		Thomas Kaminski	37881	$ 9.75		
10		Chris Nakao	29958	$11.25		
11						
12						
13						
14						

How to Format

In some programs, such as Excel 2010 or iNumber, you make formatting changes by clicking a button on a toolbar or Ribbon. In some other spreadsheet programs, you click the Format menu, click Selection, and make your choice.

Data Formats You can change the look of either labels (text and numbers) or values (numbers used in calculations) in the selected cells. You can adjust these features:

- Font—the typeface used
- Point size—the size of the font
- Font style—effects such as bold and italic applied to the font
- Color—whether the font is black or another color
- Alignment—where data is positioned in the cell

Number Formats An important set of formatting involves how numbers are displayed. You have several options:

- General—presents numbers as they are typed
- Currency—adds a dollar sign, a comma to numbers over 1,000, and two decimal places
- Comma—shows two decimal places and a comma for numbers over 1,000
- Percentage—multiplies the number in the cell by 100 to calculate the percentage and adds a percent symbol to the result
- Negative numbers—adds a minus sign or places numbers in parentheses or in red
- Decimals—includes number of decimal places chosen

Cell Formats You can also change the look of one or more cells. You can give them color backgrounds or highlight the cell borders using lines of different styles and thickness.

Adjusting Columns and Rows

To add columns or rows, go to the Insert menu and select Column or Row. The existing columns will move to the right of the active cell, and rows will move down to make room for the new column or row. To delete a column or row, click the heading in the worksheet's frame. In the Edit menu, select Delete.

You can also make columns wider or narrower or rows taller or shorter to fit data. To change column width, drag the right edge of the column's heading left or right. To change row height, drag the lower edge of the row's heading up or down.

Using Multiple Worksheets in a File

In most spreadsheet programs, a file holds several worksheets. They are arranged like pages in a book. In fact, a file is often called a workbook.

Did You Know ?

Did you know that a spreadsheet might tell you that 1 times 7 equals 6? Suppose that you had cells whose real value was 0.9 and 7 and that you had chosen to format the numbers with no decimal places. If so, the 0.9 is shown as 1 due to rounding. Now, suppose that you multiply those two numbers. The spreadsheet will use their real values and multiply 0.9 and 7 to reach the correct result, 6.3. But because decimal places are not being shown, it will seem that the program is multiplying 1 times 7 and totaling 6!

Figure 14.1.2 You can insert new rows and columns into a worksheet.

Use the Insert menu to add a new column or row.

Technology @ Work

Some Windows spreadsheet programs give you the chance to see worksheets from different files at the same time. Simply open the files and select Arrange in Excel or Tile Top to Bottom or Tile Side to Side in Quattro Pro.

Think About It!

Think about the advantages of viewing worksheets from different files at the same time. For which examples listed below would this feature be useful?

➤ move data from one file to another
➤ work on a worksheet on a different tab
➤ insert cell references into another file
➤ copy cells from one part of a worksheet to another

Figure 14.1.3 You can copy or move a worksheet within the same file or to another file.

Each worksheet is represented by a **worksheet tab** in the lower-left corner of the screen. Clicking one of these tabs opens that worksheet. Having these extra worksheets is like working in three dimensions; you can store data not only in columns and rows but also on different sheets.

Naming Worksheets   The program labels the tabs with letters ("A," "B") or numbers ("Sheet 1," "Sheet 2"). You can change the names on those worksheet tabs by double-clicking the tab and typing a new name. Suppose you were creating a year's budget. You could name each tab for each month of the year and put a month's budget on each worksheet.

Adding and Deleting Worksheets   To add another worksheet to a file in Excel, right-click on a worksheet tab, and select Insert from the pop-up menu. A new tab appears on the screen. To delete a worksheet, right-click on the tab, and select Delete from the pop-up menu.

Moving Worksheets   You can move worksheets within a file or from one file to another. There are two ways to do this:

* Pop-up Menu—Select the sheet that you want to move by clicking the sheet tab. Then, right-click to display the pop-up menu and select Move or Copy Sheet. A dialog box asks you to select the file (or workbook) and the new location.
* Click and Drag—First, click the sheet tab and then drag it to its new location in the same file or in a new one. To move a worksheet to a different file, that file must be open. As you drag, the mouse changes to a small sheet and an arrow guides you.

Creating Effective Spreadsheets

Objectives

- Outline the steps in designing an effective spreadsheet.
- Identify strategies to avoid spreadsheet errors.
- Explain reasons for using protection in spreadsheets.
- Describe how to hide cells and columns.

As You Read

Summarize Information Complete a summary chart to organize ways to create effective spreadsheets as you read.

Planning Is Important

Almost anyone can create a worksheet. But someone who simply enters labels, values, and formulas might create a worksheet that contains errors. Effective worksheets require careful planning before any data is entered.

Here are some suggestions to help you create an effective and error-free spreadsheet:

Identify the Purpose of the Worksheet What are you trying to accomplish by creating the worksheet?

Think About the End Product What results do you want to report? What individual values do you expect in columns or rows? Do you need summary statistics such as totals or averages?

Identify What Data Is Needed What information will you need? How will it be gathered? Who will put it into the worksheet? How will its accuracy be checked?

Think About What Formulas Are Needed How will you convert your input data into final results? Do you want intermediate results to appear in the worksheet or only final answers? What formulas or functions will you need? How will you test the accuracy of the formulas?

Use Cell References in Formulas How will you write formulas? Remember that it is better to write formulas that refer to cells rather than to values.

Identify Cells to Protect from Replacement What data and formulas should not be changed? You want to protect these cells from being replaced.

 Key Terms

- password
- protect

Technology @ Work

Imagine a spreadsheet that cooks can use to see if the temperatures they are using are adequate to kill different germs found in food. Cells in the spreadsheet allow cooks to input their cooking temperatures for comparison.

Think About It!

Which type of cell listed below do you think should be protected in the spreadsheet described above?

➢ column headings

➢ data

➢ formulas

➢ labels

Figure 14.2.1 You can protect an entire worksheet or just certain parts of it.

Plan How to Enhance the Worksheet Which cells are most important? Use formatting—typefaces, alignment, border, shading, and color—to make those cells stand out.

Protect Data and Formulas You can prevent errors in spreadsheets by **protecting** cells. This process blocks accidental changes.

Levels of Protection

Spreadsheet programs let you lock one or more cells, a worksheet, or all the worksheets in a file. Some programs also allow you to assign a **password**, or coded access word. Then, only people who know the password can open the file or save changes to it.

Using Protection Often users protect an entire worksheet and unlock only the cells they allow to be changed. These might include cells that will hold the values that formulas use or data like names and addresses. The rest of the worksheet remains locked until protection is removed.

How to Add Protection Programs differ in how protection is added to a worksheet. In Excel 2010, select the Review tab, Changes group, and choose the Protect Sheet command. In Quattro Pro, you select Sheet from the Format menu. In Apple's Numbers click on the Inspector button and then use options in the document inspector to apply password protection.

Hiding Cells and Columns

Another feature that can help protect data and formulas is the Hide option. By hiding certain cells or columns in a worksheet, you discourage other users from changing the information in them.

Automatic Spreadsheet Features

Objectives

- Explain how to use the automatic entry feature.
- Differentiate between series increments and decrements.
- Identify advantages of using the automatic fit and formatting features.
- Compare different types of charts.
- Summarize the advantages of using macros.

As You Read

Organize Information   Complete a concept web to identify and organize information about automatic features of spreadsheets as you read the lesson.

Automatic Data Entry

With the automatic data entry feature (often called **AutoFill**), you can enter many kinds of data series in a set of cells. A **data series** is a set of data that changes by a constant value. The series *2005, 2006, 2007, 2008* increases by one. The series *10, 8, 6, 4* decreases by two. The number by which each value increases is called the **increment**. If a series decreases, the value by which it becomes smaller is called the **decrement**. Some data series are text, such as the days of the week. Numbers and dates can also be entered as series.

To use AutoFill, you only need to enter the first one or two values in the series. Then, move the mouse to the lower-right corner of the first cell until a small plus sign or arrow appears. Drag across a row or down a column until you reach the last cell in the series. The data in the series appears in the cells.

Some programs also have a feature called **AutoComplete**. With AutoComplete, the program automatically completes a cell entry as you type, based on the data already entered in the column. For example, if you have entered the text *Yes* in a cell, and then start typing *Yes* in another cell in the same column, your program enters *Yes*. You can press Enter to accept the entry, or keep typing to change it.

Key Terms

- AutoComplete
- AutoFill
- data series
- decrement
- increment
- macro

Figure 14.3.1 Use AutoFill to automatically fill in a series of months.

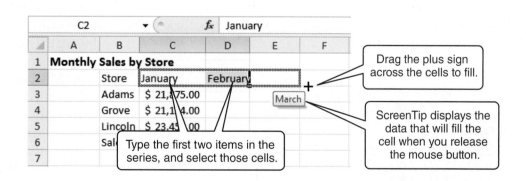

Drag the plus sign across the cells to fill.

ScreenTip displays the data that will fill the cell when you release the mouse button.

Type the first two items in the series, and select those cells.

Technology @ Home

The automatic sum feature can come in handy for some home users of spreadsheets. Some people record their valuable possessions on spreadsheets for insurance records. They can use automatic summing to add the value of these goods.

Think About It!

Think about other uses for which automatic summing might be used. For which tasks listed below do you think automatic summing would be suitable?

➤ budgeting

➤ keeping an address list

➤ keeping track of a collection

➤ tracking the amount of exercise done in a week

Automatic Summing

A very common calculation in spreadsheets is adding a group of numbers. The automatic sum function—called SUM or Auto-SUM—makes this action easy. A toolbar button with the symbol Σ controls the function. Use the following steps:

- Choose the Location—First select the cell where you want the total to appear and make it active. If you are totalling a column, choose the cell below the last number. If you are totalling a row, choose the cell to the right of the last number.

- Insert the Function—Click the Σ button.

- Finish the Sequence—In some programs, the total automatically appears. In others, a formula appears and you have to press Enter or Return to accept it. Once you do, the total appears in the cell.

Automatic Formatting

Some automatic features work on the appearance of the worksheet. They include automatic fit and formatting features.

Fitting Data in a Cell   As discussed in Chapter 13, if the data in a cell is too large for the column, you can change the column width by dragging the right edge of the column border in the frame. But, suppose you enter other data that requires you to repeat this step several times. You can choose the program's automatic fit feature to automatically adjust the column to fit the longest data in that column. Simply double-click the right edge of the column heading in the frame, and the column resizes itself.

Formatting Worksheets   You can make many formatting enhancements to worksheets. Some spreadsheet programs offer an automatic formatting feature. This feature allows you to apply preset formats to an entire worksheet or to a selected part of a worksheet.

To use the feature, select two or more cells that you want to format, and then select the AutoFormat command. For example, in Excel 2010, click Format as Table in the Styles group on the Home tab. In Quattro Pro, click the Format menu and select Speed Format. Then, select the format you want to apply. Most spreadsheets also let you apply conditional formatting, which formats cells in which the data meets certain criteria. For example, you might apply shading to cells with a value greater than 100.

Figure 14.3.2 Use the SUM function to total numbers in a worksheet.

SUM	▼	X ✓ fx	=SUM(C3:C6)						
	A	B	C	D	E	F	G	H	I
1	**Monthly Sales by Store**								
2		**Store**	**January**						
3		Adams	$ 21,875.00						
4		Grove	$ 21,154.00						
5		Lincoln	$ 23,455.00						
6		Salem	$ 27,855.00						
7		Total	=SUM(C3:C6)						
8			SUM(**number1**, [number2], ...)						

Function in formula bar

Cells to total

Function in cell

Automatic Charting

A powerful automatic tool of spreadsheet programs is the chart-creating feature. The program takes the data from a worksheet and transforms it into a chart.

- Define the data—Choose a range of cells to chart.
- Insert the command—Click the chart icon on the toolbar or select the Insert menu command.
- Choose a chart type—A dialog box will offer several different chart types as options. The dialog box explains the uses of the major types of charts.
- Finish the chart—You can then add a title and labels to the chart.

Using Macros

A **macro** is a set of mouse actions, keystrokes, or commands that you can record and put into action again and again. Once a macro is recorded, you can use it whenever you want to repeat the task. Macros save the time and effort of repeating a series of instructions. The program carries out the macro much faster than you could perform the task yourself. Also, using macros ensures that steps are done exactly the same way each time.

The formatting features of spreadsheets offer many options. Some social studies teachers have their students research details and statistics on the countries or time periods they study. By creating charts from the data they collect, students can compare information.

Think About It!

Some spreadsheet data may be easier to analyze in a chart than on a worksheet. Which topics below would be easier to interpret in a chart?

➤ area of forest
➤ population of cities
➤ climate by month
➤ forms of government
➤ main products grown in different states

Comparing Types of Charts

Chart type	Use	Example
Column	Uses vertical bars to show changes over time emphasizing fixed points in time.	Compare the number of people in a country in five different years.
Bar	Uses horizontal bars to show different amounts of the same item.	Compare the number of people in five different countries.
Line	Uses lines to show changes over time on an ongoing basis.	Show the sales of several different products over the period of twelve months.
Pie	Uses segments of a circle to show different parts in relation to the whole.	Show the percentage of a country's population in different age groups.

Using Functions in a Worksheet

Objectives

- Explain what functions are.
- Write a spreadsheet function using the correct syntax.
- Summarize how to copy a function.
- Contrast relative and absolute references.

As You Read

Summarize Information   Use a summary chart to help you summarize information about using functions in a worksheet as you read the lesson.

Key Terms

- 3-D reference
- absolute reference
- argument
- keyword
- nest
- relative reference
- syntax

Spreadsheet Functions

As you learned in Chapter 13, a function is a commonly used formula built into a program. Spreadsheets offer many different functions. Some are general, like the functions to add or average a range of numbers. Some have specialized uses, like those designed for engineering, statistics, or financial work.

Some of the most commonly used spreadsheet functions are:

- Average—averages a group of numbers
- Count—counts the number of cells that contain values
- Maximum—finds the largest value in a set of values
- Minimum—finds the smallest value in a set of values
- Sum—adds a group of numbers and displays the total

Entering Functions   Each function has its own **syntax**, or rules of wording, that specifies how it must be entered. Functions have three parts:

- An identifier, which is a symbol (such as an equal sign or the @ symbol) that identifies the formula as a function.
- A **keyword**, which is the function's name, such as SUM or AVG.
- An **argument**, which is data the function must use. This is often a reference to a cell or a range of cells but may be a number, date, or other data. A function's arguments are usually enclosed in parentheses.

Conditional Functions   Most spreadsheets lets you create formulas using an IF function. These formulas perform a calculation only *if* certain criteria are met. For example, you could apply a 10% discount if the total is less than 100, and a 15% if it is greater than 100. Using IF functions is useful for forecasting, because you can compare one possible outcome with another.

Lookup Tables Lookup functions let you locate information in a table column or row based on specific data, such as the cost of a product.

Nesting Functions You can even **nest** functions. When you nest a function, you include it within another function.

Using a Range in a Function Often the argument includes a cell range, or a group of cells. A range can include cells from one column or one row, but it also can combine cells from more than one of either.

To add a cell range to a function—or to any formula—you don't need to name every cell in the range. Instead, name the cell in the range's upper-left corner, and then name the cell in the range's lower-right corner. Depending on the program you use, you must separate the ranges' cell addresses with either a colon (:) or two periods (..).

For example, if you want to use the SUM function to add the values in the cells B4, B5, C4, and C5, your function might look like this: =SUM(B4:C5).

Relative and Absolute References

Usually, formulas (including functions) use relative cell references. A **relative reference** automatically changes when it is copied or moved so that it uses cell addresses that are specific to its new location. That means you only need to enter the formula in one location, and then copy or move it to use it someplace else.

Cost Estimator Spreadsheet functions are valuable to people who do cost estimating. Many such people work in the construction or repair industries. They have to estimate the cost of workers' labor and of materials and equipment in putting up houses, schools, and other buildings. They can use formulas and functions to find the cost of materials according to the size of the structure being built.

Figure 14.4.1 Use the Average function to find the average of a series of numbers.

Math Spreadsheets are handy for doing conversions. Suppose you need a table that shows how ounces convert to grams.

In a worksheet, type the word Ounces in cell A1, and type Grams in cell B1. Type the numbers 1 through 10 in cells A2 through A11. In cell B2, type the formula =A2*28.35 and press Enter. Because one ounce equals 28.35 grams, the answer 28.35 appears in cell B2. Copy the formula into cell B2 and paste it into cells B3 through B11. The spreadsheet automatically converts the rest of the list for you!

Figure 14.4.2 Examples of a relative cell reference, a 3-D reference, and an absolute cell reference.

Formulas can use a different kind of cell reference, called an absolute reference. An **absolute reference** does not change if you copy or move it to a different cell. You should use this type of reference when your formula or function must refer to a specific cell or range. To enter an absolute reference, you type a dollar sign ($) character to the left of the column letter and/or row number.

Suppose, for example, in cell D6 you enter the function =SUM(D1:D5). If you move the function to cell E6, the relative references change and the function becomes =SUM(E1:E5). If you want the function to use the values in cells D1:D5, no matter where you move it, you enter =SUM($D$1:$D$5); the absolute references will not change.

You can create three kinds of absolute cell references by typing a dollar sign in front of the column letter, the row number, or both, as follows:

- $A$1 uses absolute references for both column and row; neither changes when the formula is copied or moved.

- A$1 uses a relative reference for the column and an absolute reference for the row; only the column changes if the formula is copied or moved.

- $A1 uses an absolute reference for the column and a relative reference for the row; only the row changes if the formula is copied or moved.

3-D References

In a 3-D spreadsheet—one that uses multiple worksheets in the same file—you can include a **3-D reference** in your formulas and functions. A 3-D reference refers to a cell or range on a specific worksheet. That means you can include a reference to a cell on Sheet2 in a formula entered on Sheet1. To enter a 3-D reference, type an exclamation point (!) character between the worksheet name and the cell reference. For example, =SUM(Sheet2!D1:D5) totals the values in D1:D5 on Sheet2; =SUM(Sheet3!D1:D5) totals the values in D1:D5 on Sheet3.

Use the Vocabulary

Directions: *Match each vocabulary term in the left column with the correct definition in the right column.*

_____ **1.** range
_____ **2.** worksheet tab
_____ **3.** data series
_____ **4.** increment
_____ **5.** decrement
_____ **6.** syntax
_____ **7.** keyword
_____ **8.** argument
_____ **9.** relative reference
_____ **10.** absolute reference

a. function name

b. set of data that changes by a constant value

c. rules for writing a function

d. value by which numbers in a series decrease

e. value by which numbers in a series increase

f. cell reference that does not change

g. cell reference that does change

h. lets you access worksheets in a spreadsheet file

i. group of cells that might include cells from different columns and rows

j. reference to cells or range to be acted on by a function

Check Your Comprehension

Directions: *Complete each sentence with information from the chapter.*

1. To select a column, click on the _____.

2. In a spreadsheet, to record results for a race timed to the second and the tenth of a second, use the format _____.

3. To delete a column or row, highlight it, go to the _____, and choose Delete.

4. The automatic fit feature helps you when making a spreadsheet by automatically _____ a column.

5. The _____ feature formats spreadsheets so the data is clear and easy to read.

6. Both a(n) _____ and a line chart can display changes in data over time.

7. Column charts use _____ to display data.

8. _____ are ready-made formulas built into a spreadsheet.

9. A(n) _____ reference is automatically updated to reflect its new location if you move it.

10. The cell reference _____ shows an absolute reference for the column A1.

Think Critically

Directions: *Answer the following questions.*

1. Suppose you wanted to track the statistics of the basketball players for different teams. What spreadsheet feature would help you keep the teams separate from one another? How?

2. What values would you have to enter to use the automatic entry feature for a data series that started with 16 and increased by 3.5?

3. How would you write a reference to the cells in columns U through W and rows 17 through 25?

4. How would you write a function to add values in the cells D7 to D20?

5. What steps are required to copy a function?

Extend Your Knowledge

Directions: *Choose one of the following projects. Complete the exercise on a separate sheet of paper.*

A. Open a new worksheet. Title it "Town Population Growth" in cell A1. Use the AutoFill feature to fill in the years from 2001 to 2010 in cells A2 to A11. Enter these values in cells B2 to B11: 15,000; 15,700; 16,500; 17,200; 18,000; 18,700; 19,300; 20,300; 21,700; 22,900. Create a line chart of the data. Save the file, and, with your teacher's permission, print it. Delete rows B3, B4, B6, B7, and B9. Create a column chart of the new data. Save the file, and, with your teacher's permission, print it. Which type of chart is more effective for this data? Explain.

B. Use the Internet or the library to learn how spreadsheets have changed the way people do business. In what ways are spreadsheets used in businesses today? Was the same work done in the past? How is it different to do the work now? Prepare a presentation to summarize your findings.

DIRECTIONS: *You will use formulas in a spreadsheet to make an estimation of how many names are listed in a telephone book. Microsoft Excel 2010 procedures required for this activity can be found in Appendix A.*

1. Start your spreadsheet program.
2. Create a new file, and save it as **SS-1_ Phonebook_xx** in the location where your teacher tells you to store the files for this activity. Replace *xx* with your own initials or name, as directed by your teacher.
3. In cell A1, type the title, **Estimated Number of Names in a Telephone Book**.
4. Type the following column labels in row 3, beginning in column A: **Names per Inch**, **Inches per Column**, and **Columns per Page**.
5. If possible, count the number of names per inch on a page in your local telephone book, and enter the value in cell A4. If you do not have a telephone book, enter **5**, which is a typical number of names.
6. Measure a column in your local telephone book and enter the length—in inches—in cell B4. If you do not have a telephone book, enter **10**, which is a typical column length.
7. Count the number of columns per page and enter the value in cell C4. If you do not have a telephone book, enter **5**.
8. In cell D3, type the column label **Names per Page**.
9. In cell D4, enter a formula that multiplies the number of names per inch (A4) by the number of inches per column (B4), by the number of columns per page (C4) to find the number of names per page.
10. In cell E3, type the column label **Pages per Book**.
11. In cell E4, enter the number of pages displaying names in your local telephone book. If you do not have a telephone book, enter **250**, an average number of pages in a telephone book.

12. In cell A7, type the column label **Names per Book**.
13. In cell A8, enter a formula that multiplies the number of names on a page (D4) by the number of pages in a book (E4), to find the number of names in the book.
14. Select cell A1 and apply formatting to make the contents stand out. For example, apply the Title cell style, or increase the font size and make the text bold.
15. Select the column label cells in row 3 and apply bold, center alignment. Apply a fill color of your choice and a bottom border. Increase the font size to 14 points.
16. Apply the Comma Style number format to cells A4:E4 and cell A8. Decrease the decimal places to zero.
17. Apply formatting to cell A7 to make the contents stand out. For example, apply the Total cell style or apply cell borders.
18. Merge and center the data in cell A1 across A1:E1.
19. Adjust columns A through E to display all data.
20. Check the spelling in the spreadsheet.
21. Preview the spreadsheet.
22. Change the Orientation to Landscape.
23. Insert a footer with your name on the left and today's date on the right.
24. With your teacher's permission, print the spreadsheet. It should look similar to Illustration A.
25. Close the spreadsheet, saving all changes, and exit the program.
26. As a class, discuss how a spreadsheet program can help you with math. Then, discuss why it is important to know math in order to get the most out of a spreadsheet program.

Illustration A

Estimated Number of Names in a Telephone Book

Names per Inch	Inches per Column	Columns per Page	Names per Page	Pages per Book
5	10	5	250	250

Names per Book
62,500

Activity 2: Budgeting

DIRECTIONS: *You will use a spreadsheet to complete a basic budget worksheet. You will insert formulas for calculating income and expenses, create a chart so you can analyze trends, and you will format the data so it is easy to read. Microsoft Excel 2010 procedures required for this activity can be found in Appendix A.*

1. Start your spreadsheet program and open the file **SS-2_Budget**, which is located on the student CD. Save the file as **SS-2_Budget_*xx*** in the location where your teacher tells you to store the files for this activity.
2. In cell B7, enter a formula to total the values in cells B5 and B6. Fill the formula across through cell G7.
3. In cell B13, use the SUM function to total the values in cells B9:B12. Fill the formula across through cell G13.
4. Insert a blank row between rows 7 and 8.
5. Insert a blank row between rows 5 and 6.
6. Cut the data from cells A13:G13 and paste it in cells A6:G6.
7. Delete row 13.
8. In cell B15, enter a formula that subtracts the monthly expense subtotal (B14) from the monthly income subtotal (B8), and then fill the formula across through cell G15.
9. Insert a blank row between rows 14 and 15.
10. Merge and center the data in cell A1 across columns A through G, and apply formatting appropriate for a heading. For example, apply the Heading 1 cell style, or change the font color and size and apply a bottom cell border.
11. Apply bold to the cells with the labels in row 3 and column A, and apply a light blue fill.

12. Format cells B5:G16 with the Accounting number format with zero decimal places.
13. Select the range B3:G3, then select the range B16:G16, and insert a clustered 3-D column chart based on the selection.
14. Position the chart below row 16.
15. Hide the chart legend and add the chart title **Monthly Budget Surplus**.
16. Edit the value in cell F6 to **15**.
17. Display formulas in the worksheet.
18. Edit the formula in cell B8 to include the data in cell B6. Copy or fill the edited formula across through cell G8.
19. Delete sheets 2 and 3 from the workbook.
20. Check and correct the spelling.
21. Preview the sheet.
22. Insert a custom header with your name on the left and today's date on the right.
23. Scale the worksheet to fit on one page. It should look similar to Illustration B.
24. With your teacher's permission, print the worksheet.
25. Close the spreadsheet, saving all changes, and exit your spreadsheet program.
26. As a class, discuss how a spreadsheet can help you set and achieve savings goals. What other tools could you use to analyze trends?

Illustration B

DIRECTIONS: *You will research the currencies of several European countries and their current exchange rates with the U.S. dollar. You will then use formulas to calculate how much of each type of currency you would have on a trip through Europe and Russia, how much you spend, and how much you have left after the trip. Microsoft Excel 2010 procedures required for this activity can be found in Appendix A.*

1. Open the .pdf file **SS-3_Exchange**, which is located on the student CD. With your teacher's permission, print the Data Record Sheet. The sheet includes a table listing countries in Europe and Russia and space where you can record information about currencies and exchange rates. Close the file and exit the pdf reader program.

2. For each of the countries listed on the Data Record Sheet, research the currency used and the current exchange rate compared to the U.S. dollar. Use the Internet (with your teacher's permission), library resources, a daily newspaper, or information from a bank.

3. If you are using the Internet, use a search engine Web site, and search using keywords or phrases such as **exchange rates** or the currency name. You might also try a Boolean search such as **exchange rates AND the currency name**. Be sure to evaluate each Web site you visit for accuracy and validity. When you find a credible Web site with relevant information, bookmark the site, or with your teacher's permission, print the desired pages. Write the source information about each site on a separate piece of paper.

4. Start your spreadsheet program. Create a new spreadsheet file, and save it as **SS-3_Europe_xx**.

5. In cell A1, enter the title **European Vacation Budget**. Center and merge the title across columns A:G.

6. Enter the following labels in the specified cells and format them in bold:
   A2 - **Country**
   B2 - **Currency**
   C2 - **Exchange Rate (U.S. $/foreign currency unit)**
   D2 - **Budget in U.S. Dollars**
   E2 - **Budget in Local Currency**
   F2 - **Remainder**
   G2 - **Remainder in U.S. Dollars**

7. Enter the following country names in the specified cells and format them in bold:
   A3 - **England**
   A4 - **France**
   A5 - **Switzerland**
   A6 - **Poland**
   A7 - **Hungary**
   A8 - **Russia**

8. Referring to your Data Record Sheet, in columns B and C fill in the data for each country.

9. In column D, enter the following information for each country:
   England - **$200**
   France - **$300**
   Switzerland - **$100**
   Poland - **$100**
   Hungary - **$100**
   Russia - **$200**

10. In cell E3, enter a formula to calculate how much of the local currency you will receive when you exchange the dollar amount entered in cell D2. Copy the formula to cells E4:E8.

11. Assume that in each country you spend 75% of the budgeted amount. In cell F3, enter a formula to calculate how much of the local currency you have left after the trip. Copy the formula to cells F4:F8.

12. In cell G3, enter a formula to convert the remaining currency back into U.S. dollars. Copy the formula to cells G4:G8.

13. In cell G9, use the SUM function to total the amount of U.S. dollars you have left after the trip.

14. Apply appropriate formatting to the data. For example, apply the Accounting or Currency number format to all values that display U.S. dollars, and use cell borders and fills to set off labels and headings. Adjust column widths as necessary.

15. Sort the data in ascending order by the Country column.

16. Preview the worksheet. If necessary, change the margins and orientation so the data fits on one page.

17. Insert a footer with your name on the left and today's date on the right.

18. With your teacher's permission, print the worksheet.

19. Close the spreadsheet, saving all changes, and exit your spreadsheet program.

20. As a class, discuss where the U.S. dollar was strongest (where you would have received the most local currency in exchange for each U.S. dollar) and where it was weakest. Also, discuss how you might alter your trip plan if you discovered that the exchange rate had increased or decreased in one or more of your European destinations.

Spreadsheet Activities

DIRECTIONS: *You will set goals to finish a novel or book that you are currently reading. Then, you will keep track of your progress for a week. After that time, you will record the results in a spreadsheet and create a chart of the data. Microsoft Excel 2010 procedures required for this activity can be found in Appendix A.*

1. Select a novel or book that you are currently reading in your English/language arts class or at home.
2. Start your spreadsheet program and save a new workbook file as **SS-4_ReadingLog_xx**.
3. Calculate the number of pages you have left to read.
   a. In cell A1, enter the title **Reading Goal**. Apply font formatting or cell styles appropriate for a title.
   b. In cell A3, enter the label **Total Pages**. In cell A4, enter the total number of pages in the book.
   c. In cell B3, enter the label **Pages Read**. In cell B4, enter the number of pages you have already read.
   d. In cell C3, enter the label **Pages to Read**.
   e. In cell C4, enter a formula to subtract the number of pages already read from the total number of pages to find the number of pages you have left to read. Format cell C4 in bold, with a fill and border of your choice.
4. Calculate the number of pages you must read each day to complete the book.
   a. In cell D3, enter the label **Completion Date**.
   b. Using a calendar, identify the date by which you want to finish reading the book, and enter that date in cell D4.
   c. In cell E3, enter the label **Days Left**. Count the days you have until the completion date and enter the number in cell E4.
   d. In cell A2, enter the label **Goal**.
   e. In cell B2, enter a formula to divide the number of pages you have left to read (C4) by the number of days you have left until the completion date (E4).
5. Format cell A2 and cells A3:E3 with font formatting or cell styles appropriate for headings, and copy the formatting from cell C4 to cell E4 and cell B**2.**
6. Adjust column widths to display all data. Protect the worksheet so unauthorized users can select cells only, and then save and close the workbook.
7. Open the .pdf file **SS-4_Reading**, which is located on the student CD. With your teacher's permission, print the Data Record Sheet. Close the file, and exit the pdf reader program.

8. For one week, use the Data Record Sheet to record your reading time. Enter the day in column 1, the date in column 2, the daily page goal in column 3, and the actual number of pages you read in column 4. Enter the time you start reading in column 5, the end time in column 6, and write a brief summary of what you read in the column 7.
9. Open the **SS-4_ReadingLog_xx** file in your spreadsheet program. Rename Sheet2 to **Daily Log**, and make that sheet active.
10. Starting in cell A1, enter the information from your Data Record Sheet into the worksheet, including labels.
    a. Enter the first day of the week in cell A2, and then use the AutoFill feature to fill in cells A3:A8.
    b. Enter the first date in cell B2, and then use the AutoFill feature to fill in cells B3:B8.
    c. Use a formula to enter an absolute reference to cell B2 on Sheet1 in cell C2, and then copy it to cells C3:C8.
11. Apply appropriate formatting to make the data easy to read. For example, format headings and labels to stand out. Apply the MM/DD/YYYY format to the Date column. Apply the hh:mm AM/PM time format to the Start Time and End Time columns.
12. In cell A9, enter the label **Total**.
    ✔ *If you track your reading for more than one week, enter the label* Total *in the cell below the last day you are tracking.*
13. In cell C9, use the AutoSum function to calculate the total number of pages you had to read.
14. Copy the formula from cell C9 to cell D9 to calculate the number of pages you actually read.
15. Insert a column between columns F and G. In the new cell G1, enter the heading **Percentage of Goal Met**.
16. In cell G2, enter a formula that divides the number of pages read (D2) by the goal (C2) to calculates the percentage of pages you read in relation to the goal. Apply the Percent style format with no decimal places.
17. Copy the formula from G2 to G3:G9.
18. Use alignment features to rotate the labels in cells A1:H1 45 degrees, and then adjust column widths to fit the data.

19. Check the spelling in the workbook, and correct errors.
20. Change the orientation of the Daily Log worksheet to Landscape, and insert a header with your name on the left and today's date on the right.
21. Preview the worksheet. It should look similar to Illustration C.
22. Insert the same header on Sheet1, and then, with your teacher's permission, print both worksheets.
23. Close the file, saving all changes, and exit your spreadsheet program.
24. As a class, discuss why you did or did not meet your goal. Explore the benefits of setting goals and keeping track of progress. Could you use a spreadsheet and goals to forecast possibilities? Then, brainstorm for other areas in life where setting goals could be helpful.

Illustration C

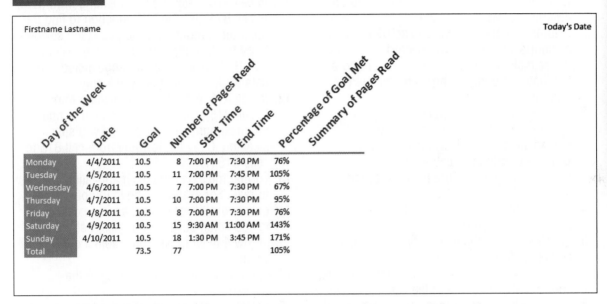

Day of the Week	Date	Goal	Number of Pages Read	Start Time	End Time	Percentage of Goal Met	Summary of Pages Read
Monday	4/4/2011	10.5	8	7:00 PM	7:30 PM	76%	
Tuesday	4/5/2011	10.5	11	7:00 PM	7:45 PM	105%	
Wednesday	4/6/2011	10.5	7	7:00 PM	7:30 PM	67%	
Thursday	4/7/2011	10.5	10	7:00 PM	7:30 PM	95%	
Friday	4/8/2011	10.5	8	7:00 PM	7:30 PM	76%	
Saturday	4/9/2011	10.5	15	9:30 AM	11:00 AM	143%	
Sunday	4/10/2011	10.5	18	1:30 PM	3:45 PM	171%	
Total		73.5	77			105%	

Firstname Lastname — Today's Date

DIRECTIONS: *You will keep track of how much time you spend on various activities during a typical week. You will use a spreadsheet program to record your data. Then, you will create charts to visually represent the information. Microsoft Excel 2010 procedures required for this activity can be found in Appendix A.*

1. Open the .pdf file **SS-5_ChartingTime**, which is located on the student CD. With your teacher's permission, print the Data Record Sheet. Close the file and the pdf reading program.

2. For one week, use the Data Record Sheet to record the amount of time you spend on different activities. Note that there are blank columns where you may add activities, such as sports and homework. Record the hours in decimals; for example, 1.5 for one-and-a-half hours. Round the hours to the nearest quarter hour.

3. When your table is complete, start your spreadsheet program. Create a new spreadsheet file, and save it as **SS-5_DailyLog_xx** in the location where your teacher tells you to store the files for this activity.

4. Apply the Aspect theme, or other theme or design of your choice.

5. In cell A1, enter the title **Daily Activity Log**, and apply formatting appropriate for a title, such as the Title cell style, or a font, font size, and font style that makes the data stand out.

6. Enter the information from your Data Record Sheet into the worksheet, including labels.
   a. In cell B3, enter the label **Activities**.
   b. In cell B4, enter **Sleeping**, then continue across row 4 entering the labels for the remaining activities.
   c. In cell A5, enter **Monday**, and then use the AutoFill feature to fill in cells A6:A11.
   d. Enter the actual times you spend on each activity, per day.

7. Apply appropriate formatting to make the data easy to read. For example, apply heading style formatting to headings and labels, or apply cell borders and fills. Merge and center the label *Activities* across the data.

8. In cell I5, use the AutoSum function to calculate the number of hours you spent on each activity on Monday. The result should be 24. Copy the formula from cell I5 to cells I6:I12.

9. In cell B12, use the AutoSum function to calculate the total hours you spent sleeping during the week. Copy the formula from cell B12 to cells C12:I12.

10. In cell A13, enter the row heading **Average**. In cell B13, use the AVERAGE function to find the average amount of time you spent sleeping. Do not include the Total Hours value in the average. Copy the formula from cell B13 to cells C13:H13.

11. In cell A14, enter the row heading **Minimum**. In cell B14, use the MIN function to find the minimum amount of time you spent sleeping. Copy the formula from cell B14 to cells C14:H14. Make sure the range includes the data for the days of the week only.

12. In cell A15, enter the row heading **Maximum**. In cell B15, use the MAX function to find the maximum amount of time you spent sleeping. Copy the formula from cell B15 to cells C15:H15.

13. Format the data to make it appealing and easy to read. For example, show numbers with only two decimal places, and use cell styles to add color, borders, and fills. Set the text in row 4 to wrap, and then adjust column widths.

14. Check and correct the spelling in the worksheet.

15. Select A4:H11 and identify the selected range as a table. Name the table **Log**.

16. Filter the Screen Time column to show days when you spent more than 3 hours on this activity. Clear the filter. Then, filter the same column to show days when you spent less than 3 hours. Clear the filter.

17. Create a Stacked Bar in 3-D chart based on the data in the table. Position the chart over cells A16:E30.

18. Add the chart title **Daily Activity Log**.

19. Create a Pie in 3-D chart to show the percentage of time you spent on each activity during the week.
   ✔ Hint: Select B4:H4 (the activities) and B12:H12 (the total hours), insert the chart, then switch the Row/Column data.

20. Title the pie chart **Weekly Activity Time**, and display data labels as percentages. Position the pie chart over the range A31:F44.

21. Delete row 2.

22. Preview the worksheet. Set the margins to Narrow (Top and Bottom 0.75" and left and right 0.25"), and add a footer with your name on the left and today's date on the right.

23. With your teacher's permission, print the worksheet. It should look similar to Illustration D.

24. Close the file, saving all changes, and exit your spreadsheet program.

Illustration D

Daily Activity Log

Column1	Sleeping	Eating	Being at School	Screen Time	Sports	Homework	Reading	Total Hours
Monday	7.50	1.00	8.00	2.00	2.00	2.00	1.50	24.00
Tuesday	8.00	1.00	8.00	2.00	2.00	3.00	0.00	24.00
Wednesday	7.75	1.00	8.00	2.00	2.00	3.25	0.00	24.00
Thursday	7.50	1.00	8.00	2.00	2.00	2.50	1.00	24.00
Friday	8.50	1.50	8.00	4.00	2.00	0.00	0.00	24.00
Saturday	10.00	1.25	0.00	7.75	4.50	0.00	0.50	24.00
Sunday	11.00	1.50	0.00	7.00	2.00	2.50	0.00	24.00
Total Hours	60.25	8.25	40.00	26.75	16.50	13.25	3.00	168.00
Average	8.61	1.18	5.71	3.82	2.36	1.89	0.43	
Minimum	7.50	1.00	0.00	2.00	2.00	0.00	0.00	
Maximum	11.00	1.50	8.00	7.75	4.50	3.25	1.50	

Activities

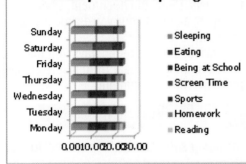

Daily Activity Log

- Sleeping
- Eating
- Being at School
- Screen Time
- Sports
- Homework
- Reading

0.00 10.00 20.00 30.00

Weekly Activity Time

- Sleeping
- Eating
- Being at School
- Screen Time
- Sports
- Homework
- Reading

36%, 5%, 24%, 16%, 10%, 8%, 1%

Firstname Lastname

Today's Date

Activity 6: Merging Price Labels

DIRECTIONS: *You will insert formulas for calculating a price markdown in an existing spreadsheet. You will then use the spreadsheet as a data source for a merge to generate price labels. Microsoft Excel 2010 procedures required for this activity can be found in Appendix A.*

1. Open **SS-6_Discount**, which is located on the student CD, and save it as **SS-6_Discount_xx** in the location where your teacher instructs you to store the files for this activity.
2. In cell D2, enter a formula that calculates the price after applying the discount.
   ✔ *Hint: Multiply the regular price by the discount. Then, subtract the discount from the regular price.*
3. Fill the formula down through cell D16.
4. Save the changes to the spreadsheet, close it, and exit your spreadsheet program.
5. Start your word-processing program and save a new blank document as **SS-6_ Labels_xx** in the location where your teacher instructs you to store the files for this activity.
6. Use the program's merge feature to start a merge for labels. For example, with Microsoft Word 2010, click the Mailings tab, click Start Mail Merge, and click Labels.
7. Select a label that is 1" high by 2.63" wide, such as Avery 6250 Easy Peel Address Labels.

8. Select to use an existing data source. For example, in Word 2010, click Select Recipients and then click Use Existing List.
9. Select Sheet 1 in the **SS-6_Discount_xx** spreadsheet as the data source.
10. In the **SS-6_Label_xx** document, click in the first cell of the table and insert the **Item** merge field.
11. Press **Enter**, type **Regular Price: $** and insert the Regular_Price merge field.
12. Press Enter, type **Discounted Price: $** and insert the New_Price merge field.
13. Update the labels, and preview the result.
14. Check the spelling, and correct any errors. Adjust the spacing, if necessary.
15. Update the labels and preview the results. Then, with your teacher's permission, print the labels. Close the document, saving all changes, and exit your word-processing program.
16. As a class, discuss other ways you might use merge to integrate data from a spreadsheet program with a document.

Activity 7: Analyzing Client Activity

DIRECTIONS: *You will use advanced spreadsheet features including subtotals and conditional formatting to complete a worksheet analyzing client activity for a landscape service company. Microsoft Excel 2010 procedures required for this activity can be found on the Student CD.*

1. Open **SS-7_Landscape**, which is located on the student CD, and save it as **SS-7_Landscape _xx** in the location where your teacher instructs you to store the files for this activity.
2. Insert a header that has your name at the left, today's date in the center, and the sheet name at the right.
3. Working in Normal view, select the range A4:D32, and convert it to a table.
4. Apply a table autoformat or style, such as the Table Style Light 20 table style.
5. Insert a total row, and adjust it so a Sum total displays for the Fee column only.
6. In cell G5, enter a formula that sums only the fees that have been paid.
7. In the range G7:G10, enter formulas that sum only the fees paid for each type of service.
8. Rename Sheet1 to **Version1**. Copy the Version1 sheet, naming the copy **Version2** and placing it after the copied sheet.
9. Delete Sheet3 and hide Sheet2.

10. On the Version2 sheet, convert the table back to a range.
11. Apply conditional formatting to the Fee column that highlights values over $100 with a yellow fill with dark yellow text.
12. Apply conditional formatting to the Paid column that highlights No entries with light red fill with dark red text.
13. To the range with the calculated paid values (G7:G10), apply a conditional format such as Blue Data Bar (either gradient or solid).
14. In both sheets, use Find and Replace to replace the Customer name *Tayson* with **Tyler**.
15. Set row 4 as the print titles on both the visible sheets.
16. Protect the Version2 sheet so unauthorized users cannot change it. Do not use a password.
17. With your teacher's permission, print both worksheets in Portrait orientation, then save and close the file and exit Excel.

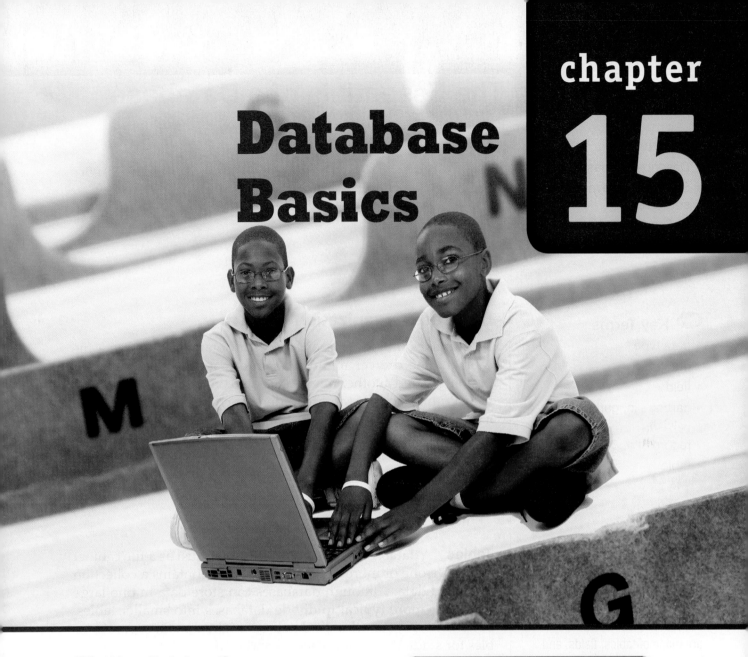

Database Basics

What Is a Database? What do the following things have in common: an address book, a telephone directory, a list of family birthdays, and a catalog of DVDs? For one thing, each can be stored in a **database**, or an organized collection of information. Databases can exist on paper or on a computer. Computerized databases can be huge, containing information on millions of items. A computerized database is an ideal tool for making use of huge amounts of existing data.

Databases make it easy to store, add, organize, and retrieve information. Suppose a worker has to find the account number for a customer. Imagine how much time that worker saves if he or she can find the information simply by typing the customer's name instead of searching through piles of paper!

Chapter Outline

 Lesson 15–1

The Essentials of a Database

 Lesson 15–2

Types of Database Programs

 Lesson 15–3

Database Techniques

The Essentials of a Database

Objectives

- Describe the basic organization of a database.
- Summarize advantages to using database software.
- Define GIGO, and explain how it relates to the quality of a database.

As You Read

Organize Information   As you read the lesson, use a concept web to help you organize basic facts about databases.

🔑 Key Terms

- data type
- database
- field
- garbage in, garbage out (GIGO)
- record
- table

Figure 15.1.1 Databases are made of tables, fields, and records.

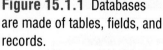

Database Organization

What makes up a database? How is it organized? Picture a file cabinet. One drawer might hold information on a company's customers, and another might have data on the company's products. Within each drawer are folders. Each folder is dedicated to a particular person or product. Finally, each folder stores different bits of information about that person or product.

A computerized database is also structured in three parts:

- tables
- records
- fields

Tables   A database has one or more **tables**, just as a file cabinet may have one or more drawers. Each table contains a collection of related data. Although databases can store data in one large table, it is more typical to divide databases into smaller tables. For example, your school's database might contain separate tables for students and for teachers and staff.

Records   The data in each table is further split into smaller units that contain related information about one individual or item. Each of these units is called a **record**. For your school's database, each unit of information, or record, is about an individual student or teacher.

Fields   Each separate piece of data that is stored in a record—a student's last name, first name, and so on—is called a **field**. Each field is set up so that only a certain type of information, called the **data type**, is permitted in that field. For example, a field for date of birth allows only dates to be entered.

Advantages of a Database

While smaller databases might just as easily be kept on paper as on a computer, computerized databases make it easier to do the following:

Enter Information   You can enter information neatly, quickly, and in an organized way with your keyboard and mouse.

Store Large Amounts of Information   If you want to keep track of 20 or 30 phone numbers, you can easily use an address book. A computerized database, however, can hold thousands, or even millions, of telephone numbers.

Find Information Quickly   A computerized database can save you time in finding information. It might take you only a minute or two to find a number in your personal address book, but a telephone directory on CD-ROM can help you find one of millions of phone numbers in even less time.

Organize Information in Different Ways   Paper filing systems can limit your ability to arrange information. For example, should you organize your personal phone book by listing each person's phone number, cell phone number, or e-mail address first? With a computerized database, you can easily switch between these different methods.

Real-World Tech

Preserving Ancient Art   Databases are often put to unexpected uses. Because databases can record and store large amounts of information, organizations have come up with creative ways to use them.

For example, at New Mexico State University, CD-ROMs store aerial views of 1,500-year-old American Indian rock art to preserve a natural art form that is vanishing due to erosion and vandalism.

How might you use a database to record information about the culture of your family or your community?

Figure 15.1.2 Students can use databases to organize information gathered for research projects.

Update Information Database software makes it easy to change or update data. Think about adding a new name to your address book. It would be difficult to re-alphabetize the list if it existed only on paper. Think about how messy the book might look after just a few changes. With a computerized database, names and numbers can be added, deleted, or changed easily and quickly. After making these changes, you have an easy-to-read, updated version of the database.

It's All About the Data

Databases can be useful tools at home and at work. They also have many different uses at school. Administrators can use them to track student performance, payroll, and supplies. Teachers can use them to record students' test scores and attendance. Students can use them to organize their grades or search for information for a project.

However, databases are useful only if they are accurate. In other words, databases are only as good as the data they contain. The acronym *GIGO* explains this principle. **GIGO** is short for "**garbage in, garbage out.**" It means that if the information placed in a database is wrong, anyone using that information will get the wrong results. When adding information to a database, it is very important to do so accurately and to check your entries.

Objectives

- Summarize the purpose of a database management system.
- Compare and contrast types of database management programs.
- Evaluate the characteristics of a well-designed database.

As You Read

Outline   As you read the lesson, use an outline to help identify types of database management systems and characteristics of good design.

Database Management Systems

A database management system, or **DBMS**, is software used to manage the storage, organization, processing, and retrieval of data in a database. There are several kinds of database management programs, including flat-file databases, relational databases, object-oriented databases, and multimedia databases.

Flat-File Databases   A **flat-file database** allows you to work with data in only one table. A computerized address book is one example. In flat-file databases, records can be retrieved randomly. That is, you can look for just one name on a list. You can also retrieve an entire table and **sort** the data, or arrange it in a different order. You might sort to find all the people living in the same town, for example.

Flat-file databases have a limitation. The data in one table cannot be linked to the data in another table. That might not be a problem with a simple address book. However, many businesses and other large organizations use databases in more complex ways, and they need added flexibility.

Relational Databases   A **relational database** can use data from several tables at the same time. This is because the tables are linked by a **key field**, a field that is found in each of the tables. A relational database is more complex than a flat-file database program. It also requires more skill to use and costs more. However, its greater power makes it more popular.

Think about a relational database a school might have. One table might hold all students' schedules. Another might have all their grades. Yet another table might include their addresses and phone numbers. All the tables can be linked by a key field: each student's name or student identification number. By using key fields, administrators can find data about a particular student from any available table.

Key Terms

- database management system (DBMS)
- flat-file database
- key field
- object-oriented database
- relational database
- sort

Businesses can link their relational databases by customer names and numbers. Companies use these databases for many purposes, including storing customer information, such as name, address, and telephone number; seeing where to ship goods the customer buys; issuing bills for purchases and receipts for payments made; and tracking what customers have bought over time and using that information to tailor ads and promotions.

Object-Oriented Databases   Another type of DBMS is called an **object-oriented database**. These databases store objects, such as documents, video clips, and audio clips. Each object contains both that data and the program needed to display that data, including showing a graphic or playing a sound.

Object-oriented databases are not yet widely used. Some experts believe that they will replace relational databases in the future.

Multimedia Databases   Traditional databases can store all kinds of text and numerical data. Today's computers also often deal with pictures, sounds, animation, or video clips. Multimedia professionals use databases to catalog media files, such as art, photographs, maps, video clips, and sound files. Media files themselves generally are not stored in databases because they are too large. Instead, a multimedia database serves as an index to all the separately stored files. Users can search through the index and then locate the particular file they want.

Figure 15.2.1 Databases are everywhere in our wired world. For example, at supermarkets, they store information about the products we buy. On our cell phones, they store the names and numbers of people we call.

Well-Designed Databases

For databases to be effective, they need to be planned carefully. Following are three characteristics of good database design:

Ensuring Data Security   The same features that make databases efficient tools make them vulnerable to invasions of privacy. Personal information can be misused. Requiring users to input a password before they can access data is one way of keeping a database secure.

Preserving Data Integrity   The accuracy and validity of the information gives a database its data integrity. Errors make the database less accurate and less useful.

Avoiding Data Redundancy   Repeating the same data in many tables wastes space by requiring a computer to store the same information more than once. It also increases the amount of work needed to update records because the data needs to be changed in more than one place. That, in turn, increases the chance of errors and slows down searches for data. Storing data in only one table and then linking the table to others enables the data to be used in various ways.

Database Administrator   One key to good database design is testing the design to make sure it works the way it is supposed to. That testing is part of the work of database administrators. They also maintain the security of the database and write manuals that explain how to use the database.

Figure 15.2.2 Protecting the database with a password.

Database Techniques

Objectives

- Give examples of how to manage information in databases.
- Compare and contrast browsing, sorting, and querying data in a database.
- Describe the features of a report template.

As You Read

Summarize As you read the lesson, use a chart to help you summarize techniques for using databases effectively.

🔑 Key Terms

- ascending order
- browse
- descending order
- information overload
- report
- report template

Figure 15.3.1 Navigation buttons allow users to move quickly through a large database table.

Information Management

Computers can produce too much information, or **information overload**. Database creators can help manage data by:

- summarizing information so that database users are not overwhelmed by details
- including in reports only the data that meets specific information needs
- arranging data in a specific order so that it is easier to view and understand

Browsing Data

Putting data into a database is of little help if you cannot retrieve it when you need it. One way to find data is to **browse**, or look through, all the records. Databases can display data like a spreadsheet, with each record occupying a row and each field in a column. You can also display each record on a separate screen.

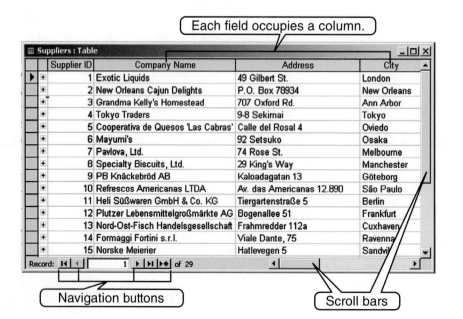

Each field occupies a column.

		Supplier ID	Company Name	Address	City
▶	+	1	Exotic Liquids	49 Gilbert St.	London
	+	2	New Orleans Cajun Delights	P.O. Box 78934	New Orleans
	+	3	Grandma Kelly's Homestead	707 Oxford Rd.	Ann Arbor
	+	4	Tokyo Traders	9-8 Sekimai	Tokyo
	+	5	Cooperativa de Quesos 'Las Cabras'	Calle del Rosal 4	Oviedo
	+	6	Mayumi's	92 Setsuko	Osaka
	+	7	Pavlova, Ltd.	74 Rose St.	Melbourne
	+	8	Specialty Biscuits, Ltd.	29 King's Way	Manchester
	+	9	PB Knäckebröd AB	Kaloadagatan 13	Göteborg
	+	10	Refrescos Americanas LTDA	Av. das Americanas 12.890	São Paulo
	+	11	Heli Süßwaren GmbH & Co. KG	Tiergartenstraße 5	Berlin
	+	12	Plutzer Lebensmittelgroßmärkte AG	Bogenallee 51	Frankfurt
	+	13	Nord-Ost-Fisch Handelsgesellschaft	Frahmredder 112a	Cuxhaven
	+	14	Formaggi Fortini s.r.l.	Viale Dante, 75	Ravenna
	+	15	Norske Meierier	Hatlevegen 5	Sandvil

Suppliers : Table

Record: 1 of 29

Navigation buttons

Scroll bars

Many database programs provide keyboard commands and other tools, such as scroll bars and navigation buttons, that help users browse quickly through records. You can also limit the browsing so that the program displays only certain records and fields. This can greatly reduce the time it takes to locate or review specific records.

Sorting Data

Another way to save time is to sort the data. Sorting lets you locate information quickly.

Types of Sorting Databases can sort data in one of three ways:

- Alphabetical sorting of letters and symbols
- Numerical sorting of numbers and values
- Chronological sorting of dates and times

Data can be sorted in **ascending order**, in which values increase, such as A, B, C or 1, 2, 3. It can also be sorted the opposite way, in **descending order**. In this order, values decrease. Letters are listed C, B, and A, and numbers are sorted 3, 2, and 1.

Single and Multiple Sorts The easiest kind of sort uses a single field, such as name. Databases can also sort data using more than one field, such as last name and first name. When two records are identical in the first field, they are sorted again based on the next field. In this case, a database would list "Williams, Serena" before "Williams, Venus."

Technology @ School

School databases contain such information as students' names, classes, health records, teachers' names, grades, and standardized test scores.

Think About It!

Think about how such data might be organized. Which fields listed below do you think could be usefully sorted in ascending order?

- names of all students in a course
- addresses
- courses offered
- telephone numbers
- student ID numbers
- teachers' names

Figure 15.3.2 Sorting lets you organize data so it best suits your needs.

ID No.	Last Name	Birthday
1	Rodriquez	10-13-89
2	Goldstein	06-03-88
3	Smith	05-15-88
4	Hernandez	11-01-87
5	Abdullah	04-21-89
6	Chung	01-03-87

Sort by ID Number

ID No.	Last Name	Birthday
5	Abdullah	04-21-89
6	Chung	01-03-87
2	Goldstein	06-03-88
4	Hernandez	11-01-87
1	Rodriquez	10-13-89
3	Smith	05-15-88

Sort by Last Name

ID No.	Last Name	Birthday
1	Rodriquez	10-13-89
5	Abdullah	04-21-89
2	Goldstein	06-03-88
3	Smith	05-15-88
4	Hernandez	11-01-87
6	Chung	01-03-87

Sort by Birthday

Technology @ Work

A database report must contain basic information so that workers can access and use it correctly.

Think About It!

Think about what kind of information a report should have. For which fields listed below do you think a report would be useful?

> on patients that is used by a hospital's medical staff.

> patient's name

> special dietary needs

> room number

> attending doctor

> diagnosis

> medicines prescribed

Querying Data

Databases can speed up the process of browsing information by finding only records that match specific criteria. A query is a user-created direction that tells the database to find specific records.

Creating Reports   A benefit that database software has over paper databases is the ease with which reports can be created. A **report** is an ordered list of selected records and fields in an easy-to-read format. Reports can display data in columns, as labels, or as single records. Reports are usually printed on paper.

To generate a report, the database software uses the appropriate data currently in its tables. If you print the same report at a later time, it might contain different data reflecting whatever changes were made when the database was updated.

Designing a Report Template   In most databases, users design a **report template**, a pattern that controls how data will be displayed. This template typically has several main features:

- a report header that appears at the beginning of a report, such as the report title
- a report footer that appears at the end of a report, such as summary totals or averages
- a page header that appears at the top of each page, such as field headings
- a page footer that appears at the bottom of each page, such as the date the report was printed and the page number
- the arrangement of the data that you want the report to include

Creating a Report

| Identify the data needed. | → | Search for the needed data. | → | Sort the data. |

| Plan the report layout, including headers and footers. | → | Preview the report. | → | Print the report. |

Use the Vocabulary

Directions: *Match each vocabulary term in the left column with the correct definition in the right column.*

_____ **1.** database
_____ **2.** record
_____ **3.** field
_____ **4.** data type
_____ **5.** GIGO
_____ **6.** database management system
_____ **7.** flat-file database
_____ **8.** relational database
_____ **9.** key field
_____ **10.** ascending order

a. smallest part of a database; holds an individual piece of data

b. term that stresses the importance of inputting accurate data

c. examples are A, B, C and 1, 2, 3

d. organized collection of information stored on computer

e. database that allows you to work with data in only one table

f. part of a database that holds data about a particular person or item

g. software used to manage the storage, organization, processing, and retrieval of data in a database

h. database in which shared key fields link data among tables

i. limited kind of information that can be entered into a field

j. element that links tables

Check Your Comprehension

Directions: *Complete each sentence with information from the chapter.*

1. Some databases have only one _____, but others can hold several, each containing a set of related data.

2. Database programs are superior to paper databases in part because the information can be _____ in different ways.

3. GIGO is a reminder that a database is of poorer quality if the _____ is not accurate.

4. The kind of database that stores and opens programs for images, video clips, and audio clips is a(n) _____.

5. A multimedia database is similar to a book _____.

6. Protecting sensitive data by requiring users to input a(n) _____ is one way to aim for data security.

7. Data _____ is usually undesirable because it wastes space and introduces the possibility of errors.

8. One way that databases can be used to reduce information overload is to _____ information so that users are not overwhelmed by details.

9. Dates and times are sorted in _____ order.

10. You can create multiple _____ to tailor the reports generated from a database.

Think Critically

Directions: *Answer the following questions.*

1. Suppose you wanted to create a database of your school's DVD collection. What fields might you include?

2. Based on efficiency, which kind of database software would you choose to create a database in which you needed to link information? Why?

3. What can you do to try to ensure the accuracy of the data you enter into a database?

4. If having a lot of information is useful, why is information overload a problem?

5. Suppose you were creating a report listing the books in a library. What headers and footers might you design for the report?

Extend Your Knowledge

Directions: *Choose one of the following projects. Complete the exercise on a separate sheet of paper.*

A. Select a magazine in your school library, and create a database of the articles featured in that issue. Include such fields as author, title, topic, and starting page number. Add another field for date of the issue, and add some records from another issue of the same magazine. Create a report that displays the data you input. With your teacher's permission, print your report. Then, find another way of presenting the data, and, with your teacher's permission, print that report. Save your database.

B. In small groups, make an appointment to visit a local business. Interview the owner or a key employee about the databases that the business uses. Find out what tables, records, and fields the databases have. Ask how the databases are used. Prepare a brief report summarizing your findings. Present it to the class.

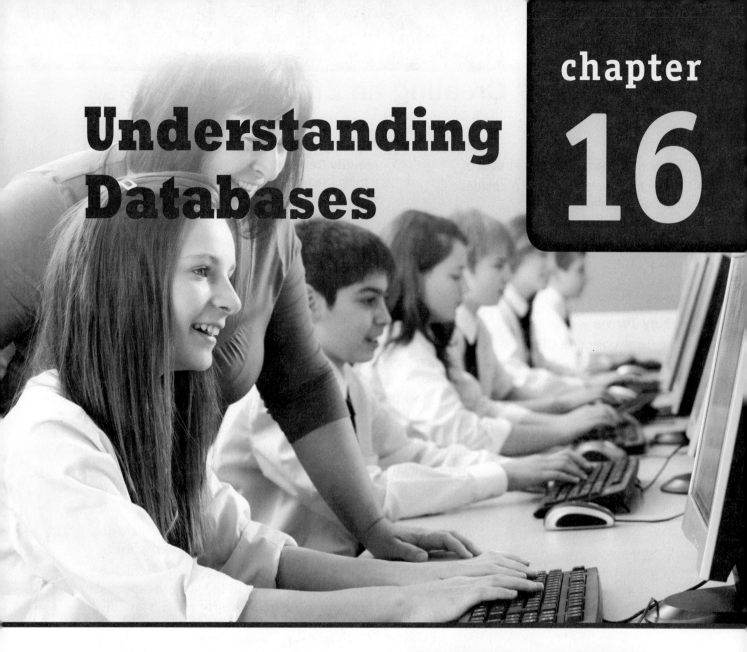

Understanding Databases

What Makes Information Valuable? Just because information can be stored in a database does not make it valuable. Information by itself has little worth. To be valuable for decision making, information needs to have these traits:

- accessibility—easily located and retrieved
- accuracy—free of errors
- relevancy—related to your purpose
- completeness—does not omit anything relevant
- economy—costs less to use than to create
- reliability—available when you need it
- security—unauthorized people denied access
- simplicity—clear and understandable
- timeliness—up-to-date
- verifiability—can be confirmed by another source

Chapter Outline

 Lesson 16–1

Creating an Effective Database

 Lesson 16–2

Maintaining Efficient Databases

 Lesson 16–3

Using Queries and Filters

Creating an Effective Database

Objectives
- Describe the parts of a data structure.
- Explain how the structure of a database influences its effectiveness.
- Sequence the steps in creating a data structure.
- Compare and contrast data types.

As You Read
Identify Details As you read the lesson, use a main idea chart to help you identify important details for creating databases.

🔑 Key Terms
- binary large object (BLOB)
- data structure
- field name
- field width

Creating a Data Structure

All structures have an underlying frame that determines their size, shape, and general appearance. Databases also have a framework, called a **data structure**. It defines the fields in the database, and thus defines what each record will contain.

Parts of a Data Structure A data structure has four parts:
- The field sequence is the order in which the fields will appear in each record.
- The **field name** is a unique identifier for each field, such as "Last Name" or "Class."
- Data type specifies the kind of information the field will contain; for example, numbers, date, text, or hyperlink.
- The **field width** is a limit on the size of the field, which is typically the number of characters in the largest expected data value. For example, a field width for a U.S. state in an address might be two characters. The field for a phone number might be 10 or 14 characters.

Customizing Data Structure Most database programs in use today allow you to design a data structure from scratch and define your fields. Many programs also have predesigned database structures that can be customized.

Benefits of Good Design Well-designed data structures can improve database effectiveness. They set up the proper amount of space for the data you will collect. They also enable you to gather the data you need and organize data so that it can be searched efficiently. Poorly designed data structures result in databases that take up unnecessary disk space. They might exclude data that you need. These problems make it more difficult to retrieve the data you need in a meaningful way.

Designing the Data Structure

Generally, a database is used by many people—not just the person who designed it. Good design is important for this reason, too. Users should find the database easy to understand and its tools easy to use. The database should be set up to encourage accurate, efficient data entry and to provide reliable results when running queries and reports. A data structure is usually designed in four steps:

1. Identify the database. You can choose an existing database in which to place the tables or you can create a new database that will contain all the tables, forms, and reports you specify.

2. Create the tables. Create each new table to be included in the database.

3. Identify each field. As you create a table, specify the name, data type, and field size of each field that will exist within the table. Many database programs give other options for fields:

   - Default values are used automatically if no data is entered in the field.

   - Input masks are formats that standardize the way data looks, such as dashes between the different parts of all phone numbers.

   - Prompt captions are messages that appear on-screen to help the person entering data understand the content of the field.

   - Validation rules are limits that determine what data is acceptable for a field. For instance, a field for test scores could be limited to values between 0 and 100.

4. Save the data structure. You can always modify a structure later, if you wish. You can add or delete fields, rearrange their order, or modify the data type or width. You can also add new tables and make changes to existing ones.

Career Corner

Librarian Librarians work with many different databases. Some catalog books, videos, and reference materials. Librarians assign numbers to the items they are cataloging based on the subjects of the items.

Reference librarians help users find the information they want in databases. Some librarians work for private companies doing this research. They have job titles such as researcher and database specialist.

Steps in Designing a Database

| Identify the database. | Create each table. | Identify each field within each table. | Save the data structure. |

Four of the United Kingdom's busiest airports, including London's Heathrow International and Manchester Airport, are using a database with a very unusual data type—eye scans. Nicknamed IRIS for "Iris Recognition Immigration System," the high-tech machines scan passengers' eyes as soon as they check in. Airport security officials hope that IRIS will make it much more difficult for illegal immigrants and criminals—particularly terrorists—to get into the country.

Common Data Types

Many databases allow you to select a data type for each field. This prevents users from typing numbers in a field that is supposed to hold names, for instance. There are several common data types:

- Text—letters, numbers, and special characters. This is used for a name or an address, for example.
- Number—numeric data that can be used in calculations, such as values that are totaled or averaged.
- Logical—data with only two possible values, such as "yes/no" or "true/false." This might be used to indicate whether a student is male or female.
- Currency—consists of number fields with special formatting to reflect the fact that they represent sums of money. This could be used for billing information.
- Date/time—used to indicate a date or time of day.
- Memo—allows for an unlimited amount of text information. This type is used for notes.
- Autonumber—automatically assigns a number to each record in the table. This could be used for assigning an identification number to each student, for instance.
- Object—any nontext object. This type is used for an image, sound, or video.
- Hyperlink—connects to a Web address.

Some database programs allow you to specify a data type to handle very large objects. This data type is known as a **binary large object (BLOB)**.

Figure 16.1.1 Assigning data types in a table of order information.

Field Name	Data Type	
OrderID	Number	Same as Order ID in Orders table.
ProductID	Number	Same as Product ID in Products table.
Product Name	Text	Same as Product Name in Products table.
UnitPrice	Currency	
Quantity	Number	
Discount	Number	

Maintaining Effective Databases

Objectives

- Describe techniques for maintaining data.
- Compare two methods of processing records.
- Explain how adding and deleting data contributes to the efficiency of a database.

As You Read

Outline As you read the lesson, use an outline to help you organize basic information about maintaining databases.

Data Maintenance

As with any tool, a database needs to be well maintained. You can make sure that a database continues to operate efficiently by performing regular **data maintenance**. This includes tasks such as adding new records, modifying existing records, and deleting those you no longer need.

You can modify databases in other ways, too. You might change the reports the database uses. You also might update the structure of the database to reflect your needs.

Keeping a Database Current

Databases typically provide for two methods of updating data: batch processing and transactional processing.

People choose a processing method based on how important it is for the data to be completely up-to-date. Batch processing was more common in the past. Most databases today use transactional processing.

Batch Processing In **batch processing**, the data is recorded as events take place, but the database itself is not updated until there is a group, or batch, of data ready to process. Each batch is processed all at once, typically when the computer is idle, such as in the late evening—this frees up memory for more extensive programs and also speeds up productivity.

Batch processing is used for tasks where updating a large database might take several hours. For example, credit card companies store customers' transaction data to be sent out in batches at the end of the month; otherwise, you'd get a paper bill for every single transaction. Batch processing is not appropriate, however, in situations where data must always be kept as current as possible.

🔑 Key Terms

- batch processing
- data maintenance
- form
- online transactional processing (OLTP)
- transactional processing

Businesses want their databases to be kept up-to-date so they can be more efficient. Suppose a business sends bills to all its customers. If some are sent to the wrong address, payments may be delayed.

Think About It!

Which reasons listed below would require a company to access up-to-date database records?

➤ send bills

➤ check inventory

➤ send catalogs

➤ pay employees

➤ ship goods

Transactional Processing   Databases that require immediate updating of data use **transactional processing**. In this method, the database is updated as events take place. For example, airline reservation systems cannot wait hours to have their records updated. They must have each new reservation entered right away. A form of transactional processing called **online transactional processing**, or **OLTP**, provides for immediate approval of Internet credit card purchases 24 hours a day.

Adding, Modifying, and Deleting Records

Databases manage the many changes made to records as they are updated.

Adding Data   Adding records to a database is a common action. When new students enroll at a school, for example, their records must be added to student tables.

Modifying Data   Data already held in records can also be modified or edited to reflect changing conditions or to correct a data entry error. For instance, when a student moves, the school's database can be updated to reflect the new address. If a grade is entered incorrectly, the student's record must be corrected. Records in a database table can be added or modified on-screen much like entering data in a spreadsheet program. The corrected data is entered and then saved.

Spotlight on...

JEFF BEZOS

❝ *Within the first few days, I knew this was going to be huge, … It was obvious that we were onto something much bigger than we ever dared to hope.* ❞

Jeff Bezos
Amazon.com Founder

Amazon.com opened its Web site worldwide on July 16, 1995. A whole new way of selling had been launched. Bezos developed his site by first hiring a programmer who developed an easy-to-use system

of searching CD-ROM databases of all books in print. That system gave Bezos—and the world—the first widely used "e-commerce" company. Customers search the company's databases to find what they want. Then, Amazon.com ships their purchases.

Using Forms to Change Data Often, databases contain forms. A **form** is a window that makes it easier for users to view, enter, and edit data. A form typically shows all the data for a given record at one time. It might also include questions or prompts to make updating the data easier. Forms also allow users to pull data from more than one table—a big advantage. A data access page, which is similar to a form, stores data in HTML format so you can view data in a Web browser.

Often, the form shown on-screen looks like the printed paper form used to gather the data. For example, a personnel form might look like a company's job application. This makes entering the data faster and more accurate because the person entering the data can look in the same place on both forms for information.

Deleting, Moving, and Linking Records Sometimes a record is removed from a database. For instance, a customer might cancel an account with a business. Although you can remove records that are no longer needed, records are typically moved from an active table into an inactive table. For example, when you graduate, your records will probably not be deleted from your school's database but will be moved to a graduate table. The main database might retain only your name, ID number, and graduation date. These will be linked to the complete record in the graduate table.

Linking is done for two reasons. First, it keeps the information available in case it is needed again. Second, it reduces the space and processing time needed when using the active records in the database.

Technology@School

Schools update their databases at least once a year. Each year, a new set of students enters the school. Another set leaves, and yet other students move to a new grade.

Think About It!

Which fields listed below do you think would be affected by the movement of students from grade to grade?

➤ lists of students by homeroom

➤ course names

➤ student emergency health contacts

➤ teachers' addresses

➤ school calendar

➤ parents' and guardians' names and addresses

Figure 16.2.1 A database form lets you view, add, or change the data in a single record.

Using Queries and Filters

Objectives

- Explain how queries make a database easier to use.
- Compare and contrast SQL and QBE.
- Compare and contrast a query and a filter.

As You Read

Summarize As you read the lesson, use a chart to help you summarize details about queries.

🔑 Key Terms

- filter
- query
- Query by Example (QBE)
- query language
- Structured Query Language (SQL)

Looking for Data

In a large database, it is inefficient to look through every record to find what you need. Many database programs have a search feature that lets you quickly locate only those records that match your search. To carry out this search, you create a query. A **query** is a question that you ask a database.

Queries are powerful tools that make databases much more efficient. You can create a query and use it once, or you can save it to use again. Queries can also be used to maintain databases. For example, you may be able to use a query to update or even delete records in the database.

Examples of Queries You can write queries constructed to find the following information:

- In a database of collector series baseball cards, you can find all new players whose careers started between 2001 and 2003 by including the word *rookie* in the query.
- In an airline database, you can find the least expensive seat from Fort Worth to Houston on a weekday evening.
- In a business database, you can find all customers who have not purchased anything in more than two years and then move these names to an inactive table.

Query Languages

The examples above are not expressed in a form that the database can understand, however. Databases use a special **query language** in which queries are written in ways similar to mathematical equations. This language allows you to specify exactly what you want to search for.

SQL A popular database query language is **Structured Query Language**, or **SQL**. It is used with most databases in operation today. Most SQL queries start with a select command. This tells the database to identify selected records that match given criteria. The SQL query also identifies the files and fields from which the data is to be selected.

For example, an SQL query to find the names and class schedules of all students in the seventh grade who have an average better than 85 looks like this:

SELECT	Name, Class
FROM	Student
WHERE	Average>85
AND	Grade=7

QBE Many database programs allow users to avoid typing SQL queries by providing a **Query by Example**, or **QBE**, feature that lets you provide an example of what you are seeking. You typically identify a field and then type the condition that explains the acceptable data limits. For example, the query for the student list might look like this:

FIELD	Name	Class	Average	Grade
FILE	Student	Student	Student	Student
SHOW	✓	✓		
CRITERIA			>85	=7

Real-World Tech

Seeing Stars One use for databases is to learn more about the stars and planets. Using a special computer program, astronomers can send queries into a database that holds pictures of the sky taken by the Hubble Space Telescope and by an earthbound observatory. By putting the information together, they can quickly find all records of objects in the same position in the sky. Then, they can study the images taken over many years to learn more about the objects. There are many other high-tech ways that scientists, government agencies, and other organizations use databases.

What databases can you think of that your local government agencies maintain?

Science Many school assignments require you to use the Internet to search for basic data. The Web site Landmarks for Schools (www.landmark-project.com) has a page called Raw Data. It offers links to government sources of basic data. Many of these sources can be used in science classes:

- Air Pollution Monitors Database

- AirNow

- FRF Wave Data

- Interactive Weather Information Network

- Soil Biological Communities

Figure 16.3.1 Creating a query in Microsoft Access.

Options Queries can search by complete data fields or parts of them. Database programs typically offer these search options:

- *Whole field* queries allow you to look for items that match the entire data value. For example, you can search for all records with a first name of "Martin."

- *Part of field* is a query that allows you to look for data that matches any part of a data value. For example, you can search for a date that includes March 2005 or a city that starts with "New."

- *Sounds like* queries allow you to look for data values that are similar to the search word. For example, if you look for "Smith," you might also find "Smyth" or "Smythe."

- *Match case* is a kind of query in which you look for data that matches the capitalization exactly as written. In this case, a search for "PowerPoint" would not find "Powerpoint," "POWERPOINT," or "powerpoint."

Filters

A **filter** helps reduce the quantity of data to be reviewed by temporarily hiding some records from view. It makes the database seem much smaller and speeds up processing.

For example, if you plan to review or edit only the records of seventh-grade students, you could filter the school's database to display only that grade. Any queries or editing would be done on this smaller record set rather than the entire database. When you no longer need the filter, you can simply cancel it to return the database to its full status.

Use the Vocabulary

Directions: *Match each vocabulary term in the left column with the correct definition in the right column.*

_____ **1.** data structure
_____ **2.** field name
_____ **3.** field width
_____ **4.** batch processing
_____ **5.** transactional processing
_____ **6.** online transactional processing
_____ **7.** form
_____ **8.** query
_____ **9.** query language
_____ **10.** filter

a. special way of phrasing queries

b. provides approval of Internet credit card purchases

c. request to search for data

d. way of limiting records being searched

e. the way a database is organized

f. identifier for each field

g. maximum number of characters in a field

h. on-screen window in which users view, enter, and edit data

i. way of changing databases that automatically keeps them up-to-date

j. way of changing databases that delays updates for a time

Check Your Comprehension

Directions: *Complete each sentence with information from the chapter.*

1. Creating a good _____ makes it easier to use a database because it promotes efficient searching.

2. In creating a data structure, you need to identify the database, create the file, and then _____.

3. In a bank database, the bank account would have a(n) _____ data type, but the balance in the account would be shown by a currency data type.

4. If a company sends weekly bills to clients, it would be reasonable for the company to use _____ processing.

5. Records can be modified in a table or by using a data _____.

6. Moving outdated information into a(n) _____ file keeps the database smaller and easier to use.

7. Making a(n) _____ is an efficient way to find complex information in a database.

8. A query made with _____ tries to identify selected records that meet particular criteria.

9. To limit a query to only those records that match the entire value, you would choose the _____ option.

10. _____ work by temporarily hiding some records from a search.

Think Critically

Directions: *Answer the following questions.*

1. What is the role of data structure in designing a database?

2. How do data types for each field affect a database?

3. Suppose a pharmacy uses a database to record the medicines it sells. Which type of processing would be most efficient? Why?

4. Why do companies tend to archive old records rather than delete them?

5. You could find a record that meets criteria you need by scanning each record. Why would you write a query to locate it instead?

Extend Your Knowledge

Directions: *Choose one of the following projects. Complete the exercise on a separate sheet of paper.*

A. With your teacher's permission, use the Internet to research the new-car inventory of an auto dealership. Review the dealer's database, or plan one of your own on paper that could be used to store information about the new cars in stock. Define or identify the fields and the report layout. Write a sample query, and share responses with your class.

B. With your teacher's permission, use the Internet to learn about database security issues. Prepare a brief written summary of the problem and possible solutions.

DIRECTIONS: *You will create a database about landforms that glaciers make as they slowly move across the land. You will create a table structure for the landform information, and use a form to enter records. Microsoft Access 2010 procedures required for this activity can be found in Appendix A.*

1. Open the .pdf file **DB-1_Landforms**, which is located on the student CD. This file contains information about glaciers and the landforms they create. With your teacher's permission, print the file. Close the file, and exit your pdf reader program.
2. Create a new, blank database file, and save it as **DB-1_Glacier_xx** in the location where your teacher instructs you to store the files for this activity. Replace **xx** with your own initials or name, as directed by your teacher.
3. Create a new table named **tblGlacial Landforms**.
4. Add the following two fields to the table:

Field Name	Data Type	Field Size
Landform	*Text*	*50*
Description	*Text*	*250*

5. Do not specify a primary key.
6. Save and close the table.
7. Create a form based on **tblGlacial Landforms**.
8. Save the form as **frmGlacial Landforms**.
9. Refer to the .pdf file **DB-1_Landforms**, and enter the data from the pdf into the database using the **frmGlacial Landforms** form.
10. Review each record carefully to be sure you enter correct information, and proofread your work for typing errors.
11. Save and close the form.
12. Open **tblGlacial Landforms**.
13. If necessary, increase the column width of the table columns to accommodate its entries.
14. Sort the table in ascending order by Landform.
15. Save the changes to your table.
16. Preview the table, and change the orientation to landscape. The table should look similar to Illustration A.
17. With your teacher's permission, print the table.
18. Close the database file, and exit the database program.

Illustration A

tblGlacial Landforms

Landform	Description
Arete	An arete is a sharp ridge separating two cirques.
Cirque	A cirque is a bowl-shaped hollow eroded by a glacier.
Drumlin	A drumlin is a long mound of till that is smoothed in the direction of the glacier's flow.
Fiord	A fiord forms when the level of the sea rises, filling a valley once cut by a glacier in a coastal region.
Glacial lake	Glaciers may leave behind large lakes in long basins eroded by plucking and abrasion.
Horn	When glaciers carve away the sides of a mountain, the result is a horn, or a sharpened peak.
Kettle lake	A kettle lake forms when a depression left in till by melting ice fills with water.
Moraine	A moraine forms where a glacier deposits mounds or ridges of till.
U-shaped valley	A flowing glacier scoops out a U-shaped valley.

Database Activities

DIRECTIONS: *You will collect and organize information relating to the climates of the United States and Canada. You will enter this information in a database, and then sort and query it to compare climates in both countries. Microsoft Access 2010 procedures required for this activity can be found in Appendix A.*

1. Open the .pdf file **DB-2_Stats**, which is located on the student CD. With your teacher's permission, print the Data Record Sheet. It has space for you to record information that you find about the climate in different regions of the United States and Canada. Close the file, and exit your pdf reader program.

2. Research the climate in at least ten states—including your home state—and three Canadian provinces.

    a. Use the Internet (with your teacher's permission), library resources, or a textbook, recording all source information as you work.

    b. If you are using the Internet, use a search engine Web site, and search using keywords or phrases such as **climate** or the name of a state or province, or use Boolean search strategies. For example, you might search for the **[name of a state] AND climate**. Be sure to evaluate each Web site you visit for accuracy and validity. When possible, find at least two sources for each fact. If two sources disagree on a fact or figure, use a third source to resolve the conflict. When you find a credible Web site with relevant information, bookmark the site, or with your teacher's permission, print the desired pages. Write the source information about each site on a separate piece of paper. When you have completed your research, close your Web browser.

    c. Record useful information on your Data Record Sheet. If you need more space, use the back of the sheet, or a separate piece of paper. Write the information about each source or site on a separate piece of paper.

3. Start your database program, create a new database, and save it as **DB-2_Stats_***xx* in the location where your teacher instructs you to store the files for this activity.

4. In a new table, change to Design View and save the table as **tblClimate Stats**.

5. In the table, include a primary key that automatically assigns a unique value to each record.

6. Create four text fields matching those in the **DB-2_Stats** Data Record Sheet: **State/Province/Territory**; **Country**; **US Region**; **Climate(s)**.

7. Save the table, and change to Datasheet view.

8. Referring to your Data Record Sheet, enter records for each of the states or provinces you researched. Fill in all of the information for each field in the table. If a state, province, or territory has multiple climates, separate the climates with commas. Adjust column widths, as necessary.

9. Sort the data in alphabetical order by country.

10. Check the spelling in the table, and correct any errors.

11. Preview the table, and adjust the page layout as necessary so the data displays properly and is easy to read. For example, change to Landscape orientation.

12. With your teacher's permission, print the table.

13. Filter the records to show only your home state. Then, remove the filter and close the table.

14. Create a new query based on **tblClimate Stats**. Include all fields except the Country field. Save the new query as **qryClimate Stats**.

15. Modify the query to show only records for states, provinces, or territories that have the same climate as your home state. To do this, enter the climate of your home state as the criteria for the Climate field. Save the new query as **qryClimate Home State**.

16. Sort the query by US Region.

17. Preview the query, and adjust the page layout so the data displays properly and is easy to read.

18. With your teacher's permission, print the query.

19. Compare tables and queries with a classmate. If you identify any errors in data entry, sorting, or querying, revise your database to correct it. With your teacher's permission, print any objects that you revise.

20. Close all open objects, saving all changes.

21. Close the database, and exit your database program.

DIRECTIONS: *You will search the Web to find ten species in your state that are on the endangered or threatened species list, as well as the reasons why they are. You will create a database to organize the information, and then design a report based on specific criteria. Microsoft Access 2010 procedures required for this activity can be found in Appendix A.*

1. Open the .pdf file **DB-3_Species**, which is located on the student CD. With your teacher's permission, print the Data Record Sheet. It has space for you to record information that you find about ten endangered species. Close the file, and exit your pdf reader program.

2. Research endangered species in your state.
   a. Use the Internet (with your teacher's permission), library resources, or a textbook, recording all source information as you work.
   b. If you are using the Internet, use a search engine Web site, and search using keywords or phrases such as **endangered species**, or use Boolean search strategies. For example, you might search for the **[name of a state] AND parks and wildlife**. Be sure to evaluate each Web site you visit for accuracy and validity. When possible, find at least two sources for each fact. If two sources disagree on a fact or figure, use a third source to resolve the conflict. When you find a credible Web site with relevant information, bookmark the site, or with your teacher's permission, print the desired pages. Write the source information about each site on a separate piece of paper. When you have completed your research, close your Web browser.
   c. Record useful information on your Data Record Sheet. If you need more space, use the back of the sheet, or a separate piece of paper. Write the information about each source or site on a separate piece of paper.

3. Start your database program, create a new database, and save it as **DB-3_Species_xx** in the location where your teacher instructs you to store the files for this activity.

4. Create a table with field names similar to the column headings on the Data Record Sheet: **Name of Species; Type; State Status; Federal Status; Reasons for Endangerment; Population Numbers; Location in State; Interesting Fact**. Be sure to define the data type for each field and to set field properties as necessary.

5. Save the table as **tblEndangered Species**.

6. Referring to the information from the Data Record Sheet, enter records for each species you researched. (You may use the abbreviations **T** for threatened and **E** for endangered in the state and federal status fields.)

7. Check the spelling, and adjust column widths to display all data.

8. Sort the table by type. Preview the table and adjust the page setup as necessary. For example, change to Landscape view.

9. With your teacher's permission, print the table.

10. Sort the table alphabetically by name, and then by state status. With your teacher's permission, print the table after each sort.

11. Create a query to find the records that have both a state and a federal status.

12. Save the query as **qrySpecies Status**.

13. Create a report based on the **qrySpecies Status** query, named **rptSpecies Status**.

14. Preview and modify the design or the report to improve the appearance and make the data easier to read.

15. Preview the report and adjust the page setup as necessary. With your teacher's permission, print the report.

16. Close all open objects, saving all changes.

17. Close the database, and exit your database program.

18. As a class, discuss why some species may be endangered at one government level but not at another. Discuss ways governments and individuals can protect and preserve wildlife.

Database Activities

DIRECTIONS: *You will create a database to track products for a garage sale and forecast the possible income you could earn. You will design a query that calculates sales of each item, and then you will generate a report that groups and summarizes the data. Microsoft Access 2010 procedures required for this activity can be found in Appendix A.*

1. Open the .pdf file **DB-4_Money**, which is located on the student CD. With your teacher's permission, print the Data Record Sheet. It has space for you to record information about a garage sale inventory. Close the file, and exit your pdf reader.

2. Choose five categories of items you might be able to gather from classmates to sell at a garage sale. Categories might include clothing, toys, entertainment, home goods, and sporting goods. List these in the wide columns in the top (gray) row of the table on the Data Record Sheet. In the rows under each category, list at least ten items you might sell. In the narrow column to the right of each item, enter the price you would charge.

3. Start your database program, and create a new database named **DB-4_Managing_Money_xx**.

4. Create a table with the following fields: **Category**, **Item Name**, **Quantity**, **Sale Price**, and an ID AutoNumber field as the primary key. Set field properties appropriate for each field.

5. Save the table as **tblGarage Sale**.

6. Use the information on the Data Record Sheet to create a record for each garage sale item. Illustration B shows a sample table with records.

7. After entering the data, check the spelling.

8. Create a query based on the table, and save it as **qrySales Total**.

9. Add a calculated field named **Sales Total** to the query that multiplies the quantity of each item by the sale price.

   ✔ Hint: Enter *Sales Total: [tblGarage Sale]![Quantity]*[tblGarage Sale]![Sale Price]*.

10. Run the query, and with your teacher's permission, print the query results.

11. Create a report based on the query that groups the records by Category, sorts them by Sale Price, and sums the Sales Total for each group and the grand total for all groups. Save the report as **rptSales Report**.

12. Apply a currency format to the totals.

13. Adjust the design and formatting of the report to improve its appearance and make it easier to read.

14. With your teacher's permission, print the report.

15. Close all open objects.

16. Close the database, and exit your database program.

17. As a class discuss how you could use the database to find ways to increase your earnings from the sale. For example, could you sell more items, or charge more per item? Brainstorm other opportunities for students to earn money.

Illustration B

DIRECTIONS: *You will collect information on several different breeds or types of pets. You will create a database to organize and sort the information. You will copy the data to a spreadsheet so you can analyze the information, perform calculations, add a picture, and print the information. Microsoft Access 2010 procedures required for this activity can be found in Appendix A.*

1. Open the .pdf file **DB-5_Costs**, which is located on the student CD. With your teacher's permission, print the Data Record Sheet. Close the file, and exit your pdf reader program.

2. With your teacher's approval, select a type of pet that you want to research, such as dogs, cats, birds, rabbits, or reptiles, and write it in the space provided on the Data Record Sheet. In column 1 on the Data Record Sheet, list five breeds or types of your selected pet.

3. Research the pet and record the facts and statistics about the average life expectancy, adult weight, and estimated annual costs for feeding, health care, and grooming in the appropriate columns on the Data Record Sheet. Look for photos or other images of the animals.
   a. Use the Internet (with your teacher's permission), library resources, or a textbook, recording all source information as you work.
   b. If you are using the Internet, use a search engine Web site, and search using keywords or phrases such as the type or breed, or use Boolean search strategies. For example, you might search for **[type of pet] AND life expectancy**. Be sure to evaluate each Web site you visit for accuracy and validity. When possible, find at least two sources for each fact. If two sources disagree on a fact or figure, use a third source to resolve the conflict. When you find a credible Web site with relevant information, bookmark the site, or with your teacher's permission, print the desired pages. Write the source information about each site on a separate piece of paper. When you have completed your research, close your Web browser.
   c. Record useful information on your Data Record Sheet. If you need more space, use the back of the sheet, or a separate piece of paper. Write the information about each source or site on a separate piece of paper.

4. Start your database program, and save a new database as **DB-5_Comparing_Costs_xx** in the location where your teacher instructs you to store the files for this activity.

5. Change to Design view and create, and save a table as **tblPet Costs**. Define fields matching the columns on your Data Record Sheet. You do not need a primary key.

6. Referring to the information from the Data Record Sheet, enter records for each breed or type of pet you researched.

7. Check the spelling, adjust column widths, and then save the table.

8. Select all of the records and copy them to the Clipboard.

9. Close the database, and exit the database program.

10. Start your spreadsheet program, and save a new file as **DB-5_Comparing_Costs_SS_xx**.

11. Select cell A2 and paste the database records into the spreadsheet.

12. In cell G2, enter the label **Total Annual Cost**.

13. In cell G3, use the SUM function to enter a formula that calculates the total annual cost of pet maintenance for the first pet. Copy this formula down to cell G7.

14. In cell H2, enter the label **Cost for Life**.

15. In cell H3, enter a formula that multiplies the life expectancy by the total annual cost. Copy this formula down to cell H7.

16. Sort the data in rows 3 through 7 in descending order based on **Cost for Life**.

17. In row 1, enter the title **Comparing Pet Costs**. Merge and center it across columns A through H.

18. Apply formatting such as number formats, styles, borders, files, and font formatting to make the data appealing and easy to read.

19. Address any errors that occur, such as numbers stored as text, or narrow column widths.

20. Insert a picture that illustrates your work and center it under the spreadsheet data.

21. Check the spelling in the spreadsheet.

22. Preview the spreadsheet. Change the orientation to landscape and add a footer with your name on the left and today's date on the right. A sample worksheet is shown in Illustration C on the next page.

23. With your teacher's permission, print the spreadsheet.

24. Close the file, saving all changes, and exit the spreadsheet program.

25. As a class, discuss what you learned from the database information. What were you able to do with the data in the spreadsheet that you could not do in the database?

Illustration C

Comparing Pet Costs

Breed or Type	Life Expectancy	Average Weight	Feeding Costs/Year	Health Care Costs/Year	Grooming Costs/Year	Total Annual Cost	Cost for Life
Cocker Spaniel	16	20	$300.00	$200.00	$250.00	$750.00	$12,000.00
Toy Poodle	16	5	$300.00	$200.00	$200.00	$700.00	$11,200.00
Golden Retriever	10	80	$500.00	$200.00	$150.00	$850.00	$8,500.00
Siberian Husky	12	70	$500.00	$200.00	$0.00	$700.00	$8,400.00
Labrador Retriever	10	85	$600.00	$200.00	$0.00	$800.00	$8,000.00

Firstname Lastname

Today's Date

Graphics Basics

What Is a Graphic? In day-to-day speech, people use the word *graphic* to refer to any visual image or object. A family photo, a road map, and a stick figure drawn on a chalkboard are all examples of graphics.

When people talk about a computer **graphic**, they usually are referring to an image. Images include drawings, painted backgrounds, and photographs. Computer graphics can be displayed in a variety of ways. They can appear on the screen as a background, or they can be placed into a document to add color and information. Thus, in the broadest sense of the term, *computer graphic* could refer to anything that can be seen on the computer screen.

Chapter Outline

Graphics and Their Uses

Objectives

- Identify two different types of graphics and explain the differences between them.
- List the advantages of each type of graphic.
- Differentiate between draw and paint programs.

As You Read

Compare and Contrast   As you read this lesson, use a Venn diagram to show the similarities and differences between bitmapped graphics and vector graphics.

🔑 Key Terms

- bitmapped graphic
- draw program
- graphic
- image editor
- paint program
- pixel
- raster graphic
- resolution
- vector graphic

Types of Graphics

There are hundreds of different uses for computer graphics. However, graphics fall into only two categories:

- raster graphics
- vector graphics

Raster Graphics   A **raster graphic**, which is commonly called a **bitmapped graphic** or bitmap, is an image formed by a pattern of dots. Imagine a sheet of graph paper with each of its squares filled in with a certain color to make a picture. If seen from far enough away, the picture will look clear, and the squares won't be noticed. But up close, you can see the individual squares of the graph paper.

Raster graphics are composed of tiny dots of different colors. Each single point in the image is a **pixel**, short for "picture element." The smaller the pixels in the image, the smoother it will look. The more colors in the image, the brighter and sharper the image will look.

Some common raster file formats include:

- Graphics Interchange Format (GIF)
- Joint Photographic Experts Group (JPG)
- Portable Network Graphics (PNG)
- Windows Bitmap (BMP)

Some formats are used for images on Web pages, while others are used for icons and images in the operating system. In Windows, these same abbreviations are used as the file extensions. A file ending in *.gif*, for example, is in the GIF file format.

Bitmaps are preferred for some types of images. They often are used for photos or images that require backgrounds.

Vector Graphics A **vector graphic** is an image that is created using paths or lines. A vector image tells the computer where a line starts and where it ends. It allows the computer to figure out how to connect the two points. The lines can form shapes, which may be filled with a color or pattern.

Encapsulated PostScript, or EPS, is one of several formats commonly used for vector art. EPS files contain the information that a printer needs in order to print a graphic correctly. The information is combined with a small sketch of what the graphic should look like. The sketch inside an EPS file allows you to preview an image on-screen. This way, you can be sure the image is correct before printing it.

Size, Resolution, and Dots Per Inch

Two basic qualities affect how every raster image will appear. Size, the height and width of the graphic, is normally measured either in pixels or in inches. **Resolution** tells how many pixels are in a certain piece of an image. Resolution also determines the quality of the computer image. Resolution is usually measured in dots per inch, or dpi. An image that is 1 inch square at 72 dpi will contain a total of 5,184 pixels (72 × 72). Generally, the higher the resolution, the sharper the image will look.

Vector graphics are created using lines or paths rather than pixels. Thus, the number of dots per inch is not a concern when changing the size of vector graphics. If a bitmapped image is enlarged to twice its normal size, it will look fuzzy and jagged. A vector image can be enlarged to any size and keep its quality.

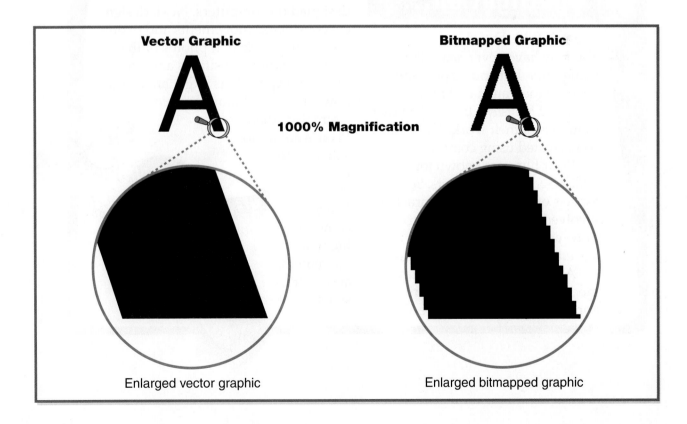

Vector Graphic Bitmapped Graphic

1000% Magnification

Enlarged vector graphic Enlarged bitmapped graphic

Multimedia designers develop Web sites and CDs using some of the same programs you use. Their jobs vary, but they often create images for programs.

Think About It!

Using the right design program is important for designers. Consider the following tasks. Which would need to be completed by a draw program?

➤ view a raster image

➤ add color to a vector image

➤ add effects to a raster image

➤ change the size of a vector image

Graphics Programs

Different programs allow you to create, edit, and view different graphic file types. Choosing the right program depends on which type of graphic you are working with and what your needs are.

Paint Programs   A **paint program** allows you to create a new raster image. Paint programs also allow you to open a raster image, view it on-screen, and make changes to it. Microsoft Windows comes with a paint program called Paint.

Draw Programs   A program that allows you to create and edit vector images is called a **draw program**. Since draw programs focus on vector images, they make editing easy. You can change the size of an image or add color to it.

Many application programs including Microsoft Word and PowerPoint come with built-in basic drawing tools. More complex programs, such as Adobe® Illustrator® and CorelDRAW®, allow you to do more.

Image Editors   An advanced paint program is called an **image editor**. Image editors are designed for editing raster images. They are also often used for adding special effects to photographs. Adobe® Photoshop® and Adobe® Photodelux® are examples of popular image editors. You can also use built-in picture editing tools in some programs, including Microsoft Word and PowerPoint.

Spotlight on...

PIXAR STUDIOS

You may have never heard the name *Pixar*, but you've probably heard of their animated films. *Toy Story* and *Monsters, Inc.* are just two examples of their work. These films were created using computers.

Pixar films are known for their realistic cartoon characters. Some aspects of creating these characters involved technology similar to the draw and paint programs and image editors discussed in this lesson.

After final drawings or clay models of the characters were approved, 3-D models were designed on computers. Next, designers considered movements and expressions. They looked at photos of live actors in various positions and with different expressions to get an idea of how each figure should move. Animators then used Pixar's animation software to make the images come to life with movements and expressions.

Exploring Graphics Programs

Objectives

- Identify the main sections of a graphics application window.
- List the different tools available in paint and draw programs.
- Determine when to use the tools in a paint or draw program.

As You Read

Summarize Information Make a table that lists tools used in paint and draw programs on the left. On the right, include the type of program(s) each tool is used in.

Exploring the Application Window

Paint and draw programs vary from one to another, but most include a workspace, toolbars, and color palettes.

Workspace Most of the screen is devoted to the **workspace**, the blank, white area which contains the graphic. This area is sometimes called the drawing area.

Toolbars A toolbar is a bar across the top or down the side of a window. It contains icons that link to the program's tools. By clicking an icon, you can create, edit, add, or remove information within the graphic. Toolbars usually appear, or are docked, on the edges of the screen. They also can be moved around, or floated, to fit your preferences.

Color Palettes The display of color options in paint and draw programs is called the **color palette**. These options allow you to choose colors for an image. Most programs also allow you to change the color palette.

 Key Terms

- color palette
- Eyedropper
- workspace
- graphics tablet
- Selection tool
- stylus
- tablet PC

Figure 17.2.1 Paint and draw programs share several basic tools, such as a workspace, toolbars, and color palettes.

Figure 17.2.2 Some tools are commonly found in Paint programs. The toolbar shown here is from Microsoft Paint.

Paint Program Tools

In paint programs, the following tools are used to place and remove color in the workspace.

Pencil The Pencil tool is used for freehand drawing. Clicking and dragging this tool across the workspace leaves a trail of the selected color. This tool is used to draw fine details. Only the color or thickness of the line drawn can be changed.

Brush The Brush tool works like the Pencil tool, but it makes a broader stroke of color. Often, the shape of the brush can be changed to create different shapes of colors. For instance, the brush can be large and square or small and circular.

Line and Shape The Line tool allows you to draw a line and use the toolbar to change its color and width. Various shapes, such as rectangles and ovals, also can be drawn using tools on the toolbar. Shape tools allow you to create shapes in three different forms: Outline, Filled With Outline, and Filled Without Outline.

Eyedropper The **Eyedropper** tool allows you to work with a specific color from an image. You place the eyedropper over the desired color in an image and click. That color becomes the selected color and can be used elsewhere in the image.

Eraser The Eraser tool removes color from an image. It is used by clicking the tool and dragging the eraser across the image. The area touched with the eraser becomes the background color.

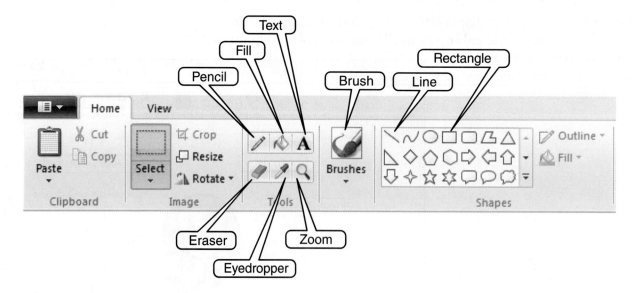

Draw Program Tools

The Line and Shape tools in draw programs are similar to those in paint programs, but with one important difference. In a draw program, you can change an image's lines and shapes without changing nearby ones. In paint programs, it is hard to change one part of an image without altering other parts that are close to it. A **Selection tool** allows you to select a portion of an image to be enlarged, moved, or edited.

Interacting with the Program

A variety of different input tools allow you to work easily with a graphics program. A mouse is used to select part of an image or to activate tools on the toolbar. By dragging, releasing, or double-clicking the mouse, a tool's function is performed.

A **graphics tablet** is a piece of hardware used for drawing. The user moves a **stylus**, or pointing device, over the drawing surface. The tablet senses the movement of the stylus and moves the cursor on-screen. As the cursor moves, it creates on the screen the image that is being drawn on the tablet. The skills for writing with a stylus on a tablet are quite different than writing with a pen and will take some time to master. An Apple iPad is a tablet PC that combines the features of a graphics tablet with the functions of a personal computer.

Figure 17.2.3 An interactive pen display combines the capabilities of a graphics tablet with an LCD monitor, so you can draw and choose commands directly on the screen by using a special pen.

Real-World Tech

Using Graphics Tools The tools in paint and draw programs have many uses. As you might expect, they often are used by newspaper and magazine publishers. What you might not expect is that students your age are using them, too.

For example, at Centennial Middle School in Boulder, Colorado, students publish an online newspaper called *The Vocal Point*. To create and edit the images in the newspaper, students rely on graphics programs.

How might you use draw and paint programs at school?

Working with Graphics

Objectives

- Explain how to modify an image with special effects.
- Compare the processes for combining vector or bitmapped graphics.
- Explain how to work with clip art.
- Describe how graphics can be converted from one format to another.

As You Read

Organize Information As you read this lesson, make an outline. Use Roman numerals for main headings. Use capital letters for subheadings, and use numbers for supporting details.

🔑 Key Terms

- alignment
- balance
- clip art
- emphasis
- export
- group
- import
- layer
- trace
- proportion
- proximity
- repetition
- ungroup
- unity
- variety

Adding Effects to Graphics

To create a new graphic, start with a blank workspace (sometimes called the background or canvas). If you are creating the graphic in a paint program, use the paint tools to add color and form to the image. If you are creating the graphic in a draw program, use the Line and Shape tools to add information to the image.

Special effects can be used to modify an image. Flipping an image turns it upside down. Mirroring the image makes it flip from left to right, as if it were being viewed in a mirror. Stretching makes the image appear longer in one direction than the other, as if it were drawn on a sheet of rubber that was stretched out. Skewing tilts the image horizontally or vertically.

Inverting reverses the colors in the graphic. In a black-and-white graphic, all the white dots will turn black, and all the black will turn white. In a color graphic, each color will change to its "opposite" color. For example, yellow will become dark blue.

Understanding the Principles of Design

An effective graphic uses the basic principles of design, including contrast, balance, and proportion.

- **Contrast**—The way different elements such as shapes and colors are placed next to or near each other provides contrast.
- **Balance**—The way objects are arranged is called balance. Symmetrically arranged objects are evenly balanced, while asymmetrically arranged objects are unevenly balanced.
- **Proportion**—The size and location of one object in relation to other objects in the graphic is called proportion.

Other elements of design include **repetition** in which a color, shape, or pattern is repeated throughout the graphic; **emphasis**, which creates a focal point; **proximity**, in which the closeness between objects indicates a relationship; **unity**, in which a third object is used to establish a connection between two other objects; **alignment**, which is the placement of text and objects so they line up within a space, and **variety**, which creates visual interest by using different colors and shapes.

Combining Images

Bringing information, such as a graphic, into a file from another file is called **importing**. Once imported, the image can then be modified or expanded.

Exporting is when data is formatted so it can be used in another application. This means that the program you are working in must be able to translate its own language to the language another program understands.

Layering Images   Raster graphics use layers, or stacks of information, to create a graphic. A powerful process known as **layering** stacks each level of an image on top of another. Imagine three or four sheets of wax paper, each with a different part of a drawing. When all of them are stacked, the complete picture is visible. Although the layers are stacked, you can still edit them separately. Any changes you make only affect the layer you touch.

The default layer is the background. You can add or delete layers as needed. The layer you're working with is usually highlighted in a color. You can hide a layer you're not using to see other parts of the image more easily.

Figure 17.3.1 Layering works by breaking an image into separate parts and stacking them.

Layers palette

Combined layers

Career Corner

Graphic Artist A graphic artist creates the design and layout of different products, such as advertisements, brochures, Web sites, and CD-ROMs/DVDs. They design or acquire images and choose and edit text features to communicate a message.

An art degree, courses in graphic arts or design, and recent experience using related software are important qualifications for this career.

Figure 17.3.2 Vector clip art may look sharper than bitmapped clip art and can be edited like any vector graphic.

Grouping Images **Grouping** is the process of combining separate vector images into one image. Once the images are grouped, they can be moved or resized as a single unit. To group images, select all of the desired items and then select the Group command. **Ungrouping** is the process of separating combined images into individual images. To ungroup an image, select a grouped image and then select the Ungroup command.

Working with Clip Art

It is not always necessary to create an image from scratch. Instead, you can start with **clip art** (graphics files that come with a program, or that you download from the Internet).

Raster Clip Art Clip art in a bitmapped format (such as GIF, JPG, or PNG) can be imported into a paint document. The art then can be edited like any other bitmapped graphic.

Vector Clip Art Vector art can be imported in a draw program and modified. If the image is complex, it can be ungrouped. Its individual parts can then be edited or moved.

Converting Graphics

If you want to use a graphic that is in a format your program does not support, you may have to convert it. You can use a file conversion program, or open the file and use the Save As command to save it in a different file format. File conversion is also required if you want to change a vector graphic to a bitmapped graphic, or vice versa.

Vector-to-Bitmapped Graphics Vector graphics must be changed to pixels before the image can be edited in a paint program.

Bitmapped-to-Vector Graphics Converting bitmapped graphics to vectors requires a special process called **tracing**. Tracing requires special software and can be complicated when an image has a lot of color and detail.

Vector Clip Art   **Bitmapped Clip Art**

Use the Vocabulary

Directions: *Match each vocabulary term in the left column with the correct definition in the right column.*

_____ **1.** bitmapped graphic
_____ **2.** vector graphic
_____ **3.** resolution
_____ **4.** paint program
_____ **5.** color palette
_____ **6.** Eyedropper
_____ **7.** graphics tablet
_____ **8.** import
_____ **9.** layer
_____ **10.** clip art

a. the number of pixels in a certain image that affects its visual quality

b. images that can be downloaded for use in a graphics program

c. images created using lines or paths

d. tool that captures and uses color from one portion of an image in another

e. input device for creating graphics

f. stacks of information on top of one another to form a more complete image

g. image created using pixels, or series of dots

h. allows you to modify bitmapped graphics

i. brings information into a file from another file

j. the display of color options in paint and draw programs

Check Your Comprehension

Directions: *Complete each sentence with information from the chapter.*

1. Sets of dots that make up an image are called _____.

2. A(n) _____ allows you to create and edit vector graphics.

3. Advanced paint programs that allow you to edit and add effects to a bitmapped graphic are _____.

4. The area of the screen where images are created and edited is the _____.

5. The set of color options in a particular paint or draw program shown in small boxes on the screen is called the _____.

6. In a draw program, a(n) _____ allows you to pick a certain portion of an image to work on.

7. A common input device in a graphics program is the _____.

8. The process of formatting data so that it can be used in another application is _____.

9. Combining separate images to form a single image is called _____.

10. The process of converting pixels to lines or paths is known as _____.

⬤ Think Critically

Directions: *Answer the following questions.*

1. What are two differences between a bitmapped graphic and a vector graphic?

2. When editing graphics, why is it important to consider the file format in which an image is created?

3. How do toolbars in draw and paint programs help you to edit and add effects to images?

4. Why are exporting and importing important functions for working with graphics?

5. How are layering and grouping similar? How are they different?

⬤ Extend Your Knowledge

Directions: *Choose one of the following projects. Complete the exercise on a separate sheet of paper.*

A. Create a comic strip using vector or bitmapped graphics. You may create your own images or edit clip art. Your comic strip should have at least four frames. Be sure to use the different tools and colors in the program. With your teacher's permission, print your comic strip to show to the class.

B. Newspapers and magazines often use graphics to capture the readers' attention or to make a point. Find three graphics (including photos with special effects) in newspapers or magazines. Next, create a three-column chart. On the chart, paste each image, identify each source and page number, and categorize the graphic as bitmapped or vector. Present your findings to the class.

Understanding Graphics

Graphics in the Real World Graphics make up everything you see on your computer screen. The images and even the letters in a word-processing document are kinds of graphics.

When working with computer graphics, there are many things to keep in mind. How many colors will an image need? How will those colors look? Will the image appear fuzzy and bumpy or smooth and sharp? How much space will it take to store the image on the computer? Can it be viewed on the Internet? How fast will images be transmitted? Graphics software helps computer users create, change, and refine the words and images we see on-screen.

Chapter Outline

 Lesson 18–1

Preparing Computer Graphics

 Lesson 18–2

Exploring Image Editing Programs

 Lesson 18–3

Draw and Animation Features

Preparing Computer Graphics

Objectives

- Compare and contrast lossless and lossy compression.
- Explain the effect of color on computer memory.
- Name and describe the four basic color modes.

As You Read

Organize Information   As you read this lesson, create an outline to help you organize the information.

🔑 Key Terms

- color depth
- compress
- lossless compression
- lossy compression

File Compression and Graphics

Graphics files can be very large. When they are stored on the computer, the images are often **compressed**, or saved in a format requiring less space. This saves disk space and decreases the time it takes to send images via the Internet.

When a file is compressed, the program performing the compression replaces certain pieces of information with shorter codes. This makes the file smaller.

Lossless Compression   In **lossless compression**, information is removed in such a way that all of it can later be fully restored without introducing errors. This process results in a perfect copy of the file that is about one third of the original size. Lossless compression is a good choice for reducing files with graphics, text, or computer code.

Lossy Compression   In **lossy compression**, some information is permanently removed from the file in such a way that it cannot be restored to its original state. Lossy compression can reduce a file to one fiftieth or less of its former size. It is best for reducing the size of video and audio files.

Figure 18.1.1 An example of a graphic before lossy compression (top) and after lossy compression (bottom).

Color Depth

The more colors or shades of gray an image contains, the sharper and more detailed it will look. The number of colors that can be displayed on a monitor at one time is the **color depth**. Most modern computer monitors can display millions of colors. Because the computer must store more bits of information for each color pixel, more memory is needed to store colors than to store black and white alone.

Color Modes   Color modes determine which and how many colors are available for creating computer graphics.

Bitmap Mode   When it comes to color modes, bitmap refers to a 1-bit, or black-and-white, image.

Grayscale Mode   When working in grayscale mode, the computer can display 256 different shades of gray to represent the colors, shades, and textures in an image.

RGB Mode   Look closely at a television picture, and you may notice that it is made up of tiny clusters of dots. Each cluster has one red, one green, and one blue dot. When these three colors are combined in various ways, they produce different colors.

RGB mode allows each of these three colors to have 8 bits of information, resulting in 256 different shades each of the colors red (R), green (G), and blue (B). Color computer monitors use RGB color to display graphics, so RGB mode is used to design on-screen graphics such as those for the Internet.

CMYK Mode   In CMYK mode, a combination of four colors in different densities produces other colors. Variations of cyan (greenish-blue), magenta (purplish-red), yellow, and black (known as K) are combined to produce new colors.

Did You Know

In Adobe® Photoshop®, its RGB mode assigns a value to each pixel. The values range from 0 to 255, for a total of 256 colors.

Black (no color) is assigned the value of 0, and white (full color) is given a value of 255. Since RGB mode is based on three colors, one value needs to be assigned to the red, another to the green, and another to the blue to make another color. For example, one shade of bright red is made using a value of 246 for red, 20 for green, and 50 for blue.

Figure 18.1.2 An image's color mode determines how many colors appear.

| Bitmap | Grayscale | RGB | CMYK |

Social Studies Printing dates back almost 1,000 years. Around 1040, wooden blocks were used for printing in China.

Printing with movable type was used by Johann Gutenberg in Germany in 1454. His printing press made books available and affordable to the general public. This is one of the advances that led to a period of history known as the Renaissance.

CMYK mode is used to design graphics that will be printed on a printing press. Each of the four color values in a CMYK graphic is assigned to one of the four inks. These inks are then used on the printing press to print a full-color piece.

But what if you wanted to display a CMYK graphic on a monitor? To view a CMYK graphic on the screen, the computer has to convert it to RGB. This is why printed graphics may look different from an on-screen preview of the image.

Resolution Issues

When creating or modifying graphics, it is important to work with the proper resolution. A graphic's resolution should be determined by how that graphic will be displayed—the output.

If a graphic is to be viewed on-screen only, the resolution need not be higher than 72 dpi or 96 dpi. A 300-dpi graphic looks the same on-screen as a 72-dpi version of the same file. Increasing the dpi does not improve on-screen appearance. Because a 72- or 96-dpi file is smaller, it will display more quickly.

If a graphic will be printed, the resolution should be as high as the device on which it will be printed. For an image to look its best on a 300-dpi printer, it should be created at 300 dpi.

Real-World Tech

Offset Printing The printing technique known as offset printing involves spreading ink on a metal plate with etched images on it. The plate is then pressed against another surface, often a rubber sheet. This transfers the ink onto the new surface, but the image now appears backward. Finally, the new surface is pressed against paper. This reverses the ink image from the surface onto the paper.

The equipment used and the cost of setting up the printing press are quite expensive. Therefore, offset printing is usually done to print a large quantity, or print run.

What types of printed materials that you read might have been printed using an offset process?

Exploring Image Editing Programs

Objectives

- Identify two different ways to bring existing images into a computer.
- Summarize how filters improve the look of an image.
- Compare and contrast image editor selection tools.

As You Read

Identify Key Concepts As you read this lesson, use a concept web diagram to help you identify tools used to edit images.

Input Devices for Graphics

While it is possible to create graphics from scratch using paint or draw programs, there are many times when images from the "real world" need to be brought into the computer. There are two main input tools that bring images into the computer: scanners and digital cameras.

Scanners As discussed in Chapter 3, a scanner is a device that copies and changes a printed image into a digital format—one the computer can process and store. A scanner divides the image into boxes and assigns each box a value representing its "darkness" or color. One type of scanner is called a flatbed scanner. Its reader—the part that actually "sees" the image—sits underneath a pane of glass, much like a copy machine. Flatbed scanners are now routinely included in All-in-One printers. The reader moves back and forth to scan the image. Another type of scanner is a handheld scanner. It is moved across an image to digitize it.

Digital Cameras A digital camera stores images digitally instead of on film. A computer chip in the camera changes light patterns from the captured image into pixels, which the camera can store. The image, or photo, can then be downloaded to the computer for storage or for printing.

Key Terms

- filter
- Lasso
- Magic Wand
- Marquee

Figure 18.2.1 A scanner (above) lets you digitize printed documents, such as photos. Digital cameras (below) store images digitally instead of on film.

Filters in Image Editors

Image editors are used to edit raster images—often, high-resolution images such as digital photographs. Image editors usually contain **filters**, preset features that alter images in a certain way. Many filters are designed to improve photos. Common filters include sharpening, blur, and noise filters.

Sharpening Filters   Image editors often contain several sharpening filters. One type of sharpening filter more clearly defines the edges of an image. It does this by finding a line of pixels that runs together as one color and is next to other pixels of other colors. The filter increases the color differences between the line of pixels of one color and those of nearby colors, making the edges more distinct.

Blur Filters   There are also many kinds of blur filters. A blur filter softens the look of an image by making hard edges look blurrier. They can be used to apply this effect to all or part of an image.

Using both sharpening and blurring techniques at the same time can add depth to an image. One way to do this is to apply sharpening effects to the area of an image that extends toward the viewer. Then, blur the areas farther away from the viewer. This produces a three-dimensional, or 3-D, effect.

Noise Filters   Filters designed to add or remove roughness from an image are called noise filters. Two types of noise filters are the despeckle and median filters. They determine the edges of an image and leave them alone. Then, they smooth out other areas with less difference in color. This is often done to remove moiré patterns, or unwanted patterns of dots, that show up in some scanned photos.

Figure 18.2.2   A blur filter was used on the left image to create the "softer" or blurred effect seen in the right image.

Image Editor Selection Tools

One powerful feature of an image editor is its ability to work with certain pixels in an image while leaving other pixels unchanged. This is done using a selection tool, a graphics tool that allows you to choose one part of an image or the objects that make up an image. For instance, you can use a selection tool to choose eyes in an image of a face. Three common selection tools are:

- Marquee tool
- Lasso tool
- Magic Wand tool

Marquee The rectangle selection tool is sometimes called the **Marquee** tool. It works just like the Rectangle tool that allows you to draw a box in Word. But instead of drawing a box, the Marquee selection tool highlights a simple shape.

Lasso The **Lasso** tool in an image editor is used to select complex, or freehand, shapes. It is well suited for selecting images that share colors with nearby pieces of an image.

Magic Wand Perhaps the most powerful selection tool is the **Magic Wand**, which selects all touching pixels of a similar color. If you select a red pixel, then all red pixels that are connected with it will automatically be selected. The Magic Wand can be adjusted for small or wide ranges of color. For instance, if set for a small range, the wand will select only exact matches. But if set for large ranges, it will select similar shades of red.

Selection tools can be useful when working on images for the school paper or to touch up yearbook photos.

Think About It!

For the following shapes, identify the right tool to use to highlight an image of each—Marquee tool, Lasso tool, or the Magic Wand.

➤ shape of a tree outside a classroom window

➤ color blue in a textbook cover

➤ lunchbox

➤ red stripes in the American flag

Figure 18.2.3 The Lasso tool is often used to select complex shapes.

Draw and Animation Features

Objectives

- Describe four advanced tools in draw programs.
- Summarize the process of computer animation.
- Explain how animation is viewed on a computer.

As You Read

Show Cause and Effect   Use a cause-and-effect chart to help you understand how advanced drawing tools create graphics.

🔑 Key Terms

- Align
- Distribute
- frame
- frame rate
- Grid
- Order
- player software
- tween

Advanced Draw Program Tools

Draw programs provide a number of tools to help you work with images.

Align Tool   The **Align** tool moves parts of an image and determines how the parts will be placed in relation to one another. It can be helpful for lining up objects of different sizes. To use this tool, select several objects in the graphic—such as lines or shapes—and then open the tool. You can arrange objects to make the tops, bottoms, sides, or middles of the objects align with one another.

Distribute Tool   The **Distribute** tool moves objects to distribute, or space, them from each other. The two kinds of distribution are fixed amount and within bounds. Fixed amount distribution puts a uniform distance between objects. For instance, you might want to put an inch of space between several objects. Within bounds distribution leaves the outermost objects exactly where they are and evenly spaces all the other selected objects between them.

Figure 18.3.1 Use the advanced drawing tools to work with images.

Order Tool   Sometimes objects in an image overlap, or lay partially on top of one another. When this happens, certain objects may be blocked from view. The **Order** tool changes the position in which objects are stacked and rearranges them to avoid this problem. Objects can be moved to the bottom, the top, or the side of a stack.

Grid Tool   Many graphics programs offer a **Grid** tool to align images properly. Grids work just like a sheet of graph paper, by showing squares on the computer screen. For objects to align, they must begin in the same column on the grid.

Many graphics programs offer a feature called snap-to-guides or snap-to-grids. When this feature is turned on, objects are automatically moved to the nearest grid line. This helps ensure that every object is in a perfectly aligned position.

Animating Images

When two or more graphics are displayed one after the other, they can appear to be in motion. Animation is the process of quickly showing many images of an object to make it appear as if it is moving.

Animating by Hand   Before computers, animation was done by hand or with cameras. Sometimes, artists drew by hand each **frame**, or individual still image in a sequence. The frames would then be flipped to simulate motion. Other times, sophisticated film cameras took one still picture at a time and sequenced them quickly to mimic movement. The more frames displayed per second, the more convincing the animation looked. The speed at which a frame moves, measured in number of images per second, is called the **frame rate**.

Animating on Computer   In computer animation, frames are created and then rapidly displayed to create the impression of motion. There is, however, a key benefit to computer animation. **Tweening** is the ability of a graphics program to determine in-between frames, so you do not need to draw every one. You just draw the starting and ending frames, and the computer draws those in-between frames in sequence.

Figure 18.3.2 Rapidly displayed frames simulate motion.

Software for Viewing Animation

Player software, a program that interprets the information in an animation file, must be installed in order to view animated graphics on a computer monitor. Player software usually can tell the computer how to interpret and convert animated graphics into images it can display.

Flash™ Player Made by the Adobe company, Flash Player is player software that allows a Web browser to view vector animation. Because vector animation downloads quickly, Flash movies have become common on the Web.

QuickTime® Player Created by Apple Computer, Quick-Time is commonly used for bitmapped animation. It provides the continuous flow of information needed to display movies, live action, and animation. QuickTime was created by Apple for Macintosh computers, but versions for Windows PCs have been available for several years.

RealPlayer® First used for streaming audio, RealPlayer® has added support for both vector and bitmapped animation.

Name ▲	Size	Type
Car chase.avi	65 KB	AVI Video
The Da Vinci Code.gvi	2,704 KB	Google Video file
dog cartoon.mov	65 KB	QuickTime Movie
Grand Canyon hike.mpg	65 KB	MPEG Video
my dance audition.mp4	65 KB	MPEG-4 File
A tree grows in Plymouth.rm	65 KB	RealAudio / RealVideo

Figure 18.3.3 There are many file formats used for displaying streaming video, animation, or live action. These various formats can be played on a variety of player software.

Use the Vocabulary

Directions: *Match each vocabulary term in the left column with the correct definition in the right column.*

_____ **1.** compress
_____ **2.** lossless compression
_____ **3.** color depth
_____ **4.** filter
_____ **5.** Marquee
_____ **6.** Magic Wand
_____ **7.** lossy compression
_____ **8.** frame
_____ **9.** tween
_____ **10.** player software

a. color selection tool

b. compression format in which all information is kept

c. compression format in which some information is permanently removed

d. saved in format that uses less space

e. one individual image in an animation

f. image editor feature that changes appearance of an image

g. program that converts animation files for viewing

h. colors shown on a monitor at one time

i. to generate middle frames of animation by computer

j. rectangle selection tool

Check Your Comprehension

Directions: *Determine the correct choice for each of the following.*

1. Which color mode is based on a combination of three colors to make new colors?

   a. bitmap

   b. grayscale

   c. RGB

   d. CMYK

2. If a graphic is to be printed, how high should its dpi rating be set?

   a. 72 dpi

   b. higher than output device

   c. lower than output device

   d. same as output device

3. Which filter will make an image's edges look softer?

   a. sharpen

   b. blur

   c. noise

   d. despeckle

4. Which tool is good for selecting complex shapes of whatever color you point out?

   a. Marquee

   b. Lasso

   c. Magic wand

   d. Distribute

5. Which tool is used to move objects so they line up in a certain way?

   a. Align

   b. Distribute

   c. Order

   d. Grid

6. Which player software views vector and bitmapped images?

   a. Flash Player

   b. RealPlayer

   c. QuickTime Player

   d. Vector Player

Think Critically

Directions: *Answer the following questions.*

1. Why do graphics files often need compression?

2. Why is RGB mode used to design computer graphics?

3. What input devices allow graphics in other formats to be digitized?

4. How has tweening changed the animation process?

5. What is one advantage of vector animation?

Extend Your Knowledge

Directions: *Choose one of the following projects. Complete the exercise on a separate sheet of paper.*

A. Experiment with the toolbars in an image editor to see what each tool does. Then, use a scanner or digital camera to capture an image and save it on your computer. Edit the image, using several of the tools. With your teacher's permission, print the images and present both your original and edited images to the class. Explain which tools you used to achieve the effects shown.

B. Several tools for working with graphics are discussed in this chapter. Research other tools for applying special effects to graphics. Create a chart identifying these tools and explaining how they are used.

DIRECTIONS: *You will use drawing tools to design a billboard for a fictitious city zoo. You will include clip art, text, and colors to create an attention-getting design for your billboard. Microsoft Office 2010 procedures required for this activity can be found in Appendix A.*

1. Start the program your teacher instructs you to use for this graphics activity. For example, you might use a presentation program, a paint program, or a word-processing program that has graphics capabilities.

2. Save the file as **GR-1_Zoo_xx** in the location where your teacher tells you to store the files for this activity. Replace *xx* with your own initials or name, as directed by your teacher.

3. Display the rulers and the gridlines. If you are working in a presentation program, change the layout of the title slide to blank.

4. In the blank file, insert a footer that includes your name and today's date.

5. Insert a clip art picture of a lion's head. If you cannot find an appropriate picture, insert the .wmf graphics file **GR-1_Lion**, which is located on the student CD.

6. Resize the picture to approximately 4.0" high by 3.0" wide.

7. Position the picture horizontally about .75" and vertically about 1.75" from the top-left corner of the document area.

8. Insert a text box approximately 3.0" high by 4.0" wide to the right of the picture.

9. Set the font in the text box to Arial, bold, 48 points, and type **Come See Our New "Mane" Attraction**.

10. Center the text in the text box.

11. Position the text box horizontally about 5.0" and vertically about 2.0" from the top-left corner of the document area.

12. Draw a rectangle with rounded corners above the other objects, centered horizontally. Size it to approximately 1.0" high by 5.0" wide.

13. Choose the command to add text to the rectangle.

14. Set the font to 26-point Arial Black, and type **Townsville City Zoo**, centered in the text box.

15. Draw another text box below the other objects, centered horizontally. Size it to approximately 0.5" high by 5.0" wide.

16. Set the font to 20-point Arial and type **123 Elm Street—Open 7 days a week!**, centered in the text box.

17. Apply a solid yellow background to the slide.

18. Select the rounded rectangle and the text box within it, and apply an orange fill and a black outline.

19. Check the spelling and grammar, and correct any errors that you find.

20. Display the file in Print Preview. It should look similar to Illustration A. If necessary, adjust the alignment and position of objects.

21. With your teacher's permission, print the file.

22. Close the file, saving all changes, and exit the program.

23. As a class, discuss the different programs available for creating graphics. Why might one be better than another?

Illustration A

DIRECTIONS: *You will use drawing tools to create a poster illustrating geometric solids. You will insert and format shapes and text boxes, and apply text effects (or WordArt). Refer to Illustration B to see a sample poster. Microsoft Office 2010 procedures required for this activity can be found in Appendix A.*

1. Start the program your teacher instructs you to use for this graphics activity. For example, you might use a presentation program, a paint program, or a word-processing program that has graphics capabilities.
2. Save the file as **GR-2_Geometry_xx** in the location where your teacher tells you to store the files for this activity.
3. Display the rulers and the gridlines. If you are working in a presentation program, change the layout of the title slide to blank.
4. In the blank file, insert a footer that includes your name and today's date.
5. If necessary, set the document or canvas to a size suitable for a poster. As you work, size and position shapes so they are appropriate for the size poster you are creating.
   ✔ *Your teacher will instruct you regarding the size that you should use.*
6. Insert a text box and type **What Is A Solid?** Position the text box 1.5" from the top of the page. Center the text in the text box and center the text box horizontally on the page.
7. Format the text box using a fill and border.
8. Insert another text box and type **A solid is a three-dimensional shape such as a cylinder, cube, or pyramid.** Center the text in the text box, and center the text box horizontally on the page.
9. Format the text box using a fill and a border.
10. Position the top of the second text box so it overlaps the first text box. Group the two text boxes.
11. Draw a cube shape.
12. Draw a cylinder shape.

13. Draw a pyramid shape.
    ✔ *If your program does not have these shapes as part of its shape gallery, you may draw a square, rectangle, and triangle and use 3-D effects to create the solids.*
14. Format the shapes using fills, borders, and effects such as shadows.
15. Size and position the three shapes so they look good on the page.
16. Insert a text box next to each shape and enter the shape name. Format, size, and position the text boxes to coordinate with the shapes.
17. Group each shape with its text box.
18. Centered along the bottom of the page, use a feature such as WordArt to create a text object using the text **Geometry**. Format the object with effects such as a shadow, border, and fill.
19. Insert other objects that you think will enhance the poster, and apply a background, page, or canvas color.
20. Check the spelling and grammar, and correct any errors that you find.
21. Display the file in Print Preview. It should look similar to Illustration B. If necessary, adjust the alignment and position of objects and the formatting to improve the effectiveness of the poster.
22. With your teacher's permission, print the file.
23. Close the file, saving all changes, and exit the program.
24. Create a display of the posters in your classroom.

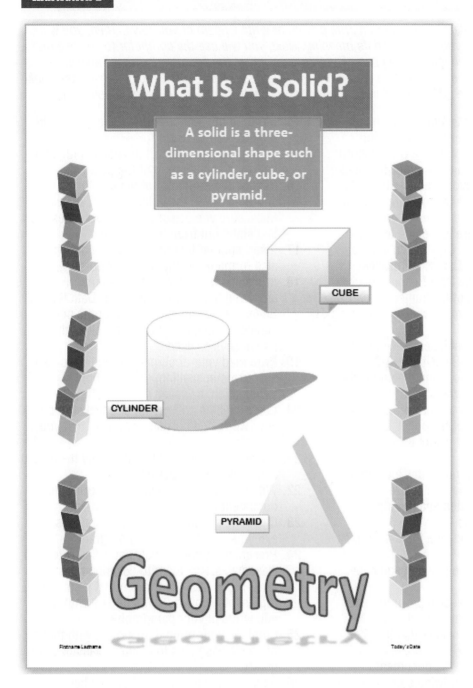

What Is A Solid?

A solid is a three-dimensional shape such as a cylinder, cube, or pyramid.

CUBE

CYLINDER

PYRAMID

Geometry

Graphics Activities

DIRECTIONS: *You will select one of your favorite poems or write a poem of your own. Then, you will analyze the poem to help you understand its meaning. Next, you will use the computer to create a drawing that illustrates the main idea of the poem. Finally, you will type the poem and write an analysis of it. When you are finished, you will combine your work with that of your classmates to create a class book of poetry. Microsoft Office 2010 procedures required for this activity can be found in Appendix A.*

1. Open the .pdf file **GR-3_Poem**, which is located on the student CD. With your teacher's permission, print the Data Record Sheet. Close the file, and exit your pdf reader.
2. Select one of your favorite poems that uses imagery and figurative language to describe something. Record the poem on your Data Record Sheet. Be sure to include the title and name of the poet. Or, you can write an original poem on the Data Record Sheet.
3. Using the table on the Data Record Sheet, record your analysis of the subject, mood, and theme of the poem, as well as the poetic devices used in it.
4. Start a program that includes drawing tools, and create a new file. Save it as **GR-3_Poem_xx** in the location where your teacher instructs you to store the files for this activity.
5. Use the drawing tools to draw a picture that reflects the meaning of the poem. Be sure to use different tools and colors as you create your drawing.
6. Preview the drawing frequently, looking for ways to improve it. Move or resize shapes to develop a coordinated image. Apply formatting and effects.
7. When you are satisfied with the drawing, save the changes.
8. Select all objects in the drawing and copy them.
9. Start your word-processing program, and create a new document. Save it as **GR-3_Analysis_xx**. Insert a header that includes your name.
10. Paste the drawing into the document.
11. Position and size the drawing so there is space for the poem on the left of the page and space for additional text on the bottom of the page.
12. Draw a text box to the left of the drawing. Format the text box so that it does not have an outside border or a fill color.
13. Using your Data Record Sheet, type the poem title, author's name, and poem in the text box.

14. Increase the font size of the title, and apply the bold font style.
15. Format the body text of the poem with a font that reflects the mood of the poem.
16. Change the font color of the text to coordinate with the colors in your drawing. Make sure you select a color that makes the text stand out from the drawing.
17. Insert another text box below the drawing, also formatted without a fill or border.
18. In the text box, type a brief paragraph analyzing the poem. Using your Data Record Sheet, include an explanation of the poem's subject, mood, and theme as well as the poetic devices used.
19. Proofread your document carefully. Correct any errors in spelling, capitalization, punctuation, or usage.
20. Use a spelling and grammar checker to check your work, and correct any errors that you find.
21. Preview the document, and modify the format and design as necessary.
22. With your teacher's permission, print the document.
23. Close the document, saving all changes, and exit your word-processing program.
24. Present your poem orally and visually to your classmates. Ask them to describe the style, tone, mood, and symbolism that your picture represents. How does it compare with what you wrote in your paragraph?
25. Combine your printed document with those of your classmates to create a class book of poetry.
26. As a class, discuss the difference between creating a work of art electronically and manually. What advantages does a computer program have over using real art supplies? What limitations does the program have? In what situations would you use a computer program?

DIRECTIONS: *In this activity, you will design a DVD case for a movie based on a book you have read. Microsoft Office 2010 procedures required for this activity can be found in Appendix A.*

1. Open the .pdf file **GR-4_Case**, which is located on the student CD. With your teacher's permission, print the Data Record Sheet. Close the file, and exit your pdf reader program.

2. Select a story or a book that you have read for which you will design the DVD case.

3. Complete the Data Record Sheet by sketching a design for the front of the case. Define space for at least one image and the areas where you want to display text. Write a summary of the plot, and include the names of actors who would play the main roles.

4. Use one of the following methods to obtain or create the image: scan an original drawing; take a photo with a digital camera; or draw the image using drawing tools.

   ✔ *If you download an image from the Internet, be sure to record the source information for a citation.*

5. Start your word-processing program, and create a new document. Save it as **GR-4_Case_xx** in the location where your teacher instructs you to store the files for this activity.

6. Change the right margin to 3" to simulate the size of a DVD case. Insert a header that includes your name and today's date.

7. Draw a text box, and type the title of the story or book at the top of the page. If necessary, remove the fill and border from the text box.

8. Draw a text box, and type a sentence introducing the actors and the parts they will play in the film. Again, remove the fill and border from the text box if necessary.

9. Draw a third text box, and type a brief statement describing the film. Format the text box without a fill or border.

10. Draw a fourth text box, type **Based on the story by**, and then type the author's name. Format the text box without a fill or border.

11. Referring to the sketch on your Data Record Sheet, size and position the text boxes on the document page the way you want them to appear on the front of the DVD case.

12. Apply font formatting effects to the text.

13. Insert your image file in the document. For example, scan a printed image and insert it as a picture or clip art, import the file from a digital camera, or copy and paste the image from a graphics or paint program.

14. Size and position the image as you want it to display on the DVD case cover.

15. Use the drawing tools in the word-processing program to draw a rectangle around the content on the page to indicate the front of the DVD case, and then save the document.

16. Insert a page break below the rectangle so you can define the back of the DVD case.

17. Draw a text box, and type the summary you wrote on your Data Record Sheet. Format the text box without a fill or border.

18. Insert text boxes and type any other information you would like to include on the back of the DVD case.

19. Format the text on the back cover.

20. Use the drawing tools in the word-processing program to draw a rectangle around the content on the page to indicate the back of the DVD case.

21. Proofread the text on both pages and make corrections. Then, run a spelling and grammar checker and correct all errors.

22. Preview the document. If necessary, adjust the size and position of the objects on the pages. Change or apply colors and font formatting to make the text more readable.

23. Preview the document again, and, with your teacher's permission, print the document.

24. Close the document, saving all changes, and exit your word-processing program.

25. Display your work for the class. Discuss your design and why you think it effectively illustrates the story or book.

Graphics Activities

DIRECTIONS: *You will measure different rooms in your home or school and use a spreadsheet to calculate their scaled measurements. Then, you will use drawing tools to draw scale versions of these rooms. Finally, you will use text tools to label these shapes with their measurements. Microsoft Office 2010 procedures required for this activity can be found in Appendix A.*

1. Open the .pdf file **GR-5_Rooms**, which is located on the student CD. With your teacher's permission, print the Data Record Sheet. Close the file, and exit your pdf reader program.

2. Measure the floor space of four different rooms in your school or home. Record the actual dimensions of each side of each room in the tables on the Data Record Sheet. Record all measurements in feet, and round to the nearest foot.

   ✔ *Although most rooms are rectangular and therefore have only four sides, some rooms may have more sides. Use the spaces labeled side 5 and 6 if you are measuring a room with more than four sides. Leave those spaces blank if your rooms have only four sides.*

3. Start your spreadsheet program. Create a new spreadsheet file, and save it as **GR-5_Scale_xx** in the location where your teacher instructs you to store the files for this activity.

4. In cell A1, enter the name of the first room you measured.

5. Starting in cell A2, and moving down to cell A7, enter the following row headings: **Side 1**, **Side 2**, **Side 3**, **Side 4**, **Side 5**, and **Side 6**.

6. Starting in cell B1 and moving across to cell D1, enter the following column headings: **Length in Feet**, **Length in Inches**, and **Scaled at 1/250**.

7. Starting in cell B2 and moving down the column, enter the measurements in feet of each side of the first room from your Data Record Sheet.

8. In cell C1, enter a formula that multiplies the number of feet by 12 to convert the value to inches. Copy the formula down the column for the remaining room sides.

9. In cell D1, enter a formula that divides the length in inches by 250. Copy the formula down the column for the remaining sides.

10. Format the measurements to show four decimal places. The worksheet should look similar to Illustration C, although your measurements will depend on the actual measurements of your room.

11. Starting in cell A9, repeat steps 4 through 10 to enter and calculate the measurements for the second room you measured. Repeat the process for the remaining two rooms.

12. Save the spreadsheet file. With your teacher's permission, print a copy of the data range.

13. Close the spreadsheet, saving all changes, and exit the program.

14. Start your presentation software program. Create a new presentation and save it as **GR-5_Scaled Rooms_xx**.

15. Enter the title **Scaled Room Drawings**. Insert your name and today's date as the subtitle.

16. Referring to the data on your spreadsheet printout, draw a scaled version of each room on a separate slide. If necessary, display gridlines and rulers to aid you in drawing. Insert a title on each slide that identifies the room.

17. On each slide, include a text box in which you enter the room's original measurements and its scaled measurements. Explain that the drawing has been scaled by a factor of 1/250.

18. Spell check the presentation.

19. With your teacher's permission, print the slides.

20. Close the presentation, saving all changes, and exit the program.

21. As a class, discuss any shortcuts you used in creating your scale drawings. Also, discuss why it might be useful to create scale drawings of rooms or buildings.

Illustration C

D5		f_x	=C5/250	
	A	B	C	D	E
1	Bedroom	Length in Feet	Length in Inches	Scaled at 1/250	
2	Side 1	8	96.0000	0.3840	
3	Side 2	5	60.0000	0.2400	
4	Side 3	8	96.0000	0.3840	
5	Side 4	5	60.0000	0.2400	
6	Side 5				
7	Side 6				

Presentation Basics

What Are Presentations?
A presentation is a visual or multimedia display. Every day, presentations are shown on overhead screens in classrooms and at meetings. They help people teach ideas, sell products, and share information with others.

Before computers, creating a professional presentation took a lot of time and involved many people. First, an artist would create graphics. Next, the graphics and wording would be organized for logical flow and visual appeal. Then, this information was transferred onto transparencies or slides.

Now, thanks to presentation software, many people create presentations more quickly. Knowing how to use presentation software is an important skill in today's world.

Chapter Outline

 Lesson 19–1

Exploring Presentation Software

 Lesson 19–2

Creating Presentations

 Lesson 19–3

Previewing Presentations

Exploring Presentation Software

Objectives

- Identify the benefits of presentation software.
- Identify three options for creating a new presentation.
- Describe six views in PowerPoint.

As You Read

Organize Information   Use a concept web to help you organize ways to create and view presentations as you read.

🔑 Key Terms

- AutoContent wizard
- Master views
- Normal view
- Notes Page view
- presentation software
- Reading view
- slide
- Slide Show view
- Slide Sorter view
- template
- thumbnails
- wizard

Introducing Presentation Software

Presentation software allows you to organize and display information visually so it can be viewed by a group of people. In most cases, this information—called a presentation—consists of both graphics and text, and may also include audio, video, and animation. Information in a presentation is organized into separate pages in an order the audience can follow easily. Each page is called a **slide**. Each slide can contain one or more main points. Information about each main point is organized into a list of short, easy-to-read key points. There are a host of good programs such as Microsoft PowerPoint, Corel Presentations and Apple's Keynote that are specifically designed to make presentations.

Creating a New Presentation   The most common presentation software is Microsoft PowerPoint. With PowerPoint 2010, you have two options for creating a new presentation:

- template
- blank presentation

Template   Work on a presentation may begin by selecting a **template**, or a preformatted version of a certain type of document. After choosing a template, you type in your information. You can also change the look and feel of the template by adjusting its settings.

Blank Presentation   This option starts by providing a plain blank slide. While this option may require more work than using a template, it does have benefits. For instance, you can create a new presentation from scratch to make your work more original by selecting your own color scheme, art, fonts, and other design elements.

Earlier versions of PowerPoint let you use the AutoContent Wizard, described below.

AutoContent Wizard   A **wizard** is a series of dialog boxes that guides you through a step-by-step procedure. The **AutoContent wizard** provides the steps for creating a presentation. It asks questions about the goals and purpose of your presentation. Once its questions are answered, the wizard creates a format for the presentation. To complete the presentation, you enter the words and images into the wizard's format.

Exploring Presentation Views

While working, you can selecting to view a presentation in many ways, depending on the task at hand. Each view has its own strength. Depending on the program you use, you may be able to choose from these views:

- Normal view
- Slide Sorter view
- Notes Page view
- Slide Show view
- Reading view
- Master views

Figure 19.1.1 Most presentation programs let you choose a theme or template to quickly apply coordinated formatting to your slides.

Technology @ Work

At work, employees may be asked to make presentations to inform others about company policies, to show the results of the company's latest research, or to sell a new product.

Think About It!

Using the right view in presentation software can make creating a presentation a little bit easier. Which views listed below would help you organize your slides?

➤ Normal view

➤ Slide Sorter view

➤ Notes Page view

➤ Slide Show View

➤ Reading View

➤ Master Views

Normal View Text and graphics can be added, removed, or edited in **Normal view**. (Versions of PowerPoint prior to 2007 have Slide view instead of Normal view.) Normal view splits the screen to show a Slide view and a Navigation pane. In the Navigation pane you can select to display an outline of the presentation or slide **thumbnails**, which are miniature versions of each slide image.

Slide Sorter View **Slide Sorter view** displays thumbnails of all of the slides in a presentation. This view allows you to change the order of the slides by dragging them to different locations.

Notes Page View In **Notes Page view**, part of the screen displays the slide and the rest of the screen shows a text box. You can type notes in the text box to use during a presentation or to print as handouts. Notes do not appear in the presentation that is shown to the audience.

Slide Show View The primary on-screen method of previewing and displaying slides during a presentation is called **Slide Show view**. Slides are displayed full-screen, one after another, in order. A slide-show presentation can be set to automatically advance slides or to wait until you—the presenter—advances the slides manually.

Reading View **Reading view** is similar to Slide Show view, except the slides are not displayed full-screen.

Master Views Many programs let you use **Master views** to make universal style changes to every slide, notes page, and/or handout pages.

You may also be able to use Black and White and/or Grayscale views to see how slides will look if printed without color. This can be helpful for previewing handouts of slides that use dark backgrounds or thin fonts.

Figure 19.1.2 Slide Sorter view (left) and Normal view (right) in Microsoft PowerPoint 2010.

Creating Presentations

Objectives

- Explain how placeholders are used in presentation software.
- Identify five steps in designing presentations.
- Summarize techniques for adding content.

As You Read

Sequence Information   Use a sequence chart to help you order steps for creating presentations as you read.

Designing Presentations

Following these five steps will help you plan and design an effective presentation.

1. Decide How Your Slides Will Be Formatted   To begin designing a presentation, choose an option for creating it. Choose either a blank presentation or a template. If none of the templates is exactly what you want, select the one that is closest. You can change much of its graphic content, format, and text. Graphics can be resized or deleted. Placeholders can be added, removed, or resized as well.

2. Choose the Slide Layout   Every slide in a presentation can be formatted in a preset layout. These layouts already have placeholders in position. This allows text and graphics to be added immediately. Some examples of slide layouts include bulleted lists, tables, grids, and flowcharts. Since each slide in a presentation can have a different layout, select a layout for each new slide you add.

3. Work with Placeholders   A **placeholder** is an area within a slide layout designed to hold data such as text or pictures. A placeholder automatically applies formatted based on the type of content. For instance, selecting a text placeholder will change the cursor to the Text tool. Selecting a picture placeholder will bring up a prompt asking which image to insert. Placeholder prompts guide you and are overwritten, or replaced, as you enter data.

4. Insert Graphics and Sound   Make your presentations come to life. Use sound, video, clip art, drawing tools, or imported images to support or illustrate a slide's text. But, be sure that the additions don't distract from the content.

Key Terms
- animation
- AutoShapes
- Clip Art task pane
- placeholder

Technology @ School

Some teachers use interactive multimedia software to help them teach. This software allows students to control the pace of the instruction.

Think About It!

Using interactive multimedia in the classroom has advantages and disadvantages. Which of those listed below could present a disadvantage for schools?

➤ expensive

➤ uses images

➤ uses sounds

➤ only some subjects available

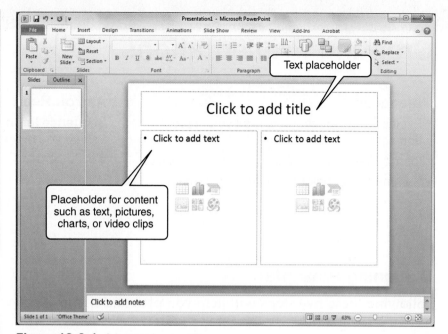

Figure 19.2.1 A two-column slide layout in Microsoft PowerPoint 2010.

5. View and Organize the Presentation Once information has been added to the slides, preview the entire presentation using the Slide Show view. Make any changes to the order of the slides in Slide Sorter view. Typos and text changes can be handled in Outline view or Normal view.

Adding Content to Presentations

Each new slide in a presentation has a layout with placeholders for adding content. For instance, a layout might contain a placeholder where you can add a title. Click (or, in some programs, double-click) the placeholder and begin typing. The program automatically formats the text to fit the area with a preselected font and alignment.

Adding Graphics You can insert many types of graphics including clip art, pictures, drawings, charts, diagrams, and tables. In PowerPoint 2010, use the buttons on the Insert tab of the Ribbon, or click the appropriate icon in a Content placeholder. PowerPoint drawing tools also include ready-to-use shapes, called **AutoShapes**. The list includes banners, arrows, borders, frames, and more.

Figure 19.2.2 The Clip Art task pane lets you find a piece of clip art to add to a PowerPoint slide.

You do not need a placeholder to insert graphics. Select the desired tool and use it in a blank area of the workspace.

Adding Animation and Sound   A multimedia presentation combines text and graphics with sound and **animation**. Both sound and animation, or moving images, are inserted using menu commands. For example, in PowerPoint 2010 you can choose to insert video or audio clips from the **Clip Art task pane** using buttons in the Media group on the Insert tab.

Adding Text   To add text, you simply type in a placeholder or in an outline. Text on a slide is often formatting as a bulleted list, which is a neat and effective way to present information.

Software Production Manager
Have you ever wondered who oversees the process of developing presentation or multimedia software? That is the job of software production managers. These are some of their job responsibilities:

➤ oversee people working on a project
➤ work with clients to develop features for the software
➤ oversee testing of the new software

Figure 19.2.3 Inserting a clip art image on a slide.

Previewing Presentations

Objectives

- Identify reasons for reviewing and previewing a presentation
- Summarize seven tips for creating effective presentations.

As You Read

Organize Information Use a main idea/detail chart to help you create useful presentations as you read.

Previewing a Presentation

Before finalizing a presentation you should review it and preview it.

Review Reviewing your presentation should include checking and correcting the spelling and grammar. Most programs include spellcheck tools that highlight possible errors and offer suggestions for correcting them. You can also send your presentation to a peer, such as a classmate or co-worker for review. He or she can point out things that are unclear and suggest ways to improve. Many programs include tools to make peer review easier, such as the ability to insert comments.

Preview Use Slide Show view to preview your presentation to check for inconsistencies such as incorrect fonts and spacing, poorly timed transitions, and animations that are out of order. During a preview you can also practice delivering your presentation to an audience.

Creating Effective Presentations

Apply these seven tips to make your presentation effective.

One Idea Per Slide Avoid crowding data onto a slide. Make as many slides as needed to present important information clearly.

Keep It Simple The audience will be listening to your speech or narration while viewing your slides. Use simple words to make key points. Include clear transitions from one topic to another.

Figure 19.3.1 In a well-designed presentation, each slide explains one key point or answers one key question.

Display Key Facts   Your slides should serve as an outline for the audience. Your speech will fill in the gaps in that outline. Displaying too much information can make a presentation hard to follow.

Mix It Up   Vary the layouts and content of your slides to help hold the audience's attention. For instance, switch between lists that appear on the right-hand and left-hand side and break up text with illustrations.

Use Color Cautiously   Select colors that are pleasing to the eye. For instance, bright pink lettering on a bright blue background will be difficult to read. Avoid using too many colors on a slide.

Watch the Fonts   Do not use more than two fonts on a single slide. This helps prevent a presentation from becoming too distracting to read. Also, be sure to use fonts that fit the tone. A presentation about the Civil War, for example, would not use fonts that seem playful or humorous.

Make It Readable   Choose readable font and color combinations. Check that your text and images can be seen from the back of the room so your presentation can be viewed by your entire audience.

Before giving a presentation, test it with an audience such as friends and family.

Think About It!

Ask your test audience to point out slides that were hard to see or to understand. Which items listed below are concerns for presentation slides?

➤ text too small

➤ animation

➤ detailed information given

➤ many colors used

Spotlight on...

DISTANCE LEARNING

Can you imagine creating presentations to show people who live hundreds of miles away? Distance learning teaches people at remote, or off-site, locations from the teacher. These students aren't seated together in a single classroom. Companies that develop distance-learning materials must create presentations students understand. It also means these presentations must keep students' interest.

Distance learning is offered by a large number of schools, colleges,

and universities. Many people are now earning college degrees through distance learning by taking classes online. Some schools also offer classes that combine some face-to-face instruction with online presentations.

Use the Vocabulary

Directions: *Match each vocabulary term in the left column with the correct definition in the right column.*

_____ **1.** presentation software
_____ **2.** slide
_____ **3.** wizard
_____ **4.** template
_____ **5.** Slide Show view
_____ **6.** placeholder
_____ **7.** AutoShapes
_____ **8.** animation
_____ **9.** thumbnail
_____ **10.** Slide Sorter view

a. preformatted version of a certain type of document

b. list of ready-to-use drawing tools

c. allows you to change the order of slides by dragging them to different locations

d. single page in a presentation

e. creates and displays visual information

f. miniature versions of each slide image

g. area in a presentation that holds data

h. can automatically show a presentation in the correct order

i. images that show movement

j. a series of dialog boxes that provides a step-by-step guide

Check Your Comprehension

Directions: *Complete each sentence with information from the chapter.*

1. Graphics designed using _____ usually are accompanied by text.

2. Using _____ view lets you make universal style changes to every slide, notes page, and/or handout pages.

3. The _____ view provides information that only the presenter can see during a presentation.

4. An on-screen method of previewing a presentation's slides is called the _____.

5. Animation can be added to some PowerPoint presentations using the _____.

6. Bulleted lists, flowcharts, and grids can be included in a slide's _____.

7. You can create a multimedia presentation with _____.

8. In a presentation, only the most _____ should be included on slides, not everything you plan to say.

9. A(n) _____ presentation combines text and graphics with sound and animation.

10. To prevent a presentation from becoming too distracting, do not use more than two _____ on a single slide.

Think Critically

Directions: *Answer the following questions.*

1. Which option for creating a new presentation works best for you? Explain.

2. What are disadvantages to adding clip art to PowerPoint presentations?

3. Why is it important to limit each slide in a presentation to a main concept or idea?

4. Why is it important to preview your presentation from the back of the room?

5. Which of the seven tips for finalizing effective presentations was the most meaningful to you? Why?

Extend Your Knowledge

Directions: *Choose one of the following projects. Complete the exercise on a separate sheet of paper.*

A. In addition to PowerPoint, other software is available to create professional-looking presentations. Conduct research online or in software catalogs to find one other presentation program. Create a Venn diagram to compare and contrast the features of this program to those of PowerPoint.

B. Work in small groups, one for each of the PowerPoint presentation views described in this chapter. In the groups, create text slides in your assigned view to summarize this chapter. Give your presentation to the class, and discuss the effectiveness of each view.

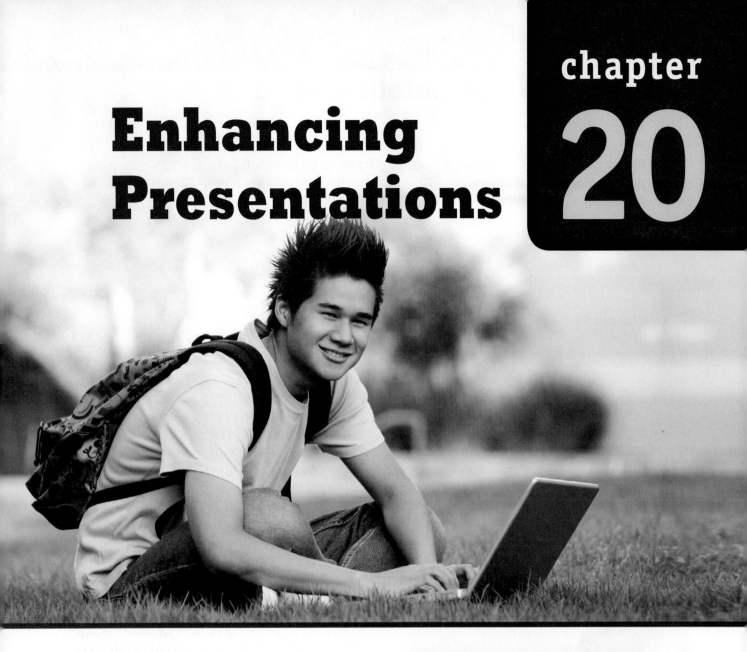

Enhancing Presentations

The Big Moment You have worked hard to assemble all the necessary tools and information. The stage is now properly set. The colors and lighting are perfect, and the script is well written. The show is about to begin.

Is this a Hollywood production? Is it a stage play? No, it's a computer presentation. Presentation software allows you to create a presentation with graphics, audio, text, animation, and more. Today, your computer screen is the stage. On other days, your show may be viewed on a large screen or on the Internet. The text, images, and sounds are your actors and props.

Learning to use presentation software is an important skill for school and work. Learning to use it effectively will benefit you for years to come.

Chapter Outline

 Lesson 20–1

Presentation Options

 Lesson 20–2

Developing Presentations

 Lesson 20–3

Enhancing and Finalizing Presentations

Presentation Options

Objectives

- Identify the purpose of presentation software.
- Explain the importance of knowing the output before developing a presentation.

As You Read

Organize Information   Use a spider map to organize tips for using presentation software effectively as you read.

Key Terms

- master slide
- viewable area
- visual aid

Using Presentation Software

The main purpose of presentation software is to provide speakers with **visual aids**, or graphics that help give information to an audience. For example, a teacher can use a chalkboard, flip chart, or handouts to illustrate ideas or provide examples.

Another way to present these concepts is by using presentation software to introduce key points either as text or images or to clarify details. Users can create slides and handouts to teach a concept or convey a message. They also can deliver presentations on-screen in an office, in a conference room, and on the World Wide Web.

Most presentations use default settings suitable for creating and displaying a full color slide show to an audience on a monitor or screen, controlled by a live presenter. You can change the presentation options. For example, you can create a self-running presentation that does not require a live presenter, or that can be controlled by an individual.

You can also make use of customization features such as designs and masters to create consistent and professional-looking presentations. For example, you can apply a design template to your presentation to give it a uniform look and color scheme.

Figure 20.1.1 Depending on which profession you choose, you may see a lot of presentations.

Working with Masters

Programs such as PowerPoint let you work with Slide, Notes, and Handout masters. Masters are default templates; changes you make to a master are applied to the components based on that master.

A **master slide** is a default template that is applied to all slides of a certain type. There are two different types of master slides in a presentation program such as PowerPoint:

- Slide Master
- Title Master

By editing a master slide, you are able to change fonts, sizes, colors, and layouts for all of the slides of that type throughout a presentation. For instance, the Slide Master controls the format for the slides. A Title Master controls the appearance of the title and subtitle of a title slide.

For example, suppose you want to change the font used for the main heading at the top of each slide. You can open the master slide, select the heading placeholder, and make your change. When you close the master slide, all the slide headings in the presentation will have changed to match the new format.

Technology @ School

When preparing a presentation for school, it may be a good idea to use Speaker Notes to help you remember what you want to say to the audience.

Think About It!

Entering notes can help remind you of details you want to share about your slides. For which of the ways listed below can Speaker Notes help you do this?

➤ help presenter remember dates and details

➤ organize layout of the slide show

➤ show thumbnails of the presentation

➤ prompt the punchline to a joke

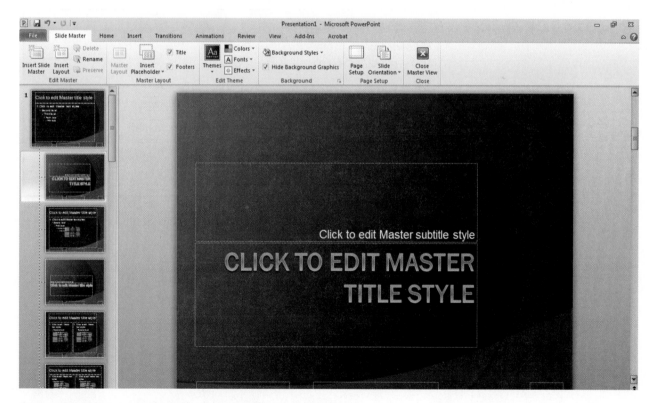

Figure 20.1.2 Like PowerPoint 2010, most presentation programs let you use a master slide to control the look of an entire presentation.

Consider the Output

The page setup options for presentation software offer choices for printing the presentation and for displaying the slides on-screen or as 35-mm slides. Other issues to consider are printer output and displays.

Printer Output If a presentation is to be printed and provided as a handout, the page setup should match the capabilities of the printer. A solid black background with green lettering might look fine on a computer screen. However, printing a colored background on every page for every person in the audience uses a lot of ink. In addition, simple color graphics lose their effect if they are printed in black. Also, dark backgrounds can make text hard to see on a printed page.

Displaying the Output For each presentation, it is important to anticipate the display's **viewable area**, or portion of the screen where an image can be shown. Different displays have different viewable areas. For instance, if the computer uses a television as an output device, some of the information may not be visible. This is also true when using an LCD (liquid crystal display) monitor to project computer-screen images for large audiences. It is important to adjust the page setup so that all of the presentation can be viewed on-screen by the audience.

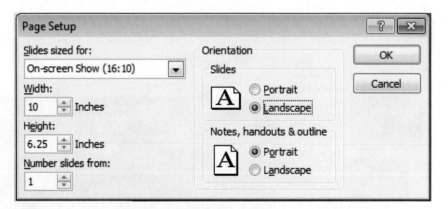

Figure 20.1.3 You can use the options in the Page Setup dialog box to set output options for a presentation.

Developing Presentations

Objectives

- Explain the use of a presentation outline.
- Identify slide layout options.
- Explain the benefit of designing the content of a slide before choosing the layout.
- Summarize the editing process that should occur after a draft presentation is complete.

As You Read

Sequence Information   Use a sequence chart to sequence the steps to organize a presentation as you read.

Using a Presentation Outline

In most presentation programs you can use an outline to develop your presentation. You can type the outline to create slide titles and bullet items, or you can import an outline from a program such as Microsoft Word.

Typing an Outline   When you type a presentation outline, the first line you type displays as the slide title. From the title, you press Ctrl+Enter to start a bulleted list, or Enter to create a new slide. From the bulleted list, you press Enter to continue the bulleted list, or Ctrl+Enter to start a new slide. You can format and rearrange outline text and increase or decrease outline levels to change the way the text displays on the slide.

Importing an Outline   If you have an existing outline in a file created with a program such as Microsoft Word, you can import it into your presentation program. Each heading 1 level in the outline becomes a slide title, and the subheadings become bulleted lists.

Key Terms

- transition effect
- self-running presentation
- rehearsed presentation

Figure 20.2.1 Like Power-Point 2010, most presentation programs let you work with a presentation outline.

Large companies often use organizational charts to identify the structure and responsibilities of employees. PowerPoint offers a template layout to help generate this information.

Think About It!

Which items listed below would be valuable to an organizational chart for a business?

➤ detailed job descriptions

➤ names of department heads

➤ telephone extensions

➤ work schedules

Figure 20.2.2 Checking the spelling in a presentation.

Choosing a Slide Layout

Each slide in a presentation can have its own layout. Consider the content of a slide before you choose a layout. By deciding the slide's key points first, you can then select the most appropriate layout for it.

The first slide in a new blank presentation usually has the Title Slide layout, with placeholders for entering a title and a subtitle. By default, new slides you add have the Title and Content layout, with placeholders for a title and content such as a bulleted list, clip art, picture, chart, table, or media clip. Other layout choices include Two Content, Comparison, Title Only, Blank, Content with Caption, Picture with Caption, and Section Header.

Editing Your Presentation

Good presenters edit drafts of their work. Be sure to fix the errors you find, reorganize the sequence of the slides, and improve the flow of ideas. If a slide is in the wrong location, use Slide Sorter or Outline view to move it. To revise the flow of text, use Outline view to adjust it.

Checking Errors Presentation software can check spelling as you type text in a placeholder. If a red, wavy line appears under a word, it might be spelled incorrectly. If so, in Windows, right-click the word to open the suggested-spellings list and see other spelling choices.

Enhancing a Presentation

Inserting Images Text-only presentations can be dull. Insert clip art, photos, and other images to clarify and enhance key points. Use charts, shapes, and drawings to help your audience better understand the information in your slides.

Adding Animation, Video, and Sound As mentioned in Chapter 19, sound, animation, and video can make a presentation more informative and interesting. Most presentation software can import and use standard animation formats, including animated .gif clips. You can also animate objects and text on a slide. For example, you can have a title slide in from the left, or set a picture to fade out or blink.

Some presentation programs, including PowerPoint 2010, include the ability to embed video clips or a link to a video from your presentation. You can insert sound files, such as music or recorded narration. When you insert sounds or video, an icon displays on the slide. You can hide the icon during a presentation, or set it so the clip only plays when a viewer clicks it.

Adding Transitional Effects A **transition effect** is a multimedia feature that adds visual interest as your presentation moves from one slide to the next. For example, one slide might suddenly appear to fade out as the next slide appears. A new slide can move into view from one side of the screen as the previous slide disappears from sight.

Adjusting the Timing You can adjust the timing of slide shows. In **self-running presentations**, each slide stays on the screen for a specified period of time. Timings are usually set by entering the number of seconds you want a slide to display. In a **rehearsed presentation**, you set the program to record how long you spend presenting a slide; the program automatically sets the timing based on your rehearsal.

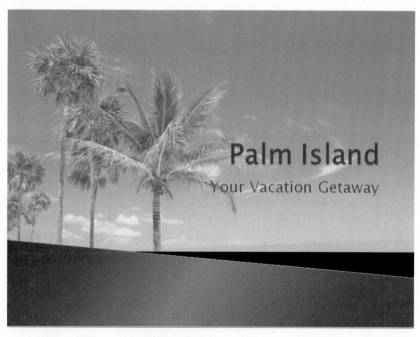

Palm Island
Your Vacation Getaway

Figure 20.2.3 Graphics can make slides more informative or more appealing.

Enhancing and Finalizing Presentations

Objectives

- Identify strategies to enhance a presentation.
- Summarize choices for presentation output.

As You Read

Draw Conclusions Use a conclusion chart to draw conclusions about finalizing a presentation as you read.

Key Terms

- digital projector
- on-screen presentation

Making Powerful Presentations

Presentation programs are effective tools for generating high-interest, engaging presentations. Here are ten tips for finalizing presentation slides so that they are easy to understand and help you meet your presentation goals.

Remember your goal. Keep your goal, and your main message, in mind as you outline your presentation. When finalizing your presentation, review your slides and the information they convey to ensure that your goal has been met.

Support your main idea. Start by stating your main idea or topic sentence. Follow it with details that are simply presented and that clarify or support your main idea.

Know your audience. Fewer words on a slide mean fewer words your audience has to read. However, make sure that you do not oversimplify the content on your slides or you run the risk of boring your audience. Finally, rehearse in clear language and make sure your slides are also clear to others.

Preview and review. A preview slide introduces the presentation for an audience. This slide usually appears after the presentation's title slide and before the first slide that addresses a point.

A review slide usually restates the presentation's main points and may be identical to the preview slide. Used together effectively, a preview and review slide can help your audience remember the most important points of your presentation.

Figure 20.3.1 The more planning you do, the better your presentations will be.

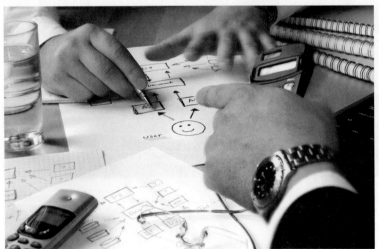

Stay on point. The purpose of slides is to highlight key facts, so it is fine to leave out supporting details. Keep your text lively but to the point.

Select and apply a consistent design. Too many different designs or too many colors and fonts can distract or confuse an audience.

Be smart with art. Use clip art, tables, charts, icons, and animations wisely to enhance a point. Don't add illustrations that do not contribute to your message.

Proofread your text. Use the spelling checker to help you eliminate typos from your work. Then, print your slides and ask someone to proofread them.

Check the output. Make sure the hardware on which you plan to display your work will be able to run your slide show. Incompatible machines can ruin your presentation.

Watch the clock. Rehearse your presentation with a timer. Make sure any timed slides are sequenced with your verbal message.

Figure 20.3.2 Badly designed slides make it hard to understand your message.

Figure 20.3.3 Well-designed slides make your message memorable.

Choosing a Delivery Method

Now that you have created your slides, how will your audience view your presentation? There are a number of ways to deliver a presentation to an audience, including:

- on-screen delivery, with or without a speaker
- interactive presentation at a kiosk or booth
- Internet broadcast

Choose the best method to meet the needs of your audience, using the available technology.

On-screen Presentations   Sometimes two or three people can comfortably gather around a single computer to view a slide-show presentation. In other cases, large groups may view a presentation on an overhead or video monitor, a presentation projector, or a "jumbo" screen. This is called an **on-screen presentation**, or a screen display of the slides.

In the past, overhead projectors were commonly used for on-screen presentations, especially in classrooms. Today, **digital projectors** have largely replaced them. Where overhead projectors worked by shining light through transparencies, digital projectors project an image directly from the computer through a lens and onto the screen.

Large-format displays require special hardware, such as a digital light projector that takes the computer's output and projects it onto a wall or other large surface. Large-scale monitors are available but are expensive and difficult to move. In large settings, other equipment is often required, such as a microphone, amplifier, and speakers, which allow the audience to hear the speaker and any sound that plays during the presentation.

Interactive Presentations   PowerPoint allows users to add interactivity to a presentation. To help promote a product at a conference sales booth or a shopping mall kiosk, for example, you can set animation effects to play when a customer clicks a specific object on-screen. Depending on the object selected, the customer is taken to different parts of the presentation and receives different information.

Internet Delivery   If the audience is in a remote place, the presentation can be exported for broadcast on a Web site. The user can then view the slide show at any time through a Web browser. This method is useful for long-distance education. Group size is not an issue, and interactivity and animation are both possible presentation features.

Audience Handouts   You can help your audience remember important information by providing audience handouts. These handouts may be printouts of your slides or a summary of your main ideas. Handouts are especially helpful when presenting difficult information.

Use the Vocabulary

Directions: *Match each vocabulary term in the left column with the correct definition in the right column.*

_____ **1.** visual aid
_____ **2.** digital projector
_____ **3.** master slide
_____ **4.** viewable area
_____ **5.** transition effect
_____ **6.** self-running presentation
_____ **7.** rehearsed presentation
_____ **8.** on-screen presentation

a. device used to display an image directly from a computer through a lens and onto a screen

b. changing the format of this slide changes all slides of this type

c. automatically switches from one slide to the next

d. uses a counter to help determine how long a slide should stay on the screen

e. graphic that is used to assist in communicating a topic

f. a display of slides on a monitor or screen

g. technique for switching from one slide to another during a presentation

h. portion of a screen on which an image can be seen

Check Your Comprehension

Directions: *Determine the correct choice for each of the following.*

1. What is the overall purpose of presentation software?
   a. show images to large audiences
   b. provide visual aids for speeches
   c. provide a way of creating art
   d. replace human presenters

2. Which color combination is best for printed handouts?
   a. white background with black letters
   b. black background with green letters
   c. dark blue background with red letters
   d. pale yellow background with white letters

3. Which slide usually restates the presentation's main points?
   a. title slide
   b. master slide
   c. review slide
   d. blank

4. Which slide layout is best for adding a two-column bulleted list?
   a. Title and Content
   b. Blank
   c. Two Content
   d. Picture with Caption

5. What kind of presentations are timed in a specific sequence?
   a. self-running
   b. rehearsed
   c. transition effect
   d. slide sorter

6. Which presentation delivery method is useful for long-distance education?
   a. on-screen delivery with a speaker
   b. Internet broadcast
   c. interactive presentation at a booth
   d. printed handouts

Think Critically

Directions: *Answer the following questions.*

1. Why are the master slides valuable to someone using presentation software?

2. Why should you know your method of output before giving a presentation?

3. What choices does a presenter have for adding a graph, table, or spreadsheet to a slide?

4. How can the use of colors, fonts, font styles, and font sizes affect the design of a presentation?

5. For what purposes might you be asked to develop a presentation using presentation software?

Extend Your Knowledge

Directions: *Choose one of the following projects. Complete the exercise on a separate sheet of paper.*

A. There are many ways to add graphics to a presentation. You can download images from the Internet; export images from digital files or paint or draw programs; or use clip art. Access to premade images makes adding images to slides easy. Using presentation software, design and create three slides—each using text and an image captured in a different way. Present your slides to the class, and explain the process you followed to create them. Document your sources.

B. Design, create, and distribute a survey to ten people of different ages to find out what kinds of presentations they have seen in the past 12 months. In your survey, include questions about the type of delivery method and the effectiveness of the presentation. Draw conclusions from the results of your survey about the use of presentation software to convey information to an audience.

DIRECTIONS: *You will prepare a presentation that defines the basic parts of speech, lists examples of each, and includes a sample sentence using one of the examples. You will format the presentation and add transitions. Microsoft Office 2010 procedures required for this activity can be found in Appendix A.*

1. Open the .pdf file **PR-1_Speech**, which is located on the student CD. With your teacher's permission, print the Data Record Sheet. Close the file, and exit your pdf reader program.
2. In the second column of the Data Record Sheet, write a definition of each part of speech listed in column 1. Use a dictionary, textbook, Internet, or other reference to gather the information as necessary. In column 3, enter three examples of words that fall into that category of speech. Then, in column 4, write a sentence using one of the three examples.
3. Start your presentation program, and save a new presentation as **PR-1_PartsofSpeech_*xx*** in the location where your teacher instructs you to store the files for this activity. Replace **xx** with your own initials or name, as directed by your teacher.
4. On the title slide, type the title **Parts of Speech**. Include your name as the author of the presentation in the subtitle, along with the current date.
5. Referring to the Data Record Sheet, prepare a slide for each part of speech listed in column 1, for a total of 8 slides. On each slide, include a title that identifies the part of speech, a text box in which you enter the definition, and a bulleted list for the three examples. A sample slide is shown in Illustration A.
6. In the Notes pane on each slide, enter the sentence from the usage column in the Data Record Sheet.
7. Insert pictures on at least three of the slides, sizing and positioning them so they enhance the appearance of the slide.

8. If necessary, include a slide at the end for listing source information.
9. When you have finished entering the slide and note text, proofread each one carefully, checking for consistency in sentence structure and placement of objects, and correct any errors you find.
10. Check the spelling and grammar in the presentation, and correct any errors.
11. Apply a theme or design to the presentation that you think helps make the content easy to read and the presentation appealing.
12. View the presentation and look for ways to improve it. For example, you might decide to change the theme colors and/or fonts, or modify the slide backgrounds.
13. Apply transitions to all slides and set timings to advance automatically after 10 seconds or on a mouse click.
14. Practice delivering the presentation.
15. With your teacher's permission, print the notes pages for yourself, and print handouts with three slides per page for the class.
16. Show your presentation to the class, and respectfully watch your classmates' presentations.
17. Close the presentation, saving all changes, and exit your presentation program.
18. As a class, discuss the effectiveness of each presentation. What were the strengths and weaknesses? Evaluate the presentations for design, content, delivery, purpose, and relevancy to the assignment.

Noun

A noun is the part of speech that is used to name or identify a person, place, thing, quality or action.

▸ Athlete
▸ Stadium
▸ Basketball

Illustration A

Presentation Activities

Presentation Activities

DIRECTIONS: *You will use presentation software to create a slide show about a book you have read. You will use the program's drawing tools to graphically illustrate the rising and falling action of the story. You will also analyze and present information about the book's characters, setting, conflict, and theme. Microsoft Office 2010 procedures required for this activity can be found in Appendix A.*

1. Open the .pdf file **PR-2_Report**, which is located on the student CD. With your teacher's permission, print the Data Record Sheet. The sheet includes a table to help you record information for your book report. Close the file, and exit your pdf reader.

2. Select a book you have read recently, and then use the Data Record Sheet to record information about the book.

3. Start your presentation program. Create a new presentation, and save it as **PR-2_ Book_xx** in the location where your teacher instructs you to store the files for this activity.

4. Apply a theme or design to your presentation.

5. On the title slide, type a title for your presentation. Use the book's title and the author's name as the presentation subtitle. Insert a footer on this slide only that reads: **Prepared by [your name]**, along with the current date. See Illustration B for a sample.

6. Insert a new slide with placeholders for a title and a bulleted list.

7. Title this slide **Characters**.

8. In the text placeholder, type a list of major characters in the book. Change the layout of the slide to two columns, if necessary.

9. Create slides for the Setting and Conflict rows in the table on your Data Record Sheet. For example, the next slide should be titled **Setting**, and the bulleted list should include information about the setting of the story. The slide after that should be titled **Conflict**, and the list should describe elements of the conflict in the story.

10. Insert a new slide with a title only layout.

11. Type the title **Plot** on the slide. Insert a flowchart diagram or use the drawing tools to create a flowchart that illustrates the major events in the book. Refer to your Data Record Sheet. If there are many events, consider extending the diagram to another slide.

12. Improve the appearance and readability of the diagram by resizing and positioning the drawing objects and by formatting the shapes in the illustration using colors, outlines, and fills. Format the text using font formatting such as color and font styles.

13. Add one more slide to the presentation for the Theme row in the Data Record Sheet. Title the slide **Theme**, and type a bulleted list explaining the theme of the story.

14. Insert graphics to illustrate your slides.

15. Proofread each slide carefully, checking for consistency in sentence structure, spelling, and grammar, and correct any errors.

16. View the presentation, and look for ways to improve it. For example, you might want to change the theme colors and/or fonts to enhance the appearance of the slides.

17. Add transitions and animations, and view the presentation again.

18. Add speaker's notes that you can refer to while delivering the presentation.

19. With your teacher's permission, print the notes pages for yourself, and print handouts with three slides per page for the class.

20. Rehearse the presentation.

21. Show your presentation to the class and respectfully watch the presentations of your classmates.

21. Close the presentation, saving all changes, and exit the presentation program.

22. As a class, discuss the effectiveness of each presentation, including the use of graphics, fonts, theme, and other elements. What features caught your attention the most? What were the strengths and weaknesses of the presentation? Evaluate the presentations for design, content, delivery, purpose, and relevancy to the assignment.

Illustration B

DIRECTIONS: *You will explore a career that interests you. You will conduct research to find out about duties, training, and salary associated with that career. You also will investigate how technology is used in the career, and how changes in technology have impacted the field. Then, you will create a presentation about the career. Microsoft Office 2010 procedures required for this activity can be found in Appendix A.*

1. Open the .pdf file **PR-3_CareerResearch**, which is located on the student CD. With your teacher's permission, print the Data Record Sheet. The sheet includes a table to help you record information about careers. Close the file, and exit your pdf reader program.
2. Research a career that interests you.
   a. Use the Internet (with your teacher's permission), library resources, or a textbook, recording all source information as you work.
   b. If you are using your library's online catalog, search for the keyword **careers**. With an Internet search engine, you might search for words or phrases such as **"career information for kids"**. Be sure to include quotation marks around the keywords. Evaluate each Web site you visit for accuracy and validity. When possible, find at least two sources for each fact. If two sources disagree on a fact or figure, use a third source to resolve the conflict. When you find a credible Web site with relevant information, bookmark the site, or with your teacher's permission, print the desired pages. Write the source information about each site on a separate piece of paper. When you have completed your research, close your Web browser.
   c. Record useful information on your Data Record Sheet. If you need more space, use the back of the sheet, or a separate piece of paper. Write the information about each source or site on a separate piece of paper.
   d. If you locate any images or photographs related to your chosen career, identify whether or not they are available for use free of charge. If they are, download and save them as files so you can use them in your presentation.
3. Start your presentation program. Create a new presentation, and save it as **PR-3_Career_xx**, in the location where your teacher instructs you to store files for this activity.
4. Apply a theme or design to your presentation.
5. Create the first slide as a title slide. Type an appropriate title that reflects the career you chose. The subtitle might include a phrase about the career that will grab your audience's attention. Insert a footer on this slide only that reads: **Prepared by [your name]**, along with the current date. The title slide should look similar to the one shown in Illustration C.
6. Insert a new slide using a layout that has placeholders for a title and a bulleted list. Type **Job Duties** as the title. Using your Data Record Sheet, type bulleted items listing the job responsibilities. If there are too many items, either modify the layout to include two columns, or continue the list on a new slide.
7. Create slides for the Required Training, Average Salary, and Job Outlook rows on your Data Record Sheet. Use a slide layout that works best with the information you have and insert any graphics or clip art you want to include.
8. Create at least one slide that summarizes how technology is used in your chosen career. For example, in the field of fashion design, computerized sewing machines are used to make clothing; an inventory control program enables retailers to order clothing as it is needed; and designers use Web sites to advertise and promote their fashions.
9. Create at least one slide that lists how changes in technology have impacted your chosen career and the way workers in that field do their jobs. For example, doctors can now fax or e-mail a prescription to a pharmacy instead of writing out prescription slips by hand; they can access medical databases to diagnose rare conditions; and as they make their rounds, they can use a wireless network to download x-rays, test results, and other information about patients to a notebook, tablet, or handheld device.
10. When you have finished entering the slide text, proofread each one carefully, checking for consistency in sentence structure, and correct any errors you find.
11. Check the spelling and grammar in the presentation, and correct any errors.
12. View the slide show and make any changes that you think will improve the presentation value, or make the presentation more effective. For example, split crowded slides into two slides, change the theme colors and/or fonts, or modify the slide background.

13. Add transitions and animations, and view the presentation again.
14. Add speaker's notes that you can refer to while delivering the presentation.
15. With your teacher's permission, print the notes pages for yourself, and print handouts with three slides per page for the class.
16. Rehearse the presentation.
17. Show your presentation to the class and respectfully watch the presentations of your classmates.

18. Close the presentation, saving all changes, and exit the presentation program.
19. As a class, discuss how changes in technology affect employment and the way people work. How do you think it impacts worker productivity? How does it influence how workers are trained? How has it changed the traditional office structure?

Illustration C

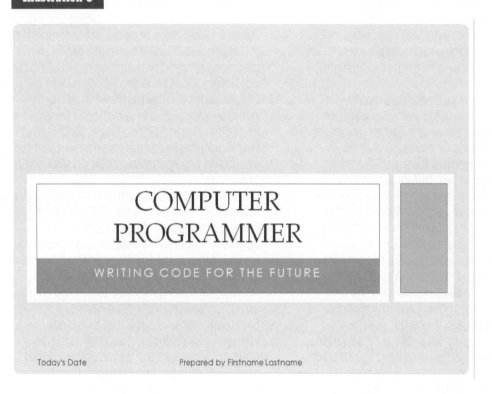

COMPUTER
PROGRAMMER

WRITING CODE FOR THE FUTURE

Today's Date   Prepared by Firstname Lastname

DIRECTIONS: *You will conduct research to learn about the newest components for personal computers. Then, you will create a slide presentation to display your findings. You will format your presentation, and then you will display your presentation and share your findings with the class. Microsoft Office 2010 procedures required for this activity can be found in Appendix A.*

1. Open the .pdf file **PR-4_Components**, which is located on the student CD. With your teacher's permission, print the Data Record Sheet. The sheet includes a table to help you record your research about technology. Close the file, and exit your pdf reader program.

2. With your teacher's permission, open a Web browser and navigate to a search engine. Search for sites that offer information about new components for personal computers. Try to identify at least ten items, such as new types of monitors, input devices, output devices, processors, or storage components. You might also look for developments in networks, processors, graphics, printers, speakers, microphones, or Web cameras.

   a. Try searching for words or phrases such as **current PC technology**, or use a Boolean search such as **Personal Computer AND Current Technology**. Evaluate each Web site you visit for accuracy and validity. When possible, find at least two sources for each fact. If two sources disagree on a fact or figure, use a third source to resolve the conflict. When you find a credible Web site with relevant information, bookmark the site, or with your teacher's permission, print the desired pages. Write the source information about each site on a separate piece of paper. When you have completed your research, close your Web browser.

   b. Use the Data Record Sheet to record the information that you find. Include the name of each component, the type of component—for example, input, output, processing, or storage—and a brief description of its features.

   c. If you locate any images or photographs related to computer components, identify whether or not they are available for use free of charge. If they are, download and save them as files so you can use them in your presentation.

   d. Record your source citation information on a separate sheet of paper, including information about sites from which you download images.

3. Start your presentation program. Create a new presentation, and save it as **PR-4_Components_xx** in the location where your teacher tells you to store the files for this activity.

4. Apply a theme or design to the presentation.

5. Format the first slide to contain a title and a subtitle. Type **What's New in the Computer World?** as the title. Type **Latest Devices for Your Computer** as the subtitle. Insert a footer on this slide only that reads: **Prepared by [your name]**, along with the current date.

6. Insert a new slide, and format it to contain a title and a bulleted list of text.

7. Refer to the Type column on your Data Record Sheet. Pick one type, and enter the name as the title of the slide. For example, you might enter **Output Devices** as a title.

8. For the bulleted list, enter the name of each component in your Data Record Sheet that fits the category, along with a brief description of the component. If you have an appropriate image, insert it on the slide.

9. Repeat this process to create slides for the remaining types of components listed on the Data Record Sheet.

10. When you have finished entering the slide text, proofread each one carefully. Correct any errors in spelling, capitalization, punctuation, or usage. Also, rearrange text if necessary to make sure the information is presented in a logical way.

11. Check the spelling and grammar in the presentation, and correct any errors.

12. View the slide show and make any changes that you think will improve the presentation value, or make the presentation more effective. For example, split crowded slides into two slides, change the theme colors and/or fonts, or modify the slide background.

13. Add transitions and animations, and view the presentation again.

14. Add speaker's notes that you can refer to while delivering the presentation.

15. With your teacher's permission, print the notes pages for yourself, and print handouts with three slides per page for the class.

16. Rehearse the presentation.

17. Show your presentation to the class and respectfully watch the presentations of your classmates.
18. Close the presentation, saving all changes, and exit the presentation program.

19. As a class, discuss some of the more interesting components you discovered during your research. What other new products do you expect to see within the next ten years? In what new ways do you think computers and/or technology will be used in the future? How are these products relevant to daily living, lifelong learning, and future careers?

Activity 5: Creating a Photo Album

DIRECTIONS: *You will use a presentation program to create a photo album for displaying photographs on a computer. Microsoft Office 2010 procedures required for this activity can be found in Appendix A.*

1. Collect at least five photographs that you can use in your album. If the photographs are not already in a digital format, convert them as necessary. For example, scan printed photos.
2. Start your presentation program. Create a new presentation.
3. Create a new photo album in your presentation program. Refer to Help if necessary. If your software does not have a photo album feature, then create a blank presentation.
4. Select the pictures to insert, and create the album.
5. Save the album as **PR-5_Album_xx**, in the location where your teacher instructs you to store files for this activity.
6. On the title slide, type a title and make sure your name displays correctly.
7. Insert a footer with your name and today's date on all slides.
8. Insert a text box on each slide, and type a description of the picture.

9. Apply a theme or design to your presentation.
10. Check the spelling and grammar in the presentation, and correct any errors.
11. Set the slides to advanced on a mouse click, or automatically after 10 seconds.
12. View the album. (A sample album displayed in Slide Sorter view is shown in Illustration D.)
13. With your teacher's permission, print handouts with one slide per page for the class.
14. Publish the album to the Web, a slide library, or a shared site so others may view it.
15. Close the presentation, saving all changes, and exit the presentation program.
16. As a class, discuss different ways of sharing photos using technology. Discuss the benefits—such as staying in touch and up-to-date with family and friends—and drawbacks—such as privacy issues.

Illustration D

Multimedia Basics

Different Media Offer Powerful Choices

For centuries, people have shared their thoughts and ideas by speaking, drawing pictures, or using written words. When you talk or write words on paper, you use one medium, or means of expressing information. Today, however, computers allow people to use many different media (the plural of *medium*) at the same time.

When you play a video game, watch a movie, or visit a Web site, you see many kinds of media, such as text, graphics, audio, video, and animation. A few years ago, it took expensive equipment and a lot of experience to combine these different media. Today, ordinary PCs and inexpensive software tools allow anyone to create entertaining and useful presentations, Web pages, interactive programs, games, and more using a combination of media types.

Chapter Outline

 Lesson 21–1

Introducing Multimedia

 Lesson 21–2

Multimedia File Formats

 Lesson 21–3

Introducing Virtual Reality

Introducing Multimedia

Objectives

- Define multimedia and compare multimedia and interactive multimedia.
- Explain how multimedia is used in various fields.
- Identify tools used to work with audio and video.

As You Read

Organize Information   Use a main idea/detail chart to help you identify details about multimedia applications as you read.

🔑 Key Terms

- frame rate
- interactive multimedia
- multimedia
- sound card
- video capture board
- video editor

Defining Multimedia

A medium is one way to communicate information or express ideas. Talking is a medium, as is writing or drawing. Different media can be combined together in many ways. An animated cartoon, for example, combines moving graphics (one medium) with sound and music (other media). This is what is meant by the term **multimedia**—combining different media to express information or ideas. A multimedia event can include text, graphics, sound, video, and animation.

Because multimedia can take so many forms and be used in so many ways, terms such as event or experience are often used to describe it. A multimedia event can be many things. Movies and television programs are common examples, but now watching videos on YouTube or Hulu, listening to an audio podcast, or using a social networking site, like Facebook, are just as common. And while many kinds of computer programs use multimedia, from games to encyclopedias, a teacher displaying slides or using a low-tech chalkboard is also creating a multimedia event.

Many, though not all, examples of multimedia are interactive. **Interactive multimedia** allows the user to make choices about what is displayed. Computer and video games, educational computer software, and some Web sites—which let you decide what you see and how you interact with information—are all examples of interactive multimedia.

To be interactive, a multimedia event must provide more than audio or video. It must also give the user a way to control the action and make choices that determine what happens next. Think of a video game that lets you direct an avatar through a series of passages and then go back again. Or think of multimedia social networking Web sites that let you update your "status," watch videos posted by others, and comment on them.

Using Multimedia

Multimedia applications are widely used today in business, education, and entertainment.

Business Multimedia technologies help businesses communicate with their customers and employees. Many corporate Web sites, for example, use sound, video, or animation to demonstrate products to customers.

Businesses also use multimedia to train employees. For example, many companies create custom multimedia programs that workers can access via CD-ROM or a network. These programs use audio and video to demonstrate products and explain procedures. These programs can be interactive, which allows workers to jump to different areas of the content at will or take tests that provide feedback about their knowledge.

Education Multimedia can make learning more fun for students and provides extra tools for teachers. Interactive software can teach lessons, present quizzes, and give students immediate feedback to help them see how well they are doing.

Multimedia programs offer audio and video to enhance learning in ways that printed text alone cannot. For instance, instructional software may use audio to teach languages. Multimedia encyclopedias can play video clips from historical events.

Entertainment Video and computer games are multimedia programs. Flight simulators use rapidly changing graphics and sound to put the player "inside the cockpit" of a plane. Action games use realistic graphics and color to create the experience. But interactivity is what gives these games their true appeal. Using a game controller or keyboard, you can direct the action from start to finish. Multimedia technologies are used in many products besides games. Movies use 3-D animation and computer-generated effects. Concerts, documentaries, and television programs also incorporate multimedia.

Technology @ School

The sales catalogs that are sent to schools these days don't just include books. They also offer a large number of multimedia programs that can be used in teaching various subjects.

Think About It!

Which benefits listed below might a school gain from purchasing multimedia programs?

➤ easier material

➤ providing immediate feedback to students

➤ capturing students' attention

➤ making an actual teacher unnecessary

➤ matching students' learning styles to material (whether they learn best through sight or sound)

Figure 21.1.1 Many schools and libraries use multimedia programs to teach all kinds of subjects to people of all ages.

Figure 21.1.2 Today's multimedia products use several kinds of data, from simple text to sound to video.

Tools for Working with Audio and Video

Audio (sound) and video (movies and animations) are essential components of multimedia. You will need these three components to create multimedia.

Sound Card As you learned earlier, a **sound card** is a special expansion board that allows the computer to input, edit, and output sounds. Audio—whether voices, music, or sound effects—is entered into the computer through the input jacks on the sound card. Once audio is captured on the computer's hard drive, you can edit and work with it. You can then play it through the computer's speakers or headphones, or save it to a disc. You can also send it to another audio device using the sound card's output jack. Full-featured cards even include optical inputs and outputs for digital sound and special software for mixing sound.

Video Capture Board Video signals, such as those from television programs or movies, have to be converted into a format that computers understand. This is done with a **video capture board**, a special card that plugs into a computer. You can transfer video to the capture board from camcorders, VCRs, digital cameras, and other sources.

Video Editor After video and audio are saved to the computer's hard drive, you can combine them in new ways. You do this work with a video editor. A **video editor** is a program that allows you to cut and paste sound and video segments and change the order in which segments appear. Video editors also allow you to define the **frame rate**, or how many still images are displayed in one second, and specify the speed at which video should be displayed.

Multimedia File Formats

Objectives

- Identify video file formats.
- Summarize audio file formats and the platforms on which they run.
- Identify programs used to play multimedia programs on a computer or the Internet.

As You Read

Outline Information   Use an outline to help you understand multimedia tools as you read.

Video File Formats

Multimedia can combine text, audio, graphics, video, and animation. To do such complicated work, designers choose from a number of file formats, each suited for a specific task.

MPEG   MPEG is a family of formats developed by the Moving Picture Experts Group. Web sites and CD-based products commonly use MPEG to display video such as movie clips, animations, and recorded television broadcasts. MPEG files offer full-motion video; thus, they give a very realistic effect. In fact, the quality of a basic MPEG file is only slightly lower than that of a VCR recording.

Different versions of the basic MPEG format have been developed. MPEG-2 is used for regular television, DVDs, and high-definition television (HDTV). The MPEG-4 format is used for interactive graphics and interactive multimedia on the Internet.

QuickTime™   Designed by Apple Computer, QuickTime is the basic file format for showing animation and video on Macintosh computers. QuickTime videos also can be viewed on Windows computers, but a special player must first be installed. The QuickTime format is often used for high-quality movie trailers shown on Web sites. It is also used for the video feeds from Web sites that provide news and weather information.

AVI   Audio Video Interleave, or AVI, is another name for Microsoft Video for Windows format. Some AVI videos are not of the best quality, but they can be played on any Windows computer. Many businesses create their multimedia in AVI format to tap into the huge market of Windows users.

 Key Terms

- encoder
- synthesize

Audio File Formats

While formats like MPEG, QuickTime, and AVI capture both pictures and sound, other formats can be the best choice when sound quality is a priority.

MP3   MPEG audio layer 3 (MP3) files are very common today, thanks to the ease of downloading music from the Internet. The MP3 format takes a large audio file and makes it very small. It does this using regular compression methods and also by removing data from the music file that the human ear cannot hear. This results in a much smaller file, with little or no loss of sound quality.

WMA   WMA is the music format of Microsoft. It stands for Windows Media Audio®.

AU   AU, or audio, is the standard format for audio files for the UNIX operating system.

WAV   The waveform audio (WAV) format is built into the Microsoft Windows operating system. WAV files can be played on almost any computer system. WAV and WMA files can be converted into MP3 files using a hardware device or special software programs called **encoders** that convert the files from one format to another.

MIDI   Musical Instrument Digital Interface, or MIDI, is a standard that allows a computer to control a musical instrument. MIDI sounds are **synthesized**. This means that sounds imitative of musical instruments are generated by the computer when they are played; no actual recorded sound is stored in the file.

Figure 21.2.1 MP3 files are one type of common music format.

Name ▲	Size	Type
A Hard Rain's A-Gonna Fall.mp3	3,998 KB	MP3 Audio
Angel Eyes.mp3	2,684 KB	MP3 Audio
Avalon.mp3	4,012 KB	MP3 Audio
Dance Away.mp3	3,512 KB	MP3 Audio
Do The Strand.mp3	2,218 KB	MP3 Audio
In The Midnight Hour.mp3	2,948 KB	MP3 Audio
Jealous Guy.mp3	4,604 KB	MP3 Audio
Love Is The Drug.mp3	3,824 KB	MP3 Audio
More Than This.mp3	3,912 KB	MP3 Audio
Oh Yeah.mp3	4,318 KB	MP3 Audio
Over You.mp3	3,234 KB	MP3 Audio
Pyjamarama.mp3	2,696 KB	MP3 Audio
Same Old Scene.mp3	3,712 KB	MP3 Audio
Sign Of The Times.mp3	2,316 KB	MP3 Audio
Slave To Love.mp3	4,030 KB	MP3 Audio
These Foolish Things.mp3	4,522 KB	MP3 Audio
Virginia Plain.mp3	2,786 KB	MP3 Audio

Multimedia Players

You use a media player program to play multimedia content on your computer, media device, or on the Internet. This can be a stand-alone media player or a browser plug-in that you download for free from the Internet.

Windows Media, QuickTime, and RealPlayer™ Players

These three players are very popular for playing streaming audio and video—that is, content that is broadcast in a continuous feed from Web sites. They are also useful for playing content from some disc-based multimedia products.

All of these players can handle a wide variety of audio and video formats, although each one has its own unique format. You can use any of these players to listen to music broadcast by online radio stations, watch news and weather reports, check out movie trailers and music videos, and enjoy many other kinds of multimedia content. Many people have all three of these players installed on their computer.

Adobe Flash™ and Shockwave® Players Multimedia developers can use special file programs called Shockwave and Flash to create interactive multimedia content, such as animated games. These programs can accept user input, use high-quality audio and graphics, and are very small so they can be downloaded quickly from a Web site or disk. To view content created in these programs you need the Flash Player and the Shockwave Player, both of which are free.

Technology @ Work

Have you heard of elevator music—that soothing background music that plays in elevators, hallways, and offices? Well now you've probably seen little digital display screens in elevators as well—elevator multimedia!

Think About It!

Think about the kinds of multimedia productions that might be appropriate in public places. Which statements below are usable ideas?

➢ an online multimedia news service

➢ a dramatic short story

➢ illustrated readings of poems

➢ a pattern of colors and shapes "matching" music

➢ a series of violent action scenes

Spotlight on...

GEORGE HARRISON

❝ *It is the first complete album of synthesized music by a major rock star, and the antithesis [direct opposite] of the rigid pop sound that put the Beatles in the spotlight: 100 percent synthesizer, no beats, no songs.* **❞**

Greg Cahill
Reviewer, Metroactive Music

That quotation is from a tribute written after the death of George Harrison in 2002. Harrison is best known as a member of the Beatles, the music

sensation of the 1960s and 1970s. But Harrison was a musical innovator in his own right. His 1969 release *Electronic Sound*, for example, led to more experimentation by other musicians and, ultimately, to the rave generation of music.

Introducing Virtual Reality

Objectives

- Explain what virtual reality is and describe some methods of presenting it.
- Discuss computer and video games.

As You Read

Organize Information   Use a concept web to help you organize details about virtual reality as you read.

Key Terms

- augmented reality
- Cave Automatic Virtual Environment (CAVE)
- head-mounted display (HMD)
- virtual reality (VR)

Forms of Virtual Reality

The terms **virtual reality**, **VR**, or Virtual Environment, VE, are used interchangeably to describe three-dimensional computer-generated environments that you can explore by using special hardware and software. Such environments simulate spaces, such as the flight deck of an airliner or the inside of an underwater cave. The purpose of all VR environments is the same: to let users explore and also manipulate every aspect of the space, moving in any direction, just as if that space or the things within it were real.

Sophisticated hardware and software are needed to create large-scale, detailed VR environments. Users can explore such environments in several different ways.

HMD   A **head-mounted display**, or **HMD**, is usually a helmet or a set of goggles that wraps around the head, blocking out light. A tiny computer monitor is located in front of each eye. Using these two separate monitors gives the illusion of three dimensions. HMDs often have headphones to provide audio to the user.

In advanced HMDs, tiny sensors can tell when the user's head tilts in any direction. The image on the monitors then shifts accordingly, in order to create a convincing illusion of being part of the action, rather than a spectator of it. HMDs today are more likely to use liquid crystal display (LCD) monitors, which are less bulky and now have improved resolution.

Figure 21.3.1 A head-mounted display is a portable, relatively inexpensive way to experience virtual reality.

CAVE   The **Cave Automatic Virtual Environment**, or **CAVE**, is an expensive and advanced form of VR. Images of a virtual world are projected on the walls of a room. Visitors wear special goggles that create the illusion of three dimensions. The result is so realistic and so convincing that most "explorers" cannot tell where reality ends and virtual reality begins without reaching out and touching something.

In many CAVEs, users wear special gloves (called data gloves) or hold special wands, either of which can detect hand movements. These devices allow users to interact with objects in the virtual world, by opening doors, for example, or picking up the pieces in a virtual chess game.

Augmented Reality   An emerging category of virtual reality is called **augmented reality**. Cameras in mobile devices are used to layer virtual information onto real information. One example is a smart phone app for translation. When you point your phone at foreign language text, the English translation displays on the screen.

Connections

Science   Many educators believe virtual reality is having a major impact on science classrooms. Students can now "visit" and explore various ecosystems—take a stroll in a rain forest, for example, or shiver on the Alaskan tundra. Students studying anatomy can get a 3-D view of the respiratory system, the digestive system, and so on. Students opposed to dissecting animals can cut apart a virtual frog, making that experiment less distasteful.

Real-World Tech

Strolling Through Comet Tails   A new virtual reality deep vision display wall at Boston University will let students and professors stroll through comet tails, walk through the sun's weather, observe an earthquake, and study how air flows around airplanes. Two IBM supercomputers and 24 projectors fill a 15 × 8-foot screen with a high-resolution stereo image. The images change as the visitors move through the room.

What other phenomena could usefully be explored in a room like this?

Computer and Video Games

The first electronic games displayed only simple, two-dimensional images with limited sounds. Today, because of virtual reality, you can choose from hundreds of games with detailed graphics, lifelike characters, and realistic environments.

Computer Games Today's PCs, with their fast processors, powerful sound and graphics cards, and large displays, let you get the most from your games. Games for PCs usually come on compact discs.

Game Consoles A game console is a device that uses a television to display a game. You interact with the game by using one or more controls, which are connected to the console. The most popular consoles in recent years have been the Nintendo Wii®, Microsoft Xbox®, and Sony Playstation III®. While consoles used to be just dedicated to game playing, now some are used to stream videos from the computer to the TV.

Online Games Many PC games, such as World of Warcraft (WoW), are available on the Internet and allow multiple players to compete in real time while keeping score. To have the best gaming experience, you often need a high speed Internet connection, a PC with multimedia features, and a new model game console. Sometimes players need to pay a monthly fee to play, and all multiple player games require you to abide by a set of rules, called an End User Licensing Agreement (EULA). These rules prevent conflicts between players, and players who violate them are banned from playing.

Figure 21.3.2 Games such as Rock Band®, available on many gaming systems, let the players use controllers that are shaped like musical instruments.

Use the Vocabulary

Directions: *Match each vocabulary term in the left column with the correct definition in the right column.*

_____ **1.** multimedia

_____ **2.** video capture board

_____ **3.** video editor

_____ **4.** frame rate

_____ **5.** encoder

_____ **6.** synthesize

_____ **7.** virtual reality

_____ **8.** head-mounted display

_____ **9.** CAVE

_____ **10.** interactive multimedia

a. allows the user to make choices about what is displayed

b. very realistic form of virtual reality that is displayed in a room

c. hardware that lets a computer work with video data

d. software that changes a WAV file into MP3 format

e. using more than one medium to express information or ideas

f. program that lets users manipulate sound and video

g. realistic, but simulated, 3-D world

h. number of still images displayed in one second

i. helmet or goggles used to display a virtual reality environment

j. the process in which a computer generates sounds

Check Your Comprehension

Directions: *Determine the correct choice for each of the following.*

1. What kind of multimedia lets users make choices about the direction a program may take?

  a. graphic multimedia

  b. animated multimedia

  c. interactive multimedia

  d. technical multimedia

2. What hardware allows a computer to input, edit, and output audio?

  a. a sound card

  b. a video editor

  c. AU

  d. 3-D

3. Which audio file format does a computer use to produce synthesized sounds?

  a. CAVE

  b. CD-ROM

  c. MIDI

  d. AVI

4. Which of the following file formats allows you to view interactive multimedia games on your computer?

  a. MPEG-2

  b. Shockwave

  c. video capture board

  d. Net video

5. Where are the monitors in an HMD located?

  a. on the wall

  b. in a helmet or a set of goggles

  c. in a room

  d. online

6. Which of the following layers virtual information with real information?

  a. CAVE

  b. virtual 3-D

  c. World of Warcraft

  d. augmented reality

Think Critically

Directions: *Answer the following questions.*

1. For what purpose might a business want to hire a computer specialist who knows QuickTime and AVI?

2. What equipment and software would you need to develop your own multiplayer online game?

3. What two file formats are commonly used for interactive games found on Web sites?

4. Why is a virtual reality simulation used to train fighter pilots an example of interactive multimedia?

5. What is an example of how an electronic textbook might make use of VR technology?

Extend Your Knowledge

Directions: *Choose one of the following projects. Complete the exercise on a separate sheet of paper.*

A. In groups of four students, choose a topic you are studying in language arts, social studies, science, math, art, or music. Plan a two-minute multimedia presentation on that topic that includes at least one example of each of these media: audio, video, text, and graphics. Assign one medium to each member to complete. Use groupware or collaborative software to review one another's work. Then, use a video editor to combine the pieces into a smooth, logical sequence.

B. Electronic games can be a lot of fun, but some people believe that youngsters spend too much time playing them. Conduct online or library research to identify some specific objections that people have to these games. Then, debate the pros and cons of electronic games, using your research and your own gaming experiences as resources. Which argument was the most persuasive? Why?

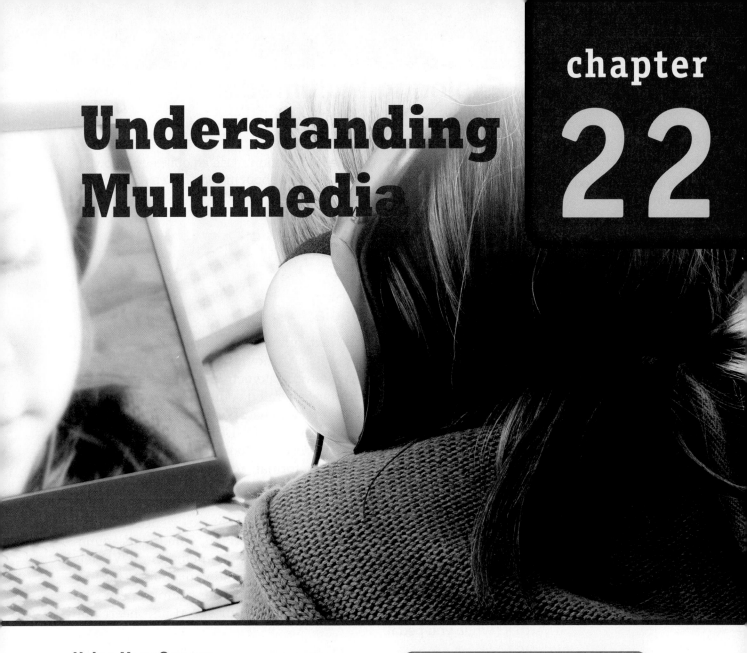

Understanding Multimedia

Using Your Senses   Human beings are sensory creatures—that is, we operate not just through what we know but through what we see and hear and feel. Reading about something brings us understanding, but our senses of sight, hearing, and touch deepen that understanding.

Multimedia—combinations of words, sounds, images, video, and animation—can provide that sensory input. Multimedia productions can take many forms, including an encyclopedia CD-ROM, a television commercial, a full-length movie, a short video within a presentation, or an animated introduction to a Web site.

Multimedia techniques are also used to create virtual worlds for us to explore, worlds that can test medical procedures, preview new buildings, and tap our imagination.

Chapter Outline

 Lesson 22–1

Exploring Multimedia

 Lesson 22–2

Developing Online Multimedia

 Lesson 22–3

Exploring Virtual Reality

Exploring Multimedia

Objectives

- Describe the forms of multimedia.
- Identify specialized tools used to produce multimedia.

As You Read

Outline Information Use an outline to help you organize details about multimedia as you read.

 Key Terms

- information kiosk
- pen-based graphics tablet

Forms of Multimedia

Multimedia combines text, graphics, video, animation, and sound. Television programs and movies are one-way multi-media—you are a passive viewer. Interactive multimedia lets you interact with the computer-generated content.

Both CDs and DVDs offer a rich opportunity for multimedia experiences. Watching a movie on DVD is no longer a passive activity because you can choose whether to view the film in letterbox or standard television format. You decide what language to hear it in. You can skip to or replay your favorite parts. Many DVD movies include interactive features such as games.

CDs and DVDs also offer educational experiences and adventures. A multimedia encyclopedia offers videos and animations that bring subjects to life. A mountain-climbing DVD lets you choose your view of the mountain and your route to the top. A DVD used with a stationary bike and your computer can give you 18 different "rides" and check your speed and heart rate while you pedal.

Information Kiosks An **information kiosk** uses an automated system to provide information or training. In effect, this is a PC-in-a-box, usually with a touch screen allowing input. At the Museum of Science in Boston, Massachusetts, for example, you can create artificial fish and watch how they behave when you release them into a simulated fish tank.

Games Computer games, home video game consoles, and arcade games offer dramatic examples of multimedia. They can simulate flying in an airplane, escaping from a dungeon, exploring outer space, or running a business.

Multimedia Development Tools

Certain tools are used to create and make use of the elements of a multimedia presentation including the following:

Pen-Based Graphics Tablets When creating still or animated graphics for use in a multimedia program, many artists find it easier to draw and sketch using a **pen-based graphics tablet** rather than a mouse. To use the tablet, you move a stylus, or electronic pen, across a sensitive touchpad, and your movements are recorded by your graphics software. The images can then be saved and edited.

A tablet PC combines the features of a graphics tablet with the functions of a personal computer. Users can create graphics as on a graphics tablet, but they can also use the tablet PC as if it were a regular laptop computer.

Microphones Audio can be recorded into a conventional recording device and then imported through a sound card. Audio can also be recorded directly into the computer using a microphone. Most sound cards have a special plug for a microphone. Using the software that comes with the sound card, you can assign a file name, click "record," and start speaking into the microphone. The sounds will be recorded to a new audio file.

Digital Cameras Digital cameras and camcorders are an easy way to aquire images and video for use in multimedia. These cameras don't require film. Images and video are stored in the camera and can then be transferred to the computer through a special cable or disk. Once on the computer, the pictures and video can be edited and used in presentations, movies, Web sites, and other applications.

Online Reporter Some online news services are affiliated with newspapers, magazines, or radio and television networks. Others exist only online. Online reporters need traditional reporting skills. But they must also be familiar with collecting news and photos in a variety of formats, including multimedia, and with presenting information and graphics effectively on a screen. The top candidates have good communication skills, work quickly and accurately, and understand how to use high-tech tools.

Figure 22.1.1 Microphones let you use a computer by talking. This student is using a PC and microphone to practice a foreign language.

Developing Online Multimedia

Objectives

- Describe how to access online multimedia.
- Explain the term "authoring" as it relates to multimedia.
- Discuss the use of authoring tools.

As You Read

Organize Information   Use a spider map to help you categorize information about online multimedia as you read.

Key Terms

- authoring tool
- rip
- stream

Accessing Online Multimedia

Multimedia presentations aren't limited to files stored on your computer's disks. With an Internet connection, you have access to an unlimited number of multimedia experiences. Many multimedia Web sites can **stream** video and audio data—that is, transmit it across a network without interruption. You don't have to wait until the entire file is downloaded to your computer for it to play. The file begins playing as soon as it starts to download from the Web site to your PC.

Net Radio   Internet radio is a method for listening to music, talk, and information over the Internet. Net radio doesn't actually use radio waves. Instead, audio programs are converted to digital format and streamed across the Internet. Streaming radio places a temporary audio file on your hard drive. This is what is heard—not the actual stream. The audio stream replenishes the file on the hard drive, continually updating the data as it plays.

Net Video   Like Net radio, Net video uses streaming, but it delivers pictures as well as sound. News sites use online video to deliver the latest news. Movie sites preview upcoming releases and offer short films and animations. In the business world, Net video is used for videoconferencing. In a videoconference, small cameras are used to allow people in different places to see and hear one another.

Ripping   If your computer has a CD-ROM drive, you can also copy music for your personal use from audio CDs onto your hard drive. This process is called **ripping**, and it requires special software. Once audio is ripped to the hard drive, it can be converted to MP3 format, which creates a much smaller file than a regular audio file.

Creating Multimedia

Authoring is the term used to describe the creation of multimedia programs. To combine audio, video, graphics, and text, you use software called **authoring tools**.

Using Authoring Tools Authoring tools let you choose which sounds, video clips, animations, text, and graphics will appear. You also control timing, transition effects, and volume. Authoring tools let you respond to questions such as the following:

- How long will an image appear on-screen?
- How will one clip fade into the next?
- How loud should a sound clip be?

Most authoring tools save data in a format for use only by the software developers and authorized users. You use a media player program to view the finished piece.

Choosing Authoring Tools The authoring tool you choose depends on how complex your project will be, the type of computer system you have, and how much time you have to spend learning the program. Some sophisticated authoring tools are for media professionals; others are simple enough that they can be used by anyone who wants to create their own multimedia CDs, videos, and presentations.

The professional version of QuickTime and some high-end desktop publishing programs include a small set of multimedia authoring tools. Adobe offers several popular products, like Director, Director/Student Edition, and Studio MX. Presentation programs such as Microsoft PowerPoint includes tools for inserting audio and video and for animating slides. Many PCs come with software such as Muvee Reveal by Muvee Technologies for creating movies that include video, images, and sound.

Technology @ School

Think about the ways your school could inform the public about school activities. Sequence each medium from 1 (lowest) to 5 (highest) to show which you think would be most effective.

➤ CD

➤ video for cable television

➤ information kiosk

➤ local newspaper article

➤ Web page

Figure 22.2.1 Use a program such as Muvee Reveal to create your own multimedia projects.

Exploring Virtual Reality

Objectives

- Explain what is meant by immersive virtual reality.
- Identify virtual reality equipment and language.
- Discuss real-world uses of virtual reality.

As You Read

Organize Information Use a concept web to help you understand the practical applications of virtual reality as you read.

🗝 Key Terms

- data glove
- simulations

The Technology of Virtual Reality

Virtual reality works by making a computer-generated scene feel as it would in the real world. It does this by using three-dimensional, or 3-D, graphics, color, texture, and sound.

In some cases, VR worlds are displayed on regular computer screens. A 3-D video game is one example. Another example is a flight simulator, which is valuable in training pilots.

Virtual reality's main potential, however, lies in immersive technologies that surround a viewer with the VR world. With immersive VR, the user feels part of the virtual environment. For example, gaming consoles such as Microsoft's Kinnect for Xbox let the player use his or her body as the controller; some museum exhibits project moving images on walls around the viewer; and arcade games let you steer a race car or ski down a mountain.

VR Gadgets In addition to a head mounted display, virtual reality often uses a device called a **data glove**. A data glove is a basic glove equipped with sensors that measure movements of the hand and fingers. One use of the data glove is to operate equipment from a distance.

VR Language To create virtual worlds on the Internet, programmers use a language called X3D. X3D allows programmers to describe objects that appear in the virtual world, such as shapes, buildings, landscapes, or characters.

Figure 22.3.1 Data gloves are an important tool in immersive virtual reality.

Practical Applications of Virtual Reality

Virtual reality has become very useful for **simulations**. Simulations are virtual reality programs that mimic a specific place, job, or function. Virtual reality is used in many design and architectural businesses. It is also used in the military to train fighter pilots and combat soldiers without the risks of live training.

In medicine, virtual reality is used to simulate complex surgery for training surgeons without using actual patients.

Easing Pain   At the University of Washington's Harborview Burn Center, virtual reality is being used to help severe burn victims deal with their pain. Patients are immersed in a virtual reality environment. There, they imagine that they are flying through icy canyons and cold waterfalls, building snowmen, and throwing snowballs. By focusing on things that are pleasant and cold, patients can focus less on their pain.

Overcoming Fear   A study by Walter Reed Army Hospital and Emory University School of Medicine showed that patients placed in virtual reality flight simulators overcame their fear of flying as successfully as patients treated using other techniques. But the VR method offers additional benefits: It is cheaper and easier than taking the patients on real airplane flights.

Technology @ Work

VR applications can help in many fields. CAD software, for example, is used by architects and building supply stores to show customers how a kitchen might look with new cabinets.

Think About It!

Think about which professions might benefit from using virtual 3-D worlds. Which professions listed below do you think would find this technology useful?

➤ museum exhibit organizer

➤ landscape designer

➤ art teacher

➤ flower arranger

➤ construction worker

Real-World Tech

Exploring Virtual Therapy   For many years, psychology resisted technology. On-line therapy seemed to lack the necessary closeness between patient and therapist. At the 2002 meeting of the American Psychological Association, however, therapists saw virtual reality equipment that can help people overcome fears or generate a group of "virtual" people with whom a patient can interact.

What practical applications of virtual reality at middle schools can you think of?

Today, people can use their computers to get help for all kinds of problems, including those that are personal, psychological, financial, and medical.

Think About It!

Think about how people might sensibly and safely use their computers to seek help. Which of the strategies listed below do you think will lead to useful advice?

> searching for factual information on the Web

> joining an online support group

> e-mailing friends about the problem

> finding an online advisor

> describing the problem on a personal Web site

Saving Lives   Heart surgeons often need to replace portions of a heart and its valves with artificial pieces. Designing replacement valves is very tricky, because even minor flaws can cause major problems.

Scientists at the University of Sheffield in England have developed a way to use virtual reality to test new heart valves before they are manufactured, using a computer to simulate how blood will flow through them. This software lets doctors predict whether or not the valve will work properly after it is in the body.

Virtual reality is also used to train doctors to perform surgery. Software can simulate open heart surgery, for instance, allowing doctors to practice without the risk of harming a patient. Someday, doctors using virtual reality interfaces may be able to operate on actual patients halfway around the world!

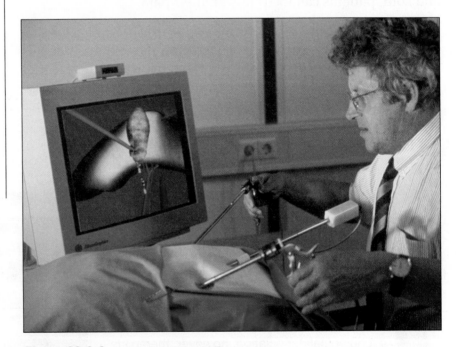

Figure 22.3.2 Using specialized VR systems, doctors can master surgical procedures without practicing on a real patient.

Use the Vocabulary

Directions: *Match each vocabulary term in the left column with the correct definition in the right column.*

_____ **1.** information kiosk
_____ **2.** pen-based graphics tablet
_____ **3.** stream
_____ **4.** rip
_____ **5.** simulation
_____ **6.** authoring tool
_____ **7.** data glove

a. copy music from an audio CD to a computer hard drive

b. computer program that mimics a specific place, job, or function

c. transmit audio or video data across the Internet without interruption

d. equipment with sensors that measure hand movements

e. automated system used for information or training

f. equipment that lets users draw images for animation and multimedia

g. software that helps in the production of multimedia

Check Your Comprehension

Directions: *Determine the correct choice for each of the following.*

1. Which input device is usually used on an information kiosk?
   a. DVD
   b. data glove
   c. keyboard
   d. touch screen

2. Which device allows you to input your voice directly into a computer?
   a. digital camera
   b. microphone
   c. CD-ROM drive
   d. media player

3. What kind of Internet video starts playing as soon as you start to download it?
   a. graphic video
   b. virtual video
   c. streaming video
   d. ripping video

4. Which of the following is NOT accomplished using authoring tools?
   a. fading one video clip into the next
   b. setting the length of time an image will display on-screen
   c. setting the price of a multimedia program
   d. setting the volume for an audio clip

5. Which of the following CANNOT be produced using an authoring tool?
   a. Web page
   b. head-mounted display
   c. multimedia presentation
   d. CD-ROM

6. Which VR application is sometimes used in pain-control therapy?
   a. simulations
   b. X3D
   c. CAD
   d. Net video

Think Critically

Directions: *Answer the following questions.*

1. What special effects might you create for a multimedia presentation if you use a stylus and a digital camera?

2. What are three ways your computer can offer you interactive multimedia experiences?

3. Why might a business want to hire someone who is skilled in using authoring tools?

4. What piece of VR equipment might be useful in training surgeons? Why?

5. How might landscapers use VR technology to plan their work and attract customers?

Extend Your Knowledge

Directions: *Choose one of the following projects. Complete the exercise on a separate sheet of paper.*

A. Digital video cameras have become popular consumer items. Also popular are easy-to-use home-movie editing programs like iMovie® for Macintosh computers. Conduct research in the library, at a store, or online to find several cameras in the same price range, and compare their features. Repeat this process with several home-video editing programs. Create a chart in which to record your findings. Then, conclude which camera and which editing program you would recommend.

B. In small groups, visit a graphic arts company and ask for a demonstration of one of the multimedia tools described in this chapter. Ask for details about how the tool works. Also ask to see some applications of the tool. Share your findings with the class.

DIRECTIONS: *You will select the appropriate program for creating a multimedia monogram. You will then design a monogram for yourself using graphics and text objects. Finally, you will animate the monogram and enhance it with sound. Microsoft Office 2010 procedures required for this activity can be found in Appendix A.*

1. Using a dictionary, look up the word *monogram*, and then sketch your own monogram on paper.

2. As a class, discuss the types of programs you could use to design a multimedia monogram. For example, you might consider a presentation program, an html editor, or a video editing program. Select the program you will use for this activity.

3. Start the program and save a new file as **MM-1_Monogram_*xx*** in the location where your teacher instructs you to store the files for this activity. Replace the initials *xx* with your own name or initials, as instructed by your teacher.

4. Create your monogram by inserting shapes, images, and/or text objects. A sample monogram created using WordArt and a shape in PowerPoint is shown in Illustration A.

5. Use the program's animation tools to animate the monogram. You might choose to animate the entire monogram as a group, or animate the individual parts of the monogram. For example, you might have each letter fly in separately, or have the entire monogram shrink and grow.

6. Insert sound to play during the animation. Be sure to check that you have permission to use sound and/or music clips. Set options to control the way the sound plays and displays.

7. Apply color to the background or canvas.

8. Preview the multimedia monogram. Make any adjustments necessary so that all transitions and animations are smooth and effective.

9. Show your monogram to the class, and respectfully watch your classmates' monograms.

10. Close the program, saving all changes, and exit.

11. As a class, discuss the multimedia components you used, and why they were effective. Discuss why multimedia is useful for some purposes but not for others.

Illustration A

DIRECTIONS: *You will use the United States Department of Agriculture Web site to learn about the MyPyramid system of nutrition. You will then use the information to create a multimedia educational presentation for children ages 9 to 13, explaining the importance of eating a healthy balance of foods every day. Microsoft Office 2010 procedures required for this activity can be found in Appendix A.*

1. With your teacher's permission, log on to the Internet and go to the Web address www.MyPyramid.gov.

   a. Read about recommendations for daily nutrition for children ages 9 to 13. Note the meaning of the colored stripes used in the pyramid, the different food groups, and the amounts that someone 9 to 13 should eat each day. Record the information that will be useful for your presentation on paper or in a word-processing file.

   b. Visit the site's News & Media section and, with your teacher's permission, download the JPG version of the full-color MyPyramid graphic. Save it as **MyPyramid.jpg** in the location where your teacher instructs you to save files for this activity.

2. Start your presentation program. Create a new presentation, and save it as **MM-2_ MyPyramid_xx** in the location where your teacher instructs you to store files for this activity.

3. Apply a theme or design to your presentation.

4. Insert a footer on all slides that displays your name and today's date.

5. On the slide 1 title slide, type the title **Nutrition and You**. In the subtitle placeholder, type your full name.

6. Also on slide 1, use the graphics tools to create a logo for your presentation. Use at least two different shapes that you combine using tools such as layering and grouping. Apply formatting such as fills, borders, and effects to the shapes.

7. Develop a presentation to show how someone age 9 to 13 can use MyPyramid guidelines to choose healthy, delicious foods.

   a. Insert slides with the following slide titles: **What Is MyPyramid?**; **Grains**; **Vegetables**; **Types of Vegetables**; **Fruits**; **Milk**; **Meat and Beans**; **Oils**; **Discretionary Calories**; and **Summary**.

   b. On each slide, enter content that explains and illustrates the title. Use the information from your research, including explanations of the colors and the daily eating guidelines.

   c. Insert the MyPyramid graphic on at least three slides, and other appropriate images on at least two slides.

   d. On the Types of Vegetables slide, use a flowchart or other diagram to list types of vegetables and examples of each. Refer to Illustration B to see a sample slide.

   e. Insert an appropriate clip art video on the title slide, such as an animated .gif of fruit or vegetables.

   f. Insert sound, such as narration, or clip art audio that plays throughout.

8. When you have finished entering the slide content, proofread each slide carefully, checking for consistency in sentence structure, spelling, and grammar, and correct any errors you find.

9. View the slide show and make any changes that you think will improve the presentation value, or make the presentation more effective. For example, split crowded slides into two slides, change the theme colors and/or fonts, or modify the slide background.

10. Add transitions and animations, and view the presentation again.

11. Set up the slide show as a self-running presentation for a kiosk or computer.

12. With your teacher's permission, print handouts with three slides per page for the class.

13. Ask your classmates to view the presentation, or make it available to younger students.

14. Close the presentation, saving all changes, and exit the presentation program.

15. As a class, discuss why healthy eating is important for maintaining energy. Discuss other ways you could encourage healthy eating habits among your peers.

Illustration B

DIRECTIONS: *You will use text, images, audio, and video to create a multimedia slide show promoting tourism in the state where you live. Microsoft Office 2010 procedures required for this activity can be found in Appendix A.*

1. Open the .pdf file **MM-3_MyState**, which is located on the student CD. With your teacher's permission, print the Data Record Sheet. The sheet includes a chart to help you record information for your tourism presentation. Close the file, and exit your pdf reader program.

2. Use the Internet (with your teacher's permission), library resources, or information obtained from your state's division of travel and tourism or convention and visitor's bureau to find information about your state's climate, special events, outdoor recreation, and tourist attractions.

3. To use the Internet, open a Web browser and navigate to a search engine. Search for sites by typing the keywords **[your state] tourist information**. You might also try a Boolean search such as **[your state] AND tourism**.

4. Evaluate each site you visit for accuracy and validity.

5. When you find a credible Web site with relevant information, bookmark the site, or with your teacher's permission, print the desired pages.

6. Use your Data Record Sheet to record relevant information you find.

7. If you locate any images or photographs related to tourism in your state, identify whether or not they are available for use by students free of charge. If they are, download them and save them as files so you can use them in your presentation.

8. Record your source citation information on a separate sheet of paper, including the sites from which you download images.

9. When you have finished your research, exit the Web browser.

10. Start your presentation program. Create a new presentation, and save it as **MM-3_ Tourism_xx** in the location where your teacher tells you to store the files for this lesson.

11. Apply a theme or design to the presentation.

12. On the title slide, type your state name as the title. For the subtitle, enter a catchy slogan. Insert a footer on this slide only that reads: **Prepared by [your name]**, along with the current date.

13. Add a slide using a layout with placeholders for a title, bulleted list, and graphics.

14. Type **Climate** as the title of the slide.

15. In the bulleted list, type information about the climate of your state.

16. Insert a related image you downloaded from the Internet, or use an appropriate clip art image. Position and size the image to enhance the slide.

17. At the bottom of the slide, insert a text box where you credit the source of the image, if necessary. Be sure to include the name of the site, its URL, and the date you visited the site.

18. Repeat this process to create a slide for Special Events, Outdoor Recreation, and Tourist Attractions. Use information from your Data Record Sheet, and insert pictures and other images to illustrate the slides.

19. Insert a new slide 2 that has the title **Contents** and a bulleted list of all the slide titles in order. Insert hyperlinks from each bullet to the corresponding slide.

20. At the end of the presentation, add a slide that identifies the ideal times of year to visit your state. Enter the slogan you used on the opening slide as the slide title.

21. Insert a video clip on the last slide that illustrates tourism in your state. You may use a video from clip art, or a free Internet clip that you download or link to. Or, with your teacher's permission, you may create your own video to insert.

22. Insert an audio clip in the presentation. You may insert music that plays during the entire presentation, or an audio clip that plays when a certain slide is displayed. Or, with your teacher's permission, you may record an appropriate audio clip to insert.

23. In the lower-right corner of all but the title slide, insert a text box, type **Home**, and format it with a hyperlink to display the title slide.

24. When you have finished entering the slide content, proofread each slide carefully. Check the spelling and grammar in the presentation. Revise and edit your work as necessary.

25. Add transitions and animations to the presentation.

26. Preview the presentation, and make any final modifications. Rehearse the presentation and then show it to the class.

27. Close the presentation, saving all changes, and exit your presentation program.

28. As a class, compare and contrast a multimedia presentation with a printed travel brochure.

DIRECTIONS: *You will create a multimedia presentation on an environmental problem. You will conduct research to identify specific actions that affect the environment in both positive and negative ways. You will present your findings in a presentation enhanced with audio and animation effects. Microsoft Office 2010 procedures required for this activity can be found in Appendix A.*

1. Open the .pdf file **MM-4_Effects**, which is located on the student CD. With your teacher's permission, print the Data Record Sheet. The sheet includes diagrams to help you identify cause and effect. Close the file, and exit your pdf reader program.

2. Use the Internet (with your teacher's permission), library resources, or a textbook to search for information on an environmental problem, such as water pollution or ozone depletion.

3. To use the Internet, open a Web browser and navigate to a search engine. For the search, type the environmental problem plus the word **causes** as the keywords. For example, you might type **water pollution causes** as your keywords. Or, use Boolean search strategies. For example, you might search for **"water pollution" AND causes**.

4. Evaluate each site you visit for accuracy and validity.

5. When you find a credible Web site with relevant information, bookmark the site, or with your teacher's permission, print the desired pages.

6. In the first diagram on the Data Record Sheet, record three causes of the environmental problem you selected in the Causes list, and record the effect(s) the causes have in the Effect circle.

7. Then, conduct research to identify three things that people can do to reduce the environmental problem you chose. Type **"ways to protect the environment"** as your keywords, making sure that you include the quotation marks. Look for sites that list specific actions people can take to reduce the problem.

8. In the Causes list in the second diagram on the Data Record Sheet, record three things people can do to reduce the environmental problem, and the effect(s) of the action in the Effect circle.

9. Record your source citation information on a separate sheet of paper.

10. When you have finished your research, exit the Web browser.

11. Start your presentation program. Create a new presentation, and save it as **MM-4_Environment_xx** in the location where your teacher instructs you to store the files for this activity.

12. Apply a theme or design to the presentation.

13. On the title slide, type **People and the Environment** as the title, and then type **By** followed by your own name as the subtitle. Insert a footer with today's date and your name on all slides.

14. Insert a slide using a title only slide layout.

15. Type the title **Main Idea**.

16. Draw a text box in the space below the title, and type a sentence that states the main idea of your presentation. Use your research and the information you wrote on your Data Record Sheet to determine the main idea.

17. Insert a video clip on the slide that illustrates the main idea. You may use a video from clip art, or a free clip downloaded from the Internet. Or, with your teacher's permission, you may create your own video to insert.

18. Insert another slide using a title only slide layout, and type the environmental problem you researched as the title.

19. In the space below the title, use the program's pre-drawn diagrams or its drawing tools to create a cause-and-effect diagram like the one on your Data Record Sheet.

20. Type the causes and the effect(s) in your diagram.

21. Duplicate this slide and edit the text to match the causes and effect(s) you listed in the second diagram on your Data Record Sheet.

22. When you have finished entering the slide content, proofread each slide carefully. Check the spelling and grammar in the presentation. Revise and edit your work as necessary.

23. Insert an audio clip in the presentation. You may insert music that plays during the entire presentation, or an audio clip that plays when a certain slide is displayed. Or, with your teacher's permission, you may record an appropriate audio clip to insert.

24. Add transitions and animations to the presentation. For example, animate the cause-and-effect diagrams.

25. Preview the presentation and make any final modifications.
26. Rehearse the presentation, and then deliver it to your class.
27. Close the presentation, saving all changes, and exit your presentation program.

28. As a class, discuss your research findings. Create a class list of things people do that harm the environment and things people can do to protect it. Then, consider how your slide presentation is similar and different from an informative essay. What are the benefits and drawbacks of presenting information in a multimedia presentation rather than in an essay?

Illustration C

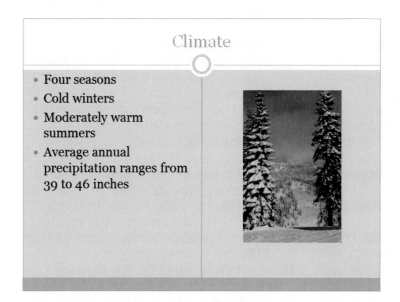

Climate

- Four seasons
- Cold winters
- Moderately warm summers
- Average annual precipitation ranges from 39 to 46 inches

DIRECTIONS: *You will write an article on how to use technology to better prepare for college and career pursuits, develop new skills, and stay informed about the changing world around you. You will publish the article in html format and then enhance it with a graphic, a video, and an audio clip. Microsoft Office 2010 procedures required for this activity can be found in Appendix A.*

Multimedia Activities

1. Open the .pdf file **MM-5_TechOutline**, which is located on the student CD. With your teacher's permission, print the Data Record Sheet. The sheet includes an outline to help you prepare your article. Close the file, and exit your pdf reader program.

2. Use the Internet (with your teacher's permission), library resources, or information from your school's guidance counselor or career center to research the importance of technology to college and career readiness, lifelong learning, and daily living.

3. To use the Internet, open a Web browser and navigate to a search engine. Search for sites by typing keywords or phrases such as **using technology to prepare for college**. You might also try a Boolean search such as **technology AND "lifelong learning"**.

4. Evaluate each site you visit for accuracy and validity.

5. When you find a credible Web site with relevant information, bookmark it, or with your teacher's permission, print the desired pages.

6. Use your Data Record Sheet to record relevant information you find. Support each point in the outline with facts and details.

7. If you locate any images or photographs related to your research, identify whether they are available for use by students free of charge. If they are, download them and save them for use in your report.

8. Record your source citation information on a separate sheet of paper, including the sites from which you download images.

9. When you have finished your research, exit the Web browser.

10. Start your word-processing program. Create a new document, and save it as **MM-5_Technology_xx** in the location where your teacher instructs you to store the files for this activity.

11. Insert the title of the article, along with your name and the current date. Using the outline on your Data Record Sheet, write your article.

12. When finished, check the spelling and grammar and proofread it carefully.

13. With your teacher's permission, print the document.

14. Exchange your printed document with a classmate. Proofread your classmate's article, correcting any errors on the printed page, and then return the printout to your classmate.

15. Review the corrections and comments that your classmate made on your article, and incorporate them into your document file.

16. When you have finalized the document, save it in html format. Name the file **MM-5_Technology_Web_xx**. Assign an appropriate page title.

17. Close the file, and then open it in your html or WYSIWYG editor. (Refer to Chapters 29 and 30 for more information.)

18. Adjust the format of the title, and insert subheadings to look good on a Web page.

19. Insert at least one image file or photograph on the page.

20. If your editor supports video, insert a video file related to the article. Or, insert an automated .gif that illustrates the article's topic.

21. Insert an audio file that reflects the tone and mood of your article.

22. For both the audio and video, set properties so viewers can turn them off if they choose.

23. Preview the page and make adjustments to improve its display.

24. View the page in your Web browser, and then close it and exit your Web browser.

25. Close your html file, saving all changes, and exit your html or WYSIWYG editor.

Communications and Networks

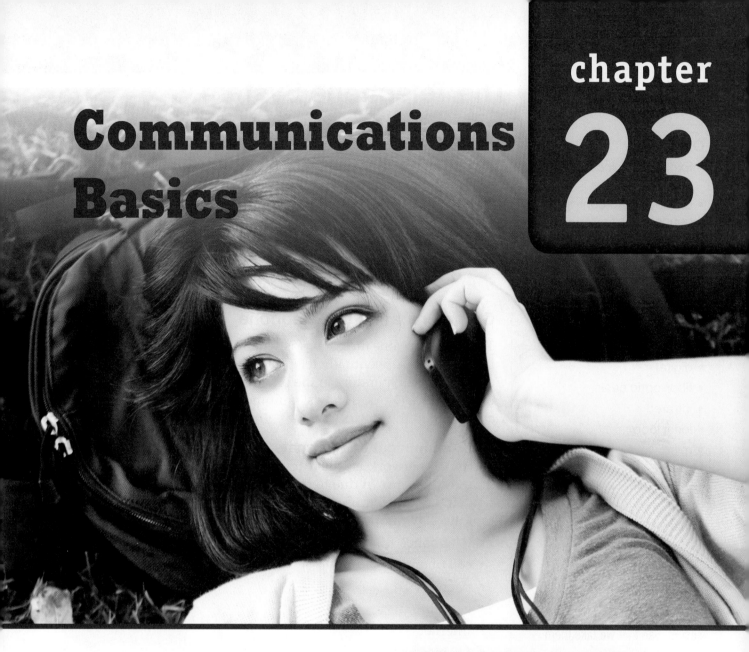

Communications Basics

chapter 23

Why Are Telcommunications Valuable?

Telecommunications is a word that means "messages exchanged over distances." The most common telecommunications device is the telephone. Think of how important the telephone is to you. Wired and wireless technology makes it possible to have conversations, send text messages, pictures, and even video.

Another important telecommunications device is your computer. You connect to the Internet through a phone or cable line, and you send and receive e-mail messages, use instant messaging, surf the Web, and even talk face-to-face.

These ways of sending and receiving messages and information are valuable to individuals, businesses, communities, and schools. All these forms of communication rely on networks.

Chapter Outline

 Lesson 23–1

The Telephone System

 Lesson 23–2

Using Telephone Communications

 Lesson 23–3

Exploring High-Speed Telecommunications

Communications Basics • 321

The Telephone System

Objectives

- Explain how local and long-distance telephone calls are made.
- Compare and contrast analog and digital connections.
- Identify the technologies that handle telephone calls.

As You Read

Organize Information   Use a spider map to help you organize ways in which the telephone system operates as you read.

🔑 Key Terms

- analog
- digital
- fiber-optic cable
- infrared
- local loop
- microwave
- telecommunications
- twisted pair

Figure 23.1.1 Today, telephones are so common and easy to use that we take them for granted.

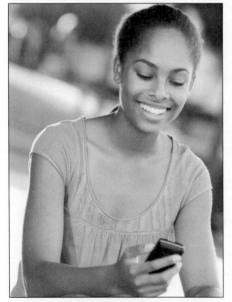

Communicating by Telephone

The first telephone message was sent in 1876 over a line connecting two rooms. Eventually telephone cables were connected to a central office. Operators in the office could connect calls to anyone on the network. Today's equipment can connect telephones anywhere in the world.

Telecommunications Formats   Sending information over a telephone network is called **telecommunications**. Telecommunications has grown due to the demand for instant communication. Today, people use many forms of telecommunications to rapidly relay information:

- telephones
- cell phones
- pagers
- e-mail
- Internet
- fax machines

Making Telephone Calls

In the past, only a few companies provided telephone services in the United States. Today, people can choose from among many phone companies that offer both local and long distance service.

Public Switched Telephone Network   Many phone calls are made through the Public Switched Telephone Network (PSTN). This network is built from copper wires and other cables and forms a circuit between the caller's telephone and another telephone.

Local Calls For local calls, your phone company provides directly wired services between the homes and businesses that belong to the local network. Within your neighborhood, telephones connect to a common network for telephone service. This common network, called the **local loop**, connects to the phone company's central office. Much of the local loop is an **analog** system. An analog system sends electrical signals that carry voice and other sounds.

Long-Distance Calls Outside the local loop, the long-distance telephone system today is mostly digital. **Digital** connections use computer code and can carry voice, data, and video on a single line. When you dial a long-distance number, computers figure out how to complete your call. To connect analog and digital networks, special equipment changes analog signals into digital signals.

Contrasting Analog and Digital Communications People often confuse the terms "analog" and "digital" when they are talking about communications or computers. The difference is important but easy to understand. In analog communications, sounds (such as a person's voice or music) start as waves or vibrations in the air. The vibrating air varies in frequency or pitch (how high or deep the sound is) and strength or loudness. A small microphone in the telephone converts the sound waves into varying patterns of electrical signals or radio waves. The pattern of electrical signals or radio waves is similar to the pattern of the sound waves. These signals are converted back into sound waves by a small loudspeaker in the receiver. In digital communications, sounds are converted into binary data (a series of 1s and 0s) at the caller's end. The stream of 1s and 0s is transmitted without any variation in the pattern of electrical or radio waves. The receiver converts the binary data back into sound waves.

Did You Know ?

Americans make almost one billion telephone calls per day. How does our system carry so many calls?

Engineers have developed a technology called multiplexing. This technology allows 24 calls at a time on a local wire and almost 50,000 at a time on a long-distance wire.

Parts of a Telephone Number

1	214	555	7804
Long Distance	**Area Code**	**Prefix**	**Line Number**
Finds the country code (1 is the code for the United States.)	Finds a geographic area (214 is the code for Dallas, Texas.)	Finds a local-rate area	Finds a specific phone line

Home appliances are among the upcoming targets of wireless communication. Appliances with *picoradios*—very small, very low-power radios built into the appliance—can communicate with one another.

Think About It!

If customers are going to be interested in them, picoradios must be useful. Which item(s) listed below would be *unlikely* to be useful?

➤ a bedroom clock that can start a coffeemaker

➤ a sensor that can close a refrigerator door

➤ a faucet that can turn on a light

The Wired—and the Wireless—World

Wires connect the phone jack in your wall to an interface box outside. Outside wires may be above or below ground. Wires also connect your local loop with distant places.

Twisted Pair   At first, the entire telephone system depended on twisted pair technology. **Twisted pair** refers to a pair of copper wires that are twisted together to reduce interference, or outside noise. In the United States today, most homes and business buildings still have twisted pair wiring.

Fiber-Optic Cables   **Fiber-optic cables** are strands of fiberglass that transmit digital data by pulses of light. These cables can carry large quantities of information. They work faster and more efficiently than copper wires. As they get lower in price, fiber optic cables will eventually replace copper

Wireless   Wireless communication frees users from traditional telephone lines. Messages are sent on radio or infrared signals. Cell phones use radio signals. **Infrared** signals are light waves that cannot be seen by the human eye. Remote control devices for TVs, VCRs, and DVD players use infrared signals.

Before fiber-optic cables, high-frequency radio waves called **microwave** signals were used to relay long-distance telecommunications. Microwaves are broadcast from repeater tower to repeater tower in a straight line.

Satellites orbiting Earth also transfer voice and data. Satellites provide an efficient means to handle large amounts of phone calls and data.

Spotlight on...

CORNING, INC.

A 161-year-old company that made its name making glass casserole dishes is at the forefront of telecommunications technology. In 1970, a team of Corning scientists developed a technology that would revolutionize telecommunications—though its impact wouldn't be felt until three decades later. Scientists Peter Schultz, Donald Keck, and Robert Maurer spun optical glass into thin strands that could transmit electrical impulses and light. The Corning Glass researchers are credited with making optical fi-

ber—capable of carrying 65,000 times more information than traditional copper wire—a practical reality. Now more than 90% of the U.S. long distance traffic is carried by optical fiber, almost all of it using the design of Schultz, Keck, and Maurer.

Exploring Telephone and High-Speed Telecommunications

Objectives

- Sequence the steps in a modem transmission.
- Explain how fax machines operate.
- Summarize how modems and fax machines have affected the ways people communicate.

As You Read

Compare and Contrast Use a Venn diagram to help you compare and contrast modems and fax machines as you read.

Using Modems

Back in the early 1990s, when the Internet was still "new," most people used phone lines to connect to it. Your computer is a digital device. The local loop that connects you to the telephone system, however, is analog. A device called a **modem** makes it possible for your computer and telephone lines to communicate, and for your computer and TV cables to communicate.

The word *modem* actually names the work the device does: *modulation* and *demodulation*. Through modulation, the modem changes the digital signal of the computer to the analog sounds used by telephones. Then, the data—in the form of pictures, audio, or video—can travel over the telephone wires. When the data gets to its destination, the receiving modem changes the analog signals back to digital. This process is called demodulation. The early dial-up modems were usually internal, housed inside the computer. Today's modems for use with DSL and cable (discussed later) are usually external.

Key Terms

- bits per second (bps)
- demodulation
- modem
- modulation

Figure 23.2.1 A 56K modem, like the one show here, is a hardware device that enables a PC to send and receive data through a standard telephone line.

The Arts Can a fax machine create art? Artist and lecturer Margaret Turner of Australia thinks so.

To demonstrate a connection between human emotions and computers, Margaret borrowed handkerchiefs—plain and fancy, white and patterned. The handkerchief represented a human element becoming art through an electronic medium.

She scanned the handkerchiefs into a computer and manipulated the images. Then, she faxed the resulting images to a gallery for a special exhibit called "Electric Hankie."

Drawbacks of Dial-Up Today only 10% of U.S. households connect to the computer using the local phone line loop, but dial-up service is still a worthwhile backup. One problem with using dial-up was that you could not be on your computer and use your telephone simultaneously, so the computer modem required a dedicated phone line. Another larger drawback was slow speed.

Modem speed is measured in **bits per second**, or **bps**, which is the amount of data that can be sent in one second. Dial-up modems can only transmit 56,600 bps, which has been surpassed by newer, speedier technologies.

Figure 23.2.2 Fax machines can send and receive documents using standard telephone lines.

Sending Faxes

While dial-up is usually a thing of the past, there is one machine that still uses telephone lines to send printed messages or visual images. A facsimile machine, or fax machine, is a device that allows you to send pages of information to a fax machine anywhere in the world. Fax machines can send hand-written documents, printed text, pictures, blueprints, or anything else on a page. Yet, even these machines are largely being replaced by e-mail, by which you can send attachments over the Internet.

How Fax Machines Work As a document enters a fax machine, a sensor scans it. The data becomes a digital signal. An internal modem in the fax machine (or in an All-in-One printer with fax capability) changes the digital signal to an analog signal. The receiving fax machine accepts the analog signal, changes it back to digital, and prints a copy of the original document.

Technology @ Work

Many stores now use special scanners at the checkout counters. These scanners read the Universal Product Code on a package and record the product and price on the sales receipt.

Think About It!

Think about the advantages store scanners offer. Which item(s) listed below would be an advantage, and which would not?

▷ Price changes can be entered in a central computer rather than stickered on a package.

▷ The computer prevents clerks from entering mistakes.

▷ The computer tracks the number of products sold.

▷ The computer cuts down on the need for employees.

Figure 23.2.3 In businesses, fax machines are still important for transmitting important documents, particularly those that have or require personal signatures.

Exploring High-Speed Telecommunications

Objectives

- Explain the importance of bandwidth.
- Identify alternatives to analog systems.
- Predict advances in telecommunications.

As You Read

Organize Information Use a chart to help you identify various new technologies as you read.

🔑 Key Terms

- bandwidth
- broadband
- Voice over Internet Protocol (VoIP)

Introducing Bandwidth

People always want faster, better, and less expensive telecommunications choices. Twisted pair copper wiring in many homes and businesses in the United States at first made it hard to increase bandwidth. Then telephone, cable, and satellite television companies began to compete in offering higher speed communications. Now, more than eight out of ten homes and businesses are using high-speed connections for Internet access.

Understanding Bandwidth **Bandwidth** is the amount of data that can be sent through a modem or network connection. The more bandwidth, the faster the connection. It is usually measured in bits per second (bps) or in Megabits per second (Mbps). The more bandwidth, the more information can be transferred in a given amount of time.

Imagine several people on different computers connecting to the Internet to visit Web pages, participate in video chats, or send e-mail. These users need a lot of bandwidth. That's why there is always a race to find a technology that offers services that transmit data faster. Currently the fastest technology is broadband transmission.

Working with Broadband Transmission

Broadband is the general term for all high-speed digital connections that transmit at least 1.5 megabits per second (Mbps), though current broadband services transmit between 10 and 30 Mbps. Several broadband technologies are available, and more are always on the drawing board. This high transmission speed is required for videoconferencing, video-on-demand, digital television services, and high-speed Internet connectivity in general.

DSL Digital Subscriber Line, or DSL, uses the same copper wires telephones use, but it transmits data in digital form rather than analog. Voice calls and DSL can exist simultaneously on copper lines, because each services has its own frequency band. Unlike the old dial-up, DSL allows for very fast connections to the Internet and features an "always-on" connection. DSL service also requires a modem, which translates the computer's digital signals into voltage sent across phone lines to a central hub. There is one drawback to DSL: A user must be within a few miles of a local telephone switching station for a connection to be made.

Different companies offer DSL at different levels of service and price. For instance, asymmetric DSL (ADSL) allows download speeds of up to 1.5 Mbps and upload speeds of 128 kilobits per second (Kbps). This means you can receive data (download) faster than you can send it (upload) with ADSL. Subscribers to a Symmetric Digital Subscriber Line (SDSL) can send data at the same speed at which they receive it. These are used usually by businesses that need to send large files, data, and programs.

SONET Telephone companies that offer DSL and other Internet connection methods rely on a digital network called SONET. SONET stands for *Synchronous Optical Network*. It uses fiber optics to provide faster connections and greater bandwidth—from 52 Mbps to up to a whopping 40 gigabits per second (Gbps).

Technology @ School

With all the ways that schools use technology these days, they need a lot of bandwidth to send and receive information electronically.

Think About It!

Think about who in your school might benefit from increased bandwidth. Which tasks listed below could use bandwidth?

➤ students participating in a class teleconference

➤ a teacher researching Mars

➤ a librarian helping a student find a book

➤ a counselor checking student records

➤ a principal answering e-mail

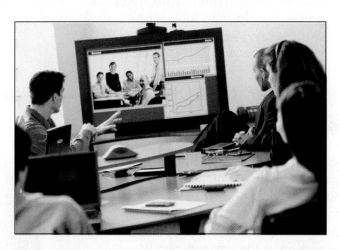

Figure 23.3.1 In a video-conference, users in different locations transmit and receive audio, video, and computer data in real time. This kind of activity requires a great deal of bandwidth.

Cable and Satellite TV Connections   Most cable and digital television companies offer high-speed Internet connection through a cable modem. Satellite television companies also offer a similar service with signals sent through the customer's satellite dish. A cable modem connects your computer to the local cable TV line and supports data transfer rates of up to 30 Mbps—over 500 times faster than the old dial-up modem. However, this number can be misleading, because most Internet Service Providers (ISPs) cap subscribers' transfer rates to less than 6 Mbps to conserve bandwidth. However, this is more than enough for the average home computer user.

Voice over Internet Protocol   Just as you can use your telephone to send and receive messages over the Internet, you can use the Internet to send and receive messages over the telephone. **Voice over Internet Protocol (VoIP)** technology allows you to have a telephone connection over the Internet. VoIP uses data sent digitally, with the Internet Protocol (IP), instead of analog telephone lines. People use VoIP to talk to each other from across the globe, sometimes without having to pay a cent. With Webcams callers can also see each other during their calls.

The Future of Bandwidth

The demand for bandwidth is growing. People want increased bandwidth for video-on-demand, meetings via the Internet, and Web-based learning. Thus, telephone and other high-tech companies continue to look for new ways to improve telecommunications services and data transmission.

Real-World Tech

Making Communication Possible   It's not just governments and huge companies that put communications satellites into orbit. Students are doing it, too.

In 2001, for example, six students at the U.S. Naval Academy built a satellite with equipment anybody could buy: A tape measure was used as the antenna, and 24 AA batteries provided the power. Both a sailor in the Atlantic Ocean and some hikers in New Zealand used signals from the students' satellite to contact family at home.

How might students fund the cost of their experiments?

Use the Vocabulary

Directions: *Match each vocabulary term in the left column with the correct definition in the right column.*

_____ **1.** telecommunications
_____ **2.** analog
_____ **3.** digital
_____ **4.** fiber-optic cable
_____ **5.** microwave
_____ **6.** modulation
_____ **7.** demodulation
_____ **8.** bits per second
_____ **9.** bandwidth
_____ **10.** broadband

a. the measure of how much data can be sent through a network connection

b. system using computer code to carry different kinds of data

c. changing digital signals to analog

d. system using electrical signals that match the human voice and other sounds

e. high-frequency radio waves that carry data

f. strand of fiberglass that transmits data by pulses of light

g. using a telephone network to send information

h. high-speed digital connection of at least 1.5 Mbps

i. measurement of the speed at which data can be sent in one second

j. changing analog signals to digital

Check Your Comprehension

Directions: *Complete each sentence with information from the chapter.*

1. The _____ consists of the local loop and long-distance lines that handle data and voice communications.

2. The _____ part of your telephone number identifies the area of the country you live in.

3. In the long-distance telephone system, _____ largely have replaced twisted pair copper wire.

4. Radio and infrared signals make _____ communication possible.

5. Within a neighborhood, telephones connect to a common network called the _____.

6. One issue DSL users face is that it is _____ to send information than to receive it.

7. A fax machine sending a document transmits data into a(n) _____ signal and changes it into a(n) _____ signal.

8. _____ offers a way for people across the globe to call each other over the Internet free of charge.

9. *DSL* stands for _____.

10. The demand for _____ will continue to grow.

Think Critically

Directions: *Answer the following questions.*

1. Why is a modem needed to access the Internet?

2. Why is faxing an order to a company an example of telecommunications in action?

3. For what types of documents might a fax machine be a better method of transmission than e-mail?

4. What challenges do you think telecommunications companies face in the near future?

5. Why might it be important for a home-office computer to have Internet service that offers a lot of bandwidth?

Extend Your Knowledge

Directions: *Choose one of the following projects. Complete the exercise on a separate sheet of paper.*

A. With the growing number of cell phones, telephone companies must assign more telephone numbers. Sometimes they even need more area codes. Contact your local telephone company to find out how many telephone numbers can be assigned to a given area code and when the phone company anticipates assigning the next new area code. Present your findings to the class.

B. Divide into two groups and have one group research VoIP service packages offered by Vonage and the other research the same service offered by Skype. Write up your findings and discuss the differences.

Understanding Communications

How Do You Use Cellphones? People all over the world rely on cellular, or cell, phones to communicate. Cell phones allow for instant access to families, friends, and—on a smart phone—the Internet. They're great for emergencies, sending messages, chatting on the go, and, for many people, they have replaced traditional landline phones.

When you're home you may call someone with your analog telephone system, your cell phone, or even your computer. Many businesses you call—or who call you—use telephones and computers together.

Cell phones and computer technology promise great things for the future. You can expect even faster access to information, better communications, and more choices of ways to stay in touch with family and friends.

Chapter Outline

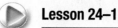

Lesson 24–1

Using Cellphone Technology

Lesson 24–2

Choosing Digital Options

Using Cell Phone Technology

Objectives

- Explain how cellular telephones make and receive calls.
- Identify advantages of cell phones to subscribers.
- Compare and contrast local and long-distance cell phone calls.

As You Read

Organize Information Use an outline to help you organize the information in the lesson as you read.

🗝 Key Terms

- cell
- cellular phone
- cell site
- leased line
- personal digital assistant (PDA)

What Are Cell Phones?

A cell phone actually is a type of radio. In fact, that's the definition: **cellular phones** are mobile phones that use radio waves to communicate. Early cellular phones were called radiotelephones and were used in ships at sea and in police cars. Radiotelephones were very useful during World War II, when they were used to send military information.

For a while after that war, only a few people in a city could use radiotelephones at one time. New technology, however, soon increased the number of possible callers by adding more radio frequencies within each city.

What Does "Cellular" Mean?

When you use a traditional phone, the call is connected through a wire. The wire from your house is connected to a telephone pole or buried cable in the local loop and from a local office to long-distance wires. Cell phones bypass part of the wired system.

Figure 24.1.1 Primarily due to their flexibility and ease of use, cell phones are quickly replacing wired telephones as the communication system of choice.

Locating Cells Cell phone systems are divided into **cells**, or geographic areas to which a signal can be transmitted. Each cell has a **cell site**, also called a base station, for all the cellular phones in that area. Each cell site has a radio tower that receives radio signals from other towers and sends them on to still other towers. As a caller moves from one area to another, a new cell site automatically picks up the call to keep the signal strong and clear. Ultimately, the signal gets to individual cell phones.

Managing Locations Each geographic area is assigned to a central base station, or Mobile Telephone Switching Office (MTSO). It, in turn, is connected to the standard Public Switched Telephone Network (PSTN) telephone system. The MTSO has several responsibilities:

- directs cellular activities at base stations
- locates cellular users in the area
- tracks users as they roam, or move, from cell to cell
- connects cellular phones to land-based phones

Providing Services Of course cell phones provide many services in addition to completing phone calls—most for an additional service fee. You can pay for sending and receiving text messages and for data service. With data service, you can access the Internet, send and receive e-mail, and stream audio and video.

Spotlight on...

RICHARD FRENKIEL AND JOEL ENGEL

❝ *It is hard for any one person to feel he is uniquely responsible for something like this. Hundreds of people were working on it in my company alone.* ❞

Richard Frenkiel

Two of the reasons people today have cell phones are Richard Frenkiel and Joel Engel. They worked on a team of more than 200 engineers at AT&T's Bell Labs in the 1960s and 1970s. As part of this team, they helped to increase the number of mobile phones that could operate at once in a city.

This was accomplished by dividing a city into small "cells" that could reuse radio channels many times and by creating the technology to "handoff" calls from cell to cell without losing the signal.

In 1987, Frenkiel and Engel were awarded the Alexander Graham Bell Medal for their contributions to the advancement of telecommunications. In 1994, President Bill Clinton awarded the partners National Medals of Technology.

Retired from Bell Labs, Frenkiel and Engel now consult for the telecommunications industry.

Mathematics Many math classes and standardized tests now require that students use calculators to solve problems. One of the features offered by most PDAs is a calculator. In addition to tracking assignments for class, PDAs can help you complete them, too!

How Cell Phones Work

When you turn on a cellular phone, it searches for a signal from the service provider's base station in the local area. When you place a call, the MTSO selects a frequency for your phone and a tower for you to use and identifies the tower you are using. Each tower sends and receives signals to and from the individual cell phones within its cell. The MTSO is connected to the local telephone network, usually by telephone cable. Cell phones are connected to the telephone network through the cell site.

Receiving a Phone Call When someone calls your cell phone, the cellular service provider locates the phone by cell. Moving from one cell into another, the phone transmits this information to the service provider's base station. The base station reports this information to the MTSO so it knows where to find you.

Placing Long-Distance Calls If you dial a long-distance number from your cell phone, the MTSO connects the call through a **leased line**. A digital leased line is a permanent connection allowing the MTSO to interact with long-distance providers.

What Else Does Cellular Technology Offer?

A **personal digital assistant**, or **PDA**, such as the Palm Tungsten E2, is a small, highly portable handheld computer. Smart phones are cell phones offering advanced capabilities that are able to function as both personal computers and cell phones. The main difference between the two is that smart phones are oriented more to mobile phone features while PDAs are heavy on the business/organizational features and do not necessarily include phone/fax service.

Figure 24.1.2 Because the cellular system stores information about your phone, it can track your location as you move. Cells often overlap, so users do not lose service if they move from one cell to another.

Cell A

Cell B

Cell C

Mobile telephone switching office

Telephone network

Choosing Digital Options

Objectives

- Identify advantages of computer telephony integration.
- Identify competitors for business in the telecommunications market.

As You Read

Draw Conclusions Use a chart to help you draw conclusions about the information in this lesson as you read.

Using Computer Telephony Integration

By working together, computers and telephones can increase the power of communications. Linking computers to telephone systems is called computer telephony integration (CTI). While uses of CTI have expanded in recent years, one of the most traditional uses is when the computer takes the place of a human and acts as a **call center**, a central place where an organization's inbound and outbound calls are received and made. A call center CTI helps businesses and other organizations become more efficient. Suppose you call your favorite pizza restaurant for a delivery order. If this restaurant uses CTI, the modem and computer software work together to identify your name and your last delivery order. It will locate your house on an area map. Many organizations use CTI including the following:

- emergency response centers in police and fire stations
- hospitals
- telemarketers (who conduct surveys or sell products or services by telephone)
- voicemail services
- banks, manufacturers, and small businesses

 Key Terms
- cable modem
- call center
- download
- upload

Figure 24.2.1 The 911 emergency telephone system is a great example of how computers and telephone systems can be integrated.

Technology @ Home

Many of us use a combination of technologies to communicate at home. We use phones, computers, and televisions to send and receive messages.

Think About It!

Conduct a class survey to identify how many of each tool below your class uses at home. Write your own answers and then compare your responses with those of your classmates. What conclusions can you draw?

➤ analog telephones

➤ cell phones

➤ ISDN or DSL connections

➤ digital satellite systems

➤ cable systems

➤ wireless networks

➤ other

Competition Brings Choices

Most telephones are analog-based and rely on twisted pair technology. For more than 100 years, telephone service was provided only by telephone companies. The Telecommunications Act of 1996, however, introduced competition into the telecommunications market. Now, satellite companies, cable television companies, and businesses offering wireless services also compete with telephone companies to provide high-bandwidth digital telecommunications. This competition has created new, affordable methods for transferring voice, video, and data.

People are no longer bound to a single choice for their telecommunications needs. Think of the different choices available to consumers at home and at work for sending and receiving text and images quickly and reliably. In addition to analog phones and DSL services, choices include:

- digital satellite systems
- cable systems
- wireless networks

Communicating Without Analog

Some people use the Internet to bypass some or all analog phone wires. Some communicate through a purely digital network that links one computer to another. Others connect a computer to a telephone or a telephone to a computer.

Many people today talk with others without using a telephone. A computer with a sound card, a microphone, speakers, and the right software allows this type of communication to take place with ease.

Direct Broadcast Satellites If you have satellite television, your family subscribes to a digital satellite system, called a Direct Broadcast Satellite (DBS) service. Satellites receive signals from a central broadcast center here on Earth and then rebroadcast them around the globe. In many areas of the country, DBS systems are now offering Internet access and data transfer services. Because satellites can only transmit data to a subscriber, a modem and telephone line are needed to send data, such as a pay-per-movie request, to the provider.

Cable Connections If your family has cable television, the cable that brings in your favorite television shows may also let you access your favorite Web site. There's plenty of bandwidth on the cable for both television programs and data. Connections usually are fast and reliable—unless too many subscribers share bandwidth in a specific area.

To connect your computer to a cable service, you need a **cable modem**. Like analog modems, cable modems can be internal or external. Cable modems catch the downstream signal from the Internet, called **downloading**, and pass it on to your computer. Some cable modems can also send information upstream, or **upload**, data from your computer back to the Internet. Not all cable modems allow two-way communication. Like DBS, they require an analog phone line and an analog modem.

Wireless Networks Cell phones are one form of wireless communication. In addition, wireless networks allow computers to communicate through radio signals, also without being wired together. Many hospitals, college campuses, businesses, hotels, and even cafes use wireless networks or "Wi-Fi." Wi-Fi is a short range network with high-bandwidth for data transfer. Multi-computer households may also use wireless networks, allowing family members to share equipment and exchange data.

With the advent of smart phones there is need for networks designed for use with cell phone technology. These networks, called 3G or 4G, provide layered transmission of data, allowing for increased network capacity, a wider range of services, and faster upload and download speeds.

Real-World Tech

Finding Your Way by Satellite
Some of the satellites that circle Earth can pinpoint any spot on the ground or at sea. Using signals from these satellites, a Geographic Positioning System (GPS) receiver can show maps and directions on a screen. GPS is widely used by the military, but it is also used by drivers, boaters, hikers, hunters, and others who may rely on directions.

How is GPS used in cars?

Use the Vocabulary

Directions: *Match each vocabulary term in the left column with the correct definition in the right column.*

_____ **1.** cellular phone
_____ **2.** cell
_____ **3.** cell site
_____ **4.** leased line
_____ **5.** personal digital assistant
_____ **6.** cable modem
_____ **7.** download
_____ **8.** upload

a. permanent connection for long-distance cell phone calls

b. handheld computer

c. geographic area to which radio signals are sent

d. phone that uses radio waves to communicate

e. base station for handling cell calls

f. to send a file from your computer to another computer

g. to receive a file from another computer

h. device that enables a computer to access the Internet through a cable television connection

Check Your Comprehension

Directions: *Complete each sentence with information from the chapter.*

1. A cell phone is a type of _____.

2. Cell phones use _____ to communicate.

3. A problem with early cell phones was a lack of _____ for making calls.

4. The central base station manages activities in assigned _____.

5. As a caller moves from one point to another, a new _____ relays the signal from MTSO to MTSO.

6. Linking computers and telephones to work together is called _____.

7. A wireless network, which may be called _____, is a short range network with high-bandwidth for data transfer.

8. DBS service relies on _____ for its transmission signals.

9. All cable modems allow downloading of data, but not all offer the ability to _____ information through the cable television connection.

10. _____ allow computers to communicate with each other without being physically connected.

Think Critically

Directions: *Answer the following questions.*

1. Why are mobile phones called cell phones?

2. What fairly common communications tools do you think use CTI to send and receive information?

3. Why do you think so many companies offer telecommunications services?

4. How are cell phones like wireless networks?

5. Which telecommunications choice do you think will offer more options to consumers in the future?

Extend Your Knowledge

Directions: *Choose one of the following projects. Complete the exercise on a separate sheet of paper.*

A. Some states and industries have developed policies to guide cell phone use. Select one of the following topics: (1) states that have banned or restricted drivers from using handheld cell phones or (2) airlines that restrict cell phone calls at certain times. With your teacher's permission, conduct online research to identify the reasons for the rules or laws, using appropriate strategies to locate the information on the Internet. Then, conclude whether or not the desired results have been achieved.

B. Some people complain that cell phone towers are unsightly. Others are concerned about possible harmful effects of the microradiation that comes from them. With your teacher's permission, conduct online or library research to find out more about these topics, and then conduct a class debate on the issues.

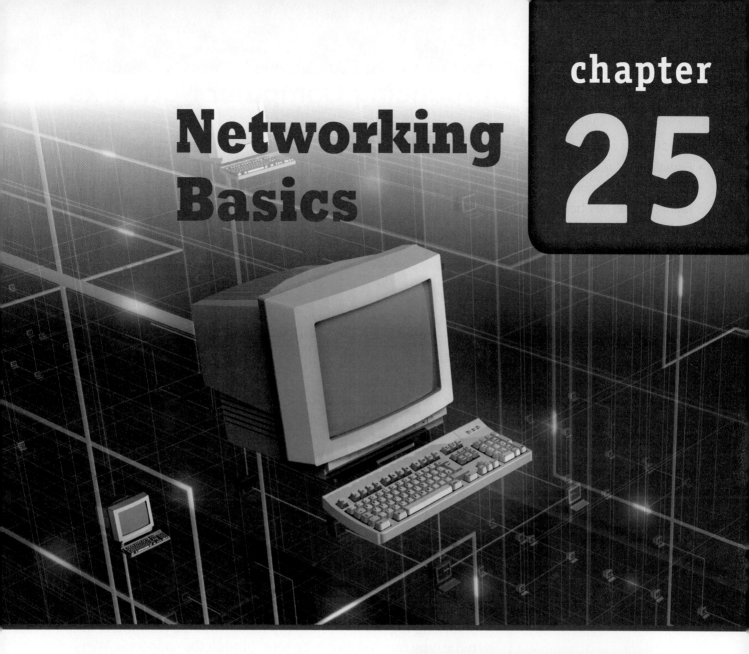

Networking Basics

What Is a Computer Network? In the simplest terms, a computer network is a group of computers and devices connected to each other so they can exchange data. The smallest network may only connect two computers; the largest—the Internet—connects millions.

In this chapter you are introduced to the concepts and terminology associated with computer networks, including the difference between local area networks and wide area networks.

Chapter Outline

 Lesson 25–1

Introducing Computer Networks

 Lesson 25–2

Local Area Networks

 Lesson 25–3

Wide Area Networks

Introducing Computer Networks

Objectives

- Explain what a computer network is.
- List media commonly used in networks.
- Identify three key benefits of using a network.
- Discuss how computers communicate.

As You Read

Organize Information Complete a chart to help you identify the details that support the main idea of the lesson.

🔑 Key Terms

- network
- network interface card (NIC)
- network traffic
- node
- open protocol
- physical media
- proprietary protocol
- protocol
- protocol suite
- synergy
- terminal
- workstation

Introducing Networks

If your family owns two computers, can they both use the same printer? They can if your computers are networked.

A computer **network** is two or more computers connected to one another to share resources. Networks allow users to access files and programs. They also let users share printers and other equipment. They allow people to work together, too. A network may be small, with just a few computers, or it may be large, with thousands of workstations. The network functions the same way, no matter how many workstations are connected.

Physical Media To create a computer network, each workstation and device must be able to communicate with the network. This requires establishing the physical connection using **physical media**. The medium can be any type of telecommunications connector: twisted pair telephone lines, coaxial cable, fiber-optic cable, or a microwave, radio, or infrared system.

Working together, the network media and the computers determine how much data can be sent through the connector. Wireless networks usually aren't as fast as wired networks.

Network Interface Cards Some computers are designed with the ability to connect to networks. Others need a **network interface card**, or **NIC**, which handles the flow of data to and from the computer in both wired and wireless networks. If the network is put together by actual cables, those cables connect to the NIC. NICs often have a light that blinks green and amber to alert you to activity it's experiencing.

Figure 25.1.1 Network interface cards enable PCs to connect to a network.

Organizing Users

If you have more than one computer at home, you probably identify them by each user's name—your computer, Mom's computer, and so on. In businesses, schools, and other organizations, a network is organized into workstations, each with its own name and address. In both home and larger networks, pieces of equipment connected together must be able to understand one another.

Network Members A **workstation** is a computer connected to a computer network. It is often set up with the same operating system, applications, and access to resources as the other computers in the network. Workstations are where individuals do their day-to-day work.

In a large network, a workstation is also called a **node** by the people who take care of the network. A node is anything connected to the network—a workstation, a printer, a fax machine, or any other piece of equipment.

Network Alternative Sometimes network users work at a **terminal**, which usually includes a keyboard, a monitor, and a mouse. A terminal can feel as if the computer is local, but it's not. Users are actually sharing time on a central computer, with their own work displayed on their terminal's monitor. (This kind of network is sometimes called a timesharing system.)

Terminals can save on the cost of purchasing workstations. They are also useful in situations with limited need for a workstation, such as a public computer in a library.

Ensuring Communication

Once a network is created, the computers and other connected equipment can communicate with one another. The communication on a network is called **network traffic**. Network traffic is the electronic pulses of information sent by the network cards to carry data through the network wires to its destination. Specifically, computers communicate with languages called protocols.

A **protocol** sets a standard format for data and rules for handling it. There are many different protocols available to use on networks. For computers to speak with one another, they must use the same protocol.

Kinds of Protocols There are two protocol categories: open and proprietary. An **open protocol** is available for anyone to use. For example, the most common open protocol is the Transmission Control Protocol/Internet Protocol. (TCP/IP), which is used by computers on the Internet.

A **proprietary protocol**, however, is not open to everyone. Instead, only people who buy certain equipment, services, or computers can use it. Some personal digital assistants, digital cameras, and even dial-up Internet services use proprietary

Connections

Literature With e-books, your next reading selection could come from a network instead of a bookstore! Today, readers download their selections onto PDAs or special reading devices. Currently in development, however, is electronic paper that displays letters in response to electrical signals.

If your school is networked, it will enjoy the same benefits all networks do—hardware, software, and people benefits.

Think About It!

Think about the benefits of a network. Sequence the value of each possible benefit using a scale of 1 (lowest) to 4 (highest). What conclusions can you draw?

➤ one expensive printer shared among 20 computers

➤ one version of a program installed on all computers

➤ a school newspaper file to which each computer user can contribute

➤ a joint science experiment conducted by two schools

Figure 25.1.2 Computers in different locations can communicate as long as they use the same network protocols.

protocols. Overall, however, open protocols are more common. Both manufacturers and consumers benefit from open protocols that allow a broad range of connections.

A Stack of Protocols The protocols networks use to communicate are often called a **protocol suite**. A protocol suite is the stack, or collection, of individual protocols that determines how the network operates. For example, TCP/IP is not just one network language, but many smaller ones. Each small protocol in this suite has a specific job to do in a specific order. Working together, protocols allow computers to communicate.

Working with Others

Everyone on a network has the ability to access programs and data stored anywhere on the network. You might use an application like Google docs which is stored on a network rather than on your own computer, or you might print a document on a printer that is located on a different floor than your computer.

Networks also let people work together in new and exciting ways. People on a network can collaborate more easily than those working on standalone systems. **Synergy** is the effect a group effort can create. People working together on a network can accomplish more than people working alone on unconnected computers.

Using a Network

The steps you use to access network resources are basically the same as those you use to work on your own computer. Your actions may seem simple enough, but behind the scenes, the network's hardware and software are performing complex tasks.

Some tasks you can accomplish using a network include:

- Scheduling a meeting
- Sending e-mail
- Exchanging documents
- Instant messaging
- Video conferencing
- Playing games.

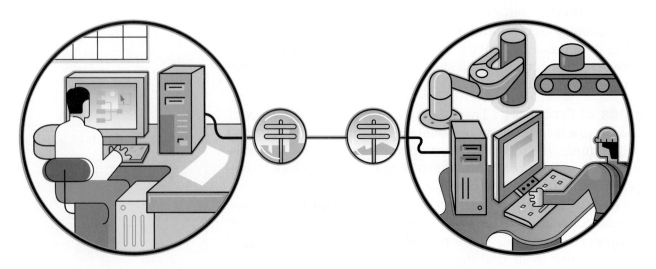

Local Area Networks

Objectives

- Describe how local area networks work.
- Define how local area networks allow information sharing.
- Compare peer-to-peer and client/server networks.

As You Read

Organize Information Complete a spider map to help you identify the basics of networking as you read the lesson.

Introducing LANs

A school lab with its ten computers networked together is an example of a **local area network**, or **LAN**. A LAN is a network in which all the workstations and other equipment are near one another. LANs can be set up in any defined area, such as a home, a school, an office building, or even a cluster of shops.

A LAN can have just a few or several hundred users. Small or large, a LAN lets its members share equipment and information, resulting in lower costs. There are three key ways to share information: sharing files, using collaborative software, and sharing peripherals.

Sharing Files Through a computer's operating system, people connected to a LAN can participate in **file sharing**. File sharing is making files available to more than one user on the network.

Using Collaborative Software **Collaborative software** enables the network to help people work together more closely. With collaborative software, users can share calendars, work on a document together, or even hold meetings through the network. Collaborative software is also called groupware.

Sharing Peripherals In addition to sharing files and software, a LAN allows users to share peripherals, such as printers, fax machines, or any other equipment.

Using a Peer-to-Peer Network

Your peers are your equals. In a **peer-to-peer network (P2PN)**, all the computers are equals. Peer-to-peer networks are usually small, made up of two to ten computers.

Key Terms

- client
- client/server network
- collaborative software
- file server
- file sharing
- local area network (LAN))
- network operating system (NOS)
- peer-to-peer network (P2PN)

Sharing Files   In a P2PN, each user decides whether any files on his or her computer will be shared. You can share the files with your neighbor, a few of your neighbors, or everyone on the network. The reverse is true, too. Other workstations may have files you'd like to access through the network—and you can if you have permission.

Creating a P2PN   A P2PN is an easy network to create, since all of the workstations are equals. The operating system of each computer typically has built-in file-sharing abilities. The workstations are connected to each other through the network cable. In some systems, the network cables all connect to a central device called a hub. A hub handles the flow of traffic from computer to computer.

Evaluating P2PNs   A peer-to-peer network is ideal for small offices and homes. In a large business, however, peer-to-peer networking has some drawbacks:

- Security problems can arise.
- Data can be hard to back up.
- With many users, file sharing can become difficult.
- Finding shared files can be difficult.
- Managing resources can be complicated.

These problems arise because resources are scattered across many computers. If one computer fails or is turned off, its resources are no longer available to the network.

Figure 25.2.1 An ethernet switch with many ports can be used to set up a local area network.

Using a Client/Server Network

Large businesses usually use a **client/server network**. With this system, one powerful computer provides information and management services to the workstation computers, the **clients**.

Creating a Client/Server Network   The main computer in a client/server system is called the **file server** or the server. It contains the network operating system, other programs, and large data files. The **network operating system**, or **NOS**, manages and secures the entire network. It controls access, permissions, and all aspects of network use. Only those who provide a username and a password can use the network. It centralizes and protects data and controls what users can do with files. Thus, a client/server network is far more secure than a P2PN.

Evaluating a Client/Server Network   For a large office, file servers are better than peer-to-peer networks, for several reasons:

- They offer a central location for files.
- Data is easy to back up and easy to recover.
- Servers are faster than workstations.
- Servers usually are powered on.
- Security is easier to maintain.

Figure 25.2.2   In a client/server network, users can share files stored on the file server and access a common printer, too.

Wide Area Networks

Objectives

- Identify the purpose and components of a wide area network.
- Compare methods organizations use to connect to a point of presence.
- Compare and contrast packet-switching networks and circuit-switching networks.
- Describe three types of WANs.

As You Read

Organize Information   Complete an outline to help you note key facts about wide area networks as you read the lesson.

🔑 Key Terms

- backbone
- circuit-switching
- congestion
- frame relay
- packets
- packet-switching
- permanent virtual circuit
- point of presence (POP)
- public data network
- router
- T1 line
- virtual private network (VPN)
- wide area network (WAN)

What Is a WAN?

A **wide area network (WAN)** connects computers and other resources that are miles or even continents apart. A business with offices in many places can use a WAN to link its LANs in different cities. Then, users from any of the locations can, with the proper permissions, access the network. Each user can access files, printers, and other resources as if they were local. As far as users are concerned, a WAN "feels like" one giant LAN.

Once a WAN is created, users may not even realize the files they are sharing are remote. And that's the way it should be. Users should not worry about the physical location of the shared files, just that the files are available.

Figure 25.3.1 A WAN can link distant LANs through telephone lines or microwave signals.

How Is a WAN Controlled?

Like a client/server LAN, a WAN is controlled by a network operating system. A NOS is especially helpful on a WAN because there are so many users and resources to manage. The NOS also helps network administrators secure the resources throughout the network.

Creating WANs

To create a WAN, LANs are connected through high-speed data lines called **backbones**. Organizations attach to the backbone at a **point of presence (POP)**. But how do they get to the POP? There are several options.

ISDN and DSL   These technologies use ordinary telephone lines to attach to the backbone. Special adapters or modems provide ways to deal with digital data.

Leased Lines   Some companies rent a private end-to-end connection, called a leased line, from a telecommunications company. Leased lines allow data to be sent at 56,000 bps.

T1 Lines   Larger companies and many school districts lease **T1 lines**. T1 lines can be either copper or fiber optic, and they allow data to be sent at more than 1.5 million bps.

Permanent Virtual Circuits   A **permanent virtual circuit (PVC)** allows multiple users' data to travel the line at once. Thus, they are cheaper than private lines. Most PVCs use a technology called **frame relay**. Frame relay allows voice, data, and video to travel on the same line and at the same time.

Sending Data Long-Distance

Packet-Switching Networks   Most networks use **packet-switching** technology. The sending computer divides information into tiny segments called **packets**. Each packet is marked with a delivery address, so packet transfers are quick and accurate. When you transfer a file, send an e-mail, or even browse a Web site, you're sending and receiving packets.

Circuit-Switching Networks   Some WANs use circuit-switching technology to transmit messages. **Circuit-switching** happens on a real, end-to-end connection between the sending computer and the receiving computer, which make up the circuit. There's no delay on circuit-switching networks, so they are ideal for sending voice messages and for teleconferencing. A telephone network uses circuit-switching.

Routers are network devices or programs that choose the best pathway for each packet. If there is **congestion**, or too much traffic, on the network, the router can delay some of the packets. The receiving computer puts the packets back together in the right order.

Career Corner

Medical Technician In addition to taking a patient's temperature and blood pressure, medical technicians are now trained to use high-tech devices, such as a new handheld device that can map a patient's DNA and provide an instant diagnosis. In addition to the high-tech training, technicians learn to use medical computer networks.

Types of WANs

Businesses and other organizations use three types of WANs.

Public Data Network   A **public data network** allows a company to set up its own network. Telecommunications companies own the public data network and charge fees for the use of the network.

Private Data Network   Some companies set up a private data network that cannot be accessed by outsiders. Having a private data network costs more than using a public data network.

Virtual Private Network   A **virtual private network (VPN)** is a private network set up through a public network. VPN users connect to an Internet service provider (ISP) to access the network.

Real-World Tech

Networking the Navajo Nation   The Navajo Nation spreads across 26,000 square miles in Arizona, New Mexico, and Utah. The Nation's Diné College has seven campuses that are hundreds of miles apart. Only about half of the Nation's households have phone lines. How could the educational system take advantage of the Internet? The solution was to create a WAN using a variety of technologies. Small satellite dishes receive information while phone and dedicated data lines send messages out. The Navajo Nation's wide area network has expanded to overcome the wide open spaces in which its people live.

What group or institution do you think would benefit from a WAN? Why? .

Use the Vocabulary

Directions: *Match each vocabulary term in the left column with the correct definition in the right column.*

_____ **1.** network
_____ **2.** workstation
_____ **3.** protocol
_____ **4.** local area network
_____ **5.** collaborative software
_____ **6.** peer-to-peer network
_____ **7.** file server
_____ **8.** backbone
_____ **9.** point of presence
_____ **10.** virtual private network

a. network in which all computers are equal

b. computer connected to a network

c. local connection to a WAN

d. standard format and rules

e. set up on a public network

f. two or more computers linked together

g. program that lets people work together closely

h. high-speed line that carries network traffic

i. network set up in a limited area

j. the central computer in one kind of network

Check Your Comprehension

Directions: *Determine the correct choice for each of the following.*

1. Which of the following is NOT an example of a physical medium used to connect a network?

a. telephone wires
b. electric cords
c. fiber-optic cables
d. radio signals

2. If a company buys one large computer instead of many workstations, which of the following will it supply for its employees to work on?

a. a file server
b. nodes
c. a point of presence
d. terminals

3. Which of the following is another name for collaborative software?

a. groupware
b. network operating system
c. local area network
d. backbone

4. Which of the following do users of a client/server network have to provide?

a. a client
b. a file
c. a protocol
d. an access control

5. Which of the following is used to control a WAN?

a. NIC
b. VPN
c. NOS
d. POP

6. Which of the following is used to provide a local connection to a WAN?

a. NIC
b. VPN
c. NOS
d. POP

Think Critically

Directions: *Answer the following questions.*

1. How are a LAN and a WAN similar? How are they different?

2. Why might a P2PN be a good choice for a small network? Why might a client/server model be a good choice for a large network?

3. Why is the Internet an example of a WAN?

4. What kinds of wires and wireless lines can be used as the backbone of a WAN?

5. Why are protocols important to LANs and WANs?

Extend Your Knowledge

Directions: *Choose one of the following projects. Complete the exercise on a separate sheet of paper.*

A. If your school library has computers, find out if the ones available for students to use are workstations or terminals and why they are organized this way. Also, find out how the computers in your public library are organized. If possible, try each system. Write a brief report comparing and contrasting the operation and purposes of a network using workstations and a system using terminals.

B. Conduct research in the library or, with your teacher's permission, on the Internet to find more details about each of the physical media used to create networks, such as twisted pair, coaxial cable, fiber-optic cable, microwaves, radio waves, and infrared rays. Present your findings in an illustrated chart. Compare the details you discovered with those your classmates found. What conclusions can you draw about the use of these media in networks?

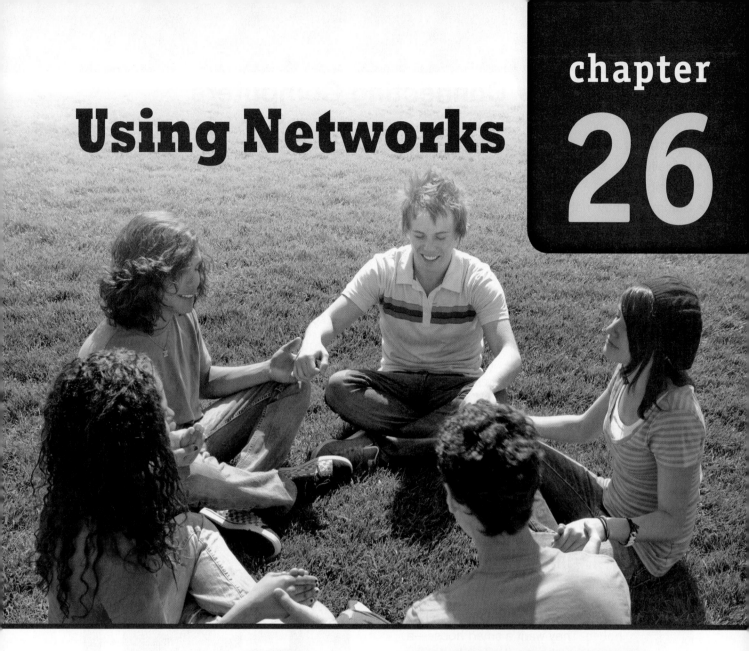

Using Networks

Can Computers Work Together? From the workstations in your classroom, to the PC at the library, and lately even in the interface on your cell phone, computers are everywhere. Today, thanks to networking, these devices can become even more useful.

Networks, and the science of network design, are becoming more important in our lives than ever before. People at home, in schools, and at work are all exploring how they can use networks in their daily activities.

In this chapter, you learn about the different designs used to create networks, and how networks are used by businesses and individuals.

Chapter Outline

Lesson 26–1

Connecting Computers

Lesson 26–2

Creating Local Area Networks

Lesson 26–3

Connecting Remote Networks

Lesson 26-1

Connecting Computers

Objectives

- Explain what is meant by network architecture.
- Explain OSI.
- Summarize how networks are designed.

As You Read

Organize Information   Use a main-idea chart to help you identify the details that support the main idea of the lesson.

 Key Terms

- collision
- contention
- network architecture
- network layer
- topology

Network Architecture

To design a network for your school, you would consider the number of students, the placement of your servers, Internet access, and more. Designing a network for a large company raises different issues.

Setting Up a Network   **Network architecture** is the science of designing a network. In many cases, a systems engineer is hired to find out what the network will be used for and to design a network the operating system can handle.

Real-World Tech

Networking the Home   For some homeowners, it's not enough to buy a house. They want a smart house—a networked house. It offers benefits such as wireless security systems and baby monitors, central control of heat and lighting, high-tech control of home entertainment systems, and more. The retail world is changing as more and more companies are able to turn houses into smart houses!

Which high-tech feature would you most like to have in your home?

Small networks are fairly easy to create. The network administrator first connects the network card of each work-station to the network cable and usually connects the cable to a hub. The administrator also has to make sure the operating system of the computer is set up to participate in the network. On larger networks, however, the job becomes more complicated.

Following Rules Recall that all network communication, large or small, is based on and must follow common rules, called protocols. These rules were developed by the International Standards Organization, or ISO.

The rules specific to computer networks are called the Open Systems Interconnection, or OSI, model, which has seven layers. These rules define what happens at each step of a network operation and how data flows through it. Each layer communicates with the layer above and below it to ensure that networking takes place.

On the sending computer, data flows from the application layer, down through each layer in the model, and out through the network. Then, it flows back up through the model on the receiving computer. Each layer has a job to do to prepare outgoing data for the network and incoming data for the operating system. All layers are important, but the **network layer** deserves special attention.

Layers of the OSI Model

Layer	Purpose
Application	Communicate with the operating system to do an actual job
Presentation	Package data from the operating system so the lower layers can understand it
Session	Create and end communication between two devices on the network
Transport	Manage the flow of data within the network and check for errors
Network	Route and address data traffic
Datalink	Choose the right physical protocols for the data
Physical	Define the actual network hardware, such as cabling and timing

The word *contention* has more than one meaning. It can mean a state of rivalry or a statement that one supports.

Think About It!

Think about the various meanings of the word *contention*. Which sentence(s) below do not use the word correctly?

▷ Sally and Tom are in contention for the job of manager.

▷ Ralph did not apply for that position because he feels contention in his present job.

▷ It is Sally's contention that her skills are ideal for the job.

Network Design

If you were to create a map of your neighborhood, you might include streets, lakes, and hills. A map of a network shows the physical structure of the network, including servers, workstations, and other network devices. The network's layout is called the network **topology**.

Topology isn't only concerned with where to put equipment, however. The design of a network must also solve another problem: Only one computer on a network may speak at a time. When two computers try to access the network at the same time, they're in **contention**. If both sent their data at once, there could be a **collision**, and the data could become all mixed together.

To avoid such collisions, each computer divides its data into very small, fast-moving packets. Network equipment or software transmits these packets. Users typically are not affected by the tiny delays this system causes as each computer must wait its turn to transmit data.

Figure 26.1.1 Like the traffic signals used on roads, networks use special means to prevent data from colliding.

Creating Local Area Networks

Objectives

- Compare and contrast LAN topologies.
- Identify network types.
- Describe the operation of an Ethernet.

As You Read

Organize Information Use an outline to help you identify types of LANs as you read the lesson.

Choosing a Network Topology

Each LAN can have a different combination of computers, printers, and other equipment. The LAN designer chooses a network type to connect the components. Each type of network can be described by its topology: bus, ring, star, and star bus.

Bus Topology An older network design, **bus topology** is rarely used now. In a bus, devices are connected to a single network line like a string of holiday lights. When one network device fails, the entire network fails, and adding new devices to the network can also be tricky.

Key Terms

- bus topology
- Ethernet
- hub
- mesh topology
- ring topology
- star bus topology
- star topology
- token

Figure 26.2.1 In a bus topology, all computers connect to a single cable.

Which topology would you use if you were in charge of networking a classroom with five computers, one printer, and one scanner?

Think About It!

Sequence the value of each topology below using a scale of 1 (lowest) to 5 (highest) to indicate which you believe would be best in the classroom.

➤ bus topology

➤ ring topology

➤ star topology

➤ star bus topology

➤ mesh topology

Ring Topology   As its name suggests, **ring topology** connects all the network devices in a circle. To control collisions, such networks pass **tokens**, or special units of data, around the ring. Only the workstation that has control of the token can send other data onto the network. Because of the token-passing technique, these networks are also called token rings, or, if the network is wireless, wireless token rings. Like bus topology, one fault can disrupt a ring network, but this network type has the advantage of not requiring a network server.

Star Topology   **Star topology** design connects each network device to a central hub. A **hub** is a connection point for all the computers, printers, and other equipment on the network.

Adding and removing devices to a star network is easy. If the hub loses power or fails, however, the network devices will not be able to communicate. Star topology avoids collisions by using strategies that manage contention.

Star Bus Topology   **Star bus topology** connects multiple star networks along a bus. It is the most common design used in LANs today.

Suppose each classroom in your school had its own network with its own hub. The hub in each classroom could then be connected to a common line, called a backbone. A backbone is a fast network medium that provides communication among all of the networks. It links all the hubs in the school, for example, expanding the reach of each network.

Mesh Topology   In **mesh topology** the components are all connected directly to other components. Because this topology connects devices with multiple paths, redundancies exist. But, because all devices are cross-connected, the best path can be taken at any time. The drawback to mesh topology is that needing at least one and a half connections for each computer makes it very expensive to construct. This topology is usually used in the Internet structure.

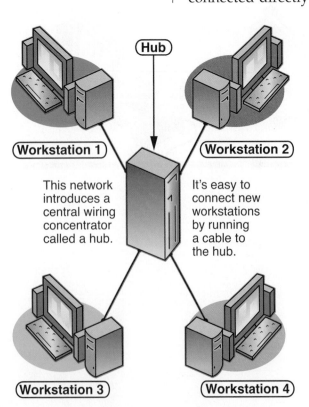

This network introduces a central wiring concentrator called a hub.

It's easy to connect new workstations by running a cable to the hub.

Figure 26.2.2 A star topology.

Exploring Ethernet

Ethernet is the most common networking technology used on LANs. Ethernet and star bus topology work together to ensure fast data transfers, logical network design, and fewer collisions. Ethernet uses a rule called Carrier Sensing Multiple Access/Collision Detection, or CSMA/CD. This protocol governs how network devices communicate and what happens if they break the rules.

Ethernet Communications Like a well mannered conversation, CSMA/CD requires each network device, also called a node, to take turns speaking. The node first listens to hear whether anyone is using the network, and then it transmits the data. When a node transmits data, every workstation on the network receives the data. However, only the device the data is intended for actually accepts it.

Ethernet Collisions If two nodes speak at the same time, a collision occurs. In that case, each of the conflicting nodes waits a random number of milliseconds and then attempts to speak again. The random waiting time helps prevent another collision.

Star bus topology expands a network's reach. As more nodes are added to a single network and as more networks are connected, the chance of multiple collisions increases. To solve this problem, Ethernet often uses bridges, switches, or routers. These devices divide the network into segments. To reduce congestion, messages are routed to the proper segment rather than to the entire network.

Spotlight on...

ROBERT M. METCALFE

"[The Association for Computing Machinery conference] aims to do more than brainstorm about the future. If we do a good job, we can change the future."

Robert M. Metcalfe

In the 1970s, Xerox® wanted a system that would let all the computers at a research center share a laser printer—the world's first laser printer, in fact. When Robert Metcalfe and his assistant, David R. Boggs, came up with Ethernet, the problem was solved.

Later, Metcalfe founded his own company, 3Com Corporation, which stands for *computers, communications,* and *compatibility.*

Connecting Remote Networks

Objectives

- Summarize the purpose of WANs.
- Specify WAN technologies.
- Identify common uses for WANs.
- Explain the use of intranets.

As You Read

Organize Information Complete a concept web to help you identify different WAN applications.

🔑 Key Terms

- electronic data interchange (EDI)
- extranet
- firewall
- intranet
- point-of-sale (POS)

Overview of WANs

As you learned in Lesson 25-3, wide area network, or WAN, is just what its name suggests: a network that links resources that are far apart from one another. Often, a WAN connects two or more LANs into one large network. Suppose a company has networks in Chicago, Illinois; Indianapolis, Indiana; and St. Louis, Missouri. A high-speed data line between Chicago and Indianapolis can connect those two networks. From Indianapolis, another high-speed data line is connected to St. Louis. Now, all three networks are connected, and the company has a WAN.

Protecting a WAN In the example network described above, the company has a problem. If the data line between St. Louis and Indianapolis fails, users in St. Louis cannot communicate beyond their LAN. Companies can solve this problem by adding more high-speed lines. For example, a data line between St. Louis and Chicago would ensure connectivity to resources in all three LANs even if one line fails.

Figure 26.3.1 WAN networks allow people spanning a large geographic area to share resources and communicate.

WANs in the Business World

The introduction of WANs allowed individuals on each network to communicate, access resources, and collaborate on projects. And as people got used to networking, they developed new forms of personal and business communications.

Groupware When the science of networking was applied to the need for collaboration, groupware was born. Groupware is another name for collaborative software.

EDI Companies can also use WANs for **electronic data interchange**, or **EDI**. EDI is a business-to-business WAN. For example, a company can use EDI to order equipment from a supplier quickly and accurately. It helps the supplier, too, because it automatically creates a bill and sends it to the buyer. Though EDI is expensive to set up, it saves both buyers and suppliers money: It saves paper and employee time, and it helps companies avoid having to stock large inventories.

WANs in Your World

You are likely exposed to WANs every day. Many of the retail stores you visit, such as grocery stores, shoe stores, or video stores, use WANs to track sales, inventory, and profits. You are also involved with WANs every time you use the Internet.

The POS System One example of a WAN in action is a **point-of-sale (POS)** system. Here's how it works:

- The cashier at a retail outlet, such as a grocery store, scans the bar code on the item you purchase. That bar code is linked to a central database.

- The POS system allows the store to order more of the product automatically, learn which day of the week customers are likely to buy the item, and compare its sales with other stores.

- Once a store has collected information on its sales, it can predict trends. Knowing these trends lets the store managers stock the shelves and set prices sensibly.

The Internet The Internet is the most common example of a WAN. You and others access the Internet through an Internet service provider (ISP). The ISP is connected to a backbone in order to reach other networks where Web servers are located.

Often, an employee who is connected to the office through a network can work from home, or telecommute.

Think About It!

Think about the advantages and disadvantages of telecommuting for the company. Which items below do you think are advantages? Which are disadvantages?

➢ You do not have to dress up to go to work.

➢ You do not travel to get to work.

➢ You can avoid people very easily.

➢ You can work at your own pace.

➢ You can take breaks whenever you want.

Figure 26.3.2 Ringing up a sale on a point-of-sale system.

What Is an Intranet?

Many companies, universities, and other organizations install intranets. An **intranet** is a private network that uses the same TCP/IP protocol as the Internet.

Comparing Intranets and the Internet   Intranets offer many of the same services the Internet does, such as e-mail and Web sites. Intranets are different from the Internet in that they are not meant for public use. **Firewall** software prevents outsiders from accessing the intranet.

Creating an Extranet   An intranet can also be converted to an **extranet**, which allows for limited public access. Companies often use extranets so employees can access the network while they travel or **telecommute**, which is when employees work from home while linked to the office by computer. Extranets are also used to share information with other businesses.

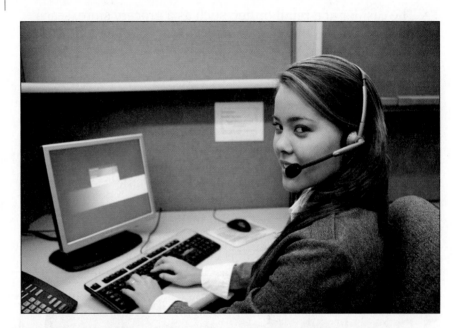

Figure 26.3.3 Company intranets enable employees to access information such as human resources forms, shared databases, and information about company policies.

Use the Vocabulary

Directions: *Match each vocabulary term in the left column with the correct definition in the right column.*

_____ **1.** network architecture

_____ **2.** topology

_____ **3.** contention

_____ **4.** bus topology

_____ **5.** hub

_____ **6.** token

_____ **7.** star topology

_____ **8.** firewall

_____ **9.** point-of-sale

a. science of designing a network

b. network designed around a hub

c. software that prevents outsiders from accessing an intranet

d. layout of a network

e. two messages trying to travel at once on a network

f. WAN to which a scanner at the checkout can be attached

g. unit of data that prevents collisions in ring topology

h. network connected to one line

i. a connection point for all the computers, printers, and other equipment on the network

Check Your Comprehension

Directions: *Determine the correct choice for each of the following.*

1. All networks follow rules developed by the _____.

   a. ISO

   b. POP

   c. EDI

   d. LAN

2. The OSI model defines how data travels through _____.

   a. a collision

   b. backbones

   c. seven layers

   d. groupware

3. Early LANs were designed with _____.

   a. bus topology

   b. ring topology

   c. star topology

   d. star bus topology

4. Ethernet deals with contention by _____.

   a. storing messages in the session layer

   b. assigning messages to a POP

   c. dumping messages that collide

   d. delaying messages that collide

5. Groupware makes all of the following possible EXCEPT _____.

   a. videoconferences

   b. e-mail

   c. electronic bulletin boards

   d. protocol stacks

6. A _____ topology is used in the Internet structure, and it is the most expensive.

   a. tree

   b. star bus

   c. mesh

   d. ring

Think Critically

Directions: *Answer the following questions.*

1. How does the existence of protocols such as the Open Systems Interconnection model make the job of designing a network easier?

2. What equipment do you think employees need to telecommute?

3. For what purposes might a big bank use both LANs and a WAN?

4. Do you think LANs and WANs will become more or less standardized in the future? Why?

5. How has networking changed the way many companies do business?

Extend Your Knowledge

Directions: *Choose one of the following projects. Complete the exercise on a separate sheet of paper.*

A. Work with a partner to find out more about Ethernet, which many schools use in their networks. With your teacher's permission, use a search engine and the keyword *Ethernet* to research three Web sites that describe this technology. Next, outline and create a chart to help you evaluate the three sites. Identify the source of each. Then develop a scale and rank each on completeness, clarity, organization, and overall value.

B. Within the next few years, the POS (point-of-sale) system could make a leap from bar codes to smart labels. The labels are also known as radio frequency identification, or RFID, tags, and they've actually been used for some time to track cattle. Conduct research in the library or, with your teacher's permission, on the Internet to find out how smart labels work and how they will affect retailers and customers. Discuss your findings with your classmates.

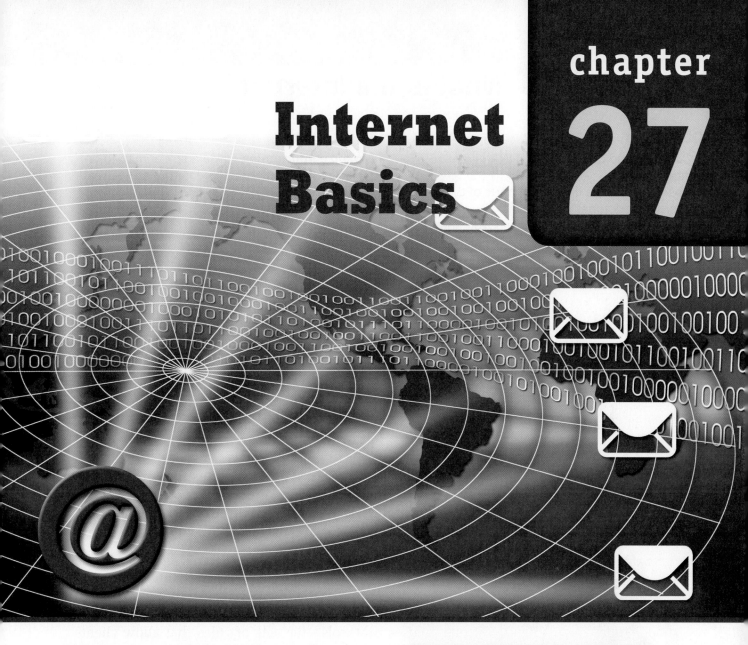

Internet Basics

A Network of Networks The Internet connects people all over the world through a huge network of computer systems. The U.S. government and university researchers began the Internet to share information. Since then, it has turned into one of the most exciting inventions in history.

As more and more people use the Internet, the demand for user-friendly online services has also grown and created new business opportunities. Additionally, electronic mail and instant messaging services have changed the way people meet and stay in touch with one another. People online can work together on projects in different locations, sharing information as if they were in the same office.

Chapter Outline

What Is the Internet?

Objectives

- Compare and contrast LANs, WANs, and the Internet.
- Describe how the three main parts of the Internet work together.
- Explain the advantages and disadvantages of the organization of the Internet.
- Identify organizations responsible for setting standards for the Internet.

As You Read

Organize Information Use a spider map to organize information about the Internet as you read.

🔑 Key Terms

- Internet
- Internet client

Figure 27.1.1 Like many networks, the Internet is made up of connected client and server computers, which use protocols to communicate.

Organization of the Internet

The **Internet** is a global WAN, a network of networks. It connects everything from single computers to large networks. The Internet can even connect computers that run different operating systems. This ability to share information with almost any computer makes the Internet a powerful tool for communication. The Internet is made up of three important parts: servers, clients, and protocols.

Servers Internet servers are the computers that provide services to other computers by way of the Internet. These services include processing e-mail, storing Web pages, or helping send files from one computer to another.

Clients and Protocols Internet clients are the computers that request services from a server. When you connect to the Internet, the computer you use is considered a client. Like other networks, the Internet uses protocols—the sets of rules that allow clients and servers to communicate.

Is the Internet a WAN?

There are three key differences between the Internet and other WANs.

Type of Access The Internet is public, while WANs are typically private.

Degree of Security While the Internet is becoming more secure, it is still not as secure as a private WAN connection. As data travels through the Internet, snoops and eavesdroppers on the public networks through which the data moves sometimes try to access it. A private WAN is more secure because it is more likely that only the organization that owns it has access to it.

Types of Information On the Internet, information is transmitted in the form of Web pages and other types of files. A WAN is used for more than just browsing Web pages. It provides access to network resources, such as printers, file servers, and databases.

Inventing the Internet

In the 1960s, people were working on ideas that later became the Internet. In 1969, the first four major computer centers in the United States were linked. By 1973, the network was international. In 1983, the Internet protocols went online for the first time. Two major groups worked on the development of the Internet: the United States military and university researchers.

United States Military In the 1960s, the United States government wanted to find a way to communicate in the event of a disaster or military attack. The military began to work on a system that would operate even if some communication connections were destroyed. The Defense Advanced Research Projects Agency (DARPA) of the U.S. Department of Defense focused on computer networking and communications. In 1968, this research led to a network of connected computer centers called the Advanced Research Projects Agency Network (ARPANET).

University Researchers With the military's leadership and funding, DARPA formed computing research centers at universities across the United States. From 1969 through 1987, the number of computers on the network increased from 4 to more than 10,000. These connections created the networks that became the Internet.

Figure 27.1.2 Today, the Internet includes millions of servers and connections all over the globe.

Internet Management

Who owns the Internet? The truth is, no specific organization or government does. Many organizations are responsible for different parts of the network. Here are some examples:

- The World Wide Web Consortium (W3C) issues standards related to the World Wide Web.
- Internet Engineering Task Force (IETF) is a large international community of network designers, operators, vendors, and researchers. This group is concerned with the future structure and smooth operation of the Internet. Like many organizations that set computing standards, the IETF is "open," meaning any interested person can participate.
- Internet Corporation for Assigned Names and Numbers (ICANN) is a nonprofit corporation with a variety of responsibilities, including the management of domain names.
- Web Standards Project (WaSP) is a coalition that supports standards for simple, affordable access to Web technologies.

Freedom of the Internet   One advantage to the open quality of the Internet is the ability to share information. Anyone can make an idea or opinion accessible to anyone else.

Pitfalls of the Internet   However, there are pitfalls to this open organization. People can post whatever point of view or information they want, even if it can sometimes be misleading or false. It is up to the users of the Internet to think critically about the information they find. If you have a question about anything you find on the Internet, ask an adult you trust about it.

Real-World Tech

Voting on the Internet?   According to the Federal Election Commission, the Internet is not ready for U.S. citizens to vote on it. Safeguarding the privacy, security, and reliability of the voting process is important to ensuring a free democratic election.

While there have been some experiments with Internet voting, experts agree that it will be a long time before it is used in general elections. The Internet, however, can improve some parts of the election process. For example, the technology is in place for secure overseas military voting. Also, registration databases and vote totals can be sent over the Internet, saving time and money.

In what other ways might you use the Internet to find out more about politics?

Connecting to the Internet

Objectives

- Identify ways to connect to the Internet.
- Compare and contrast Internet Service Providers and online services.
- Categorize access methods by temporary or permanent IP address.
- Compare and contrast the connection speed of a modem to DSL and to a fiber-optic line.

As You Read

Outline Information   Use an outline to organize information about how the Internet works as you read.

Accessing the Internet from Home

There are different ways to connect to the Internet. The reasons for various options are availability, location, speed, and price.

Dial-up, ISDN, and DSL Access   The least expensive way to get online is to use a dial-up connection between a standard phone line and a modem. These connections are called "dial-up" because your computer must connect to the Internet by using a telephone number to contact a server. Only 10% of households in the United States still use dial-up access. This type of access uses a modem and a standard phone line to connect to the Internet with **Point-to-Point protocol (PPP)**. Aside from the slow speed, a drawback of dial-up is that your computer is assigned a temporary IP address; you can't run server software without a permanent IP address. When the session is over, the connection is broken.

Some Digital Subscriber Lines (DSL) require a special telephone line. Integrated Services Digital Network (ISDN) lines require a special ISDN adapter and modem. As a result, both services cost more than regular phone service. Furthermore, DSL and ISDN are not available in all areas. One drawback of DSL is that service does not extend more than a few miles from telephone switching stations, so this service is unavailable in some areas.

Cable and Satellite   Cable television companies offer Internet access through cable modems. This access is at speeds much faster than dial-up modems. You need a network card in your computer, a cable modem, and cable access. Satellite access is also very fast for downloading files to your computer, but it requires a phone line and a modem for sending files to outside users.

Key Terms

- Internet service provider (ISP)
- navigate
- online service
- Point-to-Point protocol (PPP)
- username

Accessing the Internet from Work

Access needs of large organizations may differ from those of home Internet users.

LAN Access   If your school or library has a local area network (LAN) that is connected to the Internet, you access the Internet through the network. LAN access is generally much faster than dial-up access because LANs usually access the Internet via a high-speed connection. But the performance you experience depends on how many LAN users are trying to access the Internet at the same time. In most cases, you have a permanently assigned IP address on a LAN.

Fiber Optics   An organization that needs a high bandwidth might use a T1 line (which stands for trunkline) for Internet access. Internet service providers, who are responsible for maintaining backbones, need even faster connections, such as a T3 line. T1 and T3 lines use fiber-optic cables that are capable of handling huge amounts of data. This technology is popular for Internet backbones and LANs.

To get an idea of just how fast a modern backbone is, compare the speed of an old-fashioned dial-up modem to the speed of different types of fiber-optic lines. At one time, home computers came equipped with a 56K modem, which could transmit about 50,000 bits per second, or approximately 5,000 characters per second. The following table illustrates the amount of data that can travel across DSL, cable, and fiberoptic lines.

Type of Line	Transmission Speed
ADSL (Asymmetric digital subscriber line)	16 to 640 kilobits per second sending data 1.5 to 9 megabits per second receiving data
SDSL (Symmetric digital subscriber line)	Up to 3 megabits per second
T1	1.544 megabits per second
T3	43.232 megabits per second

Getting Online

After you have access to the Internet, you must select a way to get online. Choices include Internet service providers and online services.

Internet Service Providers An **Internet service provider (ISP)** is a company that provides a link from your computer to the Internet. For a fee, an ISP provides its subscribers with software, a password, an access phone number, and a username. A **username** identifies who you are when you access the Internet. An ISP does not guide you through the Internet—it only provides an easy-to-use connection to it. You can use either a local ISP or a national ISP.

Online Services An online service connects your computer to the Internet. **Online services** are businesses that provide tools to help you **navigate**, or move to different parts of, the Internet. Online services are not the Internet. These services are now almost all free. When you register for them on the Internet, special software is downloaded onto your computer. The software makes the connection to the service, which then guides you through content and activities. Three popular online service providers are Microsoft Network (MSN), AOL, and Verizon. The functions of online service providers, Internet portals, and search engines, which you'll read about soon, will likely overlap. Also, the term online service provider has broadened to include any business that offers services over the Internet—from Amazon.com to banks offering online banking to entertainment sites, like youtube.com.

Figure 27.2.1 Microsoft Network (MSN) is a popular online service provider with millions of subscribers.

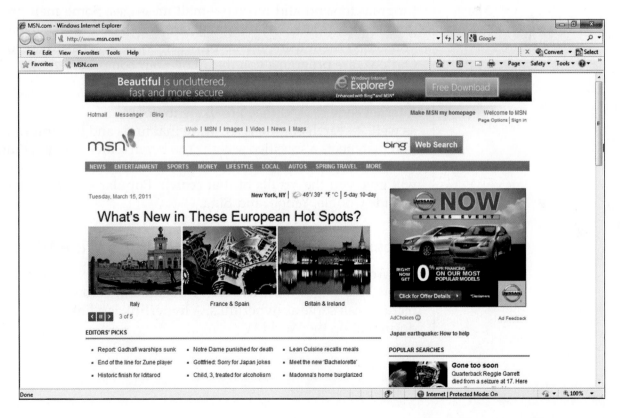

Comparing Internet Services

Objectives

- Identify and describe types of Internet services.
- Summarize how to access information on the Web.
- Analyze the usefulness of e-mail in daily living.
- Explain File Transfer Protocol.
- Discuss issues related to transferring files.

As You Read

Identify Main Idea/Details   Use a main idea/detail chart to identify the main idea and details of popular Internet services as you read.

🔑 Key Terms

- download
- file compression
- hyperlink
- hypertext
- portal
- search engine
- uniform resource locator (URL)
- upload
- virus
- Web browser

Internet Services

When you send an e-mail message to a friend, you use one kind of Internet service. Browsing the World Wide Web is done through another type of service. Different Internet services are used for accessing the World Wide Web, sending and receiving electronic mail, and conducting file transfers.

Internet Software

The protocols for delivering an e-mail message are not the same as the protocols for displaying a Web page. Typically, there is different software for each Internet service. You use a **Web browser** to view Web pages. Popular Web browsers are Mozilla Firefox, Google Chrome, and Microsoft Internet Explorer. You use a mail program to send and receive e-mail messages. Some mail programs, such as Hotmail and gmail, are Web-based, which means you access them using a Web browser. Some, such as Microsoft Outlook, are programs you install on your computer.

Portals   Internet **portals** provide organized subject guides of Internet content, and they are likely to double as search engines as well. A **search engine** is software that finds and lists information that meets a specified search. You begin searching by typing a keyword or phrase into a blank field. Then, the search engine will give you the results of that search. Popular search engines include Google, Yahoo, and Bing.

Accessing Information on the World Wide Web

The World Wide Web is a huge collection of hypertext documents called Web pages. In a **hypertext** document, certain words or pictures can serve as hyperlinks. A **hyperlink** is a link to another document on the World Wide Web.

Hyperlinks Usually hyperlinks appear underlined, in a different color, or highlighted. Sometimes there are buttons or images that can be clicked. When you move your mouse over a hyperlink, the pointer changes to an icon of a hand. You can click this hyperlink item to be transferred to another document.

URLs When you click a hyperlink, the Web browser retrieves and displays the document connected to that hyperlink. How does this work? Every document has a unique address, called a **uniform resource locator (URL)**, which tells exactly where the document is located on the Internet. A hyperlink instructs the browser to go to the URL for that document.

Electronic Mail

For many Internet users, electronic mail, or e-mail, has replaced traditional mail and telephone services. E-mail is fast and easy. If you organize your e-mail addresses into groups, you can broadcast, or send, a message to a group in just one step.

E-mail Pros and Cons E-mail is not free, and it's not instantaneous. However, you do not pay to send each e-mail, as you would a letter. The cost of your e-mail service is included in the fee you pay your Internet service provider or online service provider. In most cases, it takes minutes or more for an e-mail message to reach its destination. But it costs the same and takes approximately the same amount of time to send a message to someone in your own city as it does to send a message halfway around the world.

Spotlight on...

TIM BERNERS-LEE

❝The whole idea that you can have some idea and make it happen means dreamers all over the world should take heart and not stop.❞

Tim Berners-Lee
Creator of the World Wide Web

In the 1980s, Tim Berners-Lee turned what was a system for keeping track of his random notes into a system for linking the work of scientists anywhere in the world.

Berners-Lee designed the URL, or a scheme for locating Internet addresses; developed HTML, or a language for encoding hypertext; created HTTP, or a system to link hypertext documents; and built the first browser. Few people in history have had a greater impact on the way we communicate than Berners-Lee.

Career Corner

Director of Music Programming
Many online services sell music over the Internet, creating new business and career opportunities in this area of technology.

A Director of Music Programming for an online music subscription service needs several years of experience in the music industry and with technology. Knowledge of music copyright laws is also essential.

Figure 27.3.1 The File Download - Security Warning from Windows. If you trust the source of the file, you click Run or Save.

Transferring Files

File Transfer Protocol (FTP) lets you transfer files on the Internet. With an FTP client, you can transfer files from an FTP server to your computer in an operation called **downloading**. In **uploading**, you transfer files from the client to the server.

FTP can transfer both text files and binary files. Binary files are program files, graphics, pictures, music or video clips, and documents. Once you've stored a file on an FTP server, you can distribute the URL so that your friends can also download the file from the server.

One difference between using an FTP server and using e-mail to transfer files is that with FTP, the file stays on the server until you take it off. With e-mail, a file that has been transferred will be lost once the e-mail message has been deleted. (The file attachment remains on the computer where it was sent from— unless it is deleted from there as well. See Lesson 31–1 for more information on sending e-mail with attachments.) E-mail is considered a more secure method, however, because only the recipient of the e-mail message has access to the attached files.

File Transfer Issues

Computer Viruses It's important to exercise caution when downloading files from the Internet, especially program files. Files are commonly used to transmit viruses. A **virus** is a program created to damage computers and networks. The damage caused may be minor or serious, such as altering or destroying data. It's a good idea to check all downloaded files for viruses before saving them. Most antivirus programs will do this for you automatically. You should update your antivirus program regularly to be protected from the newest viruses. The Windows operating system helps by giving a security warning when a download is about to begin. You may want to review the advice provided by clicking the *What's the Risk?* link.

File Compression The larger a file is, the more time it takes to travel over a network. **File compression** is a way of reducing file size so it can travel more quickly over a network. If you are sending a large file, it is important to compress it. It can also be convenient to compress multiple files into one when you are sending them to someone in an e-mail attachment. Some compressed files are set to decompress automatically. Others must be decompressed using decompression software. The most widely used compression software for a Windows system is WinZip®. Macintosh computers use a program called StuffIt™ to compress files and a utility called StuffIt Expander to decompress files.

Use the Vocabulary

Directions: *Match each vocabulary term in the left column with the correct definition in the right column.*

_____ **1.** Internet
_____ **2.** Internet client
_____ **3.** Internet service provider
_____ **4.** username
_____ **5.** search engine
_____ **6.** portal
_____ **7.** hyperlink
_____ **8.** uniform resource locator
_____ **9.** download

a. highlighted text or graphic in a Web site that directs browser to another URL

b. software that finds and lists information that matches criteria

c. computer that requests services from a server

d. identification while on the Internet

e. address of documents on the Web

f. vast network of connected computers

g. a company that provides access to the Internet

h. to transfer a file from a server to a client

i. Internet service that provides a guide to Internet content

Check Your Comprehension

Directions: *Complete each sentence with information from the chapter.*

1. A network that covers a large area is called a(n) _____.

2. The three main parts of the Internet are _____, servers, and protocols.

3. The two main groups responsible for inventing the Internet are the U.S. military and _____ .

4. A(n) _____ is the least expensive way to access the Internet.

5. _____ are businesses that provide special software to guide users through Internet content and activities.

6. A(n) _____ enables someone to search for a Web site with a keyword.

7. In a(n) _____ document, certain words or pictures serve as hyperlinks.

8. File _____ is a way of reducing file size.

9. A(n) _____ is used to view Web pages.

10. You can send a(n) _____ to someone by attaching it to an e-mail message.

Think Critically

Directions: *Answer the following questions.*

1. Why did the U.S. Department of Defense begin to research computer networking and communications?

2. Why do you think it is important to think critically about the accuracy and validity of information you find on the Internet?

3. Why might someone use an online service rather than an Internet service provider?

4. Compare and contrast the use of e-mail and file transfer protocol for transmitting files over the Internet.

5. Why do you think e-mail is so popular for daily communication at home, school, and work?

Extend Your Knowledge

Directions: *Choose one of the following projects. Complete the exercise on a separate sheet of paper.*

A. Because the Internet is so easily accessible, it is important to learn how to protect yourself when you are online. With permission from your teacher, conduct research using the Internet to compile a list of Web safety tips. Include information about any acceptable use policy your school may have. Publish your findings, with permission from your teacher, on your school's Web site.

B. With permission from your teacher, in small groups, conduct online research using keyword strategies to learn what kinds of Internet access are available in your area. Find out how much the services cost and the benefits of each. If possible, get information from companies competing for the same services so you can compare prices. Compile your research in a chart. Then, summarize your findings as a class.

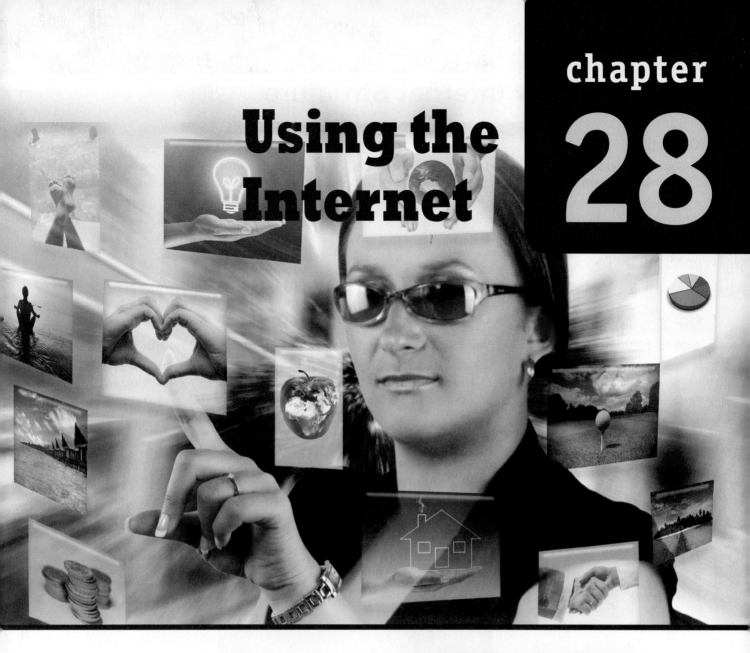

Using the Internet

Expanding Our Horizons Are you interested in Japanese animation? Hiking trails in the Australian Outback? Sending pictures of your family to a pen pal in another country? Each day more resources are available on the Internet. The ability to send data faster and faster allows people to more easily share ideas, information, and entertainment with people all over the world.

Every day more people connect to the Internet, using whatever form of technology is available to them. As demand for Internet access increases, even remote areas of the globe will be able to connect to the Internet and contribute to the ever-changing, diverse collection of information and services that can be found there.

Chapter Outline

Internet Structure

Objectives

- Compare and contrast the Internet and the telephone system.
- Sequence how information travels through the hierarchy of networks on the Internet.
- Summarize the advantages of a cross-platform network

As You Read

Identify Key Information   Use a concept web to help you identify six key phrases to describe what the Internet is as you read.

🔑 Key Terms

- cross-platform
- platform

Figure 28.1.1 When you make a telephone call, the line is all yours until you hang up.

Organization of the Internet

You can pick up a phone, dial a number, and, within a few seconds, communicate with any other person on a phone connected to the telephone system. This is similar to the Internet, in that any computer can communicate with any other computer on the network.

Internet Versus Telephones   The Internet, however, does work on different principles than the phone system does. Rather than a telephone number, every computer on the Internet has an Internet address, also called an IP address. It can contact any other computer on the Internet by "dialing" the other computer's address.

Another difference is that the Internet works on packet-switching technology rather than the circuit-switching technology of the telephone system.

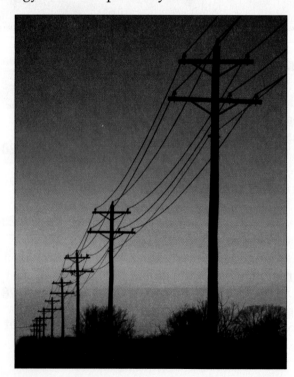

Internet Infrastructure

When you use your computer to connect to the Internet, the computer is called a client. A client uses a browser to request access to a Web page stored on an Internet server computer. Your request travels by local connections to your Internet service provider's (ISP) local point of presence (POP). From there, your ISP sends your request to a regional backbone, which uses high-speed lines that connect your city to a larger metropolitan area. Your request then travels to a network access point, or NAP.

On the Internet, dozens of large ISPs connect with one another at NAPs in various cities. Trillions of bytes of data flow between the individual networks at these points. This is how your computer at home connects to another computer in a completely different region.

Cross-Platform Network

One amazing thing about the Internet is that you can exchange information with computers that are different from your own. When you connect to the Internet, you may connect to an Internet server on a Macintosh, a Windows PC, a Linux PC, a UNIX machine, or a mainframe computer.

Connections

Science Vinton Cerf, one of the developers of TCP/IP protocol, is working with scientists on parcel transfer protocol, which will send data to other planets and space-craft. It is hoped that this new technology will help pave the way for manned missions to Mars by 2099. The plan for wiring Earth to Mars includes using an existing international antenna system, a six-satellite constellation around Mars, and a new protocol for transferring data between the planets.

Figure 28.1.2 All kinds of computers can communicate with one another through the Internet, as long as they use the same protocols.

In the United States, one employment benefit on the rise is telecommuting, or working from home on a computer.

Think About It!

Networks are needed to allow employees to work efficiently between their home and their office. Which type(s) of networks listed below would a telecommuter likely use to conduct work from home?

➤ LAN

➤ WAN

➤ Internet

A **platform** is a kind of computer that uses a certain type of processor and operating system, such as an Intel-based Windows PC. Software or hardware is said to have **cross-platform** capability when it can run the same way on more than one platform. When you are using the Internet, you don't know which type of computer platform you are accessing, and it doesn't matter. This is because all computers on the Internet use TCP/IP protocols. As a result, they all look and behave the same way online, regardless of their platform.

Compatibility Cross-platform compatibility is one of the major reasons for the increasing popularity of private intranets. Many organizations, such as schools, use computers that run on different platforms. They may use computers running the Macintosh operating system in one part of the school and computers running Windows in another. Yet, they still need to share information. After the computers are connected with the Internet's TCP/IP protocols, the computers can exchange data and even control one another's operations. For instance, someone could create a file on a Macintosh computer and then send it to a printer connected to a computer running Windows.

Spotlight on...

KATHRYN C. MONTGOMERY

66 *We believe this . . . balances the need for effective safeguards with the goal of providing children with the full benefits of interactivity on the World Wide Web.* **99**

Kathryn C. Montgomery, Ph.D. Co-founder, Center for Media Education

Dr. Montgomery is one of the co-founders of the Center for Media Education (CME). This nonprofit organization focuses on creating a safe and high-quality online culture for young people and their families.

Montgomery's work helps frame national public policy, such as the Children's Online Privacy Protection Act (COPRA) of 1998. COPRA states that personal information requested of children under 13 years of age online must be limited and necessary.

Accessing Data on the Internet

Objectives

- Distinguish between Internet Protocol addresses and domain names.
- Explain how the domain names are organized.
- Identify the different parts of a URL.
- Describe how to locate the owner of a domain name.

As You Read

Outline Information   Use an outline to organize information about how the Internet works as you read.

Accessing Data

The Internet has revolutionized access to data. Anyone with an Internet connection can find information on virtually any topic. Many local governments insure access to all citizens by making Internet access available at public locations such as libraries. That means even those who are disabled or disadvantaged have the same access as everyone else.

Requesting Data on the Internet

To understand how a data request is sent on the Internet, it might be helpful to compare the process to taking a road trip. Recall that when you request a Web page through your Web browser, the request travels by local connections—like streets in a town—to your ISP's local POP. From there, your ISP sends your request to a regional backbone—a type of data highway.

Your Web page request then travels to a NAP, which is like a freeway. As your request nears its destination, it moves off the information freeway. It travels back through other regional highways and local roads until its trip is complete and the Web page you requested is displayed on your computer screen.

Domain Names

Each computer that connects to the Internet has to be uniquely identified. To do this, every computer is assigned a four-part number separated by periods called the **Internet Protocol (IP) address**. For example, the IP address for your computer might be 123.257.91.7. The administrator of the network to which your computer connects assigns your IP address.

🔑 Key Terms

- domain name
- domain name system
- Internet Protocol (IP) address
- top-level domain
- WHOIS database

Technology @ Work

Alex Jarrett started a nonprofit organization called the Degree of Confluence Project to have people visit each of the latitude and longitude markers in the world. They then send his company pictures of each location to post on the Web.

Think About It!

If a company has Internet access, it can start its own Web site. But first it has to get a domain name. Which top-level domain name(s) listed below do you think would be most appropriate for Jarrett's company?

➢ .org
➢ .gov
➢ .edu
➢ .com
➢ .mil

Figure 28.2.1 Using the VeriSign® service to search for an available domain name.

A **domain name** identifies one or more IP addresses and is used to locate information on the Internet. For example, an Internet server computer's domain name might be whitehouse.gov, but its numeric IP address might be 206.166.48.45. The domain name and the IP address are simply two ways to identify the same computer on the Internet.

Top-Level Domains   Every domain name has a suffix that tells which type of organization registered the name. The most common domains are .com (commercial), .edu (education), .org (nonprofit organizations), .gov (government), .mil (military), and .net (network organizations). These are called **top-level domains**. New top-level domain names such as .biz (business), .museum (arts and culture), .pro (professionals), .info (information services), and .name (individuals) are coming online to meet the growing demand for new classifications.

Acquiring a Domain Name   A special server called a **Domain Name System (DNS)** server matches the domain name to the correct IP address. To get a domain name, you or your ISP must contact a registering organization, which then contacts InterNIC. InterNIC is a service organization that maintains a central database of domain names in the United States. Other countries maintain their own network information centers.

When you register a domain name, you pay a fee to keep it in the database of domain names. If you do not pay the renewable registration fee, the domain becomes available for someone else to register in his or her name.

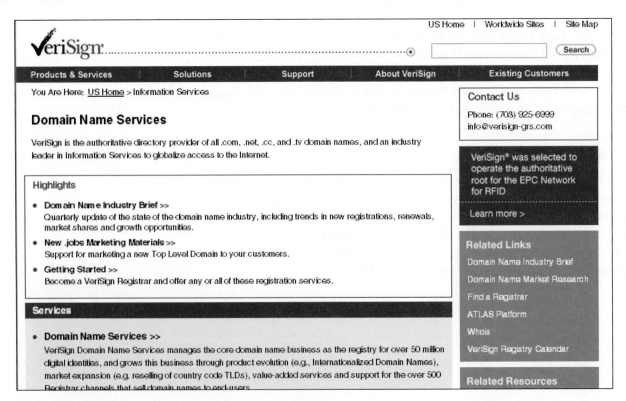

Domain Names and WHOIS Searches

Within the Domain Name System, each computer on the Internet must have a unique name, or the browser would not know to which server to go.

The InterNIC The organization responsible for maintaining the list of the registered domain names is the InterNIC. When you register a domain name, you pay an accredited registrar to insert an entry into a directory of all the domain names and their corresponding computers on the Internet. An Accredited Registrar Directory provides a listing of accredited domain name registrars available on the InterNIC Web site.

The central database of domain names is called the **WHOIS database.** You can look up information about the owner and servers of a certain domain on this database.

Branding Consultant Branding consultants work with businesses to define their image to their target customers. Everything from the colors on a logo to the domain name communicate a company's personality to a customer. Brand consultants use both research and creativity in the building of a company's brand.

Figure 28.2.2 Access the WHOIS database at Whois.net.

Internet Communications

Objectives

- Identify different ways to communicate online.
- Identify advantages and disadvantages of electronic communication.
- Identify how to find information about Internet etiquette.
- Discuss the future of the Internet.

As You Read

Organize Information   Use a spider map to help you organize key details about Internet services as you read.

Key Terms

- alt newsgroup
- blog
- channel
- hierarchy
- Internet 2 (I2)
- podcast
- social networking
- Usenet
- Web feed
- wiki

Figure 28.3.1 Internet newsgroups let you participate in online discussions with other people who share your interests.

Communicating Online

The Internet is fast becoming the main means by which people communicate over distances. If you have an Internet connection and an account with a communication service, there are many ways to communicate. Communication can be formal, through e-mailing (see Chapter 27) and newsgroups, or it can be more informal, through online chat channels or forums, instant messaging, and social networking sites.

Newsgroups

The **Usenet** is a discussion system computer users can access through the Internet. It has thousands of newsgroups on many subjects and contains messages newsgroup users have posted. Usenet newsgroups are organized into categories called **hierarchies**.

These hierarchies are divided into subcategories: 1) standard newsgroups or world newsgroups, which feature high-quality discussions on any topic; 2) biz newsgroups, which are devoted to discussing commercial uses of the Internet; and 3) **alt newsgroups**, which can be created by anyone to discuss a specific topic and often feature odd or offensive discussions. Usenet servers are not required to carry alt newsgroups.

Internet Relay Chat

Internet Relay Chat (IRC) is an Internet service that enables users to join chat groups, called **channels**, and enter into live, or real-time, conversations. Some cover a specific topic, and others are gathering places for groups of friends. When you join a channel, you'll find others chatting away with messages that appear on-screen, prefaced by the senders nickname. Normally, messages are seen by everyone in the channel, but it is possible to send a "whisper," which can only be seen by the person you send it to. In addition to IRC channels, most ISPs offer chat forums as well. Sometimes chat rooms are not friendly places, but they are not entirely without rules. Every channel has a moderator who can remove a sender from the channel for any reason. The standards of behavior differ from channel to channel, so it is best to practice respectful online behavior.

Instant Messaging (IM)   Instant messaging is when you send real-time messages to another Internet user. Instant messaging is like a chat room, except you get to choose your chat partners. For most young people, instant messaging, along with texting on their cell phones, has replaced phone calls as the quickest, most satisfying way to communicate in real time. With a webcam, IMers can even video chat.

Social Networking   Sites like Facebook and Myspace are **social networking** sites, or virtual communities that offer real-time chatting options. On Facebook everyone has a "wall," and people you've invited to be your "friends" can see your wall and write on it. If you have something personal to say to a friend, it's better to send a message through Facebook, which is like sending an e-mail, or to see if they are online to chat in real time. Facebook has a default setting that not only lets everyone on Facebook see your wall, your profile (the information you post about yourself), and your photos, but it also lets marketers see and use your information. It's up to the individual user to change the default privacy settings so that only friends can see your wall.

Podcasts   A **podcast** is an audio or video file that is created for downloading to an iPod or an MP3 player, such as Microsoft's Zune. Many radio stations create podcasts of popular programs or parts of them. College teachers create podcasts and upload them to a special Apple Web site called iTunes U or to other Web locations. Students can download the podcasts to their iPods or MP3 player, or they choose to listen to them on their own computers.

Web Feed   A **Web feed** is a service that automatically downloads Web page content that a user has signed up for. The content may include the text of news or opinions or audio/video files. A site that offers a Web feed has a symbol such as RSS to indicate that a feed is available. When a browser detects a feed on a Web page, it may also display a special Web feed icon. When you click on the button, the site asks the user to indicate how and where the content is to be downloaded. Yahoo!, Google, AOL, and other Web services offer to manage Web feeds for users.

Did You Know ?

Emoticons are combinations of certain keystrokes used to express feelings in informal online conversations, but there are many more emoticons out there than frowns, smiles, and winks. Here are some less common emoticons. Can you guess what they signal? (Turn the book upside down to see the answers.)

:-o   Oh!

:'-)   So happy I'm crying.

:-0   No yelling!

:-#   My lips are sealed.

Some services safeguard students on the Internet at school. For example, some allow teachers to create password-protected Web pages that include secure chat rooms and discussion forums.

Think About It!

Participating in online communities can be a great way to gain information, but it is not without risks. Circle the suggestions below that can help you to stay safe online.

▶ Chat only on monitored channels.

▶ Refuse to give out any personal information.

▶ Practice good netiquette (Internet etiquette).

Blogs and Wikis A **blog**—or Weblog—is a type of Web page diary. People create blogs to share their thoughts and opinions. A blog is stored on a Web server, like a Web page, and the owner usually updates it on a regular basis. Anyone with access to the Internet can read the blog. Often, blogs provide a way for readers to comment on the blog content. A **wiki** is a collaborative Web page. Anyone can edit or create content on the page. The most notable wiki is Wikipedia.org, an encyclopedia Web site with user-generated content. It is important to keep in mind that blogs and wikis reflect the opinions of the people who write or edit the content; they may not always be accurate or up-to-date.

Advantages and Disadvantages Electronic communication helps create and maintain bonds between people. It is also available around the clock, making it possible to communicate at any time of day. These same advantages also cause problems. Constant electronic communication can get in the way of face-to-face communication and hurt personal relationships. It also leaves room for misunderstandings.

Internet Growth

Over the next decade, millions of new users will connect to the Internet. Can the Internet handle this kind of growth? Internet experts say that improvements must take place to make certain the Internet doesn't become overwhelmed by its own success.

More Internet Addresses IP protocol allows for about 4 billion IP addresses. Surprisingly, that is not enough. One solution lies in a new version of the Internet Protocol called IPv6. However, the problem with this solution is that existing Internet equipment must be modified to work with the new protocol.

More Bandwidth With growing Internet use, new technologies to increase bandwidth must be developed. The **Internet 2 (I2)** project will develop and test high-performance network and telecommunications techniques. These improvements will eventually find their way to the public Internet, allowing faster access for all users.

Use the Vocabulary

Directions: *Match each vocabulary term in the left column with the correct definition in the right column.*

_____ **1.** domain name
_____ **2.** IP address
_____ **3.** social networking
_____ **4.** WHOIS database
_____ **5.** Usenet
_____ **6.** hierarchy
_____ **7.** Domain Name System
_____ **8.** channel
_____ **9.** platform
_____ **10.** Internet 2 (I2)

a. domain name lookup
b. a special server that matches a domain name to the correct IP address
c. project that tests new network technologies
d. an individual IRC chat group
e. identifies one or more IP addresses and is used to locate information on the Internet
f. virtual communities that offer real-time chatting options
g. hosts thousands of newsgroups
h. a kind of computer that uses a certain type of processor and operating system
i. a four-part number separated by periods used to identify a computer connected to the Internet
j. Internet newsgroup categories

Check Your Comprehension

Directions: *Complete each sentence with information from the chapter.*

1. After your Web page request goes to your ISP's POP, it goes to a(n) _____.

2. Software or hardware is said to have _____ platform capability when it can run the same way on more than one platform.

3. The _____ domain identifies which type of organization registered the domain name.

4. _____ is a service organization that maintains a central database of domain names in the United States.

5. When you use your computer to connect to the Internet, the computer is called a(n) _____.

6. The _____ of the network to which your computer connects assigns your IP address.

7. In the Domain Name System, each name has to be _____.

8. You can search the _____ database for the owner and servers of a particular domain.

9. By using _____ people can effectively create their own personal chat channels.

10. In the future, the Internet will need to increase bandwidth and create more _____.

Think Critically

Directions: *Answer the following questions.*

1. How does information travel through the hierarchy of networks on the Internet?

2. Compare and contrast the telephone system with the Internet.

3. Why is it important to have no duplication of domain names? How is this goal accomplished?

4. What are advantages and disadvantages of chatting with IRC?

5. How might the increasing popularity of the Internet become a problem?

Extend Your Knowledge

Directions: *Choose one of the following projects. Complete the exercise on a separate sheet of paper.*

A. With your teacher's permission, use Internet research, including keyword searches, and personal observation to find out about some interesting technology-related projects students are conducting in schools across the country. Create a Web page describing these projects. Add links to any relevant sites. Publish the Web site on the Internet. Be sure to check the page on multiple computer platforms to be sure it displays properly and adjust it, if necessary.

B. Work in small groups to simulate a chat room. Hold a conversation about a topic you are studying by writing messages to each other in random order on one sheet of paper. Pass the paper to anyone who has something to say. Do not speak, and only write one message at a time. After five minutes, discuss your experiences. What advantages and disadvantages did you find to this form of communication?

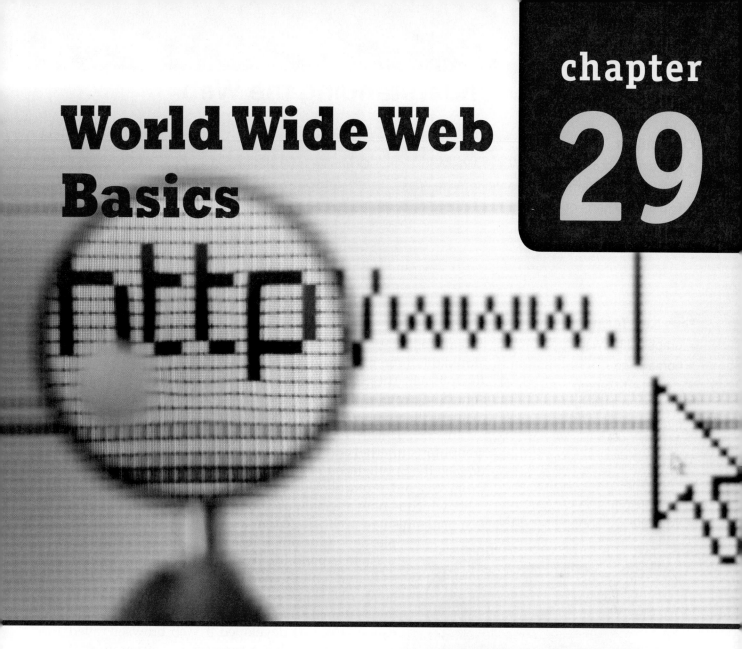

World Wide Web Basics

A Global Source of Information

Think about a comprehensive source of information—one that grows by thousands of new documents every day. Such a resource would contain a wealth of information.

Actually, you don't have to suppose such a resource into existence. It already exists—it's the World Wide Web. You can turn to the World Wide Web to check out products, get help with schoolwork, find out about current events, and do many more tasks.

However, along with offering a lot of wonderful information, the Web is also home to some inaccurate and potentially harmful information. It is up to you to evaluate the information you find on the Web.

Chapter Outline

Understanding the Web

Objectives

- Explain the creation of the World Wide Web.
- Contrast the Internet and the World Wide Web.
- Explain the parts of a URL.

As You Read

Organize Information Use a summary chart to help organize details as you read.

🔑 Key Terms

- graphical browser
- home page
- Hypertext Markup Language (HTML)
- hypertext transfer protocol (HTTP)
- tag
- Web page
- Web server
- Web site

Creating the Web

As early as 1980, a few people were trying to connect documents stored on different computers by means of a private network or the Internet. These connected documents, it was thought, could someday create a "web" of information that would be instantly available to anyone.

In 1989, Tim Berners-Lee developed a way to retrieve one computer's Internet address while working on another computer. (See the Spotlight on . . . feature on page 375.) The resulting programs and protocols led to the creation of the World Wide Web, which is now a widely used part of the Internet. Berners-Lee made this new technology freely available to everyone and pleaded with other researchers to help develop ways to expand the World Wide Web, or the Web, as it is commonly called.

In 1992, Marc Andreesen and other students at the National Center for Supercomputing Applications (NCSA) developed a Web browser called Mosaic®. Recall that a browser is a program that enables users to navigate the Web and locate and display Web documents. Mosaic was the first **graphical browser** that could display graphics as well as text.

In 1994, Andreesen introduced Netscape Navigator. A year later, Microsoft released Internet Explorer, and that same year the Web was opened up to public and commercial use. Navigator and Explorer soon became the most popular Web browsers.

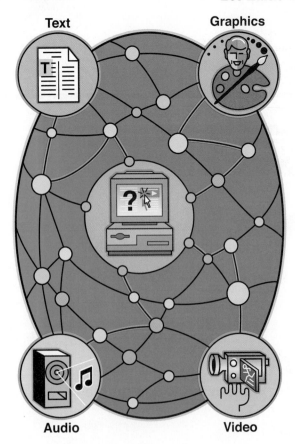

Text **Graphics** **Audio** **Video**

Figure 29.1.1 The Web gets its name from the web of connections it creates between computers all over the planet.

The Internet and the Web

Many people use the terms *Internet* and *World Wide Web* as synonyms. In fact, the World Wide Web is just one part of the Internet. Recall that every computer on the Internet has a unique IP, or Internet Protocol, address and that every document on the Web has a unique address, too, called its uniform resource locator, or URL.

Like e-mail, newsgroups, and file transfer, the Web is a service supported by the Internet. Although these services share the Internet and many of its resources, each is different, with its own set of protocols and applications.

A Web of Documents The World Wide Web is a huge collection of documents linked by hypertext. Writers format documents and add the hyperlinks by using **Hypertext Markup Language**, or **HTML**. People all over the world create and format Web documents by using standardized HTML codes called **tags**. These documents are saved, or "published" to a server on the Internet. Then, when the documents are accessed by a Web browser, each portion—text, images, sound, or animation—appears with its intended formats.

Spotlight on...

MARC ANDREESEN

❝ *I think the browsers are obviously important. I think also the servers are important. And the single most important thing that has happened is the thousands of people that have created applications using this stuff that none of us thought of or ever would have thought of.* ❞

Marc Andreesen
Web browser developer

That's Marc Andreesen's perspective, in 1995, on the popularity of the Web. Browsers existed before Andreesen's work on linking documents. The graphical browsers he helped develop, however, were a real breakthrough. With graphical browsers, Web documents could include illustrations, photos, animation, sounds, and videos. Through his work on Mosaic and Netscape Navigator, Andreesen greatly contributed to the growth of the World Wide Web.

Technology @ Work

Companies and organizations try to obtain a domain name that will easily lead people to their Web site's home page. The address of specific pages is not as important because the home page can provide navigation aids, such as a row or column of subject buttons.

Think About It!

Below are the parts of the URL of the popular PBS (Public Broadcasting System) program Nature. Sequence from 1 (first) to 4 (last), the order in which the parts of the URL should be listed.

➤ www.pbs.org

➤ /index.html

➤ http://

➤ wnet/nature

Figure 29.1.2 The parts of a URL.

Understanding Web Sites

A **Web page** is a document on the Web. A **Web site** is a collection of related pages. Moving from one Web page to another is called browsing. When you type a URL or click a link in your Web browser, it sends a request to the computer on the Internet that contains the page identified by the URL. That computer is called a **Web server**. It stores Web pages and responds to requests from Web browsers. When the server receives your request, it sends the document to your computer, and your browser displays the page on your screen.

Most Web sites have a primary page called the **home page** or index page which appears when you first enter the site's URL. A URL can also contain other information to identify a specific page on a Web site.

Protocol   The first part of a URL specifies the protocol required to access the document. Web documents use http://, indicating that the file should be retrieved using **hypertext transfer protocol (HTTP)**. Some URLs might have other protocols, such as ftp, which shows that the file should be retrieved with file transfer protocol.

Domain Name   The next part of a URL, such as www.fbi.gov, is the domain name of the server that stores the Web site. This part of the URL usually takes you to the site's home page.

Path   The remainder of a URL, if any, defines the path to the document's location on the Web server. Like any computer, a Web server stores files in folders, so the path lists the folder and subfolders, if any, containing the desired document. Thus, a URL such as http://www.fbi.gov/employment/ identifies a folder named "employment" on the site's Web server.

Resource File Name   At the end of a URL, you may see the name of a file—the specific Web resource for which you are looking. The resource may be an HTML document or a Web page, a video clip, a text file, or another type of resource. The file name extension identifies the type of resource.

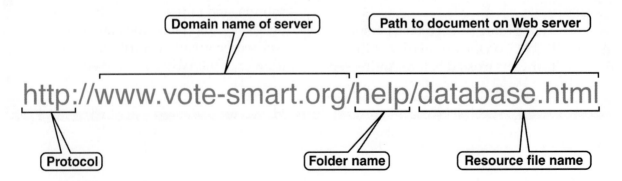

Web Browsing

Objectives

- Explore Web navigation tools.
- Describe how to customize a Web browser.
- Explain the difference between a subject guide and a search engine.

As You Read

Organize Information   Use an outline to organize ways of accessing and evaluating Web pages as you read.

Browsing the Web

You use a Web browser application to display Web information on your computer. Although their look is different, most Web browsers, including the popular Mozilla Firefox, Google Chrome, and Microsoft Internet Explorer, share some common features.

Navigation Buttons   Located on the browser's toolbar, **navigation buttons** let you perform certain operations quickly. When you click Refresh or Reload, the browser again downloads the page you are viewing. When you click the **Back button**, the browser reloads the previous page. The **Forward button** moves ahead to pages previously viewed before Back was activated.

Address Box   If you type a URL in the Address box and press Enter, the browser will take you to the Web page located at that URL. In some browsers, if you type a search phrase and press Enter, the browser displays a page of search results.

Favorites or Bookmarks   The Favorites feature in Internet Explorer and the Bookmarks feature in Netscape Navigator and Mozilla Firefox let you create a list of frequently visited Web pages. Then, rather than retyping the URL, you can return to any bookmarked or favorite page by clicking its name in the list.

 Key Terms
- Back button
- cookie
- Forward button
- navigation buttons
- tracking

Figure 29.2.1 All popular browsers feature navigation buttons, an Address box, and tools for creating a list of frequently visited Web sites.

Customizing a Web Browser

When you use a Web browser, you'll see the default start page of your browser, or one developed by your Internet service provider. Usually, you can customize your browser to suit your preferences. Most customization options can be found in a dialog box such as Internet Options in Internet Explorer.

Changing the Start Page You can customize your browser by making any Web page your start page. You can also set your browser to display a blank page when it launches. That way, you don't have to wait for a start page to load before you begin to work.

Security and Privacy You can select different levels of security and privacy. For example, set a high security level to disable all Internet file downloads, or a high privacy level to block **cookies**—small files that store identification information—from being automatically stored on your computer. Most browsers include options for preventing **tracking**, which is when a Web site gathers information about your Web browsing activity.

Organizing Favorites or Bookmarks You can use the browser's organization tools to create folders and subfolders to organize your preferred links. You can also add and remove sites to your Favorites or Bookmark list.

Finding Information on the Web

Because the Web is so vast, it can be hard to locate information on a specific topic. Subject guides and search engines can help.

Subject Guides Many Web sites offer subject guides to the Web, pages grouped together under headings like Careers, News, or Travel. These guides include only pages that provide useful information about the subject.

Search Engines If you cannot locate what you are looking for in a subject guide, use a search engine. A search engine is a program or Web site designed to search the Web looking for documents that match specified criteria, such as keywords. In a matter of moments, the search engine displays a list of links to pages that match. General search engines, such as Google, Yahoo, or Bing, search throughout the Web to find matches. Some search engines are customized for a certain topic. For example, the Web site www.fedworld.gov, maintained by the U.S. Department of Commerce, lets you search U.S. government documents.

Figure 29.2.2 Search engines and search tools help users find information on specific topics.

Introducing E-commerce

Objectives

- Compare and contrast methods of e-commerce.
- Identify reasons for the success of online shopping.
- Discuss how e-postage works to deliver postage across the Internet.

As You Read

Organize Information   Use a spider web to help you organize ways to use e-commerce as you read.

Electronic Commerce

Electronic commerce, or **e-commerce**, is the use of telecommunications networks or the Internet to conduct business. E-commerce is not new; companies have used wide area networks, or WANs, to do business for years.

Thanks to the Internet and affordable computers, e-commerce has become accessible to anyone who has an Internet connection and a Web browser. More and more Internet users are researching products, shopping, opening bank accounts, and trading stocks online. Many businesses realize that they may lose customers if they do not have an online presence.

Online Banking

In **online banking**, customers use a Web browser to access their accounts, balance checkbooks, transfer funds, and pay bills online.

Personal Finance Programs   Programs such as Microsoft Money or Intuit's Quicken® have features that can help you budget your money, analyze your spending habits, balance your checkbook, and make account transactions. One drawback to these programs is that you can access your online account only from the computer on which you keep your Microsoft Money® or Quicken data. Another potential problem is that anyone with access to that computer and your password can view this data.

Web-based Banking   Web-based banking allows users to access their accounts in financial institutions. All the data is stored on the bank's computer, not your own, so you can access your account from any computer that has an Internet connection. You can learn about different types of services and interest rates, transfer funds, check your statements, reconcile your accounts, or even pay bills online. This service allows you to set up accounts for the businesses you want to pay. When you receive a bill in the mail, you log on to your bank account, enter the amount to be paid, and pay online instead of writing a check and mailing the payment.

 Key Terms
- e-commerce
- online banking

Figure 29.3.1 Amazon.com is a popular e-commerce Web site.

Online Shopping

When many people think of e-commerce, they think of shopping online. Online shopping has grown in popularity due to security features built into popular Web browsers.

The Buyer's Point of View The World Wide Web is an excellent resource for researching products, services, and prices. At many sites, buyers can read product reviews posted by other buyers. At other sites, they can find vendors and product ratings.

The Seller's Point of View One of the main advantages of online business is low startup cost. For a small investment, a vendor can open a Web storefront and sell products online to a wider variety of customers than one physical location offers.

Amazon.com, for example, was launched by Jeff Bezos in 1995. Rather than visit a bookstore that stocks from 10,000 to 40,000 titles, consumers around the globe can log on to Amazon.com and search a database of millions of titles. What started out as "The Earth's biggest bookstore," has morphed into the Earth's biggest store—period. The Web site not only offers millions of books, music, and movies, but it also sells everything from auto parts, toys, and electronics to cosmetics, prescription drugs, and groceries. In 2010 the company had sales of $13 billion.

Getting Postage Online

The United States Postal Service®, or USPS, is a major participant in e-commerce. You can still buy stamps and postal money orders at a post office, of course, but the USPS Web site now features The Postal Store, where you can order stamps or send money to others.

E-stamps   The USPS has teamed up with other private companies to sell postage to anyone with a computer, an Internet connection, and a printer. After a user addresses an envelope, the service adds a printed mark indicating that the appropriate postage was paid. The companies charge users for the postage plus a service fee. Businesses can integrate the service with other software that directs and keeps track of mailings.

Another service lets you print postage that can be used just like regular stamps. NetStamps™, offered by Stamps.com™ in cooperation with the USPS, can be printed and used for personal mail anytime.

Did you know that as you follow interesting links on the Web you are setting up a clickstream—a record of every Web site and every Web page that you visited? Your Internet service provider and the Web sites can track your clickstream. Internet marketers and advertisers are interested in that information. Some use it to target ads to you. You can avoid this by turning on the tracking protection or private browsing features in your Web browser.

Figure 29.3.2 You can save a trip to the post office by buying stamps online.

Use the Vocabulary

Directions: *Match each vocabulary term in the left column with the correct definition in the right column.*

_____ **1.** graphical browser
_____ **2.** HTML
_____ **3.** Web server
_____ **4.** Web page
_____ **5.** Web site
_____ **6.** navigation button
_____ **7.** cookie
_____ **8.** e-commerce
_____ **9.** tracking
_____ **10.** online banking

a. tool that lets users perform routine operations with a browser

b. a small file that stores identification information

c. computer that houses Web sites and sends documents to users

d. a collection of related documents on the Web

e. using a Web browser to access accounts, balance checkbooks, transfer funds, and pay bills online

f. conducting business through a network on the Internet

g. Web navigation program that shows pictures and text

h. when a Web site gathers information about your Web browsing activity

i. single document on the Web

j. markup language used to format Web documents

Check Your Comprehension

Directions: *Determine the correct choice for each of the following.*

1. Which was the first browser that could display graphics as well as text?

  a. Explorer
  b. Mosaic
  c. Firefox
  d. Chrome

2. Which of the following is NOT part of a complete URL address?

  a. protocol
  b. server
  c. path
  d. author

3. Which of the following browser tools will most easily help you revisit a Web site you enjoyed?

  a. Favorites or Bookmarks
  b. Forward
  c. Refresh or Reload
  d. Address box

4. By which of the following does a search engine search?

  a. URL addresses
  b. Favorites
  c. Bookmarks
  d. keywords

5. Which of the following has contributed the most to the growth of e-commerce?

  a. traditional stores
  b. advanced Web browsers
  c. affordable computers
  d. personal finance programs

6. Which of the following is the language used to create Web pages?

  a. FTP
  b. HTTP
  c. HTML
  d. LINUX

Think Critically

Directions: *Answer the following questions.*

1. Why is the URL of a page describing a particular book available on Amazon.com more detailed than the URL of the company's home page?

2. Explain the difference between the Internet and the World Wide Web.

3. Which Web browser features or tools do you find most useful? Why?

4. How might you identify an online bank with which you would like to do business?

Extend Your Knowledge

Directions: *Choose one of the following projects. Complete the exercise on a separate sheet of paper.*

A. Browsers provide other features and functions in addition to those listed in this lesson. For example, as you begin to type an address, most browsers reveal a list of sites you've already visited that begin with the same letters. With your teacher's permission, work with a partner and explore the functions of a browser. Position the mouse over other buttons to see what appears. Click the buttons to see what happens. Visit the online Help feature to find out more about it. Create a chart in a word-processing program and enter your findings.

B. The Web has been praised for the wealth of knowledge it provides for users around the world. It is also criticized for the dangers it makes possible and for the temptation it offers some people. With your teacher's permission, conduct on-line or library research to learn the praises and objections people have for the World Wide Web, and take notes. Participate in a debate on the advantages and disadvantages of the resource.

Using the Web

Finding Your Way Around the Web   The World Wide Web is fast becoming the preferred source for information on news, weather, products, and much more. Knowing how and where to find this information is the key to successfully using the Web.

As a student, you probably search for information to help with schoolwork, to learn more about things you are interested in, or to decide which products you want to own. Others seek information about careers, about places they might want to live in or travel to, or about the issues in an election. At home, people track their finances, pay bills, and make investments online.

Learning how to find your way around the World Wide Web will prepare you to take advantage of the variety of resources it offers.

Chapter Outline

 Lesson 30–1

Understanding Hypertext

 Lesson 30–2

Designing for the Web

 Lesson 30–3

Working on the Web

 Lesson 30–4

Conducting Business Online

Understanding Hypertext

Objectives

- Discuss how hypertext has changed the way people read.
- Compare and contrast traditional writing methods and writing for the Web.

As You Read

Organize Information Use a table to help you organize what hyperlinks do as you read the lesson.

🔑 Key Terms

- dead link
- hypermedia system

A New Way to Read

Documents displayed on the World Wide Web are created in hypertext, a way of organizing and linking information. Hypertext uses hyperlinks, or links, to take you to and from one location to another on the Web. The new location might be another part of the page you are on, another page on the same Web site, or another Web site.

Text and Graphic Hyperlinks The most common links are underlined or highlighted words, but graphic images can also be links. Graphic links aren't always highlighted, so watch the mouse pointer. If it changes to a hand icon, it's positioned over a hyperlink.

Hypermedia Links A **hypermedia system** lets you retrieve multimedia resources, such as sounds and videos. The next time you visit an online news site, look for any icons that resemble videotapes. Clicking one of these icons retrieves a video clip. If you have the right software loaded on your system—and, in some cases, are a subscriber—you can view the clip.

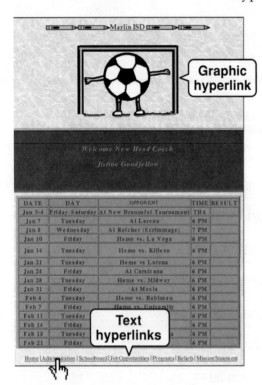

Graphic hyperlink

Text hyperlinks

Figure 30.1.1 On a Web page, text and graphics can be used as hyperlinks.

Dead Links Pages on the Web can be added, moved, or deleted easily by their creators. **Dead links**, also called stale links, are links to documents that are invalid. This means that the URL does not link to an actual document or the document has been moved or deleted. If you click a dead link, you may see a message that the page no longer exists in that location or you may reach a page that obviously is not one you want. Click the Back button to return to the document you were reading.

A New Way to Write

Well designed Web pages usually are not crammed with information. Authors break their documents into smaller pieces. Then they create a master document in hypertext that lets them create links to the pieces.

Using Links for Explanation Hypertext authors don't have to explain everything on one page. Instead, they can define links to other documents containing additional information. If readers want to know more about the topic, they can click the links. When they're done exploring the new page, they can jump right back to the original document.

Using Links for Reference Have you ever had to write a research paper using footnotes? Web page authors cite references differently. Rather than identifying the source at the bottom of a page, they set up a link to the original source. Likewise, bloggers include links to related pages on their posts.

Spotlight on...

MAKONNEN DAVID BLAKE HANNAH

At age 13, Makonnen David Blake Hannah began acting as an official advisor for Jamaica's Web site. He got the job while visiting the office of the Minister of Technology with his mother. The nation's Web site needed updating and this student came to the rescue.

Makonnen researches ideas, uploads information, and makes suggestions for expanding computer education in Jamaica.

Someday Makonnen would like to have his own computer-game design company. But, he says, "I have many goals. I would like to change the world—especially Jamaica."

Designing for the Web

Objectives

- Discuss Web page design tools.
- List six major steps in creating a Web site.
- Identify advanced design and browser tools.

As You Read

Organize Information   Use an outline to help you organize details about Web page design as you read.

 Key Terms

- applet
- Dynamic Hypertext Markup Language (DHTML)
- plug-in program
- Web host
- Webmaster
- WYSIWYG

Choosing Web Page Design Tools

To publish documents on the Web, you must use Hypertext Markup Language, or HTML, to format the text and define links to other documents. Each section of text is enclosed in tags that mark it as a heading, a paragraph, a link, and so on. Several kinds of programs allow you to work with HTML tags.

Text Editors   Programs like Notepad and SimpleText are simple tools you can use to enter both text and codes. Using these programs can be tedious, though. If you want your Web page to include a menu, for example, you have to write the HTML code for each detail of that menu.

HTML Editors   These programs feature text editing and an easier way to add HTML tags. Examples include HomeSite™ and BBEdit™. These kinds of programs require the user to do most or all of the HTML coding manually.

Word-Processing Programs   You can use a word-processing program to create a Web page. However, it must be a program, such as Microsoft Word 2010, that allows you to save your work as an .htm or .html file.

WYSIWYG Web Page Editors   WYSIWYG stands for "What You See Is What You Get." These sophisticated editing programs let you create a page without entering tags yourself. They are almost as easy to use as a word processor and feature many of the same kinds of editing and formatting tools. The difference, however, is that these programs automatically handle the HTML coding for you. You set up the page to look the way you want, including graphics or hyperlinks. Adobe® Dreamweaver® is an example of a program that automates the process of formatting documents for the Web.

Content Management Systems (CMS)   These programs let you create blogs and simple Web sites. Sometimes called a Web Management System, they are software or a suite of tools and applications that allow an individual or organization to create, edit, review, and publish electronic text. Most of these systems provide a Web-based GUI, which allows you to use a Web browser to access the CMS online. Examples of CMS are Tumblr and Wordpress.

Creating a Web Site

Are you interested in having your own Web site? You'll need a **Web host**, a company that provides space on a Web server for Web sites, either for free or for a small monthly fee. The following list describes the main steps for creating a Web site:

1. Plan the Web site. Think about your purpose and audience.

2. Choose your design tools. Do you want to learn HTML and code the site manually, or can you access software that will walk you through the process?

3. Design the Web site. A fast way to build a Web site is to use a pre-coded template that includes titles and navigation bars.

4. Upload the Web site. To put your Web site on the Internet, you have to upload, or publish, your files to the server of your Web host. This is usually done through a utility program provided by your Web host.

5. Test the Web site. This means viewing your pages in a Web browser to see if they look and work as you intended.

6. Maintain the Web site. Don't just build a Web site and forget about it. You are the **Webmaster**, the person responsible for the look and maintenance of the site.

Figure 30.2.1 A finished Web page (right) and its underlying HTML code (left).

Exploring Advanced Tools

To create some of the dramatic effects you see on the Web, designers use advanced design tools and upgraded browsers to display the pages as they intended.

Advanced Design Tools   Designers can use **Dynamic Hypertext Markup Language**, or **DHTML**, to add interactivity to Web pages. You might see butterflies flying across a screen or a personal greeting when you visit an online store. Some designers use JavaScript, a cross-platform programming language, to create **applets**, or small applications for the Web.

Advances like DHTML, JavaScript, and others have made it possible to have internal search engines, animation, downloadable audio and video clips, and streaming audio and video on the Web.

Advanced Browser Tools   Web users may like to access splashy features, but their browsers must be able to process them. Browsers can be upgraded with **plug-in programs**—small, downloadable programs that add new features to an application. RealPlayer® and Windows Media® Player play streaming media. Shockwave®/Flash™ supports interactive documents and animation. Sometimes sites are done all in Macromedia Flash, but the main drawback is that they are not as searchable and take longer to load than sites done in HTML. Finally, Adobe® Acrobat® Reader makes it possible to view documents on-screen in the same format as they appear when printed.

Spotlight on...

WIREDWOODS

66 *The key of this program is to get kids excited about computers. When they are looking for a job or at school, they will realize that with the experiences they have they can do much more in life.* 99

Paul Deninger
WiredWoods Founder
Chairman and CEO
Broadview Holdings

WiredWoods is a summer camp program for middle school students designed to foster in them a lifelong interest in technology. Campers learn how to create their own Web pages, use HTML animation, and work with digital cameras. The result? One example is the creative online brochure of the camp created by 12-year-old Tyneshia. Her work includes photos of the camp and streaming video of various activities.

Working on the Web

Objectives

- Demonstrate how to use inclusion or exclusion operators and wildcards to find information on the Web.
- Explore methods to critically evaluate information found on the Web.

As You Read

Identify Information   Use an outline to help you identify effective ways to use the Web as you read.

Getting More from Web Searches

Search engines index keywords in Web pages and maintain a database of those words. You can search for Web sites by typing one or more key words in the search engine; the engine then displays a list of pages that contain your keyword or words.

Often, a keyword search can yield too many search results. You can improve search effectiveness by using advanced search tools such as Boolean operators and special symbols.

Inclusion Operators   An **inclusion operator** is a plus sign (+) or the word AND. It indicates that you want to find only pages that contain a match for all the specified words. Searching for *dog+husky* finds only pages that contain both words.

Exclusion Operators   An **exclusion operator** is a minus sign (-) or the word NOT. Use it to find pages that contain certain words but not others. Searching for *"dog+husky-sled"* returns a list of pages with the words *dog* and *husky* but not *sled*.

Key Terms

- inclusion operator
- exclusion operator
- proximity operator
- wildcard

Figure 30.3.1 Conducting a search using the Boolean operators + and -.

Many younger workers know more about the Web than their older colleagues. Can they use their skills to help their co-workers find information on the Web?

Think About It!

Which of the online tasks listed below could you teach a co-worker to perform?

➤ use a search engine

➤ conduct a keyword search

➤ use a hyperlink

➤ comparison-shop online

➤ make an online purchase

Proximity Operator   Use the operator NEAR to search for words that appear close together in a document.

Exact Phrase Search   Use quotation marks around a phrase to find the phrase exactly as typed. For example, searching for *"Austin, Texas"* finds only pages that contain the exact phrase. It won't find pages with just *Austin*, or just *Texas*.

Parentheses   Use parentheses to nest one expression within another. For example searching for (*growth OR increase*) NEAR (*Internet OR Web*) find documents that mention the words *growth* or *increase* within a few words of *Internet* or *Web*.

Wildcards   Many search engines let you use **wildcards**, or symbols that stand for other characters. The most common wildcard is the asterisk (*). A single asterisk can represent one or more characters. If you search for *harvest**, you get pages with variations on the word, such as *harvests* and *harvester*.

Another common wildcard is the question mark (?). A single question mark represents a single character. If you search for *to?*, you get pages containing words such as *top* or *toy*.

Advanced Searches   Many popular search engines feature special pages with tools for advanced searches. These pages often appear as forms; instead of constructing complex keyword searches yourself, you can use the form's text boxes and options to create very sophisticated searches. Nearly all such advanced search pages support Boolean operators, special symbols, and wildcards.

Evaluating Information on the Web

Whether you're doing schoolwork or pursuing your own interests, it is important to evaluate the information you find on the Web for accuracy before you use it. Consider these criteria:

Author   The author should be identified in the site. If you can't locate this information, there may be a reason the author chooses to remain anonymous. If you do locate a name, conduct a search to find out more about the person or organization responsible for the content in the site.

Language and Purpose   Evaluating whether the information is well-written and presented in a balanced, factual manner or if it is biased or argumentative and filled with spelling and grammatical errors can help you determine the author's purpose.

Content Validity   Does the author indicate the sources of the information? Do those sources appear to be respected, valid, and authoritative? Run a search on the references or other sources to see what you can learn.

Relevancy   Most search engines list results in the order of hits received. Thus, search engines sometimes place popular sites before relevant sites. Don't be fooled into thinking that a page is relevant simply because it appears at the top of a list of results.

Home-computer users often search the Web for information they need to finish a project or draw a conclusion.

Think About It!

For which of the reasons listed below might you or a family member conduct online research at home?

- ▶ research doctors in your community
- ▶ determine a reason for a rash
- ▶ find a babysitter
- ▶ learn to roast a turkey
- ▶ locate a local air-conditioning repair service

Figure 30.3.2 Searching for 3D television returns a list that's almost all advertisements.

Figure 30–4

Conducting Business Online

Objectives

- Analyze online shopping.
- Compare and contrast online and traditional stores.
- Explain the process of securing online transactions.

As You Read

Organize Information Use a chart to help you organize main ideas and details about e-commerce as you read.

🔑 Key Terms

- click-and-mortar store
- encryption
- e-tailer
- secure electronic transaction

Figure 30.4.1 Clothing is one type of merchandise that sells successfully online.

Online Shopping

The World Wide Web has become a global market. Most things are available for sale online.

What Sells Online Merchandise that sells successfully online ranges from clothing to jewelry, electronics to vacations, and furniture to homes and cars. Amazon.com is a successful, high-profile company that started out selling books and moved into many other product lines. The company tries out new products in a "test" store to see if they will sell well. If they don't, that link is shut down.

Many popular Web sites offer shopping channels to help you locate items and check the latest prices. Buyers can also access a directory of online vendors, or **e-tailers**, organized by category.

Challenges of Selling Online Not every business can successfully sell products online, and some face unique challenges. For example, there are very few successful online knitting and yarn stores, because knitting and crochet enthusiasts like to see and feel the yarn. Companies that sell perishable items, such as fresh fruit or baked goods, must have a system in place that lets them deliver products quickly and safely. A book can travel for days without suffering any quality problems, but red velvet cupcakes must be delivered before they become stale. While grocery store consumers like to talk to the butcher or squeeze the melons to see if they are ripe, some online grocers have found a niche by tailoring their offerings to hurried consumers who don't want to take the time to shop.

Click-and-Mortar Versus Bricks-and-Mortar

A traditional retail outlet is known as a bricks-and-mortar store. Businesses that also sell products online are called **click-and-mortar stores**. Some online businesses have bricks-and-mortar counterparts, while others only sell online.

Online-only Stores Online shopping sites like eBay and Amazon.com do not sell in traditional stores. This saves the company money on salaries and overhead, so prices can be lower. Although online shopping is convenient, if you have a problem with your purchase, you can not talk to someone about it face-to-face. If you want to return something, you have to ship it back and sometimes pay for shipping costs, too.

Click-and-Mortar Online stores that also have bricks-and-mortar locations have an advantage over companies that do business only online. If you are not satisfied with a product, you may be able to take it back to a store location for a refund or replacement. You can speak with someone face-to-face and get the problem resolved right away.

Secure Electronic Transactions

One of the keys to the growth of e-commerce is **secure electronic transactions**. Originally a standard that relied on digital signatures, secure electronic transaction now refers to a variety of measures e-tailers use to secure online transactions so customers can bank and shop online without worrying that their private information will be misused, lost, or stolen, which could result in identify theft and fraud.

Real-World Tech

E-pinionated Online Shoppers Word-of-mouth spreads fast on the Internet. In fact, when it is unstoppable, we say that a product, a video, or phenomenon has gone "viral." One way to get reliable word-of-mouth opinions of products you want to purchase online is to go to Epinions.com, which offers unbiased reviews of products and services. They are written by average people—even teens—so you can review your latest electronic gadget or piece of clothing. Most e-commerce sites, however, offer customer reviews and a five-star rating system for all products.

Check them out before you put items into your virtual shopping cart.
What would prompt you to write a product review online? A good or a bad experience and why?

Technology @ School

Schools, too, can place orders for merchandise online.

Think About It!

Which item(s) listed below do you think your school might order online?

➤ costumes for a school play

➤ school supplies

➤ textbooks

➤ electronic equipment

➤ athletic equipment

Secure Sites A secure Web site uses **encryption**—coding—and authentication standards to protect online transaction information. That means your personal information including debit card numbers and personal identification numbers (PINs) are safe when you shop online. You can tell that you are viewing a secure Web site because the letters "https" display to the left of the Web site name in the Address bar of your browser. On an unsecured site, there is no "s." Also, a small lock icon displays in your Web browser's status bar. You can double-click the lock icon to display details about the site's security system.

Secure Payment Services PayPal®, which started out as a service for eBay buyers and sellers, is now the most popular secure online payment service. It is used by millions of buyers and sellers on thousands of e-commerce sites. PayPal lets you avoid repeatedly entering your credit card number and other personal data when making transactions online. Instead, you can designate an amount to be used for PayPal purchases, and, when you make an online purchase, the money is deducted directly from your bank account. To use PayPal, or any other secure online payment service, you sign up directly and provide your payment information only once. The service keeps your records secure and handles payments to online vendors for you, using only secure methods.

How PayPal Works

Step 1
Buyer registers on PayPal.com.

Step 2
Buyer enters credit card information, seller's e-mail address, and the amount to be sent.

Step 3
Buyer's credit card is charged the sale amount and an account in seller's name is credited with that amount.

Step 4
Seller is notified of transaction and linked to the new account.

Step 5
Seller registers by entering name and address.

Step 6
Seller can withdraw funds by direct deposit to bank or by check from PayPal.

Use the Vocabulary

Directions: *Match each vocabulary term in the left column with the correct definition in the right column.*

_____ **1.** hypermedia system
_____ **2.** dead link
_____ **3.** WYSIWYG
_____ **4.** e-tailer
_____ **5.** encryption
_____ **6.** inclusion operator
_____ **7.** exclusion operator
_____ **8.** wildcard
_____ **9.** click-and-mortar store
_____ **10.** Web host

a. lets users retrieve audio and video online
b. symbol that stands for another character
c. sophisticated Web-page editing programs
d. business that offers products online
e. someone who primarily uses the Web to sell goods or services
f. plus sign or the word AND
g. connection to a document that no longer exists or has been moved
h. minus sign or the word NOT
i. coding used to protect data
j. a company that provides space on a Web server for Web sites

Check Your Comprehension

Directions: *Determine the correct choice for each of the following.*

1. Which of the following indicates that a particular graphic on a Web page is actually a link?

    a. The mouse pointer turns into a hand.
    b. The mouse pointer changes color.
    c. The graphic moves across the screen.
    d. The graphic is underlined.

2. Which of the following can you use to upgrade a browser to add new features to an application?

    a. plug-in program
    b. cookie
    c. DHTML program
    d. WYSIWYG program

3. Which of the following is NOT an indicator that a Web site is an accurate source?

    a. author is identified on the site
    b. information is balanced and factual
    c. the link displays at the top of a list of search results
    d. spelling and grammar are correct

4. Which of the following might yield a list of pages with *travel, travels, traveled,* and *traveling*?

    a. wildcard
    b. database
    c. inclusion operator
    d. exclusion operator

5. What term is used to describe a traditional retail outlet that does not sell products online?

    a. online stores
    b. test stores
    c. bricks-and-mortar stores
    d. click-and-mortar stores

6. Which of the following is a secure payment service that consumers can use to complete online transactions?

    a. eBay
    b. Secure Payment Service
    c. PayPal
    d. ASCII

Directions: *Answer the following questions.*

1. What problems related to links do you think might increase as use of the World Wide Web increases?

2. What does a hyperlink do?

3. What are several ways to find information quickly on the Web?

4. How can window shopping on the Web benefit consumers?

5. Which products might you avoid buying online? Why?

Extend Your Knowledge

Directions: *Choose one of the following projects. Complete the exercise on a separate sheet of paper.*

A. Find out what differences there are between a bricks-and-mortar company and a click-and-mortar company that have the same name but conduct themselves as two separate companies. What are the advantages and disadvantages of this arrangement for the company? For the customer?

B. With your teacher's permission, with a partner, try using several Web browsers. Discuss the advantages, disadvantages, and features of each. Then, create and complete a Venn diagram to summarize your preferences.

DIRECTIONS: *You will search the Internet to learn about what types of information are protected by copyrights and what you legally can and cannot use. Then, you will use a word-processing program to make a top-ten list of facts about copyright laws to display in your school library. Microsoft Office 2010 procedures required for this activity can be found in Appendix A.*

1. Open the .pdf file **Web-1_CopyrightInfo**, which is located on the student CD. With your teacher's permission, print the Data Record Sheet. The sheet includes a K-W-L chart and forms for recording source information. K-W-L stands for What I **K**now, What I **W**ant to Know, and What I **L**earned. Close the file, and exit your pdf reader program.

2. In the K-W-L chart, fill in the K column with what you already know about copyright laws, and fill in the W column with what you want to know.

3. With your teacher's permission, open your Web browser and navigate to a search engine.

4. Use the search engine to find information about copyright laws. Search for keywords from the W column of your K-W-L chart. Use Boolean search strategies such as AND, NOT, or OR to fine-tune the search results list. Look for sites that explain what information you can and cannot use according to copyright laws. Research illegal acts such as software piracy, as well as patent and trademark infringement. Find sites that explain the consequences of violating these copyright laws in simple, easy to understand language.

5. Evaluate each site you visit for accuracy and validity.

6. Write the source information about each Web page that you use on the bottom portion of the Data Record Sheet, or on a separate piece of paper.

7. With your teacher's permission, print relevant information from the Web sites you find most helpful. You may want to copy the information from the Web page into a word-processing or notes program, along with the page's URL, and then print it.

8. Using your browser's History list, go back to one of the sites that explained the consequences of copyright violations.

9. Mark the site as a favorite or bookmark it. With your teacher's permission, print the Web page if you have not already done so.

10. When you have finished your search, exit your Web browser.

11. Read the information you printed. As you read, use a highlighter to identify the main ideas of each article.

12. Use your findings to write ten facts about copyright laws in the "What I Learned" column of the K-W-L chart.

13. Start your word-processing program, and create a new document. Save it as **Web-1_Copyrights_xx**. Replace **xx** with your own initials or name, as directed by your teacher. Insert a footer that includes your name and the current date.

14. At the top of the document, type the title **Ten Things to Remember About Copyrighted Materials**. Increase the font size of the title to 18 points, center it, and make it bold, or apply the Title style.

15. Leave a blank line below the title, and type the ten facts you learned from the K-W-L chart. Format the items as a numbered list.

16. Leave a blank line below the last fact, type **Source Sites** and format it in bold with a solid underline.

17. On the next line, type a list of the Web sites or other sources you recorded on your Data Record Sheet. Format the sources in a smaller font size than the rest of the document text, and leave one line space between sources. Remove all hyperlink formatting.

18. Proofread the document carefully. Check the spelling and grammar, and correct any errors.

19. Preview the document.

20. With your teacher's permission, print the document.

21. Close the document, saving all changes, and exit your word-processing program.

22. As a class, brainstorm scenarios that do or do not violate copyright laws. Write the scenarios on the board or an overhead transparency. Discuss which scenarios are legal under current copyright laws.

23. With permission, share your work by displaying it in the school library.

Web Activities

DIRECTIONS: *You will use a search engine to research one of the original thirteen colonies. You will then use a word-processing program to create a written report about the colony, including images. Then, you will save the document as an HTML file so you can publish it on the Web. Microsoft Office 2010 procedures required for this activity can be found in Appendix A.*

1. Open the .pdf file **Web-2_ColonyInfo**, which is located on the student CD. With your teacher's permission, print the Data Record Sheet. The sheet includes a table where you can record information about a colony and a checklist you can use to make sure you complete your report correctly. Close the file, and exit your pdf reader program.

2. As a class, list the thirteen colonies on the board. Then, choose one colony to research.

3. Use the Internet (with your teacher's permission), library resources, or a textbook to find information about the foundation and early history of the colony you chose.

4. To use the Internet, open a Web browser and navigate to a search engine. Search for sites by typing keywords or phrases such as the name of your colony, or use a Boolean search phrase such as AND.

   a. Look for information about the key individuals or groups who helped establish the colony, the basis for the colony's economy, the hardships that colonists encountered, and important dates in the history of the colony.

   b. In addition, locate at least three images related to the colony. The images might include maps, paintings, photographs of artifacts, or portraits of the colony's leaders. If you find the images online, download them in a format that is compatible with the computer you are using. If you find the images in a print source, scan the images and save them as .pdf or .jpg files. If necessary, obtain permission to use images that you download or scan.

5. Evaluate each site you visit for accuracy and validity.

6. When you find a credible Web site with relevant information, bookmark the site, or with your teacher's permission, print the desired pages, or copy the information from the Web page into a word-processing or notes file for saving and printing. Write the source information about each site on a separate piece of paper.

7. Record the details and facts that you find on the Data Record Sheet.

8. When you have finished your search, exit your Web browser.

9. Start your word-processing program, and create a new document. Save the document as **Web-2_Colonies_xx** in the location where your teacher instructs you to store the files for this activity. Insert a footer on all but the first page that includes your name, the page number, and the current date.

10. Create a cover page that includes a descriptive title for the report, formatted in bold and centered, or apply the Title style. Include your name, today's date, and an appropriate picture.

11. Use the information on your Data Record Sheet to write a report on the colony you researched. Your report should be at least two pages. Use a font and font formatting that is easy to read and not distracting.

12. Insert images to illustrate the report. Select appropriate text wrapping options. Size and position the images so they integrate with and enhance the text.

13. Insert a caption below each image. You may do this using your program's Insert > Caption command, or by inserting a text box in which you type a caption. Format the text box so that text will wrap around it, and format the caption text with a smaller font size than you use in the body of the document.

14. At the end of the report, insert a Works Cited page or Bibliography listing your sources.

15. Proofread your report carefully. Use your program's thesaurus feature to find interesting synonyms for common words in order to improve your writing. Check the spelling and grammar in the document and correct any errors that you find.

16. Format all paragraphs with a first-line Indent and justified alignment.

17. Preview the document and make modifications to the page layout, as necessary. For example, you may want to adjust the margin width.

18. With your teacher's permission, print the report.

19. Close the document, saving all changes.

20. Exchange reports with a classmate, either electronically or in print. Use the criteria on the Data Record Sheet to evaluate your classmate's work. Does the report meet the requirements of the assignment? If not, how can it be improved? What if any changes are needed to make the report more effective for presentation on the Web? If you are reviewing a file, use your program's revision tracking and commenting features, or handwrite your comments and edits on the print out to provide feedback and corrections. Then, return the report to your classmate.

21. Revise your report based on your classmate's comments and suggestions.

22. Save the changes to the report.

23. Save the document as a single file Web page.

24. View the document as it will display on the Web. If necessary, adjust the position and formatting of the text and images on the page to improve its appearance and readability.

25. Insert hyperlinks from the report page to your source Web sites.

26. With your teacher's permission, publish your Web page on your school's Web site so other students can access it.

27. Open your Web browser and view your Web page and those of your classmates. Then, close all open documents, saving all changes, and exit all open programs.

28. As a class, discuss how publishing documents to the Web makes information more accessible, and how you can use the HMTL documents to encourage other students to learn more about the thirteen colonies.

Illustration A

Massachusetts

The Second of the Thirteen Original Colonies

By

Firstname Lastname

Today's Date

Web Activities

DIRECTIONS: *Working in teams, you will use wiki collaboration to develop an anti-bullying campaign for your school. You will collect information on types of bullying and how to respond to it. You will then create content on the topic and collaborate with others to develop the content. Microsoft Office 2010 procedures required for this activity can be found in Appendix A.*

1. Open the .pdf file **Web-3_Bullying**, which is located on the student CD. With your teacher's permission, print the Data Record Sheet. It has space for you to record information that you find about types of bullying. Close the file, and exit your pdf reader program.

2. Working individually or with your team members, use the Internet (with your teacher's permission), library resources, or your school's student handbook or code of conduct to locate information about the three main types of bullying: physical, verbal, and cyber.

3. To use the Internet, open a Web browser and navigate to a search engine. Search for words or phrases such as **bullying**, or use Boolean search strategies. For example, you might search for **bullying AND physical** or **bullying AND cyber**.

4. Evaluate each site you visit for accuracy and validity.

5. When you find a credible Web site with relevant information, bookmark the site, or with your teacher's permission, print the desired pages, or copy the information from the Web page into a word-processing or notes file for saving and printing. Write the source information about each site on a separate piece of paper.

6. Use the information you find to complete the first table on the Data Record Sheet.

7. When you have finished your search, exit your Web browser.

8. Access the wiki space that your teacher has created.

9. Working cooperatively with your team members, create the following for the wiki:
   - Photo of your school
   - List of team members
   - Slogan or title for the anti-bullying campaign
   - Brief introduction to the topic of bullying
   - Summary paragraph on each of the three types of bullying—physical, verbal, and cyber—based on the information you recorded on the Data Record Sheet.

10. Working independently, develop your own recommendations on how to respond to each type of bullying. Record your advice in the second table on the Data Record Sheet.

11. Access the wiki space where you can post your individual contributions. Create a heading or new page on the space and enter the information.

12. Collaborate with team members to combine and edit the recommendations on the wiki space.

13. With your teacher's permission, share your wiki with others, and read and comment on other teams' wikis.

14. As a class, discuss the different types of bullying, and how you can expand the anti-bullying campaign in your school.

DIRECTIONS: *You will develop a blog on one of your hobbies or interests. You will gather information and statistics on the hobby and create content to post on the blog. You will customize the blog with images, links, and other design elements. Microsoft Office 2010 procedures required for this activity can be found in Appendix A.*

1. Open the .pdf file **Web-4_Blog**, which is located on the student CD. With your teacher's permission, print the Data Record Sheet. Close the file, and exit your pdf reader program.

2. Use the Data Record Sheet to summarize information on a hobby or interest. Be as detailed and informative as possible. Use your own experience, as well as research resources such as Web sites, other blogs, publications, and books.

3. With your teacher's permission, access the designated blogging service. To register with a blogging service, you will typically be required to provide an e-mail address and password. You may then be asked to provide a blog title (which is the title that appears on the published blog) and a blog address, or URL.

4. If available, select a design template for your blog.

5. Using the information on your Data Record Sheet, write a blog post about your hobby or interest. Be sure to use complete sentences, proper subject-verb agreement, and correct verb tense. Also, use only one space after punctuation marks.

6. When you have finished writing your blog post, proofread it carefully. Check the spelling and grammar and correct errors.

7. Preview your post if the blogging service provides that option.

8. When you have finalized the post, publish it, and then view your blog.

9. Edit the blog post by inserting a picture or image that represents your hobby or interest.

10. Publish the post again, and view it.

11. Refer to the information about resources that you listed in your Data Record Sheet. Create a new post that describes at least one of the Web sites you listed where you can obtain helpful information about your hobby or interest. Create a link in the post to the Web site.

12. Publish the post, and view your blog.

13. Log out of your blog service when finished.

Web Activities

DIRECTIONS: *You will research a natural disaster and its effects on the surrounding ecosystems. You will use a word processor to write a description of the disaster. You will also add images that you download from the Web. Then, you will save and publish your work as a Web page. Finally, you will view the page in your Web browser, upload it to your school's network, and bookmark it so it can be retrieved and viewed easily. Microsoft Office 2010 procedures required for this activity can be found in Appendix A.*

1. Open the .pdf file **Web-5_EvaluationForm**, which is located on the student CD. With your teacher's permission, print the rubric. The rubric identifies points on which your research will be evaluated. Close the file, and exit your pdf reader program.

2. Use the Internet (with your teacher's permission), library resources, or a textbook to research a natural disaster that occurred at least ten years ago. You might research wildfires in California, the Galveston hurricane of 1900, Hurricane Andrew, Mississippi River flooding, or tornadoes in Texas and Oklahoma. Find out how, where, and when the disaster happened. Find examples of the ecosystems that were disrupted and how they recovered.

3. To use the Internet, open a Web browser and navigate to a search engine. Search for sites by typing keywords or phrases such as the type or name of the natural disaster, or use a Boolean search to narrow your focus.

4. When you find information about the disaster, carefully evaluate it to make sure it is valid and relevant to the topic.

5. During your research, locate before and after photos of the event. Remember to obtain permission to use the photos.

6. Find at least three helpful URLs, one of which contains a photo, and save them as Favorites or bookmarks in your Web browser.

7. Start your word-processing program, and save a new file as **Web-5_Research_xx** in the location where your teacher instructs you to store the files for this activity.

8. Make your Web browser active and return to the sites you bookmarked. Refresh the pages, if necessary. Select relevant text and images from each site and copy them to the word-processing document for saving or printing. Copy the source URL and type the page title for all content you copy.

9. Save the changes to the word-processing document, and with your teacher's permission, print it.

10. When you have completed your research, exit your Web browser.

11. In your word-processing program, create a new document, and save it as a Web page with the name **Web-5_Equilibrium_xx** and the page title **Ecosystem Equilibrium**, in the location where your teacher instructs you to store files for this activity.

12. Insert a footer on the page that includes your name and the current date.

13. Apply a theme or design to the page, or apply a page background color.

14. Enter a descriptive title on the page. Use a readable font and center and boldface it. Increase the font size to make it stand out, or apply an appropriate style.

15. Using the information in your **Web-5_Research_xx** document, write a description in your own words of the natural disaster. Include examples of the ecosystems that were affected and the natural succession, or recovery, which occurred afterward.

16. Apply ½" first line indents to each paragraph.

17. Copy at least one image from the **Web-5_Research_xx** file to your Web page document to illustrate the content. Select appropriate text wrapping options. Size and position the image so it integrates with and enhances the text, but does not overwhelm it.

18. At the end of the document, type a list of URLs hyperlinked to your source pages, so readers can use the links to access the pages for more information.

19. Proofread the document carefully. Check the spelling and grammar and correct any errors that you find.

20. Preview the document as it will look in a Web browser, and test the links. Make corrections and modifications to the page layout so it looks good and is easy to read.

21. With your teacher's permission, print the document.

22. With your teacher's permission, publish your Web page on your school's Web site so other students can access it.

23. Open your Web browser and view your Web page and those of your classmates. Then, close all open documents, saving all changes, and exit all open programs

24. As a class, evaluate one another's Web page reports for relevancy to the task. Is the information relevant to the topic? Are the images good quality? Is the role of ecological succession and equilibrium clear?

Personal Communications Basics

Staying in Touch How do you stay in touch with friends after school, on weekends, or during school vacations? How do you stay in contact with friends who have moved? You could make phone calls and hope someone answers, or send letters and then wait for a response. Today, however, many people use their computer to stay in touch with friends, family, and co-workers.

Computer technology allows you to stay connected with people who are both close by and far away. You can communicate through text messages. You can chat online with several friends at once. With the right technology, you can even chat face-to-face through a computer network. There's no need to feel out of touch!

Chapter Outline

 Lesson 31–1

Using E-mail

 Lesson 31–2

Avoiding E-mail Problems

 Lesson 31–3

Other Electronic Communications

Using E-mail

Objectives

- Describe e-mail systems.
- Identify the purpose of a unique identifier.
- Explain the parts of an e-mail address
- Identify the key components of an e-mail message.
- Describe the process of creating, sending, and replying to messages.

As You Read

Sequence Information   Use a sequence chart as you read to help you outline the process of receiving a message and responding to it.

🔑 Key Terms

- alias
- attachment
- e-mail client
- e-mail server
- mailbox name
- server address

Evaluating E-mail

E-mail allows people to send an unlimited number of messages quickly and easily to anyone with an e-mail address. It is also less expensive than standard mail and voice, fax, and telephone messages. To use e-mail, all you need is a computer, an Internet connection, e-mail software, and an e-mail account.

E-mail also lets you attach files to a message. Anything sent with an e-mail message is called an **attachment**. Common attachments include word-processing documents, spreadsheets, photos, artwork, and movies.

Understanding E-mail Addresses

Like a computer on a network, every communication service user must have a unique identifier, usually called a username. The system uses the identifier to differentiate one user from another in order to deliver services, such as mail. For e-mail, the identifier is the e-mail address. All e-mail addresses have two parts. The **mailbox name** is the part of the address before the "at" symbol (@) that identifies the user. The **server address** follows the symbol. It gives the domain name of the e-mail server where the mailbox is stored. An **e-mail server** is a computer, operated by your Internet service provider (ISP), that handles three key jobs:

- accepts incoming messages
- sends outgoing messages
- delivers incoming messages

Figure 31.1.1 Every e-mail address has two basic parts—a mailbox name and a server address.

Sending, Receiving, and Forwarding E-mail

To send or receive e-mail, you use an **e-mail client**, which is a program that lets you create, send, receive, and manage e-mail messages. You may get the program from your ISP, as part of a productivity suite, or with a Web browser. For example, Microsoft Outlook 2010 is the e-mail client that comes with the Microsoft Office 2010 productivity suite.

Composing E-mail   To compose a new message, you click a button within the e-mail client. The client displays a form for you to complete. The form includes two main parts—the header, which includes places for entering the recipient(s) and the subject, and the body, which is where you type the message.

First, you must specify the message's recipient in the To: line of the message form. Depending on your e-mail client's features, you may select someone's name from an address book. You may also type the e-mail address, which can be a name or a combination of letters and numbers. For example, the e-mail address for Chris Rodriguez might be chris_rodriguez@isp.net or cjr615@isp.net. Instead of typing a complete address, you may be able to type an alias, or select it from a list. An **alias** is an easy-to-remember nickname for the recipient, such as Chris_R. If you want to send a copy of the message to other recipients, you can add their names or addresses to the To: line or place them in the Cc: line. (The characters Cc stand for "carbon copy.")

Next, fill in the Subject line. The Subject line gives the recipient an idea of the message's content and may help the recipient decide whether to open it or delete it. Some e-mail clients will not accept messages with blank Subject lines. When the header is complete, type the text message. You can add attachments by clicking a button and then clicking the name of the file you want to attach to the e-mail. Finally, click Send.

Netiquette are the rules for polite online behavior.

Think About It!

Which of the following online rules help make e-mail more useful?

- ▷ Type a lengthy description in the Subject line.

- ▷ Vary fonts and type sizes in the message.

- ▷ Edit the original message so only the part you are answering appears in your reply.

- ▷ Don't write in anger.

- ▷ Be brief, but be polite.

Figure 31.1.2 Creating an e-mail message with Google's gmail.

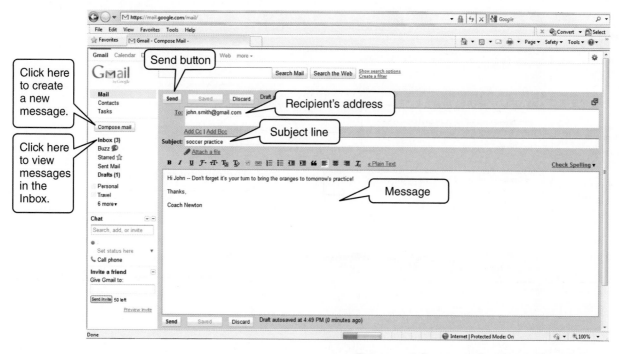

Replying to E-mail You can respond to the person who sent a message by clicking Reply. You can also click Reply All, which responds to all the people who received the original message. Several things occur when a response is prepared:

- The client displays a reply form with the original sender's address shown in the To: field.
- The subject field may show Re: in front of the subject of the original message. (Re stand for "regarding.")
- The original message is copied into the body of the reply. Most e-mail programs give you the option of excluding the original text in your reply.
- You can type your reply above or below the original text, and then click Send.

Forwarding E-mail When you receive a message, you can pass it along to someone else. This is called forwarding a message. The Subject line of a forwarded e-mail may include the characters *FW:* before the subject text to show that the message has been forwarded. You can add your comments before the original message's text.

Before you hit "send" on any e-mail, it's good to remember that your e-mail can be forwarded to other people. Don't write anything that you don't want other friends, parents, or teachers to see!

Figure 31.1.3 Replying to an e-mail message.

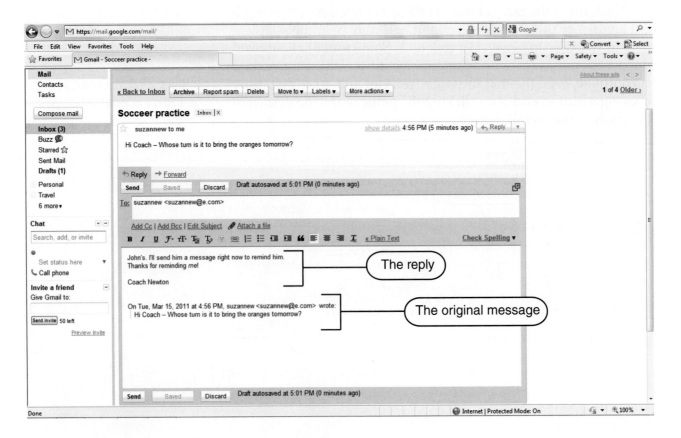

Avoiding E-mail Problems

Objectives

- Examine problems related to e-mail.
- Define bounce messages and spam.
- Explain the use of digital signatures with e-mail.

As You Read

Compare and Contrast   Use a Venn diagram as you read to help you compare and contrast various e-mail problems.

Failed E-mail

It is easy to send e-mail messages, but it is also easy to make mistakes. What happens when you make a mistake?

Using the Wrong Address   One of the most common e-mail mistakes is entering an incorrect address in the To: field. When you do this, one of two things will happen:

- Your message will go to the wrong person if the incorrect address is someone else's valid address. Unless that person replies, you may never know what happened to your message.
- The e-mail server will return the e-mail to you with a bounce message.

A **bounce message** is a notice from the e-mail server telling you that your message could not be delivered. Bounce messages are often a result of an incorrect e-mail address. You sometimes see "MAILER-DAEMON@..." as the "From" address of a bounce message. Also, a message may not be delivered if the recipient's mailbox is full. This happens because many ISPs limit the amount of server space available for each user's messages. Never attempt to reply to a bounce message.

Avoiding Bounce Messages   If you or your family changes ISPs, your e-mail address will change. In that case, be sure to tell everyone in your address book about your new e-mail address. Otherwise, people sending messages to your former address will receive a bounce message when they write to you.

 Key Terms
- bounce message
- digital signature
- spam

Bounce messages are a part of e-mail use. But what should you do when you get one?

Think About It!

Suppose you e-mail the school photographer to find out whether your class pictures are ready. However, you get a bounce message. Which actions listed below might then be helpful?

➤ Retrieve the message from your Sent Items folder and check your typing.

➤ Confirm the e-mail address of the photographer.

➤ Resend the message to the same address.

➤ Send a reply to the bounce message asking for help.

Figure 31.2.1 A bounce message, due to an incorrect e-mail address.

Junk E-mail, or Spam

Many e-mail users complain about the flood of **spam**, a term used to describe unwanted, or junk, e-mail messages and advertisements. Like physical junk mail, spam usually tries to sell something to the recipient. Spam can cause several problems:

- The recipient wastes time reviewing and deleting spam.
- Spam clogs e-mail servers, slowing Internet traffic.
- Spam often contains incorrect or misleading information.
- Sometimes you unknowingly generate the spam you get.

When you make an online purchase, you might agree to get e-mails from the company about future sales. You might have signed up for e-mail newsletters at many Web sites or joined a group (as in Yahoo Groups) that lets you exchange messages about a topic.

Blocking Unwanted E-mail Most newsletters and user groups give easy directions to unsubscribe to the e-mail. For e-mail newsletters, you will usually find an "unsubscribe" link at the bottom of the page in tiny print. Yet, stopping spam from reaching e-mail servers and clients is an ongoing battle. Some servers use technology to block "spammers" or automatically puts spam in a "spam folder." Some e-mail clients provide special spam filters that users can configure to automatically delete junk mail. It is worthwhile checking your spam folder regularly, because sometimes personal or important e-mail is mistakenly re-routed there.

E-mail Risks

Because you cannot see who is actually sending you a message, e-mail is often used to commit crimes. Someone can send you a message and pretend it is from someone else. The message could contain a virus or request personal information. Because you trust the person or organization you believe sent the message, you open it or reply.

Using Digital Signatures   One way to secure e-mail messages is by using a **digital signature**—an electronic identifier which verifies that the message was created and sent by the person whose name appears in the From field.

Most current e-mail programs support digital signatures, which you purchase from a vendor, such as Symantec's VeriSign Authentication Services. Once the certificate is installed on your computer, you can use it to "sign" any message you send by embedding the certificate in the message. The signature proves that the message comes from you.

Connections

Language Arts   Did you know you can use e-mail to improve your reading and writing? There are online magazines to which you can submit your work for publication. One of these sites, WritingDEN (www2.actden.com/writ_den), also has language-building exercises on words, sentences, and paragraphs. You complete the exercises, e-mail your answers, and receive your scores shortly.

Real-World Tech

Getting Career Advice by E-mail   What do you think you want to do when you "grow up?" It's not too early to start exploring careers and find out what conduct, dress, and behaviors are acceptable in the workplace. Career advice that appears in newspaper or magazine columns exists online as blogs. Some are geared toward specific careers and some to general career advice, like how to be a good team member, solve problems, or get organized.

Search out some career question-and-answer forums available online. Look for ones that offer general advice on how to dress and behave in the workplace. Remember, as with all online resources, be cautious about where you send e-mail and any information you share.

Personal Communications Basics   •   **429**

Other Electronic Communications

Objectives

- Compare and contrast technology-enabled conferences.
- Describe one key advantage of teleconferencing for business.
- Examine the technical aspects of videoconferences.
- Summarize goals of Web-based training.
- Explain distance learning.

As You Read

Organize Information   Use an outline as you read to help you organize information about advanced communications methods.

🔑 Key Terms

- blended learning
- teleconference
- videoconference
- Web-based training

Meeting Through Technology

E-mail communication has advantages. It allows you to quickly send a message and, later, receive a reply. But what if you need to communicate with others right away? What if you need the benefits of a conversation? What if you need to talk to many people at once?

Teleconferencing   Imagine a company with 50 salespeople located around the world. Getting all these people together to discuss a new product would be helpful. Flying them all to one city for a meeting would be very expensive, however.

In cases such as this, teleconferencing may be the solution. A **teleconference** uses computers that are connected by a network or the Internet. These connections allow people to communicate with one another in real time through their computers. Depending on the software they use, the participants may be able to speak to one another as if they were using telephones, and every participant can hear all the others. Teleconferencing software may allow users to "chat" by typing messages that appear on everyone's screen. Participants may also be able to share documents on-screen, as well, using a special feature called a whiteboard to view and edit the documents in real time. Teleconferences help companies in several ways:

- They save time and money.
- They are similar to in-person meetings.
- They are convenient.
- They allow all participants to communicate in real time.

Videoconferencing   A **videoconference** is a meeting at which the participants can see and hear one another without being physically together. Videoconferences require equipment such as cameras, a fast network connection, and video screens or computer monitors. A Web-based videoconference allows participants to connect to a Web server, identify themselves, and then join the meeting.

Types of Videoconferences   Videoconferences can serve many purposes. Depending on the goal, they are set up in one of three delivery methods.

- One-to-one videoconferences allow two people to see and talk to each other on their computers. This type of conference is easy to set up through applications such as Microsoft NetMeeting or through using Voice over Internet Protocol (VoIP) with Skype, software that lets you use your computer to make voice or video phone calls.

- One-to-many videoconferences are similar to watching television programs. Many people can watch the presentation, but usually only one person speaks to the group.

- Many-to-many videoconferences are like a face-to-face meeting. Any of the participants can speak and be seen and heard at any time in the conversation.

 Spotlight on...

TELEMENTORING

66 *Students get a chance to work with people who are proof of the value of education. Academic performance improves as a result of a renewed motivation to learn. Started in 1995, ITP has served more than 11,000 students in nine countries in grades 4 through college.* **99**

David Neils
Founder,
International Telementor Program

The International Telementor Program, or ITP, matches students with workplace mentors who help them

complete projects. Students and their mentors communicate online. Students at Eisenhower Middle School in Topeka, Kansas, developed their school's first Web site with help from ITP mentors. And students in Pleasant View School in Baldwin Park, California, worked with mentors to create multimedia presentations on their state's history.

Technology @ School

Many students and teachers use distance learning.

Think About It!

Think about some of the ways schools might use distance learning. Which statement(s) listed below identify a sensible use?

➤ Small schools could offer a wider range of courses.

➤ Schools could let individuals or small groups pursue their interests.

➤ Schools could pair a sports team with a coach.

➤ A teacher in one school could share lessons with teachers on other campuses.

Learning from a Distance

Distance learning allows you to learn anytime, anywhere—as long as you are on a computer connected to the Internet. Many schools offer classes via distance learning, and they use a variety of technologies to deliver instruction to their students. In many cases, the instructor provides lectures and displays slides through a one-to-many videoconference, which students can watch on their home computers. Reading assignments can be done; tests and quizzes can be done via the Internet; and students can work together via teleconference and e-mail. It is possible to study many different subjects through distance learning. You can even earn a complete college degree online.

Web-based Training   One of the newest methods of distance learning is **Web-based training**. Schools, colleges, and businesses are using the speed and technology of the Internet to deliver educational programs and activities.

This method of education offers anytime, anywhere learning, as long as you have an Internet connection. Research has shown that the most successful Web-based training, or e-learning, has these features:

• colorful and well designed classes

• accurate and well written information

• activities that involve students in learning

• activities that help students remember the information

Blended Learning   Some students find the best method of learning combines traditional classroom education with Web-based education. **Blended learning** offers opportunities for students to interact with others face-to-face and at a distance.

Computer-based Training   Online instruction is one form of computer-based training, or CBT. But the first method for delivering computer-based training—the CD—remains popular among teachers and students. Many companies use CD tutorials to train employees on policies, products, and procedures. The advantage of this type of CBT is that the user can carry it around, and it does not require a network or Internet connection.

Use the Vocabulary

Directions: *Match each vocabulary term in the left column with the correct definition in the right column.*

_____ **1.** attachment
_____ **2.** mailbox name
_____ **3.** e-mail client
_____ **4.** alias
_____ **5.** e-mail server
_____ **6.** bounce message
_____ **7.** spam
_____ **8.** digital signature
_____ **9.** teleconference
_____ **10.** videoconference

a. part of an e-mail address

b. a meeting that provides audio and visual contact for people in different locations

c. a notice that e-mail could not be delivered

d. junk e-mail

e. anything sent with an e-mail

f. a meeting via computers and a network or the Internet, which lets participants talk or exchange text messages

g. an electronic identifier used to verify the identity of an e-mail sender

h. an ISP computer that accepts, sends, and delivers e-mail messages

i. software that lets you create, send, receive, and manage e-mail messages

j. nickname by which an e-mail user is known

Check Your Comprehension

Directions: *Complete each sentence with information from the chapter.*

1. In an e-mail address, the symbol @ represents the word _____.

2. The _____ is an Internet service provider's computer that routes e-mail.

3. In an e-mail message form, the _____ field identifies people other than the main recipient who should receive the message when it is sent.

4. When you _____ an e-mail message you have received, you send it to another person.

5. You will not get a bounce message if you enter an incorrect but _____ address.

6. Some e-mail clients have _____ that you can configure to delete unwanted e-mail.

7. Sometimes, _____ can clog e-mail servers, slowing Internet traffic.

8. Teleconferences and videoconferences save money because people don't have to _____ to attend a meeting.

9. One-to-one _____ allow two people to see and talk to each other on their computers.

10. Many schools now offer classes through the Internet, a practice known as _____.

Think Critically

Directions: *Answer the following questions.*

1. How do an e-mail client and an e-mail server work together to handle e-mail?

2. What steps can you take to avoid receiving junk e-mail?

3. What advantages do e-mail, teleconferences, and videoconferences offer to workgroups in different locations?

4. What is one way to avoid receiving a bounce message?

5. Could distance learning make use of a videoconference? How?

Extend Your Knowledge

Directions: *Choose one of the following projects. Complete the exercise on a separate sheet of paper.*

A. Picture phones allow you to see the person at the other end of a telephone call. A video camera that clips on your computer allows you to see the person with whom you communicate on the Internet. With your teacher's permission, research these technologies on the Internet. Compare and contrast their cost, features, and uses. Assess which, if either, you think will become more popular.

B. In small groups, brainstorm for the advantages and disadvantages of face-to-face communications, traditional letters, e-mail, telephone calls, teleconferencing, and videoconferencing. Then, create a list of situations for which each of these media might be the most appropriate communications choice.

Understanding
Personal
Communications

We Need to Communicate Thanks to technology, today we can stay in touch more easily than ever before. We have many communications options, from speaking face to face or talking on the phone to using computers to exchange ideas and information.

Technology also gives us more freedom in communicating. We no longer have to sit by the phone waiting for a call or stay by a computer to check our e-mail; phone calls and e-mail messages can travel with us.

Advances in science and technology help us communicate anytime, almost anywhere. However, the virus programmers who deliberately interfere with communications systems continue to cause millions of dollars of damage to computers each year.

Chapter Outline

 Lesson 32–1

The Science of E-mail Systems

 Lesson 32–2

E-mail Benefits and Hazards

The Science of E-mail Systems

Objectives

- Describe how e-mail travels through networks.
- Summarize the key e-mail protocols.
- Explain how e-mail can be organized.

As You Read

Organize Information Use a concept web as you read to help you organize ideas about e-mail systems as you read the lesson.

 Key Terms

- authentication
- e-mail folder
- message header

Figure 32.1.1 E-mail protocols enable clients and servers to exchange messages smoothly.

What Happens When You Send and Receive E-mail?

When you send and receive e-mail messages, you participate in a client-server network. Your e-mail software is the client. The computer that accepts and forwards messages for its users is the e-mail server. Internet service providers (ISPs), companies and institutions, and other mail services maintain the servers. Because e-mail servers and clients use the same protocols, you can send messages to and receive messages from anyone with an e-mail address, as long as the computers have access to the same network or the Internet.

Sending Messages When you click Send, most messages travel first to your ISP's e-mail server via Simple Mail Transfer Protocol, or SMTP. The e-mail server then examines the recipient's address. If the person you are e-mailing uses the same server you do, the message is delivered instantly. The recipient's e-mail client retrieves the message from the server by using another protocol, called the Post Office Protocol (POP). Most current e-mail programs use a version of POP called POP3, which can work with or without SMTP.

Different Servers Often, however, you and the recipient use different ISP e-mail servers. For example, you may use AOL, while your friend uses Mindspring. In this case, the AOL server, using SMTP, sends your e-mail message to the Mindspring server via the Internet. The Mindspring server then delivers the message to your friend. Attachments to a message are translated by a protocol called Multipurpose Internet Mail Extensions, or MIME.

Receiving Messages What happens to incoming messages sent to you? Usually, your server stores them. When you open your e-mail client and get your mail, the server sends you your messages and, depending on your settings, erases them from the server.

Securing Your Account

To handle your e-mail, your client needs your username and password. The server also uses this information to identify you as a valid user. In a process called **authentication**, the e-mail server confirms that you are a valid user.

Password Protection Guard your username and password, and change your password frequently. It should be easy for you to remember but difficult for others to guess. If someone learns your password, change it. Never allow others to log on with your password.

Organizing Your E-mail

E-mail programs provide you with an address book, where you can store the names and e-mail addresses of frequent e-mail contacts. You may be able to create group contact lists in your address book. If you and several friends are working on a project, you might create a list called Project and add the e-mail address of each group member to the list. This feature lets you send a message to all the contacts at once, saving you the time of typing each address separately.

Storing Messages The list of messages in your Inbox can grow quickly. You should delete unimportant messages after you read them. You can, however, save important messages in folders you create for this purpose. Like a manila folder, an **e-mail folder** stores related messages. For example, you can create a folder to hold messages relating to a specific topic or which come from a certain person. A Folder List identifies the folders you have created. Folders make it easy to find and manage messages.

To retrieve a message saved in the Inbox, click it. To store a message in a folder, drag the message from the Inbox to the desired folder. To open a message saved in a folder, click the name of the folder, and then click the message you wish to read.

Viewing Messages in the Inbox   Incoming messages appear in your Inbox. Depending on your setup, you may see just a list of messages, or you may see the actual contents of the messages, too. At the top of the message is the **message header**. The message header contains information that identifies the sender of the message, other recipients, the date sent, and the subject.

Sorting Messages   Most e-mail clients allow you to sort messages—that is, arrange them in a certain order, by senders' names, date received, and so on. To view the messages by sender, click the From heading. To sort by Subject or Date, click either of those headings.

Configuring E-mail Options   All e-mail clients allow you to customize your e-mails. You can usually do this by clicking on the "settings" option. For instance, you can use settings to create a signature that will appear on every e-mail message you create, even with a quote or image you like. When you are not available, you can use a "mail away" option to alert senders to your absence, and you can use your SPAM filter to block unwanted messages.

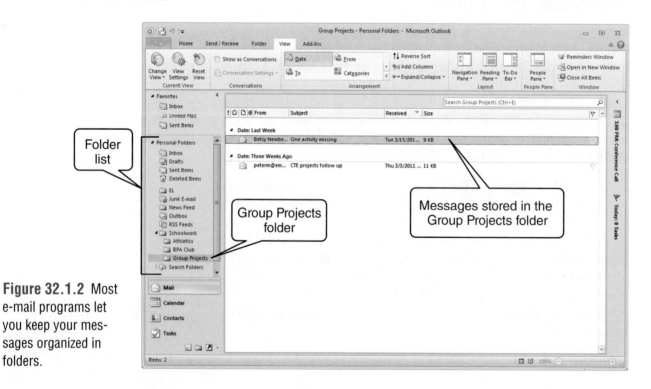

Figure 32.1.2 Most e-mail programs let you keep your messages organized in folders.

E-mail Benefits and Hazards

Objectives

- Explain how e-mail attachments work.
- Discuss the hazards of e-mail viruses.
- Assess the value of virus detection software.

As You Read

Organize Information Use an outline to help you identify the advantages and dangers of e-mail as you read the lesson.

Tapping the Power of E-mail

A useful feature of e-mail is the ability to send attachments. An attachment is a computer file that is added to an e-mail message. There are two important issues about attachments that you should be aware of:

- Your recipients may have a different e-mail program or computer platform. They also may not have the program you used to create an attached file. They may not be able to retrieve or use the attachment.

- Large files, such as photo or video files, can take a long time to download. Be sure your recipients want them: Some recipients' e-mail servers or clients may reject large attachments.

Common Uses of Attachments What if you are on vacation and want to share photos you took with your digital camera? You can copy them onto your laptop and send them to your friends as e-mail attachments. Are you and your friends working together on a school report? Perhaps you wrote the text for the document and a friend created the artwork, while another created a video explaining the report. Each of you could attach your work to an e-mail message and let the others review your progress.

Business Uses of Attachments Companies no longer need to print, package, and ship documents. Instead, with just a few clicks, documents can be sent as e-mail attachments. E-mailing attachments can also replace faxing documents to other locations. In both cases, e-mailing documents saves time and money.

Key Terms

- e-mail virus
- executable file
- macro virus
- replicate

Figure 32.2.1 An e-mail message with an attachment.

The paper-clip icon usually means there is an attachment.

Double-click the file icon to open the attachment.

Viruses appear in many forms, ranging from prank messages to system failure and erasure of the information on a hard drive.

Some Web sites provide free virus scanning and, at the same time, test the performance of your Internet connection.

The Dangers of E-mail Attachments

Some attachments can contain **e-mail viruses**—scripts or programs that cause harm, such as changing or deleting files. The worst viruses **replicate**, or copy themselves. They locate your address book and send themselves to every address listed in it. Since your name appears in the message header, the friends and family whom you e-mail do not suspect a problem until they open the message and their computers become infected.

E-mail viruses can do great harm to businesses, too. Imagine that a virus replicated on the computers listed in employees' address books. The e-mail servers would become overloaded, and files would be destroyed.

Executable Files   One way of spreading a virus is through an executable file. An **executable file** is one that carries out instructions that might destroy files on your computer, change its settings, or cause Internet traffic jams.

You can recognize an executable file by the extension at the end of the file name: .COM, .EXE, .VBS, .BAT. If you get an e-mail message that has one of these files attached, beware. You may be asking for trouble if you open it.

Macro Viruses   Another type of virus is called a macro virus. A **macro virus** is a series of commands that takes advantage of the programming language built into everyday application software, such as Microsoft Word. The virus might add words or phrases to documents, or do additional damage.

Real-World Tech

Catching a Virus   Anyone can be vulnerable to viruses—even people who know a lot about the risks. Josh Quittner is a columnist for an online technology magazine. But that didn't protect him when he received an e-mail with an attachment from a friend. He opened it and then watched in horror as his screen began to shimmer. Quittner's computer had been infected by a virus.

What steps can you take to help protect your computer from a virus?

Protecting Yourself

E-mail attachments aren't the only source of viruses. Viruses have been found in:

- files downloaded from the Internet
- files created on public computers, such as those in libraries
- infected media, such as CDs or DVDs

Antivirus Software   A good antivirus software program will run all the time on your computer. It looks for any application or script that tries to manipulate the system. Some antivirus software can also scan incoming and outgoing e-mail for viruses.

Automatic Updates   Virus programmers continually try to create new viruses and make changes to existing ones, with a primary goal of making viruses more difficult to detect and eliminate. The developers of antivirus software, however, are never more than a step behind the virus programmers. Most good antivirus programs can be updated regularly via the Internet. Some of the programs can update themselves automatically, without the user even knowing about it. By regularly updating your antivirus software, you can protect yourself against the most current viruses.

Can home computers catch a virus just as business computers can? Of course!

Think About It!

Think about how home computers might be at risk for a virus. Which activities listed below might spread a virus?

➤ typing a document on a home computer
➤ downloading a game from the Internet
➤ opening an attachment labeled "birthday.exe" on an e-mail from your cousin
➤ using a CD-ROM your friend gave you
➤ using a home computer that isn't connected to the Internet

Figure 32.2.2 An antivirus program helps protect your computer from malicious software that might damage your data.

Use the Vocabulary

Directions: *Match each vocabulary term in the left column with the correct definition in the right column.*

_____ **1.** message header
_____ **2.** authentication
_____ **3.** e-mail folder
_____ **4.** replicate
_____ **5.** executable file
_____ **6.** macro virus
_____ **7.** e-mail virus

a. part of an e-mail that identifies the sender, among other information
b. series of commands hidden in a document
c. to copy or reproduce, as a virus makes copies of itself
d. process by which an e-mail server identifies valid users
e. place to store saved messages
f. can launch a program; sometimes used by viruses
g. a script or program that causes harm

Check Your Comprehension

Directions: *Complete each sentence with information from the chapter.*

1. The _____ helps your e-mail messages reach your e-mail server.

2. With most e-mail clients, you can organize the messages in your Inbox by _____ different headers at the top of the Inbox.

3. Your _____ should be easy for you to remember but hard for someone else to guess.

4. An e-mail folder stores _____.

5. You can send photos with an e-mail message as _____.

6. You can recognize some executable files by the _____ at the end of the file name.

7. _____ software checks for viruses and alerts you to them.

8. An e-mail server uses _____ to confirm that you are a valid user.

9. Incoming messages are listed in your _____.

10. Some e-mail servers or clients may reject attachments that are too _____.

Think Critically

Directions: *Answer the following questions.*

1. What is the overall purpose of SMTP, MIME, and POP3?

2. How can you secure both your outgoing and incoming e-mail?

3. How might your antivirus software help others?

4. Summarize the reasons for organizing e-mail into folders.

5. Explain ways you can customize e-mail options.

Extend Your Knowledge

Directions: *Choose one of the following projects. Complete the exercise on a separate sheet of paper.*

A. Two well-known e-mail viruses are "Here you have" virus, which spread in 2010, and Code Red, which made its way through networks in 2001. Conduct library or, with your teacher's permission, online research to find out what problems each of these invaders caused, how they spread, and how they were defeated. Also, identify a more recent virus and describe its effects and how computer users might have protected themselves from the destruction the virus caused. Present your findings in a report.

B. E-mail is one type of electronic communication, but there are many others, include texting, instant messaging, blogging, and social networking. Compare and contrast the advantages and disadvantages of different types of electronic communication. Summarize your findings in a report and present it to your class.

DIRECTIONS: *You will use e-mail to exchange information about e-mail etiquette. You will create a new contact to which you will send the e-mail. You also will reply to and forward an e-mail message. Microsoft Office 2010 procedures required for this activity can be found in Appendix A.*

1. Open the .pdf file **EM-1_Etiquette**, which is located on the student CD. With your teacher's permission, print the Data Record Sheet. It has space for you to record information that you find about e-mail etiquette. Close the file, and exit your pdf reader program.

2. Use the Internet (with your teacher's permission), library resources, or your school's acceptable Internet use policy to locate information about e-mail etiquette.

3. To use the Internet, open a Web browser and navigate to a search engine. Search for words or phrases such as **"e-mail etiquette"**.

4. Evaluate each site you visit for accuracy and validity.

5. When you find a credible Web site with relevant information, bookmark the site, or with your teacher's permission, print the desired pages. Complete the Data Record Sheet.

6. Start your e-mail program.

7. Open your address book or contacts list, and with your teacher's permission, enter the name and e-mail address of a classmate or other recipient.

8. In your e-mail program, create a new mail message. Alternatively, with your teacher's permission, complete this activity using an instant messaging service or electronic bulletin board.

9. In the To box, select the recipient's e-mail address that you entered in step 7.

10. In the Subject box, type **E-mail Etiquette Guidelines**.

11. In the body of the e-mail message, write a greeting to the recipient, followed by a list of tips or guidelines you create based on the information you recorded on your Data Record Sheet. Ask the recipient to reply with his or her opinion on your etiquette guidelines. At the end of the message, enter your name or signature. A sample message is shown in Illustration A.

12. Check the spelling and grammar in the e-mail message, and correct any errors.

13. With your teacher's permission, send the e-mail.

14. When you receive the e-mail reply from the recipient, open it and read it.

15. With your teacher's permission, print the e-mail message from the recipient.

16. With your teacher's permission, forward the e-mail with the recipient's reply to your teacher.

17. With your teacher's permission, send a reply to the recipient, thanking him or her for the response.

18. Exit the e-mail program.

19. As a class, discuss the e-mail guidelines. Why do you think it is important to use e-mail etiquette when corresponding with e-mail? Do you think you must use the same guidelines when you communicate with friends as when you communicate with teachers, parents, and other adults?

Illustration A

DIRECTIONS: *You will practice using e-mail to send a document. You will write a persuasive essay about an interesting topic in your school or community. You will include specific facts and examples to support your opinion. Then, you will send your essay as an e-mail attachment to the editor of a local newspaper or your school newspaper. Microsoft Office 2010 procedures required for this activity can be found in Appendix A.*

1. Obtain a recent edition of a local or regional newspaper. Locate an article about an issue that relates to your school or community, and read it. If possible, locate other articles about the same issue in a different newspaper, or a different edition of the same paper. As you read, formulate an opinion about the issue.

2. Open the .pdf file **EM-2_Outline**, which is located on the student CD. With your teacher's permission, print the Data Record Sheet. Close the file, and exit your pdf reader program.

3. Use the Data Record Sheet to outline a persuasive essay on the topic of the article. List reasons, facts, and details that support your opinion about the issue.

4. Locate the e-mail address for the editor of the newspaper you read or for your school newspaper. Write the e-mail address on your Data Record Sheet.

5. Start your word processor, and create a new document. Save it as **EM-2_Opinion_xx** in the location where your teacher instructs you to store the files for this activity. Replace the initials *xx* with your own name or initials, as instructed by your teacher.

6. At the top of the page, write a title that makes it clear what issue you are writing about. Format the title appropriately and center it.

7. Using the outline on your Data Record Sheet, write a persuasive essay about the topic. Be sure to use proper keyboarding posture and techniques, including typing only one space after punctuation marks.

8. When you have finished writing your essay, proofread it carefully, check the spelling and grammar, and make improvements.

9. With your teacher's permission, print the document.

10. Exchange documents with a classmate according to your teacher's instructions. For example, you may print the document to exchange, copy it to a removable drive, or send it via e-mail. Proofread your classmate's essay by marking errors on the printed page or by using comments and revision marks. Return the essay to your classmate.

11. Review the corrections and comments that your classmate made on your essay, and incorporate them into your document file.

12. Finalize your essay, and, with your teacher's permission, print the document. Then, close the file, saving all changes, and exit your word-processing program.

13. Open your e-mail program, and create a new mail message.

14. In the To box, type the e-mail address of the newspaper that you wrote on your Data Record Sheet. With your teacher's permission, include your teacher's e-mail address in the Cc box.

15. In the Subject box, type a subject related to the issue that is the topic of your essay.

16. Type a brief e-mail message to the editor, explaining that you are attaching an essay that expresses your opinion about the issue. Explain that you are submitting the essay to be considered for publication. Include a respectful greeting at the beginning of the message and your name and school name at the end.

17. Attach the **EM-2_Opinion_xx** file to the message. A sample e-mail message is shown in Illustration B.

18. With your teacher's permission, send the message and attachment. Alternatively, print the message.

19. Exit the e-mail program.

20. As a class, discuss why it is important to voice your opinion about issues in your school or community. Discuss other ways you can make your opinions known.

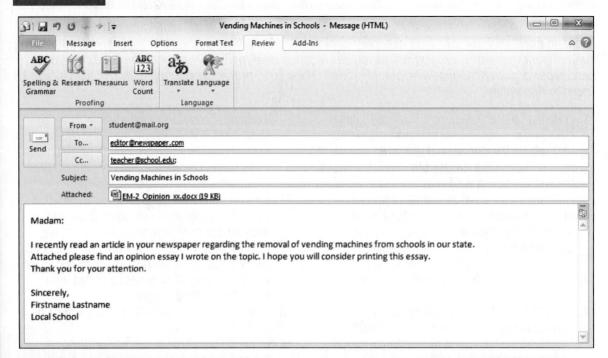

Activity 3: Attaching a Spreadsheet to an E-mail Message

DIRECTIONS: *You will practice using e-mail to send a spreadsheet that contains survey results data. You will open an existing spreadsheet, insert a formula to perform a calculation, and create a chart to illustrate the data. You will then create an e-mail message and attach the spreadsheet file before sending. Microsoft Office 2010 procedures required for this activity can be found in Appendix A.*

1. Start your spreadsheet program and open **EM-3_Survey**. Save the file as **EM-3_ Survey_xx** in the location where your teacher instructs you to store the files for this activity.
2. In cell B5, use the SUM function to enter a formula totaling the responses.
3. Select cells A2:B4 and create an Exploded pie in 3-D chart.
4. Insert the chart title **Vending Machine Survey Results**.
5. Display percentages in the data labels.
6. Position the chart over cells A7:F21.
7. Insert a footer with your name on the left and today's date on the right.
8. Preview the spreadsheet. It should look similar to Illustration C.
9. With your teacher's permission, print the spreadsheet, and then exit your spreadsheet program, saving all changes.
10. Start your e-mail program, and create a new mail message.
11. In the To box, type the e-mail address approved by your teacher, such as a classmate, a family member, or a teacher.
12. In the Subject box, type **Survey Results**.

13. In the message area, type a greeting and then type: **Attached is a spreadsheet illustrating the results of the survey on vending machines in schools. Please reply to this message telling me if you think the chart is easy to read.**
14. After the message, type your name.
15. Check the spelling and grammar in the e-mail message, and correct any errors.
16. Attach the **EM-3_Survey_xx** file to the message.
17. With your teacher's permission, send the e-mail.
18. When you receive the e-mail reply from the recipient, open it and read it.
19. With your teacher's permission, print the e-mail message from the recipient.
20. With your teacher's permission, forward the e-mail with the recipient's reply to your teacher.
21. Exit the e-mail program.
22. As a class, discuss when it is appropriate to send an attachment to an e-mail message. Discuss whether there are other methods for sharing information such as survey results and charts.

Illustration C

Vending Machine Survey	
Agree with the decision to remove vending machines	45
Disagree with the decision to remove vending machines	68
Do not have an opinion	22
Total	135

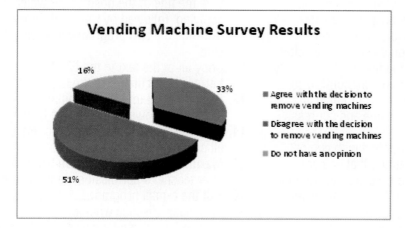

Vending Machine Survey Results

16%

33%

51%

- Agree with the decision to remove vending machines
- Disagree with the decision to remove vending machines
- Do not have an opinion

Firstname Lastname

Today's Date

DIRECTIONS: *You will use a word-processing program to compose a cover letter for a job application. You will then copy the text of the letter into your e-mail program to send to a potential employer. Microsoft Office 2010 procedures required for this activity can be found in Appendix A.*

1. Begin by looking for summer jobs or internships in your area. For example, you might look into being a camp counselor, babysitting in your neighborhood, or any type of employment for students your age. For resources, look in local newspapers and their Web sites, your school career office, or a local government bulletin board. Identify the name, title, mailing address, and e-mail address of the person responsible for hiring.

2. Start your word-processing program and create a new file based on a simple letter template. Save the file as **EM-4_Cover Letter_xx** in the location where your teacher instructs you to store the files for this activity.

3. Replace sample text or content controls in the letter to enter the date, your name and address, the recipient's name and address, and the salutation.

4. Replace the sample letter text with two or three paragraphs explaining that you are applying for the position. Be sure to state the position title, where you heard about it, and why you think you are qualified.

5. Proofread the letter carefully and make improvements.

6. Check the spelling and grammar in the letter, and make corrections.

7. Preview the letter. It should look similar to the one shown in Illustration D (right).

8. With your teacher's permission, print the letter.

9. Start your e-mail program, and create a new mail message.

10. In the To box, type the recipient's e-mail address. If you do not have an actual employer's address, enter the address of a classmate, family member, or teacher. With your teacher's permission, include his or her address in the Cc box. In the Subject box, type the title of the position for which you are applying, followed by the word **Application**.

11. Arrange the two program windows side by side.

12. Copy all of the text in the **EM-4_Cover Letter_xx** document to the Clipboard.

13. Paste the text into the e-mail message area. A sample is shown in Illustration D (left).

14. Exit your word-processing program, saving all changes.

15. Maximize the e-mail program window. With your teacher's permission, send the e-mail.

16. Exit the e-mail program.

17. As a class, discuss whether it is always appropriate to send a cover letter by e-mail. Discuss the types of documents you might include as an attachment to a cover letter, and how you can make your documents stand out in a positive way.

Illustration D

E-mail Activities

DIRECTIONS: *You will conduct research about volcanoes. As part of your research, you will send an e-mail message to an expert. You will use the research information to create a presentation, which you will send as an e-mail attachment. Microsoft Office 2010 procedures required for this activity can be found in Appendix A.*

1. Open the .pdf file **EM-5_VolcanoResearch**, which is located on the student CD. With your teacher's permission, print the Data Record Sheet. You will record notes about volcanoes to create a draft for your presentation. Close the file, and exit your pdf reader program.

2. Use the Internet (with your teacher's permission), print, or CD-ROM resources to find information about a specific volcano of your choice.

3. If you are researching online, search for terms and phrases such as the name of the volcano. You may also use Boolean searches, such as **volcanoes AND volcanologists**.

4. Compare and evaluate each site you find for its accuracy and validity. Use information from only those sites relevant to your purposes.

5. Locate information about the volcano's location and height, how often it erupts, date of most recent eruption, and at least two interesting or unusual facts about the volcano.

6. Record the information you find on the Data Record Sheet. On a separate sheet of paper, cite sources for all information you use.

7. Search for several photos of the volcano. Download and save them. If a scanner is available, you can scan images from print resources and save them to a storage device. Remember to check on whether you need permission to use the photos.

8. Locate information about volcanologists. Find information about the following and record it on the Data Record Sheet:
   - How close scientists get to a volcano
   - What precautions they take
   - What kinds of protective equipment they use
   - Which instruments they use to take measurements
   - What kinds of information they gather
   - The e-mail address of a volcanologist or other volcano researcher, such as a professor at a local college or someone at the United States Geological Survey (www.usgs.gov)

9. Start your e-mail program and create a new message. Address it to the researcher. As the subject, type **Volcano Research**. In the message, introduce yourself as a student and request brief answers to the questions in step 8. Mention that you will be creating an informational presentation on a volcano and would like to e-mail it to the scientist for review. Check the spelling and grammar in the message and correct errors. A sample message is shown in Illustration E.

10. With your teacher's permission, send the message. If you receive a timely reply from the researcher, with your teacher's permission, print the e-mail message. Record any additional notes on the Data Record Sheet.

11. When you have completed your research, close the Web browser.

12. Start your presentation program, and create a new presentation. Save it as **EM-5_Volcano_xx**.

13. Create the first slide as a title slide, and enter the title for the presentation. Insert a subtitle that includes your name, school name, and school address.

14. Insert a new slide using a layout that has placeholders for a title, text, and a picture. Enter a title and the information about the volcano's location, height, and last eruption. Insert a picture of the volcano.

15. Create slides for the interesting facts, equipment used by volcanologists, types of information volcanologists research, and precautions. Include a slide to cite your sources. For each slide, select a slide layout that works best with the information you have and any graphics or clip art you want to include.

16. When you have finished entering the slide text, proofread each one carefully, checking for consistency in sentence structure, and correct any errors you find.

17. Check the spelling and grammar in the presentation, and correct any errors.

18. Apply a theme or design to your presentation.

19. Add transitions and animations to the presentation.

20. Add notes to reference while you deliver the presentation.
21. Preview the presentation, and make any final modifications.
22. With your teacher's permission, print the notes pages for yourself, and print handouts with three slides per page for the class.
23. Rehearse the presentation, and then show it to the class.
24. Close the presentation file, saving all changes, and exit your presentation program.
25. Start your e-mail program and create a new e-mail message. Address it to the researcher or volcanologist, if possible, or address it to a classmate.
26. In the subject line, type **Volcano Presentation**. Type a brief message explaining that this is the presentation you created with the information he or she provided. Check the spelling and grammar in the message and correct any errors.
27. Attach the presentation to the message, and then, with your teacher's permission, send it.
28. Exit your e-mail program.
29. As a class, discuss volcanoes and predict how volcanic eruptions change the land features of the surrounding area. Compare and contrast the information students found about specific volcanoes.

Illustration E

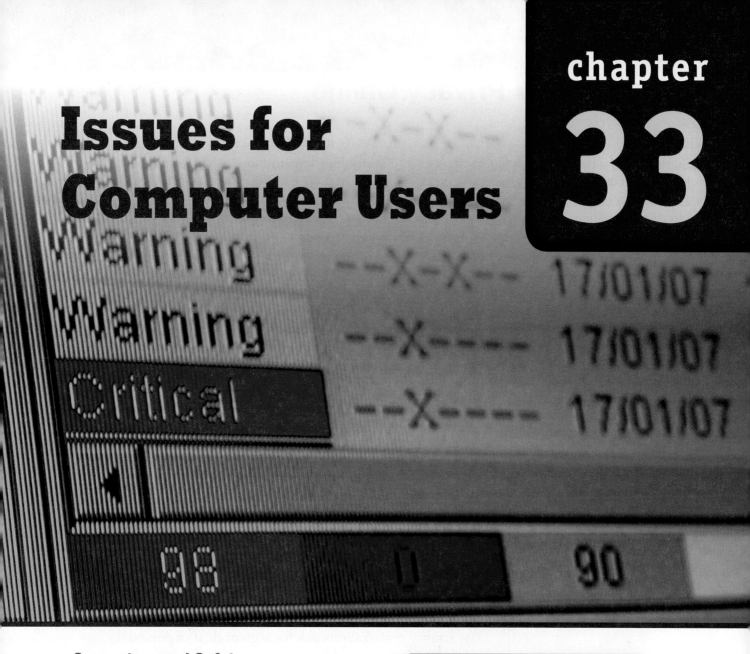

Issues for Computer Users

Computers and Safety Computers are tools and, like other tools, they are controlled by the person using them. People can use computers to learn, to communicate, and to have fun. However, people can also use computers to snoop into another person's private life or to commit crimes. Careless computer users can pass computer viruses from their machines to those of other users. What can make computers dangerous is the same thing that makes them helpful: They can store vast amounts of data.

When people learn to use tools, they learn to use them with care and to protect themselves and others from harm. Computer users need to learn ways to protect themselves, too.

Chapter Outline

 Lesson 33–1

Privacy Online

 Lesson 33–2

All About Cybercrime

 Lesson 33–3

Avoiding Cybercrime

Privacy Online

Objectives

- Summarize the danger of sharing personal information on the Internet.
- Explain how cookies and global unique identifiers endanger privacy.

As You Read

Organize Information   As you read the lesson, use an outline to help you organize basic information about privacy and ethical issues.

 Key Terms

- global unique identifier (GUID)
- infringe

Privacy in Cyberspace

Many consumers share personal information about themselves, their habits, and their finances. Sometimes, however, such information is gathered without a person's knowledge or approval.

How Businesses Obtain Personal Information   Some businesses gather information from public records kept by the government. They may also access information that people volunteer about themselves in several ways:

- Web site registration—Many Web sites require visitors to fill out registration forms.
- Online purchases—Some Web sites gather information about people who buy their goods or services.
- Warranty registration—Products of all kinds come with a warranty that enables the user to get help if the product breaks or fails. To take advantage of a product warranty, you usually must register with the manufacturer. Some warranty registrations ask for a great deal of personal information.
- Sweepstakes entries—Many people fill out sweepstakes entry forms hoping to win a prize. In doing so, they provide important personal information.

What consumers may not know is that companies that gather personal information often sell it to other organizations, such as marketing companies, whose job is to sell products and services to consumers. As a result, marketing companies have access to enormous quantities of data about people. This information is stored in large computerized databases.

Protecting Privacy   Some people say that individuals should have the right to refuse to provide information about themselves, as well as the right to have information about themselves removed from a database. Although such a guarantee does not yet exist in the United States, you can protect your privacy. The main thing you can do is be careful to whom you give out personal information about yourself.

Respecting Others' Privacy   Not only do you have to guard your own privacy, but you also need to make sure not to **infringe** on the privacy and rights of others. That means you should not take steps that interfere with the privacy of others. Do not breach friends' or teachers' privacy by posting personal information about them online, via texts, or in e-mails.

Expectations of Privacy   Remember that everything you send by e-mail can be forwarded and is on record. Employees of a company have no right of privacy for their e-mail when they use their employer's computer system. Although the employer may not say so, every message might be read by someone who alerts management if anything seems amiss. Employees may face serious consequences if they disclose inside information to competitors, threaten or harass other employees, or tell jokes.

New Technology and Your Privacy

The Internet has generated new methods for tracking what people do. Even if you do not buy anything online, outsiders can use different hardware and software to learn about your habits and interests. Some people worry that these technologies—and your personal information—can be misused.

Cookies   A cookie is a small file that is saved to your hard drive when you visit some Web sites. Cookies give Web sites a way of storing information about you so it is available when you return. Cookies are meant to make your Web experience more pleasurable by personalizing what you see. However, they can also be used to gather data on your browsing and shopping habits without your consent.

If you wish, you can set your browser to reject cookies or warn you about them. Several programs and Web browsers let users see what the purpose of a cookie is. Then you can decide whether or not to accept the cookie.

Global Unique Identifiers   A **global unique identifier**, or **GUID**, is a unique identification number that is generated by a piece of hardware or by a program. Companies that place GUIDs in their products generally do not say so openly. Some people worry that GUIDs can be used to follow a person's online activity, invading his or her privacy.

Figure 33.1.1 Most Web-browser programs let you select Privacy settings to control cookies.

The Web is not the only way others can learn about you on the Internet. Visitors to newsgroups can reveal facts about themselves to other visitors.

Think About It!

Think about what you might say in a newsgroup. Which statement(s) below might reveal too much personal information?

➤ "In my town, people often leave their doors unlocked."
➤ "We always go to the shore on weekends in the summer."
➤ "I don't like being alone."
➤ "Our porch light doesn't work."
➤ "My parents get home an hour after I arrive from school."

All About Cybercrime

Objectives

- Identify techniques that intruders use to attack computer systems.
- Discuss different types of cybercrime.
- Summarize how computer crime costs businesses money.

As You Read

Identify Key Points   As you read, use a conclusion chart to help you identify key points about computer-related crime.

🔑 Key Terms

- computer crime
- cybercrime
- downtime
- identity theft
- memory shave
- phishing
- scanning
- software piracy
- spoof
- superzapper
- time bomb
- trap door
- virus
- worm
- Trojan horse

Cybercrime Techniques

Many cybercrimes are based on the ability of people to tap illegally into computer networks. They may create a **virus**, **worm**, or **Trojan horse** program to infiltrate computers and damage or delete data. Or, they may use a variety of other criminal techniques.

Scanning   Some intruders develop programs that try many different passwords until one works. This is called **scanning**, or probing. Networks can be blocked from scanners by limiting the number of failed attempts to log onto the system. After three password failures, for instance, the network can refuse access.

Superzapping   A program called a **superzapper** allows authorized users to access a network in an emergency situation by skipping security measures. In the hands of an intruder, a superzapper opens the possibility of damage to the system.

Spoofing   Some intruders **spoof**, or use a false Internet Protocol (IP) or e-mail address to gain access. Intruders assume the IP address of a trusted source to enter a secure network and distribute e-mails containing viruses.

Phishing   **Phishing** criminals try to lure victims into giving them user names, passwords, bank account numbers, or credit card details, usually by using an e-mail that looks like it comes from an official and legitimate source. For example, in a typical phishing scam, a thief sends an e-mail message that looks as if it is from your bank, asking you to verify or update your account information. The thief captures the information you enter and can then steal from your account.

Time Bombs   A **time bomb** is a program that sits on a system until a certain event or set of circumstances activates the program. For example, an employee could create a time bomb designed to activate on a certain date after he or she resigns from the company. Although a time bomb is not necessarily a virus, these malicious programs are often categorized or described as viruses.

Trap Doors   Some employees may create a **trap door**, or a secret way into the system. Once they quit working for the employer, they can use this to access the system and damage it. Not all trap doors are viruses, but some viruses are trap doors. Many Trojan horse programs, for example, act as trap doors.

Scams   Some criminals use advertisements and e-mail messages to scam you into sending them money. For example, they might claim you have won a lottery, and if you pay a tax or fee, they will send you the winnings.

Types of Cybercrime

Crimes using the Internet can take many different forms. They affect individuals, businesses, and government agencies.

Fraud   When someone steals your personal information, he or she can impersonate you and make credit card purchases in your name or access your bank accounts. This is called **identity theft.** The criminal leaves you with bills and a damaged credit rating.

Piracy   **Software piracy** is the illegal copying of computer programs. It is estimated that about one third of all software in use is pirated.

As discussed in Lesson 9–2, most programs that people buy are licensed only to the purchaser. In other words, it is illegal for you to copy such a program and give it to a friend. It is also illegal to accept a copy of software from someone else.

Software piracy affects software publishers. They lose money when people use illegal copies of programs to avoid paying for legitimate copies.

Theft   The vast majority of computer thefts occur "on the inside" (by employees), leaving no signs of forced entry. The hardest crime to detect is **memory shaving**. In this act, a thief steals some of a computer's memory chips but leaves enough so the computer will start. The crime might go unnoticed for days or weeks.

Vandalism   Some Web servers are not properly secured. As a result, intruders can vandalize a Web site by placing prank material on it.

Figure 33.2.1 Identity theft is a growing problem in the United States, and the Department of Justice is taking steps to help consumers avoid this problem.

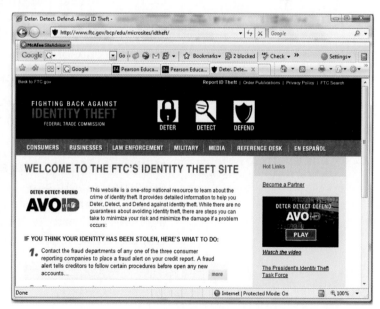

The High Cost of Computer Crime

The Internet has opened the door to new kinds of crime and new ways of carrying out traditional crimes. **Computer crime** is any act that violates state or federal laws and involves using a computer. The term **cybercrime** often refers specifically to crimes carried out by means of the Internet. Computer crime causes businesses to lose money in the following ways.

Staff Time   Even if intruders steal nothing from a business, they still cost companies money. Staff must make the network secure again and consider how to stop security breaches.

Downtime   Security breaches also cost a company in terms of **downtime**, or a temporary stop to work. System administrators sometimes shut a network down to prevent the loss of data. While the system is down, workers cannot do their jobs. A company can lose business if customers are affected by downtime.

Bad Publicity   When security problems become known, the public image of a company may suffer. Even if no personal information is lost, customers lose confidence that the company's security is trustworthy. Customers then take their business elsewhere.

Fighting Cybercrime

Law enforcement officials are using technology to catch cybercriminals. Several groups have taken part in this effort.

Computer Crime and Intellectual Property Section (CCIPS)
The Department of Justice created a special group known as CCIPS to advise and train federal prosecutors and local law enforcement on cybercrime. They review and propose new laws. They coordinate international efforts to combat computer crime and prosecute offenders.

Computer Hacking and Intellectual Property Project (CHIP)
In the CHIP project, law enforcement officials and prosecutors work closely together to pursue cybercrime. CHIP offices are in areas with a heavy concentration of computer companies.

National Infrastructure Protection Center (NIPC)   In 1998, government officials became worried about terrorist attacks on U.S. computer systems. Staffed by people from intelligence agencies and private companies such as Internet service providers, the NIPC ensures that the nation's computer system could continue to operate in the case of an attack.

Avoiding Cybercrime

Objectives
- Describe ways criminals obtain passwords.
- Discuss ways to protect your computer from being accessed by others.
- Explain the criteria of a strong password.
- Summarize ways to stay safe online.

As You Read

Summarize As you read the lesson, use a chart to help you summarize ways to protect information on your computer.

Password Theft

Many computer crimes start when an unauthorized user hacks, or gains unauthorized entry, into a computer network. This often happens when the intruder learns the password to access the victim's computer and the network. Following are ways such criminals learn passwords.

Guessing Too often, computer users choose passwords that are easy for them to remember, such as birthdates, names of pets, names of celebrities, and names of family members. Unfortunately, these passwords are also easy for intruders to guess.

Finding Sometimes people keep passwords written on pieces of paper near their computer. Other times, criminals simply look over someone's shoulder as he or she types the password and use it later. An intruder can also search the trash in the hopes of finding user IDs and passwords.

"Sniffing" Some criminals may use **packet sniffers**. A packet sniffer is a program that examines data streams on networks to try to find information, such as passwords and credit card numbers.

Pretending Some intruders pretend to be network administrators. They call network users and ask for their passwords, claiming that the passwords are needed to solve a problem in the system.

Modifying Network software makes the people who administer a system into superusers. Intruders who have superuser access can modify virtually any file on the network. They also may change user passwords to ones they know.

 Key Terms
- packet sniffer

One way companies generate mailing lists for spam messages is by checking the addresses of people in chat rooms and in Web discussion groups. If you use these services, you can minimize spam at your primary e-mail address by using a secondary e-mail address for these chats. You can then trash the spam when you want.

Think About It!

Which contacts listed below would you give your secondary e-mail address to?

➤ friend

➤ movie promotional site

➤ Web site from which you ordered a DVD

➤ chat room

➤ Web site where you receive support for your computer

Protecting Your Personal Data

It is in your best interest to protect your computer and its data. Here are some ways to help protect personal information.

Use Strong Passwords   Whenever you create a password, don't use things like family names, nicknames, or birth dates. Use a combination of at least six upper- and lowercase letters, numbers, and symbols. Often the site will let you know if your password is strong enough. Remember to change your password every so often. Do not keep a record of your passwords on your computer or on a piece of paper near your computer. Never give our your passwords to anyone, and never type a password while someone is watching.

Browse Anonymously   When you go online, surf from sites that protect your identity. Anonymizer and IDZap are two sites offering this service.

Use a Different E-mail Address   Although you may not be able to do this at school, on a home computer you can sign up for a free e-mail account from a Web site such as Hotmail or gmail. Use that address when you register at Web sites or participate in other public Internet spaces. This will protect you from receiving unwanted mail, or spam, at your primary e-mail address.

Avoid Site Registration   Be careful of Web sites that require you to register. Do not fill out a registration form unless the site clearly says that the data will not be shared with other people without your approval.

Figure 33.3.1 You may be required to provide a user name and password before accessing a computer network. Be sure to use a "strong" password.

Be Smart Online

You can avoid most computer crime simply by being a smart computer user. You can make sure your Internet browser settings are at the highest level for security and privacy, you can delete e-mail from unknown senders without opening it, and you can be wary of offers that seem too good to be true. Make sure you do business only with established companies that you know and trust. No reputable company or bank will ever ask you to send them your username, password, account information, or social security number. You should never reveal financial or other personal information, even if the request sounds legitimate.

Safe Social Networking   Here are some safety tips for online social networking:

- Do not add just anyone as a "friend." This person will see everything you post, including pictures and status updates.
- Check your settings. If you don't understand how to manage your account, get an adult to help you make sure you maintain your privacy.
- Give your parents or other trusted adult access to monitor your social networking activity.
- Don't write or post anything online that you would not want your grandparents or teachers to see or that you would not want posted about yourself.
- Never give out private information such as your phone number or address.
- Never agree to meet a new online friend in person.
- If you feel uncomfortable about an online experience, immediately tell a trusted adult.
- Don't download or install programs without parental permission.

Connections

Language Arts   Where did all the unusual names for destructive software come from?

- A computer virus is named for the kind of virus that causes infectious diseases like the cold and the flu.

- A worm is named for a tapeworm, a kind of organism that lives in the intestines of another creature and lives off the food that creature eats.

- A Trojan horse takes its name from an ancient Greek story about soldiers who entered a fortress by hiding inside the body of a giant replica of a horse, which the defenders allowed in. The soldiers hidden inside the horse attacked and defeated the defenders.

Figure 33.3.2 Facebook lets you customize your privacy settings. Why is it safer to allow "Friends Only" rather than "Everyone" to see your personal information and photos?

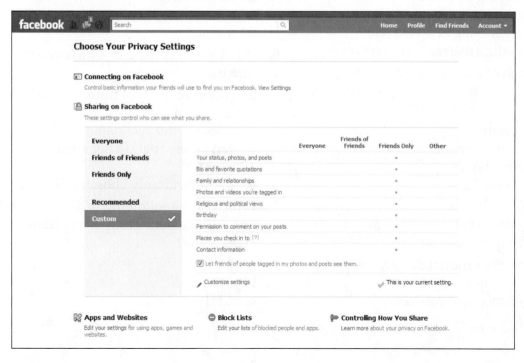

Use the Vocabulary

Directions: *Match each vocabulary term in the left column with the correct definition in the right column.*

_____ **1.** identity theft
_____ **2.** phishing
_____ **3.** global unique identifier
_____ **4.** computer crime
_____ **5.** cybercrime
_____ **6.** downtime
_____ **7.** software piracy
_____ **8.** packet sniffer
_____ **9.** scanning
_____ **10.** spoof

a. using a program to try different passwords until one works
b. using a computer to break the law
c. using the Internet to break the law
d. when workers cannot work because a network is temporarily not available
e. illegal copying of software programs
f. identification number generated by a piece of hardware or by a program
g. use a false IP or e-mail address to gain access to a network
h. impersonating someone in order to commit fraud
i. using an official-looking e-mail to lure victims into providing personal data
j. method of finding another's password

Check Your Comprehension

Directions: *Determine the correct choice for each of the following.*

1. Which of the following should you do cautiously because it could result in sharing personal information without your approval?
   a. buying software
   b. copying software
   c. registering at a Web site
   d. getting warranty protection

2. Which of the following malicious programs is activated by an event or set of circumstances?
   a. worm
   b. e-mail virus
   c. time bomb
   d. Trojan horse

3. Which of the following might cause a business to lose money as a result of computer crime?
   a. faulty product design
   b. downtime
   c. economic recession
   d. fire

4. Which kind of destructive computer program can move from one operating system to another?
   a. macro virus
   b. Trojan horse
   c. virus
   d. worm

5. What is an example of a password that is easy to guess?
   a. a combination of numbers and letters that makes no sense
   b. a four-letter nickname
   c. ten letters that do not spell a word
   d. eight randomly chosen numbers

6. Which of the following is NOT a law enforcement group for fighting cybercrime?
   a. CCIPS
   b. FDA
   c. CHIP
   d. NIPC

Think Critically

Directions: *Answer the following questions.*

1. Why is it a good idea to keep personal information confidential?

2. Summarize the components of a strong password.

3. Give examples of computer crime and cybercrime that illustrate the difference between the two terms.

4. What are the consequences of software piracy? How can you help prevent piracy?

5. Which methods of protecting your privacy and your data do you follow?

Extend Your Knowledge

Directions: *Choose one of the following projects. Complete the exercise on a separate sheet of paper.*

A. Create a poster illustrating one way you can be a smart computer user. Present your poster to the class, and then, with permission, display the poster in a public area of your school, such as a hallway or cafeteria.

B. With your teacher's permission, use the Internet to investigate a cybercrime. Write a brief report outlining what happened, what damage resulted, and whether the criminal was caught. If he or she was caught, describe how. State what consequences the criminal must face.

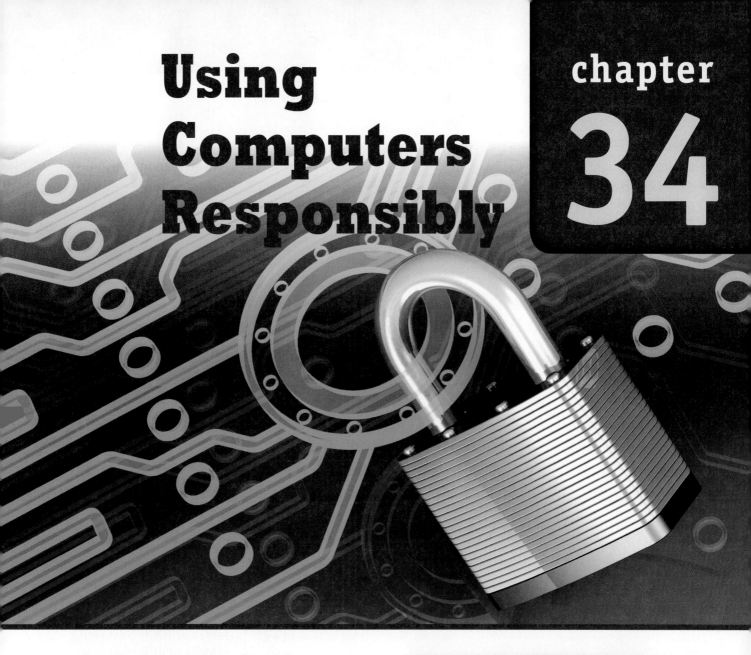

Using Computers Responsibly

Keeping Information Secure In the past, criminals needed to break into a building to steal money or goods. Today, computers offer new avenues to crime. Criminals can steal data stored on a computer without going anywhere near a home or office building. They simply use an Internet connection and special software to cover their tracks. With these tools, they can drain money out of a company's accounts or steal its secrets. They can steal a person's credit card information and use it to generate huge bills that cause severe financial problems for the innocent person.

Some people and many businesses have electronic security systems to prevent break-ins to homes and offices. Fortunately, there are also tools available to protect the data on your computer.

Chapter Outline

Computer Ethics

Objectives

- Explain copyright laws.
- Give examples of rules in acceptable use policies (AUPs).
- Summarize netiquette.

As You Read

Organize Information As you read the lesson, use a chart to help you organize details about privacy and ethics.

Key Terms

- acceptable use policy (AUP)
- citation
- copyright
- ethics
- fair use
- intellectual property
- patent
- plagiarism
- trademark

Figure 34.1.1 Your school district's AUP provides guidelines for using your school's computers, network, and Internet access.

Ethical Computer Use

How people use computers, including networks and e-mail, can affect other people. People who practice **ethics** behave morally. Ethical computer users respect others, and make sure their actions do not harm anyone.

Acceptable Use Policies

One way you can act ethically is to follow your school district's **acceptable use policy,** or **AUP.** These policies identify the responsibilities of Internet use. They spell out certain rules of behavior and explain the consequences of breaking those rules. Many businesses use AUPs, too, to govern the way workers use company-owned computers.

Policy Guidelines An AUP may include the following ethical guidelines:

- Users agree not to visit objectionable Web sites that contain content that does not meet community standards.
- Users agree not to use inappropriate language, such as language that is profane, abusive, or impolite.
- Users agree not to copy copyrighted material or to damage computer equipment belonging to the school.
- Users agree to respect the privacy of other people.

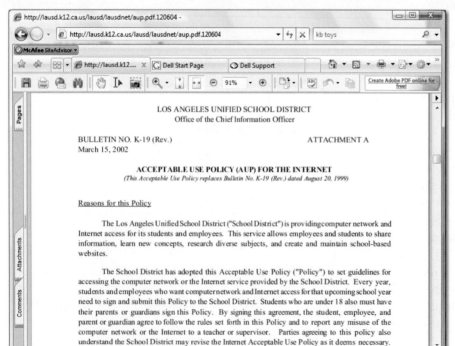

Possible Penalties Users of school computers who do not follow these rules may face consequences. They might lose privileges or be suspended from school activities. Very serious violations, such as using a school computer to threaten someone, may require police involvement.

Copyright Laws

Laws that involve **copyright** protect individuals and companies from the theft or misuse of their **intellectual property**, such as creative, literary, or artistic work. It is a crime to copy this kind of work without the permission of the person who owns the copyright to it.

Cite Your Source If you use information you find on the Web in your work, you must give credit to the source. You do this by inserting a reference to the source, called a **citation**, in a footnote, endnote, or bibliography. A proper citation gives credit to the source, and provides the tools a reader needs to locate the source on his or her own. Some Web sites have features that automatically generate the citation information for you.

Plagiarism If you do not cite your sources you are guilty of **plagiarism**, which is the unauthorized use of another person's idea's or creative work without giving that person credit. You should insert a citation when you quote, summarize, or paraphrase someone else, use someone else's idea, or reference someone else's work.

Copyright and Fair Use Doctrine If the content is protected by copyright, you must have permission from the copyright holder to use the work. However, part of copyright law called the **Fair Use Doctrine** allows you to use a limited amount of copyrighted material without permission for educational purposes. For example, you can quote a few lines of a song or a passage from a book.

Trademarks and Patents Some intellectual property is protected by trademark or patent. A **trademark** is a symbol that indicates that a brand or brand name is legally protected and cannot be used by other businesses. A **patent** is the exclusive right to make, use, or sell a device or process. Many types of inventions can be patented.

Gestures, facial expressions, and tones of voice—which people use in conversation to add meaning—are missing from e-mail.

Think About It!

Which items listed below do you think would be clearly communicated through the text in an e-mail? Which could be miscommunicated?

➤ fact

➤ sarcasm

➤ anger

➤ question

➤ joy

Practicing Netiquette

The Internet has an informal set of rules for expected behavior called netiquette. As an ethical computer user, you have a responsibility to use netiquette at all times. Some ways to practice netiquette include:

- Send e-mails only to people who really need to see a message.
- Keep e-mail messages short.
- Avoid sending extremely large files via e-mail.
- Do not use impolite or rude language when communicating online.
- Do not pretend to be someone else when communicating online.
- Do not use someone else's work without citing the source.
- Do not share files illegally.

The rules of netiquette are similar to general standards for good behavior. If you go to a search engine and type "netiquette," you will find many Web sites on the topic.

Spotlight on...

CYBERBULLYING

It's easier to fight online, because you feel more brave and in control. On Facebook you can be as mean as you want.
8th grade girl,
Benjamin Franklin Middle School,
Ridgewood, NJ

With the explosion of tweens and teens using cell phones and social networking sites on the Internet, there has been an explosion of cyberbullying. According to the Cyberbullying Research Center, "cyberbullying is when someone repeatedly harasses, mistreats, or makes fun of another person online or while using cell phones or other electronic devices."

Cyberbullies hurt their victims by doing things like sending threatening or harassing messages or texts, posting private pictures online or via cell phones, and creating hurtful Web sites, like fake Facebook sites.

Cyberbullying is hard to fight, because it happens anonymously and away from school. However, it has led to many high profile cases of teen suicide, spreading unstoppable rings of grief through whole communities. If you are the victim of cyberbullying, you should tell someone you trust right away, your Internet or mobile phone service provider, your school—or even the police.

Protecting Your Data

Objectives

- Explain how to prevent data loss.
- Describe how to use antivirus programs.
- Discuss ways of backing up data.

As You Read

Organize Information As you read the lesson, use a sequence chart to help you explain ways to protect yourself, your system, and your data.

Protecting Your Computer

Although corporations and government agencies are far more likely to be targeted than an individual or a school, any system is vulnerable. You should protect your computer now.

Antivirus Programs Often called virus protection programs, or virus checkers, **antivirus programs** protect computers from viruses. These programs use a special technique to examine program and data files. Once they find a virus, they delete it or at least quarantine the virus so it can do no harm.

 Key Terms

- antivirus program
- full back-up
- incremental back-up
- power surge
- uninterruptible power supply (UPS)

Figure 34.2.1 An antivirus program scanning a hard drive. Today's antivirus programs can automatically look for viruses whenever your computer is on.

If your computer equipment is not properly maintained, you can run into problems ranging from slower data access speeds to lost data. Using preventive maintenance to stop problems before they occur can help keep your system running at maximum efficiency. You can:

➤ Clear dust from internal components and peripherals

➤ Delete unused files and programs, including temporary Internet files and cookies

➤ Run a defragmenter utility to clean up fragmented files

Think About It!
What other preventive maintenance techniques can you use to protect your computer system?

Simply installing an antivirus program is not enough to protect your computer. New viruses are created every day. Software publishers update their antivirus programs to defeat each new attack. You must update your version of the program to take advantage of these changes. Fortunately, the companies generally make it easy to download updates over the Internet.

To protect yourself from viruses, follow these simple rules:

- Install an antivirus program on your computer.
- Be sure to keep this program up-to-date.
- Always check files that you download from the Internet for viruses before saving them to your hard drive.
- If your antivirus program can do so, set it to monitor incoming e-mail messages and to check files.
- Always check the disks you borrow from someone else before using them on your computer.

Firewalls To help block unauthorized users from accessing your computer through a network, you can install and activate a firewall. A firewall is a program that restricts unauthorized access. Most operating systems, including Microsoft Windows, come with a firewall, and so do many antivirus programs.

Protecting Your Computer Data

Computers are subject to problems other than viruses and security breaches. One such problem concerns the computer's hard drive, where data is stored. Hard drives are reliable pieces of equipment, but they do sometimes crash, or shut down improperly. When that happens, they can no longer read or write data. If that happens to you, you will be unable to access any of the information stored on your computer.

Backing Up Data A hard drive crash is a problem, but it does not have to be a disaster as long as you have backed up your data. As discussed in Lesson 2–2, backing up is simply creating a copy of the data on your hard drive that is stored separately from the hard drive.

To back up data, you can use an external hard drive, a shared network drive, an online storage service, a flash drive, or a recordable CD or DVD. Online storage, in which data is stored on multiple virtual servers hosted by third parties, is sometimes called cloud storage. No matter which method you choose, you can back up data to different degrees:

- **Full back-ups** copy everything stored on your computer. They should be done at least once a month.
- **Incremental back-ups** copy only those files that have changed since the last full back-up. These should be made regularly, such as once a week. Some back-up programs, such as Apple's Time Machine, perform them every hour automatically.

Power-Related Problems Just like any other device that runs on electricity, a computer can be affected by power fluctuations or outages. These problems can lead to the loss of data. A **power surge**, or a sharp increase in the power coming into the system, can destroy a computer's electrical components.

You can help protect your computer from power problems by attaching an **Uninterruptible Power Supply**, or **UPS**, between your computer and the power source. This battery powered device goes to work when it detects an outage or critical voltage drop. It powers the computer for a period of time. A UPS can also protect against power surges by filtering sudden electrical spikes.

Figure 34.2.2 An Uninterruptible Power Supply unit, such as this one from APC, has outlets for all your computer's components, phone, and cable lines. The unit will prevent a power surge from damaging your computer. In event of a power outage, the unit will keep your computer running long enough for you to shut it down properly.

Backing up can be done by simply copying files. However, special back-up programs offer advantages. They compress data as they back it up, making the files smaller.

Think About It!

Think about the advantages of compressing data. Which item(s) listed below do you think are an advantage of compressing data in a back-up?

➤ Data will take up less space.

➤ Back-up will take less time.

➤ Labor costs will be lower.

➤ You need the back-up software in order to restore the data.

➤ Back-up programs cost money.

Real-World Tech

The Wireless Problem Communicating with wireless devices such as cell phones creates a major security issue. This kind of communication can be monitored by outsiders, who can intercept and overhear what is being said. That is why the U.S. Department of Defense has banned the use of most wireless devices from defense establishments.

Does knowing that other people can overhear cell phone conversations affect whether or not you use a cell phone? Why or why not?

Troubleshooting Your Computer

Objectives

- Identify troubleshooting techniques.
- Explain the difference between a hard reboot and a soft reboot.
- Identify the purpose of starting in safe mode.
- Identify how to stay informed about changes and advancements in technology.

As You Read

Identify Key Points   As you read the lesson, use a conclusion chart to help you identify key points about troubleshooting.

🔑 Key Terms

- command prompt
- reboot
- safe mode
- troubleshooting

Figure 34.3.1   You can find troubleshooter utilities for many system components in the Windows Control Panel.

Simple Troubleshooting Techniques

Troubleshooting, the act of diagnosing and, hopefully, solving a computer or software problem, can help you get a stalled computer system back up and running quickly.

Check the Connections   Many problems occur when cables or wires become loose. When your monitor goes dark or your keyboard won't respond, turn the system off and check to make sure all cables are securely connected. Many computers are plugged in to a power strip. Make sure the power strip is on. When you have reestablished all connections, turn your system back on and see if the problem is resolved.

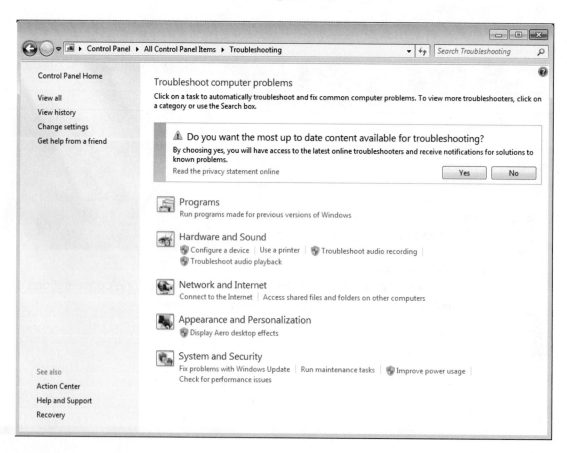

Refer to the Documentation All your computer products come with product manuals. The manuals may be printed books, or they may be available on the manufacturer's Web site. These manuals will always have a troubleshooting section. In addition, many systems come with built-in troubleshooter utilities. Usually these prompt you through a series of questions to diagnose the problem, and they may offer suggestions for action you should take. For example, you can find Windows 7 troubleshooters through the Control Panel. Click the Start button, click Control Panel, and then click Find and fix problems.

Reboot Many computer problems—such as a program freezing—can be solved by a simple **reboot**. When you reboot your computer, you turn it off and then on again.

There are two kinds or reboots: a *hard reboot* is when you turn off all power by pushing the power button or unplugging your computer. A *soft reboot* is when you use the computer's own software to allow your computer to shut down properly. You can click on the main menu and choose the "shut down" option. Once the computer shuts down, you can turn it back on with the power button. If, in contrast, your computer is not frozen, you can try the "restart" option, in which the computer goes through the shut-down sequence and powers back up again. However, if the screen is frozen, a hard reboot may be your only option.

If your computer is unresponsive and you cannot reboot, you may be able to use a key combination to access a troubleshooting menu or restart the computer. On a Windows PC, you can press Ctrl+Alt+Delete. For computers using a Mac OS, you should check your troubleshooting guide, because there are several key combinations.

Repair Utilities

Most computers come with programs that let you check, diagnose, and repair your computer. The programs may be utility programs installed with the operating system, or they may be provided on separate discs.

System Restore You can often use a utility to restore your system to the state it was in before it stopped working. For example, Windows comes with a Restore utility. You select the date and time which you want to revert to, and Windows runs a program to restore that configuration. Changes that occurred since that date and time are undone, including new software installation or modified system settings.

Figure 34.3.2 On a Windows system, you can use System Restore to restore your computer to an earlier configuration.

System Recovery   Some computers come with recovery CDs or DVDs that you insert into the appropriate drive before rebooting. You may then select from a menu of options for checking and repairing problems.

Safe Mode   Most computers let you start in **safe mode**, which means they start with only a limited set of files and drivers. Safe mode lets you identify and fix problems with software that is interfering with the operating system and other components. To start a Windows computer in safe mode, restart your computer, and press the F8 key before the Windows logo displays. On the menu, use the arrow keys to highlight the Safe Mode option, and press Enter.

Access the Command Prompt   Before there were graphical user interfaces such as Windows, you typed commands at the **command prompt**. You can still access the command prompt to type commands if necessary. In Windows, the command prompt is available by clicking Run on the Start menu, by clicking Command Prompt in the Accessories folder, or by restarting your computer, pressing F8 before the Windows logo displays, and choosing the Command Prompt option.

Get Help   If you exhaust all basic troubleshooting techniques, you may need to get professional help. If your computer or your software is still under warranty, you can often get help from the manufacturer's tech support team over the phone or through an online live chat. If your computer or software is out of warranty, you may need to hire a computer technician or bring your system to a local repair shop.

Stay Informed   One of the best ways to solve computer problems is to avoid them. Staying informed about issues, such as new computer viruses, changes, such as software updates, and advancements, such as new products or services, can help you anticipate and avoid trouble. It also helps you make informed decisions such as when to purchase new products. You can stay informed by reading technology news articles on reputable sites such as Cnet.com, or by subscribing to technology news feeds.

Use the Vocabulary

Directions: *Match each vocabulary term in the left column with the correct definition in the right column.*

_____ **1.** copyright
_____ **2.** power surge
_____ **3.** fair use
_____ **4.** plagiarism
_____ **5.** uninterruptible power supply
_____ **6.** ethics
_____ **7.** reboot
_____ **8.** Safe Mode
_____ **9.** full back-up
_____ **10.** troubleshoot

a. behaving morally
b. unauthorized use of another person's ideas or work without credit
c. a systematic attempt to analyze and diagnose computer or software problems
d. duplicate all files on a hard drive
e. laws that protect creative, literary, or artistic work
f. a sharp increase in the power coming into the system
g. turning a computer system off and then on again
h. device that protects a computer from power problems
i. starting the system with a limited set of files and drivers
j. allowed use of a limited amount of creative work without permission

Check Your Comprehension

Directions: *Determine the correct choice for each of the following.*

1. What is stolen in copyright infringement ?
   a. back-up files
   b. GUIDs
   c. someone's work
   d. someone's identity

2. What should you use to give credit to a source?
   a. citation
   b. plagarism
   c. infringement
   d. netiquette

3. Which of the following is used to identify the responsibilities of a user on an organization's computer system?
   a. copyright laws
   b. Fair Use Doctrine
   c. acceptable use policy
   d. antivirus program

4. Why is copyright infringement a crime?
   a. It is illegal to make back-up copies of your work.
   b. It violates the rights of a software publisher to its work.
   c. It results in identity theft.
   d. It is theft of another's work.

5. Which of the following can help protect your computer system from a power surge?
   a. copyright laws
   b. acceptable use policy
   c. device driver
   d. uninterruptible power supply

6. Which of the following lets you revert your system configuration to a previous date and time?
   a. system restore
   b. system recovery
   c. safe mode
   d. command prompt

Think Critically

Directions: *Answer the following questions.*

1. Summarize netiquette.

2. Compare and contrast a full data back-up with an incremental data back-up.

3. Which one rule would you recommend making part of an AUP?

4. Summarize troubleshooting techniques you can use to diagnose and solve computer problems.

5. What advice can you share with others about using an antivirus program effectively?

Extend Your Knowledge

Directions: *Choose one of the following projects. Complete the exercise on a separate sheet of paper.*

A. Review rules your school district may have for computer use as part of its acceptable use policy. Categorize policies based on appropriate use, vandalism or destruction, and consequences of violations.

B. With your teacher's permission, use the Internet to look up a user manual for a hardware device. Locate troubleshooting or problem-solving information and read it. Exit your browser. With a partner, select a problem that someone might encounter using a computer at home. Use a word-processing application to create a document in the manner and style of a user's manual. Provide the necessary information for identifying and solving the selected problem. With your teacher's permission, print or publish the document and discuss it with your class.

Microsoft Office 2010 Reference Skills

This reference lists key skills for completing the activities in the book. A more comprehensive list, along with procedures for earlier versions of Microsoft Office, can be found on the Student CD and Companion Web site.

Index to Skills

Common Office 2010 Skills A-19

Microsoft Office 2010 Reference Skills • A-3

Microsoft Office 2010 Reference Skills • A-7

Starting the Computer

- Press the on switch.

Shutting Down the Computer

1. Click the Start button.
2. Click **Shut down**.

Restarting the Computer

1. Click the **Start** button.
2. Click the right-pointing arrow to the right of Shut down, and click **Restart**.

Logging on to a User Account

1. Click the desired user account to log on as that user.

OR

1. Click the **Start** button.
2. Click the right-pointing arrow to the right of Shut down, and click **Switch user**.
3. Click the desired user account to log on as that user.

Starting a Program

1. Click the **Start** button.
2. Click **All Programs**.
3. Click the program to start.

OR

- Click to open the folder containing the program, and then click the program to start.

OR

- Double-click the program icon in the desktop.

OR

- Click the program icon on the Windows taskbar.

Exiting a Program

- Click the program's **Close** button at the right end of the title bar.

OR

1. Click **File**
2. Click **Exit**.

Logging off a User Account

1. Click the **Start** button.
2. Click the right-pointing arrow to the right of Shut down, and click **Log off**.

Navigating Storage Locations

1. Click the **Start** button.
2. Click **Computer**.

OR

- To navigate to a network location, click **Network**.

3. In the Content pane, double-click the storage location.
4. Do any of the following:

    - Click the **Back** button to display the previous storage location.

    - Click the **Forward** button to move forward to the last window you had opened.

    - Click a location in the Navigation pane to display its contents.

    - Click a location in the Address bar to open it.

    - Click an arrow between locations in the Address bar to display a menu, then click a location on the menu to open it.

Displaying a ScreenTip

- Rest the mouse pointer on a window element.

Controlling Windows

Minimizing a Window

- In the window, click the **Minimize** button.

Maximizing a Window

- In the window, click the **Maximize** button.

√ *The Maximize button does not display if the window is already maximized.*

Restoring a Maximized Window

- In the Window, click the Restore Down button.

Closing a Window

- In the window, click the **Close** button.

Resizing a Window

1. Position the mouse pointer over the window border.

√ *The pointer will change to a horizontal double-headed arrow over a side border, a vertical double-headed arrow over a top or bottom border, or a diagonal double-headed arrow over a corner.*

2. Press and hold the left mouse button and drag the border to resize the window.

Displaying Open Windows Side by Side

1. Right-click a blank area of the taskbar.
2. On the shortcut menu, click **Show windows side by side**.

Cascading Open Windows

1. Right-click a blank area of the taskbar.
2. Click **Cascade windows**.

Changing the Active Window

- Click in the window you want to make active

OR

- Click the taskbar button of the window you want to make active.

OR

1. Press and hold the **Alt** key on your keyboard.
2. Press **Tab** repeatedly to scroll through the open windows.
3. Release all keys when the window you want to make active is selected.

Capturing a Screen Image

1. Press the **Prt Scr** key on your computer keyboard.
   √ *On a notebook computer, press* ***Fn+Prt Sc***.
2. Position the insertion point in a word processing or paint program file.
3. Click the **Paste** button .

Capturing an Image of the Active Window

1. Press **Alt+ Prt Scr** key on your computer keyboard.
   √ *On a notebook computer, press* ***Alt+Fn+Prt Sc***.
2. Position the insertion point in a word processing or paint program file.
3. Click the **Paste** button .

Managing the Desktop

Viewing and Arranging Desktop Icons

1. Right-click the desktop and click **View**.
2. To change the icon size click:
   - Large icons
   - Medium icons
   - Small icons
3. Select **Auto arrange icons** to automatically arrange icons.

OR

   - Deselect **Auto arrange icons** to arrange icons manually by dragging.
4. Select **Align icons to grid** to automatically arrange icons in columns and rows.
5. Deselect **Show desktop icons** to hide all icons.

Sorting Desktop Icons

1. Right-click the desktop and click **Sort by**.
2. Click property to sort by.

Creating a Desktop Shortcut

1. Right-click the desktop and click **New**.
2. Click **Shortcut**.
3. Type the path to the program, file, folder, computer, or Internet address, or click **Browse** and navigate to the desired location; click **OK** after selecting the desired object.
4. Click **Next**.
5. Type a name for the shortcut.
6. Click **Finish**.

Creating a Folder or File on the Desktop

1. Right-click the desktop and click **New**.
2. Click the item to create.

Deleting a Folder, File, or Shortcut from the Desktop

1. Right-click the item to delete.
2. Click **Delete**.
3. Click **Yes** to confirm deletion.

Managing Files and Folders

Creating a Folder

1. Navigate to the location where you want to create the new folder.
2. Click **New folder** in the toolbar.
3. Type the folder name.
4. Press **Enter**.

Creating a File

1. Right-click the location in which you want to create the new file.
2. Click **New** on the shortcut menu.
3. Click the file type to create.
4. Type the file name.
5. Press **Enter**.

Copying a Folder or File

1. Navigate to the folder where the item is stored.
2. Right-click the item to copy.
3. Click **Copy**.
4. Navigate to the folder where you want to store the copy.
5. Right-click a blank area of the folder window.
6. Click **Paste**.

OR

1. Navigate to the folder where the item is stored.
2. Click the item to select it.
3. Press and hold down **Ctrl** while you drag the item to the new location.

Renaming a Folder or File

1. Right-click the item to rename.
2. Click **Rename** on the shortcut menu.
3. Type new name.
4. Press **Enter**.

Deleting a File or Folder

1. Right-click the item to delete.
2. Click **Delete** on the shortcut menu.
3. Click **Yes** to confirm the deletion or **No** to cancel the operation.

Moving a Folder or File

1. Navigate to the folder where the item is stored.
2. Right-click the item to move.
3. Click **Cut**.
4. Navigate to the folder where you want to move the item.
5. Right-click a blank area of the folder window.
6. Click **Paste**.

OR

1. Navigate to the folder where the item is stored.
2. Click the item to select it.
3. Drag the item to the folder to which you want to move it.

√ *If you drag files or folders from one drive to another, they are automatically copied. To move them, hold down* **Shift** *as you drag.*

Restarting in Safe Mode

1. Click the **Start** button.
2. Click the right-pointing arrow to the right of Shut down, and click **Restart**.
3. Press and hold the F8 key as the computer restarts.

√ *Begin pressing F8 before the Windows logo appears and continue pressing until the desktop appears.*

4. If the computer has started correctly in Safe mode, the desktop screen displays Safe Mode in the corners.

Working with Files

Displaying File Extensions

1. Click **Windows Explorer** on the taskbar.
2. Click **Organize** in the toolbar.
3. Click Folder and search options.
4. In the Folder Options dialog box, click the **View** tab.
5. In the Advanced settings list, scroll down if necessary and clear the checkmark from **Hide extensions for known file types**.

Opening (Retrieving) a File

1. Click **Windows Explorer** on the taskbar.
2. Click the right-pointing triangle of the appropriate section, such as Libraries, if necessary to display all folders in that section.
3. Continue to click triangles to open folders, or double-click a folder to open it.
4. When the desired file displays in the file list, double-click the file to open the file and its application.

Saving a New File

1. Click **File**.
2. Click **Save As**.
3. In the File name box, type a file name.
4. Navigate to the location where you want to store the file.
5. Click **Save**.

Saving Changes to a File

1. Click **File**.
2. Click **Save**.

Printing a File

1. Display the location where the file is stored.
2. Right-click the file.
3. Click **Print**.

Displaying File Properties

1. Click **Windows Explorer** on the taskbar.
2. Navigate to the folder that contains the file.
3. In the file list, right-click the file and click **Properties**.
4. Click **OK** when finished.

Changing the Folder View

1. Navigate to a storage location
2. Click the **Change your view** button to rotate through the view options.

OR

■ Click the **Change your view** down arrow and select one of the view options:

- **Extra Large Icons**
- **Large Icons**
- **Medium Icons**
- **Small Icons**
- **List**
- **Details**
- **Tiles**
- **Content**

Shutting Down and Restarting a Nonresponsive Program

1. Press and hold down the Ctrl + Alt + Del keys.
2. Click **Start Task Manager**.
3. On the Applications tab, click the nonresponsive program in the Task list.
4. Click **End Task**.
5. Restart the application in the usual way.

Modifying Display Properties

1. Display the desktop, right-click on the desktop, and click **Personalize**.
2. Modify display in any of these ways:
   - Select a preformatted theme from the Change the visuals and sounds on your computer gallery.
   - Click **Desktop Background**, select the desired picture, and click **Save changes**.
   - Click **Window Color**, select a color for window borders from the gallery; then click **Save changes**.
   - Click **Screen Saver**, select a screen saver option, and click **OK**.
   - Click **Display** near the bottom of the left pane and choose a different text size; click **Apply** to apply the new size.
3. If desired, click **Save theme** to save personalized settings.

Displaying System Information

1. Click the **Start** button.
2. Click **Control Panel**.
3. Click **System and Security**.
4. Click **View amount of RAM and processor speed**.

Accessing the Command Prompt

1. Click the **Start** button.
2. Click **All Programs** and scroll to display the **Accessories** folder.
3. Click the **Accessories** folder and then click **Command Prompt**.

Changing Simple Settings

Changing Date and Time

1. Click the **Start** button.
2. Click **Control Panel**.
3. Click **Clock, Language, and Region**.
4. Click **Date and Time**.
5. Click the **Change date and time** button.
6. Select a new date or adjust the time using the spin arrows below the clock.
7. Click **OK** twice.

√ *You may need permission from an administrator to make this change.*

Changing Audio Settings

1. Click the **Start** button.
2. Click **Control Panel**.
3. Click **Hardware and Sound**.
4. Select any of the following sound options:
   - Click **Adjust system volume** in the Sound list and then drag the sound level arrow for installed devices such as speakers or for system sounds.
   - Click **Change system sounds** in the Sound list and, in the Sound dialog box, select a new sound scheme or click a program event and select a new sound for it.
   - Click **Manage audio devices** in the Sound list and in the Sound dialog box, select the **Playback** or **Recording** tab, select the desired device, and click the **Configure** button to change device setup.

Changing Security Settings

1. Click the **Start** button.
2. Click **Control Panel**.
3. Click **System and Security**.
4. To adjust firewall settings:
   a. Click **Windows Firewall**.
   b. Adjust settings as desired.
5. Modify User Account Control settings:
   a. In the Action Center list, click **Change User Account Control settings**.
   b. Drag the slider to adjust how often to notify if potentially harmful actions occur.
   c. Click **OK**.

√ *You may need permission from an administrator to make this change.*

Verifying Network Connectivity

1. Click the **Start** button.
2. Click **Control Panel**.
3. Click **Network and Internet**.
4. In the Network and Sharing Center section, click **View network status and tasks**.
5. View the current active network connections.

Safely Removing Hardware and Eject Media

1. On the right end of the Windows taskbar, click the **Safely Remove Hardware and Media** icon .
2. Click the name of the device to remove or eject.
3. When Windows displays a message that it is safe to remove or eject the device, do so.

Checking Power Issues

Ensuring the Computer Has Power

1. Check that the computer's power cord is plugged correctly into a power outlet or power strip.
2. Check that the outlet is receiving power from the circuit and/or that the power strip is on.
3. Check that the power cord is plugged correctly into the computer.

Adjusting Power Settings

1. Click the **Start** button.
2. Click **Control Panel**.
3. Click **Hardware and Sound**.
4. Click **Power Options**.
5. Modify power settings in any of these ways:
   - Click **Change plan settings** for the current selected Preferred plan, then select new settings for turning off the display and putting the computer to sleep.
   - Click **Choose when to turn off the display** in the left panel and select a time from the Turn off the display drop-down list.
   - Click **Change when the computer sleeps** in the left panel and select a time from the Put the computer to sleep drop-down list.
6. Click **Save changes** to put the new power plan into effect.

Displaying and Updating a List of Installed Printers

1. Click the **Start** button.
2. Click **Devices and Printers**.
3. Right-click anywhere on the screen and click **Refresh** to update the current list of printers and devices.

Managing Printing and Print Jobs

1. Click the **Start** button.
2. Click **Devices and Printers**.
3. To view current print jobs:
   a. Right-click the image of the current printer.
   b. Click **See what's printing** to display the printer's current print queue.
4. To pause a print job, with the print queue displayed, right-click the job to pause and then click **Pause**.
5. To resume a print job, with the print queue displayed, right-click the job to resume and then click **Resume**.
6. To cancel a print job, with the print queue displayed, right-click the job you wish to cancel and click **Cancel**.
   OR
   - Click **Printer** and then click **Cancel All Documents**.
7. To restart a print job, with the print queue displayed, right-click the job to restart and click **Restart**.

Identify and Solve Common Printing Problems

1. Click the **Start** button.
2. Click **Control Panel**.
3. Under System and Security, click **Find and fix problems**.
4. Under hardware and Sound, click **Use a printer**.
6. Click **Next** to start the Troubleshooter, and then follow the instructions to identify and solve the problem.

Connecting to a Remote Resource

Connecting to a Remote Windows 7 Computer

√ *To use this feature, the remote computer must be turned on, connected to the network, and running Windows 7. You must also have permission to connect to the remote computer.*

1. Click the **Start** button.
2. In the *Search programs and files* box, type **Remote Desktop Connection.**
3. Click **Remote Desktop Connection** in the Programs area of the pop-up menu.
4. In the Remote Desktop Connection dialog box, in the Computer box, type the name of the computer to which you want to connect.
5. Click **Connect**.
6. Enter your user name and password and click **OK**.
7. You now have access to the remote computer.
8. When finished, click the **Start** button and then click **Log off**.

Creating a New Network Location

1. Click the **Start** button.
2. Click **Computer**.
3. Right-click on any blank area of the screen and click **Add a network location**.
4. Click **Next** to start the Add Network Location Wizard.
5. Click Choose a custom network location and click Next.
6. Type the address of the Internet or network address, or click **Browse** button and browse for the desired folder.
7. If you have been supplied with a user name, deselect **Log on anonymously** and type the user name.
8. Click **Next**.
9. Type a name for the network connection.
10. Click **Next** and then click **Finish**.

Converting Content into Digital Files

Scanning Content into Microsoft Clip Organizer

1. Click **Start**.
2. Point to **All Programs**.
3. Click **Microsoft Office**, click **Microsoft Office 2010 Tools**, and then click **Microsoft Clip Organizer**.
4. In the Microsoft Clip Organizer, click **File**.
5. Click **Add Clips to Organizer** and then click **From Scanner or Camera**.
6. Click **Insert**.

Acquiring Files from a Camera

1. Connect the camera to the computer, and, if necessary, install the camera's device driver software.
2. Follow the prompts in the Camera Wizard to acquire the files.

OR

1. Click **Start**.
2. Click **Computer**.
3. Double-click the camera device icon.
4. Navigate to the location where the camera files are stored.
5. Right-click the file to copy and click **Copy**.
6. Navigate to the location where you want to store the copied file.
7. Right-click a blank area of the window and click **Paste**.

Starting Windows Help

1. Click the **Start** button.
2. Click Help and Support.

Using Help to Search for Information

1. Click the **Start** button.
2. Click Help and Support.
3. In the *Search Help* box, type a brief description of what you are looking for. For example, type *Printer trouble*.
4. In the list of results, click a result. For example, click **Open the Printer troubleshooter**.
5. Read the information, or click another link for more information. For example, click the link **Click to open the Printer troubleshooter**.
6. Continue to click links. For example, click **Next** to begin, and then follow instructions for the troubleshooter to resolve the problem.

Identify and Solve Hardware Problems

1. Click the **Start** button.
2. Click **Control Panel**.
3. Under System and Security, click **Find and fix problems**.
4. Click **Hardware and Sound**.
5. Click a category.
6. Click **Next** to start a Troubleshooter, and then follow instructions to identify and solve the problem.

Installing and Uninstalling Software

Install Software from a CD or DVD

1. Insert the disk into the appropriate drive in your system.

   √ *You may be prompted for administrator permission to start the installation process.*

2. Follow the instructions on the screen provided by the software to install the program.

Installing Software from the Internet

1. Use your Web browser to navigate to the Web page that contains the link to the software.

2. Choose one of these options:

   - Click **Open** or **Run** to install the program immediately; follow directions on the screen and provide an administrator password or confirmation if prompted.

   - Click **Save** to download the program so you can install it later; to install later, double-click the downloaded file and follow directions on the screen.

Uninstalling Software

1. Click the **Start** button ⊞.
2. Click Control Panel.
3. Click **Uninstall a program** in the Programs list.
4. Select the program in the list of installed programs.
5. Click **Uninstall** on the toolbar.
6. Click **Yes** if asked to confirm and follow instructions on the screen.

Installing Updates from Online Sources

Manually Installing Updates for Windows

1. Click the **Start** button ⊞.
2. Click **Control Panel**.
3. Click **System and Security**.
4. Click **Windows Update**.
5. To check for updates, click **Check for updates** in the left pane.
6. To install updates:

   a. Click the link for any update in the *Updates are available for your computer* list.

   b. Click the checkbox of any update to install.

   c. Click **OK**.

   d. Click **Install updates** button and follow any instructions.

Adjusting Automatic Update Settings for Windows

1. Click **Start** button ⊞.
2. Click **Control Panel**.
3. Click **System and Security**.
4. Click **Windows Update**.
5. Click **Change settings** in the left pane.
6. Choose from the following options:

   - Click the drop-down arrow for **Important updates** and select a different option for downloading and installing updates.

   - Click the **Install new updates** drop-down arrow and select a day on which to install updates.

   - Click the **at** drop-down arrow and select a time to install updates.

   - Deselect options for recommended updates, who can install updates, Microsoft updates, and software.

7. Click **OK**.

Troubleshooting Installing Applications

1. Check program documentation to verify Windows 7 compatibility.
2. If the program is not Windows 7-compatible, try steps in the *Resolve Software Compatibility* procedure.

OR

1. If you have administrator rights, right-click on the installation file and click **Run as administrator**.
2. If you do not have administrator rights, obtain the necessary password to log in as an administrator.

OR

1. If the program installs but does not run, right-click the program icon, click **Properties**, click the **Compatibility** tab, and click **Run this program as an administrator**.

OR

1. If you cannot install from Internet:

   a. Save the program to your computer as directed in *Install Software from the Internet*.

   b. Double-click the program icon to start the installation.

OR

1. If the disk containing the software to install does not start:

   a. Click **Windows Explorer** 🗐 and browse to the location of the installed program.

   b. Locate the setup file and double-click to start setup.

OR

- Contact the manufacturer for assistance.

Resolving Software Compatibility

1. Click the **Start** button .
2. Click **Control Panel**.
3. In the System and Security list, click **Review your computer's status**.
4. At the bottom of the left pane, click **Windows Program Compatibility Troubleshooter**.
5. Click **Next** to start scan to detect issues.
6. Select the program you want to run in Windows 7 and click **Next**.
7. Select the desired troubleshooting option and click **Next**.
8. Click **Start the program**.
   √ *You may need to authorize Windows to start the program.*
9. After running the program, click **Next** and then choose to save settings or try again with different settings.
10. Click **Close**.

Troubleshooting Running Programs

1. Make sure you have the appropriate permission to run the program.
   a. Obtain the necessary administrator password and log in as an administrator.
   b. Right-click the program icon, click **Properties**, click the **Compatibility** tab, and click **Run this program as an administrator**.
2. Try to run the program in safe mode to see if any other settings are interfering with the program's operation.
   a. Click the **Start** button.
   b. Click the right-pointing arrow to the right of Shut down, and click **Restart**.
   c. Press and hold the **F8** key as the computer restarts.
   √ *Begin pressing F8 before the Windows logo appears and continue to press until the desktop displays.*
   d. Once Windows has started in safe mode, start the program.
3. Repair the program. Steps for repair differ by application, but may be similar to the following:
   a. Insert the application's installation disk and start the process of installing.
   b. Select an option to detect and repair problems and then follow specific instructions.
4. Uninstall and reinstall the program.
5. If the program does not run after taking these steps, contact the manufacturer for further troubleshooting.

Backing Up Files Using Automatic Backup

√ *Using Windows 7 automatic back-up feature.*
1. Click the **Start** button .
2. Click Control Panel.
3. In the System and Security list, click **Back up your computer**.
4. If you do not have backup settings in place, click **Set up backup**.
5. Follow the steps in the wizard to create back-up settings.
√ *You can have Windows choose what files to back up or you can select the folders and files you want to back up to include only your working files.*
√ *You may need permission from an administrator to create these settings.*
√ *Do not back up to the same drive on which Windows is installed.*
6. Click **Back up now** to create a backup any time after setting up the backup options

Solving Common File Problems

Making Programs and Files Compatible with Windows 7

1. Click the **Start** button.
2. Click **Control Panel**.
3. In the System and Security list, click **Review your computer's status**.
4. At the bottom of the left pane, click Windows Program Compatibility Troubleshooter.
5. Click **Next** to start scan to detect issues.
6. Select the program you want to run in Windows 7 and click **Next**.
7. Select the desired troubleshooting option and click **Next**.
8. Click **Start the program**.
   √ *You may need to authorize Windows to start the program.*
9. After running the program, click **Next** and then choose to save settings or try again with different settings.
10. Click **Close**.

Dealing with Corrupted Files

If a file has become corrupted and will not open, you have the following options:

- Delete the file.
- Use a software program external to Windows to repair the corrupted file.
- If you have backed up the computer, try to retrieve a previous version of the file.

Retrieving a Previous Version

1. Right-click the file or folder and then click **Restore previous versions**.
2. In the Tracking and Flagging Messages dialog box, click the previous version in the list of File versions and click **Open** to verify that it is the version you want.
3. Select the previous version again and click **Restore**.

Accessing a File or Folder to Which Access Has Been Denied

1. Check permissions on the file or folder:
   a. Right-click the file or folder and click **Properties**.
   b. Click the **Security** tab.
   c. Click **Continue**, provide the necessary administrator password, and click **Yes**.
   d. In the Group or user name list, click your name and review your permissions in the Permissions for Users list.
2. To change permissions, click the **Edit** button.
3. Click your name in the Group or user names list, and then select the appropriate permission check boxes in the Permissions for System panel.
4. Click **OK** and then click **OK** again.

Starting an Office Program

1. Click the **Start** button 🔘.
2. Click **All Programs**.
3. Click the **Microsoft Office** folder icon.
4. Click the program to start.

Exiting an Office Program

- Click the program's **Close** button ▄️Ⓧ▄️ at the right end of the title bar.

OR

1. Click the **File** tab.
2. Click **Exit**.

Opening a File *(Ctrl +O)*

Opening a Saved File
1. Click **File**.
2. Click **Open**.
3. Navigate to file's location.
4. Click the file.
5. Click **Open**.

Opening a Recently Used File
1. Click **File**.
2. Click **Recent**.
3. Under Recent, click the file to open.

Opening Compatible File Types
1. Click **File**.
2. Click **Open**.
3. In the Open dialog box, click the **File Type** button.
   The text on the File Type button changes depending on your most recent selection.
4. Select the desired file type.
5. Select the file to open.
6. Click **Open**.

Creating a File

Creating a New, Blank File (Ctrl+N)
1. Click **File**.
2. Click **New**.
3. Click the **Blank *filetype*** icon.
4. Click the **Create** button.

Creating a File Based on a Template
1. Click **File**.
2. Click **New**.
3. Click **Sample templates**.
4. Click the desired template.
5. Click the **Create** button.

Exploring Templates on Office.com
1. Click **File**.
2. Click **New**.
3. Under **Office.com Templates**, search for and select the desired template.
4. Click **Download**.

Saving Files *(Ctrl + S)*

Saving a New File
1. Click the **File** tab.
2. Click **Save**.
3. In the File name text box, type the name of the file.
4. Navigate to the location where you want to save the file.
5. Click **Save** or press **Enter**.

Saving Changes to a File

- Click the **Save** button 💾 on the Quick Access Toolbar.

OR

1. Click the **File** tab.
2. Click **Save**.

Saving a File with a New Name or in a New Location

1. Click **File**.
2. Click **Save As**.
3. Type the file name in the File name text box.
4. Navigate to the location where you want to save the file.
5. Click **Save**.

Saving in a Compatible File Format
1. Click **File**.
2. Click **Save As**.
3. In the Save As dialog box, click the **Save as type** button to display a list of compatible file types.
4. Select the desired file type.
5. Enter the file name and select the location where the file will be saved.
6. Click **Save**.
7. Click **OK** in the File Conversion dialog box.

Saving a File as a Template
1. Click **File**.
2. Click **Save As**.
3. In the Save As dialog box, enter the file name and select the location where the file will be saved.
4. Click the **Save as type** button.
5. Click ***program name* Template**.
6. Click **Save**.

Viewing Application Options

1. Click the **File** tab.
2. Click **Options**.
3. In left pane, click the category of options to display:
   - General
   - Display
   - Proofing
   - Save
   - Language
   - Advanced
   - Customize Ribbon
   - Quick Access Toolbar
   - Add-Ins
   - Trust Center
4. Select or clear options.
5. Click **OK**

Minimizing the Ribbon

- Click the **Minimize the Ribbon** button ⌃.

OR

- Double-click any tab on the Ribbon.

Expanding the Ribbon

- Click the **Expand the Ribbon** button ⌄.

OR

- Double-click any tab on the Ribbon.

Adding Commands to the Ribbon

1. Right-click a Ribbon tab.
2. Click **Customize the Ribbon**.
3. In left pane, select command to add.
4. In right pane, select the tab where you want the command to display.

OR

   Click **New Tab** to create a new Ribbon tab.
5. Click **New Group**.
6. Click **Add**.
7. Click **OK**

Renaming a Custom Ribbon Tab or Group

1. Right-click a Ribbon tab.
2. Click **Customize the Ribbon**.
3. In right pane, select item to rename.
4. Click **Rename**.
5. Type the new name.
6. Click **OK**.
7. Click **OK**.

Removing Commands, Groups, or Tabs from the Ribbon

1. Right-click a Ribbon tab.
2. Click **Customize the Ribbon**.
3. In right pane, select item to remove.
4. Click **Remove**.
5. Click **OK**

Adding Buttons to the Quick Access Toolbar

1. Click the **Customize Quick Access Toolbar** button ▾.
2. Click the command to add.

OR

1. Right-click any button on any Ribbon tab.
2. Click **Add to Quick Access Toolbar**.

Removing Buttons from the Quick Access Toolbar

1. Click the **Customize Quick Access Toolbar** button ▾.
2. Click the command to remove.

OR

1. Right-click any button on the Quick Access toolbar.
2. Click **Remove Quick Access Toolbar**.

Moving the Quick Access Toolbar

1. Click the **Customize Quick Access Toolbar** button ▾.
2. Click **Show Below the Ribbon**.

OR

   Click **Show Above the Ribbon**.

Scrolling in a Window

√ *The scroll bars and boxes are only active when there is more content than can display at once in the window.*

Scroll Down

In the window, click the **down arrow** ▾ at the bottom of the vertical scroll bar.

OR

Drag the **vertical scroll** box down.

Scroll Up

In the window, click the **up arrow** ▴ at the top of the vertical scroll bar.

OR

Drag the **vertical scroll** box up.

Scroll Left

In the window, click the **left arrow** ◂ at the left of the horizontal scroll bar.

OR

Drag the **horizontal scroll** box left.

Scroll Right

In the window, click the **right arrow** ▸ at the right of the horizontal scroll bar.

OR

Drag the **horizontal scroll** box right.

Changing the Zoom Percentage

1. Click the **View** tab.

   Zoom Group

2. Click the **Zoom** button 🔍.
3. In the Zoom dialog box, click the desired magnification.
4. Click **OK**.

OR

- Click the Zoom Out ⊖ or Zoom In ⊕ on the status bar.
- Drag the Zoom slider ▯ on the status bar.

Selecting

With the Mouse

- Drag across text to select it.

With the Keyboard

1. Click to left of the first character to select.
2. Press and hold the Shift key.
3. Click to the right of the last character to select.

Selecting Noncontiguous Text

1. Select first block.
2. Press and hold the Ctrl key.
3. Select next block.

Selecting and Replacing Text

1. Select text it.
2. Type the replacement text.

Canceling a Selection or Command

- Click anywhere outside selected text to cancel the selection.
- Press **Escape** to cancel a command or close a dialog box.
- Click anywhere outside a displayed menu to close it without making a selection.

Moving a Selection

Using Drag-and-Drop

1. Select item to move.
2. Move the mouse pointer anywhere over the selection.
3. Press and hold the left mouse button.
4. Drag to the desired location and release the mouse button.

Using Cut *(Ctrl+X)* and Paste *(Ctrl+V)*

1. Select the item to move.
2. Click the **Home** tab.

   Clipboard Group

3. Click the **Cut** button ✂.
4. Click where you want to move the item.
5. Click the **Home** tab.

   Clipboard Group

6. Click the **Paste** button 📋.

OR

- Click the **Paste** button drop-down arrow 📋.

7. Click the desired paste option on the menu.

Copying a Selection

Using Drag-and-Drop

1. Select the item to copy.
2. Move the mouse pointer anywhere over the selection.
3. Press and hold **Ctrl**.
4. Press and hold the left mouse button.
5. Drag to the desired location and release the mouse button.

Using Copy *(Ctrl+C)* and Paste *(Ctrl+V)*

1. Select the item to copy.
2. Click the **Home** tab.

   Clipboard Group

3. Click the **Copy** button 📋.
4. Click where you want to copy the text.
5. Click the **Home** tab.

   Clipboard Group

6. Click the **Paste** button 📋.

OR

- Click the **Paste** button drop-down arrow 📋.

7. Click the desired paste option on the menu.

Using Paste Special

1. Select the item to copy or move.
2. Click the **Home** tab.
   Clipboard Group
3. Click the **Cut** button ✂.

OR

- Click the **Copy** button ⧉.

4. Click where you want to paste the item.
   Clipboard Group
5. Click the **Paste** button drop-down arrow ⧉.
6. Click **Paste Special**.
7. In the Paste Special dialog box, click the desired paste option.

Using Undo *(Ctrl + Z)*, Redo *(Ctrl + Y)*, and Repeat *(Ctrl + Y)*

- Click the **Undo** button ↺ on the Quick Access Toolbar to reverse a single action or series of actions.

- Click the **Redo** button ↻ on the Quick Access Toolbar to reinstate any action that you reversed with Undo.

- Click the **Repeat** button ↻ on the Quick Access Toolbar to repeat the most recent action.

√ *Repeat is not available in all programs.*

Working with Themes

Applying a Theme
1. Click the **Design** tab.
   Themes Group
2. Click the Themes **More** button ▾.
3. From the gallery, click the desired theme.

Changing Theme Colors
1. Click the **Design** tab.
   Themes Group
2. Click the **Colors** button ▪.
3. From the gallery, click the desired color scheme.

Creating Custom Theme Colors
1. Click the **Design** tab.
   Themes Group
2. Click the **Colors** button ▪.
3. From the gallery, click **Create New Theme Colors**.
4. In the Create New Theme Colors dialog box, select the colors as desired.
5. Enter a name for the new theme colors.
6. Click **Save**.

Changing Theme Fonts
1. Click the **Design** tab.
   Themes Group
2. Click the **Fonts** button Ⓐ.
3. From the gallery, click the desired font scheme.

Creating Custom Theme Fonts
1. Click the **Design** tab.
   Themes Group
2. Click the **Fonts** button Ⓐ.
3. From the gallery, click **Create New Theme Fonts**.
4. In the Create New Theme Fonts dialog box, select the fonts as desired.
5. Enter a name for the new theme fonts.
6. Click **Save**.

Applying Custom Theme Effects
1. Click the **Design** tab.
   Themes Group
2. Click the **Effects** button ◎.
3. Click one of the built-in theme effects options.

Working with Fonts

Applying Font Styles
1. Click the **Home** tab.
   Font Group
2. Click the desired font style:
   - **Bold** (Ctrl + B) **B**
   - **Italic** (Ctrl + I) *I*

OR

1. Click the **Home** tab.
2. Click the **Font** group dialog box launcher ⬒.
3. In the Font style list, click the desired style.
4. Click **OK**.

Changing the Font
1. Click the **Home** tab.
   Font Group
2. Click the **Font** button drop-down arrow | Calibri (Body) ▾ |.
3. Click the desired font.

OR

1. Click the **Home** tab.
2. Click the **Font** group dialog box launcher ⬒.
3. In the Font list, choose your font.
4. Click **OK**.

Changing the Font Color
1. Click the **Home** tab.
   Font Group
2. Click the **Font Color** button drop-down arrow **A ▾**.
3. Click the desired font color.

OR

1. Click the **Home** tab.
2. Click the **Font** group dialog box launcher ⬒.
3. Click the **Font color** drop-down arrow.
4. Click the desired font color.
5. Click **OK**.

Changing the Font Size

1. Click the **Home** tab.
   Font Group
2. Click the **Font Size** button drop-down arrow ⎵11 ▾⎵.
3. Click the desired font size.

OR

- Click the **Home** tab.
  Font Group
  - Click the **Grow Font** ⎵A'⎵ button to increase the font size.
  - Click the **Shrink Font** ⎵A˙⎵ button to decrease the font size.

OR

1. Click the **Home** tab.
2. Click the **Font** group dialog box launcher ⎵⎵.
3. In the Size list, click the desired font size.
4. Click **OK**.

Applying Font Effects

1. Click the **Home** tab.
2. Click the **Font** group dialog box launcher ⎵⎵.
3. Under Effects, click the desired effect.
4. Click **OK**.

Applying Underlines

1. Click the **Home** tab.
   Font Group
2. Click the **Underline** button drop-down arrow ⎵U ▾⎵.
3. Click the desired underline style.

OR

1. Click the **Home** tab.
2. Click the **Font** group dialog box launcher ⎵⎵.
3. Click the **Underline** style drop-down arrow.
4. Click the desired underline style.
5. Click **OK**.

Using the Clip Organizer

Scanning Content into Microsoft Clip Organizer

1. Click **Start** 🔘.
2. Point to **All Programs**.
3. Click **Microsoft Office**, click **Microsoft Office 2010 Tools**, and then click **Microsoft Clip Organizer**.
4. In the Microsoft Clip Organizer, click **File**.
5. Click **Add Clips to Organizer** and then click **From Scanner or Camera**.
   √ *Follow the prompts for your scanner to select resolution and other options.*
6. Click **Insert**.

Inserting a Picture from the Clip Organizer

1. Click **Start** 🔘.
2. Point to **All Programs**.
3. Click **Microsoft Office**, click **Microsoft Office 2010 Tools**, and then click **Microsoft Clip Organizer**.
4. In the Microsoft Clip Organizer, navigate in the Collection List to the picture you want to insert.
5. Click the selected clip's drop-down arrow and click **Copy**.
6. Click in the document where you want to insert the selected clip.
7. Click the **Home** tab.
   Clipboard Group
8. Click the **Paste** button ⎵⎵.

Inserting Objects

Inserting a Picture File

1. Click the **Insert** tab.
   Illustrations Group
2. Click the **Picture** button ⎵⎵.
3. In the Insert Picture dialog box, navigate to and select the picture you want to insert.
4. Click **Insert**.

Inserting Clip Art

1. Click the **Insert** tab.
   Illustrations Group
2. Click the **Clip Art** button ⎵⎵.
3. In the Clip Art task pane, type the keyword(s) for the clip art you want to insert in the Search for box.
4. If desired, click the **Results should be** drop-down arrow and specify the media.
5. Click the **Go** button.
6. Click a picture in the task pane to insert it.

Inserting a Shape

1. Click the **Insert** tab.
   Illustrations Group
2. Click the **Shapes** button ⎵⎵.
3. Click the desired shape from the gallery.
4. Click and drag to draw the shape as desired.

Inserting a Text Box

1. Click the **Insert** tab.
   Text Group
2. Click the **Text Box** button ⎵⎵.
3. Click the desired style from the gallery.

OR

1. Click the **Insert** tab.
   Text Group
2. Click the **Text Box** button ⎵⎵.
3. Click **Draw Text Box** on the menu.
4. Click and drag to draw the text box as desired.

Inserting WordArt

1. Click the **Insert** tab.

   Text Group
2. Click the **WordArt** button 🔳.
3. Click the desired WordArt style from the gallery.
4. Type the WordArt text.

Inserting a SmartArt Graphic

1. Click the **Insert** tab.

   Illustrations Group
2. Click the **SmartArt** button 🔳.
3. Click the desired SmartArt from the Choose a SmartArt Graphic dialog box.
4. Click **OK**.

Formatting Objects

Deleting an Object

1. Click the object to select it.
2. Press **Delete** or **Backspace**.

Resizing an Object

1. Click the object to select it.
2. Drag a sizing handle to adjust the size as desired.

OR

1. Click the object to select it.
2. Click the *objectname* **Tools Format** tab.

   Size Group
3. Use the **Shape Height** 🔳 increment arrows and the **Shape Width** 🔳 increment arrows to adjust the object's size.

Moving an Object

1. Position the mouse pointer over the selected picture until the mouse pointer changes to a four-headed arrow 🔳.
2. When the vertical bar in the move pointer displays in the position where you want to move the object, release the mouse button to move the picture.

Applying a Style to an Object

1. Click the shape to select it.
2. Click the *objectname* **Tools Format** tab.

   Shape Styles Group
3. Click the **More** button 🔳.
4. Click the desired style in the gallery.

Applying a Fill, Outline, and Effects to a Shape

1. Click the shape to select it.
2. Click the *objectname* **Tools Format** tab.

   Shape Styles Group
3. Click to apply the desired format, as follows:

   - Shape Fill 🔳
   - Shape Outline 🔳
   - Shape Effects 🔳

Wrapping Text Around an Object

1. Click the object to select it.
2. Click the *objectname* **Tools Format** tab.

   Arrange Group
3. Click the **Wrap Text** button 🔳.
4. Click the desired wrap option from the menu.

Cropping a Graphic

1. Click the graphic to select it.
2. Click the *objectname* **Tools Format** tab.

   Size Group
3. Click the **Crop** button 🔳.
4. Click and drag a cropping handle to crop out a portion of the graphic.
5. Click the **Crop** button 🔳 again to complete the crop.

Modifying a Picture

1. Click the picture to select it.
2. Click the **Picture Tools Format** tab.

   Adjust Group
3. Click an option to make the desired modification, as follows:

   - **Corrections** 🔳 to adjust the contrast and brightness
   - **Color** 🔳 to change the color
   - **Artistic Effects** 🔳 to add special effects
   - **Compress Pictures** 🔳 to reduce the file size
   - **Change Picture** 🔳 to change to a different picture, preserving the formatting and size of the current picture
   - **Reset Picture** 🔳 to remove all formatting applied to the picture

Changing the Direction of Text in a Text Box

1. Click the text box to select it.
2. Click the **Drawing Tools Format** tab.

   Text Group
3. Click the **Text Direction** button 🔳.
4. Click the desired rotation option.

Adding Text to a Shape

1. Right-click the shape.
2. Click **Add Text** on the shortcut menu.
3. Type the text and apply formats as desired.

Grouping Objects

1. Click an object to select it.
2. Hold down **Shift** to select other objects to include in the group.
3. Click the ***objectname*** **Tools Format** tab.
   ### Arrange Group
4. Click the **Group** button 🔳.
5. Click **Group** on the menu.

Positioning an Object

1. Click the ***objectname*** **Tools Format** tab.
   ### Arrange Group
2. Click the **Position** button 🔳.
3. Select the desired position from the gallery.

OR

1. Click the ***objectname*** **Tools Format** tab.
   ### Arrange Group
2. Click the **Align** button 🔳.
3. Select the desired alignment option from the menu.

OR

1. Click the object to select it.
2. Press the up, down, left, or right arrow keys to nudge the object in the desired direction.

Rotating an Object

1. Click the object to select it.
2. Position the mouse pointer over the object's green rotation handle so it resembles a circular arrow 🔳.
3. Drag to rotate the object as desired.

OR

1. Click the object to select it.
2. Click the ***objectname*** **Tools Format** tab.
   ### Arrange Group
3. Click the **Rotate** button 🔳.
4. Click the desired rotation option from the menu.

Layering Objects

1. Click an object to select it.
2. Click the ***objectname*** **Tools Format** tab.
   ### Arrange Group
   - Click the **Bring Forward** button 🔳 to move the object forward one layer at a time.
   - Click the **Bring Forward** drop-down arrow and click **Bring to Front** to move the object all the way to the top of the stack.
   - Click the **Send Backward** button 🔳 to move the object back one layer at a time.
   - Click the **Send Backward** drop-down arrow and click **Send to Back** to move the object all the way to the bottom of the stack.

Duplicating an Object

1. Click the object.
2. Press **Ctrl+C**.
3. Press **Ctrl+V** to paste a duplicate copy.

Aligning and Distributing Objects

1. Select the objects you want to align and distribute.
   *Hold down **Ctrl** to select multiple objects.*
2. Click the ***objectname*** **Tools Format** tab.
   ### Arrange Group
3. Click the **Align** button 🔳.
4. From the menu, click the desired option.

Using Office Help

Starting the Help Program

- Click the **Help** button 🔳 in the upper-right corner of the window.

OR

- Press F1.

OR

1. Click the **File** tab.
2. Click **Help**.
3. Click the **Help** button 🔳 in the upper-right corner of the window

OR

Click the **Help** button 🔳 under the heading Support.

Navigating in Help

- Click a topic or subtopic until the information you need is displayed.

OR

- Type a word or topic in the Search box and click the **Search** button 🔳.

OR

- Use the buttons on the Help window toolbar:
  - **Back** 🔳 to display the previously viewed page.
  - **Forward** 🔳 to return to a viewed page.
  - **Stop** 🔳 to cancel a search
  - **Refresh** 🔳 to update the current page.
  - **Home** 🔳 to display the Help Home page.
  - **Print** 🔳 to print the current page.
  - **Change Font Size** 🔳 to change the size of the Help window characters.
  - **Show Table of Contents** 🔳 to display the Help table of contents.
  - **Keep on Top** 🔳 to keep the Help window on top.

Showing or Hiding Nonprinting Characters

1. Click the **Home** tab.
   Paragraph Group
2. Click the **Show/Hide ¶** button ¶.
3. Click the **Show/Hide ¶** button ¶ again to toggle off.

Showing or Hiding the Ruler

- Click the **View Ruler** button 🗔 above the vertical scroll bar.

OR

1. Click the **View** tab.
   Show Group
2. Click the **Ruler** check box.
√ *A check in the check box indicates the ruler is displayed.*

Changing the View

1. Click the **View** tab.
   Document Views Group
2. Click the desired View button:
   - Print Layout 🗒
   - Full Screen Reading 📖
   - Web Layout 🖳
   - Outline 🗒
   - Draft 🗒

OR

- Click a View icon on the status bar:
   - Print Layout 🗒
   - Full Screen Reading 📖
   - Web Layout 🖳
   - Outline 🗒
   - Draft 🗒

Splitting a Word Window

1. Click the **View** tab.
   Window Group
2. Click the **Split** button 🗔.
3. Drag the resize pointer ↔ to the location where you want the split to occur and click.

Removing a Split

1. Click the **View** tab.
   Window Group
2. Click the **Remove Split** button 🗔.

Switching between Open Documents

- Click in the document window you want to make active.

OR

- Click the program's taskbar button and click the document you want to make active.

OR

1. Click the **View** tab.
   Window Group
2. Click the **Switch Windows** button 🗗.
3. Click the document you want to make active.

Arranging Multiple Documents

1. Open all documents.
2. Click the View tab.
   Window Group
3. Click the **Arrange All** button 🗕.

Closing a Document

- Click the **Close** button 🗙.

OR

1. Click **File**.
2. Click **Close**.

Entering Text and Data

Typing in a Document

- Type letters, numbers, and other characters using the keyboard.
- Press **Enter** to start a new paragraph.
- Press **Backspace** to delete one character to the left of the insertion point.
- Press **Delete** to delete one character to the right of the insertion point.
- Press **Escape** to cancel a command or close a dialog box.

Using Click and Type

- Position the mouse pointer so it changes to indicate the horizontal alignment of the new text, as follows:
   - I🗕 Text will be flush left with the margin.
   - 🗕 Text will be centered.
   - 🗕I Text will be flush right with the margin.
   - I🗕 The first line of text will be indented 0.5".

Using Overtype Mode

1. Right-click the status bar.
2. Click **Overtype** on the shortcut menu.
√ *A check mark next to the command on the shortcut menu indicates it is selected.*
3. Click **Insert** on the status bar to change to overtype mode.

Setting the Insert Key to Toggle Overtype Mode

1. Click **File**.
2. Click **Options**.
3. In the Word Options dialog box, click the **Advanced** tab.
4. If necessary, click the **Use the Insert key to control overtype mode** check box.
5. Click the **Use overtype mode** check box.
6. Click **OK**.
7. Right-click the status bar.
8. Click to mark **Overtype** on the shortcut menu.
9. Press the **Insert** key to toggle overtype mode on and off.

Finding and Replacing

Using Find

1. Click the **Home** tab.
   Editing Group
2. Click the **Find** button .
3. In the text box at the top of the Navigation pane, enter the text you want to find. Word displays a list of occurrences in the Navigation pane.

Using Advanced Find

1. Click the **Home** tab.
   Editing Group
2. Click the **Find** button drop-down arrow .
3. Click **Advanced Find**.
4. In the Find and Replace dialog box, enter the text to find in the Find what text box.
5. Click **Find Next**. A message box appears when all occurrences have been found.

Using Find and Replace

1. Click the **Home** tab.
   Editing Group
2. Click the **Replace** button .
3. In the Find and Replace dialog box, enter the text to find in the Find what text box.
4. Enter the replacement text in the Replace with text box.
5. Click the **Replace** button to replace each separate occurrence; click **Replace All** to replace all occurrences.

Using Go To

1. Click the **Home** tab.
   Editing Group
2. Click the **Find** button drop-down arrow .
3. Click **Go To**.
4. On the Go To tab of the Find and Replace dialog box, select the desired option from the Go to what list box.

Using the Navigation Pane

1. Click the View tab.
   Show Group
2. Click the **Navigation Pane** check box.
3. Choose to browse the headings in the document, browse the pages, or browse the search results.

Browsing by Object

1. Click the **Select Browse Object** button at the bottom of the vertical scroll bar.
2. Select the object you want to browse by from the gallery of browse objects.

Changing Case

1. Select the text whose case you want to change.
2. Click the **Home** tab.
   Font Group
3. Click the **Change Case** button .
4. On the menu, click the desired case option.

Applying Text Effects

1. Select the text.
2. Click the **Home** tab.
   Font Group
3. Click the **Text Effects** button .
4. Click the desired effect from the gallery.

Using the Format Painter to Copy Formats

1. Select the text whose format you want to copy.
2. Click the **Home** tab.
   Clipboard Group
3. Click the **Format Painter** button .
4. Select the text to which you want to apply the copied format.

Copying Formatting to Multiple Selections

1. Select the text whose format you want to copy.
2. Click the **Home** tab.
   Clipboard Group
3. Double-click the **Format Painter** button .
4. Select the text to which you want to apply the copied format, and repeat for additional blocks of text.

Highlighting Text

1. Select the text you want to highlight.
2. Click the **Home** tab.
   Font Group
3. Click the **Text Highlight Color** drop-down arrow.
4. Click the desired highlight color.

OR

1. Click the **Home** tab.
   Font Group
2. Click the **Text Highlight Color** drop-down arrow.
3. Click the desired highlight color.
   √ *The mouse pointer changes to the Highlight Text pointer.*
4. Drag across the text you want to highlight.
5. Click the **Text Highlight Color** button again to turn off the feature.

Clearing Formatting

1. Click the **Home** tab.
   Font Group
2. Click the **Clear Formatting** button.

Revealing Formatting

1. Click the formatting text.
2. Click the Home tab.
   Styles Group
3. Click the **Styles** group dialog box launcher.
4. In the Styles task pane, click the Style Inspector button.
5. In the Style Inspector task pane, click the Reveal Formatting button.

Setting Alignment

Aligning Text Horizontally

1. Click the **Home** tab.
   Paragraph Group
2. Click the desired alignment button:
   - Align Text Left
   - Center
   - Align Text Right
   - Justify

Aligning a Document Vertically

1. Click the **Page Layout** tab.
2. Click the **Page Setup** group dialog box launcher.
3. Click the **Layout** tab.
4. Click the **Vertical alignment** drop-down arrow.
5. Select the desired alignment from the menu.
6. Click **OK**.

Printing a File

Previewing and Printing a File

1. Click the **File** tab.
2. Click **Print**.
   √ *In Backstage view, print settings display on the left, and a preview of the file displays on the right.*
2. Use the **Next Page** and **Previous Page** arrows under the preview to view other pages
3. Use the **Zoom** controls under the preview to adjust the preview magnification.
4. Click the **Print** button.

Changing Print Options

1. Click the **File** tab.
2. Click **Print**.
   √ *In Backstage view, print settings display on the left, and a preview of the file displays on the right.*
3. Under Print, enter the number of copies.
4. Under Printer, select the printer to use.
   √ *Click Printer Properties to set options for the selected printer.*
5. Under Settings, select options:
   - What to print.
   - Pages to print.
   - One sided or two sided printing
   - Collated or Uncollated
   - Landscape or Portrait orientation
   - Page Size
   - Margin width
   - Pages per sheet
   √ *Click Page Setup to open the program's Page Setup dialog box for additional options.*
6. Click the **Print** button.

Setting Document Spacing

Setting Paragraph Spacing

- Click the **Page Layout** tab.
  Paragraph Group
  - Use the **Spacing Before** box increment arrows to set the spacing before the paragraph.
  - Use the **Spacing After** box increment arrows to set the spacing after the paragraph.

OR

1. Click the **Page Layout** tab.
2. Click the **Paragraph** group dialog box launcher ⌷.
3. Click the **Indents and Spacing** tab.
4. Under Spacing, enter the desired spacing in the **Before** and **After** boxes.
5. Click **OK**.

Setting Line Spacing

1. Click the **Home** tab.
   Paragraph Group
2. Click the **Line and Paragraph Spacing** button ⌷.
3. Click the desired line spacing option.

OR

1. Click the **Home** tab.
2. Click the **Paragraph** group dialog box launcher ⌷.
3. Click the **Indents and Spacing** tab.
4. Click the **Line spacing** drop-down arrow.
5. Select the desired spacing option.
6. Click **OK**.

Inserting a Non-Breaking Space

1. If necessary, delete space between the words you do not want to break.
2. Press **Ctrl + Shift + Space** to insert a non-breaking space.

Controlling Hyphenation

1. Click the **Page Layout** tab.
   Page Setup Group
2. Click the **Hyphenation** button ⌷.
3. On the menu, select from None, Automatic, Manual, or Hyphenation Options.

Formatting Pages

Selecting a Preset Margin

1. Click the **Page Layout** tab.
   Page Setup Group
2. Click the **Margins** button ⌷.
3. Click the desired margin setting.

Setting Custom Margins

1. Click the **Page Layout** tab.
   Page Setup Group
2. Click the **Margins** button ⌷.
3. Click **Custom Margins**.
4. Under Margins, set the margins as desired.
5. Click **OK**.

Selecting a Paper Size

1. Click the **Page Layout** tab.
   Page Setup Group
2. Click the **Size** button ⌷.
3. Click the desired page size.

Setting Page Orientation

1. Click the **Page Layout** tab.
   Page Setup Group
2. Click the **Orientation** button ⌷.
3. On the menu, click the desired orientation.

Applying a Page Border

1. Click the **Page Layout** tab.
   Page Background Group
2. Click the **Page Borders** button ⌷.
3. In the Borders and Shading dialog box, click the **Page Border** tab.
4. Select the Setting, Style, Color, and Width as desired.
5. Click **OK**.

Setting Indents

Adjusting the Left Indent by 0.5"

1. Click the **Home** tab.
   Paragraph Group
2. Click one of the following:
   - Decrease Indent button ⌷
   - Increase Indent button ⌷

Setting a Left or Right Indent Precisely

- Click the **Page Layout** tab.
  Paragraph Group
  - Use the **Indent Left** box increment arrows to set the left indent.
  - Using the **Indent Right** box increment arrows to set the right indent.

Setting Indents Using the Paragraph Dialog Box

1. Click the **Page Layout** tab.
2. Click the **Paragraph** group dialog box launcher ⌷.
3. Click the **Indents and Spacing** tab.
4. Under Indentation, use the **Left** and **Right** increment arrows to set the left and right margins, respectively.
5. If desired, click the **Special** drop-down arrow to set the indent on the first line.
6. Click the **By** increment arrows to adjust the indent on the first line, if desired.

Setting a Hanging Indent

1. Click the **Page Layout** tab.
2. Click the **Paragraph** group dialog box launcher ⌷.
3. Click the **Indents and Spacing** tab.
4. Click the **Special** drop-down arrow and click **Hanging**.
5. Click the **By** increment arrows to adjust the indent on the hanging indent, if desired.

Setting Tabs

Setting Tabs Using the Horizontal Ruler

1. To select a tab type, click the Tab selector box at the left end of the horizontal ruler until the tab you want to use displays, as follows:

   - Left ⌊L⌋
   - Right ⌊⌟⌋
   - Center ⌊⊥⌋
   - Decimal ⌊⊞⌋
   - Bar ⌊⏐⌋

2. Click at the position on the horizontal ruler where you want to set the tab.

Setting Tabs in the Tab Dialog Box

1. Click the **Home** tab.
2. Click the **Paragraph** group dialog box launcher ⌊⌐⌋.
3. Click the **Tabs** button.
4. Type the tab stop position in the **Tab stop position** text box.
5. From the Alignment option, select the desired tab type.
6. Click **Set**.
7. Click **OK**.

Using the Horizontal Ruler to Adjust and Clear Tab Stops

- Position the insertion point in the line of text for which the tab has been set.

  - To clear a tab stop, drag the tab stop off the horizontal ruler.
  - To adjust a tab stop, drag it to the desired position on the horizontal ruler.

Selecting a Tab Leader

1. Click the **Home** tab.
2. Click the **Paragraph** group dialog box launcher ⌊⌐⌋.
3. Click the **Tabs** button.
4. In the Leader section, click the desired leader style.
5. Click **OK**.

Working with Breaks

Inserting a Hard Page Break

1. Position the insertion point where you want to insert the page break.
2. Click the **Insert** tab.
   Pages Group
3. Click the **Page Break** button ⌊▭⌋.
OR
2. Click the **Page Layout** tab.
   Page Setup Group
3. Click the **Breaks** button ⌊▤⌋.
4. From the Breaks gallery, click **Page**.

Deleting a Hard Page Break

1. Position the insertion point on the page break.
2. Press **Delete**.

Inserting a Section Break

1. Position the insertion point where you want to insert the break.
2. Click the **Page Layout** tab.
   Page Setup Group
3. Click the **Breaks** button ⌊▤⌋.
4. From the Breaks gallery, click the desired break type.

Deleting a Section Break

1. Position the insertion point on the break.
2. Press **Delete**.

Inserting Symbols

1. Position the insertion point where you want to insert the symbol.
2. Click the **Insert** tab.
   Symbols Group
3. Click the **Symbol** button ⌊Ω⌋.

√ *If the symbol you want displays in the Symbols gallery, click it to insert it in the document.*

4. Click **More Symbols**.
5. In the Symbol dialog box, select a font if necessary, and then click the desired symbol.
6. Click **Insert**.

Inserting Special Characters

1. Position the insertion point where you want to insert the character.
2. Click the **Insert** tab.
   Symbols Group
3. Click the **Symbol** button ⌊Ω⌋.
4. Click **More Symbols**.
5. In the Symbol dialog box, click the **Special Characters** tab.
6. Click the desired character.
7. Click **Insert**.

Creating Lists

Creating a Bulleted List
1. Click the **Home** tab.
   Paragraph Group
2. Click the **Bullets** button drop-down arrow.
3. Click the desired bullet style from the Bullet Library.

OR

1. Click the **Home** tab.
   Paragraph Group
2. Click the **Bullets** button drop-down arrow.
3. Click **Define New Bullet** on the menu.
4. In the Define New Bullet dialog box, click the **Symbol** button, **Picture** button, and/or **Font** button to define a new bullet.

Creating a Numbered List
1. Click the **Home** tab.
   Paragraph Group
2. Click the **Numbering** button drop-down arrow.
3. Click the desired numbering style from the Numbering Library.

Changing an Item Level in a Numbered List
1. Click the **Home** tab.
   Paragraph Group
2. Click the **Decrease Indent** button to promote the item one level, or click the **Increase Indent** button to demote the item one level.

Creating a Multilevel List
1. Click the **Home** tab.
   Paragraph Group
2. Click the **Multilevel List** button.
3. In the List Library, click the desired list style.
4. Type first item in list.
5. Press **Enter**.
6. Press **Tab** to increase indent one level.

OR

Press **Shift + Tab** to decrease indent one level.
7. Type next item in list.
8. Repeat until list is complete.

Changing the Bullet or Number Formatting
1. Right-click the bullet or number.
2. On the shortcut menu, click **Font** or **Paragraph** to open the corresponding dialog box and change formats as desired.

Inserting Page Numbers
1. Click the **Insert** tab.
   Header & Footer Group
2. Click the **Page Number** button.
3. On the menu, click the desired location for the page number.
4. On the gallery, click the desired format for the page number.

Changing the Page Number Format
1. Double-click in the header or footer containing the page number.
2. On the Header & Footer Tools Design tab, click the **Page Number** button.
3. On the menu, click **Format Page Numbers**.
4. In the Page Number Format dialog box, set the formatting as desired.

Working with Headers and Footers

Typing in the Header or Footer
1. Double-click in the header or footer area to make it active.
2. Type and format the header or footer information.
3. Double-click in the main document area.

OR

1. Click the **Header & Footer Tools** tab.
   Close Group
2. Click the **Close Header & Footer** button.

Inserting a Header or Footer
1. Click the **Insert** tab.
   Header & Footer Group
2. Click the **Header** button 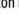.

OR

Click the Footer button.
3. Click the desired style.
4. Type and format the header or footer information.
5. Click the **Header & Footer Tools** tab.
   Close Group
6. Click the **Close Header & Footer** button.

Modifying a Header or Footer
1. Click the **Insert** tab.
   Header & Footer Group
2. Click the **Header** button .

OR

Click the **Footer** button.
3. Click **Edit Header**.

OR

Click **Edit Footer**.
4. Modify the header or footer information.
5. Click the **Header & Footer Tools** tab.
   Close Group
6. Click the **Close Header & Footer** button.

Working with Styles

Applying a Built-In Style
1. Click within the line of text.
2. Click the **Home** tab.
   Styles Group
3. Click the desired style from the Styles gallery.

Creating a Custom Style
1. Format text.
2. Select formatted text.
3. Right-click selection.
4. On the shortcut menu, click **Styles**.
5. Click **Save Selection as a New Quick Style**.
6. Type a style name.
7. Click **OK**.

Modifying a Style
1. Apply the style to text.
2. Make changes or modifications.
3. Select formatted text.
4. Right-click selection.
5. On the shortcut menu, click **Styles**.
6. Click **Update** *stylename* **to Match Selection**.

Changing the Style Set
1. Click the **Home** tab.
   Styles Group
2. Click the **Change Styles** button ⒜.
3. Click **Style Set**.
4. Click the desired style set.

Using Desktop Publishing Features

Creating Newsletter Columns
1. Select the text or click in the section of text that you want to format in columns.
2. Click the **Page Layout** tab.
   Page Setup Group
3. Click the **Columns** button ▱.
4. From the gallery, select the desired number of columns.

Setting Column Width
1. Click the **Page Layout** tab.
   Page Setup Group
2. Click the **Columns** button ▱.
3. Click **More Columns**.
4. In the Columns dialog box, set the column width and spacing as desired.
5. Click **OK**.

Inserting a Column Break
1. Position the insertion point where you want to insert the break.
2. Click the **Page Layout** tab.
   Page Setup Group
3. Click the **Breaks** button ▱.
4. From the Breaks gallery, click **Column**.

Balancing Columns
1. Position the insertion point at the end of the text in the last column on the page.
2. Click the **Page Layout** tab.
   Page Setup Group
3. Click the **Breaks** button ▱.
4. From the Breaks gallery, click **Continuous**.

Applying a Page Background
1. Click the **Page Layout** tab.
   Page Background Group
2. Click the **Page Color** button ▱.
3. Click the desired color from the color palette.
OR
3. Click **Fill Effects** on the menu.
4. In the Fill Effects dialog box, select the gradient, texture, pattern, and picture formats as desired.
5. Click **OK**.

Inserting Dropped Capitals
1. Click in the paragraph where you want to insert the dropped capital.
2. Click the **Insert** tab.
   Text Group
3. Click the **Drop Cap** button ▱.
4. From the menu, click the desired format.

Customizing a Dropped Capital
1. Click in the paragraph where you want to insert the dropped capital.
2. Click the **Insert** tab.
   Text Group
3. Click the **Drop Cap** button ▱.
4. From the menu, click **Drop Cap Options**.
5. In the Drop Cap dialog box, click the desired position for the drop cap.
6. Under Options, set the desired font, lines to drop, and distance from text.
7. Click **OK**.

Enhancing a Paragraph with Borders

1. Position the insertion point in the paragraph to which you want to add a border.
2. Click the **Page Layout** tab.
   Page Background Group
3. Click the **Page Borders** button ▯.
4. In the Borders and Shading dialog box, click the **Page Border** tab.
5. In the Style list box, click the desired line style for the border.
6. Click the **Color** drop-down arrow and click the desired color for the border.
7. Click the **Width** drop-down arrow and click the desired line width for the border.
8. In the Setting list, click the desired effect for the border.
9. Click **OK**.

Enhancing a Paragraph with Shading

1. Position the insertion point in the paragraph to which you want to add shading.
2. Click the **Page Layout** tab.
   Page Background Group
3. Click the **Page Borders** button ▯.
4. In the Borders and Shading dialog box, click the **Shading** tab.
5. Click the **Fill** drop-down arrow and click the desired color for the shading.
6. Under Patterns, click the **Style** drop-down arrow and click the desired patterns for the shading.
7. Under Patterns, click the **Color** drop-down arrow and click the desired color for the pattern.
8. Click **OK**.

Inserting the Date and Time

1. Click the **Insert** tab.
   Text Group
2. Click the **Date & Time** button ▣.
3. In the list of Available formats, select the desired format.
   √ *Click the Update automatically check box if you want the date and time to update automatically every time you save or print the document.*
4. Click **OK**.

Sorting Paragraphs

1. Click the **Home** tab.
   Paragraph Group
2. Click the **Sort** button ▣.
3. In the Sort dialog box, click the **Ascending** button or the **Descending** button.
4. Click **OK**.

Creating Tables

Inserting a Table

1. Click the **Insert** tab.
   Tables Group
2. Click the **Table** button ▣.
3. On the menu, highlight the number of rows and columns in the grid.
OR
3. Click **Insert Table**.
4. In the Insert Table dialog box, set the number of rows and columns and the AutoFit options.
5. Click **OK**.

Entering Text in a Table

- Click in a cell and type the entry.
OR
- Press **Tab** or an arrow key to move to a cell and type an entry.

Converting Text to a Table

1. Select the text to convert.
2. Click the Insert tab.
   Tables Group
2. Click the **Table** button ▣.
3. On the menu, click **Convert Text to Table**.
4. In the Convert Text to Table dialog box, click **OK**.

Drawing a Table

1. Click the **Insert** tab.
   Tables Group
2. Click the **Table** button ▣.
3. Click **Draw Table**.
   √ *The mouse pointer changes to ✎.*
4. Drag to create table cells.

Changing Table Structure

Viewing Gridlines

1. Click in the table to select it.
2. Click the **Table Tools Layout** tab.

   Table Group
3. Click the **View Gridlines** button ▦.

Selecting in a Table

1. Click in the table.
2. Click the **Table Tools Layout** tab.

   Table Group
3. Click the **Select** button ⟍.
4. Click the desired selection on the menu.

Selecting a Table

- To select the table, click the **Table Selector** button ⊞ that appears outside the upper left corner of the table.

Selecting a Row

1. To select a row, position the mouse pointer outside the table, to the left of the row.
2. When the mouse pointer changes to →, click to select the row.

Selecting a Column

1. To select a column, position the mouse pointer outside the table, just above the column.
2. When the mouse pointer changes to ↓, click to select the column.

Selecting a Cell

1. To select a cell, position the mouse pointer outside the cell, at the bottom left corner.
2. When the mouse pointer changes to ◥, click to select the cell.

Selecting Multiple Components in a Table

- To select contiguous cells, drag across them.

OR

- Select the first cell and press and hold **Shift** to select additional cells.

- To select noncontiguous cells, select the first cell and press and hold **Ctrl** to select additional cells.

Inserting Rows and Columns

1. Click where desired in the table.
2. Click the **Table Tools Layout** tab.

   Rows & Columns Group
3. Click the options, as follows:
   - Insert Above ▦
   - Insert Below ▦
   - Insert Left ▦
   - Insert Right ▦

Deleting in a Table

1. Click in the cell, row, or column to be deleted.
2. Click the **Table Tools Layout** tab.

   Rows & Columns Group
3. Click the **Delete** button ▦.
4. Click the desired option to delete on the menu.

Deleting a Table

1. Click in any cell of the table.
2. Click the **Table Tools Layout** tab.

   Rows & Columns Group
3. Click the **Delete** button ▦.
4. Click **Delete Table** on the menu.

Merging Cells

1. Select the cells to merge.
2. Click the **Table Tools Layout** tab.

   Merge Group
3. Click the **Merge Cells** button ▦.

OR

1. Click the **Table Tools Design** tab.

   Draw Borders Group
2. Click the **Eraser** button ▦.
√ *The mouse pointer changes to* ⬦.
3. Click on a cell divider to merge the cells.

Splitting Cells

1. Select the cell to split.
2. Click the **Table Tools Layout** tab.

   Merge Group
3. Click the **Split Cells** button ▦.
4. In the Split Cells dialog box, set the number of columns and rows for the split cell.
5. Click **OK**.

Formatting a Table

Applying a Table Style
1. Click in the table to select it.
2. Click the **Table Tools Design** tab.

Table Styles Group
3. Click the Table Styles **More** button ▾.
4. Click the desired style.

Applying Formats to Cell Contents
1. Select the text to be formatted.
2. Click the **Home** tab.
3. Apply formats from the Font and Paragraph groups as desired.

Applying Cell Borders
1. Select the cell(s).
2. Click the **Table Tools Design** tab.

Draw Borders Group
3. Click the **Line Style** button.
4. From the Line Style gallery, click the desired line style.
5. Click the **Line Weight** button.
6. From the Line Weight gallery, click the desired line weight.
7. Click the **Pen Color** button drop-down arrow.
8. From the palette, click the desired color.
9. Click the **Table Tools Design** tab.

Table Styles Group
10. Click the **Borders** button drop-down arrow.
11. From the Borders gallery, click the desired border style.

Applying Cell Shading
1. Select the cell(s).
2. Click the **Table Tools Design** tab.

Table Styles Group
3. Click the **Shading** button drop-down arrow.
4. From the color palette, click the desired shade.

Setting Column Width and Row Height
1. Click a cell in the column or row you want to adjust.
2. Click the **Table Tools Layout** tab.

Cell Size Group
3. Click the **AutoFit** button.
4. Click the desired option from the menu.

OR

1. Rest the pointer on the column divider or row divider.
2. Drag to the desired width or height.

OR

1. Click a cell in the column or row you want to adjust.
2. Click the **Table Tools Layout** tab.

Cell Size Group
3. Click the **Table Row Height** increment arrows or the **Table Column Width** increment arrows to adjust the size as desired.

OR

1. Click the **Table Selector** button to select the table.
2. Click the **Table Tools Layout** tab.

Cell Size Group
3. Click the **Distribute Rows** button to distribute the rows evenly, or the **Distribute Columns** button to distribute the columns evenly.

Setting Alignment in a Table Cell
1. Click in the cell(s) in which you want to set the alignment.
2. Click the Table Tools Layout tab.

Alignment Group
3. Click from the alignment options, as follows:
   - Align Top Left
   - Align Top Center
   - Align Top Right
   - Align Center Left
   - Align Center
   - Align Center Right
   - Align Bottom Left
   - Align Bottom Center
   - Align Bottom Right

Setting Tabs in a Table Cell
1. Click in the cell in which you want to set the tab.
2. Click the Tab selector box at the left end of the horizontal ruler until the tab you want to use displays, as follows:
   - Left
   - Right
   - Center
   - Decimal
   - Bar
3. Click at the position on the horizontal ruler where you want to set the tab.
4. Press **Ctrl + Tab** to advance to the tab stop.

Setting Cell Margins

1. Click in any cell.
2. Click the **Table Tools Layout** tab.

Alignment Group

3. Click the **Cell Margins** button.
4. In the Table Options dialog box, use the increment arrows to set the top, bottom, left, and right margins as desired.
5. Click **OK**.

Aligning a Table Horizontally on the Page

1. Click anywhere in the table.
2. Click the **Table Tools Layout** tab.

Table Group

3. Click the **Properties** button.
4. In the Table Properties dialog box, click the **Table** tab if necessary.
5. Select the desired alignment option.
6. Click **OK**.

Changing Text Direction in a Table Cell

1. Click in the cell.
2. Click the **Table Tools Layout** tab.

Alignment Group

3. Click the **Text Direction** button to rotate through the different options.

Moving a Table

1. Click the **Table selector** button to select the table.
2. Drag the mouse pointer to the new location and release.

Resizing a Table

1. Rest the mouse pointer over the table so the sizing handle displays in the lower right corner.
2. Click and drag the sizing handle to the desired size.

Setting Text Wrapping Around a Table

1. Click in any cell in the table.
2. Click the **Table Tools Layout** tab.

Table Group

3. Click the **Properties** button.
4. In the Table Properties dialog box, click the **Table** tab if necessary.
5. In the Text wrapping section, select the desired option.
6. Click **OK**.

Performing Addition in a Table

1. Click in the cell that will contain the formula.
2. Click the **Table Tools Layout** tab.

Data Group

3. Click the **Formula** button.
4. Verify that the Formula box contains =SUM(ABOVE).
5. Click **OK**.

Applying a Number Format

1. Click in the cell that contains, or will contain, the formula.
2. Click the **Table Tools Layout** tab.

Data Group

3. Click the **Formula** button.
4. In the Formula dialog box, click the **Number format** drop-down arrow.
5. Click the desired format.
6. Click **OK**.

Sorting Rows in a Table

1. Select the column to sort by.
2. Click the **Table Tools Layout** tab.

Data Group

3. Click the **Sort** button.
4. In the Sort dialog box, verify the column(s) to sort by and the sort order.

Using Mail Merge

1. Click the **Mailings** tab.

Start Mail Merge Group

2. Click the **Select Recipients** button.
3. On the menu, click the desired type of recipient list.
4. Click the **Mailings** tab.

Write & Insert Fields Group

5. Click the **Address Block** button to insert the desired address block.
6. Click **Greeting Line** button to insert the desired greeting line.
7. Click the **Insert Merge Field** drop-down arrow to insert other fields, as desired.
8. Click the **Mailings** tab.

Preview Results Group

9. Click the **Preview Results** button to preview the letters if desired.
10. Click the **Mailings** tab.

Finish Group

11. Click the **Finish & Merge** button.
12. On the menu, click **Edit Individual Documents**.
13. In the Merge to New Document dialog box, click **OK**.

Creating a New Address List

1. Click the **Mailings** tab.
   Start Mail Merge Group
2. Click the **Select Recipients** button .
3. On the menu, click **Type New List**.
4. In the New Address List dialog box, enter recipient names and addresses as desired.
5. Click **OK**.
6. In the Save Address List dialog box, enter the file name for the list and select the location where you want to save it.
7. Click **OK**.

Using an Existing Data Source

1. Click the **Mailings** tab.
   Start Mail Merge Group
2. Click the **Select Recipients** button .
3. On the menu, click the desired type of data source.

Adding Records to the Data Source

1. Click the **Mailings** tab.
   Start Mail Merge Group
2. Click the **Edit Recipient List** button .
3. In the Data Source box, click the data source you want to edit.
4. Click **Edit**.
5. In the Edit Data Source dialog box, click **New Entry**.
6. Enter new recipients as desired.

Using an Excel File as a Data Source

1. Click the **Mailings** tab.
   Start Mail Merge Group
2. Click the **Select Recipients** button .
3. On the menu, click **Use Existing List**.
4. Navigate to and open the desired Excel file.
5. In the Select Table dialog box, click the sheet to be used as the data source.
6. Click **OK**.

Matching Fields to a Data Source

1. Click the **Mailings** tab.
   Write & Insert Fields Group
2. Click the **Match Fields** button .
3. In the Match Fields dialog box, match the fields in the data source as desired.
4. Click **OK**.

Starting an Envelope Mail Merge

1. Click the **Mailings** tab.
   Start Mail Merge Group
2. Click the **Start Mail Merge** button .
3. Click **Envelopes**.
4. In the Envelope Options dialog box, click OK to accept the default settings.

Starting a Labels Mail Merge

1. Click the **Mailings** tab.
   Start Mail Merge Group
2. Click the **Start Mail Merge** button .
3. Click **Labels**.
4. In the Label Options dialog box, click the **Label vendors** drop-down arrow and click the desired label type.
5. In the Product number list, click the desired label size.
6. Click **OK**.

Using Language Tools

Correcting Spelling as You Type

1. Right-click the misspelled word.
   √ *A red wavy line under a word indicates a possible spelling error. A blue wavy underline indicates a possible word choice error.*
2. Click the desired option on the shortcut menu.

Correcting Grammar as You Type

1. Right-click the misspelled word.
   √ *A green wavy line under a word indicates a possible grammatical error.*
2. Click the desired option on the shortcut menu.

Checking Spelling and Grammar

1. Click the Review tab.
   Proofing Group
2. Click the **Spelling & Grammar** button .
3. Click options to correct or ignore errors identified in the Spelling & Grammar dialog box.

Using the Thesaurus

1. Select the word you want to research.
2. Click the **Review** tab.
   Proofing Group
3. Click the **Thesaurus** button .
4. In the Research task pane, select the desired synonym or antonym.

Using AutoCorrect

Reversing AutoCorrect Changes

1. Rest the mouse pointer on the blue rectangle that appears below the corrected text.
2. When the **AutoCorrect Options** button ⌐ appears, click it to display the options from which you can choose.

Editing the AutoCorrect List

1. Click **File**.
2. Click **Options**.
3. In the Word Options dialog box, click **Proofing**.
4. Click **AutoCorrect Options** to open the AutoCorrect Options dialog box.
5. In the Replace text box, type the text you want replaced.
6. In the With text box, type the AutoCorrect replacement text.
7. Click **Add**.
8. Click **OK**.

Using Content Controls

1. Click a content control to select it.
2. Type replacement text as desired.

Removing a Content Control

1. Right-click the content control.
2. On the shortcut menu, click Remove Content Control.

Managing Document Properties

1. Click **File**.
2. On the Info tab, in the Preview pane under Properties, review the document's properties or click available content controls as desired.
3. If desired, click **Show All Properties** to display all properties.

OR

1. Click **File**.
2. On the Info tab, in the Preview pane, click **Properties**.
3. Click **Show Document Panel** to display the panel below the Ribbon.
4. Add or modify properties as desired.

Viewing a Properties Dialog Box

1. Click **File**.
2. On the Info tab, in the Preview pane, click **Properties**.
3. Click **Advanced Properties** to display the document's Properties dialog box.
4. Add or modify properties as desired.
5. Click **OK** to close the dialog box.

Printing Document Properties

1. Click **File**.
2. Click **Print**.
3. Under Settings, click the top button.
4. On the menu, click **Document Properties**.
5. Click the **Print** button 🖨.

Managing Sources and Citations

Inserting Footnotes

1. Position the insertion point where you want to insert the footnote marker.
2. Click the **References** tab.
   Footnotes Group
3. Click the **Insert Footnote** button AB¹.
4. Type the footnote.

Inserting Endnotes

1. Position the insertion point where you want to insert the endnote marker.
2. Click the **References** tab.
   Footnotes Group
3. Click the **Insert Endnote** button.
4. Type the endnote.

Inserting Citations

1. Position the insertion point where you want to insert the citation.
2. Click the **References** tab.
   Citations & Bibliography Group
3. Click the **Style** button drop-down arrow.
4. Click the desired style.
5. Click the **Insert Citation** button.
6. From the menu, click **Add New Source**.
7. In the Create Source dialog box, select the type of source and enter the source information.
8. Click **OK**.

Creating a Reference Page

1. Position the insertion point at the end of the document and insert a hard page break.
2. Click the **References** tab.
   Citations & Bibliography Group
3. Click the **Bibliography** button.
4. Click the desired format.

Tracking Revisions

Turning Tracking On or Off
1. Click the **Review** tab.
   Tracking Group
2. Click the **Track Changes** button.

Accepting or Rejecting Changes
1. Click the **Review** tab.
   Changes Group
2. Click the **Next** button ➡ to move to the next tracked change in the document.
   OR
   Click the **Previous** button ⬅ to move to the previous tracked change.
   Changes Group
3. Click the **Accept** button ✐ to accept the change.
   OR
   Click the **Reject** button ✐ to reject the change.

Accepting all Changes
1. Click the **Review** tab.
   Changes Group
2. Click the **Accept** button drop-down arrow .
3. Click **Accept All Changes in Document**.

Rejecting all Changes t
1. Click the **Review** tab.
   Changes Group
2. Click the **Reject** button drop-down arrow ✐ Reject ▾.
3. Click **Reject All Changes in Document**.

Working with Comments

Inserting a Comment
1. Position the insertion point.
   OR
   Select text
2. Click the **Review** tab.
   Comments Group
3. Click the **New Comment** button.
4. Type the comment text.

Displaying or Hiding the Reviewing Pane
1. Click the **Review** tab.
   Tracking Group
2. Click the **Reviewing Pane** button.

Editing a Comment
1. Position the insertion point within the comment text.
2. Edit text.

Moving through Comments
1. Click the **Review** tab.
   Comments Group
2. Click the **Next** button.
   OR
   Click the **Previous** button.

Deleting a Comment
1. Click comment to delete.
2. Click the **Review** tab.
   Comments Group
3. Click the **Delete** button.

Deleting All Comments
1. Click first comment to delete.
2. Click the **Review** tab.
   Comments Group
3. Click the **Delete** button drop-down arrow.
4. Click **Delete All Comments in Document**.
   OR
   Click the **Previous** button.

Protecting a Document

Applying a Password and Encryption to a Document
1. Open the document to protect.
2. Click the **File** tab.
3. Click **Info**, if necessary.
4. In the Permissions area, click the **Protect Document** button .
5. Click **Encrypt with Password**.
6. Type the password.
7. Click **OK**.
8. Type the password again.
9. Click **OK**.

Open an Encrypted and Password-Protected Document
1. Open the document to protect.
2. In the Password dialog box, type the password.
3. Click **OK**.

Restricting Editing

1. Click the **Review** tab.

   Protect Group

2. Click the **Restrict Editing** button.

3. In the Restrict Formatting and Editing task pane, click to select the **Allow only this type of editing in the document** check box.

4. Click the drop-down arrow and click one of the following:

   - **Tracked changes**, to allow editing with revision marks.

   - **Comments**, to allow the insertion of comments.

   - **Filling in forms**, to allow editing in form fields,

   - No changes (Read only) to allow no editing.

5. Click **Yes, Start Enforcing Protection**.

6. In the Start Enforcing Protection dialog box, click **OK**.

   OR

   Type a password, press Tab, type the password again, and click **OK**.

Restricting Formatting

1. Click the **Review** tab.

   Protect Group

2. Click the **Restrict Editing** button.

3. In the Restrict Formatting and Editing task pane, click to select the **Limit formatting to a selection of styles** check box.

4. Click the **Settings** link.

5. In the Formatting Restrictions dialog box, select desired options.

6. Click **OK**.

7. In the Restrict Formatting and Editing task pane, click **Yes, Start Enforcing Protection**.

8. In the Start Enforcing Protection dialog box, click **OK**.

   OR

   Type a password, press Tab, type the password again, and click **OK**.

Canceling Editing and Formatting Restrictions

1. Open protected document.

2. In the Restrict Formatting and Editing task pane, click **Stop Protection**.

Working with Excel Data in Word

Inserting an Excel Worksheet

1. Position the insertion point in the Word document.

2. Click the **Insert** tab.

   Tables Group

3. Click the **Table** button.

4. Click **Excel Spreadsheet**.

5. Enter and format data in the worksheet object.

6. Click anywhere outside the worksheet object to deselect it.

Copying Worksheet Data from Excel to Word

1. In the Excel workbook, select the worksheet data.

2. Click the **Home** tab.

   Clipboard Group

3. Click the **Copy** button.

4. In the Word document, position the insertion point where you want to insert the data.

5. Click the **Home** tab.

   Clipboard Group

6. Click the **Paste** button.

Creating a Chart in Word

1. Position the insertion point in the Word document.

2. Click the **Insert** tab.

   Illustrations Group

3. Click the **Chart** button.

4. In the left pane of the Insert Chart dialog box, click the chart type.

5. In the right pane of the Insert Chart dialog box, click the chart subtype.

6. Click **OK**.

7. In the displayed Excel workbook, replace the sample data with the data you want to chart.

8. If necessary, drag the lower-right corner of the chart data range to display the data you want to chart.

Saving a Word Document as a PDF

1. Click **File**.
2. Click **Save As**.
3. In the Save As dialog box, enter the file name and select the location where the file will be saved.
4. Click **Save as type**.
5. Click **PDF**.
6. Click **Save**.

OR

1. Click **File**.
2. Click **Save & Send**.
3. Click **Create PDF/XPS Document**.
4. Click **Create PDF/XPS**.
5. Enter the file name and select the location where you want to save the file.
6. Click the **Save as type** drop-down arrow.
7. Click **PDF**.
8. Click **Publish**.

Saving a Word Document as XPS

1. Click **File**.
2. Click **Save & Send**.
3. Click **Create PDF/XPS Document**.
4. Click **Create PDF/XPS**.
5. Enter the file name and select the location where you want to save the file.
6. Click the **Save as type** drop-down arrow.
7. Click **XPS**.
8. Click **Publish**.

Saving a Word Document as a Web Page

1. Click **File**.
2. Click **Save As**.
3. In the Save As dialog box, enter the file name and select the location where the file will be saved.
4. Click the **Save as type** button.
5. Click **Single File Web Page**.
6. Click **Change Title**.
7. In the Page title text box, enter the desired page title and click **OK**.
8. In the Save As dialog box, click **Save**.

Changing a Web Page Title

1. Click **File**.
2. Click **Save As**.
3. Click the **Change Title** button.
4. In the Enter Text dialog box, type the title text.
5. Click **OK**.
6. Click **Save**.

Opening a Web Page in Word

1. Click **File**.
2. Click **Open**.
3. Navigate to the Web page file.
4. Double-click the file.

OR

1. Use your operating system to locate the Web page file.
2. Right-click the file.
3. On the shortcut menu, point to **Open With** and click **Microsoft Word**.

Sending a Word Document as an E-mail Attachment

1. Click **File**.
2. Click **Save & Send**.
3. Under Send Using E-mail, click **Send as Attachment**.
4. Enter the e-mail information as necessary.
5. Click **Send**.

Working with Hyperlinks

Inserting a Hyperlink

1. Select text or object to hyperlink.
2. Click the **Insert** tab.
   Links Group
3. Click the **Hyperlink** button.
4. In the Insert Hyperlink dialog box, locate and select the hyperlink destination.
5. Click **OK**.

Creating a Hyperlink to a Web Site

1. Click the **Insert** tab.
   Links Group
2. Click the **Hyperlink** button.
3. In the Insert Hyperlink dialog box, type the Web site address in the Address text box.
4. Click **OK**.

Creating an E-mail Hyperlink

1. Click the **Insert** tab.
   Links Group
2. Click the **Hyperlink** button.
3. In the Insert Hyperlink dialog box, in the Link to section, click **E-mail Address**.
4. Enter the e-mail information as necessary.
5. Click **OK**.

Testing a Hyperlink

- Hold down the **Ctrl** key and click the hyperlink.

Editing a Hyperlink

1. Right-click the hyperlink.
2. On the shortcut menu, click **Edit Hyperlink**.
3. Edit the link as desired.
4. Click **OK**.

Removing a Hyperlink

1. Right-click the hyperlink.
2. On the shortcut menu, click **Remove Hyperlink**.

Creating a Blog

Starting a Blog Post

1. Click **File**.
2. Click **New**.
3. Click **Blog Post**.
4. Click **Create**.
5. Register your blog service.
6. Type the blog text.

Registering a Blog Server

√ *You must have a blog account in order to register a blog server.*

1. In your blog file, click the **Blog Post** tab.
   Blog Group
2. Click the **Manage Accounts** button.
3. In the Blog Accounts dialog box, click **New**.
4. In the New Blog Account dialog box, click the **Blog** drop-down arrow and click your provider.
5. Click **Next**.
6. Enter your user name and password, and click **OK**.
7. Click **Yes**.
8. Click **OK**.
9. Click **Close**.

Publishing to Your Blog

√ *You must have a blog account in order to register a blog server.*

1. In your blog file, click the **Blog Post** tab.
   Blog Group
2. Click the **Publish** button.
3. If prompted, type your user name and password for your blogging service in the boxes provided.
4. Click **OK**.
5. If prompted to confirm, click **Yes**. (You may see this prompt more than once.)

√ *When the post is successfully published, a message appears in an information bar at the top of the document in Word.*

Navigating a Worksheet

- Press **Ctrl + Home** to return to cell A1.
- Click the **up** or **down** scroll arrows on the vertical scroll bar to scroll one row up down.
- Click the **right** or **left** scroll arrows on the horizontal scroll bar to scroll one column right or left.
- Click above or below the scroll box on the vertical scroll arrow to scroll one screen up or down.
- Click to the left or right of the scroll box on the horizontal scroll arrow to scroll one screen left right.
- Drag the scroll box on either scroll bar to bring the desired portion of the worksheet into view.
- Use the mouse wheel to scroll up or down in the worksheet.

Freezing Labels While Scrolling

1. Position the insertion point in the column to the right and/or the row below the data to be frozen.
2. Click the **View** tab.
   Window Group
3. Click the **Freeze Panes** button.
4. Click the desired freeze option on the menu.

Unfreezing Labels

1. Click the **View** tab.
   Window Group
2. Click the **Freeze Panes** button.
3. Click **Unfreeze Panes** on the menu.

Changing the Worksheet View

Showing and Hiding Worksheet Elements

1. Click the **View** tab.
   Show Group
2. Click to mark the check box for **Ruler**, **Gridlines**, **Formula Bar**, and **Headings**.
   √ *A check in the check box indicates the element is displayed.*

Hiding the Ribbon

1. Double-click the selected tab to hide the Ribbon.
2. Double-click the tab to redisplay the Ribbon.

Changing the View

1. Click the **View** tab.
   Workbook Views Group
2. Click the desired View button:
   - Normal
   - Page Layout
   - Page Break Preview
   - Custom Views
   - Full Screen

OR

- Click a View icon on the status bar:
   - Normal
   - Page Layout
   - Page Break Preview

Changing the Active Worksheet

- Click the sheet tab of the sheet you want to display.

Splitting a Worksheet into Panes

1. Click the cell to the right and below where you want the split to occur.
2. Click the **View** tab.
   Window Group
3. Click the **Split** button.

OR

- Click and drag the split box at the top of the vertical scroll bar to split the window horizontally.
- Click and drag the split box at the right end of the horizontal scroll bar to split the window vertically.

Removing a Split

1. Click the **View** tab.
   Window Group
2. Click the **Split** button.

Switching between Open Workbooks

- Click in the window you want to make active.

OR

- Click the program's taskbar button and click the workbook you want to make active.

Arranging Multiple Workbooks

1. Open all workbooks.
2. Click the View tab.
   Window Group
3. Click the **Arrange All** button.

Closing a Workbook

- Click the **Close** button.

OR

1. Click **File**.
2. Click **Close**.

Entering and Editing Data

Entering Data

- Click in the cell and type.
- Press **Enter** to complete the entry and move to the cell below.
- Press **Tab** to complete the entry and move to the cell to the right.
- Press an arrow key to complete the entry and move to the cell in the desired direction.

Editing Data

- Click a cell and type to replace the existing data.
- Double-click in the cell and edit the data.
- Select the cell, click in the formula bar, and edit the data.
- Press **Backspace** to delete one character to the left of the insertion point.
- Press **Delete** to delete one character to the right of the insertion point.

Using AutoComplete

- When an AutoComplete suggestion appears in a cell, press **Enter**, **Tab**, or an arrow key to accept the entry.

Using Pick From List

1. Right-click the desired cell.
2. On the shortcut menu, click **Pick From Drop-down List**.
3. In the list that appears, click the desired entry.

Using AutoCorrect

- To accept an AutoCorrect entry, press **Enter**, **Tab**, or an arrow key.

Editing the AutoCorrect List

1. Click **File**.
2. Click **Options**.
3. In the Excel Options dialog box, click **Proofing**.
4. Click **AutoCorrect Options** to open the AutoCorrect Options dialog box.
5. In the Replace text box, type the text you want replaced.
6. In the With text box, type the AutoCorrect replacement text.
7. Click **Add**.
8. Click **OK**.

Clearing Cell Contents

1. Click the desired cell(s).
2. Click the **Home** tab.
   Editing Group
3. Click the **Clear** button.

Inserting and Deleting Columns and Rows

Inserting a Column

1. Click the heading of the column that will be to the right of the new column.
2. Click the **Home** tab.
   Cells Group
3. Click the **Insert** button drop-down arrow.
4. Click **Insert Sheet Columns**.

Inserting a Row

1. Click the heading of the row that will be below the new row.
2. Click the **Home** tab.
   Cells Group
3. Click the **Insert** button drop-down arrow.
4. Click **Insert Sheet Rows**.

Deleting a Column or Row

1. Click the heading of the column or row that you want to delete.
2. Click the **Home** tab.
   Cells Group
3. Click the **Delete** button.

Filling in a Series

1. Select the beginning entries in the series.
2. Drag the fill handle in the lower right corner to complete the series as desired.

Using Find and Replace

1. Click the **Home** tab.
   Editing Group
2. Click the **Find & Select** button.
3. On the menu, click **Replace**.
4. In the Find and Replace dialog box, enter the text or values you want to find in the Find what box.
5. Enter the replacement text or values in the Replace with box.
6. Click the **Options** button to further specify the search.
7. Click **Find Next** to find each occurrence and then **Replace** to replace each occurrence. Click **Replace All** to replace all occurrences.
8. Click **Close**.

Checking the Spelling in a Worksheet

1. Click the **Review** tab.
   Proofing Group
2. Click the **Spelling** button.
3. Misspelled words are displayed in the Spelling dialog box, where you can choose to ignore or change them.

Applying Number Formats

1. Click the **Home** tab.
   Number Group
2. Click the **Number Format** drop-down arrow
   | General ⌄ |
3. From the gallery, select the desired format.

Aligning Data in a Cell

Setting Horizontal Alignment

1. Click the **Home** tab.
   Alignment Group
2. Click the alignment option as follows:
   - Top Align ▤
   - Middle Align ▤
   - Bottom Align ▤
   - Align Text Left ▤
   - Center ▤
   - Align Text Right ▤

Rotating Cell Entries

1. Click the cell or range of cells whose entries you want to rotate.
2. Click the **Home** tab.
   Alignment Group
3. Click the **Orientation** button ⯗⌄.
4. On the menu, click the desired rotation.

Wrapping Text in Cells

1. Click the **Home** tab.
   Alignment Group
2. Click the **Wrap Text** button ▤.

Formatting Cells

Applying Cell Styles

1. Click the **Home** tab.
   Styles Group
2. Click the **Cell Styles** button ▦.
3. From the gallery, click the desired style.

Applying Borders

1. Right-click selection to format.
2. Click **Format Cells**.
3. Click the **Border** tab.
4. Under Style, click the border line style.
5. Click the **Color** drop-down arrow and click the border color.
6. Click a **Presets** button.

OR

   - Click one or more **Border** buttons.
7. Click **OK**.

Applying Fills

1. Right-click selection to format.
2. Click **Format Cells**.
3. Click the **Fill** tab.
4. Under Background Color, click the fill color.
5. Click **OK**.

Entering Dates

- Press **Ctrl+;** to insert the current date in the *mm/dd/yyyy* format.

OR

1. Click the **Home** tab.
   Number Group
2. Click the **Number Format** drop-down arrow
   | General ⌄ |
3. From the gallery, select **Short Date** or **Long Date**.

Merging Cells

Merging and Centering Across Cells

1. Select the cells that you want to merge and center.
2. Click the **Home** tab.
   Alignment Group
3. Click the **Merge & Center** button ▦.

Merging Across Cells

1. Select the cells that you want to merge.
2. Click the **Home** tab.
   Alignment Group
3. Click the **Merge & Center** drop-down arrow ▦.
4. Click **Merge Across**.

Merging Cells

1. Select the cells that you want to merge.
2. Click the **Home** tab.
   Alignment Group
3. Click the **Merge & Center** drop-down arrow ▦.
4. Click **Merge Cells**.

Removing a Merge

1. Select the cells that you want to unmerge.
2. Click the **Home** tab.
   Alignment Group
3. Click the **Merge & Center** drop-down arrow ▦.
4. Click **Unmerge Cells**.

Copying Formats

1. Click the cell whose formats you want to copy.
2. Click the **Home** tab.
   Clipboard Group
3. Click the **Format Painter** button ⬧.
4. Click the cell to which you want to copy the formats.

OR

3. Double-click the **Format Painter** button ⬧.
4. Click each cell to which you want to copy the formats.
5. Press **Esc** to turn off the Format Painter.

Inserting Comments

1. Click the cell where you want to insert the comment.
2. Click the **Review** tab.
   Comments Group
3. Click the **New Comment** button ▭.
4. Type the comment text.

Deleting a Comment

1. Click the cell containing the comment.
2. Click the **Review** tab.
   Comments Group
3. Click the **Delete** button ⊠.

Changing Column Width and Row Height

Changing Column Width

1. Position the mouse pointer on the right border of a column header.
2. When the pointer changes to ⊞, drag to the desired width as indicated in the ScreenTip.

OR

1. Click the **Home** tab.
   Cells Group
2. Click the **Format** button ▦.
3. Click **Column Width** on the menu.
4. In the Column Width dialog box, enter the desired width.
5. Click **OK**.

Changing Row Height

1. Position the mouse pointer on the bottom border of a row header.
2. When the pointer changes to ⊞, drag to the desired height as indicated in the ScreenTip.

OR

1. Click the **Home** tab.
   Cells Group
2. Click the **Format** button ▦.
3. Click **Row Height** on the menu.
4. In the Row Height dialog box, enter the desired width.
5. Click **OK**.

Resolving a #### Error Message

1. Double-click the right border of the column header to resize the column to the longest entry.

OR

1. Click the **Home** tab.
   Cells Group
2. Click the **Format** button ▦.
3. Click **AutoFit Column Width** on the menu.

Working with Ranges

Selecting a Contiguous Range

1. Click the cell in the top left corner of the range.
2. Drag to select the remaining cells to be included in the range.

OR

Press and hold **Shift** and use the arrow keys to extend the selection as desired.

OR

Press **Shift** and click the cell that's at the lower-right corner of the range.

Selecting a Noncontiguous Range

1. Select the first portion of the range using one of the methods previously described.
2. Press and hold **Ctrl** to select additional portions.

Filling Range Cells with the Same Entry

1. Select the range.
2. Type the entry.
3. Press **Ctrl + Enter**.

Filling a Range with a Series

1. Select the cells with the series starting value(s).
2. Click the **Home** tab.
   Editing Group
3. Click the **Fill** button ▦.
4. Click **Series** on the menu.
5. In the Series dialog box, specify if the series will fill a row or column, the type of series, and the step and stop values.
6. Click **OK**.

Making a Range Entry Using a Collapse Dialog Box Button

1. In the dialog box, click the **Collapse** button ▦, which normally appears at the end of the text box in which you are to enter the range address.
2. In the worksheet, select the range.
3. Click the **Expand** button ▦ to redisplay the dialog box.

Defining a Range Name

1. Select the range you want to name.
2. Click in the **Name Box**.
3. Type the desired range name and press **Enter**.

OR

1. Select the range you want to name.
2. Right-click the selected range.
3. Click **Define Name** on the shortcut menu.
4. In the New Name dialog box, type the desired range name in the Name text box.
5. Click **OK**.

OR

1. Select the range you want to name.
2. Click the **Formulas** tab.
   Defined Names Group
3. Click the **Define Name** button [image].
4. In the New Name dialog box, type the desired range name in the Name text box.
5. Click **OK**.

Using AutoFill

Using AutoFill to Complete a Series

1. Select the range that will begin the series.
2. Click the AutoFill handle [image] and drag to the desired cell to complete the series.

Using AutoFill to Create a Trend

1. Select the range that will begin the series.
2. Right-click the AutoFill handle [image] and drag to the desired cell to complete the series.
3. When you release the mouse button, click the desired trend on the shortcut menu.

Using the Fill Button to Create a Linear Trend

1. Select the range that will begin the series.
2. Click the **Home** tab.
   Editing Group
3. Click the **Fill** button [image].
4. Click **Series**.
5. In the Series dialog box, click **Rows** or **Columns** for the direction to fill.
6. Click the **Linear** type of series
√ *Enter a step and stop value if desired.*
7. Click **OK**.

Using Formulas

Entering a Formula

1. Click the cell.
2. Type =.
3. Type the formula using parentheses and operators such as:
   - + for addition
   - - for subtraction
   - * for multiplication
   - / for division
4. Press **Enter**, **Tab**, or an arrow key to complete the entry.

OR

- Click the **Enter** button ✓ on the formula bar.

Using Parentheses in a Formula

- Excel calculates the part of the formula enclosed in parentheses first.
- When there are multiple nested pairs of parentheses in a formula, Excel calculates from the innermost pair to the outermost.

Editing a Formula

- Click in the cell and type a new formula to replace the existing formula.
- Double-click in the cell and edit the formula.
- Select the cell, click in the formula bar, and edit the formula.
- Select the cell, press **F2**, edit the formula.

Entering a Cell Reference in a Formula

1. Click the cell to contain the formula.
2. Type =.
3. Begin entering the formula.
4. At the location where you want to enter a cell reference, type the cell or range reference.

OR

- Click the cell or select the range to reference.
- √ *You may click a cell or select a range on any worksheet.*
5. Continue entering the formula until it is complete.
6. Press **Enter**, **Tab**, or an arrow key to complete the entry.

OR

Click the **Enter** button ✔ on the formula bar.

Entering an Absolute Cell Reference

- Type a dollar sign (**$**) before the column letter and again before row number of the cell you want to make an absolute reference.

OR

- Press **F4** to insert the dollar signs.

Copying a Formula Using the Fill Handle

1. Click the cell.
2. Drag the fill handle 🔲 to copy the formula to the desired cells.

Creating a 3-D Reference in a Formula

1. Click the cell where you want to enter the formula.
2. To enter a cell reference or range from another worksheet, click the sheet tab, select the cell or range of cells, and press **Enter**.

OR

- Type the sheet name and cell reference or range address directly in the formula using the following guidelines:

    - Use an exclamation point (!) to separate the sheet name(s) from the cell reference(s); for example, *April!G41+September!G41*.

    - Use a colon (:) between sheet names to indicate a range of worksheets; for example, *April:June!B23:D45 or Sheet2:Sheet3!C21*.

    - Use single quotation marks surround a sheet name that contains a space for example, *'NW Region'D14+'SW Region'D14 or 'Tax 2001':'Tax 2003'G23*.

Displaying and Hiding Formulas

1. Click the **Formulas** tab.
   Formula Auditing Group
2. Click the **Show Formulas** button 🔳.
3. Click the **Show Formulas** button 🔳 again to hide formulas.

OR

- Press **Ctrl+`** to toggle formulas on and off.

Working with Functions

Using AutoSum Functions (SUM, AVERAGE, MAX, MIN, and COUNT)

1. Click the cell that will contain the function.
2. Click the **Home** tab.
   Editing Group
3. Click the **AutoSum** button Σ drop-down arrow.
   √ *To use the SUM function, simply click the AutoSum button.*
4. Click the function to use:

    - **Sum** to add a range.

    - **Average** to return the average of a range.

    - **Count Numbers** to return the number of entries in a range.

    - **Max** to return the greatest value in a range.

    - **Min** to return the lowest value in a range.

5. Type or select the range.
   √ *Range must be enclosed in parentheses.*
6. Press **Enter**, **Tab**, or an arrow key to complete the entry.

OR

- Click the **Enter** button ✔ on the formula bar.

Inserting Other Functions

1. Click the cell in which you want to enter the function.
2. Click the **Formulas** tab.
   Function Library Group
3. Click one of the function category buttons and click the desired function from the menu.

OR

- Click the **More Functions** button 🔳, point to a category, and click the desired function.

Using the NOW Function to Display a System Date

1. Click the cell in which you want to insert the date.
2. Type **=NOW()**.
3. Press **Enter**.

Inserting an IF Function

1. Click the cell in which you want to enter the function.
2. Click the **Formulas** tab.
   Function Library Group
3. Click the **Logical** button 🔲.
4. Click **IF**.
5. Complete the Function Arguments dialog.
6. Click **OK**.

Using SUMIF() and SUMIFS() Functions

1. Click the cell in which you want to enter the function.
2. Click the **Insert Function** button 🔲 on the formula bar.
3. Click the **Or select a category** drop-down arrow.
4. Click **Math & Trig**.
5. In the Select a function list, click **SUMIF** or **SUMIFS**.
6. Click **OK**.
7. Complete the Function Arguments dialog box.
8. Click **OK**.

Using COUNTIF() and COUNTIFS() Functions

1. Click the cell in which you want to enter the function.
2. Click the **Insert Function** button 🔲 on the formula bar.
3. Click the **Or select a category** drop-down arrow.
4. Click **Statistical**.
5. In the Select a function list, click **COUNTIF** or **COUNTIFS**.
6. Click **OK**.
7. Complete the Function Arguments dialog box.
8. Click **OK**.

Inserting the VLOOKUP Function

1. Click the cell where you want to enter the function.
2. Type **=VLOOKUP(**.
√ *The function's syntax appears in a ScreenTip underneath the selected cell.*
3. Type the desired values for each argument.
√ *Type a comma to separate arguments.*
4. Type the closing parenthesis and press **Enter**.

Inserting an HLOOKUP Function Using the Function Wizard

1. Click the cell where you want to enter the function.
2. Type **=HLOOKUP(**.
3. Click the **Insert Function** button 🔲 on the formula bar.
4. In the Function Arguments dialog box, enter the desired values for each argument.
5. Click **OK**.

Using the GROWTH Function

1. Click the cell where you will enter the function.
2. Type **=GROWTH(**.
3. Enter the function arguments as necessary.
4. Type the closing parenthesis and press **Enter**.
8. Click **OK**.

Using the FORECAST Function

1. Click the cell where you will enter the function.
2. Type **=FORECAST(**.
3. Enter the function arguments as necessary.
4. Type the closing parenthesis and press **Enter**.

Using the TREND Function

1. Click the cell where you will enter the function.
2. Type **=TREND(**.
3. Enter the function arguments as necessary.
4. Type the closing parenthesis and press **Enter**.

Using the PMT Function

1. Click the cell where you will enter the function.
2. Type **=PMT(**.
3. Enter the interest rate per period for the loan as the first argument.
√ *Type a comma to separate arguments.*
4. Enter the total number of payments for the loan as the second argument.
5. Enter the present value, or total amount that a series of future payments is worth now, as the third argument.
6. Press **Enter**.

OR

1. Click the cell where you will enter the function.
2. Click the **Formulas** tab.
   Function Library Group
3. Click the **Financial** button 🔲.
4. Click **PMT** on the menu.
5. In the Rate text box, enter the interest rate per period for the loan.
6. In the Nper text box, enter the total number of payments for the loan.
7. In the Pv text box, enter the present value, or total amount that a series of future payments is worth now.

Previewing and Printing a Worksheet

Previewing and Printing a File

1. Click the **File** tab.
2. Click **Print**.
   √ *In Backstage view, print settings display on the left, and a preview of the file displays on the right.*
3. Use the **Next Page** and **Previous Page** arrows under the preview to view other pages
4. Use the **Zoom** controls under the preview to adjust the preview magnification.
5. Click the **Print** button .

Changing Print Options

1. Click the **File** tab.
2. Click **Print**.
   √ *In Backstage view, print settings display on the left, and a preview of the file displays on the right.*
3. Under Print, enter the number of copies.
4. Under Printer, select the printer to use.
   √ *Click Printer Properties to set options for the selected printer.*
5. Under Settings, select options:
   - What to print.
   - Pages to print.
   - One sided or two sided printing
   - Collated or Uncollated
   - Landscape or Portrait orientation
   - Page Size
   - Margin width
   - Pages per sheet
   √ *Click Page Setup to open the program's Page Setup dialog box for additional options.*
6. Click the Print button .

Printing a Selection

1. Select the range you want to print.
2. Click **File**.
3. Click **Print**.
4. In Backstage view, under Settings, click the first drop-down arrow.
5. Click **Print Selection**.
6. Click the **Print** button .

Printing Titles

1. Click the **Page Layout** tab.
   Page Setup Group
2. Click the **Print Titles** button .
3. In the Page Setup dialog box, on the Sheet tab, click in the **Rows to repeat at top** text box or the **Columns to repeat at left** text box.
4. Type the range address of the row(s) or columns to repeat.
   OR
   a. Click the **Collapse Dialog** button and select the range to repeat.
   b. Click the **Expand Dialog** button to return to the dialog box.
5. Click **OK**.

Printing All the Worksheets in a Workbook

1. Click **File**.
2. Click **Print**.
3. In Backstage view, under Settings, click the first drop-down arrow.
4. Click **Print Entire Workbook**.
5. Click the **Print** button .

Setting the Print Area

1. Switch to Page Break Preview.
2. Select the range to print.
3. Click the **Page Layout** tab.
   Page Setup Group
4. Click the **Print Area** button .
5. Click **Set Print Area**.

Clearing the Print Area

1. Click the **Page Layout** tab.
   Page Setup Group
2. Click the **Print Area** button .
3. Click **Clear Print Area**.

Repeating Row and Column Labels

1. Click the **Page Layout** tab.
   Page Setup Group
2. Click the **Print Titles** button .
3. In the Page Setup dialog box, on the Sheet tab, click the **Collapse Dialog** button on the Rows to repeat at top box.
4. Select the rows to repeat.
5. Click the **Expand Dialog** button .
6. Repeat steps 3-5 to specify the columns to repeat in the Columns to repeat at left box.
7. Click **OK**.

Printing Gridlines

1. Click the **Page Layout** tab.
   Sheet Options Group
2. Under Gridlines, click to mark the **Print** box.

Working with Page Breaks

Setting Manual Page Breaks
1. Click the cell below and to the right of where you want to insert the page break.
2. Click the **Page Layout** tab.
   Page Setup Group
3. Click the **Breaks** button.
4. Click **Insert Page Break**.

Using Page Break Preview
1. Click the **View** tab.
   Workbook Views Group
2. Click the **Page Break Preview** button.

OR

- Click the **Page Break Preview** button on the status bar.

Changing a Page Break Manually
1. Switch to Page Break Preview.
2. Drag the dashed line to the desired location.

Removing Page Breaks
1. Switch to Page Break Preview.
2. Drag the solid line to the margin and off the worksheet.

OR

1. Click the cell below or to the right of the page break.
2. Click the **Page Layout** tab.
   Page Setup Group
3. Click the **Breaks** button.
4. Click **Remove Page Break**.

Formatting Worksheets

Selecting a Preset Margin
1. Click the **Page Layout** tab.
   Page Setup Group
2. Click the **Margins** button.
3. Click the desired margin setting.

Setting Custom Margins
1. Click the **Page Layout** tab.
   Page Setup Group
2. Click the **Margins** button.
3. Click **Custom Margins**.
4. Under Margins, set the margins as desired.
5. Click **OK**.

Selecting a Paper Size
1. Click the **Page Layout** tab.
   Page Setup Group
2. Click the **Size** button.
3. Click the desired page size.

Setting Page Orientation
1. Click the **Page Layout** tab.
   Page Setup Group
2. Click the **Orientation** button.
3. On the menu, click the desired orientation.

Scaling to Fit
1. Click the **Page Layout** tab.
   Scale to Fit Group
2. Click the **Scale to Fit** dialog box launcher.
3. In the Page Setup dialog box, on the Page tab, click the **Fit to** button.
4. Adjust the Fit to settings as desired.
5. Click **OK**.

Inserting a Built-in Header or Footer

Using the Insert Tab
1. Click the **Insert** tab.
   Text Group
2. Click the **Header & Footer** button.
3. Click in the placeholders and type the desired header or footer text.

OR

3. Click the **Header & Footer Design Tools** tab.
4. Click the **Header** button or the **Footer** button.
5. From the gallery, select the desired style.

OR

3. Click the **Header & Footer Design Tools** tab.
   Header & Footer Elements Group
4. Click an element to insert it as desired.

Using Page Layout View
1. Switch to Page Layout view, if necessary.
2. Click a placeholder in either the header or footer area.
3. Click the **Header & Footer Tools Design** tab.
   Header & Footer Group
4. Click the **Header** button or the **Footer** button.
5. Click the desired built-in option from the menu.

Using the Page Setup Dialog Box
1. Click the **Page Layout** tab.
2. Click the Page Setup dialog box launcher ▣.
3. In the Page Setup dialog box, click the **Header/Footer** tab.
4. Click the **Header** drop-down arrow or the **Footer** drop-down arrow.
5. Click the desired header or footer.
6. Click **OK**.

Inserting a Custom Header and Footer

Using Page Layout View
1. Switch to Page Layout view, if necessary.
2. Click the desired placeholder in either the header or footer area.
3. Type the desired text in the placeholder.

OR

3. Click the **Header & Footer Tools Design** tab.
   Header & Footer Elements Group
4. Click a button to insert the desired element.

Using the Page Setup Dialog Box
1. Click the **Page Layout** tab.
2. Click the Page Setup dialog box launcher ▣.
3. In the Page Setup dialog box, click the **Header/Footer** tab.
4. Click the **Custom Header** button or the **Custom Footer** button.
5. In the Header dialog box or the Footer dialog box, type the desired text or use the buttons to enter information in the Left section, Center section, and Right section boxes as desired.
6. Click **OK**.

Changing the Font of a Header or Footer
1. Switch to Page Layout view.
2. Select the text in the header or footer section whose font you want to change.
3. Click the **Home** tab.
   Font Group
4. Use buttons in the Font group to change the font and other formatting as desired.

Working with Excel Tables

Creating a Table
1. Click in the range of data that will make up the table.
2. Click the **Insert** tab.
   Tables Group
3. Click the **Table** button ▦.
4. In the Create Table dialog box, verify the range containing the table data.
5. Click **OK**.

Applying a Table Style
1. Click any cell in the table.
2. Click the **Table Tools Design** tab.
   Table Styles Group
3. Click the Table Styles **More** button ▾.
4. Click the desired table style.

Inserting a Total Row
1. Click any cell in the table.
2. Click the **Table Tools Design** tab.
   Table Style Options Group
3. Click the **Total Row** check box.

Converting a Table to a Range
1. Click any cell in the table.
2. Click the **Table Tools Design** tab.
   Tools Group
3. Click the **Convert to Range** button ▣.
4. Click **Yes** in the dialog box to confirm the conversion.

Sorting and Filtering Data

Sorting Rows
1. Click anywhere in column by which you want to sort.
2. Click the **Home** tab.
   Editing Group
3. Click the **Sort & Filter** button ⧖.
4. Click **Sort A to Z** to sort in ascending order.

OR

- Click **Sort Z to A** to sort in descending order.

Filtering Rows
1. Click anywhere in column by which you want to filter.
2. Click the **Home** tab.
   Editing Group
3. Click the **Sort & Filter** button ⧖.
4. Click **Filter**.
5. Click the down arrow on column header.
6. Click to select the column entries you want to display and to clear those you want to hide.
7. Click **OK**.

Sorting a Table
1. Click the down arrow on the desired table column header.
2. From the menu, click the desired sort option.

OR

1. Click the **Data** tab.
   Sort & Filter Group
2. Click the **Sort** button ▦.
3. In the Sort dialog box, set the sort options as desired.
4. Click **OK**.

Filtering a Table
1. Click the down arrow on the desired table column header.
2. From the menu, click to mark the desired column entries you want included in the filter.

Managing Worksheets

Inserting a Worksheet

1. Click the **Insert Worksheet** tab [icon] next to insert a new sheet that follows the existing sheets.

OR

1. Click the **Home** tab.
   Cells Group
2. Click the **Insert** drop-down arrow [icon].
3. Click **Insert Sheet**.

Renaming a Worksheet

1. Right-click the sheet tab.
2. Click **Rename** on the shortcut menu.
3. Type the new sheet name.

Deleting a Worksheet

1. Click the **Home** tab.
   Cells Group
2. Click the **Delete** drop-down arrow [icon].
3. Click **Delete Sheet**.

OR

1. Right-click the sheet tab.
2. Click **Delete** on the shortcut menu.

Moving or Copying a Worksheet

1. Right-click the sheet tab.
2. Click **Move or Copy** on the shortcut menu.
3. In the Move or Copy dialog box, specify where you want to move the sheet and if you want to create a copy of the sheet.
4. Click **OK**.

Changing the Color of a Worksheet Tab

1. Right-click the sheet tab.
2. Point to **Tab Color** on the shortcut menu.
3. Click the desired color in the color palette.

Hiding a Sheet

1. Click the tab of the sheet you want to hide.
2. Click the **Home** tab.
   Cells Group
3. Click the **Format** button [icon].
4. Click **Hide & Unhide**.
5. Click **Hide Sheet**.

Unhiding a Sheet

1. Click the **Home** tab.
   Cells Group
2. Click the **Format** button [icon].
3. Click **Hide & Unhide**.
4. Click **UnHide Sheet**.

Grouping Worksheets

1. Click the tab of the first sheet in the group.
2. Hold down **Shift** and click adjacent sheets you want to include in the group.

OR

- Hold down **Ctrl** and click noncontiguous sheets you want to include in the group.

Working with Charts

Creating a Chart

1. Select the range of data you want to chart.
2. Click the **Insert** tab.
   Charts Group
3. Click the desired chart category button.
4. In the gallery, click the chart style.

Deleting a Chart

1. Click the chart to select it.
2. Press **Delete**.

Resizing a Chart

1. Click the chart to select it.
2. Position the pointer on a corner handle.
3. When the pointer changes to [icon], drag to the desired size.

Moving a Chart

1. Click the chart to select it.
2. When the pointer changes to [icon], drag to the desired location.

Moving a Chart to a Chart Sheet

1. Click the chart to select it.
2. Click the **Chart Tools Design** tab.
   Location Group
3. Click the **Move Chart** button [icon].
4. In the Move Chart dialog box, click **New Sheet**.
5. Type the name of the sheet, if desired.
6. Click **OK**.

Copying a Chart

1. Click the chart to select it.
2. Click the **Home** tab.
   Clipboard Group
3. Click the **Copy** button [icon].
4. Click the location to which you want to copy the chart.
5. Click the **Home** tab.
   Clipboard Group
6. Click the **Paste** button [icon].

Changing Chart Type

1. Click the chart to select it.
2. Click the **Chart Tools Design** tab.

Type Group

3. Click the **Change Chart Type** button 📊.
4. In the Change Chart Type dialog box, click the type of chart to which you want to change.
5. Click the chart style.
6. Click **OK**.

Applying a Chart Layout

1. Click the chart to select it.
2. Click the **Chart Tools Design** tab.

Chart Layouts Group

3. Click the Chart Layouts **More** button ▾.
4. Click the desired layout from the gallery.

Applying a Chart Style

1. Click the chart to select it.
2. Click the **Chart Tools Design** tab.

Chart Styles Group

3. Click the Chart Styles **More** button ▾.
4. Click the desired layout from the gallery.

Resizing a Chart Element

1. Click the chart to select it.
2. Click the chart element you want to resize.
3. Drag a corner sizing handle to resize the element as desired.

Moving a Chart Element

1. Click the chart to select it.
2. Click the chart element you want to move.
3. Position the mouse pointer on the border of the element.
4. When the pointer changes to 📍, drag the element to the desired location.

Deleting a Chart Element

1. Click the chart to select it.
2. Click the chart element.
3. Press **Delete**.

Changing Chart Text

1. Click the placeholder for the chart title you want to change.
2. Click the **Chart Tools Layout** tab.

Labels Group

- To change the chart title, click the **Chart Title** button 📊.

- To change the axis titles, click the **Axis Titles** button 📊.

3. Click the desired option on the menu.

Enhancing the Chart Plot Area

1. Click the chart to select it.
2. Click the **Chart Tools Layout** tab.

Current Selection Group

3. Click the **Chart Elements** drop-down arrow.
4. Click **Plot Area**.
5. Click the **Chart Tools Layout** tab.

Current Selection Group

6. Click the **Format Selection** button 📊.
7. In the Format Plot Area dialog box, click the formats as desired.
8. Click **Close**.

Formatting Category and Value Axes

1. Click the chart to select it.
2. Click the **Chart Tools Layout** tab.

Axes Group

3. Click the **Axes** button 📊.
4. Point to the desired axis on the menu.
5. Click the desired format for the axis on the submenu.

Changing Data Series Orientation

1. Click the chart to select it.
2. Click the **Chart Tools Design** tab.

Data Group

3. Click the **Switch Row/Column** button 📊.

Creating a Line Chart to Compare Data

1. Select the ranges to be charted.
2. Click the **Insert** tab.

Chart Group

3. Click the **Line** button 📊.
4. Click the **Line with Markers** line chart style.

Printing a Chart

1. Click the tab of the sheet containing the chart.
2. Click **File**.
3. Click **Print**.
4. Examine the preview and adjust print settings as desired.
5. Click the **Print** button 📊.

Publishing a Chart to the Internet/Intranet

1. Click the tab of the sheet containing the chart.
2. Click **File**.
3. Click **Save As**.
4. In the Save As dialog box, navigate to the location where you want to save the file.
5. Click the **Save as type** drop-down arrow.
6. Click **Single File Web Page**.
7. If desired, click the **Change Title** button.
8. Type the page title and click **OK**.
9. In the Save As dialog box, click **Selection: Chart**.
10. Click **Publish**.
11. In the Publish as Web Page dialog box, verify the publish settings.
12. Click **Publish**.

Pasting a Picture of a Chart

1. Click the chart to select it.
2. Click the **Home** tab.
   Clipboard Group
3. Click the **Copy** button.
4. Click in the destination where you want to paste the chart.
5. Click the **Paste** button.
6. Click the **Paste Options** button at the lower right of the chart.
7. Click the **Picture** button.

Creating an Organization Chart

1. Click the **Insert** tab.
   Illustrations Group
2. Click the **SmartArt** button.
3. In the Choose a SmartArt Graphic dialog box, click **Hierarchy**.
4. Click the desired layout.
5. Click **OK**.
6. Use the Text Pane if desired to enter text in the placeholders.

Using Sparklines to Chart Trends

1. Select the range containing the trend data.
2. Click the **Insert** tab.
   Sparklines Group
3. Click the desired Sparkline button as follows:
   - **Insert Line Sparkline** to show the trend in a line chart
   - **Insert Column Sparkline** to show the trend in a column chart
   - **Insert Win/Loss Sparkline** to show the trend in a Win/Loss chart.
4. In the Create Sparklines dialog box, click in the **Location Range** text box and type the cell address where you want to place the Sparkline.
5. Click **OK**.

Embedding and Linking Charts

Embedding a Chart in another File
1. Click the chart to select it.
2. Click the **Home** tab.
   Clipboard Group
3. Click the **Copy** button.
4. Click in the destination document where you want to paste the chart.
5. Click the **Home** tab.
   Clipboard Group
6. Click the **Paste** button.
7. Click the **Paste Options** button.
8. Click the **Keep Source Formatting & Embed Workbook** button.

Linking a Chart
1. Click the chart to select it.
2. Click the **Home** tab.
   Clipboard Group
3. Click the **Copy** button.
4. Click in the destination document where you want to paste the chart.
5. Click the **Home** tab.
   Clipboard Group
6. Click the **Paste** button.
7. Click the **Paste Options** button.
8. Click the **Use Destination Theme & Link Data** button.

Editing a Linked or Embedded Chart
1. Double-click the chart.
2. Edit the chart.
OR
1. Right-click a linked or embedded chart and click **Edit Data**.
2. Edit the data.

Updating Links Manually
1. Right-click the linked data.
2. Click **Update Link** on the shortcut menu.

Saving a Worksheet or Workbook as a Web Page

1. Click **File**.
2. Click **Save As**.
3. In the Save As dialog box, navigate to the location where you want to save the file.
4. Type the file name in the File name box.
5. Click the **Save as type** drop-down arrow.
6. Click **Single File Web Page**.

OR

   Click **Web Page**.
7. If desired, click the **Change Title** button, type the title, and click **OK**.
8. Click **Publish**.
9. In the Publish as Web Page dialog box, verify the item to publish, and click **Publish**.

Embedding Excel Data in a PowerPoint Presentation

1. Select the Excel data you want to embed.
2. Click the **Home** tab.
   Clipboard Group
3. Click the **Copy** button ▣.
4. Click the slide in the presentation on which you want to embed the data.
5. Click the PowerPoint **Home** tab.
   Clipboard Group
6. Click the **Paste** button drop-down arrow ▣.
7. Click **Paste Special**.
8. In the Paste Special dialog box, click **Microsoft Excel Worksheet Object**.
9. Click **OK**.

Linking Excel Data in a PowerPoint Presentation

1. Select the Excel data you want to embed.
2. Click the **Home** tab.
   Clipboard Group
3. Click the **Copy** button ▣.
4. Click the slide in the presentation on which you want to embed the data.
5. Click the PowerPoint **Home** tab.
   Clipboard Group
6. Click the **Paste** button drop-down arrow ▣.
7. Click **Paste Special**.
8. In the Paste Special dialog box, click **Microsoft Excel Worksheet Object**.
9. Click the **Paste link** button.
10. Click **OK**.

Editing Embedded Data

1. Double-click the embedded data.
2. The source program's Ribbon appears which you can use to edit the data as desired.

Editing Linked Data

1. Double-click the linked data.
2. The source program opens in which you can edit the data as desired.

Linking Workbooks Using Paste Link

1. Select the data to copy.
2. Click the **Home** tab.
   Clipboard Group
3. Click the **Copy** button ▣.
4. Click where you want to paste the data.
5. Click the **Home** tab.
   Clipboard Group
6. Click the **Paste** drop-down arrow ▣.
7. Click the **Paste Link** button ▣.

OR

7. Click **Paste Special**.
8. In the Paste Special dialog box, click the **Paste link** button.
9. Click **OK**.

Starting Access and Creating a New Database

1. Click **Start** 🌐.
2. Point to **All Programs**.
3. Click **Microsoft Office**.
4. Click **Microsoft Access 2010**.
5. In the File Name box in the right pane, type the name of the new database.
6. Click the **Browse** button 📂and navigate to the location where you want to save the file.
7. Click **Create**.

Creating a Database

Creating a New, Blank Database

1. Click **File**.
2. Click **New**.
3. If necessary, click **Blank database**.
4. In the File Name box in the right pane, type the name of the new database.
5. Click the **Browse** button 📂and navigate to the location where you want to save the file.
6. Click **Create**.

Creating a New Database Using a Template

1. Click **File**.
2. Click **New**.
3. In Backstage view, click **Sample templates**.
4. Click the desired template.
5. In the File Name box, type the name for the new file.
6. Click the **Browse** button 📂 and navigate to the location where you want to save the database.
7. Click **Create**.

Changing the View

Collapsing and Expanding the Navigation Pane

1. In the database window, click ⫷ to collapse the Navigation pane.
2. Click ⫸ to expand the Navigation pane.

Changing the View of the Navigation Pane

1. If necessary, click ⫸ to expand the Navigation pane.
2. Click the down arrow button ⊙ at the top of the Navigation pane.
3. On the menu, click the desired view option.

Closing and Reopening the Field List

1. With the table open in Datasheet view, press **Alt+F8** to open the Field List task pane.
2. Click the **Close** button ⊠ to close the Field List task pane.

Saving a Database

Saving Changes to a Database

- Click the **Save** button 💾 on the Quick Access Toolbar.

OR

1. Click the **File** tab.
2. Click **Save**.

Saving a Copy of a Database

1. Click **File**.
2. Click **Save Database As**.
3. In the Save As dialog box, navigate to the location where you want to save the file.
4. In the File name box, type the database file name.
5. Click **Save**.

Opening a Database

Opening a Recently Used Database

1. Click **File**.
2. Click **Recent**.
3. Click the desired database to open it.

Opening a Saved Database

1. Click **File**.
2. Click **Open**.
3. In the Open dialog box, navigate to the file you want to open and select it.
4. Click **Open**.

Opening a Database Exclusively

1. Click **File**.
2. Click **Open**.
3. In the Open dialog box, navigate to and select the file to open.
4. Click the **Open** drop-down arrow.
5. Click **Open Exclusive**.

Closing a Database

1. Click **File**.
2. Click **Close Database**.

Managing Tables

Saving and Closing a Table
1. Right-click the table tab.
2. On the shortcut menu, click **Close**.

OR

- Click the **Close** button ☒ in the upper right corner of the datasheet.
3. In the message box, click **Yes** to save the table.
4. In the Save As box, type the table name.
5. Click **OK**.

Opening a Table
- In the Navigation pane, double-click the table.

Renaming a Table
1. In the Navigation pane, right-click the table you want to rename.
2. On the shortcut menu, click **Rename**.
3. Type the new table name and press **Enter**.

Creating Additional Tables
1. Click the **Create** tab.
   Tables Group
2. Click the **Table** button ▦.

Creating a Table with a Template
1. In the open database, click the **Create** tab.
   Templates Group
2. Click the **Application Parts** button ▤.
3. From the gallery, click **Tasks**.
4. In the Create Relationship dialog box, click the desired option.
5. Proceed through the dialog box prompts as necessary.

Creating a Field in a Datasheet
1. In the open datasheet, click **Click to Add**.
2. Click the desired field type on the menu.
3. Type the field name and press **Enter**.

Adding Records to a Table
1. Click in the first field.
2. Type the field entry.
3. Press **Tab** to move to the next field.

Editing Field Data
- Double-click the field entry and type the replacement entry.
- Click the field entry, position the insertion point where desired, and type the edits or press **Backspace** or **Delete** to delete characters.
- Position the mouse pointer in the upper left corner of the field entry. When it changes to ⊕, click to select the entire field. Press **Backspace** or **Delete** to delete the entry, or type the replacement entry.

Selecting Records
- Click the record selector ➡ to select the desired record.
- To select multiple records, click the record selector ➡ of the first record, hold **Shift**, and click the record selector of adjacent records.
- Press **Ctrl+A** to select all records.

Deleting Records
1. Click the record selector ➡ of the record you want to delete.
2. Press **Delete**.
3. In the message box, click **Yes** to confirm the deletion.

Managing Fields in Datasheet View

Changing the Field Type
1. In Datasheet view, click in the desired field.
2. Click the **Table Tools Fields** tab.
   Formatting Group
3. Click the **Data Type** drop-down arrow.
4. On the menu, click the desired field type.

Making a Field Required
1. In Datasheet view, click in the desired field.
2. Click the **Table Tools Fields** tab.
   Field Validation Group
3. Click the **Required** check box.

Making a Field Unique
1. In Datasheet view, click in the desired field.
2. Click the **Table Tools Fields** tab.
   Field Validation Group
3. Click the **Unique** check box.

Adding a Field by Right-Clicking
1. Right-click the field that will be to the right of the new field.
2. On the shortcut menu, click **Insert Field**.

Adding a Field from the Ribbon
1. Click in the field that will be to the left of the new field.
2. Click the **Table Tools Fields** tab.
   Add & Delete Group
3. Click the button for the desired field type.

Renaming a Field

1. Double-click the field column heading.
2. Type the new name for the field and press **Enter**.

OR

1. Right-click the field column heading.
2. On the shortcut menu, click **Rename Field**.
3. Type the new name for the field and press **Enter**.

Moving a Column

1. Click the column heading of the field you want to move.
2. Click and hold the mouse button down and drag the field to the desired location.

Deleting a Field

1. Click the column heading of the field you want to delete.
2. Click the **Table Tools Fields** tab.

   Add & Delete Group

3. Click the **Delete** button ⬇.
4. In the message box, click **Yes** to confirm the deletion.

Hiding and Unhiding Columns

1. Right-click the column heading of the field you want to hide.
2. On the shortcut menu, click **Hide Fields**.
3. To unhide a column, right-click the column heading of any field.
4. On the shortcut menu, click **Unhide Fields**.
5. In the Unhide Columns dialog box, click to select the field you want to unhide.
6. Click **OK**.

Changing Datasheet Column Widths

1. Position the mouse pointer on the right border of the column heading.
2. When the pointer changes to ⬌, drag the column to the desired width.

OR

- Double-click the right border of the column heading to automatically resize the column width to accommodate the longest entry.

OR

1. Right click the column heading.
2. On the shortcut menu, click **Field Width**.
3. In the Column Width dialog box, enter the desired width.
4. Click **OK**.

Freezing Fields

1. Select the fields you want to freeze.
2. Right-click the selected fields.
3. On the shortcut menu, click **Freeze Fields**.
4. To unfreeze the fields, right-click the column heading of a field.
5. On the shortcut menu, click **Unfreeze All Fields**.

Importing Data

To an Existing Table

1. In the database window, click the **External Data** tab.

   Import & Link Group

2. Click the button for the type of data you want to import.
3. In the Get External Data dialog box, click the **Browse** button and navigate to the file you want to import.
4. Click the **Append a copy of the records to the table** button.
5. Click the drop-down arrow and select the desired table.
6. Click **OK**.
7. Select options as desired in the Import Wizard dialog boxes.

To a New Table

1. In the database window, click the **External Data** tab.

   Import & Link Group

2. Click the button for the type of data you want to import.
3. In the Get External Data dialog box, click the **Browse** button and navigate to the file you want to import.
4. Click the **Import the source data into a new table in the current database** button.
5. Click **OK**.
6. Select options as desired in the Import Wizard dialog boxes.

Working with Tables in Design View

Opening a Table in Design View
1. Right-click the table name in the Navigation pane.
2. On the shortcut menu, click **Design View**.

OR

1. With the table open in Datasheet view, right-click the table tab.
2. On the shortcut menu, click **Design View**.

Creating a Table in Design View
1. In the open database, click the **Create** tab.
   #### Tables Group
2. Click the **Table Design** button 🗔.
3. Set the field names, data types, and field properties.

Setting a Primary Key
1. Open the table in Design view.
2. Click the field you want to set as the primary key.
3. Click the **Table Tools Design** tab.
   #### Tools Group
4. Click the **Primary Key** button 🗝.

Inserting a Field
1. In Design view, click the field selector → of the field that will follow the new field.
2. Click the **Table Tools Design** tab.
   #### Tools Group
3. Click the **Insert Rows** button ⊒.

Moving a Field
1. In Design view, click the field selector → to the left of the desired field.
2. Holding the mouse button down, drag the field selector to the desired location in the field list.

Deleting a Field
1. In Design view, click the field selector → of the field you want to delete.
2. Click the **Table Tools Design** tab.
   #### Tools Group
3. Click the **Delete Rows** button ⊒.

Changing a Field's Data Type
1. In Design view, click the Data Type drop-down arrow of the desired field.
2. On the menu, click the desired data type.

Modifying a Field's Properties
1. In Design view, click the field selector → of the field whose properties you want to modify.
2. In the Field Properties pane, modify the properties as desired.

Previewing a Datasheet
1. Click **File**.
2. Click **Print**.
3. Click **Print Preview**.

Printing a Datasheet
1. Click **File**.
2. Click **Print**.
3. Click the **Print** button.
4. In the Print dialog box, select options as desired.
5. Click **OK**.

Modifying Database Properties
1. Click **File**.
2. In the right pane of Backstage view, click **View and edit database properties**.
3. In the Properties dialog box, modify properties as desired.
4. Click **OK**.

Protecting a Database

Setting a Database Password
1. Open the database exclusively (see preceding procedure).
2. Click **File**.
3. Click **Info**.
4. Click **Encrypt with Password**.
5. In the Set Database Password dialog box, type the password in the Password box.
6. Type the password again in the Verify box.
7. Click **OK**.

Opening a Password-Protected Database
1. Click **File**.
2. Click **Open**.
3. In the Open dialog box, navigate to and double-click the file to open.
4. In the Password Required dialog box, type the password.
5. Click **OK**.

Removing the Password from a Database
1. Open the database exclusively.
2. Click **File**.
3. Click **Info**.
4. Click **Decrypt Database**.
5. In the Unset Database Password dialog box, type the password.
6. Click **OK**.

Creating a Simple Query

1. In the open database, click the **Create** tab.
   Queries Group
2. Click the **Query Wizard** button.
3. In the New Query dialog box, click **Simple Query Wizard**.
4. Click **OK**.
5. In the Simple Query Wizard dialog box, click the **Tables/Queries** drop-down arrow.
6. Click the table or query on which the new query will be based.
7. Select fields from the Available Fields list box to move to the Selected Fields list box.
8. Click **Next**.
9. Enter the title for the query.
10. Click **Finish**.

Creating a Quick Form

1. In the Navigation pane, click the table on which you want to base the form.
2. Click the **Create** tab.
   Forms Group
3. Click the **Form** button.

Creating a Split Form

1. In the Navigation pane, click the table on which you want to base the form.
2. Click the **Create** tab.
   Forms Group
3. Click the **More Forms** button.
4. On the menu, click **Split Form**.

Creating a Multiple-Items Form

1. In the Navigation pane, click the table on which you want to base the form.
2. Click the **Create** tab.
   Forms Group
3. Click the **More Forms** button.
4. On the menu, click **Multiple Items**.

Entering Records in a Form

1. Click in the first field and type the field data.
2. Press **Tab** to move to the next field.

Sorting

Sorting Records in a Table

1. With the table open in Datasheet view, click in the field by which you want to sort the records.
2. Click the **Home** tab.
   Sort & Filter Group
3. Click the **Ascending** button to sort in ascending order or the **Descending** button to sort in descending order.

Removing a Sort

1. Click the **Home** tab.
   Sort & Filter Group
2. Click the **Remove Sort** button.

Sorting Using Multiple Fields

1. With the table open in Datasheet view, arrange the fields in the order you want to sort them.
2. Select the fields by which you want to sort.
3. Click the **Home** tab.
   Sort & Filter Group
4. Click the **Ascending** button to sort in ascending order or the **Descending** button to sort in descending order.

Filtering

Filtering by Selection

1. With the table open in Datasheet view, select the field value for which you want to filter.
2. Click the **Home** tab.
   Sort & Filter Group
3. Click the **Selection** button.
4. On the menu, click the desired filter option.

Removing a Filter

1. Click the **Home** tab.
   Sort & Filter Group
2. Click the **Toggle Filter** button.

Filtering by Form

1. With the table open in Datasheet view, click the **Home** tab.
   Sort & Filter Group
2. Click the **Advanced** button.
3. On the menu, click **Filter By Form**.
4. In the form, set filter options as desired.
5. Click the **Toggle Filter** button.

Saving a Filter as a Query

1. With the table open in Datasheet view, click the **Home** tab.

   Sort & Filter Group
2. Click the **Advanced** button ⊞.
3. On the menu, click **Filter By Form**.
4. In the form, set filter options as desired.
5. Click the **Toggle Filter** button ⊞.
6. Click the **Home** tab.

   Sort & Filter Group
7. Click the **Advanced** button ⊞.
8. On the menu, click **Save As Query**.
9. In the Save As Query dialog box, type the name of the query in the Query Name box.
10. Click **OK**.

Finding Data

1. With the table open in Datasheet view, click the **Home** tab.

   Find Group
2. Click the **Find** button ⊞.
3. In the Find and Replace dialog box, type the text you want to find in the Find What box.
4. Set the Look In, Match, and Search options as desired.
5. Click **Find Next**.

Replacing Data

1. With the table open in Datasheet view, click the **Home** tab.

   Find Group
2. Click the **Replace** button ⊞.
3. In the Find and Replace dialog box, type the text you want to find in the Find What box.
4. Type the replacement text in the Replace With box.
5. Set the Look In, Match, and Search options as desired.
6. Click **Find Next**.
7. Replace found text as desired.

Working with Queries

Creating a Query in Design View

1. In the database window, click the **Create** tab.

   Queries Group
2. Click the **Query Design** button ⊞.
3. In the Show Table dialog box, click the table or query on which the new query will be based.
4. Click **Add**.
5. In Query Design view, drag fields from the table window to the grid as desired.

   OR

   Click in the Field row in the query grid, click the drop-down arrow, and click the field to add.

   OR

   Double-click a field in the table window to add it to the grid.

Removing Fields from the Query

1. In the query grid, click on the thin gray bar above the desired field to select the column.
2. Press **Delete**.

   OR
1. In Query Design view, click on the thin gray bar above the desired field to select the column.
2. Click the **Query Tools Design** tab.

   Query Setup Group
3. Click the **Delete Columns** button ⊞.

Running a Query

1. In Query Design view, click the **Query Tools Design** tab.

   Results Group
2. Click the **Run** button ⊞.

Saving a Query

1. In Query Design view, click the **Save** button ⊞ on the Quick Access Toolbar.
2. In the Save As dialog box, type the query name.
3. Click **OK**.

Saving a Query with a Different Name

1. Open the query.
2. Click **File**.
3. Click **Save Object As**.
4. In the Save As dialog box, type the new name.
5. Click **OK**.

Printing a Query

1. With the query open in Datasheet view, click **File**.
2. Click **Print**.
3. Click the **Print** button.
4. In the Print dialog box, set the print options as desired.
5. Click **OK**.

Creating a Multi-Table Query

1. In the database window, click the **Create** tab.
   Queries Group
2. Click the **Query Design** button.
3. In the Show Table dialog box, double-click the tables on which the new query will be based.
4. Drag fields from the table windows to the grid as desired.

Sorting Query Results

1. Open the query in Design view.
2. In the query grid, click in the **Sort** row for the field on which you want to sort.
3. Click the drop-down arrow and click **Ascending** or **Descending**.

Reordering Fields in a Query

1. Open the query in Design view.
2. In the query grid, click the gray bar above the field you want to move.
3. Drag the field to the desired location.

Using All Fields of a Table

1. In the database window, click the **Create** tab.
   Queries Group
2. Click the **Query Design** button.
3. In the Show Table dialog box, double-click the table on which the new query will be based.
4. In the table window, double-click the asterisk (*****) at the top of the table field list.

Changing a Column Name

1. Open the query in Design view.
2. In the query grid, click in the **Field** row of the column you want to rename.
3. Position the insertion point to the left of the current field name.
4. Type the new name followed by a colon.

Specifying Criteria in a Query

1. Open the query in Design view.
2. In the query grid, click in the **Criteria** row for the desired field.
3. Type the criteria.

Filtering by an Undisplayed Field

1. Open the query in Design view.
2. In the query grid, click in the **Criteria** row for the desired field.
3. Type the criteria.
4. Click to clear the field's **Show** box .

Filtering for Null Values

1. Open the query in Design view.
2. In the query grid, click in the **Criteria** row for the desired field.
3. Type **Is Null**.

Using Wildcards and Operators in a Query

Using Wildcards

1. Open the query in Design view.
2. In the query grid, click in the **Criteria** row for the desired field.
3. Type the criteria, using:

   - asterisk (*****)to specify any number of characters
   - question mark (**?**)to specify a single character.

Using the Like Operator

1. Open the query in Design view.
2. In the query grid, click in the **Criteria** row for the desired field.
3. Type **Like**, followed by the criteria.

Using the Between…And Operator

1. Open the query in Design view.
2. In the query grid, click in the **Criteria** row for the desired field.
3. Type the criteria in the format, **Between** *criteria* **and** *criteria*.

Using the In Operator

1. Open the query in Design view.
2. In the query grid, click in the **Criteria** row for the desired field.
3. Type the criteria in the format, **In (criteria)**.

Using the Or Operator

1. Open the query in Design view.
2. In the query grid, click in the **Criteria** row for the desired field.
3. Type the criteria in the format, *criteria* **Or** *criteria*.

Using a Comparison Operator in a Query

1. Open the query in Design view.
2. In the query grid, click in the **Criteria** row for the desired field.
3. Type the criteria with comparison operator.

Creating a Calculated Field in a Table

1. Open the table in Design view.
2. Add a blank field where desired.
3. Click the **Data Type** drop-down arrow and click **Calculated**.
4. In the Expression Builder, select from the Expression Elements, Expression Categories, and Expression Values as desired.
5. Click **OK**.

Using Calculated Fields in a Query

1. Open the query in Design view.
2. In the query grid, click in a blank column and type the field name followed by a colon (:).
3. Click the **Query Tools Design** tab.
   ### Query Setup Group
4. Click the **Builder** button.
5. In the Expression Builder, select from the Expression Elements, Expression Categories, and Expression Values as desired.
6. If necessary, delete the Expr text.
7. Click **OK**.

Summarizing Data in Query Design View

1. Open the query in Design view.
2. Click the **Query Tools Design** tab.
   ### Show/Hide Group
3. Click the **Totals** button ∑.
4. In the query grid, click the **Total** row for the field whose values you want to summarize.
5. Click the drop-down arrow and click the desired summary option.

Summarizing with the Simple Query Wizard

1. In the database window, click the **Create** tab.
   ### Queries Group
2. Click the **Query Wizard** button.
3. In the New Query dialog box, click **Simple Query Wizard**.
4. Click **OK**.
5. In the Simple Query Wizard dialog box, click the **Tables/Queries** drop-down arrow.
6. Click the table or query on which the query will be based.
7. Select fields from the Available Fields list box to move to the Selected Fields list box.
8. Click **Next**.
9. Click **Summary**, and then click **Summary Options**.
10. In the Summary Options dialog box, click the options as desired.
11. Click **OK**.
12. Click **Next**.
13. Enter the desired title for the query.
14. Click **Finish**.

Creating a Form

Creating a Form with a Wizard

1. In the database window, click the **Create** tab.
   ### Forms Group
2. Click the **Form Wizard** button.
3. In the Form Wizard dialog box, select the table on which you want to base the form.
4. Select fields in the Available Fields list box and move them to the Selected Fields list box.
5. Click **Next**.
6. In the next dialog box, select the layout for the form.
7. Click **Next**.
8. In the next dialog box, enter the title for the form.
9. Click **Finish**.

Creating a Form in Layout View

1. In the Navigation pane, click the table on which you want to base the form.
2. Click the **Create** tab.
   ### Forms Group
3. Click the **Blank Form** button.
4. Drag the fields from the field list to the form layout as desired.

Creating a Form in Design View

1. Click the **Create** tab.
   ### Forms Group
2. Click the **Form Design** button.
3. Click the **Form Design Tools Design** tab.
   ### Tools Group
4. Click the **Add Existing Fields** button.
5. In the Field List pane, click **Show all tables**.
6. Expand the fields of the table that you want to add to the form.
7. Double-click the desired fields to add them to the form.

Managing Records in a Form

Adding a Record to a Table by Using a Form

1. In Form view, click the **New (blank) record** button ▶⃰ at the bottom of the form.
2. Type the record data in the fields.

Navigating Records in a Form

- Click the navigation buttons as follows:
  - First record ◄⃒
  - Previous record ◄
  - Next record ▶
  - Last record ▶⃒

Deleting a Record from a Form

1. In Form view, click in the record you want to delete.
2. Click the **Home** tab.
   Records Group
3. Click the **Delete** button ✕.
4. On the menu, click **Delete Record**.
5. In the message box, click **Yes** to confirm the deletion.

Applying a Theme to a Form

1. Open the form in Layout view.
2. Click the **Form Layout Tools Design** tab.
   Themes Group
3. Click the **Themes** button 🅰.
4. Click the desired theme from the gallery.

Printing a Form

1. In Form view, click **File**.
2. Click **Print**.
3. Click the **Print** button 🖶.
4. In the Print dialog box, set printing options as desired.
5. Click **OK**.

Modifying a Form

Selecting Form Fields in Layout View

1. Open the form in Layout view.
2. Click the desired field's text box to select it.
3. Hold down the Ctrl key to select multiple fields.

Changing the Form's Layout

1. Open the form in Layout view.
2. Click the **Format Layout Tools Arrange** tab.
   Table Group
3. Click the button of the desired layout as follows:
   - Gridlines 🎛
   - Stacked 🎛
   - Tabular 🎛

Changing the Form Size

1. Open the form in Design view.
2. Position the mouse pointer at the right edge of the form.
3. When the pointer changes to ⬌, drag to the desired size.

Resetting Tab Order

1. Open the form in Design view.
2. Click the **Form Design Tools Design** tab.
   Tools Group
3. Click the **Tab Order** button 🎛.
4. In the Tab Order dialog box, click a field and drag it to the desired position in the list.
5. Click **OK**.

Adding a Date Code

1. Open the form in Design view.
2. Click the **Form Design Tools Design** tab.
   Header/Footer Group
3. Click the **Date and Time** button 🗓.
4. In the Date and Time dialog box, select the desired format for the date and the time.
5. Click **OK**.

Inserting an Unbound Label

1. Open the form in Design view.
2. Click the **Form Design Tools Design** tab.
   Controls Group
3. Click the **Label** button 𝐴𝑎.
4. Click in the form where you want to insert the label.

Working with Form Sections

Selecting Sections of a Form

1. Open the form in Design view.
2. Click the bar of the section you want to select.

Displaying Sections

1. Open the form in Design view.
2. Right-click the form.
3. On the shortcut menu, click **Page Header/Footer** or **Form Header/Footer** to display the respective sections.

Resizing a Section

1. Click the bar of the section you want to resize.
2. Position the pointer on the top border of the bar.
3. When the pointer changes to ⬍, drag to the desired size.

Moving Controls Between Sections

1. Open the form in Design view.
2. Click the control you want to move.
3. Press **Ctrl+X**.
4. Click where you want to move the control.
5. Press **Ctrl+V**.

Managing Controls

Sizing a Control
1. Open the form in Layout view.
2. Click the control you want to resize.
3. Position the mouse pointer on the control's border.
4. When the pointer changes to ↔or ↕, drag to the desired size.

Moving Controls in a Layout
1. Open the form in Layout view.
2. Click the control you want to move.
3. Position the mouse pointer on the control's border.
4. When the pointer changes to ⬚, drag to the desired location.

Deleting a Control
1. Open the form in Layout view.
2. Click the control you want to delete.
3. Press **Delete**.

Adjusting the Control Margins
1. Open the form in Layout view.
2. Select the control you want to adjust.
3. Click the **Form Layout Tools Arrange** tab.
   Position Group
4. Click the **Control Margins** button ▣.
5. On the menu, click the desired setting.

Adjusting the Control Margins
1. Open the form in Layout view.
2. Select the control you want to adjust.
3. Click the **Form Layout Tools Arrange** tab.
   Position Group
4. Click the **Control Padding** button ▣.
5. On the menu, click the desired setting.

Changing Control Formatting
1. Open the form in Layout view.
2. Click the **Home** tab.
   Text Formatting Group
3. Select the formatting options from the Text Formatting group as desired.

Resizing Fields in Design View
1. Open the form in Design view.
2. Click the control you want to resize.
3. Position the mouse pointer on the control's sizing handle.
4. When the pointer changes to ↔or ↕, drag to the desired size.

Moving Fields on a Form
1. Open the form in Design view.
2. Click the control you want to move.
3. Position the mouse pointer on the control's border.
4. When the pointer changes to ⬚, drag to the desired location.

Creating a Report

Creating and Viewing a Tabular Report
1. In the Navigation pane, click the table or query on which you want to base the report.
2. Click the **Create** tab.
   Reports Group
3. Click the **Report** button ▤.
4. Click the **Report Design Tools Design** tab.
   Views Group
5. Click the **View** button drop-down arrow ▣.
6. Click **Report View**.

Creating a Report in Layout View
1. Click the **Create** tab.
   Reports Group
2. Click the **Blank Report** button ▢.
3. Click the **Report Layout Tools Design** tab.
   Tools Group
4. If necessary, click the **Add Existing Fields** button ▦.
5. In the Field List pane, click **Show all tables**.
6. Expand the fields of the table that you want to add to the report.
7. Double-click the desired fields to add them to the report.

Deleting Fields from a Report Layout
1. In Layout view, click the field you want to delete.
2. Click the **Report Layout Tools Arrange** tab.
   Rows & Columns Group
3. Click the **Select Column** button ▥.
4. Press **Delete**.

Changing Column Widths in a Report

1. In Layout view, click the field whose width you want to change.
2. Position the mouse pointer on the right edge of the selected field.
3. When the pointer changes to ↔, drag to the desired width.

Creating a Report Using the Report Wizard

1. Click the **Create** tab.
   ### Reports Group
2. Click the **Report Wizard** button.
3. In the Report Wizard dialog box, select the table on which you want to base the form.
4. Select fields in the Available Fields list box and move them to the Selected Fields list box.
5. Click **Next**.
6. In the next dialog box, select a grouping field if desired.
7. Click **Next**.
8. In the next dialog box, set a sort order if desired.
9. Click **Next**.
10. In the next dialog box, click the desired layout and orientation for the report.
11. Click **Next**.
12. In the next dialog box, enter the title for the report.
13. Click **Finish**.

Previewing and Printing a Report

1. With the report open, right-click its tab.
2. On the shortcut menu, click **Print Preview**.
3. Click the **Print Preview** tab.
   ### Print Group
4. Click the **Print** button.
OR
1. With the report open, click **File**.
2. Click **Print**.
3. Click the **Print** button.
4. In the Print dialog box, set print options as desired.
5. Click **OK**.
OR
1. With the report open, click **File**.
2. Click **Print**.
3. Click the **Quick Print** button.

Working with Report Sections

Selecting Sections of a Report
1. Open the report in Design view.
2. Click the bar of the section you want to select.

Resizing a Section
1. Click the bar of the section you want to resize.
2. Position the pointer on the top border of the bar.
3. When the pointer changes to ⊥, drag to the desired size.

Moving a Control Between Sections
1. Open the report in Design view.
2. Click the control you want to move.
3. Press **Ctrl+X**.
4. Click where you want to move the control.
5. Press **Ctrl+V**.

Modifying a Report

Adding Page Number Codes
1. Open the report in Design view.
2. Click the **Report Design Tools Design** tab.
   ### Header/Footer Group
3. Click the **Page Numbers** button.
4. In the Page Numbers dialog box, set the form, position, and alignment of the page numbers as desired.
5. Click **OK**.

Adding Sorting and Grouping
1. Open the report in Design view.
2. Click the **Report Design Tools Design** tab.
   ### Grouping & Totals Group
3. Click the **Group & Sort** button.
4. In the Group, Sort, and Total pane, select the sorting and grouping options as desired.

Adding a Calculated Field to a Report
1. Open the report in Design view.
2. Click the **Report Design Tools Design** tab.
   ### Controls Group
3. Click the **Text Box** button.
4. Click in the section where you want to insert the calculated field and drag to create the control.
5. If desired, delete the label associated with the text box.
6. Click in the text box and type the formula for the calculation you want to perform.

Changing the View

1. Click the **View** tab.
   Presentation Views Group
2. Click the desired View button:
   - **Normal** 🔳.
   - **Slide Sorter** 🔳.
   - **Notes Page** 🔳.
   - **Reading View** 📖.

OR

- Click a View icon on the status bar:
  - **Normal** 🔳.
  - **Slide Sorter** 🔳.
  - **Reading View** 📖.
  - **Slide Show** 🔳.

Showing and Hiding On Screen Elements

1. Click the **View** tab.
   Show Group
2. Click to select the checkbox for the element(s) to display:
   - **Ruler**
   - **Gridlines**
   - **Guides**
   √ *A check in the check box indicates the element is displayed.*

Adjusting Grid and Guide Settings

1. Click the **View** tab.
   Show Group
2. Click the **Show** dialog box launcher 🔳.
3. In the Grid and Guides dialog box, adjust the settings.
4. Click **OK**.

Using the Navigation Pane

Displaying Slides

- In the Navigation pane, click the **Slides** tab.
√ *Use the Navigation pane scroll bar to scroll up or down through the slides.*

Displaying the Outline

- In the Navigation pane, click the **Outline** tab.

Closing the Navigation Pane

- In the Navigation pane, click the **Close** button ⊠.

Displaying the Navigation Pane

1. Click the **View** tab.
   Presentation Views Group
2. Click the **Normal** button 🔳.

Navigating in the PowerPoint Window

Navigating in Slides View

1. In the Navigation Pane, click the **Slides** tab.
2. Click a slide to display it.
√ *Use the Navigation pane scroll bar to scroll up or down through the slides.*

OR

- On the bottom of the vertical scroll bar:
  - Click the **Previous Slide** button ⊡.
  - Click the **Next Slide** button ⊡.

OR

- Click the up or down scroll arrows on the vertical scroll bar.

Navigating in Reading View

1. On the status bar, click the **Reading View** button 🔳.
2. To scroll through the presentation, click the **Next** button ➡ or **Previous** button ⬅.

OR

1. Click the **Menu** button 🔳.
2. From the menu, click the desired option.

Switching between Open Presentations

- Click in the presentation window you want to make active.

OR

- Click the program's taskbar button and click the presentation you want to make active.

OR

1. Click the **View** tab.
   Window Group
2. Click the **Switch Windows** button 🔳.
3. Click the presentation you want to make active.

Arranging Multiple Presentations

1. Open all presentations.
2. Click the View tab.
   Window Group
3. Click the **Arrange All** button 🔳.

Entering and Editing Text

General Typing

- Press **Enter** to start a new paragraph.
- Press **Backspace** to delete one character to the left of the insertion point.
- Press **Delete** to delete one character to the right of the insertion point.

Typing in a Placeholder

1. Display the slide.
2. Click in the desired placeholder.
3. Type.

Typing in an Outline

1. Display the outline.
2. In the Navigation pane, click the slide where you want to enter text.
3. Type to enter a title.
4. Press **Ctrl + Enter** to start a new bullet line.

OR

- Press **Enter** to insert a new slide.

Typing Notes

1. Display the slide.
2. Click in the **Notes pane**.
3. Type.

OR

1. Display the slide.
2. Change to **Notes Page** view.
3. Click in the **Notes placeholder**.
4. Type.

Inserting a New Slide

Inserting a New Slide Using the Previously-Used Layout

1. Click the **Home** tab.
   Slides Group
2. Click the **New Slide** button ⬚.

Inserting a New Slide with a Different Layout

1. Click the **Home** tab.
   Slides Group
2. Click the **New Slide** button drop-down arrow ⬚ New Slide ▾.
3. From the gallery, click the desired layout.

Selecting in Presentation

Selecting Text

- Click and drag across the text you want to select.

Selecting Placeholders

- Click the placeholder you want to select.

Selecting Objects

- Click the object you want to select.

Selecting a Slide

- In the Navigation pane, click the slide you want to select.

Checking Spelling in a Presentation

1. Click the **Review** tab.
   Proofing Group
2. Click the **Spelling** button 🔤.
3. In the Spelling dialog box, click to **Change** or **Ignore** the suggestions.
4. Click **Close**.

OR

1. Right-click a word that has been identified as misspelled.
2. On the shortcut menu, click the desired spelling.

Finding and Replacing Text

Finding Text

1. Click the **Home** tab.
   Editing Group
2. Click the **Find** button 🔍.
3. In the Find dialog box, type the text you want to find.
4. Click **Find Next**.

Replacing Text

1. Click the **Home** tab.
   Editing Group
2. Click the **Replace** button 🔁.
3. In the Replace dialog box, enter the text to find in the Find what text box.
4. Enter the replacement text in the Replace with text box.
5. Click the **Replace** button to replace each separate occurrence; click **Replace All** to replace all occurrences.

Copying Text Formatting

1. Select the text or placeholder whose formatting you want to copy.
2. Click the **Home** tab.
   Clipboard Group
3. Click the **Format Painter** button 🖌.
4. Select the text or placeholder to which you want to copy the formatting.

Clearing Formatting

1. In the Slides tab, click the slide from which you want to clear the formatting.
2. Click the **Home** tab.
   Slides Group
3. Click the **Reset** button 🔄.

Aligning Text

1. Select the text or placeholder.
2. Click the **Home** tab.
   Paragraph Group
3. Click the desired alignment button:
   - Align Text Left
   - Center
   - Align Text Right
   - Justify

Adjusting Paragraph Spacing

1. Select the text.
2. Click the **Home** tab.
   Paragraph Group
3. Click the Paragraph Group dialog box launcher.
4. In the Paragraph dialog box, in the Spacing section, set the Before and After spacing as desired.
5. Click **OK**.

Adjusting Line Spacing

1. Select the text.
2. Click the **Home** tab.
   Paragraph Group
3. Click the **Line Spacing** button.
4. From the menu, click the desired spacing option.

OR

1. Select the text.
2. Click the **Home** tab.
   Paragraph Group
3. Click the Paragraph Group dialog box launcher.
4. In the Paragraph dialog box, click the **Line Spacing** drop-down arrow, and click the desired line spacing.
5. Click **OK**.

Using AutoFit Options

1. Select the placeholder.
2. Click the **AutoFit Options** button.
3. From the menu, click the desired option.

Adjusting and Formatting Placeholders

Adjusting Placeholders

1. Click the placeholder.
2. Click and drag a sizing handle to resize the placeholder.

Formatting Placeholders

1. Click the placeholder.
2. Click the **Home** tab.
   Drawing Group
3. Click the **Quick Styles** button.
4. From the gallery, click the desired style.

Inserting Symbols

1. Position the insertion point where you want to insert the symbol.
2. Click the **Insert** tab.
   Symbols Group
3. Click the **Symbol** button.
4. In the Symbol dialog box, click the **Font** drop-down arrow and click the desired font.
5. Click the desired symbol.
6. Click **Insert**.
7. Click **Close**.

Working with Lists

Changing a List Level

1. In the Navigation pane, click the **Outline** tab.
2. Click the line to change.
3. Click the **Home** tab.
   Paragraph Group
4. Click the **Decrease List Level** button to decrease the level.

OR

   - Click the **Increase List Level** button to increase the level.

Removing a Bullet

1. Click in the bulleted item you want to remove.
2. Click the **Home** tab.
   Paragraph Group
3. Click the **Bullets** button.

Changing a Bulleted List to a Numbered List

1. Drag across the entire bulleted list to select it.

OR

   - Click in the bulleted list and press **Ctrl+A**.
2. Click the **Home** tab.
   Paragraph Group
3. Click the **Numbering** button.

Modifying the Bulleted List Style

1. Drag across the entire bulleted list to select it.

OR

   - Click in the bulleted list and press **Ctrl+A**.
2. Click the **Home** tab.
   Paragraph Group
3. Click the **Bullets** drop-down arrow.
4. From the gallery, click the desired style or click **Bullets and Numbering**.
5. In the Bullets and Numbering dialog box, customize the list style as desired.
6. Click **OK**.

Using a Picture as a Bullet Character

1. Drag across the entire bulleted list to select it.

OR

- Click in the bulleted list and press **Ctrl+A**.

2. Click the **Home** tab.

Paragraph Group

3. Click the **Bullets** drop-down arrow ⬚.
4. From the gallery, click **Bullets and Numbering**.
5. In the Bullets and Numbering dialog box, customize the **Picture** button.
6. In the Picture Bullet dialog box, click the desired picture.
7. Click **OK**.

Changing the Bullets on a Slide Master

1. Click the **View** tab.

Master Views Group

2. Click the **Slide Master** button ⬚.
3. On the Slide Master slide, click the placeholder for the bulleted list.
4. Click the **Home** tab.

Paragraph Group

5. Click the **Bullets** drop-down arrow ⬚.
6. From the gallery, click the desired style or click **Bullets and Numbering**.
7. In the Bullets and Numbering dialog box, customize the list style as desired.
8. Click **OK**.

Changing the Bullets on a Layout Master

1. Click the **View** tab.

Master Views Group

2. Click the **Slide Master** button ⬚.
3. In the Slides pane, click the layout master whose list you want to change.
4. Click the placeholder for the bulleted list you want to change.
5. Click the **Home** tab.

Paragraph Group

6. Click the **Bullets** drop-down arrow ⬚.
7. From the gallery, click the desired style or click **Bullets and Numbering**.
8. In the Bullets and Numbering dialog box, customize the list style as desired.
9. Click **OK**.

Formatting the Slide Background

Changing a Slide Background Style

1. Click the **Design** tab.

Background Group

2. Click the **Background Styles** button ⬚.
3. From the gallery, click the desired style.

Hiding Background Graphics

1. Click the **Design** tab.

Background Group

2. Click the **Hide Background Graphics** button ⬚.

Applying a Background Fill Color

1. Click the **Design** tab.

Background Group

2. Click the Background Group dialog box launcher ⬚.
3. In the Format Background dialog box, click **Fill** in the left pane.
4. Select the fill options as desired.
5. Click **Close**.

Formatting a Slide Background with a Picture

1. Click the **Design** tab.

Background Group

2. Click the Background Group dialog box launcher ⬚.
3. In the Format Background dialog box, click **Fill** in the left pane.
4. From the Fill options, click **Picture or texture fill**.
5. Under Insert from, click the **File** button.
6. Navigate to the location where the picture file is stored.
7. Click the picture and click **Insert**.
8. In the Format Background dialog box, click **Close**.

Resetting the Slide Background

1. Click the **Design** tab.

Background Group

2. Click the **Background Styles** button ⬚.
3. From the gallery, click **Reset Slide Background**.

Changing a Slide Layout

1. In Navigation pane, select the slide to change.
2. Click the **Home** tab.

Slides Group

3. Click the **Layout** button ⬚ Layout ▾.
4. From the gallery, click the desired layout.

Printing a Presentation

Previewing and Printing All Slides
1. Click the **File** tab.
2. Click **Print**.
   √ *In Backstage view, print settings display on the left, and a preview of the current slide displays on the right.*
2. Use the **Next Page** and **Previous Page** arrows under the preview to view other pages
3. Use the **Zoom** controls under the preview to adjust the preview magnification.
4. Click the **Print** button ⎙.

Changing Print Options
1. Click the **File** tab.
2. Click **Print**.
3. Under Print, enter the number of copies.
4. Under Printer, select the printer to use.
   √ *Click **Printer Properties** to set options for the selected printer.*
5. Under Settings, select options:
   - Which slides to print.
   - What to print (Slides, Notes, Outline, or handouts).
   - One sided or two sided printing
   - Collated or Uncollated.
   - Landscape or Portrait Orientation (not available when printing full page slides).
   - Color, Grayscale, or Pure Black and White
   √ *Click **Edit Header & Footer** to open the Header and Footer dialog box for additional options.*
6. Click the **Print** button ⎙.

Managing Slides

Copying Slides
1. In Slide Sorter view or in the Navigation pane, click the slide you want to copy.
2. Click the **Home** tab.
   Clipboard Group
3. Click the **Copy** button 🖻.
4. Click between the slides where you want to place the copy.
5. Click the **Home** tab.
   Clipboard Group
6. Click the **Paste** button 📋.

Duplicating Slides
1. In Slide Sorter view or in the Navigation pane, click the slide you want to duplicate.
2. Click the **Home** tab.
   Clipboard Group
3. Click the **Copy** drop-down arrow 🖻.
4. On the menu, click **Duplicate**.

Deleting Slides
1. In Slide Sorter view or in the Navigation pane, click the slide you want to delete.
2. Press **Delete**.

Rearranging Slides

In Slide Sorter View
1. In the status bar, click the **Slide Sorter** button ▦.
2. In Slide Sorter view, click the slide you want to move.
3. Drag the selected slide to the new location.

In the Navigation Pane
1. In the Navigation pane, click the slide you want to move.
2. Drag the selected slide to the new location.

Creating Slides from Existing Sources

Creating a Presentation from an Existing Outline
1. Click **File**.
2. Click **Open**.
3. In the Open dialog box, click the **All PowerPoint Presentations** drop-down arrow.
4. Click **All Files**.
5. Navigate to the outline file you want to open.
6. Click the file and click **Open**.

Adding Slides from an Outline to a Presentation
1. Click the **Home** tab.
   Slides Group
2. Click the **New Slide** drop-down arrow 🖼.
3. Click **Slides from Outline**.
4. In the Insert Outline dialog box, navigate to the location where the outline file is stored.
5. Click the outline file and click **Insert**.

Reusing Slides from Other Presentations
1. Click the **Home** tab.
   Slides Group
2. Click the **New Slide** drop-down arrow 🖼.
3. Click **Reuse Slides**.
4. In the Reuse Slides task pane, click the **Browse** button.
5. On the menu, click **Browse File**.
6. Navigate to the location where the file containing the slides you want to reuse is stored.
7. Click the file and then click **Open**.
8. In the Reuse Slides task pane, click the slide you want to reuse to insert it in the presentation.

Resetting a Slide

1. Select the slide(s) you want to reset.
2. Click the **Home** tab.
   Slides Group
3. Click the **Reset** button ⊞.

Adding Slide Transitions

1. Click the slide to which you want to add the transition.
2. Click the **Transitions** tab.
   Transition to This Slide Group
3. Click the Transition to This Slide **More** button ⊡.
4. From the gallery, click the desired transition.

Adding Transition Effects

1. Click the slide with the transition.
2. Click the **Transitions** tab.
   Transition to This Slide Group
3. Click the **Effect Options** button.
4. From the menu, click the desired effect.

Controlling Slide Advance

1. Display the presentation in Slide Sorter view.
2. Click the **Transitions** tab.
   Timing Group
3. From the Advance Slide options, click **On Mouse Click**, or click the **After** box and set the timing as desired.

Applying Animations

Applying Entrance Effects Using the Animation Gallery

1. Select a placeholder or object to which you want to apply the animation.
2. Click the **Animations** tab.
   Animation Group
3. Click the Animation **More** button ⊡.
4. From the gallery, click the desired animation.

Setting Effect Options

1. Select the placeholder or object to which you have applied the animation.
2. Click the **Animations** tab.
   Animation Group
3. Click the **Effect Options** button ☆.
√ *The graphic on your Effect Options button will depend on the animation already applied to the object or placeholder.*
4. From the gallery, click the desired effect.

Using the Animation Painter

1. Select the placeholder or object with the animation you want to copy.
   Advanced Animation Group
2. Click the **Animation Painter** button ✦.
3. Click the placeholder or object to which you want to apply the animation.

Applying Animation to Objects and SmartArt Graphics

1. Select the graphic or object to which you want to apply the animation.
2. Click the **Animations** tab.
   Animation Group
3. Click the Animation **More** button ⊡.
4. From the gallery, click the desired animation.

Previewing a Slide Show

- Click the **Slide Show** button on the Status bar ⊡.

OR

1. Click the **View** tab.
   Start Slide Show Group
2. Click **From Beginning** button ⊡.

OR

   Click **From Current Slide** button ⊡.

3. Click the screen to manually advance through the slides.
4. Right-click the screen and use the shortcut menu to control the slide show preview.
5. Press **Esc** to stop the preview.

Working with Notes Pages

Typing Notes Pages

1. In the Slides pane, click the slide to which you want to add speaker notes.
2. Click the **View** tab.
   Presentation Views
3. Click the **Notes Page** button ⊡.
4. Click in the Notes placeholder and type the desired notes text.
5. Use the vertical scroll bar arrows to move to the next or previous notes page.

Printing Notes Pages

1. Click the **File** tab.
2. Click **Print**.
3. Under Settings, click the second option button (what to print).
4. Under Print Layout, click **Notes Pages**.
5. Select additional options as necessary.
6. Click the Print button ⊡.

Printing Handouts

1. Click the **File** tab.
2. Click **Print**.
3. Under Settings, click the second option button (what to print).
4. Under Handouts, click the handout layout you want to print
5. Select additional options as necessary.
6. Click the Print button .

Changing Slide Size and Orientation

Changing Slide Size

1. Click the **Design** tab.
   Page Setup Group
2. Click the **Page Setup** button .
3. In the Page Setup dialog box, select the desired size settings.
4. Click **OK**.

Changing Slide Orientation

1. Click the **Design** tab.
   Page Setup Group
2. Click the **Slide Orientation** button .
3. On the menu, click the desired orientation.

OR

1. Click the **Design** tab.
   Page Setup Group
2. Click the **Page Setup** button .
3. In the Page Setup dialog box, click the desired orientation.
4. Click **OK**.

Inserting Headers and Footers

1. Click the **Insert** tab.
   Text Group
2. Click the **Header & Footer** button .
3. In the Header and Footer dialog box, click the desired options on the Slide tab.
4. Click **Apply to All** to insert the header and/or footer on all slides.

OR

- Click **Apply** to insert the header and/or footer on the current slide only.

Inserting Graphics

Inserting a Picture from a File

1. Select the slide on which you want to insert the picture.
2. In the content placeholder, click the **Insert Picture from File** icon .
3. In the Insert Picture dialog box, navigate to the location where the picture file is stored.
4. Click the picture and then click **Insert**.

OR

1. Select the slide.
2. Click the **Insert** tab.
   Images Group
3. Click the **Picture** button .
4. In the Insert Picture dialog box, navigate to and select the picture you want to insert.
5. Click **Insert**.

Inserting Clip Art

1. Select the slide on which you want to insert clip art.
2. In the content placeholder, click the **Clip Art** icon .
3. In the Clip Art task pane, type the keyword(s) for the clip art you want to insert in the Search for box.
4. If desired, click the **Results should be** drop-down arrow and specify the media.
5. Click the **Go** button.
6. Click the desired clip art to insert it on the slide.

Working with Text Boxes

Inserting a Text Box

1. Click the slide where you want to insert the text box.
2. Click the **Insert** tab.
   Text Group
3. Click the **Text Box** button .
4. On the slide, drag to draw the box the desired size.
5. Type the text as desired.

Creating a Multiple Column Text Box

1. Click the outer border of the text box to select it.
2. Click the **Home** tab.
   Paragraph Group
3. Click the **Columns** button .
4. On the menu, click the desired column setting.

Working with Video

Inserting a Movie from a File

1. In the slide's content placeholder, click the **Insert V Clip** icon.

OR

   a. Click the **Insert** tab.

       Media Group

   b. Click the **Insert Video** button.

2. In the Insert Video dialog box, navigate to the location where the video file is stored.
3. Click the file and then click **Insert**.

Inserting a Clip Art Video

1. Click the slide on which you want to insert the video.
2. Click the **Insert** tab.

       Media Group

3. Click the **Video** button drop-down arrow.
4. Click **Clip Art Video**.
5. In the Search for box in the Clip Art task pane, type the keyword(s) for the video you want to insert.
6. Click the **Go** button.
7. Click the desired clip to insert it on the slide.

Adjusting Video Color

1. Click the video to select it.
2. Click the **Video Tools Format** tab.

       Adjust Group

3. Click the **Color** button.
4. From the gallery, click the desired color option.

Previewing a Movie in Normal View

1. Click the video to select it.
2. Click the **Video Tools Playback** tab.

       Preview Group

3. Click the **Play** button.

OR

- Click the **Play/Pause** button on the video itself.

Viewing Videos in a Slide Show

1. In the status bar, click the **Slide Show** button.
2. Hover the mouse over the video.
3. Click the **Play** button.

OR

1. Click the **Slide Show** tab.

       Start Slide Show Group

2. Click the **From Current Slide** button.

Working with Sound

Inserting Sounds or Music from a File

1. Click the slide on which you want to insert the sound.
2. Click the **Insert** tab.

       Media Group

3. Click the **Audio** button.
4. Click **Audio from File**.
5. In the Insert Audio dialog box, navigate to the location where the audio file is stored.
6. Click the file and then click **Insert**.

Inserting a Clip Art Sound

1. Click the slide on which you want to insert the sound.
2. Click the **Insert** tab.

       Media Group

3. Click the **Audio** button drop-down arrow.
4. Click **Clip Art Audio**.
5. In the Search for box in the Clip Art task pane, type the keyword(s) for the sound or music you want to insert.
6. Click the **Go** button.
7. Click the desired clip to insert it on the slide.

Hiding the Audio Icon

1. Click the audio icon on the slide.
2. Click the **Audio Tools Playback** tab.

       Audio Options Group

3. Click to select the **Hide During Show** check box.

Setting Audio to Play Continuously

1. Click the audio icon on the slide.
2. Click the **Audio Tools Playback** tab.

       Audio Options Group

3. Click to select the **Loop until Stopped** check box.

Setting Audio to Rewind

1. Click the audio icon on the slide.
2. Click the **Audio Tools Playback** tab.

       Audio Options Group

3. Click to select the **Rewind after Playing** check box.

Setting the Playback Volume

1. Click the audio icon on the slide.
2. Click the **Audio Tools Playback** tab.

       Editing Group

3. Click the **Volume** button.
4. Click the volume level.

Trimming an Audio Clip

1. Click the audio icon to select it.
2. Click the **Audio Tools Playback** tab.

       Editing Group

3. Click the **Trim Audio** button.
4. Drag the green handle on the left to trim the beginning of the audio.
5. Drag the red handle on the right to trim the end of the audio.
6. Click **OK**.

Working with WordArt

Applying WordArt Styles to Existing Text

1. Select the text you want to format as WordArt.
2. Click the **Drawing Tools Format** tab.

   WordArt Styles Group

3. Click the WordArt Styles **More** button ⌄.
4. From the gallery, click the desired style.

Inserting WordArt

1. Click the Insert tab.

   Text Group

2. Click the **WordArt** button 𝓐.
3. From the gallery, click the desired style.
4. Select the placeholder text and type your text.

Formatting WordArt

1. Click the WordArt object.
2. Click the **Drawing Tools Format** tab.

   WordArt Styles Group

3. Click the desired format buttons as follows:
   - **Text Fill** 𝐀⌄
   - **Text Outline** ✏⌄
   - **Text Effects** 𝐀⌄
4. From the menu, click the desired option.

Working with SmartArt

Converting a Bulleted List to SmartArt

1. Select the entire bulleted list.
2. Right-click the selected list.
3. On the shortcut menu, click **Convert to SmartArt**.
4. From the gallery, click the desired SmartArt.

Inserting a New SmartArt Object

1. On a blank slide, click the **Insert SmartArt Graphic** icon 📊 in the content placeholder.
2. In the Choose a SmartArt Graphic dialog box, click the category from the left pane.
3. In the middle pane, choose the SmartArt style.
4. Click **OK**.

Removing a Shape from a SmartArt Object

1. Click the shape you want to remove.
2. Press **Delete**.

Adding a Shape to a SmartArt Object

1. Click a shape in the SmartArt object.
2. Click the **SmartArt Tools Design** tab.

   Create Graphic Group

3. Click the **Add Shape** button 🔳.

Resizing a Shape

1. Click the shape you want to resize.
2. Click and drag a sizing handle to resize as desired.

Reordering Diagram Content

1. Click the shape within the diagram that you want to move.
2. Click the **SmartArt Tools Design** tab.

   Create Graphic Group

3. Click the reorder options as follows:
   - **Promote** ⬅ to increase the level of the shape.
   - **Demote** ➡ to decrease the level of the shape.
   - **Right to Left** 🔁 to switch the layout.
   - **Move Up** ⬆ to move the current selection forward in the sequence.
   - **Move Down** ⬇ to move the current selection backward in the sequence.

Changing the SmartArtStyle

1. Click the SmartArt to select it.
2. Click the **SmartArt Tools Design** tab.

   SmartArt Styles Group

3. Click the SmartArt Styles **More** button ⌄.
4. From the gallery, click the desired style.

Changing the SmartArt Colors

1. Click the SmartArt to select it.
2. Click the **SmartArt Tools Design** tab.

   SmartArt Styles Group

3. Click the **Change Colors** button ⚬.
4. From the gallery, click the desired color.

Working with Photo Albums

Creating a Photo Album

1. Click the **Insert** tab.
   Images Group
2. Click the **Photo Album** button.
3. In the Photo Album dialog box, click the **File/Disk** button.
4. In the Insert New Pictures dialog box, navigate to the picture files.
5. Click the files you want to insert, holding down the **Ctrl** key to select multiple files.
6. Click **Insert**.
7. In the Photo Album dialog box, edit the pictures as desired.
8. Click **Create**.

Editing a Photo Album

1. Click the **Insert** tab.
   Images Group
2. Click the **Photo Album** drop-down arrow.
3. On the menu, click **Edit Photo Album**.
4. In the Edit Photo Album dialog box, click the photo you want to edit.
5. Edit the photo as desired.
6. Click **Update**.

Applying a Theme to a Photo Album

1. Click the **Insert** tab.
   Images Group
2. Click the **Photo Album** drop-down arrow.
3. On the menu, click **Edit Photo Album**.
4. In the Edit Photo Album dialog box, click the **Browse** button next to Theme.
5. In the Choose Theme dialog box, click the desired theme.
6. Click **Select**.
7. Click **Update**.

Working with Tables

Inserting a Table

1. Click the slide on which you want to insert the table.
2. In the content placeholder, click the **Insert Table** icon.
3. In the Insert Table dialog box, specify the number of columns and rows.
4. Click **OK**.

OR

1. Click the **Insert** tab.
   Tables Group
2. Click the **Table** button.
3. On the menu, drag the pointer over the grid to specify the desired number of columns and rows.

Applying Table Formats

1. Click the table to select it.
2. Click the **Table Tools Design** tab.
   Table Styles Group
3. Click the Table Styles **More** button.
4. From the gallery, click the desired style.

Applying Shading Formats

1. Click the table to select it.
2. Click the **Table Tools Design** tab.
   Table Styles Group
3. Click the **Shading** drop-down arrow.
4. From the palette, click the desired color.

Applying Border Formats

1. Click the table to select it.
2. Click the **Table Tools Design** tab.
   Table Styles Group
3. Click the **Borders** drop-down arrow.
4. From the menu, click the desired border.

Inserting a Row

- Click the **Table Tools Layout** tab.
  Rows & Columns Group
  - Click the **Insert Above** button to insert the row above the selected table cell.
  - Click the **Insert Below** button to insert the row below the selected table cell.

Inserting a Column

- Click the **Table Tools Layout** tab.
  Rows & Columns Group
  - Click the **Insert Left** button to insert the column to the left of the selected table cell.
  - Click the **Insert Right** button to insert the column to the right of the selected table cell.

Deleting Part of the Table

1. Click the **Table Tools Layout** tab.
   Rows & Columns Group
2. Click the **Delete** button.
3. On the menu, click the desired part of the table you want to delete.

Merging Table Cells

1. Select the cells you want to merge.
2. Click the **Table Tools Layout** tab.
   Merge Group
3. Click the **Merge Cells** button.

Distributing Rows and Columns Evenly

1. Click the **Table Tools Layout** tab.

   ### Cell Size Group

   - Click the **Distribute Rows** button ⊞ to distribute rows evenly.
   - Click the Distribute Columns button ⊞ to distribute columns evenly.

Working with Charts

Inserting a Chart

1. Click the slide on which you want to insert the chart.
2. In the content placeholder, click the **Insert Chart** icon 📊.

OR

   - Click the **Insert** tab.

   ### Illustrations Group

   - Click the **Chart** button 📊.

3. In the Insert Chart dialog box, click the type of chart in the left pane.
4. In the right pane, click the style of chart.
5. Click **OK**.
6. Enter data in the Excel worksheet as desired.

Changing the Chart Type

1. Click the chart to select it.
2. Click the **Chart Tools Design** tab.

   ### Type Group

3. Click the **Change Chart Type** button 📊.
4. In the Change Chart Type dialog box, click the type of chart in the left pane.
5. In the right pane, click the style of chart.
6. Click **OK**.

Applying a Chart Style

1. Click the chart to select it.
2. Click the **Chart Tools Design** tab.

   ### Chart Styles Group

3. Click the Chart Styles **More** button ▾.
4. From the gallery, click the desired style.

Editing the Chart Data

1. Click the chart to select it.
2. Click the **Chart Tools Design** tab.

   ### Data Group

3. Click the **Edit Data** button 📊.
4. Edit the data as desired.

Switching Rows and Columns

1. Click the chart slide
2. Click the **Chart Tools Design** tab.

   ### Data Group

3. Click the **Edit Data** button 📊.
4. Click the **Chart Tools Design** tab.

   ### Data Group

5. Click the **Switch Row/Column** button 📊.

Selecting Data to Chart

1. Click the chart to select it.
2. Click the **Chart Tools Design** tab.

   ### Data Group

3. Click the **Select Data** button 📊.
4. In the Select Data Source dialog box, click in the **Chart data range** box and type the range address.

OR

   - Click the **Collapse Dialog** button 📊.
   - In the spreadsheet, select the range of data to chart.
   - Click the **Expand Dialog** button 📊 to return to the dialog box.

5. Click **OK**.

Changing Chart Layout

1. Click the chart to select it.
2. Click the **Chart Tools Layout** tab.
3. Click options in the Labels, Axes, and Background groups as desired.

Animating a Chart

1. Click the chart to select it.
2. Click the **Animations** tab.
3. Click the Animation **More** button ▾.
4. From the gallery, click the desired animation.

Inserting an Excel Worksheet

Inserting a New, Blank Worksheet

1. Click the slide on which you want to insert the worksheet.
2. Click the **Insert** tab.

   ### Tables Group

3. Click the **Table** button ▦.
4. On the menu, click **Excel Spreadsheet**.

Inserting an Existing Worksheet

1. Click the slide on which you want to insert the worksheet.
2. Click the **Insert** tab.

   ### Text Group

3. Click the **Object** button 📷.
4. In the Insert Object dialog box, click **Create from file**.
5. Click the **Browse** button and navigate to the location where the Excel file is stored.
6. Click **Open** and then click **OK**.

Resizing a Worksheet Object
1. Click the worksheet to select it.
2. Click a corner sizing handle to resize the worksheet as desired.

OR

1. Double-click the worksheet object.
2. Position the mouse pointer on a side handle.
3. When the pointer changes to a double-headed arrow, drag to crop out empty rows or columns.

Inserting and Editing Data in a Worksheet
1. Double-click the worksheet object.
2. Enter and edit data in the worksheet cells as desired.

Linking Excel Worksheet Data
1. In the Excel worksheet, select the data you want to copy and link.
2. Press **Ctrl+C** to copy the data to the Clipboard.
3. In the PowerPoint slide, click the slide on which you want to copy the data.
4. Click the **Home** tab.
   Clipboard Group
5. Click the **Paste** drop-down arrow.
6. On the menu, click **Paste Special**.
7. In the Paste Special dialog box, click **Paste link**.
8. Click **OK**.

Editing Data in a Linked Worksheet
1. Double-click the worksheet object.
2. Edit the data as desired.

Working with Slide Masters

Opening the Slide Master
1. Click the **View** tab.
   Master Views Group
2. Click the **Slide Master** button.

Customizing Slide Master Elements
1. Click the **View** tab.
   Master Views Group
2. Click the **Slide Master** button.
3. In Slide Master view, click the slide master you want to customize.
4. Click the desired element.
5. Customize the element as desired.

Creating a Custom Layout in Slide Master View
1. Click the **View** tab.
   Master Views Group
2. Click the **Slide Master** button.
3. In Slide Master view, click the **Slide Master** tab.
   Edit Master Group
4. Click the **Insert Layout** button.
   Master Layout Group
5. If desired, click the **Title** box to show the title placeholder and the **Footers** box to show the footer placeholder.
6. Click the **Insert Placeholder** button and on the menu, click the desired placeholder.

Working with the Notes and Handouts Masters

Working with the Notes Master
1. Click the **View** tab.
   Master Views Group
2. Click the **Notes Master** button.
3. Click a placeholder and modify as desired.

Working with the Handout Master
1. Click the **View** tab.
   Master Views Group
2. Click the **Handout Master** button.
3. Click a placeholder and modify as desired.

Creating Links in a Presentation

Inserting Hyperlinks on Slides
1. Click the slide on which you want to insert the link.
2. Click the placeholder or object for the link.
3. Click the **Insert** tab.
   Links Group
4. Click the **Insert Hyperlink** button.
5. In the Insert Hyperlink dialog box, click the desired option in the Link to box.
6. Fill in the linking information as necessary and click **OK**.

Inserting an Action Button
1. Click the slide on which you want to insert the button.
2. Click the **Home** tab.
   Drawing Group
3. Click the Shapes **More** button.
4. Under Action Buttons, click the desired button.

Sending a Presentation for Review

1. Click **File**.
2. Click **Save & Send**.
3. In Backstage view, click the desired option for sending the presentation.

Using Comments

Inserting a Comment

1. Click the slide on which you want to insert the comment.
2. Click the **Review** tab.
   Comments Group
3. Click the **New Comment** button.
4. Type the comment text.

Viewing Comments

1. Click the **Review** tab.
   Comments Group
2. Click the **Previous** button to move to the previous comment.
   - Click the **Next** button to move to the next comment.

Deleting a Comment

1. Click the comment to select it.
2. Click the **Review** tab.
   Comments Group
3. Click the **Delete** button.

Hiding Slides

1. On the status bar, click the **Slide Sorter** button.
2. Click the slide you want to hide.
3. Click the **Slide Show** tab.
   Set Up Group
4. Click the **Hide Slide** button.

Controlling Slides During a Presentation

1. Click the **Slide Show** tab.
   Start Slide Show Group
2. Click the **From Beginning** button.
3. Right-click the screen and from the shortcut menu, click the desired option for controlling the slide show.

OR

- Press the following keys to advance one slide:
  - N
  - Down arrow
  - Right arrow
  - Enter
  - PgDn
  - Spacebar
- Press the following key to go back one slide:
  - P
  - Up arrow
  - Left arrow
  - PgUp
  - Backspace

Preparing a Presentation for Delivery

Rehearsing Timings

1. Click the **Slide Show** tab.
   Set Up Group
2. Click the **Rehearse Timings** button.
3. Advance from slide to slide at the desired pace.
4. At the end of the show, click **Yes** to keep the slide timings, or **No** to discard them.

Setting Slide Show Options

1. Click the **Slide Show** tab.
   Set Up Group
2. Click the **Set Up Slide Show** button.
3. In the Set Up Show dialog box, click the options as desired.
4. Click **OK**.

Creating a Looping Presentation that Runs Automatically

1. Click the **Slide Show** tab.
   Set Up Group
2. Click the **Set Up Slide Show** button.
3. In the Set Up Show dialog box, under Show type, click **Browsed at a kiosk**.
4. Under Show Options, click **Loop continuously until 'Esc'**.
5. Click **OK**.

Check a Presentation for Issues

1. Click **File**.
2. Click **Info**.
3. Click the **Check for Issues** button.
4. On the menu, click **Inspect Document**.
5. In the Document Inspector, click to mark options as desired.
6. Click **Inspect**.
7. Review the inspection results and then click **Close**.

Sending a Presentation as a PDF via E-mail

1. Click **File**.
2. Click **Save & Send**.
3. In Backstage view, click the **Send as PDF** button.
4. In the e-mail message window, type in the information as desired.
5. Click the **Send** button.

Finalizing a Presentation

1. Click **File**.
2. Click **Info**.
3. Click the **Protect Presentation** button.
4. From the menu, click **Add a Digital Signature**.
5. In the message box, click **OK**.
6. Click **Create your own digital ID**.
7. Click **OK**.
8. Complete the Create a Digital ID dialog box.
9. Click **Create**.
10. In the Sign box, type the desired digital signature.
11. Click **Sign**.
12. Click **OK**.

Saving a Presentation as a Show

1. Click **File**.
2. Click **Save As**.
3. In the Save As dialog box, navigate to the location where you want to store the show.
4. Type the name for the presentation.
5. Click the **Save as type** drop-down arrow and click **PowerPoint Show**.
6. Click **Save**.

Saving a Presentation as a Video

1. Click **File**.
2. Click **Save & Send**.
3. Click **Create a Video**.
4. In the Create a Video pane, click **Computer & HD Displays**.
5. Click the desired resolution.
6. If desired, change the number of seconds for each slide.

OR

  a. Click **Don't Use Recorded Timings and Narrations**.
  b. Click **Record Timings and Narration**.
  c. In the Record Slide Show dialog box, click **Start Recording**.

7. Click **Create Video**.
8. In the Save As dialog box, navigate to the location where you want to store the video.
9. Type the name for the video.
10. Click **Save**.

Saving a Presentation to a Windows Live SkyDrive

1. Click **File**.
2. Click **Save & Send**.
3. Click **Save to Web**.
4. Sign in to Windows Live SkyDrive or sign up for a Windows Live account.
5. Click to select the Public or another SkyDrive folder.
6. Click **Save As**.
7. Click the **Save as type** drop-down arrow and click the format you wish to use.
8. Change the name of the presentation, if necessary.
9. Click **Save**.

Broadcasting a Presentation via the Internet

1. Click the **Slide Show** tab.
   Start Slide Show Group
2. Click the **Broadcast Slide Show** button 🖳.

OR

  a. Click **File**.
  b. Click **Save & Send**.
  c. Click **Broadcast Slide Show**.
  d. Click the **Broadcast Slide Show** button.

3. In the Broadcast Slide Show dialog box, click **Start Broadcast**.
4. In the next dialog box, click the option for how to send the URL to attendees.
5. Click **Start Slide Show** when you and your attendees are ready to begin the presentation.
6. Click **End Broadcast** when the slide show ends.

Packaging a Presentation

Creating the Package for CD

1. Insert a recordable CD in the computer.
2. Click **File**.
3. Click **Save & Send**.
4. Click **Package Presentation for CD**.
5. Click the **Package for CD** button.
6. In the Package for CD dialog box, type the CD name.
7. Click **Options**.
8. Set the options as desired.
9. Click **OK**.
10. Click **Copy to CD**.
11. When asked if you want to use linked files, click **Yes**.
12. Click **Close**.

Copying to a Folder

1. Insert a recordable CD in the computer.
2. Click **File**.
3. Click **Save & Send**.
4. Click **Package Presentation for CD**.
5. Click the **Package for CD** button.
6. In the Package for CD dialog box, type a presentation package name.
7. Click **Copy to Folder**.
8. In the Copy to Folder dialog box, type the folder name.
9. Click the **Browse** button and navigate to the location where you want to store the files.
10. Click **OK**.
11. When asked if you want to copy linked files, click **Yes**.
12. Click **Close**.

Unpacking and Running a Presentation

1. Insert the packaged CD in the computer.
2. In the AutoPlay dialog box, open the Presentation Package folder if necessary, and then click **Presentation Package.html**.
3. Click **Download Viewer**.
4. Click **Download** to download the PowerPoint 2010 Viewer.

OR

   a. Click **Start**.
   b. Click **Computer**.
   c. Click the CD drive to see files on CD.

5. Double-click **PowerPointViewer.exe**.
6. Accept the terms of use for the PowerPoint Viewer, if necessary and click **Continue**.
7. Click **Next** as necessary throughout the installation. When the installation completes, click **OK**.
8. Go back to the browser window and click the name of show.
9. Click **Open** to start the show.

Creating a New Mail Message

1. Click **Mail** in the Navigation pane.
2. Click the **Home** tab.
   New Group
3. Click the **New E-mail** button 🔲.

OR

1. Click the **New Items** drop-down arrow 🔲.
2. On the menu, click **E-mail Message**.

Creating and Sending a Mail Message

1. In the e-mail message window, click in the **To** box and type the recipient's e-mail address.
2. If desired, click in the **Cc** box and type the e-mail address of the copied recipient.
3. Click in the **Subject** box and type the subject of the message.
4. Click in the message window and type the message text.
5. Click the **Send** button 🔲.

Receiving Messages

1. Click the **Send/Receive** tab.
   Send & Receive Group
2. Click the **Send/Receive All Folders** button 🔲.

Reading Mail

1. In the Navigation pane, click **Inbox**.
2. In the middle pane, click the message you want to read to display it in the Reading pane.

OR

- In the middle pane, double-click the message you want to read to display it in the message window.

Formatting Message Text

1. In the e-mail message window, select the message text you want to format.
2. Click the **Format Text** tab.
3. Click the button or its drop-down arrow to apply the desired format. Some of the more commonly used formats are listed below:
   Font Group
   - **Font** Calibri (Body) ▾
   - **Font Size** 11 ▾
   - **Bold** B
   - **Italic** I
   - **Underline** U ▾
   - **Text Highlight Color** 🔲 ▾
   - **Font Color** A ▾
   Paragraph Group
   - **Align Text Left** 🔲
   - **Center** 🔲
   - **Align Text Right** 🔲
   - **Justify** 🔲
   - **Bullets** 🔲 ▾
   - **Numbering** 🔲 ▾

Check Spelling in a Message

1. Click the **Review** tab.
   Proofing Group
2. Click the **Spelling & Grammar** button 🔲.
3. In the Spelling & Grammar dialog box, click the desired option to change or ignore the word.
4. When the spelling check is complete, click **Yes** in the message box.

Creating a Folder for Storing Mail

1. Click the **Folder** tab.
   New Group
2. Click the **New Folder** button 🔲.
3. In the Create New Folder dialog box, type the name of the new folder.
4. Select where you want to place the folder.
5. Click **OK**.

Printing an E-mail Message

1. Select the message you want to print.
2. Click **File**.
3. Click **Print**.
4. In Backstage view, set the print options as desired.
5. Click the **Print** button 🔲.

Replying to Mail

1. Select the message to which you want to reply.
2. Click the **Home** tab.
   Respond Group
3. Click the **Reply** button ⬚.

OR

- Click the **Reply All** button ⬚.

4. Type your reply.
5. Click the **Send** button ⬚.

Forwarding a Message

1. Select the message you want to forward.
2. Click the **Home** tab.
   Respond Group
3. Click the **Forward** button ⬚.
4. In the message window, enter the e-mail address in the To and Cc boxes of the recipient to which you want to forward the message.
5. Type a message if desired.
6. Click the **Send** button ⬚.

Working with Attachments

Attaching a File to a Message

1. Compose the e-mail message.
2. Click the **Message** tab.

OR

   Click the **Insert** tab.
   Include Group
3. Click the **Attach File** button ⬚.
4. In the Insert File dialog box, navigate to the location where the file is stored.
5. Click the file and then click **Insert**.

Opening an E-mail Attachment

1. Display the message in the Reading pane.
2. Double-click the attached file in the message header to open the file in its native program.

Previewing an Attachment

1. Display the message in the Reading pane.
2. Click the attached file in the message header to display its contents in the Reading pane.

Saving an Attachment

1. Display the message in the Reading pane.
2. Click the attached file in the message header that you want to save.
   Actions Group
3. Click the **Save All Attachments** button ⬚.
4. In the Save All Attachments dialog box, verify the file to save.
5. Click **OK**.
6. In the Save Attachment dialog box, navigate to the location where you want to save the file.
7. Enter a file name and set the file type, if desired.
8. Click **Save**.

Managing Messages

Deleting a Message

1. Select the message you want to delete.
2. Press **Delete**.

OR

1. Click the **Home** tab.
   Delete Group
2. Click the **Delete** button ⬚.

Moving a Message

1. In the middle pane of the mail window, select the message you want to move.
2. Drag the message to the desired folder in the Navigation pane.

OR

1. Click the **Home** tab.
   Move Group
2. Click the **Move** button ⬚.
3. From the menu, click the desired folder.

Copying a Message

1. In the middle pane of the mail window, select the message you want to copy.
2. Hold down **Ctrl** and drag the message to the desired folder in the Navigation pane.

OR

1. Click the **Home** tab.
   Move Group
2. Click the **Move** button ⬚.
3. From the menu, click **Copy to Folder**.
4. In the Copy Items dialog box, click the folder to which you want to copy the message.
5. Click **OK**.

Flagging a Message for Follow-up

1. Select the message to flag.
2. Click the **Home** tab.
   Tags Group
3. Click the **Follow Up** button ⬚.
4. From the menu, click the desired follow-up deadline.

Adding an Entry to the Address Book

1. Click the **Home** tab.
   New Group
2. Click the **New Items** drop-down arrow.
3. On the menu, click **Contact**.
4. Complete the contact form as desired.
5. Click the **Save & Close** button.

OR

1. Click the **Home** tab.
   Find Group
2. Click the **Address Book** button.
3. In the Address Book dialog box, click **File**.
4. Click **New Entry**.
5. In the New Entry dialog box, click **New Contact**.
6. Click **OK**.
7. Complete the contact form as desired.
8. Click the **Save & Close** button.

Entering an E-mail Address Using the Address Book

1. Create a new e-mail message.
2. Click the **To** button.
3. In the Select Names dialog box, click the recipient's address.
4. Click **To**.
5. Click **OK**.

Searching Mail

1. In the Navigation pane, click the folder you want to search.
2. In the Search text box at the top of the middle pane, type the text for which you want to search.
3. Press **Enter**.

Creating a Distribution List

1. Click the **Home** tab.
   Find Group
2. Click the **Address Book** button.
3. In the Address Book dialog box, click **File**.
4. Click **New Entry**.
5. In the New Entry dialog box, click **New Contact Group**.
6. Click **OK**.
7. In the Contact Group window, click in the **Name** box and type the name for the contact group.
8. Click the **Contact Group** tab.
   Members Group
9. Click the **Add Members** button.
10. From the menu, click the desired resource from which you will add members.
11. In the Select Members dialog box, double-click member names.
12. When you have selected all the members, click **OK**.
13. Click the **Save & Close** button.

Viewing a Web Page in a Browser

1. In Internet Explorer, click in the **Address bar**.
2. Type the Web page address.
3. Press **Enter**.

Navigating Web Pages

- Click the **Back** button to return to the previously viewed page.
- Click the **Forward** button to go to the page you were on when you clicked the Back button.
- Click the down arrow to the right of the Forward button to display a menu of sites you have visited during the browser session with the most recently visited site listed at the top of the menu.
- Click the **Home** button to return to the page that displays when you start Internet Explorer.

Using a Web Site's Navigation Bar

1. Locate the navigation bar, typically located at the top of the Web page or along the left side.
2. Click a link within the navigation bar to go to that Web page.
3. Click the **Home** link within the navigation bar to return to the Web site's home page.

Finding Specific Information on a Web Site

- Use the Web site's navigation bar to go to pages with more specific information.
- Click in the site's Search box and type the keyword(s) for which you are searching.
- Click the **Edit** menu and click **Find on this Page**. In the Find dialog box, type the text you want to find and click **Next**.

Refreshing a Web Page

1. Click the **View** menu.
2. Click **Refresh**

OR

- Click the **Refresh** button.

OR

- Press **F5**.

OR

1. Right-click the page's tab.
2. On the shortcut menu, click **Refresh**.

Opening a New Tab

1. Point to the new tab and click the **New Tab** button.
2. Click in the **Address bar** and type the address of the Web page you want to open.

Viewing Tabs

- Click the **Quick Tabs** button to display thumbnails of all open tabs.
- Click the **Tab List** button to display a menu of all open tabs.

Closing a Tab

1. Right-click the tab you want to close.
2. On the shortcut menu, click **Close**.

Copying Data from a Web Page

Copying Text

1. Display the Web page in Internet Explorer.
2. Select the text you want to copy.
3. Press **Ctrl+C**.
4. Click in the file where you want to paste the copied text.
5. Press **Ctrl+V**.

Copying Graphics

1. Display the Web page in Internet Explorer.
2. Right-click the graphic you want to copy.
3. On the shortcut menu, click **Copy**.
4. Click in the file where you want to paste the graphic.
5. Press **Ctrl+V**.

Printing a Web Page

1. Display the Web page in Internet Explorer.
2. Press **Ctrl+P**.

OR

- Click **File**.
- Click **Print**.

3. In the Print dialog box, set the printing options as desired.
4. Click **Print**.

Showing History of Recently Visited Web Sites

1. Click the **View** menu.
2. Click **Explorer Bar**.
3. Click **History**.

Navigating to a Recently Visited Site

1. Click the desired timeframe in the History pane to list the sites visited during that time.
2. Click a site to list the Web pages visited at that site.
3. Click a page to display it.

Sorting the History List

1. Click the **History** drop-down arrow History.
2. On the menu, click the desired sort order.

Deleting an Item on the History List

1. Right-click the item you want to delete.
2. On the shortcut menu, click **Delete**.

Using Favorites in Internet Explorer

1. Display the desired Web page in Internet Explorer.
2. Click the **Favorites** menu.
3. Click **Add to Favorites**.

OR

- Click the **Add to Favorites** button.
- Click **Add to Favorites**.

4. In the Add a Favorite dialog box, enter a name for the favorite if desired.
5. If desired, click the **Create in** drop-down arrow and select a folder in which to store the site address.
6. Click **Add**.

Managing Favorites

1. Click the **Favorites** menu.
2. Click **Organize Favorites**.
3. In the Organize Favorites dialog box, select from the following options:

   - **New Folder**: create a new folder on the Favorites list
   - **Move**: move a selected site into a Favorites folder
   - **Rename**: rename the selected site shortcut
   - **Delete**: delete the selected site.

Using a Search Engine

1. In the Address bar, type the address for the desired search engine and press **Enter**.
2. In the Search box, type the subject for which you are searching and press **Enter**.
3. In the list of Web sites that meet the search criteria, click the site you want to visit.

Selecting a Default Search Engine

1. In Internet Explorer 9, click **Tools**.
2. Click **Internet options**.
3. On the General tab, under Search, click the **Settings** button.
4. In the list of search providers, click the one you want as the default.
5. Click the **Set as default** button.
6. Click **Close**.
7. Click **OK**.
√ *To add search providers to the list, click the **Find more search providers** link, click a search provider, and follow the prompts to install it.*

Set Internet Explorer 9 to Search from the Address Bar

1. In Internet Explorer 9, click **Tools**.
2. Click **Internet options**.
3. On the General tab, under Search, click the **Settings** button.
4. Click to select the **Search in the address bar** check box.
5. Click **Close**.
6. Click **OK**.

Working with Search Tools

Using Keywords

- In the Search box, type as specific a keyword as possible to help focus the search.

Using Quotation Marks

- In the Search box, type the search string enclosed in quotation marks to return only those pages with an exact match.

Using Boolean Operators

- Use the AND operator to find pages that include more than one search term; for example, type **dogs AND terriers** to find pages that contain both "dogs" and "terriers."

- Use the OR operator to find pages that include one search term or another; for example, type **dogs OR terriers** to find pages that contain either of the terms.

- Use the NOT operator to find pages that contain one search term but exclude other terms; for example, type **Harvard NOT University** to find pages that contain the word "Harvard," but not the word "University."

Using Wildcard Characters

- Use the asterisk (*) wildcard character to substitute for any number of characters;."
- Use the question mark (?) wildcard character to substitute for a single character"

Using Natural Language

- In the search box, type a question or phrase describing what you are searching for; for example, type **conducting effective Internet searches** to return pages that contain information on the topic.

Using Subject Directories

- In the Address bar, type the address of the subject directory you want to search. If you do not know the Web address, use a search engine to find a subject directory.

Controlling Pop-ups

Turning Off Pop-up Blocker

1. In Internet Explorer, click the **Tools** menu.
2. Point to **Pop-up Blocker**.
3. On the submenu, click **Turn Off Pop-up Blocker**.

Turning On Pop-up Blocker

1. In Internet Explorer, click the **Tools** menu.
2. Point to **Pop-up Blocker**.
3. On the submenu, click **Turn On Pop-up Blocker**.

Identifying Pop-up Exceptions

1. In Internet Explorer, make sure Pop-up Blocker is turned on.
2. Click the **Tools** menu.
3. Point to **Pop-up Blocker**.
4. On the submenu, click **Pop-up Blocker Settings**.
5. In the Pop-up Blocker Settings dialog box, type the address of the Web site whose pop-up you want to allow.
6. Click **Add**.
7. Click **Close**.

Downloading a File from the Internet

1. Display the Web page from which you want to download the file.
2. Click the file to download and then click the **Download** button.
√ *You may see a message box asking you to accept a service agreement concerning the download.*
3. Proceed through the installation steps.

Display Internet Explorer Settings

1. Start Internet Explorer.
2. Click the **Tools** menu.
3. Click **Internet options**.
4. In the Internet Options dialog box, click each tab to view and select settings.
5. Click **OK**.

Resolving Page Not Found Errors

- Retry the Web page by using the Refresh option: Press **F5**; or click the Refresh button ⟳; or click the **View** menu and then click **Refresh**; or right-click the tab and click **Refresh**.
- Check for errors in the URL and/or retype the URL in the Address bar.
- Move up one directory level at a time in the URL until you connect to a page.
- If available, click a link that redirects you to the site's Home page and use the site's Search feature to find the desired page.

Keyboarding Essentials

appendix B

LEARNING TO KEY CORRECTLY

The human body is not designed for long sessions of repetitive movement. You might even know someone who has strained their hands and fingers by playing video games. Keyboarding can present similar dangers. When you key, you repeat many small movements with your hands and fingers. You might be keying for a long time. If you position yourself correctly, however, you can avoid strain and fatigue.

Even if you do not practice healthy keying techniques, you might not experience any problems while you are young and flexible. However, over the years, if you don't begin to key correctly, you will repeat thousands of stressful movements. You risk painful long-lasting injury that can reduce the quality of your life and your ability to work. It pays to develop healthy keying habits now.

ADJUSTING YOUR WORKSTATION

In a classroom you do not usually have much choice in the equipment you must use. However, flexible equipment and a little imagination can help you adjust your workstation.

Adjusting Your Keyboard and Mouse   You want your fingers to gently curve over the keys while your wrist is in a flat, neutral position.

- If wrist rests are available, place one in front of the keyboard as a guide. Never rest your arms, hands, or wrists while you are keying.
- Place your mouse or trackball at the same height as your keyboard, in easy reach of your preferred hand.

Adjusting the Slope of Your Keyboard   If your keyboard slants toward you, you need to adjust it so it is flat or slopes down away from you.

- Flatten the kickstand at the back of the keyboard.
- Alternatively, raise the front of the keyboard about ¾" by using door wedges, a wood strip, or a box.

Figure B-1 At the beginning of each class, adjust your workstation.

TECHNIQUE TIP

Never rest your arms, hands, or wrists on anything while you are keying.

CORRECT KEYING POSTURE

After you have adjusted your workstation, you need to maintain the correct keying posture. Following are some guidelines for keying correctly:

- Center your body on the J key, about a hand's length from the keyboard and directly in front of the monitor.
- Hold your head straight over your shoulders, without straining forward or backward.
- Position the monitor at eye level, about arm's length away, so you look down about 10 degrees.
- Elongate and relax your neck.
- Keep your shoulders down.
- Tilt your keyboard slightly down toward the monitor. This helps you keep your wrists neutral and your fingers relaxed and curled.
- Adjust your chair and keyboard so your elbows bend at right angles.
- Keep your arms close to your sides, but free to move slightly.
- Keep your wrists relaxed and straight in a "neutral" position.
- Keep your back upright or tilted slightly forward from the hips. Keep the slight natural curve of your lower back. Use a cushion or adjust the chair to support your lower back.
- Keep your knees slightly lower than your hips.
- Adjust your chair so your feet are well supported. Use a footrest, if needed.

AVOIDING STRESS WHEN KEYING

There are two ways to avoid stress when keying. First, you need to maintain the correct keying posture as you key. Second, you need to take a short break every 20 to 30 minutes and perform stretching exercises designed to help you avoid strain, fatigue, and injury.

Maintaining a Correct Keying Position It's easy to start keying by using the correct keying position. As we key, however, many of us lose our focus, and bad habits begin to creep in. It's important to check your keying position to make sure you are still keying correctly. The following figures show some guidelines for maintaining correct keying positions.

Figure B-2 (Left) Maintain a correct upright posture. (Right) Avoid slouching, extending your elbows, or bending your wrists.

Figure B-3 (Left) Maintain a neutral position with your hands. (Right) Avoid twisting your hands inward or outward.

Figure B-4 (Left) Maintain a neutral wrist position with gently curled fingers. (Right) Avoid bending your wrists or using an upward-sloping keyboard.

Stretching and Resting When you key for a long time, your muscles stiffen. You become fatigued and risk injury. You build tension in many parts of your body, including your neck, arms, and wrists. To relieve the tension and reduce the threat of injury, you should stretch before you start keying. You should also take short breaks from keying every 20 to 30 minutes and stretch.

Stretch 1: Neck Stretch

Sitting tall, bring your chin toward your chest, stretching the back of your neck. Slowly repeat two times. See Figure B-5.

Figure B-5 Neck stretch.

Stretch 2: Head Turn

Begin with your head in a neutral position. Look all the way to the right without moving your chest or upper back. Then, look to the left. Slowly repeat two times. See Figure B-6.

Figure B-6 Head turn.

Stretch 3: Head Tilt

Begin with your head in a neutral position. Bring your ear toward your shoulder without turning your head or lifting your shoulder. Hold for a count of five. Reverse directions. See Figure B-7.

Figure B-7 Head tilt.

Stretch 4: Downward Wrist Stretch

With your left fingers pointing down and your palm in, place your right hand over your left knuckles. Extend your arms straight out. Gently press back with your right hand to a count of ten. Reverse hands. Repeat the stretches using a fist. See Figure B-8.

Figure B-8 Downward wrist stretch.

Stretch 5: Upward Wrist Stretch

With your left fingers pointing up, place your right hand over your left palm. Extend your arms straight out. Gently press back with your right hand to a count of ten. Reverse hands. Repeat the stretches with fingers pointing down and the palm out. See Figure B-9.

Figure B-9 Upward wrist stretch.

BENEFITS OF KEYING CORRECTLY

Training takes effort and time. If you already use a keyboard, you might have to re-teach your body to use correct techniques. You might ask yourself "Why make the effort? I'm already keying fast enough."

Just imagine you will probably be using a computer for the rest of your life. If you don't learn now, you will probably need to learn later. There's really no escaping it. Besides, if you learn to key correctly, you will:

- Increase your speed.
- Increase your efficiency, making fewer errors.
- Increase your effectiveness because you can see your work and screen while your hands are free to work.
- Stay healthy, avoid injury, and remain productive over your lifetime.

BREAKING BAD HABITS

Many of you might have been keying for years. However, without any formal training, you could easily have developed bad habits.

The best way to correct bad habits is to use natural breaks as checkpoints. For instance, look at your own habits at the end of each exercise, paragraph, or page you type. Consider your posture, sitting position, hand position, keying technique, and work habits.

To help you break your bad habits, consult the following "Bad Habits Checklist." Check it when you start keying and when you take a break. If you know you have a particular bad habit, try to focus on the correction at the beginning of every keying session. Eventually the bad habit will be replaced by the good habit. It takes work, but it's worth it.

Bad Habit	Correction
Slouching	Sit up straight with your feet flat and well supported.
Reaching too far for the keyboard or the mouse	Sit one hand's length from the keyboard. Keep elbows at right angles.
Leaning your hand on the keyboard or the wrist support	Hover your hands over the keyboard; curl your fingers slightly.
Bending your wrists forward, back, left, or right	Keep your forearms and wrists straight and in the neutral position.
Pounding the keys	Strike keys lightly.
Looking at the keyboard	Position the workstand close to the monitor at eye level. Keep your eyes on your work.
Raising your elbows	Keep your arms close to your body.
Raising your shoulders	Keep your shoulders relaxed, with your chest open and wide.
Keying with the wrong fingers	Practice with correct fingers until you establish the right habit. Your speed will then improve.

Figure B-10 Many of us have developed bad habits that we need to break.

Learn the Home Keys

HOME KEYS

A Use the **A** finger.

S Use the **S** finger.

D Use the **D** finger.

F Use the **F** finger.

J Use the **J** finger.

K Use the **K** finger.

L Use the **L** finger.

Use the finger.

The semicolon (;) is typically used between two independent clauses in a sentence. In a sentence, key one space after a semicolon.

KEYBOARDING TIP

On ⬛ only the semicolon is colored. This is because the key is used for two different characters. In this lesson, you learn how to key the semicolon. In a later lesson you will learn how to key a colon.

LEARN AND PRACTICE

Begin keying by placing your fingers on the eight keys—called the *home keys*— **A S D F J K L** and semicolon ⬛ as shown below.

The index finger of your left hand should rest on **F**, your second and third fingers rest on **D** and **S**, and the little finger of your left hand rests on **A**. For your right hand, your index finger should rest on **J**, your second and third fingers rest on **K** and **L**, and your little finger rests on ⬛.

From now on, the finger you use to press a key will be named for its home-key letter. For example, your left little finger is the **A** finger Your right index finger is the **J** finger.

From the home keys, you can reach all the other keys on the keyboard. The keyboard diagram shows which homekey finger is used for each key. For example, you use the **D** finger to key all the keys in the band of green on the left. You use the **L** finger to key all the keys in the band of red on the right, and so on. When any finger is not actually pressing a key, you should keep it resting lightly on its home key.

The row of keys containing the home keys is called the *home row*. The row below the home row is the *first row*. The row above the home row is the *third row*.

Learn and Practice the Spacebar

Learn and Practice the Spacebar Notice that on the keyboard diagram, the keys you have learned are darker and tinted with their background color. Now locate the Spacebar on the diagram. You use the Spacebar to insert spaces between letters and words. You press it by using the thumb of your writing hand (that is, the hand you use for writing). You do not use the thumb of your other hand.

Key the home-key letters, inserting a space after each letter by pressing the Spacebar quickly and lightly. (Drill lines are numbered. Do not key the green numbers.)

```
1 a s d f j k l ;
```

Learn and Practice Enter You do not have to wait for a text line to be "full" before starting a new line. Pressing the Enter key starts a new line of text whenever you need one. You press Enter by using the [;] finger. Try to keep the [J] finger on its home key when you press Enter.

Now press Enter (↵) to start a new line. Key each of the lines below twice. Press Enter (↵) after each line.

```
2 asdf jkl; asdf jkl; asdf jkl;↵
3 ;lkj fdsa ;lkj fdsa ;lkj fdsa↵
4 fd jk sa l; fds jkl dsa kl;↵
5 dfsa l;kj ddss kkll ffaa ;;jj fjdk ls;a↵
```

Learn and Practice Double-Space You can add a blank line between lines of text by pressing Enter twice. This is how you *double-space* text. (Two consecutive Enters are sometimes referred to as a double line-space.)

Key a line of text, press Enter, and then key it again. After you key a line the second time, press Enter twice before keying a new line. Using this method, key each line twice, and double-space after each pair of lines.

```
6 adfs jlk; aj sk dl f; aaa jjj sd kl ldsk↵
7 fjjf dkkd slsl da l; ks fj ;f sss lll dl↵
8 kkd dlk ds ddd ;f ff ;; fdl; sl f; ds kl↵
9 a as dad sad fads lads lass falls flasks↵
```

TECHNIQUE TIP

Begin with your fingers curled and lightly touching the home keys.

TECHNIQUE TIP

Make sure your back is straight or tilted slightly forward from the hips.

Review the Home Keys

REVIEW

The keyboard shows the keys you have learned so far. This lesson focuses on the keys highlighted in dark blue.

WARM UP

Key each line twice. Double-space after each pair of lines (remember, that means pressing Enter after you key the line the first time and pressing Enter twice after you key the line the second time).

```
1 asdf jkl; asdf jkl; asdf jk l; as df jkl↵
2 ;lkj fdsa ;lkj fdsa a;sl dkfj fdjk sa l;↵
3 fk dk sl a; fds jkl asd ;lkj k fd asf lj↵
4 sdl fdk kls ad; jfd salk klas dsf; flks;↵
```

PRACTICE

Key each line twice. Double-space after each pair of lines.

Left-Hand Focus
```
5 fdsa asdf ff dd ss aa fd sa ds af asf fd↵
6 asdf df df sd sd as as fa af das fad saa↵
7 fads df as dfaa ddfs fada dada fafa sasa↵
```

Right-Hand Focus
```
8 jkl; ;lkj jj kk ll ;; jk l; kl j; jk; jk↵
9 jkl; l; l; kl kl jk jk ;j j; ;lk ;lk kjj↵
10 jlkj l; jk jll lkjj kkjl klk jkkl; kllj; ↵
```

Home Keys
```
11 asdf jkl; fjdk l;sa fjk jfd dkl kds; all↵
12 jk df dk jf sl a; fjd kds; akl kdsl dkll↵
13 adkl dajk kads lfds; ljds jfds lks; jdlk↵
14 as a dad; all lads; all fads; as a lass;↵
15 lads; dads; as sad; lass; as all; a fad;↵
```

Learn E and H

WARM UP

Key each line twice. Double-space after each pair of lines. Do not look at the keyboard when you are keying.

```
1  a dd aaa as asd sdf j jj jjj jk jkl jkl;↵
2  as ads ask; lass dada jask fads dads sad↵
3  lads dada daff; jajs ja salad dads; saks↵
4  jakk jall; jadd dajs ladd saddl aja had;↵
```

LEARN

Reach your **D** finger up and slightly left when you key **E**. Keep your **A** and **S** fingers anchored on their home keys. Reach your **J** finger directly left to key **H**. Keep the other right-hand fingers anchored on their home keys.

PRACTICE

Key each line twice. Double-space after each pair of lines.

Practice e
```
5  d e d ddd eee de ede eed lee eel del eel
6  eee ddd lll eel led eee dell lee led lee
7  eee ddd elk elf sell eee ddd see lee fee
```

Practice h
```
8  j h jjj hhh jh hj jhj hjh jjj hhh jj hhh
9  aaa hhh ash sss ash hh ss aa has sa sash
10 ha had aha has heel she hee half hah has
```

Practice e and h
```
11 he he eh eh hhh eee she he eh she eh hee
12 hhh eee easel feed seed heed lead she he
13 jade desks head sake head lead seal jade
14 has heed; lad had; heel hale; seek sale;
```

NEW KEYS
E Use the **D** finger.

H Use the **J** finger.

KEYBOARDING TIP
Press Enter at the end of every line unless you are told specifically to use word-wrap. From this point on, the Enter symbol (↵) is not shown.

Learn R and I

WARM UP

Key each line twice. Double-space after each pair of lines. Concentrate on pressing the correct key each time.

```
1  ff fff ddd fd df jj jkj lkj fjk fdjk hhj
2  fed fej fek dek dell jade dale fake keel
3  lease lash lake ladle leak led leek feel
4  flea fled sea seal sell sleek shake heel
```

NEW KEYS

R Use the F finger.

I Use the K finger.

LEARN

Reach your F finger up and slightly left when you key R. Keep the other left-hand fingers anchored on their home keys. Reach your K finger up and slightly left to key I. Keep the other right-hand fingers anchored on their home keys.

PRACTICE

Key each line twice. Double-space after each pair of lines.

Practice r
```
5  fff frf frf fff rfr rffr fff rrr fff rrr
6  ra are far raf dare reef fear free freed
7  red jar lard reel dark darker hares rare
```

Practice i
```
8  k kk iii kik kkk ikki iki kk ii kkk kiki
9  ii ll jj kij sill jik ilk fill dill kids
10 if is silk kid hid kill ilk kiss hi hide
```

Practice r and i
```
11 ri ire ride sir rife fire dire sire rise
12 if ride hire hare hers rides fries dries
13 lair fair hair raid rid dill drill frill
14 riff sheared shire sear fire liars fried
```

TECHNIQUE TIP

Adjust your chair and keyboard so your elbows bend at right angles.

Review E H R and I

REVIEW

The keyboard shows the keys you have learned so far. This lesson focuses on the keys highlighted in dark blue.

WARM UP

Key each line twice. Double-space after each pair of lines.

```
1  all ale ad else sled sell sale lass less
2  sheer shear share ail air rile lair fair
3  hash flea his head lead lease deals dash
4  here hares hire hair jars jeer rear dear
```

PRACTICE

Key each line twice. Double-space after each pair of lines.

Practice e and h

```
5  ddd dde ded dde eed ed deeds sea eel see
6  hhh hjh jhj jjj jjh hh ja had he has she
7  had shed he she jade lake head ease heed
8  deed heed seed heal seal fed easel lease
```

Practice r and i

```
9   rrr ffr frf rfr re are red her fair here
10  iii iki kik kki if ire dire kid lie like
11  rise iris frail rail err dear dire fires
12  sire fire liar lair rail hail jail riser
```

Practice e h r and i

```
13  heir hare hair heard hire here rare rear
14  lairs said share shire red her idea dare
15  jeers; sir fir hear; fare hare hair lair
16  sear shared; liars rails hired fired ire
17  hailed fresher fished rides herds shades
```

BREAKING BAD HABITS
Do not look at the keyboard. Keep your eyes on the screen or on your work.

Learn **T** and **O**

WARM UP

Key each line twice. Double-space after each pair of lines. Keep your fingers anchored on the home keys.

```
1 f ff fff fir fire fir fire fff ff fff ff
2 l ll lll lad lade lad lade lll ll lll ll
3 fall fell fill earl leaf field fife life
4 hall hall lire dire rare rash dash flash
```

NEW KEYS

T Use the **F** finger.

O Use the **L** finger.

LEARN

Reach your **F** finger up and right to key **T**. Keep your **A**, **S**, and **D** fingers anchored on their home keys. Reach your **L** finger up and slightly left to key **O**. Keep the other fingers of your right hand anchored on their home keys.

PRACTICE

Key each line twice. Double-space after each pair of lines.

Practice t

```
5 f ff ttt ftf tft fftt the that this tree
6 this tall tree; tear it; lift the tires;
7 at all; third three first; at tea three;
```

Practice o

```
 8 o ll o oo lol olo old lot soak sold told
 9 ode doe rot dot lot lost slot joke joker
10 oars are solid; oats look food; a lot of
```

Practice o and t

```
11 ff tt trt ll oo lo ol ooo of to too toto
12 foot fool tools loot took jots lots soot
13 hoot; odes to; store; lots of lost tools
14 hold those; if told; he dotes; too short
```

BREAKING BAD HABITS

Do not rest your hands or arms on any support. Keep your hands over the keyboard as you key.

Learn G and N

WARM UP

Key each line twice. Double-space after each pair of lines. Keep your wrists and fingers relaxed.

```
1  f ff fff fit file fail fir fr ftr ftt tf
2  j jj jjj jar jail has hill jhj jj hhj jj
3  feel foil life half heal this that those
4  joke hers rake fast haste hoist lash lid
```

LEARN

Reach your F finger directly right to key G. Keep the other fingers of your left hand anchored on their home keys. Reach your J finger down and left to key N. Keep the other fingers of your right hand anchored on their home keys.

PRACTICE

Key each line twice. Double-space after each pair of lines.

Practice g

```
5  g gg ggg fgf fgtg tgf go gal got get lag
6  sag sage stag stage gas rag egg edge leg
7  dog ledge keg grog get tiger grade grail
```

Practice n

```
8  n nn nnn jnj jnhn hnjn no on in kin none
9  rind seen lane train lane lean nine lion
10 tan ten ton tin tones none nasal tinnier
```

Practice n and g

```
11 ff gg gg jj nn nn gn ng ing ing nag ring
12 nag anger gnarl range longer green grind
13 ring grand glean grin gone gentle ginger
14 tangle dangle strange slings and strings
```

NEW KEYS

G Use the F finger.

N Use the J finger.

TECHNIQUE TIP

When keying, hold your head straight, without tilting it forward or backward.

Lesson 8

Learn Left Shift and >.

WARM UP

Key each line twice. Double-space after each pair of lines. Keep your fingers curved.

```
1  a aa aaa j jj jjj; a aa aaa j kk lll jkl
2  l ll lll lag lags land doll dill toil in
3  all lie like kite kin of ode or ore idea
4  lashes slides knell soil sails rill roil
```

NEW KEYS

 Use the **A** finger.

Use Left Shift for right-hand capital letters (and for all other shifted right-hand characters).

>. Use the **L** finger.

A period is used in abbreviations and to mark the end of a sentence. Typically, one space follows a period.

LEARN

Reach your **A** finger down and left to press the Left **Shift** key. With Left **Shift** pressed, you can strike any right-hand key. Then, release Left **Shift**. Reach your **L** finger down and slightly right to key **>.** Keep your **J** finger on its home key.

PRACTICE

Key each line twice. Double-space after each pair of lines.

Practice Left Shift

```
5  jJ Jj Jd kK Kk Kf lL Ll Ls JdJ fKKf sLLs
6  hH Hj Ha aHHa; Jill Hill Lee; Hall Iris;
7  Hi there Hello; Here he is; Leo the lion
```

Practice Period

```
8  a. l. s. k. d. j. f. e. r. t. i. o. n. a
9  adj. alt. art. e.g. gal. i.e. inf. sing.
10 in. ft. kil. gr. lit. orig. transl. del.
```

Practice Left Shift and Period

```
11 Kan. La. OH OK HI N.H. N.J. Jos. I. Kant
12 Long. Lat. N.H.L. Joe and Jed; King Lear
13 I see. I said. I sit. I sat. I do. I do.
14 Ode to Leo. Oh. His is. No. One. Listen.
```

BREAKING BAD HABITS

Do not slouch. Sit up straight with your feet flat and supported.

Review Left [Shift] [T] [O] [G] [N] and [.>]

REVIEW

The keyboard shows the keys you have learned so far. This lesson focuses on the keys highlighted in dark blue.

WARM UP

Key each line twice. Double-space after each pair of lines. Concentrate on pressing the correct key each time.

```
1  t to to tot toe not note got gotten tote
2  jJ kK lL hH iI oO. Joke; Kids like Jake.
3  Joanne is terse. Nora nods. Kane is kin.
4  Kirk tends to the garden. Lana looks on.
```

PRACTICE

Key each line once. Double-space after each group of lines.

Practice t and o
```
5  ttt ooo fff lll to too toot tot toe tote
6  to tone toner foot oat lot jot rote goat
7  toast knots trots lost stones toes ghost
```

Practice g and n
```
8   ggg nnn ggg nnn no go; gone; genes; sign
9   long longer longest longing song singing
10  no nod node; note done; gig agog; gotten
```

Practice Left Shift and Period
```
11  JKL; IO. KNOLL. Jr. Kg. Lg. Kg. Jds. Hd.
12  Kin are kind. Logan Hotel. Otis loiters.
13  L. L. H. H. K. K. J. J. I. I. I. Hi. No.
```

Practice t o g n Left Shift and Period
```
14  to go to. Nine tons. No one going. Ogden
15  green gnarl great gross gnats grain gilt
16  N.J.L. L.J.K. J.I.N.; Old Ohio. Old Hat.
```

TECHNIQUE TIP

Center your body on [J], about a hand's length from the keyboard, directly in front of your monitor.

Learn C and U

WARM UP

Key each line twice. Double-space after each pair of lines. Strike the keys with a light tap.

```
1  d dd ddd sad sat dot dog done dotes adds
2  j jj jjj Jill Join hill her his hat hits
3  Lili held on. Jade is green. Jess holds.
4  does he dial one or three; drifted east;
```

NEW KEYS

C Use the D finger.

U Use the J finger.

LEARN

Reach down and slightly right with your D finger to key C. Keep the A and S fingers anchored on their home keys. Reach up and slightly left with your J finger to key U. Keep the K, L, and ; fingers anchored on their home keys.

PRACTICE

TECHNIQUE TIP

Hold your head up and relax your neck.

Key each line twice. Double-space after each pair of lines.

Practice c
```
5  d dd c cc dc dc dcd cad cat cater decade
6  lacks class clicks coins; Nick can cook.
7  lace cask flock shock Jack likes cheese.
```

Practice u
```
8  j jj u uu ju ju juj ujuj us use sue uses
9  due hue hurt huge urge; He is Uncle Kurt.
10 Used lutes and flutes; noun run nuts hut
```

Practice c and u
```
11 cur cue cut cud curt cute cuff cure curd
12 cull could cough couch accuse occur ouch
13 curls cushion curious cluck scour ruckus
14 such clubs culture course cruel function
```

Learn W and Right Shift

WARM UP

Key each line twice. Double-space after each pair of lines. Keep your arms close to your sides but free to move.

```
1  s ss sss sash ski skits sour sell sister
2  so; does; sun; stars; sass; losses; dust
3  Hugh shares his fish. He leads us south.
4  sack; cast; usage; soccer; lesson; sense
```

LEARN

Reach up and slightly left with your S finger to key W. Keep your F and D fingers anchored on their home keys. Reach your ; finger down and right to press the Right Shift key. (Keep your J and K fingers anchored on their home keys.) With Right Shift pressed, you can strike any left-hand key. Then, release Right Shift.

PRACTICE

Key each line twice. Double-space after each pair of lines.

Practice w

```
5  s w ss ww sss ws sws wsw sss www sws wsw
6  saw awe dew draw jaw law wall well wills
7  sag wad owe we wan wall week wear wealth
```

Practice Right Shift

```
8   S; St; SA; W.A.G. F Fa Go Ta Da Ed We Fr
9   Fast Far Face Dad Dash Deal Sad Sash Add
10  AHA; Cold Drinks; Fine Sand; Grills Fish
```

Practice w and Right Shift

```
11  The Fresh Air Fund; The Far East; C.O.D.
12  WAAF Go slowly. Walt thinks; Tess walks;
13  Glow Aware Flaw Waist Rower Ewe Chew Few
14  Raw Flow Worn Waif Grown Stew Stow Worth
```

NEW KEYS

W Use the S finger.

Shift Use the ; finger.

Use Right Shift for left-hand capital letters (and for all other shifted left-hand characters).

TECHNIQUE TIP

Remember to use the Right Shift key for left-hand capital letters and the Left Shift key for right-hand capital letters.

Learn X and M

WARM UP

Key each line twice. Double-space after each pair of lines. Keep your wrists relaxed.

```
1  s ss sss w ww www sw wsw sw saw sew swat
2  j jj u uu jiujitsu Julio jingle just jaw
3  Chris Wes Wendi sacks socks clock roasts
4  as is was SST Sid idle snack snake straw
```

NEW KEYS

X Use the S finger.

M Use the J finger.

LEARN

Reach down and slightly right with your S finger to key X. As you make the reach, keep your F finger anchored on its home key. Reach down and slightly right with your J finger to key M. Keep your K, L, and ; fingers anchored on their home keys.

TECHNIQUE TIP

Keep your shoulders down.

PRACTICE

Key each line twice. Double-space after each pair of lines.

Practice x

```
5  s ss x xx sx xsx xs xss S X XSX six axis
6  ax axe axel ox oxen fox flex sax sox FAX
7  Rex hoax nix next index annex Saxons XXI
```

Practice m

```
8  j jj jm mj jmmj mmjm mm mmm JM MJ me mom
9  Milk makes more might. gamma mailman mum
10 mammoth makes mole mire magma Mark merge
```

Practice x and m

```
11 wax tax lax gum gem exam remix minx coax
12 mold mile mere more magic marred maximum
13 Tom Mix; Max; Mr. Maxwell; Ms. M. Maxine
14 maxim mixture axiom Manx matrix exclaims
```

Review C U W X M
and Right Shift

REVIEW

The keyboard shows the keys you have learned so far. This lesson focuses on the keys highlighted in dark blue.

WARM UP

Key each line twice. Double-space after each pair of lines.

1 Dd Ss Cc Jj Uu Ww Xx Mm cue cruel tuxedo
2 sugar smudge mail male malls urges under
3 Ursa Essex Tom mow met metric metal axle
4 Caitlin wash wish wells waxes masc. fem.

PRACTICE

Key each line twice. Double-space after each pair of lines.

Practice c and u
5 muck duck duct tuck luck lucid cull cuss
6 cute could crush crust touch truck scull
7 deuce stuck stack sticks success custard

Practice w and Right Shift
8 William Washi Wen Winslow Woodrow Wilson
9 Wolfgang Winona Wade Wheeler Wilma Wendi
10 Willow Wallace Wanda Ward Wes Walt Willa

Practice x and m
11 mix Mexican maximum maximal Maddox moxie
12 mixer Alex examined axmen taxman Maxwell
13 mass exits extremes exhumes sixth summer

Practice c u w Right Shift x and m
14 Cellist Cancels a Concert. Felix meowed.
15 Dexter Wexler Chuck chum chew chow exits
16 Sammie worries that few hear much music.

TECHNIQUE TIP
Key by using the correct reach; other fingers should remain in their home positions.

Learn B and Y

WARM UP

Key each line twice. Double-space after each pair of lines. Do not look at the keyboard.

```
1  if elf fast fill fun effort effect faded
2  end hen den jail Julie hale hinge jogger
3  gas sash fish half fresh joshes freshman
4  Edward jest heft cleft gash grass jagged
```

NEW KEYS

B Use the **F** finger.

Y Use the **J** finger.

LEARN

Reach your **F** finger down and right to key **B**. Keep your **A** finger anchored on its home key. Reach your **J** finger up and left to key **Y**. Keep the other right-hand fingers anchored on their home keys.

BREAKING BAD HABITS

Do not reach far for the keyboard. Keep elbows at right angles, but free to move slightly.

PRACTICE

Key each line twice. Double-space after each pair of lines.

Practice b

```
5  fff fbf bfb bbb fbf bbb fb bf baa be fib
6  bee bib bat bar rub dub cub club tub but
7  been bias bunt tuba stub beef bark about
8  cable rabbit cabbie ribbon rubber bubble
```

Practice y

```
9   jjj jyj yyj jjy jyj yyy jy yj yd jay hay
10  you yet yes say sty dry day aye fly away
11  joy jay jury ray rely yolk yen nosy body
12  Young York Yak yam yummy tiny teeny tidy
```

Practice b and y

```
13  Bryce buys a bulb to brighten the lobby.
14  Buddy the bulldog labors to bury a bone.
15  Brody yearns for a yacht; bye bye money.
```

Learn V and P

WARM UP

Key each line twice. Double-space after each pair of lines. Key by using the correct reach.

```
1 ff gg bb fbf fans feels Biff baffles bye
2 j; Jill; lo; hi; his; hers; their; lake;
3 good friend; forge ahead; lost messages;
4 ironclad; tea for two; title match; I.D.
```

LEARN

NEW KEYS
V Use the F finger.
P Use the ; finger.

Reach your F finger down and slightly right to key V. Keep your A and S fingers anchored on their home keys. Reach your ; finger up and slightly left to key P. Keep the other right-hand fingers anchored on their home keys.

PRACTICE

Key each line twice. Double-space after each pair of lines.

TECHNIQUE TIP
When using your ; finger to reach for P, keep your right elbow close to your side.

Practice v

```
5 fff fv fv vf fvv vfv vgf fvf fvv vet eve
6 vow van vat vex vote vast vase vest vary
7 ivy ever even envy eave avid alive above
```

Practice p

```
8 ;; ;p; pp; ;pp p; pp; ;p ppp pat pad ape
9 pep papa pass pond pane pick paste price
10 sap clap tape press supper paddle puddle
```

Practice v and p

```
11 pave peeve prove privy vamp VIP provider
12 vapors viper verve pivot private prevail
13 evil powers oval pools develop viewpoint
14 vampire approve overlap overpaid popover
```

Learn Q and ,

WARM UP

Key each line twice. Double-space after each pair of lines. Strike each key with the correct finger.

1 as aim aide avid aster ashes adapt adept
2 key kid king kit kiss kiln milks kippers
3 okay lanes lake like lamb Luke live long
4 all alarm call rail raffle river Alabama

NEW KEYS

Q Use the **A** finger.

, Use the **K** finger.

The comma is used to separate words and phrases for clearness.

LEARN

Reach your **A** finger up and slightly left to key **Q**. Keep your **D** and **F** fingers anchored on their home keys. Reach your **K** finger down and slightly right to key the comma **,**. Keep your **L** and **;** fingers anchored to their home keys.

BREAKING BAD HABITS

Do not bend your wrists forward, back, left, or right. Keep them relaxed and straight.

PRACTICE

Key each line twice. Double-space after each pair of lines.

Practice q

5 aa aq aqqa qqaa aqa qqa qa qua aqua quad
6 quit quay quite quick quill quilt quaint
7 equip equal squid squad quest quack Que.

Practice ,

8 k, kk, ki, jk, A, B, C, D, E, F, G, H, I
9 one, two, three, four; red, white, blue,
10 Joaquin owned a cat, a dog, and a mouse.

Practice q and ,

11 quiet, quota, quote, squat, squaw, squib
12 Raquel, quail, squirrel, sequel, conquer
13 equate, equator, Quincy, squares, squirt
14 Queen, quake, quasi, qualm, quirk, quash

Review B Y V P Q and ,

REVIEW

The keyboard shows the keys you have learned so far. This lesson focuses on the keys highlighted in dark blue.

WARM UP

Key each line twice. Double-space after each pair of lines.

```
1 fad frail Frank Alfred bug bud bush vast
2 hen Hanna vary very your young yell yelp
3 bevy; pamper; prove; pixie; posh; gladly
4 year, ache, acre, squish, piquant, quint
```

PRACTICE

Key each line twice. Double-space after each pair of lines.

Practice b and y

```
5 byte ruby abyss shabby tabby bygone days
6 bay birthday yellow belly bully boundary
7 gabby cubby abbey bubbly burly hobby buy
```

Practice v and p

```
8 vapor vapid pensive pave preview prevent
9 Vice President V.I.P. overpaid passivity
10 Pablo plays the vibraphone very happily.
```

Practice q and ,

```
11 Quite, squab, quickens, quibble, quantum
12 Queens, quits, toque, quarrels, quantity
13 Quinn squashed it quickly and then quit.
```

Practice b y v p q and ,

```
14 pay pry bypass bumpy pebbly pygmy opaque
15 brave, vinyl, brevity, behave very badly
16 Bowery Boys, Marquis, Beverly, Quasimodo
```

TECHNIQUE TIP

Make sure your back is straight or tilted slightly forward from the hips.

Learn Z and ⦂

WARM UP

Key each line twice. Double-space after each pair of lines. Keep your wrists relaxed and straight.

```
1  debut past perk park chances dares tries
2  flurry hurry scurry enjoy delays happens
3  salve settles vessel vassal caste create
4  Frasier will pursue a career in finance.
```

NEW KEYS

Z Use the **A** finger.

⦂ Use Left **Shift** and the **;** finger.

The colon (:) is used in numerical expressions and to direct attention to information that follows (as in "For example:").

LEARN

Reach your **A** finger down and slightly right when you key **Z**. Keep the left-hand fingers anchored on their home keys. Keying the colon is like keying a capital letter. Hold down the Left **Shift** key and strike **⦂**. Then, release Left **Shift**.

PRACTICE

Key each line twice. Double-space after each pair of lines.

Practice z

```
5  a az aza zza zaz aqza za azq zza zap zoo
6  zoom zest zeal Zen zinc zone cozy zipper
7  Zuni fizz fuzz zigzag zebra zero pizzazz
8  zip quiz lazy mezzo muzzle zenith frozen
```

Practice :

```
9  ; ;: :: ;: :; ::: Sirs: Ext: As follows:
10 Memo To: From: Date: Subj: RE: CC: ATTN:
11 To Whom It May Concern: Dear Madam: Ref:
```

Practice z and :

```
12 Dear Elizabeth: To: Mrs. Dezanne Ziegler
13 Puzzle answer: ZIP Code: Zone: Size: NZ:
14 Zoe: Zora: Oz: Ziggy: Ezra: Zelda: Buzz:
```

SPACING TIP

In a sentence, you use one space after a colon.

Learn

WARM UP

Key each line twice. Double-space after each pair of lines. Keep your eyes on the page and not on the keyboard.

```
1 fizz fuzz dizzy gaze buzzer prized gizmo
2 Abbot alley fast has lasts dash flag lab
3 play; pram; pads; my pals; swamps; pique
4 Name: Address: FAX: cars, planes, trains
```

LEARN

Reach your ⌗ finger right to key an apostrophe ⌗. Keep the J, K, and L fingers anchored on their home keys. To key a quotation mark, hold down Left **Shift**, reach your ⌗ finger right, and strike ⌗.

PRACTICE

Key each line twice. Double-space after each pair of lines.

Practice '
```
5 ;' ;';' ';'; 's s' it's I'm isn't aren't
6 Jill's Dave's Omar's didn't don't aren't
7 isn't hadn't should've would've could've
```

Practice "
```
 8 ;" ";"; "x" "y" "A" "B" "My Way" "Okay."
 9 "Not me." "Maybe soon." "See you later."
10 "Just enough," she said. "Oh, we agree."
```

Practice ' and "
```
11 "It's Magic" "Let's Dance" "That's Life"
12 "Don't hang up." "I'll call." "I'm Sue."
13 "Malcolm's moved the boxes," Rubin said.
14 It's the book "Emma" for Mr. Hu's class.
15 "Lillie won't travel on New Year's Eve."
```

NEW KEYS

⌗ Use the ⌗ finger.

The apostrophe (') has many purposes. Use it to form contractions (don't) and possessives (John's).

⌗ Use Left **Shift** and the ⌗ finger.

Use quotation marks (" ") to enclose direct quotations, to emphasize words, and to display certain titles.

BREAKING BAD HABITS

Do not key with the wrong fingers. Practice with correct fingers until you establish the right habit.

Lesson 20

Learn and ❓

WARM UP

Key each line twice. Double-space after each pair of lines. Hold your head straight, without leaning it forward or backward.

```
1  "Let's go pick apples," Sophie proposed.
2  Paul's parrot piped up, "I'm not Polly."
3  Shipped to: Paul Lopez; PS: Please RSVP.
4  Piper liked papaya; Piper's aunt didn't.
```

NEW KEYS

 Use the ⦂ finger.

A hyphen (-) is used for compound words. It is also used to divide words between lines, although most word-processing programs do this automatically.

❓ Use the ⦂ finger.

A diagonal (/), often called a forward slash, is used in abbreviations, in fractions, and to express alternatives or relationships.

LEARN

To key a hyphen, reach your ⦂ finger up and slightly right and strike ➖. Keep the J finger anchored on its home keys. To key a diagonal, reach your ⦂ finger down and slightly right and strike ❓. Keep the other right-hand fingers anchored on their home keys.

PRACTICE

Key each line twice. Double-space after each pair of lines.

Practice -

```
5  ;p; ;p-p; ;-; ;-; -er one-on-one T-shirt
6  side-by-side, after-effects, part-timers
7  toll-free, good-humored, close-captioned
```

Practice /

```
8  ;/; ;//; ;//;/ a/b I/we he/she East/West
9  true/false, owner/manager, and/or, AM/FM
10 his/her, on/off, either/or, input/output
```

Practice - and /

```
11 best-case/worst-case, high-rise/low-rise
12 left-hand/right-hand, mid-week/mid-month
13 paper-thin/see-through, ice-cold/red-hot
14 tax-exempt/tax-sheltered one-way/two-way
```

SPACING TIP

In normal use, do not space before or after the diagonal.

Review Z ⬛ ⬛ ⬛ and ⬛

REVIEW

The keyboard shows the keys you have learned so far. This lesson focuses on the keys highlighted in dark blue.

WARM UP

Key each line twice. Double-space after each pair of lines. Begin with your fingers curled and lightly touching the home keys.

```
1  brazen shilly-shally sizzle crazy quartz
2  Don's fez, Via: tilt-a-whirl willy-nilly
3  mightn't hadn't "Don't say such things."
4  http://www.si.edu "wall-to-wall" mi./hr.
```

PRACTICE

Key each line twice. Double-space after each pair of lines.

Practice z and :
```
5  Price per dozen: Prize: Size: Zookeeper:
6  Zone: Bronze medal: Tarzan: Waltz: Czar:
```

Practice ' and "
```
7  "Neither a borrower nor a lender be." S.
8  "Don't just say 'Don't' like that's it."
```

Practice - and /
```
9  street-smart/quick-witted/sharp-sighted;
10 He/she must give a blow-by-blow account.
11 She provides on-site support for E-mail.
```

Practice z : ' " - and /
```
12 "door-to-door" 'self-employed' in-house:
13 log-jam low-flying "Long-Range" two-term
14 Zig Lenz: Writer/Producer; life-or-death
15 A day of dappled sea-born clouds. -Joyce
```

SPACING TIPS

Remember: Do not key a space before or after a hyphen in a hyphenated word. Do not key a space before or after a diagonal.

Lesson 22

Learn Caps Lock and ?/

WARM UP

Key each line twice. Double-space after each pair of lines. Focus on your technique, not on speed.

1 AR append alternate Aswan Dallas daisies
2 Q.E.D. client-server peer-to-peer hi-res
3 Pass/Fail E/G/B/D/F play-by-play on-site
4 La Paz quizzical A-OK on-again/off-again

NEW KEYS

Caps Lock Use the **A** finger.

Use Caps Lock to key capital letters without pressing Right Shift or Left Shift.

?/ Use Left **Shift** and the **;** finger.

Use a question mark (?) at the end of a sentence that asks a question.

LEARN

Reach your **A** finger left to press **Caps Lock**. Keep all other fingers on their home keys. (Once you press **Caps Lock**, it stays on until you press it again.) The question mark is a shifted diagonal. Press Left **Shift**, reach your **;** finger down and slightly right and strike **?/**.

PRACTICE

Key each line twice. Double-space after each pair of lines.

Practice Caps Lock

5 NBA, NFL, AND NCAA ANNOUNCE RULE CHANGES
6 ASPCA FINDS LOST DOG; ROVER RETURNS HOME
7 IMAGINE: MEN WALK ON MOON; READ ABOUT IT

Practice ?

8 ;/; ;?; :?? ?:? ?;? ?/?/? Who? How? Why?
9 Me? When? Soon? What day? Are you going?
10 Can you? Would you? Could you? Call me?

Practice Caps Lock and ?

11 VISITOR FROM SPACE? AN ECONOMIC SETBACK?
12 PRESIDENT'S TRIP ON HOLD? TWO TEE TIMES?
13 VIKINGS IN THE NEW WORLD? KENNEWICK MAN?
14 MASSIVE CALCULATION ERRORS TO BLAME? US?

TECHNIQUE TIP

The Caps Lock key works only on letter keys. You still have to press Left Shift to key punctuation such as a question mark, a colon, or a quotation mark.

Learn Tab

WARM UP

Key each line twice. Double-space after each pair of lines.

1 adamant ACADEMIA adzuki AARDVARK amalgam
2 Alabama Havana Agra Qatar Panama Jamaica
3 La Salle, La Mancha, La Plata, La Spezia
4 aquatic AQUARIUS aqueous AQUILA aqueduct

LEARN

Reach up and left with your **A** finger to key Tab. Keep the **F** finger on its home key. Keep your elbows close to your sides.

PRACTICE

Key each line twice. Press Tab where you see an arrow. Double-space after each pair of lines.

Practice Letters and Tab

5 aba→ bcc→ cdd→ dee→ efe→ ghh→ hii→ ijj
6 jkk→ llm→ mnn→ opo→ qrr→ stt→ uvw→ xyz
7 DMA→ UPS→ CPU→ CRT→ LCD→ IRQ→ KBD→ I/O

Practice Short Words and Tab

8 all→ ad→ cat→ cot→ dot→ lot→ rot→ not
9 be→ bit→ bat→ do→ to→ tot→ in→ the
10 if→ so→ then→ who→ call→ to→ tell→ me
11 TO→ BE→ OR→ NOT→ TO→ BE→ THAT→ IS

Practice Indenting with Tab

Key the following text as a paragraph. Use word wrap. To indent the paragraph, press Tab where you see the arrow.

12 →Qatar is an independent Arab state
13 in the Middle East, bordering the
14 Persian Gulf. It is a major exporter of
15 oil and natural gas.

NEW KEYS

Tab Use the **A** finger.

Press Tab to align items into columns or to indent text for paragraphs. Tabs are automatically set every half-inch.

SPACING TIP

Do not key a space before or after pressing Tab.

Review Caps Lock ? / and Tab

REVIEW

The keyboard shows the keys you have learned so far. This lesson focuses on the keys highlighted in dark blue.

WARM UP

Key each line twice. Double-space after each pair of lines.

```
1 A diller a dollar, a ten o'clock scholar
2 Everyone's seen a movie, no? We did not.
3 a/b/c/d/e/f/g/h/i/j/k/l/m/n/o/p/q/r/s/t/
4 Del thinks he's all that. Al thinks not.
```

PRACTICE

BREAKING BAD HABITS

Do not raise your elbows. Keep your arms close to your body.

Key each line twice. Double-space after each pair of lines. Where you see an arrow, press Tab.

Practice Caps Lock

```
5 PHASE One; PHASE Two; PHASE Three; RESET
6 MONDAYS, WEDNESDAYS, and FRIDAYS AT NINE
7 Jamal: WISHING YOU A VERY HAPPY BIRTHDAY
```

Practice ?

```
8 Who said that? Why? Where is Paul going?
9 Well, which is it? What? You don't know?
10 How are you? Yes? No? Do you? Won't you?
```

Practice Tab

```
11 eucalyptus→ hemlock→ sycamore→ larch
12 hickory→ dogwood→ chestnut→ willow
```

Practice Caps Lock ? and Tab

```
13 TO:→ FR:→ RE:→ CC:→ FAX:→ EXT:→ FL:→ DEPT:
14 VOL→ HIGH→ LOW→ DATE→ OPEN→ CHG→ YTD→ INT
15 ADRIANA, did ALEJANDRO call the station?
16 Narrator: WHO KNOWS WHICH WAY THEY FLED?
```

Learn the Ten Key

LEARN

If you are doing something—like a science fair project—that requires you to enter lots of numbers, you will benefit from using the ten key pad or "ten key." This is the number pad to the right of the letters on your keyboard or the ten keys on calculators and adding machines. (Most laptop computers do not have a ten key pad. Numbers are on the top row of the keyboard.) Good ten key skills may help you get your work done faster and more accurately.

Your home row is now a home key 5 in the middle of the 4 5 6 row. This key usually has a small raised line to guide you, so you don't have to look when placing your right hand lightly on the keys. Even lefties must use the right hand for the ten key, unless they have a specially designed keyboard with the number pad on the left.

You will use your index finger for 4, your middle finger for 5, and your ring finger for 6. The same arrangement goes for the 1 2 3 row below, and the 7 8 9 row above. You use your thumb for the 0 Ins on the bottom and your pinkie for the / * - and + and Enter keys.

PRACTICE

Rest your right hand lightly on 4 5 6 and + keys, with your index finger on 4, your middle finger on 5 (the home key), your ring finger on 6, and your pinkie on + .

Double-space after each line, using your pinkie on the Enter key to return:

```
1   4,5,6 and +
2   0456++65400
3   6645+455650
4   400+566+450
5   5+566465++4
```

Keyboarding Activities

DIRECTIONS: *You will build your keyboarding skill. Each group of five strokes is considered a "word" (spaces and Enter count as strokes). Your speed is measured by how many five-stroke words you can type in a minute. For example, if you type ten five-stroke "words" in a minute, your "words per minute" (abbreviated WPM) is 10. Each of the following exercises is a one-minute drill with the focus on the alphabet keys. It is important that you do these drills in sequential order since they build on one another; do not skip around.*

1. Start a word-processing program. Save the new, blank word-processing document as **KB-1_Drills_xx**. Replace **xx** with your own initials or name, as directed by your teacher, and type your name and today's date in the header.

2. Key the text in each of the following speed drills for one minute. Press Enter after each line. If you reach the end of a drill before time is up, press Enter and start over immediately from the beginning of the drill.

3. Take these speed drills for home keys:

Drill 1 (Goal: 8 WPM)
```
lads fall; as a fad
lass adds; sad lads
```
Drill 2 (Goal: 8 WPM)
```
as a lass; all dads
alas as a lad falls
```
Drill 3 (Goal: 10 WPM)
```
as a sad lass; add a lad
lads fall; fads; add all
```

4. Take this speed drill for keys E and H (Goal: 10 WPM).
```
he has a sled; she asked
she has a sash; he sells
```

5. Take this speed drill for keys R and I (Goal: 11 WPM).
```
she shares a fare; he is fair
her red dress has real frills
```

6. Take this speed drill for keys E, H, R, and I (Goal: 12 WPM).
```
he fries fish; she feels fair
free idea; he likes fresh air
```

7. Take this speed drill for keys T and O (Goal: 13 WPM).
```
those tools are foolish; these too
jets dot the air; lift off so fast
```

8. Take this speed drill for keys G and N (Goal: 14 WPM).
```
sitting in this light; long nights
golden raisins and grains are good
```

9. Take this speed drill for Left Shift and Period (Goal: 14 WPM).
```
Ken likes Jen. He said John is in.
Hold on. OK. I see. No one has it.
```

10. Take this speed drill for keys T, O, G, N, Left Shift, and Period (Goal: 15 WPM).
```
Nikki greets Lara. I told Ossie a joke.
He kids Les. Nan is Irish. Lea led Nat.
```

11. Take this speed drill for keys C and U (Goal: 16 WPM).
```
Julia hugs her cousin Lucie once again.
Urge Louis to accrue one hundred coins.
```

12. Take this speed drill for keys W and Right Shift (Goal: 16 WPM).
```
Shawn wanted to write. Rowan went west.
Dan is a D.A. in D.C. He was a witness.
```

13. Take this speed drill for keys X and M (Goal: 17 WPM).

```
Mr. Marx meets Xena in March.
Tim fixes machines in Mexico.
Matt Solomon mined metal ore.
```

14. Take this speed drill for keys C, U, W, X, M, and Right Shift (Goal: 18 WPM).

```
Michi locates the crux of it.
Dr. Dux makes music on a sax.
Her hat is crushed in a rush.
```

15. Take this speed drill for keys B and Y (Goal: 18 WPM).

```
Moby brings Ben a toy rabbit.
Becky enjoyed yoga yesterday.
Rob blabbed about your story.
```

16. Take this speed drill for keys V and P (Goal: 19 WPM).

```
Vince has one pet peeve. Liv appeared very peppy.
View Venus and the moon. Buy very purple violets.
```

17. Take this speed drill for keys Q and Comma (Goal: 19 WPM).

```
Quentin quips about age. Buy quarts, not gallons.
She asks for equal time. Do not quibble with him.
```

18. Take this speed drill for keys B, Y, V, P, Q, and Comma (Goal: 20 WPM).

```
Jane bought a new Viper.
I provided yellow paper.
Pave your patio, please.
Quit playing that piano.
```

19. Take this speed drill for key Z (Goal: 21 WPM).

```
A piazza is an Italian public square.
Zika saw lots of zebras at the zoo.
Zanesville is located in Ohio.
```

---

20. Save the document. With your teacher's permission, print it, and then close it.

21. Exit your word-processing program.

22. Evaluate your speed and accuracy. Assess your posture and keyboarding technique. Did you remember to maintain your correct keyboarding posture and to keep your eyes on the copy?

DIRECTIONS: *You will increase your keyboarding speed. Each group of five strokes is considered a "word" (spaces and Enter count as strokes). Your speed is measured by how many five-stroke words you can type in a minute. For example, if you type ten five-stroke "words" in a minute, your "words per minute" (abbreviated WPM) is 10. Always use the correct techniques when you type. It is important that you do these drills in sequential order since they build on one another; do not skip around.*

1. Start a word-processing program, and create a blank document. Save the word-processing document as **KB-2_Drills_xx**. Type your name and today's date in the header.

2. The first three of the following drills are in pairs. For the first drill in each pair, press Enter at the end of each line. For the second drill in each pair, start with a tab and use word wrap. If you reach the end of a drill before time is up, press Enter and start over immediately from the beginning of the drill.

3. Take these speed drills using keys 4, 5, 6, and 7:
   One-Minute Drill (Goal: 12 WPM)
   ```
   You can get 4 of the 5 items.
   Wait, 5 and 6 do not match.
   ```
   One-Minute Drill (Goal: 26 WPM)
   ```
      The Moai statues on Easter Island average over fourteen feet tall.
   The builders of these stone statues thought they were sacred.
   ```

4. Take these speed drills using keys 8, 9, and 0:
   One-Minute Drill (Goal: 13 WPM)
   ```
   I let 9 kids make 8 tents at camp.
   Jo hit 80 of 90 balls in the game.
   ```
   One-Minute Drill (Goal: 27 WPM)
   ```
      The blue pike once swam the cool waters of Lake Erie. With
   overfishing, changes in habitat, and pollution, the fish has become
   extinct.
   ```

5. Take these speed drills using keys 1, 2, and 3:
   One-Minute Drill (Goal: 14 WPM)
   ```
   There are 21 men and 3 women here.
   I found 32 rocks on my trip today.
   ```
   One-Minute Drill (Goal: 27 WPM)
   ```
      Most students do not look forward to exams. It feels great when an
   exam is over, but the best feeling of all is when you ace an exam.
   ```

6. Review the number keys. One at a time, key each sentence of the following drill as many times as you can in 30 seconds (Goal: 14 WPM for each line).
   ```
   He has 2 birds, 4 dogs, and 1 cat.
   Of the 63 hours, 20 were overtime.
   All 8 students had 50 or 75 cents.
   It is 85 or 90 degrees in the sun.
   ```

7. Key the following paragraph for 2 minutes. Start with a tab, and use word wrap. If you reach the end before time is up, start again from the beginning (Goal: 27 WPM).
   ```
      Of all the people in the public eye, think of someone who you feel
   is a good role model for you and your friends. It might be someone in
   the arts, in sports, or even in your town. It might be someone you know.
   List things about this person that makes him or her special.
   ```

8. Save the document. With your teacher's permission, print it, and then close it.

9. Exit your word-processing program.

10. Evaluate your speed and accuracy. Assess your posture and keyboarding technique. Did you maintain your correct keyboarding posture and to keep your eyes on the copy?

DIRECTIONS: *You will improve your keyboarding skill. Each group of five strokes is considered a "word"(spaces and Enter count as strokes). Your speed is measured by how many five-stroke words you can type in a minute. For example, if you type ten five-stroke "words" in a minute, your "words per minute" (abbreviated WPM) is 10. Always use the correct techniques when you type. This activity consists of 30-second, 60-second, and 2-minute drills.*

1. Start a word-processing program, and create a blank document. Save the word-processing document as **KB-3_Drills_xx**. Type your name and today's date in the header.

2. For each of the following drills, key each paragraph for the specified amount of time. Start each paragraph with a tab and use word wrap. If you reach the end of a drill before time is up, press Enter and start over immediately from the beginning of the drill.

3. Take these 30-second drills (Goal: 35 WPM for each sentence):

    A river is a natural stream of water that empties into an ocean, lake, or other river. A delta is a landmass that forms at the mouth of a river by layers of sand and gravel.

4. Take these 60-second drills (Goal: 35 WPM for each paragraph):

    A reef is a ridge of sand, coral, or rock lying at or near the surface of the water. Coral reefs are found in tropical climates. They are made of the remains of sea animals.

    Sally had to change a flat tire. She had never done it before, but had seen other people do it. She found the spare tire and the tools, and made the switch in twenty minutes.

5. Take this 2-minute drill (Goal: 35 WPM):

    Jerry always wanted to write a mystery novel. He had all the details in his head before he even sat down to start writing. He knew the names of all the people in the story. He had the plot worked out. He knew how it would start and end. When he began writing on his laptop, the words flowed like water. Before long, he was ready to write the sequel.

6. Save the document. With your teacher's permission, print it, and then close it.

7. Exit your word-processing program.

8. Evaluate your speed and accuracy. Assess your posture and keyboarding technique. Did you remember to maintain your correct keyboarding posture and to keep your eyes on the copy?

Keyboarding Activities

21st Century Skills

As the future leaders of our families, communities, government, and workforce, it is imperative that you develop the skills you need to succeed in work and life. This appendix covers these 21st Century skills in the following sections:

- Making Decisions
- Setting Goals
- Solving Problems
- Managing Time
- Thinking Critically

- Communicating Effectively
- Cooperating and Collaborating
- Behaving Ethically
- Using Technology
- Suggested Activities

Figure C-1 Some decisions are easy to make, and others are more difficult. What is one of the more difficult decisions that you've had to make? What were the consequences of your decision?

Making Decisions

Any time you make up your mind about something, or choose one option over another, you are making a decision. Some decisions are simple—what time will I leave for school? Some are more difficult—should I tell my friend I don't like her hair style? The results—or consequences—of your decisions affect you in big and small ways.

- If the consequences of a decision are positive and contribute to your well-being, it means you made a healthy—or good—choice.
- If the consequences are negative and interfere with your well-being, that means you made an unhealthy—or poor—choice.

Most decisions actually have both long-term and short-term consequences. Long-term, what you eat for breakfast might affect your health and wellness. Short-term, it might affect how you do on a test.

Sometimes consequences have both positive and negative results. The good news is that you can learn how to make healthy decisions that turn out positive more often than they turn out negative. Decisions give you power and control over your life. When you make a decision, you are showing yourself and others that you are independent and responsible.

Six Steps to a Decision   You can take some of the uncertainty and doubt out of decision-making by turning it into a process. A process is a series of steps that leads to a conclusion.

1. *Identify the decision to be made.* Make sure you recognize and understand the choice. Define the decision as a goal—what do I want to achieve with this choice?

2. *Consider all possible options.* You usually have lots of options for each decision. Try to think of as many as you can, and write them down. Don't just consider the obvious choice; some of the best options might seem pretty bizarre at first. Consider your available resources, and what you are trying to achieve.

3. *Identify the consequences of each option.* Each option will have consequences— some positive and some negative; some long-term and some short-term. Recognizing all the consequences will help you predict the outcome of your decision.

4. *Select the best option.* Once you consider the options and identify the consequences, you have the information you need to make your decision.

5. *Make and implement a plan of action.* Making the decision is not the end of the process. You must take steps to make it happen. Until you do, the decision is just an idea or thought in your head.

6. *Evaluate the decision, process, and outcome.* After you have acted on your decision, you can look back and evaluate it, based on your values and standards. Did you achieve the goal you defined in step 1? Did you miss any possible options? Did you correctly identify the consequences? Did you make use of your resources? Was the outcome what you hoped for?

Thoughtful Decision-Making   We all make mistakes. Despite our best intentions, we make poor choices. Most of the time, it doesn't matter too much. If you cut your hair too short, it will grow back. Sometimes, though, we must live with the consequences of our actions for a long time—maybe even our whole lives. For example, if you text while driving and get into an accident, that's your responsibility.

But, even when we make a poor choice with long-term consequences, we can learn from our mistakes and try to make better choices going forward.

It is important that you consider how your decisions will affect other people. When you are evaluating your options while making a decision, consider these questions:

- Is it hurtful to me?
- Is it hurtful to someone else?
- Is it fair?
- Is it honest?
- Is it legal?
- Is it practical?

If the answer is to the first two questions is "Yes," you might want to look for other alternatives. If the answer to the remaining questions is "Yes," you are on the right track.

Setting Goals

A goal is something you are trying to achieve. Goals help direct your actions and guide your decision-making because they give you something to work toward. They help give your life meaning, because you know that there is a purpose in what you do. When you achieve a goal, you can be proud and express satisfaction.

If all you do is think about a goal, it's just a dream. You make goals real by deciding what you want to achieve and then planning how to get there. While you should set goals that are within reach, there is nothing wrong with challenging yourself to push harder.

Short-Term and Long-Term Goals   When you want to achieve something quickly, you set short-term goals. You can accomplish short-term goals in the near future—maybe even today. For example, finishing your homework on time is a short-term goal. It is usually easy to define short-term goals because they are specific and not very complicated. If you keep a to-do list, it is full of short-term goals—meet friends at the mall, call your grandmother, make your bed.

A long-term goal is something you want to achieve in the more distant future—maybe a year from now, or maybe even more distant than that. Graduating from college is a long-term goal. So is buying a car. Defining long-term goals may be more difficult than defining short-term goals. You might know you want to travel, but you don't know where or how.

Sometimes it's harder to stay focused on a long-term goal—it seems far away. Breaking the long-term goal down into a series of short-term goals—or milestones—makes it easier to stay on track. Becoming a computer programmer might be a long-term goal. To achieve that goal, you can set short-term goals of:

- Taking programming classes
- Graduating from high school
- Attending college

Five Steps to a Goal   There's a process you can use to help identify, assess, and set goals:

1. *Identify the goal.* Write down the goal using as much detail as you can. This helps you understand and recognize the goal. Be positive, not negative: I will attend the club meeting rather than I won't skip the club meeting.

2. *Assess whether the goal is something you really want.* It might be a fad, or something that sounds good, or even something someone else wants for you.

3. *Make a plan for achieving the goal.* This step will help you identify whether or not the goal is reasonable and attainable. What resources will you need? If you cannot come up with a plan that works, you may need to go back to step 1.

4. *Write down your action plan for achieving the goal, being as specific as possible.*

5. *Every once in a while, reevaluate your goals.* Make sure they are still important to you and, if so, that you are on track to achieve them.

Solving Problems

Any barrier or obstacle between you and a goal is a problem. Problems pop up all the time. Mostly, we come up with a solution without thinking too hard. Say you want to go to the movies Saturday night, but your mother says you can't go out until you clean your room.

- The problem: Your messy room is an obstacle between you and the movies.
- The solution: You clean your room.

Figure C-2 How can you reduce the stress you feel when you must make a choice?

Some problems sneak up on us over time, sometimes hidden by something else. You might want to do well in Social Studies, but you fall asleep in class every day. Is the problem that your teacher is boring, that your classroom is too warm, or is it that you are staying up late at night playing video games?

Taking Responsibility   One difficulty with solving problems is figuring out whose problem it really is. Generally, the person who is blocked from a goal is the one who owns the problem. If your friend loses his math book and wants to borrow yours, is it your problem or his? What if you loan him the book and he loses it?

If you own the problem, you are responsible for solving it. If someone else owns the problem, you may be able to help solve it, but ultimately it is not your responsibility.

Taking responsibility for your own problems, and working to find solutions, shows that you are independent and capable.

Six Steps to a Solution   When problems are harder to identify, or harder to solve, you can use the decision-making process to figure out the best solution:

1. *Identify the problem.* This is your chance to be honest, acknowledge the problem, and determine what goal it is blocking.

Figure C-3 Why is it important to be able to solve problems at home, in school, and in the workplace?

2. *Consider all possible solutions.* There may be one obvious solution, or there may be many possible solutions. Write down as many as you can think of. You will need to consider your values, standards, and resources, too. Some solutions might be harder to make happen, or take longer than others. Some might cost money and some might be free. Some might solve only part of the problem.

3. *Identify the consequences of each solution.* Like decisions, each solution will have consequences, and it is important to recognize how the consequences will affect you and others. Again, write them down.

4. *Select the best solution.* The best solution offers the best possible opportunity for you to continue your progress toward your goal.

5. *Make and implement a plan of action.* Recognizing and selecting a solution are only part of the process. You must take the necessary steps to make the solution real.

6. *Evaluate the solution, process, and outcome.* Did your solution work? Did you achieve your goal? Would you do anything differently if you had the same problem again?

Managing Time

Time management means organizing your schedule so you have time to complete tasks and meet your responsibilities. Combining goal-setting with time management is a very effective way to make sure you get things done.

- Create a time journal or log to figure out exactly how you currently spend your time.

- Set specific, realistic, and attainable goals using schedules. Scheduling helps you plan ahead, so you know when you will do something, and you can be ready for it. You can schedule by any time period, but the most useful are by month, week, and day. Different schedules can help you identify tasks that must be accomplished within a specific timeframe.

- Make use of the calendar program on your computer or handheld. You can enter schedules, phone calls, and appointments. Use the tasks list feature to record and prioritize the things you need to accomplish. Set the program to display a message or make a sound to remind you of deadlines.

- Create to-do lists, and rank list items in order of importance.

- Learn to say no. Some people may ask for too much of your time. They may expect you to take on more responsibility than you can handle. It is OK to say no. Be polite and respectful, but explain that your schedule is full.

- Ask for help. If you are having trouble completing tasks that are part of your assigned responsibilities, you will need to find a way to get them done. Ask your teacher, a counselor, a family member, or a friend to help you learn how to organize your time, or find ways to be more efficient.

Managing Resources   Keeping your time and to-do list organized is critical, but if the resources you need are not organized, you will not succeed at the task at hand. For example, if you complete the research for a project on time, but cannot find it in order to write the report, you will be unable to complete the assignment. Set up a system of folders—both on your computer and, if you deal with paper, in a filing cabinet—that you keep organized so that you can always find the resources that you need.

Figure C-4 Would your friends be happy if you said you'd meet them at 4:00 but you didn't show up until 4:45? Employers and co-workers expect you to honor and respect time in the workplace, too.

Thinking Critically

Critical thinking can help you evaluate your options in many situations. You can use it when you are making decisions, setting goals, and solving problems. When you think critically, you are honest, rational, and open-minded about your options. You consider all possibilities before rushing to judgment.

- Being honest means acknowledging selfish feeling and preexisting opinions.
- Being rational means relying on reason and thought instead of on emotion or impulse.
- Being open-minded means being willing to evaluate all possible options—even those that are unpopular.

You can think critically about a lot of things, not just decisions and problems. You don't have to believe everything you hear or read. You can question a news report, look deeper into the meaning of a magazine article, or investigate the truth behind a rumor.

When you think critically, you consider all possible options and other points of view. You look objectively at information. Objective means fairly, without emotion or prejudice. Then, you use your values, standards, and ethics to interpret the information subjectively. Subjective means affected by existing opinions, feelings, and beliefs.

Looking at things both objectively and subjectively can help you make choices that are right for you. For example, you can look at a candidate for class president objectively and see that she is smart, hard-working, and honest. Subjectively, you can disagree with everything she stands for, and vote for someone else.

Figure C-5 Communicating with people of different backgrounds or from different countries helps you build global awareness and understanding. How can you find ways to interact with students from different cultures?

Communicating Effectively

Communicating is how people connect with others. Communication prevents misunderstandings. It gives you a way to share ideas. It even makes it easier for you to appreciate and respect other people's opinions. At its most basic, communication is an exchange between a sender and a receiver. The sender transmits the message with a specific intent. The receiver interprets the message and responds. Effective communication is when the receiver interprets the message the way the sender intended. Ineffective communication is when the receiver misinterprets the message.

Sometimes barriers get in the way of effective communication. When you recognize any potential communication barriers, such as language barriers, cultural barriers, or value/belief barriers, you can take steps to overcome them—both when you listen and when you speak.

Verbal Communication   Verbal communication is the exchange of messages by speaking or writing. For most of us, verbal communication is the most common way we stay in touch with other people in our lives. We talk face-to-face or on the phone. We send text messages, e-mails, and instant messages. We write blogs, pass notes, and send cards.

Talking is usually a very effective form of verbal communication. When you speak clearly and use language the receiver understands, he or she almost always gets the message the way you intend it.

Nonverbal   Communication   Nonverbal communication helps put words into context. This form of communication includes visual messages that the receiver can see, such as a smile when you are talking. It also includes physical messages, such as a pat on the back. During a conversation, the tone of your voice and the language you use combine to provide context for the words. When you write, you lose some of the context, which can make the communication less effective. Exchanging written messages doesn't take the place of face-to-face communication. When the receiver can't hear your voice, he or she might misinterpret the message.

Active Listening   Active listening is an important part of effective communication. When you are an active listener, you pay attention to the speaker, and make sure you hear and understand the message. Active listening is a sign of respect. It shows you are willing to communicate and that you care about the speaker and the message. When you listen actively, the other person is more likely to listen when you speak, too.

Use these skills to be an active listener:

- Show interest using eye contact and positive nonverbal messages.
- Let the other person finish speaking before you respond.
- Ignore distractions such as cell phones and other people.
- Set your predetermined opinions and emotions aside.
- Repeat the message that you hear out loud, to make sure you received it correctly.

The Communication Process   You can communicate effectively by using a six-step process:

1. *Be clear.* Use words and body language that the other person can understand, and that send a clear message.
2. *Be personal.* Address the other person by his or her name or title. Use "I" statements to show that you take responsibility for your role in the conflict.
3. *Be positive.* State your message in positive terms directed at how to achieve your common goal.

4. *Get to the point.* Explain why you feel or think this way.

5. *Use active listening.* Be sure you hear the response.

6. *Think before you respond.* Use critical thinking instead of emotions.

Cooperating and Collaborating

Any group that works together to achieve a common goal is a team. When you are part of a team, you have access to all the knowledge, experience, and abilities of your teammates. Together you can have more ideas, achieve more goals, and solve more problems. A successful team relationship depends on all team members working together. They depend on each other. They trust one another. If one team member does not do his or her share, the entire team suffers. The challenges of a team relationship come from having different people working together. Even if everyone agrees on a common goal, they may not agree on how to achieve that goal.

Developing a Team Relationship   Teams are influenced by different things, including the personal qualities of the team members, the resources available, and the purpose or goals of the team. When a team first forms, team members might feel nervous or uncomfortable. You might not know each other very well. You might wonder what to expect.

At first, you might misunderstand each other, or misinterpret communications. One teammate might say she can't come to a meeting, and you might think she means she doesn't want to be part of the team. Another teammate might have lots of plans and ideas, and the rest of you might think he is trying to take over and be the boss.

As you get to know each other, and learn how to communicate, you might feel a sense of belonging. You might develop common bonds. You might give your team a name and identify with your teammates. You will be able to work together to achieve your goal.

Being a Leader   Teams benefit from strong leadership. Leaders exhibit positive qualities that other people respect, such as self-confidence. They use skills such as goal setting and critical thinking to make healthy decisions for the benefit of the team. Being the leader does not mean you are always right. The leader's opinion does not count more than the opinions of the other team members. An effective leader keeps the team on track and focused on achieving its goals.

Being a Team Member   While a strong leader is important to the success of a team, team members must also be committed to the group's success. An effective team member helps teammates if they need help, does not blame teammates for problems or

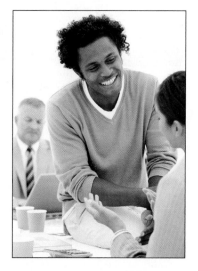

Figure C-6 How does cooperating with teammates make it easier to achieve your common goals?

mistakes, and offers ideas and suggestions instead of criticism. You are a good team member if you are:

- Open minded
- Willing to compromise
- Cooperative
- Friendly
- Trustworthy

Bullying   A bully is someone who tries to hurt others on purpose, not just once but over and over. Bullies can be boys or girls, big or small, young or old. Bullies can be found at school, but they can also turn up in other areas of your life, including in your neighborhood, at work, and even at home.

Bullies behave badly because it gets them attention. Bullies respond when witnesses laugh by bullying more. They respond when victims cry by bullying more. The more people react, the worse the bullying gets.

Some of the things bullies do include:

- Physically hurting others by tripping, pushing, kicking, pinching, or punching
- Calling people names
- Teasing people about the way they look, the way they act, or their values
- Excluding someone—leaving someone out
- Spreading rumors
- Stealing or breaking personal belongings
- Using threats or violence to make people do things they don't want to do

Bullies tend to pick on people who are smaller, who don't know how to stand up for themselves, who are easily upset, and who don't have a lot of friends. If you are being bullied, you need to take action right away.

- Tell someone!
- Avoid the bully as much as you can.
- Refuse to do what the bully says.
- Stand up for yourself!

Cyber bullies, are bullies who use technology such as the Internet, cell phones, and interactive gaming devices to hurt others. They might:

- Send threatening or harassing messages
- Steal passwords and pretend to be someone else online
- Use blogs or social networking sites to spread rumors
- Send private pictures through e-mail or cell phones
- Create hurtful Web sites
- Distribute someone else's personal information

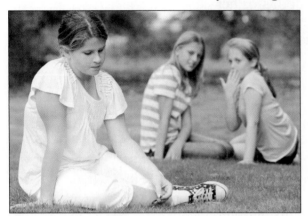

Figure C-7 Avoiding or ignoring a bully is one way to stand up for yourself.

Cyber bullying can be tricky to stop, because it is anonymous and takes place away from school. If you are being cyberbullied, you can take many of the same steps you would take with a face-to-face bully. But, if the cyber bully doesn't stop, you may have to report it to the Internet or telephone service provider. If the behavior is illegal, you may have to report it to the police.

Behaving Ethically

Ethics are a set of beliefs about what is right and what is wrong. Some ethics are established by society. They determine how people are supposed to behave, usually in terms of human rights, responsibilities, and justice. They may be based on customs or on law. Some ethics are established by groups of people, such as the members of certain professions. For example, doctors and lawyers must abide by strict ethical standards, or they can lose their licenses to practice. Some ethics are personal and usually measure virtues—or positive character traits—such as honesty, compassion, and loyalty.

People don't always agree on what is ethical. One student may think it is ethical to let a friend copy his homework, while another student may think it is unethical. Even when there are laws defining what is ethical, some people still don't agree. For example, one person might think it is ethical to download movies or share music files, even though it is illegal.

Using Technology

Technology is a varied resource that impacts all areas of your life. It makes everyday life easier, more fun, and more rewarding. As with any resource, knowing when and how to use technology can help you be more productive. Using technology just because it's there or seems cool might be fun; it can also end up wasting other resources, such as time, energy, or money.

For example, the Internet is a technology we use all the time. It can provide many benefits when you use it wisely. You can find information to complete a homework assignment, communicate with friends, or shop. If you don't use the Internet wisely, you might waste time looking at Web sites that provide incorrect or misleading information. You might spend so much time online that you put your real relationships at risk. Or, you might accidentally send personal information to identity thieves.

Critical thinking can help you recognize how best to use technology in your own life. You can decide whether technology will be a solution to a problem you are facing, or if it will cause new problems.

Types of Technology   Technology can be classified into many different categories. You might use or encounter the following common types of technology.

Figure C-8 Videoconferencing uses technology to make long-distance meetings and education possible. How do you think changes in technology have impacted areas of study throughout history?

- Information technology is likely to be the type of technology you use and that impacts your daily life the most. It refers to the use of computers to collect, store, and distribute information. For example, you use information technology to write, edit, and print a letter, or to store a name and address in a computerized contact list. You also use information technology to search the Internet or read a news story online, or for online shopping.
- Communications technology is part of information technology. It refers to the use of technology to make communication easier and more efficient. It includes cell phones, as well as video conferencing, voice over Internet protocol (VoIP), and social networking.

Figure C-9 Technology affects our food supply in many ways. How would a farmer plant and harvest crops without technology?

- Agricultural technology is the use of technology to control the growth and harvesting of animal and plant products. It includes a wide range of areas, such as soil preparation, harvesting and planting techniques, and the use of chemicals for growth or pest control.
- Medical technology is the use of technology to improve the management and delivery of health care. It includes areas such as medical imaging technology, nuclear medicine technology, and veterinary medical technology.
- Banking technology also stems from information technology. It includes areas such as software for managing online banking, controlling access to accounts, and technology for automated teller machines, as well as debit and credit card readers.

Benefits and Drawbacks of Technology   Is it always better to use technology? There are obvious benefits to using technology, but there are also drawbacks. Most new technologies have both positive and negative effects.

- Manufacturing is faster when you use assembly lines, robots, and automated management systems, than when you build products by hand. But, manufacturing processes may release chemicals into the environment, causing pollution.
- Water filtration systems, access to electricity, and advancements in medical care are a few ways technology has improved health and the quality of life. Technology also creates ethical dilemmas, such as testing medical products on animals, or genetically modifying food products.

- Jet engines make it possible for people to travel quickly and easily. But, passengers on airplanes are exposed to radiation, and can rapidly transmit disease from one country to another.

- Computers provide access to information and keep people connected. They also store personal information that can lead to invasions of privacy or identity theft.

Some newer technologies can help reverse problems caused by older technologies. For example, pollution caused by technology brought some animals to the brink of extinction. Genetic technology is helping animal breeding programs to restore the animal populations. Understanding the positive and negative effects can help you make choices about how best to use technology.

Cyberspace Is a Risky Place   Using the Internet is usually fun. It can also lead to risk. Consider the following:

- How much do you really know about someone online who you've never met? You can't see him. You can't hear his voice. An adult can pretend to be a teen, and you would never know.

- How much information do you want everyone to know? Everything you put on the Internet—including messages sent from a cell phone—is public, and it never goes away. A blog you post today will still be around ifive years from now.

- How much control are you willing to give up? As soon as you put information online, you no longer control it. You might send a picture or message to a friend, who forwards it to someone else, who forwards it to someone else, who posts it on a social networking site.

Suggested Activities

- Write down three decisions you have faced in the last two days. As a class, discuss the decisions. If more than one of you faced the same decision, discuss the different—or similar—choices you made and why. Compare the outcomes of the choices made by different people.

- For a week, keep track of how you spend your time—how much time you spend socializing with friends, doing homework, spending time with your family, etc. Write a short paragraph on ways in which you can improve your time-management skills. If you have access to an electronic bulletin board, post your paragraphs to the board.

- How much does peer pressure influence decisions?
  1. Think of a question you could ask your classmate, such as whether she wants a test on Thursday or Friday.
  2. Ask five people the question, without saying anything else: "Do you want the test on Thursday or Friday?"
  3. Ask five other people the question, but add a comment that indicates their peers have already made a choice: "Do you want the test on Thursday or Friday? Most people have been picking Thursday."
  4. Make a chart comparing the results, and discuss it as a class.
- As a class, develop a list of positive personal qualities such as flexibility, open-mindedness, initiative, listening attentively to speakers, and willingness to learn new knowledge and skills. Consider which of these personal qualities you have and which ones you need to develop. For a week, keep a journal and describe events where you exhibited the qualities listed. At the end of week, use the documentation to make a poster or presentation.
- Being able to lead a team is an important skill. Working with a partner, brainstorm the qualities that it takes to be a good leader. Make a two-column chart listing the qualities on the left and describing the ways you exhibit the quality on the right. Present your findings to the class in a multimedia presentation, a song or rap, or a poster.
- Technology is constantly changing and improving. Not that long ago, students would have to type up their reports and schoolwork using a typewriter. This meant that if they made a major error, they would have to start all over again. Write a short report describing ways in which technology impacts how students learn and study.

Career Skills

Planning for a career is a job in itself. It takes time, energy, and careful management. So why do it? Putting effort into career planning can help you set realistic and attainable goals for education. It can help you identify your strengths and weaknesses, so you focus your resources on finding a career that you will enjoy. Spending time exploring career opportunities can also be fun and exciting, because you experience new situations and activities.

This appendix covers these career planning skills in the following sections:

- Identifying Types of Careers
- Individual Assessment
- Occupational Research
- Employability Skills

- Recognizing the Value of School
- Safety in the Workplace
- Suggested Activities

Identifying Types of Careers

A career is a chosen field of work in which you try to advance over time by gaining responsibility and earning more money. Another word for career is occupation. A job is any activity you do in exchange for money or other payment. A job does not necessarily lead to advancement.

The career you choose has a major impact on the kind of life you will lead. Your career determines the type of training and education you will need. It might impact where you live and even who you will marry. Your career choice affects how much money you earn and how you spend most of your time. Most workers in the U.S. spend between 40 and 50 hours each week at work.

- Where will you be? In a large office, a hospital, or on a construction site?
- Who will you be with? Will you work alone or have coworkers? Will you be supervising children, helping animals, or caring for the elderly?

Even if you have no idea what career you want in the future, you can start now to identify different types of careers. Learning about careers now will help prepare you to choose the career that is right for you.

Individual Assessment

The first step in identifying a career is self-assessment. That means taking a close, objective look at your interests, values, and abilities. You then use that information to select careers or career clusters to investigate further. There are many ways to perform a self-assessment. There are Interest Surveys and Self-Assessment Worksheets that you can obtain from a teacher, career counselor, or online. You can also develop your own worksheet using the following steps:

1. List your two favorite school subjects.
2. List at least four specific skills you have acquired in your favorite subjects.
3. List at least four achievements in your favorite subjects.
4. List at least four of your abilities.
5. List at least two interests.
6. List at least four work values.
7. Analyze the information to identify connections that point to a career.
8. List the two career clusters or pathways that best match your interests and abilities. (See page D-5 for information on Career Clusters.)

Interests Your interests tell what you like to do and what you do not like to do. They are the subjects or activities that attract your attention and that you enjoy doing or learning about. There are six general interest categories: the arts, business, crafts, office operations, science, and social.

Knowing your interests helps you identify a career that you will find interesting. For example, if you have an interest in growing plants, you might enjoy a career as a botanist, farmer, or florist. If you have an interest in automobiles you might enjoy a career as an auto mechanic, auto salesperson, or automobile designer. When you know your interests early in your career search, you can identify careers that use those interests. If you discover that many of the tasks listed in an occupation are not interesting to you, reconsider your choice, and research careers that match your interests.

Figure D-1 What types of interests and values might someone have who wants to be a firefighter?

Values A value is the importance that you place on various elements in your life. Knowing what values you feel most strongly about helps you avoid compromising the things that are most important to you. Recognizing your values also helps you prioritize what matters most to you in a career. Money might be more important to you than leisure time. Working with people might be more important to you than what shift you work. Work-related values include the following:

- Job security. Is it important that you find a job immediately upon the completion of your training program? How important is job availability?

- Leisure time. Is it important for you to have extra time for leisure activities?

- Wages. Is an average wage acceptable if you like your work, or is a very high wage necessary?

- Recognition. Is it important that the job you choose is respected by the people in your community?

- Creativity. Do you like to come up with new ideas to solve problems, or do you prefer a job in which there is exactly one way to do things?

- Advancement. Do you want a career that provides opportunities for promotion?

- Working environment. Do you prefer to work indoors or outdoors?

- Home life. Do you want to work a daytime schedule (9 to 5) with some overtime and with weekends and holidays off, or are you willing to do shift work (all hours, any day of the week)?

- Responsibility. Do you want a job that requires you to make a number of decisions?
- Management. Do you want to be responsible for supervising the work of other people or for organizing many tasks at once?

All of these factors affect your job choice. Make a list of these work values and put them in order of their importance to you. When you research an occupation, refer to your list so you do not choose a job that conflicts with your values.

Abilities An ability, or skill, is something you do well. You have many abilities. For example, you may work well with your hands, or you may be very good at mathematics. It is much more pleasant to work in an occupation that uses your abilities. If you choose an occupation that is too far below your ability level, you will be bored. If it is too far above your ability level, you will be frustrated. It is important to evaluate your abilities during your career search. List your abilities, and use the list when researching an occupation. Match your abilities to the job description.

There are fourteen general categories of abilities: artistic, clerical, interpersonal, language, leadership, manual, mathematical/numerical, musical/dramatic, organization, persuasive, scientific, social, visual, and technical/mechanical. You might have abilities in more than one category.

Occupational Research

By conducting occupational research, you learn details about a career, including tasks performed, the job outlook, the education required, the working environment, and many other things. It requires time and effort to research the occupations that interest you and to prepare for a specific career. If possible, find a mentor who performs this occupation. Spend time following them on the job site. Remember, your efforts allow you to find a job that gives you satisfaction.

There are many resources you can use in your research. Two of them are the *Dictionary of Occupational Titles* (http://www.occupationalinfo.org/), which lists job titles, tasks, and duties for 20,000 occupations, and the *Occupational Outlook Handbook* (http://www.bls.gov/oco/), which discusses the nature of the work, employment outlook, training and qualification requirements, earnings, and working conditions for a variety of occupations. *Work Briefs* by Science Research Associates, the *Career Exploratory Kit*, the *Encyclopedia of Careers*, and computer programs are also good resources. In addition, check career-related pamphlets, microfilm, and videos. You can find all of these resources in libraries and career centers. Also, interview individuals who are already working in an occupation that you are interested in.

The Career Clusters The U.S. Department of Education organizes careers into 16 clusters, listed below. The careers in each cluster are in related industries or business areas. Each cluster is organized into pathways. Each pathway leads to a set of specific careers. The careers in a cluster require a similar set of skills and the same core training and education. You can narrow your career search by identifying a cluster that interests you. You can investigate the career clusters and pathways at www.careerclusters.org.

- Agriculture, Food & Natural Resources
- Architecture & Construction
- Arts, Audio/Video Technology & Communications
- Business Management & Administration
- Education & Training
- Finance
- Government & Public Administration
- Health & Science
- Hospitality & Tourism
- Human Services
- Information Technology
- Law, Public Safety, Corrections & Security
- Manufacturing
- Marketing
- Science, Technology, Engineering & Mathematics
- Transportation, Distribution & Logistics

Employment Trends Employment trends influence the number of available jobs in a certain industry as well as where the jobs are. A trend is a general move in a certain direction. An employment trend is one way the job market is changing over time. Sometimes trends in a specific field or industry are called the job outlook, which means it is a forecast or prediction about trends affecting that job. Knowing how to identify employment trends can help you choose a career in a growing industry with a positive outlook.

Technology has a strong influence on employment and job outlook. It creates new jobs, replaces old jobs, and changes the way some people perform their existing jobs.

- The development of new technology such as mobile phones and handheld devices creates new jobs in areas such as application development, sales, and research and development.

Figure D-2 Careers in information technology are on the rise due to our growing reliance on technology in the workplace.

- The trend toward smaller computers has shifted the manufacturing of systems from desktops to notebooks and e-books.
- Improvements in robotics have made it possible to use robots in positions that people once held, such as on automobile assembly lines.
- Electronic recordkeeping in fields such as healthcare has changed the way medical professionals enter patient information, order prescriptions, and access patient records.
- The trend toward storing information and applications on the Internet instead of on local computers has eliminated the need for some information technology managers at large companies.
- The trend toward using video conferencing instead of traveling to meetings impacts travel agents, hotel workers, and people who work in restaurants where travelers might eat.

A good source for information about employment trends is the Occupational Outlook Handbook, which is published by the U.S. Bureau of Labor Statistics. It describes more than 200 occupations, including responsibilities, working conditions, education requirements, salary ranges, and job outlook. Look it up at www.bls.gov/oco.

Nontraditional Occupations A nontraditional occupation is any job that a man or woman does that is usually done by someone of the other gender. Try not to rule out a nontraditional career because you associate it with one gender or another; it might be a good match for your skills and abilities. Some nontraditional careers include:

Men:
- Nurse
- Administrative assistant
- Flight attendant
- Hair stylist
- Childcare worker
- Elementary school teacher

Figure D-3 Would you be surprised to see a woman engineer? What jobs might you consider that would be nontraditional?

Women:
- Construction worker
- Auto mechanic
- Detective
- Architect
- Chemical engineer
- Pilot

Employability Skills

Employability means having and using skills and abilities to be hired and stay hired. Even if you are capable of diagnosing and repairing the most complex networking problems, if clients think you are unfriendly, or co-workers resent that you come in late every day, you might lose your job. Once you recognize the skills that make you employable, you can practice and develop them in school and at home, so you are ready to use them on the job.

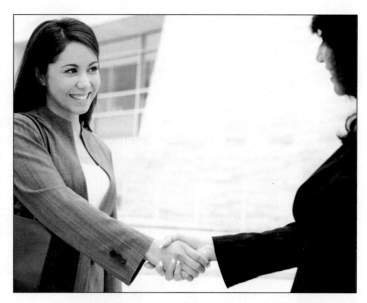

Figure D-4 If you were an employer, what characteristics would you look for in someone you were going to hire?

Transferable Skills Employability skills can generally be placed into two groups: hard skills and transferable skills. Employers often look for people with hard skills to fill specific jobs. For example, a software development company looks to hire people skilled at writing code.

Transferable skills can be used on almost any job. They are called transferable skills because you can transfer them from one situation or career to another. The foundation skills you use to succeed in other areas of your life, such as decision-making and problem-solving, are transferable skills. You can practice and develop these skills in school and at home.

Some computer skills are also transferable. There are very few jobs today that do not require basic computer use. If you have these basic skills, you can take them wherever you go:

- Turn a computer on and start a program.
- Type on a computer keyboard without making many mistakes.
- Access the Internet and move from one Web site to another.
- Use a search engine to do basic Internet research.
- Write and send e-mail.

Professional Qualities Professionalism, or work ethic, is the ability to show respect to everyone around you while you perform your responsibilities as best you can. It includes a basic set of personal qualities that make an employee successful. These qualities include:

- Integrity
- Courtesy
- Honesty
- Dependability
- Punctuality
- Responsibility

- Cooperative
- Positive
- Open-minded
- Flexibility

Professional Appearance   Dress standards vary depending on the career that you choose. For example, you wouldn't expect your car mechanic to be wearing a suit and tie, and you wouldn't want your lawyer to be wearing grease-covered clothing. However, good grooming habits are required in all professions. The following are recommendations for maintaining a well-groomed, professional appearance:

- Dress according to your workplace's dress code. This usually means that clothes will be clean, neat, and in good repair. They should not be of extreme fashion.
- Wear clean and appropriate shoes every day.
- Keep your hair neat and clean. For males, this includes your beard and/or moustache.
- Brush your teeth at least twice a day.
- Floss daily.
- Use mouthwash or breath mints.
- Bathe daily.
- Use unscented deodorant. Remember that odors can be offensive and some people may be allergic to perfumes and scented deodorants.
- For women, keep makeup conservative (e.g., no dark, heavy makeup).
- Keep jewelry to a minimum. Body piercings do not indicate a professional appearance and can cause infections.
- Do not use perfume or cologne.
- Keep nails clean.

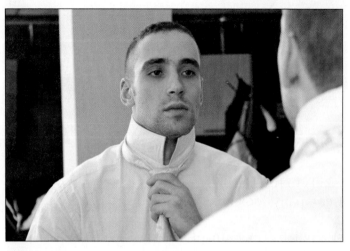

Figure D-5 How could a well-groomed appearance affect your job performance?

Recognizing the Value of School

Finishing school is an investment in your future. Most companies will not hire an employee who has not graduated from high school, and many will not hire an employee who has not graduated from college. If a company does hire dropouts, it usually pays them less than it pays graduates.

School also provides an opportunity to prepare for a career. Core subjects such as reading, writing, and math are vital for the career search process. Science, social studies, music, art, technology, family and consumer sciences, and sports all help you gain knowledge and build skills you will need to succeed at work, such as teamwork, leadership, and problem-solving. School clubs and organizations also help you build skills for future success.

Most of the classes you take in school are required. But, as you move into higher grades, there will be more opportunity to take electives—classes you choose because you are interested in the subject—and advanced level courses. Electives allow you to explore new subjects outside the standard core courses. Advanced courses can help you learn more about a subject and prepare for college.

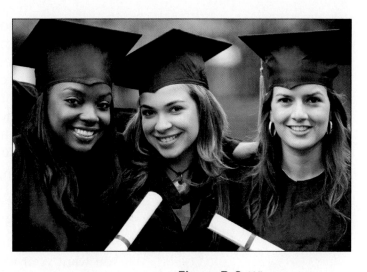

Figure D-6 What are your goals beyond high school? What types of further skills or experiences do you think a future employer might look for?

Personal Academic Plan A personal academic plan is a document that you use to set goals for the things you want to accomplish while you are in school. Some schools call it a personal career plan. It serves as a map that helps you achieve your educational goals. You create a personal academic plan with help from your school counselor. Some things that you might put in your plan include:

- Goals beyond high school
- Assessment of your skills, knowledge, and experience
- Assessment of factors that will contribute to your success
- Assessment of factors that might interfere with your success
- Basic skills assessment
- Graduation requirements
- Plan for achieving graduation
- Plan for achieving goals beyond high school

Developing a Portfolio Some academic plans include a portfolio. A portfolio is a collection of information and documents that show the progress you make in school and in your career planning. It helps you stay on track to achieve your educational and career goals. You can also take it to interviews and job fairs so you have the information you need to fill out applications and the documents you want to show to potential employers.

A portfolio may be an actual folder that holds printed documents and other materials, or it may be electronic and stored on a computer. Some things to include in a portfolio are:

- Resume
- Sample cover letters
- List of references
- Letters of recommendation
- Examples of achievement
- Awards and certificates

Creating a Resume   Your resume may be your most important job search document. It is a written summary of your work-related skills, experience, and education. It provides a snapshot image of your qualifications. It summarizes you, your skills, and your abilities. It is a statement of who you are, what you have done in your life, and what you hope to do next. Your resume may be the first communication between you and a potential employer. You will make a positive impression if your resume is:

- Neatly printed on white paper
- True and accurate
- Free of any typographical, grammatical, or spelling errors
- Direct and to the point

You want your resume to describe you in a way that makes the employer want to meet you. A well-written resume will help you to get an interview.

There are many ways to organize or format a resume. Most word-processing programs come with resume templates— sample documents. You can also find sample resume designs in books and on the Internet. Choose a format that highlights your experience and skills so they stand out to someone who might just glance at the resume quickly. You may also want to consider these tips:

- Make it easy to read. Leave space between lines so it is not crowded or overloaded.
- Use one, easy-to-read font, and apply different font styles and sizes for emphasis.
- Bullets are effective for making lines of text stand out.
- Use proper spelling, punctuation, and grammar.
- Keep it to one page, if possible; two pages at the most. (If you use two pages, be sure to put your name in the header or footer on page 2, in case it becomes separated from page 1.)

Sometimes you will mail your resume in an envelope with a cover letter. Sometimes you will send it electronically by e-mail. Make sure it looks professional when it is printed, as well as when you view it on a computer.

Lifelong Learning   Lifelong learning means continually acquiring new knowledge and skills throughout the course of your life. It can help you achieve your career goals and find career satisfaction. Education and training are not limited to learning new skills for the workplace. You should consider educational opportunities to enrich your life at home, with friends, and in your community.

Ways to achieve lifelong learning include enrolling in educational classes, developing hobbies and interests, joining clubs, and joining professional development groups. You can also stay informed by reading newspapers, news magazines, and Web

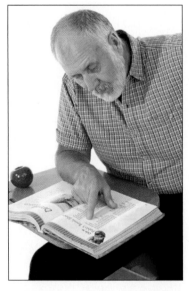

Figure D-7 Continuing education can lead to all kinds of rewards. How could going back to school later in life give you an advantage over other co-workers in your workplace?

sites, discussing current events with family and friends, paying attention to government policies and actions, and volunteering for organizations that support your goals, values, and beliefs.

Safety in the Workplace

In 1970, the federal government passed a law called the Occupational Safety and Health Act. This law requires all employers to provide a safe and healthful workplace. Workers must be provided with safe equipment, protective clothing when needed, and education about safety practices. The Occupational Safety and Health Administration (OSHA) was formed to inspect companies and enforce safety laws. Even so, more than 5,000 Americans die from on-the-job accidents every year. As a worker under the Occupational Safety and Health Act, you have the following rights and responsibilities:

- Right to know. You have the right to know about hazards in your workplace, as well as the right to training to learn how to identify workplace hazards and what to do if there is an incident.

- Right to refuse unsafe work. If you have reasonable grounds to believe the work you do or the piece of equipment you use is unsafe, you can stop work immediately. You cannot be laid off, suspended, or penalized for refusing unsafe work if you follow the proper procedures.

- Responsibility to follow safety rules. It is your employer's responsibility to teach you the safety rules; it is your responsibility to follow the rules.

- Responsibility to ask for training. If you feel that you need more training than your employer provides, it is your responsibility to ask for it.

- Responsibility to speak up. It is your responsibility to report incidents and unsafe work practices as well as unsafe conditions.

Part of your responsibility as a worker is to make sure that you keep your work environment safe for yourself and for others. You can practice this at school and at home. You have to take some responsibility for your own safety. That means using equipment properly, according to instructions. If you are a new worker, enroll in any safety classes offered by the company. If you work around chemicals, poisons, or dangerous machinery, ask how they can be handled safely. If a company offers you hard hats or other safety equipment, use them. Read your manuals and handbook, and don't take shortcuts if it means endangering your safety or the safety of customers or co-workers. Remember—failure to follow safety guidelines is cause for dismissal.

Suggested Activities

- Careers in technology range from software programmers to aircraft mechanics. The skills, abilities, and interests required are just as broad. Use the Internet, library, or your school's guidance resources to learn more about careers in technology. Make a list of five industries that offer careers in technology, and then list five types of jobs in each industry. Select one job that interests you, and prepare a presentation on it. Include the educational requirements, job responsibilities, career pathway, potential salary range, and more.

- Take turns role playing a job interview with a classmate. Take turns being the interviewer and the interviewee. After, write a note thanking the "interviewer" for his or her time.

- Select and research a business in your community. If possible, obtain an application form from the business. Identify the different parts of the application, and practice completing the form.

- Use a word-processing application template to create a resume.

- A career plan is a map that shows you the way to reach your goal. You can develop a career plan on your own, or with help from your parents, teachers, or school counselor. Start your career plan by writing a statement that describes your long-term ultimate career goal. For example, write: *I will be an occupational physical therapist in California by the time I am 30 years old.* Add short-term career goals that define how you will gain the skills, knowledge, and experience that you need to achieve your ultimate career goal. Include a timeline for achieving each one.

- Working with a partner, research ethics, behavior, and legal responsibilities in the workplace.

- You can practice safety in school or at home. Working with a partner, brainstorm safety guidelines for your computer lab, classroom, or other area of the school. Write a booklet outlining the guidelines and illustrate it with a poster.

- As mentioned earlier in this section, even if you're good at your job, it takes more than that to succeed. Employers take note of people who are, among other things, considerate of others, proud of their work, punctual, and observant of safety procedures. In small groups, brainstorm the behaviors and qualities that enhance your employability. Prepare and present a skit showing how you can model those behaviors and qualities in school and at home.

Glossary

Numerals

@ in an e-mail address, a symbol used to separate the user name from the name of the computer on which the user's mailbox is stored (for example, frodo@bagend.org); pronounced "at"

10 baseT an Ethernet local area network capable of transmitting 10 megabits of data per second through twisted-pair cabling

3-D graphics adapter a video adapter that can display images that provide the illusion of depth as well as height and width

3-D reference a reference to a cell or range on a specific worksheet in a 3-D spreadsheet

3-D rendering transforming graphic images by adding shading and light sources so that they appear to be three-dimensional

3-D spreadsheet a spreadsheet that uses multiple worksheets in the same file

3-D video accelerator a computer card that helps display graphics quickly

40-bit encryption a minimal level of encryption supplied with most Web browsers

A

absolute reference the method of copying or moving a formula that keeps its cell references exactly as they are

acceptable use policy (AUP) a policy—published by a school district, business, or other organization—that identifies rules of behavior that must be followed by anyone using that organization's telecommunications equipment, computers, network, or Internet connection

access time the amount of time required for a disk drive's read/write head to locate data on the surface of a disk

active cell the highlighted cell in use in a spreadsheet application

advanced intelligent tape (AIT) magnetic tape with very high storage capacity

alert box a dialog box that warns users that an action cannot be completed or will result in an error

alias an informal name by which an e-mail user is known

Align the tool in a draw program that determines how images will be placed in relation to one another

alignment the placement of text and objects so they line up within a space

All-in-One printer a printer that combines printing, scanner, copying, and faxing capabilties

alt newsgroup a newsgroup formed to discuss very specific topics

American Standard Code for Information Interchange (ASCII) a system that uses eight-bit codes to represent 256 characters

analog a type of system that sends electrical signals that match the human voice and other sounds

animation the process of showing many images in rapid sequence to make them appear as if they are in motion

anonymity the state of being out of the public spotlight

antivirus program a program that protects computers from viruses

applet a small application with limited features and functions

application software a program that allows you to create documents, listen to music, or play games on the computer

application workspace the large area of a program's window that displays the document in use

apps third-party software programs developed specifically for smart phones, tablet computers such as iPad, and other handheld devices such as iPod Touch

archival storage a storage device for information that is not frequently used

argument the data that a function will use

ascending order the sorting of data by increasing value

aspect ratio the relative proportion of an image's height and width

asynchronous training Web-based training without a live instructor

attachment a file sent with an e-mail message

augmented reality an emerging technology in which cameras and mobile devices are used to layer virtual information on to real information

authentication the process of confirming a valid user

authoring program a program that allows interactive programs and Web sites to be created

AutoContent wizard in some applications, a series of dialog boxes that helps the user create a new presentation

Autocorrect a feature that fixes common spelling mistakes as they are typed

AutoFill a spreadsheet command that automatically enters related, sequential data (such as the days of the week) into a connected set of cells

Autosave the feature in an application program that saves the current file after a specified amount of time has elapsed

AutoShapes a list of ready-to-use shapes in the Draw tool

avatar graphic icon that represents a user in the virtual reality world

B

Back button a tool that lets users reload the previously viewed page in a browser

backbone high-speed lines that carry data through a network

back-up utility a program that automatically copies data from the hard drive to a back-up storage device

balance the way objects are arranged in an image or on a page; symmetrically arranged objects are evenly balanced; asymmetrically arranged objects are unevenly balanced

bandwidth the amount of data that can travel through a network connection

bar-code reader a device used to scan product labels

Basic Input/Output System (BIOS) a set of programs, built into a PC's ROM chips, that controls the function of the computer's keyboard, disk drives, monitor, and several other components; the programs also help the computer start itself when the power is turned on

batch processing a way of changing a database that delays updates until a group of data is ready to process

beta version a working copy of a program from early in the development of an application

binary large object (BLOB) a database feature that allows the user to specify a data type to handle large objects

bit the smallest unit of information with values of either 0 or 1; a number that is a building block for computer languages; short for *binary digit*

bitmapped graphic an image formed by a pattern of dots; also called raster graphic

bits per second (bps) the amount of data that can be sent in one second

blended learning a method of learning by combining traditional classroom and Web-based training

blog short for "Web log," a Web page that a writer updates regularly with news or opinions

Boolean search a type of search that uses an operator to link keywords

boot to start a computer

bounce message a notice that e-mail could not be delivered

brightness a measure of how much black is added to a color

broadband the general term for all high-speed digital connections of at least 1.5 megabits per second

browse to find information in a database by looking at records one at a time

browser a program that enables users to navigate the World Wide Web and locate and display Web documents

buddy list a list of people with whom a person with an instant messaging program interacts

bus topology a network design that connects the network to a single line

business-to-business (B2B) a transaction between companies

byte a group of bits combined into groups of eight or more

C

cable modem a device that allows a computer to access the Internet through a cable television connection

cache memory hardware that stores program commands and data that are accessed often to save processing time

canvas size in a paint or draw program, the size of the workspace on which an image is placed

cathode ray tube (CRT) a type of monitor that produces images by making phosphors glow

Cave Automatic Virtual Environment (CAVE) a virtual reality environment where images of the virtual world are projected on the walls of a real room

CD-ROM drive a read-only optical storage device

cell the box in a table or worksheet where a column and row meet; also, a geographic area to which a signal can be transmitted

cell address a unique name by which each cell on a worksheet is identified

cell reference the shorthand command that tells a spreadsheet program to use the information inside a certain cell

cell site the location of the radio tower that sends and receives radio signals for a particular cellular phone

cellular phone a mobile phone that uses radio waves to communicate

central processing unit (CPU) a piece of the computer's hardware that processes and compares data and completes arithmetic and logical operations

certificate authority (CA) a third-party organization that validates digital signatures

channel a chat group

character set a system for coding letters and numbers

chart a graphical image, such as a pie or a set of columns, used to visually display numerical data, making it easy to understand and analyze

chat room an informal, public, real-time teleconference

check-screening system a system that compares checks to a database with information about problem accounts

circuit an end-to-end connection between two computers

circuit-switching a technology that provides an unbroken connection between two computers, enabling them to exchange data quickly; also used in telephone networks to open a dedicated line (a circuit) for a phone call and leave the circuit open for the duration of the call

click-and-mortar store a business that offers products online

client a workstation computer attached to a network, which is controlled by a server

client/server network a network system that uses a central server computer

clip art a graphic that has already been created for use by others

Clip Art Gallery a collection of images and sound that is ready to use

Clipboard a tool that temporarily stores cut or copied data

close tag the end of a Hypertext Markup Language (HTML) code

cloud computing using the Internet and central remote servers to host, or store, data and/or applications

cloud storage areas on Internet servers where data and applications can be stored and accessed

collaborative software application software designed to be used by a group of people working together

collision a problem in networking that occurs when two computers try to transmit data across a network at the same time, causing data packets to collide and both transmissions to fail

color depth the number of colors that can be displayed on a monitor at one time

color palette a display of options in a paint or draw program that allows the user to choose the color a tool will place in an image

command an instruction that tells a software program what action to perform

command button an icon on a toolbar or Ribbon that tells the computer to perform an action when the icon is clicked

commercial software copyrighted software that must be purchased before it can be used

compatibility the ability to share files between two different application programs or operating systems

compiler a program used to translate the source code of a computer program into binary form using only 0s and 1s

compress to reduce the size of a file

computer a machine that changes information from one form into another by performing input, processing, output, and storage

computer crime any act that violates state or federal laws involving use of a computer

computer system several different parts of a computer that perform the four basic functions of computing: input, processing, output, and storage

computer-assisted design/computer-assisted manufacturing (CAD/CAM) a method of creating a 3-D model that links 3-D design to the manufacture of that object

congestion delay caused by too much traffic on a network

contention the condition that occurs when two computers try to access a network at the same time

contrast the difference between the colors of the pixels in an image

convergence the process that enables previously separate tools to take on functions and features of the others

cookie a file left on a hard drive by a Web site that the user visits

Copy to place a duplicate of a selection on the Clipboard

copy protection a physical device or software tool that keeps users from making unauthorized copies of the software

copyright the right to control use of creative, literary, or artistic work

corrupted describes a computer file that has been damaged

cracker a cybercriminal who tries to access and damage secure networks

crash to suddenly stop working

crop to trim the edges from a graphic to make it fit a space or to remove an unwanted part of the image

cross-platform a type of software or hardware capable of running the same way on more than one platform

cross-platform compatibility ability to share files across operating systems

Cut to remove a selection from a document and place it on the Clipboard

cybercrime the use of the Internet or private networks to violate state or federal laws

cyberstalking to use electronic communications to threaten or harass someone

cylinder the same track location on the platters of a hard drive

D

data decay the loss of information due to the gradual wearing down of a storage medium

data glove a glove equipped with sensors to measure movements of the hand and fingers

data integrity describes the availability and usability of data stored on a computer

data loss occurs when information on a storage device is damaged or made unusable

data maintenance the upkeep of a database that includes regular updates, modifications, and deletions

data mining to find valuable information by examining trends in large amounts of data

data projector a device that shows a computer's video output on a screen

data series a set of data that changes by a constant value

data source a file containing variable data used for customizing a mail merge document

data structure the way a database is organized

data transfer rate the number of bits per second at which data is transferred

data type settings applied to a database field, which allow the field to store only information of a specific type and/or format

data warehouse a large collection of data

database an organized collection of information that may or may not be stored in a computer

database management system (DBMS) a software program used to manage the storage, organization, processing, and retrieval of data in a database

dead link a connection to a Web document that no longer works

decrement the number by which each value in a series decreases

default the preset options in a program

demodulation the process that changes the analog signal received by a modem to the digital signal used by a computer

denial of service attack a method used by hackers which prevents legitimate users from accessing a service, such as a Web site

deregulate to remove government regulations

descending order the sorting of data by decreasing value

desktop the workspace on a computer screen

desktop computer an individual's personal computer

desktop publishing a program with expanded design options to create high-quality documents

device a hardware component installed for use with a computer system

device driver the software utility that allows the operating system to communicate with a device

dialog box on-screen message box for users to supply information or convey requests

digital a connection that uses computer codes to send voice, data, and video on a single line

digital audio tape (DAT) a storage medium that uses high-capacity magnetic tape enclosed in a cartridge; originally used to store audio in digital format, but now used primarily for storing computer data

digital camera a camera that records and stores photos in a digital form that the computer can work with

digital signature a method to verify the source and content of an e-mail message

digital video camera a camera that records moving images in digital form

digitize to change information of any kind into digital format

disk cache software that uses space on the hard drive to store data that is used most frequently

disk operating system (DOS) an operating system that uses a keyboard to type specific commands into the computer

disk scanner a utility that checks magnetic disks for errors

Distribute the tool in a draw program that determines the distance between two objects

document map an outline of a word-processing document that can be seen in a separate pane

documentation instructions on how to install a program, use the application, and troubleshoot any problems

document-centered approach the view that focuses on a document's content rather than the software that created it

Domain Name Server a server used to match a domain name to the correct Internet protocol (IP) address

Domain Name System (DNS) a naming system using letters as well as numbers to identify one or more computers on the Internet

domain name the phrase used to identify one or more Internet protocol (IP) addresses

dot pitch the width of an individual pixel on a monitor

download to transfer copies of files from a remote computer to a local computer by means of a modem or network

downtime a temporary stop to all work on a network

drag handle one of the eight small rectangles or circles that appears at a graphic's four corners and four edges that is used to resize the image

draw program a program used to create and edit vector images

driver utility software that contains information needed by application programs to properly operate input and output devices

Dynamic Hypertext Markup Language (DHTML) a programming language that adds interactivity to a Web page

E

e-commerce the use of telecommunications networks or the Internet to conduct business

electronic data interchange (EDI) a business-to-business wide area network

e-mail an electronic communication method in which messages are sent and received over the Internet

e-mail client a program, on a user's computer, that enables the user to create, send, receive, and manage e-mail messages

e-mail folder a folder used to store and organize related messages from your Inbox

e-mail server a program, on an Internet service provider's server computer, that sends, receives, and delivers e-mail messages to client computers

e-mail virus a program sent in an e-mail message to deliberately cause computer problems for the recipient

embed to copy an object into a document; both the object and the document remain independent when changes are made to either one

emphasis in graphic design, creating a visual focal point

emulator software program that allows two incompatible computers to work with each other

encoder a software program that converts a file

encryption the process of encoding data so that it cannot be used without first being decoded

enterprise storage system technology that allows networked computers to access one or many different types of storage devices

ergonomic designed to provide comfortable use and avoid stress or injury

e-tailer a retailer that primarily uses the Web to sell goods or services

Ethernet a networking technology used for local area networks

ethics moral principles

exclusion operator a minus sign or the word NOT used to search for Web pages that do not contain certain words

executable file a file that carries out instructions as part of a program

expert system a complex program that uses artificial intelligence techniques to manipulate a large, detailed database

export to format data so it can be used in another program

Extensible Markup Language (XML) the code that describes the format for constructing Web queries and processing database queries

extension an additional set of up to four letters that is separated from the file name by a period and that generally identifies the type of data in the file

extranet a wide area network designed to look and work like the Internet that allows for limited public access

Eyedropper a tool that picks up and works with a specific color from an image

F

fair use the use of copyrighted material in a review, in research, in schoolwork, or in a professional publication, which does not necessarily require permission from the material's owner

fax machine a device that makes a digital copy (a "facsimile") of a document, then transmits the data to another device, such as a computer modem or other fax machine

fax modem a computer modem that can send and receive faxes

fiber-optic cable strands of pure glass that transmit digital data by pulses of light

field the part of a database that holds an individual piece of data

field name identifier for a database field

field width maximum number of characters a field can contain

file a unit or grouping of information that has been given a unique name

file compression a way of reducing file size so that large files can travel more quickly over a network or consume less disk space

file compression utility a software program that reduces the size of a file for storage or transmission purposes

file extension two or three letters following a period that indicate the application a file was created in

file format standards used to write data to a disk

file fragmentation the allocation of a file to noncontiguous sectors on a floppy disk or hard drive

file name a series of characters that gives each document in a folder a separate name

file server the main computer in a client/server system

file sharing making files available to more than one user on a network

filter to select or display items based on whether they meet or match specific criteria; also, a feature in some e-mail programs that can delete certain messages or file messages in folders

find and replace a feature that locates a word or word combination and then changes it to a different word or combination

firewall hardware or software that prevents access to a network

flash drive a small storage device that uses flash memory and connects to the computer through a USB port; also called a pen drive, jump drive, or thumb drive

flash memory storage medium that has no moving parts and stores data in electronic cells

flat-file database a database that can work with only one file at a time

floating image a graphic that appears on a specific place on the page, regardless of text

floppy disk an older removable, portable magnetic disk used with a floppy drive

floppy disk drive an older storage device that reads floppy disks

form an on-screen window for users to view, enter, and edit data

format prepare a storage medium to be used by a specific type of computer

formula a mathematical expression used to link and perform calculations on numbers in worksheet cells

Forward button a tool that lets users move ahead to previously viewed pages in a browser

frame an empty section in a document that will eventually hold text or graphics; or a section of a Web page window; also, an individual still image in an animated sequence

frame rate the number of still images displayed every second in a full-motion video or animation

frame relay a communications technology used by most permanent virtual circuits that allows voice, data, and video to travel on the same line at the same time

freeware copyrighted software given away for free

full back-up to duplicate all files on a hard drive

function a commonly used formula that is built into a spreadsheet program

function key a shortcut key at the top of a keyboard that is labeled with the letter F and a number

G

garbage in, garbage out (GIGO) a phrase that stresses the importance of inputting accurate data in a database

global unique identifier (GUID) a unique identification number generated by hardware or by a program

grammar checker a word-processing tool that identifies problems with verb tense, sentence structure, pronouns, punctuation, and capitalization

graphic anything that can be seen on a computer's screen

graphical browser a Web navigation program that shows pictures and text

graphical user interface (GUI) a visual display that allows the user to interact with the computer by using graphical objects on the screen

graphics tablet a hardware device used for drawing

Grid an advanced graphics tool that displays a grid onscreen to assist with alignment

gridline a line extended from chart axis to body so data will be clearer; also, non-printing lines displayed onscreen to help align and format objects on a page

group to combine separate vector images into one image; also part of the Ribbon (Microsoft Office), each tab contains groups of related tasks

groupware software that supports multiple users working on related tasks

H

hacker a computer hobbyist who tampers with systems to find mistakes and weaknesses

handheld computer a small palm-size computer mainly used for personal assistance

handwriting-recognition software software that converts handwritten text to digital format

haptic interface a method of communicating with a computer through a device that senses body movement through touch

hard drive the most commonly used type of secondary storage device, which stores bits of data as aligned particles on the surface of a magnetic disk

hardware the physical parts of a computer

head-mounted display (HMD) a helmet that wraps around the head; used for virtual reality experiences

hierarchy the categories in which Usenet newsgroups are organized

high definition television (HDTV) a type of television that produces a sharper image than regular television

holographic data storage system (HDSS) a future storage technology in which data is stored in images called holograms on optical cubes

home page the front page of a Web site

horizontal application a type of application software that is designed to meet the needs of many different users

hub a connection point for computers, printers, and other equipment on a network

hue the actual color as shown in the spectrum or range of colors

hyperlink a link to another document on the World Wide Web

hypermedia system a system of connecting resources online (via the Internet, for example) that lets users click links to access resources in different types of media, such as text, audio, or video

hypertext a type of document that is published on the World Wide Web

Hypertext Markup Language (HTML) the code that describes the format, layout, and structure of a document for publication on the World Wide Web

hypertext transfer protocol (HTTP) the protocol that governs how Web pages are transmitted across the Internet

I

icon an on-screen picture that represents an object, resource, or command

identity theft the taking of another person's identity for the purpose of committing illegal acts

image editor an advanced paint program that edits bitmapped images

image processing system technology for scanning documents so that records can be stored

image size the actual size of a graphic

imagesetter a printer that offers high-quality output at 1,200 dots per inch

impact printer a printer that uses keys or pins to strike an ink ribbon to create an image on paper

import to bring information into a program from another program

inclusion operator a plus sign or the word AND; used to search pages to find a match for specified words

increment the number by which each value in a series increases

incremental back-up to copy only the data files that have changed since the last full back-up

information kiosk an automated system that provides information or training; usually has a touch screen to allow input

information overload the result of a computer user being overwhelmed by the amount of information generated by his or her computer

infrared light waves that cannot be seen by the human eye

infringe undermine or interfere with; also, to actively break the terms of a law or agreement

infringement to break copyright law by stealing others' work

inline image a graphic that is anchored to some text so that if the text moves, the image will move as well

input raw information, or data, that is entered into a computer

insertion point a mark that indicates where entered text will appear in a document

install to prepare to run application software by copying all or part of the program onto the computer's hard drive

instant messaging (IM) the system on the Internet that allows two people who are online to communicate by typing messages

integrated software a program that combines the basic features of several applications into one package

intellectual property someone's creative, literary, or artistic work

interactive multimedia a program that uses different types of media (such as text, sound, animation, and others) to convey its message, and which allows the user to choose the content that will be displayed next or direct the flow of the content

interface a means for users to control or operate the computer

Internet a vast network that links millions of computers around the world

Internet 2 (I2) high performance network to test new technologies

Internet client the computer and related software that requests a service on the Internet

Internet protocol (IP) address a four-part number separated by periods that identifies each computer connected to the Internet

Internet Relay Chat (IRC) an Internet service that enables the user to join chat groups

Internet service provider (ISP) a company that provides the actual link between a computer and the Internet

Internet telephony the use of the Internet to complete real-time voice communication

interpreter a program used to translate source code directly into actions

intranet a private network that uses the same protocol as the Internet

K

key field an element that links tables in a relational database

keyboard shortcut a combination of keys that carries out a specific action

keyword in a spreadsheet function's syntax, the name of the function; also, text or a phrase used in a search

L

label text or a combination of numbers and text typically used for titles or explanation in a worksheet

land a flat, reflective area on the surface of an optical disc

laser sensor a laser-operated tool in an optical drive that reads information

Lasso the tool in an image editor program that selects complex or freehand shapes

launch to start an application program

layer to stack parts of a bitmapped image on top of another level

layout an on-page arrangement of text, graphics, backgrounds, images, and other design elements

leased line a permanent connection between the mobile telephone switching office (MTSO) and the long-distance providers that will complete the call

level the numerical values with which image editors are able to quickly change every pixel in an image

link to create a connection between an object's source application (the program in which an object was created) and a destination application (a program into which the object is copied), allowing the object to be edited in either program

liquid crystal display (LCD) monitor panel that produces color by using an electric field to combine crystals of different colors

list server a program that handles e-mail messages automatically

local area network (LAN) a network in which all workstations and equipment are near each other

local loop the network that connects to the phone company's central office

LocalTalk a Macintosh topology that allows Macintosh computers to be networked quickly

lossless compression a method of reducing the size of a file so that it can be returned to its original state without losing any data

lossy compression a method of reducing the size of a file so that some data may be lost when the file is decompressed;

M

macro a set of mouse actions, keystrokes, or commands recorded for repeated use

macro virus a series of commands that is hidden in a document

Magic Wand the tool in an image editor program that selects all the touching pixels of a similar color

mailbox name a part of an e-mail address before the "at" sign

mail merge a process that inserts variable information into a standardized document to produce a personalized or customized document

mainframe a type of computer used by many people at the same time to allow access to the same secure data

maintenance release a minor revision to correct errors or add minor features to a software program

markup language a set of codes used to format online text

Marquee a tool in an image editor program that highlights a simple shape

master page the pattern that sets the basic features of a document's look for all the other pages to follow

master slide a default template that is applied to all slides of a certain type

maximize to make an application window as large as possible

memory specialized chips, connected to the computer's motherboard, which store data and programs as they are being used by the processor

memory shave to steal some of a computer's memory chips

menu a list of commands

menu bar the bar generally located below an application's title bar where a set of commands is listed

mesh topology a network design in which all components are connected directly to other components

message header information located at the top of an e-mail that identifies the sender, other recipients, the date, and the subject

message priority the rating of an e-mail's importance

microwave a high-frequency radio wave

minimize to make an application window as small as possible

modem a device that allows a computer to transmit data to other computers through telephone lines

modulation the process that changes the digital signal from a computer to the analog signal of a telephone

motherboard the primary circuit board in a computer to which all devices are connected and through which all data passes

multimedia describes a program that uses different types of media (such as text, graphics, video, animation, or sound) at the same time

multitask to work with more than one computer application at a time

Musical Instrument Digital Interface (MIDI) a special type of interface that connects a computer to electronic musical instruments, enabling the computer to control the instruments and record their output

N

navigate to move to different parts of a network or program to find resources or files

navigation button a tool that lets users perform routine operations with a browser

netbook a computer approximately 10 inches across designed primarily for accessing the Internet

netiquette an informal set of rules for how to behave online

network two or more computers connected to each other to share resources

network architecture the science of designing a network

network interface card (NIC) a hardware device that physically connects a computer to a network

network layer a subset of protocols that govern how data is handled and transmitted over a network

network operating system (NOS) a set of programs that manages and secures a network

network traffic the electronic pulses of information that carry data through a network to its destination

newsgroup a discussion group in which users communicate by posting messages about a particular topic

node anything connected to a network, such as a computer, printer, or fax machine

nonimpact printer a printer that uses spray or powder to create an image on paper

O

object a piece of data such as an image, chart, video or sound clip, or a section of text

object code readable instructions created by compilers translating the source code into binary form

object linking and embedding (OLE) the feature that copies objects from one application into another and enables the data to remain linked to its original application

object-oriented database a database that stores objects, such as sound, video, text, and graphics

object-oriented programming a method of programming that provides rules for creating and managing objects

online banking using a Web browser to pay bills and access accounts online

online service a business that provides access to the Internet as well as to custom content, discussion groups, news, shopping services, and other information that is available only to its paying subscribers

online support Internet-based service that provides answers or other help

online transactional processing (OLTP) a way to immediately approve Internet credit-card purchases

on-screen presentation a display of slides on a computer screen

open protocol a standard that anyone can use

open source software software for which the source code is made available to the public

operating system (OS) a system that allows hardware devices to communicate with one another, run efficiently, and support software programs

optical character recognition (OCR) software used by most scanners that turns text into a digital file

optical storage device a storage device that uses laser beams to read the information stored on the reflective surface of a disc

Order a tool that changes the position in which objects are stacked or layered

order of evaluation the rule that tells a spreadsheet program which operation to do first in a multiple-operation formula

organic light emitting diode (OLED) a technology used for monitors and screens that is made from sheets of organic material that glows when an electrical field is applied; OLED monitors do not require backlighting or diffusers

output the result of a computer's processing, displayed on-screen, printed on paper, or heard through a speaker

output device any piece of hardware that shows the result of computer processing

P

packet tiny segment of information transmitted over a network

packet sniffer a program that examines data streams on networks to find information such as passwords and credit-card numbers

packet-switching a method of transmitting data across a network by breaking it into tiny segments called packets

page format the arrangement of text on a page

pagination the automatic division of a document into pages

paint program a basic program for working with a raster or bitmapped image

pane a section of a document after the window has been split

paragraph any amount of text up to a forced new line

parse a spreadsheet feature that breaks down data into parts that will fit into the spreadsheet cells

password a word, or a string of letters and/or numbers, that is used to gain access to a computer system or network and that is usually known only to the user and an administrator

Paste to insert an item copied or cut to the Clipboard

patent the exclusive right to make, use, or sell a device or process

peer-to-peer network (P2PN) a small network that usually includes from two to ten computers but no server

pen computing a pen used on handheld computers that sends electronic signals through a touch screen

pen-based graphics tablet a touchpad that uses a stylus to create images

peripheral separate input, output, and storage hardware

permanent virtual circuit (PVC) a circuit that allows multiple users' data to travel at the same time on the same line

personal digital assistant (PDA) a small, highly portable handheld computer that is used for taking notes or keeping track of appointments

personal information manager (PIM) a program responsible for storing phone numbers and addresses and creating schedules

personal productivity program a horizontal application used to help people work more effectively

phishing a method by which cybercriminals lure users into revealing account codes and passwords by pretending to be a legitimate Web site

photo checkout system database of customer photos to verify credit-card use

photo printer a printer that produces a high-resolution image, used for photos

physical media the wires, cables, or wireless transmitters and receivers used to connect the computers in a network

pit an indented area on the reflective surface of an optical disc that scatters light from a laser

pixel a single point in a bitmapped graphic

placeholder an area within a slide layout designed to hold data, such as text or pictures

plagiarism illegal copying of creative material owned by another person

platform a kind of computer that uses a certain type of processor and operating system

platter one of a stack of metal disks that store information in the hard drive

player software a program that plays audio or video files

Plug and Play (PnP) capability of Windows-based PC operating systems to detect new, compatible devices

plug-in program a program that adds new features to an application on the computer

podcast an audio or video file that is created for downloading to an iPod or an MP3 player such as Microsoft's Zune

point of presence (POP) a local connection to a wide area network

pointer a cursor that shows your location on a computer screen

pointing device a device such as a mouse used to point to elements on a monitor

point-of-sale (POS) a type of system used at retail checkout counters (the point of sale), which scans product codes for items being purchased, verifies the items' prices, and usually updates inventory and customer information through a connection to the seller's network

Point-to-Point Protocol (PPP) a method of connecting to the Internet in which Transmission Control Protocol/Internet Protocol (TCP/IP) packets are sent from a computer to a server that puts them on the Internet

pop-up menu a list of shortcut commands that appears when an area of the screen is right-clicked or the mouse button is held down

portal an Internet service that provides an organized subject guide to Internet content, news, weather, sports, e-mail, etc.

power surge a sharp increase in power coming into the computer system

power-on self test (POST) series of tests a computer performs while booting

Pre-designed slide PowerPoint 2007 online offers a variety of pre-designed slides to make it easy to create good presentations

preference a choice for the way a program will operate

presentation software a specialized software that is used to create and display visual information

primary storage memory chips that are built into a computer, such as random access memory (RAM)

print area a portion of a worksheet intended to be printed

Print Layout view the view of a word-processing document that shows how the document will appear when printed

Print Preview the feature in a program that shows how a document will look when printed

procedural programming a method of programming that uses step-by-step instructions

processing a task a computer carries out with data in response to a command

product update a new release of an existing software product, with enhancements that correct existing flaws or that make the new version superior to all previous versions

productivity suite a program that combines several programs and all of their features

program to write the instructions, or code, for software; also, an application

programmer an expert who writes the instructions for software

programming language a coded language used to write instructions for a computer

property a piece of data attached to or associated with a file, folder, program, or device; also called metadata

proportion the size and location of one object in relation to other objects

proprietary protocol a standard that only certain people can use

protect to block accidental changes in a file or on a device

protocol standard format and rules for handling data

protocol stack a set of small protocols used to set standards for the Internet

protocol suite a collection of individual protocols that determines how a network operates

proximity in graphic design, using the closeness between objects to indicate a relationship

proximity operator a Web query that searches for words that appear close together

public data network a network that allows different companies to set up their own networks

public domain software a program distributed for free without a copyright

pull-down menu a list of options

Q

quarter-inch cartridge (QIC) a storage medium that uses quarter-inch-wide magnetic tape housed in a cassette

query a request to search a database

query language a set of characters, terms, symbols, and rules used in the construction of database queries

query-by-example (QBE) to request information from a database by providing an example

R

random access memory (RAM) special chips that store data and instructions while the computer is working

random access storage device a storage device that lets the computer go directly to the needed information

range in a spreadsheet, a group of cells that are next to each other

raster graphic an image formed by a pattern of dots; also called bitmapped graphic

ray trace a method to determine how a source of light would affect an image

read/write device a storage device that allows users to access information and save it to the device

read/write head in a disk drive, the component that writes data to and reads data from the surface of a disk

read-only device a storage device that allows users to access information but not save or change it

read-only memory (ROM) chips on the motherboard that contain the instructions that start the computer and control some input and output devices

record a part of a database that holds data about a particular individual or item

record match to gather information about another person by searching databases

Redo allows the user to put a change back in effect after cancelling it with Undo

reel-to-reel tape a type of storage tape that moves between two large, open reels, which are not enclosed in a case or cartridge

registry in Microsoft Windows, a database of information about a computer's users, hardware settings, and software configurations, which enables Windows to run applications correctly

rehearsed presentation a slide show timing method that changes from one slide to the next according to the will of the creator so that the presentation moves at the exact desired speed

relational database a database in which shared key fields link data among tables

relative reference the method of copying or moving a formula that changes the values in the formula depending on its new location

render to create a 3-D model from a wireframe

repetition when color, shape, or pattern is repeated throughout a graphic

repetitive strain injury (RSI) nerve damage in the hand caused by continued use of a keyboard or mouse

replicate to copy

Reply to respond to the sender of an e-mail message

Reply All to respond to all people who received an e-mail message

report an ordered list of selected database records and fields in an easy-to-read format

report template a pattern that controls how data will be displayed in a database report

resolution for a raster image, the number of pixels in a certain section of the image; for a monitor, the number of pixels that are displayed on the screen at any given time, used as a measure of sharpness of picture quality

Ribbon a toolbar area in Microsoft Office applications since 2007

right to privacy the right to be free of interference of outsiders in one's personal affairs

ring topology a network design that connects all devices into a circle

rip to copy music from any source, such as an audio compact disc, to a hard drive

router a network device or program that determines which path a packet will follow to reach its destination

runtime version a limited version of authoring software

S

sans serif font a font that has no serifs, or lines, projecting from its ends

saturation the intensity of a color

scale the range of values against which data is measured; also, to change the size of an object, proportionately

scan in computer crime, to search for an unknown password using a software program created to probe computer systems; also, to convert printed content to digital format, using a scanner

scanner a device that converts printed images into a digital form

screen saver a utility program that changes the screen display after a preset period

screen-magnifier software software that makes images larger and changes colors to make text easier to see on a monitor

scroll to move from one part of a document to another on the screen

search engine software that finds a list of Web sites that meet a specified search

secondary storage computer disk drives such as the hard drive and CD-ROM drive used to store large amounts of data

section a part of a document that contains specific format settings

sector a section of a track on a computer disk

Secure Electronic Transactions (SET) a standard that uses digital signatures to protect buyers and sellers online

select a feature that allows the user to highlight, or select, data such as text or objects on-screen

selection tool a tool that can select a portion of an image to be moved, enlarged, or edited

self-running presentation a slide show timing method that changes from one slide to the next at a given increment of time

sequential storage device a storage device that requires a computer to scan from the beginning to the end of stored information

series a range

serif font a font that has serifs, or lines, projecting from its ends

server a computer that manages data and programs used in a network

server address a part of an e-mail address after the "at" sign

set-top appliance a device that allows Internet access using a television as a display

shareware copyrighted software that can be sampled before it is purchased

signature capture system a database of digitized signatures to verify credit-card purchases

simulation a virtual reality program that mimics a specific place, job, or function

site license a license that allows a group to install software on a specific number of computers for internal use only

slide a separate page in a presentation program on which information is organized smart phone

smartcard a credit-card-size electronic device, which contains built-in memory and can store information about a person, such as the information required to give the person access to a company's network

software programs that tell a computer what to do and how to do it

software license the document that contains permission for a buyer to install and use a program

software piracy the illegal copying of computer programs

solid state disk (SSD) a high-capacity storage device that contains high-speed random access memory

sort to arrange data in a specific order

sound card a circuit board chip that converts sounds in analog form into digital form and vice versa

source code the instructions that programmers write

source file the location from which data was collected

source note a way to acknowledge an information source

spam unrequested e-mail messages and advertisements

speech synthesis software a type of software that lets a computer read text files aloud

speech-recognition software software used for inputting text or commands by speaking into a microphone

spelling checker a tool that checks each word in the text against a dictionary built into the program to identify potential errors

spoof to use a false IP or e-mail address

spreadsheet a software program used for processing numbers that are stored in tables, such as budgets or financial statements

standalone program application software that specializes in one task

star bus topology a network design that connects multiple star networks in a local area network

star topology a network design that connects each network device to a hub

start tag the beginning of a Hypertext Markup Language (HTML) code

status bar the area below the application workspace that shows information about the program or document

storage devices, such as hard drives and CD-ROM drives, that permanently hold data and program instructions for a computer to use

storage area network (SAN) a network of storage devices that can be accessed by multiple computers

storage device a computer component that retains data even after the power is turned off

storage media the material that retains the stored information in a computer storage device

stream to transmit data over a network or Internet connection without interruption

Structured Query Language (SQL) a standard database query language

style a set of formats for similar elements in a document

style checker a tool that suggests ways to improve the writing style in a document

style sheet a collection of predefined formats that can be applied to a document

stylus a pointing device used for drawing on a graphics tablet

supercomputer a large and powerful scientific computer that can process large amounts of data quickly

superzapper a program that accesses data by avoiding security measures

Synchronized Multimedia Integration Language (SMIL) code that makes it easier to view multimedia content online

synchronous training a Web-based classroom to which students log on at a preset time to watch a recorded lecture

synergy the combined effect group effort can create

syntax the rules for wording a spreadsheet function

synthesize to create sounds imitative of actual musical instruments using a computer

system administrator person responsible for maintaining a computer system

system requirement the minimum equipment a computer needs to run an application

system software programs that help the computer work properly

T

T1 line copper or fiber-optic lines that allow data to be sent at more than 1.5 million bits per second

tab a part of the Ribbon in Microsoft Office applications since 2007 that contains related groups of commands

table data organized into rows and columns

tablet computer a computer that combines the features of a graphics tablet with the functions of a personal computer

tag a code used in HTML for formatting Web pages

telecommunications the process of sending information over a telephone network

telecommute to work from home by communicating with a workplace through a network

teleconference a live meeting using computers and telecommunications equipment that allows two or more people in different locations to participate

template a preformatted version of a certain type of document

terminal a keyboard and monitor attached to a shared, central computer

theme a collection of fonts, colors, and other design features used to apply consistent formatting to documents; also called a design template

thermal transfer printer a printer that uses heat to transfer color dyes or inks onto paper

thread a series of messages that make up a continuous conversation on the same general subject

thumbnail a small, representative version of a graphic

time bomb a computer virus programmed to perform a task (often a destructive one) at a specific date and time

time-limited trial a type of software that stops working after a certain number of uses or days

title bar the top row of an application window where the program name and often the name of the document is shown

token a unit of data used in ring topology to prevent collisions; or a handheld electronic device that generates a log-on code

toolbar a row of icons that represent the program's most commonly used commands

topology the layout of the physical structure of a network

trace to convert pixels into lines

Track Changes a feature that marks each editing change made by one or more members of a group working on the same document

track one of a set of uniform circles made on a disk

tracking when a Web site gathers information about your Web browsing activity

trademark a symbol that indicates that a brand or brand name is legally protected and cannot be used by other businesses

transactional processing a way of changing a database that keeps its records up to date at all times

transition effect in a presentation program, a special effect that adds visual interest when the current slide disappears and the next slide appears on the screen

Transmission Control Protocol/Internet Protocol (TCP/IP) the set of rules for formatting and transmitting data over the Internet, used by every computer that is connected to the Internet

transparency a see-through sheet of acetate that is laser-printed; also, a measure of opacity in a graphic

trap door a type of virus that enables an unauthorized user (such as a hacker) to secretly gain access to a computer

Trojan horse a program disguised as useful but that is destructive to the data on a hard drive

troubleshoot to correct a problem with a piece of hardware or a software program

tween the ability of a graphics program to determine in-between frames

twisted pair a pair of copper wires that are twisted together and commonly used as a networking medium

U

Undo a command that reverses the previous action

ungroup to separate combined vector images into individual images

Unicode a system using 16 bits to encode characters, creating more codes for foreign languages

uniform resource locator (URL) the unique address given to a document on the Internet

uninstall to remove a program from a computer

uninterruptible power supply (UPS) a device that aims to prevent interruption of power to a computer

unity in graphic design, when a third object is used to establish a connection between two other objects

universal product code (UPC) a pattern of bars printed on packages or labels to indicate price

universal serial bus (USB) a standard that allows communication between devices, such as between a flash drive and a computer

universal service the idea that all areas of the country and people of all income levels should have telephone service

upgrade to install a new and improved version of an operating system or program

upload to send data from a client computer to a server computer through a network or Internet connection

USB flash drive a small storage device that uses flash memory and connects to the computer through a USB port; also called a pen drive, jump drive, or thumb drive

Usenet a discussion system computer users can access through the Internet

user account a collection of information used to identify a person and grant him or her access to a computer system or network

username the online identity of a person who is accessing a system or network

utility software programs that are used to maintain and repair the computer

V

value a number, such as a whole number, a fraction, or decimal; also, a numerical representation of a color in a graphics program

vanishing point the point in 3-D art at which perspective makes an image disappear

variety in graphic design, the use of different colors and shapes to create visual interest

vector graphic an image that is created using paths or lines

version a release of a software program, usually identified by a unique number to distinguish it from previous releases

vertical application a type of application software that is designed for a very limited purpose in a field or business

video adapter circuit board that creates the images seen on a monitor

video capture card a circuit board chip that converts analog video images into a digital file

video editor a program that combines and edits video and audio files

video memory (VRAM) video adapter's memory used to store video images

videoconference a meeting that provides audio and visual contact for participants in different locations

viewable area a portion of the screen where an image can be shown

virtualization physical storage pooled from multiple network storage devices into what seems to be one single storage device managed from a central console

virtual memory space set aside on the hard drive for the operating system to temporarily store data

virtual private network (VPN) a private network set up through a public network

virtual reality (VR) a realistic, three-dimensional world a user can "enter" and explore

virus a program whose purpose is to damage or destroy computer data, cause a computer to behave in unexpected ways, or interfere with the operation of a network, all while concealing and replicating itself

visual aid a graphic that helps convey information to an audience

W

waveform a digitized piece of actual sound

wavetable synthesis technology for producing high-quality sound output

Web browser a program used to view Web pages

Web bug a tiny graphic image that makes it possible to record the surfing habits of a computer user

Web feed a service that automatically downloads Web page content that a user has signed up for

Web host a company that leases Web space for Web sites

Web integration a tool that makes it possible for a file created in one application to be saved in Hypertext Markup Language

Web Layout view the view in a word-processing program that shows how a document will appear when published on the World Wide Web

Web page a single document on the Web

Web server a computer that maintains Web sites

Web site a collection of related pages on the Web

Web-based training educational courses available via the Internet

Webcam a digital camera used to capture and transmit video over the Internet or other network

Webcast a live broadcast of audio and video over the Internet

Web-database integration a technique that makes databases accessible over the Internet or an intranet

Webmaster the person responsible for the creation and maintenance of a Web site

whiteboard an electronic equivalent of a chalkboard

WHOIS database the central database of domain names

wide area network (WAN) a network that connects computers and other resources over great distances

wiki a Web site that contains information created and updated by anyone who has access to the site

wildcard a symbol that stands for one or more characters; used to search pages with variations of a word in the search

window a rectangular, on-screen frame used to view a program or document

wizard a series of dialog boxes that gives a step-by-step guide through a procedure

word wrap the automatic starting of a new line of text when the previous line is full

word-processing program a program used to create documents through typing, editing, formatting, and printing functions

worksheet a grid made of vertical columns and horizontal rows in a spreadsheet program

worksheet tab a tag that identifies each worksheet in a spreadsheet program

workspace the blank area where a graphic will display in a paint or draw program

workstation a computer connected to a computer network

World Wide Web (Web) part of the Internet comprised of linked documents

worm a computer virus that spreads over a network without user execution

write the process of storing information on a storage device

write-protect switch a sliding bar on a USB flash drive that can be set to prevent changes to the data stored on the drive

write-protect tab a safety feature that prevents data from being written onto a floppy disk

WYSIWYG behind-the-scenes programming that stands for "What You See Is What You Get"

Z

zoom to focus on a part of a document

Index

Figures and photographs are indicated by an italic "*f*" following the page number.

E

F

G

M

Macintosh operating system, 10*f*, 11, 20, 77
macro viruses, 440
macros, 187
Magic Wand tool, 249
magnetic storage devices, 53, 54–55, 63, 67
magneto-optical (MO) drives, 55
magnify feature, 145, 145*f*
mail merge, 133
mailbox names, 424
"MAILER-DAEMON," 427
mainframes, 23
maintenance releases, 119
Marquee tool, 249
master page, 138
master slides, 275, 275*f*
Master views, 264
Maurer, Robert, 324
maximize, 109
media, 50
medical technicians, 351
megabytes, 8
Megahertz (MHz), 11
memory, 50
    see also RAM; ROM
memory cards, 39
memory shaving, 455
menu, 109, 122
menu bar, 110
mesh topology, 360
message headers, 438
Metcalfe, Robert M., 361
MHz (Megahertz), 11
microphones, 38, 305, 305*f*
microscopes, 79
Microsoft Corporation, 11
Microsoft Network (MSN), 373, 373*f*
Microsoft Publisher, 137
Microsoft Windows
    adaptive technology of, 21, 21*f*
    compatibility of, 20
    desktop, 20*f*, 76*f*
    market leader OS, 77
    start menu, 109*f*
    system software, 11
    viewing available devices, 52*f*
Microsoft Works, 103
microwave signals, 324
MIDI (Musical Instrument Digital Interface), 43, 296
MIME (Multipurpose Internet Mail Extensions), 437

minicomputers, 23
minimize, 109
MO (magneto-optical) drives, 55
Mobile Telephone Switching Office (MTSO), 335
modems, 30, 325–326, 325*f*, 330
modulation, 325
monitors, 21, 32–33
Montgomery, Kathryn C., 382
morality. *see* ethics
Mosaic, 392
motherboards, 17, 17*f*
Motorola processors, 20
mouse, 16, 29
Moving Picture Experts Group (MPEG) format, 295
MP3, 296
MPEG (Moving Picture Experts Group) format, 295
MSN (Microsoft Network), 373, 373*f*
MTSO (Mobile Telephone Switching Office), 335
multimedia activities, 313–317
multimedia applications, 116–117
multimedia databases, 206
multimedia events
    creating, 304–307
    definition of, 292, 294*f*
    file formats for, 295–296
    players for, 295, 297
    uses for, 293
    see also virtual reality
multiple device ports, 9
multiple sorts, 209
multiplexing technology, 323
Multipurpose Internet Mail Extensions (MIME), 437
multitasking, 75, 124, 124*f*
multi-user operating systems, 75
Musical Instrument Digital Interface (MIDI), 43, 296
Muvee Reveal, 307, 307*f*
Myspace, 387

N

NAP (network access point), 381, 383
National Center for Supercomputing Applications (NCSA), 392
National Infrastructure Protection Center (NIPC), 456
natural language databases, 206
navigate, 373

T

Art Credits

Charts and Graphs: Keithley & Associates: 28, 49, 50, 55, 136, 138, 139, 147, 164, 168, 171, 187, 202, 210, 215, 233, 240, 244, 250, 323, 326, 357, 372, 392
Illustrations: Hank Osuna/Rep. Lori Nowicki: 41, 60, 65, 294, 336, 346, 349, 350, 358, 359, 360, 368, 381

Photo Credits

Cover © Rick Fischer/Masterfle Stock Image Library; **Title Page** © Rick Fischer/Masterfle Stock Image Library; **1** Shutterstock; **3** Shutterstock; **6** Kevin HoranStock Boston; **7** Courtesy of Intel Corporation; **8** Seagate Technology; **10** "Macintosh Operating System screen shot." Screen shot reprinted with permission from Apple Computer, Inc.; **11 top:** © Bob Daemmrich/CORBIS Sygma; **bottom:** AP/World Wide Photos; **12** Courtesy of www.ifoAppleStore.com; **15** Earl Harper/EcoStock; **17** Shutterstock; **19** U.S. Navy News Photo; **22** AP/Wide World Photos; **23** Shutterstock; **24** Courtesy of www.apple.com; **27** Shutterstock; **29 top:** Shutterstock; **bottom:** Douglas Engelbart and Bootstrap Alliance; **30** CORBIS; **31** Getty Images; **32** Shutterstock; **33** Epson America, Inc.; **37** Shutterstock; **38** Photo courtesy of Creative Labs. Inc.; **39 left:** Courtesy of www.apple.com; **right:** www.usa.canon.com © Canon, Inc. Canon and PowerShot are registered trademarks of Canon, Inc. in the United States and may be registered trademarks or trademarks in other countries.; **40** Shutterstock; **42** Shutterstock; **43** Michael J. Lutch; **47** Shutterstock; **48** Shutterstock; **51** Shutterstock; **53** © Bill Aron/PhotoEdit; **54** Shutterstock; **55** © David A. J. Ripley; **56** Shutterstock; **59** Shutterstock; **64** Shutterstock; **66** Shutterstock; **67** Shutterstock; **68** Shutterstock; **69** Shutterstock; **73** Shutterstock; **75** Getty Images; **83** Kevin Radford/SuperStock; **86** Shutterstock; **87** AP/World Wide Photos; **89** AP/World Wide Photos; **90** "McAfee Security Center screen shot." Copyright McAfee, Inc. All rights reserved. Used with permission.; **99** Shutterstock; **101** Shutterstock; **103** Shutterstock; **105 left:** office.microsoft.com. Microsoft product box shot reprinted with permission from Microsoft Corporation; **right:** www.Adobe.com; **107** © Mark Richards/PhotoEdit; **115** Shutterstock; **117** Shutterstock; **119** "About QuickTime PictureViewer screen shot" © Apple, Inc.; **120** Photo courtesy of Easter Seals Massachusetts; **123** "Adobe Reader screen shot" © Adobe Systems Incorporated; **127** Shutterstock; **143** Shutterstock; **163** Shutterstock; **166** © Louis Fabian Bachrach; **175** Will Hart; **179** Shutterstock; **201** Shutterstock; **203** Canyon de Chelly National Monument, National Park Service/Photo courtesy Rupestrian CyberServices; **206** Shutterstock; **213** Shutterstock; **218** AP/Wide World Photos; **221** NASA; **231** Shutterstock; **234** PRNewsFoto/Walt Disney Television Animation; **237 top:** Shutterstock; **bottom:** Pearson Education/PH School; **239** "Adobe Photoshop screen shot." Adobe product screen shot reprinted with permission from Adobe Systems Incorporated; **243** Shutterstock; **245** Corel Professional Photos CD-ROM™; **246** © Doug Mazell; **247 top:** PhotoDisc, Inc./Getty Images; **bottom:** Images of Canon A560 PowerShot Digital Camera © Canon, Inc., used with express written permission of Canon U.S.A., Inc. Canon and PowerShot are registered trademarks of Canon, Inc. in the United States and may be registered trademarks or trademarks in other countries.; **248** PhotoDisc, Inc./Getty Images; **249** Corel Professional Photos CD-ROM™; **261** Shutterstock; **268** Shutterstock; **269** © Bob Daemmrich Photo, Inc.; **273** Shutterstock; **274** Shutterstock; **280** Shutterstock; **291** Shutterstock; **293** David Young-Wolff/PhotoEdit; **297** © Rex USA; **298** Shutterstock; **299** Laura Giannitrapani, Scientific Computing and Visualization, Boston University; **300** Shutterstock; **303** Shutterstock; **305** © Mark C. Burnett/Stock, Boston; **307** "muvee Reveal™ screen shot" © muvee Technologies; **308** © David A. Wagner/Phototake; **309** The Virtual Reality Medical Center; **310** Markus Matzel/Fotoarchive/Stockphoto.com; **319** Shutterstock; **321** Shutterstock; **322** Shutterstock; **324** © Rick Fischer/Masterfle Stock Image Library; **325** © 3Com Corporation; **327** © Jose L. Pelaez/CORBIS; **329** © Jon Feingersh/CORBIS; **330** AP/Wide World Photos; **333** Shutterstock; **334** ImageState; **337** © Michael Newman/PhotoEdit; **338** Sony Ericsson Mobile Communications; **339** Image courtesy of Lowrance Electronics, Inc.; **343** Shutterstock; **344** © 3Com Corporation; **348** Shutterstock; **352** Photo by Ed McCombs; **355** Shutterstock; **356** Shutterstock; **361** Photo courtesy of Polaris Ventures; **362** Shutterstock; **363** © Michael Newman/PhotoEdit; **364** Shutterstock; **367** Shutterstock; **369** © Matrix NetSystems, Inc., www.matrixnetsystems.com; **370** Shutterstock; **375** AP/Wide World Photos; **379** Shutterstock; **380** Shutterstock; **382** © Corbis Images/PictureQuest; **384** Verisign.com "Verisign Authentication Services homepage screen shot" © Symantec Corp.; **385** Whois.net "Whois Lookup – Domain Name Search screen shot" © Verio, Inc.; **386** Shutterstock; **390** Shutterstock; **393** AP/Wide World Photos; **396** Bing.com "Homepage screen shot" © Microsoft Corporation; **398** Amazon.com "Homepage screen shot" © Amazon.com, Inc.; **399** The Postal Store "Homepage screen shot" © USPS; **403** Shutterstock; **405** © Fridmar Damm/zefa/Corbis; **407** Irs.gov "Homepage screen shot" © IRS.gov | Internal Revenue Service | United States Department of the Treasury; **408** Used with permission of WiredWoods, Inc., www.wiredwoods.org; **409** Google.com "Boolean search results screen shot" © Google. **410** Bing.com "Search results screen shot" © Microsoft Corporation; **413** Shutterstock; **423** Shutterstock; **425** Mail.google.com "Google gmail screen shot" © Google; **426** Mail.google.com "Google gmail screen shot" © Google; **429** Shutterstock; **431** Photo courtesy of International Telementor Program; **435** Wonderfile; **440** AP/World Wide Photos; **441** "Trend Micro Internet Security screen shot" © Trend Micro Incorporated; **451** Shutterstock; **455** Ftc.gov "Fighting Back Against Identity Theft screen shot" © Federal Trade Commission, U.S. Federal Government; **459** "Facebook Privacy Settings screen shot" © Facebook; **463** Shutterstock; **464** "Acceptable Use Policy screen shot" from the Los Angeles Unified School District Bulletin K-19 (REV.), "Acceptable Use Policy (AUP) for the Internet," dated March 15, 2002. Reprinted with permission.; **467** "McAfee Security Center screen shot" © McAfee, Inc. All rights reserved. Used with permission.; **469 top:** © American Power Conversion Corp.; **bottom:** Shutterstock

Acknowledgments

Microsoft Corporation, pp. 20, 21, 52, 63, 76, 78, 79, 85, 88, 108, 109, 118, 121, 122, 123, 124, 128, 129, 130, 132, 133, 134, 135, 144, 145, 146, 148, 149, 150, 152, 153, 154, 155, 165, 167, 169, 170, 172, 174, 180, 181, 182, 184, 185, 186, 189, 190, 204, 207, 208, 216, 219, 222, 235, 236, 252, 263, 264, 266, 267, 275, 276, 277, 278, 279, 281, 296, 373, 376, 384, 395, 396, 398, 399, 407, 409, 410, 425, 426, 428, 438, 439, 441, 453, 455, 458, 464, 470, 471. Microsoft product screen shots reprinted with permission from Microsoft Corporation.

Note: Every effort has been made to locate the copyright owner of material reprinted in this book. Omissions brought to our attention will be corrected in subsequent editions.

Derivative Source Credits:

Chapter 1 taken from Chapter 1, Lessons 1-1 through 1-3, from *Prentice Hall Technology Applications Student WorkText, Level I* Revised Edition, Copyright © 2008 by Pearson Education, Inc.

Chapter 2 taken from Lessons 1-1 through 1-3 from *Prentice Hall Technology Applications Student WorkText, Level II* Revised Edition, Copyright © 2008 by Pearson Education, Inc.

Chapter 2, Lesson 2 also taken from Lesson 1-2 from *Prentice Hall Technology Applications Student WorkText, Texas Grade 8* Revised Edition, Copyright © 2008 by Pearson Education, Inc.

Chapter 3 taken from Lessons 2-1 through 2-2 from *Prentice Hall Technology Applications Student WorkText, Level I* Revised Edition, Copyright © 2008 by Pearson Education, Inc.

Chapter 4 taken from Lessons 2-1 through 2-2 from *Prentice Hall Technology Applications Student WorkText, Level II* Revised Edition, Copyright © 2008 by Pearson Education, Inc.

Chapter 5 taken from Lessons 3-1 through 3-3 from *Prentice Hall Technology Applications Student WorkText, Level I* Revised Edition, Copyright © 2008 by Pearson Education, Inc.

Chapter 6 taken from Lessons 3-1 though 3-3 from *Prentice Hall Technology Applications Student WorkText, Level II* Revised Edition, Copyright © 2008 by Pearson Education, Inc.

Chapter 6, Lesson 1 also taken from Lesson 3-1 from *Prentice Hall Technology Applications Student WorkText, Texas Grade 8* Revised Edition, Copyright © 2008 by Pearson Education, Inc.

Chapter 6, Lesson 3 also taken from Lesson 3-3 from *Prentice Hall Technology Applications Student WorkText, Texas Grade 8* Revised Edition, Copyright © 2008 by Pearson Education, Inc.

Chapter 7 taken from Lessons 4-1 thorugh 4-2 from *Prentice Hall Technology Applications Student WorkText, Level I* Revised Edition, Copyright © 2008 by Pearson Education, Inc.

Chapter 8 taken from Lesson 4-1 through 4-2 from *Prentice Hall Technology Applications Student WorkText, Level II* Revised Edition, Copyright © 2008 by Pearson Education, Inc.

Chapter 8, Lesson 1 also taken from Lesson 4-1 from *Prentice Hall Technology Applications Student WorkText, Texas Grade 8* Revised Edition, Copyright © 2008 by Pearson Education, Inc.

Chapter 9 taken from Lessons 5-1 through 5-3 from *Prentice Hall Technology Applications Student WorkText, Level I* Revised Edition, Copyright © 2008 by Pearson Education, Inc.

Chapter 10 taken from Lessons 5-1 through 5-3 from *Prentice Hall Technology Applications Student WorkText, Level II* Revised Edition, Copyright © 2008 by Pearson Education, Inc.

Chapter 11 taken from Lessons 6-1 through 6-3 from *Prentice Hall Technology Applications Student WorkText, Level I* Revised Edition, Copyright © 2008 by Pearson Education, Inc.

Chapter 11, Lesson 4 also taken from Lesson 6-3 from *Prentice Hall Technology Applications Student WorkText, Texas Grade 8* Revised Edition, Copyright © 2008 by Pearson Education, Inc.

Chapter 12 taken from Lessons 6-1 through 6-3 from *Prentice Hall Technology Applications Student WorkText, Level II* Revised Edition, Copyright © 2008 by Pearson Education, Inc.

Chapter 12, Lesson 4 also taken from Lesson 6-2 from *Prentice Hall Technology Applications Student WorkText, Texas Grade 8* Revised Edition, Copyright © 2008 by Pearson Education, Inc.

Chapter 13 taken from Lessons 7-1 through 7-3 from *Prentice Hall Technology Applications Student WorkText, Level I* Revised Edition, Copyright © 2008 by Pearson Education, Inc.

Chapter 13, Lesson 4 also taken from Lesson 7-3 from *Prentice Hall Technology Applications Student WorkText, Texas Grade 8* Revised Edition, Copyright © 2008 by Pearson Education, Inc.

Chapter 14, Lessons 1, 3, and 4 taken from Lessons 7-1 through 7-3 from *Prentice Hall Technology Applications Student WorkText, Level II* Revised Edition, Copyright © 2008 by Pearson Education, Inc.

Chapter 14, Lesson 2 taken from Lesson 7-1 from *Prentice Hall Technology Applications Student WorkText, Texas Grade 8* Revised Edition, Copyright © 2008 by Pearson Education, Inc.

Chapter 15 taken from Lessons 8-1 through 8-3 from *Prentice Hall Technology Applications Student WorkText, Level I* Revised Edition, Copyright © 2008 by Pearson Education, Inc.

Chapter 16 taken from Lessons 8-1 through 8-3 from *Prentice Hall Technology Applications Student WorkText, Level II* Revised Edition, Copyright © 2008 by Pearson Education, Inc.

Chapter 17 taken from Lessons 9-1 through 9-3 from *Prentice Hall Technology Applications Student WorkText, Level I* Revised Edition, Copyright © 2008 by Pearson Education, Inc.

Chapter 18 taken from Lessons 9-1 through 9-3 from *Prentice Hall Technology Applications Student WorkText, Level II* Revised Edition, Copyright © 2008 by Pearson Education, Inc.

Chapter 19 taken from Lessons 10-1 through 10-3 from *Prentice Hall Technology Applications Student WorkText, Level I* Revised Edition, Copyright © 2008 by Pearson Education, Inc.

Chapter 20 taken from Lessons 10-1 through 10-3 from *Prentice Hall Technology Applications Student WorkText, Level II* Revised Edition, Copyright © 2008 by Pearson Education, Inc.

Chapter 21 taken from Lessons 11-1 through 11-3 from *Prentice Hall Technology Applications Student WorkText, Level I* Revised Edition, Copyright © 2008 by Pearson Education, Inc.

Chapter 22 taken from Lessons 11-1 through 11-3 from *Prentice Hall Technology Applications Student WorkText, Level II* Revised Edition, Copyright © 2008 by Pearson Education, Inc.

Chapter 23 taken from Lessons 12-1 through 12-3 from *Prentice Hall Technology Applications Student WorkText, Level I* Revised Edition, Copyright © 2008 by Pearson Education, Inc.

Chapter 24 taken from Lessons 12-1 through 12-2 from *Prentice Hall Technology Applications Student WorkText, Level II* Revised Edition, Copyright © 2008 by Pearson Education, Inc.

Chapter 25 taken from Lessons 13-1 through 13-3 from *Prentice Hall Technology Applications Student WorkText, Level I* Revised Edition, Copyright © 2008 by Pearson Education, Inc.

Chapter 26 taken from Lessons 13-1 through 13-3 from *Prentice Hall Technology Applications Student WorkText, Texas Grade 8* Revised Edition, Copyright © 2008 by Pearson Education, Inc.

Chapter 27 taken from Lessons 15-1 through 15-3 from *Prentice Hall Technology Applications Student WorkText, Level I* Revised Edition, Copyright © 2008 by Pearson Education, Inc.

Chapter 28 taken from Lessons 15-1 through 15-3 from *Prentice Hall Technology Applications Student WorkText, Texas Grade 8* Revised Edition, Copyright © 2008 by Pearson Education, Inc.

Chapter 29 taken from Lessons 16-1 through 16-3 from *Prentice Hall Technology Applications Student WorkText, Level I* Revised Edition, Copyright © 2008 by Pearson Education, Inc.

Chapter 30, Lessons 1, 3, and 4 taken from Lessons 16-1 through 16-3 from *Prentice Hall Technology Applications Student WorkText, Level II* Revised Edition, Copyright © 2008 by Pearson Education, Inc.

Chapter 30, Lesson 2 taken from Lesson 16-1 from *Prentice Hall Technology Applications Student WorkText, Texas Grade 8* Revised Edition, Copyright © 2008 by Pearson Education, Inc.

Chapter 31 taken from Lessons 14-1 through 14-3 from *Prentice Hall Technology Applications Student WorkText, Level I* Revised Edition, Copyright © 2008 by Pearson Education, Inc.

Chapter 32 taken from Lessons 14-1 through 14-2 from *Prentice Hall Technology Applications Student WorkText, Level II* Revised Edition, Copyright © 2008 by Pearson Education, Inc.

Chapter 33, Lessons 1 and 3 taken from Lessons 17-1 and 17-3 from *Prentice Hall Technology Applications Student WorkText, Level I* Revised Edition, Copyright © 2008 by Pearson Education, Inc.

Chapter 33, Lesson 2 taken from Lesson 17-2 from *Prentice Hall Technology Applications Student WorkText, Level II* Revised Edition, Copyright © 2008 by Pearson Education, Inc.

Chapter 34 taken from Lessons 17-1 through 17-4 from *Prentice Hall Technology Applications Student WorkText, Level II* Revised Edition, Copyright © 2008 by Pearson Education, Inc.

Keyboarding Essentials taken from pp. K1-K32 from *Prentice Hall Technology Applications Student WorkText, Level II* Revised Edition, Copyright © 2008 by Pearson Education, Inc.